Lynda Weinman's | Hands-On Training

Includes CD-ROM with Exercise Files and Demo Movies

Photoshop® Elements 2

H·O·T ™

Hands-On Training

lynda.com/books

By **Shane Rebenschied**
developed with **Lynda Weinman**

Design: Ali Karp

Photoshop Elements 2 | H·O·T
Hands-On Training

By Shane Rebenschied (developed with Lynda Weinman)

lynda.com/books | Peachpit Press
800 East 96th Street • Indianapolis, IN • 46240
800.571.5840 • 317.428.3000 •
317.428.3280(fax)
http://www.lynda.com/books
http://www.peachpit.com

lynda.com/books is published
in association with Peachpit Press,
a division of Pearson Education
Copyright ©2004 by lynda.com

ISBN: 0-321-20300-3

0 9 8 7 6 5 4 3 2 1

Printed and bound in the
United States of America

H•O•T | Credits

Original Design: Ali Karp, Alink Newmedia (alink@earthlink.net)

Editor: Jennifer Eberhardt

Copyeditor: Darren Meiss

Compositors: Rick Gordon, Deborah Roberti

Beta testers: Grace Hodgson, Laurie Burruss-Myers

Proofreader: Karen Gill

Cover Illustration: Bruce Heavin (bruce@stink.com)

Indexer: Cheryl Lenser

H•O•T | Colophon

The original design for *Learning Adobe Photoshop Elements 2 H•O•T* was sketched on paper. The layout was heavily influenced by online communication—merging a traditional book format with a modern Web aesthetic.

The text in *Adobe Photoshop Elements 2 H•O•T* was set in Akzidenz Grotesk from Adobe and Triplex from Emigre. The cover illustration was painted in Adobe Photoshop 7.0.

This book was created using QuarkXPress 4.1, Adobe Photoshop 7.0, Microsoft Office X, Microsoft Office XP, and Adobe Photoshop Elements 2 on a PC using Windows XP and on an Apple Macintosh using Mac OS X 10.2.6. It was printed on 60 lb. Influence Matte at CJ Krehbiel in Cincinnati, Ohio.

Dedications

For my wife:
Thank you for continually
reminding me that
there's life beyond
the computer screen.

For my kids,
Eva and Ethan (the E's):
Without knowing it,
you make me strive to
be better than I am.

For my family.

Photoshop Elements 2 | H•O•T ———————————— **Table of Contents**

Introduction —————————————————————— **x**

I. **Background** ———————————————————— **2**

What Is Adobe Photoshop Elements?   3

Elements versus Photoshop   3

Image Size and Resolution   5

What's New in Version 2.0   6

Updates   11

2. **Interface** ———————————————————— **12**

The Welcome Screen   13

Photoshop Elements Interface   15

Menu Bar   15

Toolbox   16

Shortcuts Bar   18

Palettes   20

The Palette Well   21

Options Bar   23

3. **Opening and Importing Images** ——————— **24**

Supported Image Formats   25

Exercise 1_Importing Images from a Scanner   26

Exercise 2_Importing Images from a Digital Camera   28

Exercise 3_Opening Images   30

Exercise 4_Using the File Browser Palette   34

Exercise 5_Place   39

Video Formats Supported by Elements 2.0   46

Exercise 6_Frame From Video   47

Exercise 7_Creating a New Image   51

What Are Image Modes?   53

Exercise 8_Working with Image Modes   54

4.   **Layers** _____ **58**

What Are Layers?   59

Exercise 1_Layer Basics–Part One   60

Exercise 2_Layer Basics–Part Two   67

Non-Destructive Editing   71

Exercise 3_Fill and Adjustment Layers   72

What Are Layer Blending Modes?   80

Exercise 4_Using Blending Modes   85

5.   **Selecting** _____ **88**

About Selections   89

Pre-Selecting Advice   90

Exercise 1_Using and Choosing Proper Selection Tools   91

How Do I Add or Subtract from a Selection?   103

Exercise 2_Moving and Saving Selections   105

Exercise 3_Building an Image   108

6.   **Painting and Colors** _____ **114**

Exercise 1_Painting and Drawing   115

Exercise 2_Erasing   127

Exercise 3_Modifying Colors   136

7.   **Shapes and Layer Styles** _____ **144**

Bitmaps and Vectors   145

Exercise 1_Creating Shapes   147

About Layer Styles   154

Exercise 2_Layer Styles   155

8.   **Type** _____ **164**

Exercise 1_Adding Text   165

Exercise 2_More Text   173

Exercise 3_Warping Text   178

9. **Correcting Photos** _____ **182**

Exercise 1_Adjusting the Value of a Photo 184

Exercise 2_Automatic Value Adjustments 192

Exercise 3_Dodge and Burn Tools 195

Exercise 4_Color Adjustments 201

Exercise 5_More Color Adjustments 207

Exercise 6_Automatic Color Adjustments 215

Exercise 7_The Sponge Tool 216

10. **Retouching Photos** _____ **222**

Exercise 1_Removing Red Eye 223

Exercise 2_Removing Dust, Scratches, and Imperfections 229

Exercise 3_Sharpening a Photo 243

Exercise 4_Blurring a Photo 251

11. **Photo Manipulation** _____ **258**

Exercise 1_Photomerge 259

Exercise 2_Smudge Tool 269

Exercise 3_Liquify 274

12. **Elements and the Web** _____ **282**

Image Sizes, Resolutions, and the Web 283

Exercise 1_Attach to Email 285

Exercise 2_Save for the Web 292

Exercise 3_PDF Slideshow 305

13. **Printing** _____ **312**

Exercise 1_Print Preview 313

Exercise 2_Contact Sheet 318

A. **Online Resources** ———————————— 324

A Few Elements-Related Web Sites 325

Stock Photo and Clip Art Sites 327

B. **Technical Support** ———————————— 328

Adobe Technical Support 329

Peachpit Press 329

lynda.com 329

Index ———————————————————— 330

Introduction

A Note from Lynda	About the Author	Our Team
Acknowledgments	How to Use This Book
Interface Screen Captures	System Differences
A Note to Windows Users
Making Exercise Files Editable on Windows Systems
Elements System Requirements
H•O•T CD-ROM Contents

H•O•T

Photoshop Elements 2

A Note from Lynda Weinman

In my opinion, most people buy computer books in order to learn, yet it is amazing how few of these books are actually written by teachers. In this book, you will find carefully developed lessons and exercises to help you learn Adobe Elements 2.0. This book was written by one of lynda.com's most popular instructors, Shane Rebenschied, who not only works professionally as a digital illustrator/artist, but has years of teaching experience at our now-closed training center and works as a current CD-ROM instructor for our products and online training movie subscription library. Shane is a respected teacher for a reason: He knows his stuff, he has patience and respect for his students, he makes you laugh, and he teaches you really cool stuff.

This book is written for beginning Adobe Elements learners who are looking for a great tool to edit photographs and create images for print or screen. The premise of the hands-on exercise approach is to get you up to speed quickly in Adobe Elements while actively working through the book's lessons. It's one thing to read about a product, and another experience entirely to try the product and get measurable results. Our motto is, "Read the book, follow the exercises, and you will know the product." We have received countless testimonials to this fact, and it is our goal to make sure it remains true for all of our hands-on training books.

Many exercise-based books take a paint-by-numbers approach to teaching. Although this approach works, it's often difficult to figure out how to apply those lessons to a real-world situation, or to understand why or when you would use the technique again. What sets this book apart is that the lessons contain lots of background information, advice, and insights into each given subject, designed to help you understand the process as well as the exercise.

At times, pictures are worth a lot more than words, and moving pictures are even better! When necessary, we have also included short QuickTime movies to show any process that's difficult to explain with words. These files are located on the **H·O·T CD-ROM** inside a folder called **movies**. It's our style to approach teaching from many different angles, since we know that some people are visual learners, others like to read, and still others like to get out there and try things. This book combines a lot of teaching approaches so you can learn Adobe Elements as thoroughly as you want to.

In this book, we didn't set out to cover every single aspect of Adobe Elements. The manual and many other reference books are great for that! What we saw missing from the bookshelves was a process-oriented tutorial that taught readers core principles, techniques, and tips in a hands-on training format.

We welcome your comments at **elm2faq@lynda.com**. Please visit our Web site at **http://www.lynda.com**. The support URL for this book is **http://www.lynda.com/products/books/elm2hot/**.

–Lynda Weinman

NOTE | About lynda.com/books and lynda.com

lynda.com/books is dedicated to helping designers and developers understand tools and design principles. **lynda.com** offers hands-on books, CD-ROMs, online subscription-based movie training, conferences, and "expert tips" for design and development. To learn more about our training programs, books, and products, be sure to give our site a visit at **http://www.lynda.com**.

About Shane Rebenschied

Shane Rebenschied graduated from the Art Center College of Design in 1998 with an emphasis on traditional and digital media. Since then, his work has appeared in the Society of Illustrators Los Angeles and New York annuals as well as on numerous book covers and magazines. He is a fan of old paper and stains, and can often be found staring at pieces of corroded, rusted metal. Shane is a professional freelance Illustrator and Macromedia Flash designer/developer/consultant living somewhere in the Arizona desert. He maintains an illustration portfolio site at **www.blot.com**.

Past clients include Scholastic, D'Arcy Masius Benton & Bowles, Tor, Harper Collins, Harlequin, Hodder Headline Plc, Summertime Publishing, Harcourt Brace, Ziff Davis, Hanley-Wood LLC, Spirit IC, *Backpacker* Magazine, *X-Files* Magazine, McGraw-Hill, Vanderbilt University, Flashforward, *Phoenix New Times*, *Miami New Times*, *San Francisco Weekly*, and *Cleveland Scene*.

Our Team

Shane frowning at the camera. (I like to take pictures, not have them taken of me!)

Acknowledgments from Shane

My deepest thanks and appreciation to:

Does anyone ever read this? Oh, they do? Hmmm… ;-)

Lynda Weinman, thank you for being my friend and supporter in my personal and professional life.

Garo Green, for heckling me at 2 a.m. and periodically messaging me "*burp*" over AIM. Your caffeinated ramblings have kept me in good spirits. Thank you for inviting me to your home so your dog could scare my daughter and your bird could bite my son…twice. You're a true friend and mentor.

Darren Meiss, the copy editor at New Riders, for turning my confusing, muddled thoughts into crystal clear, razor sharp statements of genius.

Grace Hodgson and Laurie Burruss-Myers, my beta testers for this book, for making sure that left is left, and what's up is down…err…rather…oh, never mind. Your comments and criticisms have made this a better book than I could have written alone.

New Riders, for being so cool to work with, catering to my every whim, and FedEx-ing me bon-bon's to keep me going at 3 a.m. What? That wasn't you? Hmm…

Apple Computer, for making the coolest computers and software in the world.

Adobe, for allowing me to make images I only dreamed of as a kid.

The Universe, for existing. Is this place cool or what?

You, the reader, for buying this book. Congratulations on wanting to further your knowledge and yourself. Keep learning!

How to Use This Book

Please read this section—it contains important information that's going to help you as you use this book. The following chart outlines the information I cover:

Learning Adobe Photoshop Elements 2 H•O•T

Information in this section:

The Formatting in This Book

Macintosh and Windows Interface Screen Captures

Mac and Windows System Differences

• "Choose" for Mac and "OK" for Windows

A Note to Windows Users

• Making Exercise Files Editable on Windows Systems

• Making File Extensions Visible on Windows Systems

Elements System Requirements

What's on the CD-ROM?

NOTE | The Formatting in This Book

This book has several components, including step-by-step exercises, commentary, notes, tips, warnings, and movies. Step-by-step exercises are numbered, and filenames and command keys are shown in bold so they pop out more easily. Captions and commentary are in italicized text: *This is a caption.* Filenames/folders, command keys, and menu commands are bolded: **images** folder, **Ctrl+S**, and **File > Open**. And URLs are in bold: **http://www.lynda.com**.

Macintosh and Windows Interface Screen Captures

Most of the screen captures in this book were taken on a PC using Windows XP. The only time I used Macintosh shots was when the interface differed from the PC under Windows XP. I made this decision because most of the audience for this book and Adobe Photoshop Elements is running Windows, and I wanted to show the images in this book in a format that the majority of the readers would be familiar with. I also own and use numerous Macintosh systems, so I noted important differences when they occurred and took screen captures accordingly.

Mac and Windows System Differences

Adobe has done a great job of ensuring that Photoshop Elements 2 looks and works the same between the Macintosh and Windows operating systems. However, there are still some differences that should be noted. If you are using this book with one of the Windows operating systems, please be sure to read the following section, titled "*A Note to Windows Users,*" carefully.

WARNING | "Choose" for Mac and "OK" for Windows

Throughout this book, you will be instructed to click the **OK** button. This is the correct way to do it on the PC using Windows XP. On a Macintosh running OS X, you will instead see a **Choose** button. The two buttons are interchangeable and do the same thing.

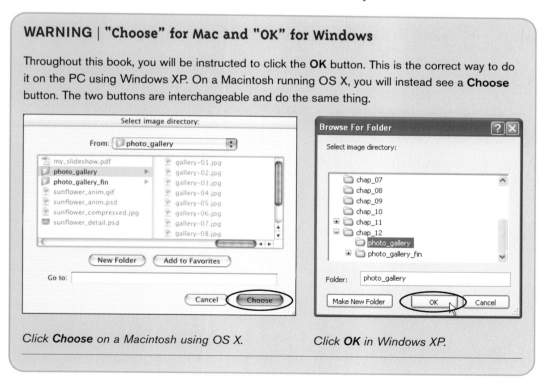

Click **Choose** on a Macintosh using OS X.   Click **OK** in Windows XP.

A Note to Windows Users

This section contains essential information about making your exercise folders editable, and making file extensions visible.

Making Exercise Files Editable on Windows Systems

By default, when you copy files from a CD-ROM to your Windows 98/2000 hard drive, they are set to read-only (write protected). This will cause a problem with the exercise files, because you will need to write over some of them.

Note: *You do not need to follow these steps if you are using Windows NT, Windows XP Home Edition, or Windows XP Professional Edition.*

1. Copy the chapter folder from the **H•O•T CD-ROM** to your hard drive.

2. Open the chapter folder and press **Ctrl+A** to select the folder's entire contents.

3. Right-click on one of the selected items and choose **Properties**.

4. In the Properties window, uncheck **Read-only**. This will change the setting for all of the selected files.

5. Click **OK**.

6. If there are other folders inside the chapter folder, Windows 2000 has the option of selecting **Apply changes to the selected items, subfolders and files** to make the contents of all folders editable. Users of earlier Windows systems will have to open each subfolder and repeat Steps 2 through 5.

Making File Extensions Visible on Windows Systems

In this section, you'll see how to turn on file extensions for Windows systems. By default, Windows 98/2000 users cannot see file extensions, such as .gif, .jpg, or .html. Fortunately, you can change this setting!

Windows Users:

1. Double-click on the **My Computer** icon on your desktop. **Note:** If you (or someone else) have changed the name, it will not say **My Computer**.

2. Select **View > Folder Options** (or **Tools > Folder Options** in Windows 2000/XP). This opens the **Folder Options** dialog box.

3. Click on the **View** tab at the top. This opens the **View** options screen so you can change the view settings for Windows.

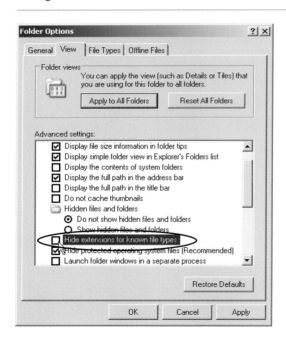

4. Uncheck the **Hide extensions for known file types** check box. This makes all of the file extensions visible.

Photoshop Elements 2 System Requirements

This book requires that you use either a Macintosh operating system (Power Macintosh running System 9.1 or later) or Windows 98, Windows 2000, or Windows NT 4.0, Windows ME, or Windows XP. You also will need a color monitor capable of 800 x 600 resolution and a CD-ROM drive. I suggest that you have at least 256 MB of RAM in your system, because that way you can open Elements and one or two other necessary programs at the same time. More RAM than that is even better, especially on Macintosh computers, which do not dynamically allocate RAM, as Windows does. Although Mac OS X does dynamically allocate RAM, more is always better, *especially* when dealing with high-resolution digital images. Here's a little chart that cites Adobe's RAM requirements, along with our recommendations:

Elements 2 System Requirements		
	Elements Requires	**I Recommend**
Mac	128 MB	256 MB
Windows	128 MB	256 MB

What's on the CD-ROM?

Exercise Files and the H•O•T CD-ROM

Your course files are located inside a folder called **exercise_files** on the **H•O•T CD-ROM**. These files are divided into chapter folders, and you will be instructed to copy the chapter folders to your hard drive during many of the exercises. Unfortunately, when files originate from a CD-ROM, under some Windows operating systems, it defaults to making them write-protected, meaning that you cannot alter them. You will need to alter them to follow the exercises, so please read the "Note to Windows Users" on pages xvi and xvii for instructions on how to convert them to read-and-write formatting.

Demo Files on the CD-ROM

In addition to the exercise files, the **H•O•T CD-ROM** also contains free 30-day trial versions of several software applications for the Mac or Windows. All software is located inside the **software** folder on the **H•O•T CD-ROM**. I have included trial versions of

• Adobe Photoshop Elements 2 (trial version)

• Adobe Reader

• QuickTime 6.3

1.

Background

| What Is Adobe Photoshop Elements |
| Elements versus Photoshop | Image Size/Resolution |
| What's New in Version 2 | Updates |

chap_01

Photoshop Elements 2
H•O•T CD-ROM

This chapter offers a quick overview of some important topics that you'll be dealing with as you read this book and learn Adobe Photoshop Elements 2.0. You need to understand the basic concepts behind digital imaging and Photoshop Elements before you jump in and start working on the exercises. I know you're probably itching to get started, but taking a few minutes to read this chapter will give you a better understanding of many of the topics that I will be addressing later in this book.

What Is Adobe Photoshop Elements?

Simply put, Photoshop Elements is an application that takes many of the features of Adobe's flagship, professional image editing program, Photoshop, and stuffs them into a consumer-level, easy-to-use program. Although Photoshop Elements is geared primarily towards novice computer users, I think you'll find a whole slew of fantastic features that will make your life on the computer easier. Not to mention that Photoshop Elements is "easy on the wallet" as well, oftentimes coming bundled with other items such as scanners and digital cameras. Oh sure, you can use Photoshop Elements to scan in a picture of your sister and give her a few extra eyes and some hairy warts, but its usefulness and capabilities go way beyond that.

Photoshop Elements gives you the ability to easily and quickly do everything from correcting "red-eye" in that otherwise great family photo, to making those old and torn family photos look new again, to easily emailing your favorite photos to friends and family, to automatically creating a Web site with your favorite photos for the whole world to see.

Adobe has certainly outdone itself with this latest version of Elements by adding even more features and capabilities. Whether you are new to the whole computer scene or an advanced Photoshop user, after reading through this book you'll see how Photoshop Elements is a great tool to add to your graphics arsenal.

Elements versus Photoshop

Because Photoshop Elements and Photoshop are similar in name and purpose, understanding which program does what and when you should use one over the other can be confusing. To help clear up some of this confusion, here is a list of some of the things you could do with Photoshop Elements and some things that are better suited for Photoshop. The following chart identifies some common tasks and which program is best suited to complete those projects.

Elements versus Photoshop		
Task	**Elements 2.0**	**Photoshop 7.0**
Getting help; integrated Help such as a Glossary, Hints and How To Windows, Dialog Tips, Smart Messages, and a Help search field in the toolbar	X	
Correcting images; easy-to-use "Quick Fix" window	X	
Extracting images from a video source; "Frame from video" feature	X	
Working with "print quality" image modes; support for CMYK, Lab, and Multichannel images		X

continues on next page

Elements versus Photoshop *continued*		
Task	**Elements 2.0**	**Photoshop 7.0**
Selecting images with a Selection brush	X	
PDF slideshow export	X	
Attach to E-mail button	X	
Remove red-eye	X	X
Correcting images (change the color, brightness, and so on)	X	X
"Recipes" to guide you through simple image editing tasks	X	
Batch processing images	X	X
Utilizing a File Browser	X	X
Photomerge feature to create panoramic photos	X	
Utilizing Layers	X	X
Ability to save files for the Web	X	X
Utilizing Channels		X
Auto straighten and crop image features	X	

If you are new to image editing or graphics creation, Elements offers a great way to get up and running quickly. The learning curve isn't as steep with Elements as it is with Photoshop, and many features in Elements can be done easily with one click. Let's also not forget cost. After you buy that expensive digital camera, you will be looking to save all the spare change you can. For the price of one Photoshop, you could buy almost seven copies of Elements! (Not to mention the copies of Elements that are bundled with various hardware items such as scanners and digital cameras.) That cost difference isn't just for hoots, however.

But what can Photoshop do that Elements can't? Why would someone want to spend the extra cash to buy Photoshop? *The* main reason (in my opinion) is that Photoshop is geared more towards professionals who require the capability of creating images for high-quality printing (for those of you "in-the-know," that means that Photoshop can create CMYK, Lab, and Multichannel images—a feature Photoshop Elements lacks). Photoshop also gives you more options when preparing to put your images on a Web site and other nifty ways of selecting and modifying an image. Other than that, and the increased power and flexibility of a few different features and tools, Elements is—for the most part—Photoshop with an easy-to-use, helpful, and intuitive interface (and lower price tag!).

Image Size and Resolution

As you work with images from your digital camera, from your scanner, from a frame of video, or from the Web, you are going to be dealing with images that are all different sizes and resolutions (the amount of detail—or pixels—in an image). All of the images you will be working with in Elements are comprised of pixels—tiny squares of color and value (that's brightness/darkness, not tiny squares of high morals).

Throughout this book I refer to the *size* of an image and the *resolution* of an image. You need to understand what these two disparate terms mean because they play an essential role in how detailed the image is and how big it is when you print it.

The quantity of those pixels in an image determines how detailed the image actually is. Pixels are measured by a specific unit; in the United States, it is usually inches. So an image that you bring in from your scanner may be 200ppi (pixels per inch), whereas an image that you get off a Web page is most likely 72ppi. Separate from the *resolution* of an image is the *size* of the image—the actual dimensions of the image in inches, centimeters, millimeters, and so on. The size of the image is obviously important because it determines how big your image will be when it is printed, posted onto a Web site, or emailed to your friends and family. The size and resolution of an image are related because changing one affects the other. You'll learn more about that in Chapter 3, "*Opening and Importing Images*."

What's New in Version 2.0

Version 2.0 of Photoshop Elements added a few new and greatly helpful features:

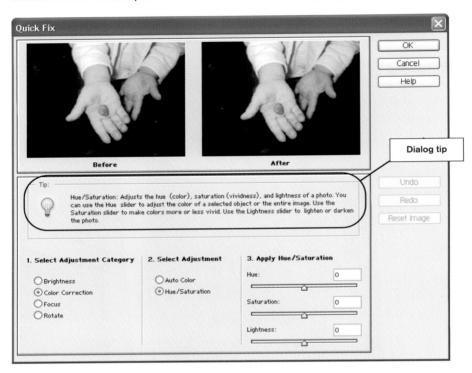

- **Dialog tips:** In Elements, certain complex windows (dialog boxes), or those that offer many options, have dialog tips. Dialog tips are little bits of handy information, relevant to whatever you are trying to accomplish and built right into the dialog window. How useful is that?!

- **Smart Messages:** This is one of those features that makes you say "Now why don't all programs have this?". When you are working in Elements and you trigger an error message for one reason or another, that error message will oftentimes have a link in it. Clicking on the link will give you more detailed information about what that error message means in plain, easy-to-understand terms. Thank goodness!

• **Help search field:** Built in to one of the toolbars is a help search field. Entering in a word or words that you are confused with will provide you with a detailed explanation. I wish life had a built-in search field. *Sigh*

• **Quick Fix:** Quick Fix borrows the same name as my morning ritual of pounding down four cups of black tea in under an hour, and it is a great timesaving feature to boot! Nicely consolidated within one window, you can perform a multitude of color correction and manipulation tasks such as modifying the brightness, color, focus, and rotation of an image, which is a great feature when you're "on the run."

- **Frame From Video:** This feature allows you to select a video file and quickly and easily extract one or more still pictures from that video source. Turn that video camera into a still-shot digital camera with the click of a button! Frame From Video is great for extracting those perfect frames from your home movies.

- **Selection Brush:** Quickly and easily select a portion of your image just by painting! The new Selection Brush tool allows you to select just a portion of your image by painting with your paintbrush, which is a great way to very easily and quickly create a selection. I use this feature many more times throughout this book.

• **PDF Slideshow:** Now you can take a collection of your photos and automatically create an interactive PDF (**P**ortable **D**ocument **F**ormat) slideshow! PDFs are read by the Adobe Reader, which comes bundled for free with many different software packages. As a matter of fact, a free installer for the Adobe Acrobat Reader is on your Photoshop Elements installer CD-ROM. This feature is a great way to spice up that photo trip to the Utah Salt Flats, ensuring complete attention from whoever is viewing it. Because it's a PDF, you're also nearly guaranteed that the recipient probably already has the necessary software (Adobe Acrobat Reader) installed to view it.

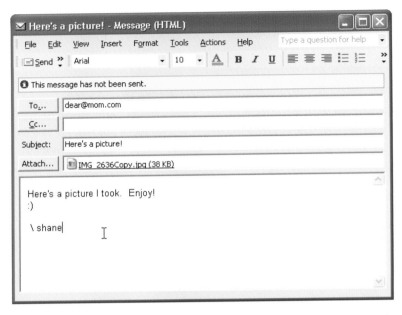

- **Attach to E-mail:** This one-click button allows you to take one of your photos and attach it to an e-mail. Photoshop Elements eliminates all the guesswork by automatically resizing your image to something more suitable for sending via email and compresses it for you as a JPEG. This ensures that the person on the receiving end of the email can download it quickly and will be able to view it with minimal difficulty.

- **Optimization:** Last but certainly not least, Photoshop Elements has been optimized for Mac OS X and Windows XP operating systems. Hurray!

Updates

At the time of writing this book, only three updates to Photoshop Elements 2.0 are available. The first two updates are for Mac users only. The first update addresses an issue with color and certain digital cameras, and the second update addresses an issue with localized language versions of Elements (if you're using Elements in a language other than English) and an automated feature called the WebContactSheet plug-in. The third update is for Windows users and addresses performance issues with certain plug-ins for users with Pentium 4 computers. You can download these updates (as well as any future program updates) from Adobe's Web site at **http://www.adobe.com/support/downloads**.

Now that you have a better understanding of Photoshop Elements, how it compares to Photoshop 7.0, and the differences between image size and resolution, you are going to move on to learning the interface of Adobe Elements in the next chapter.

2.

Interface

Welcome Screen	Interface	Menu Bar
Toolbox	Shortcuts Bar	Palettes
Palette Well	Options Bar

chap_02

Photoshop Elements 2
H•O•T CD-ROM

This chapter offers an introduction to the main items of the Photoshop Elements interface. If you have used other Adobe programs before, such as Photoshop, Illustrator, InDesign, and so on, you should feel right at home in the interface of Photoshop Elements thanks to the commonality of the interface design in the majority of Adobe's applications. You'll be dealing with most of the major interface items as you build projects and work through exercises in later chapters, but this chapter offers a brief tour of a few essential items that comprise the Elements interface.

The Welcome Screen

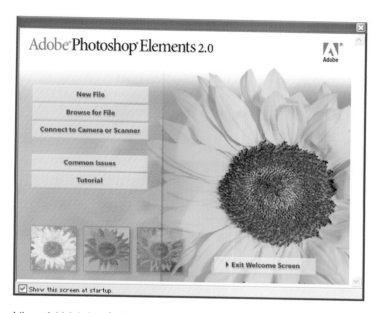

Like a faithful dog (without the slobber and bad breath, of course), Photoshop Elements happily greets you with a welcome screen every time you start the program. From this window you can easily do a variety of common tasks with a single click.

New File

The **New File** button will prompt you with settings to create a new, blank file. (You'll find more about creating new files in Chapter 3, "*Opening and Importing Images*.")

Browse for File

The **Browse for File** button will open up the powerful **File Browser** window, where you can quickly browse through all of the images on your hard drive and get information about each one *before* you open it (a great timesaving feature).

Connect to Camera or Scanner

The **Connect to Camera or Scanner** button brings up the **Select Input Source** window. If you have installed the drivers correctly for your digital camera or scanner, and if those devices are connected and turned on, you should see their names appear from the Import pull-down menu. Simply select a device, and Elements will launch the camera or scanner software, which will take over from there.

Common Issues

The **Common Issues** button will open the **How To** window with links to articles on…well…common issues that you may need resolved when working in Photoshop Elements. Clicking on one of the **Common Issues** links will show you step-by-step instructions (Adobe calls these "Recipes") on how to complete that particular task. It will even offer to complete many of the steps for you if you need extra help!

Tutorial

The **Tutorial** button launches your Web browser to display the help files on tutorials. The tutorials are similar to the How To window (described briefly in the preceding paragraph) but are more in-depth and usually revolve around completing a specific task, such as animating with layers, creating a greeting card, and so on.

▶ Exit Welcome Screen

The **Exit Welcome Screen button** causes a hot tub to appear in your living room and…oh wait. That's in Elements version 3. ;-)

The **Exit Welcome Screen** is pretty self-explanatory. Clicking on it just closes the window and deposits you in the Elements interface.

☑ Show this screen at startup.

Lastly, as you become more familiar with Elements, you may not need the assistance that the welcome screen provides and may grow tired of clicking on the Exit Welcome Screen button each time Elements launches. Adobe realized this and has put a **Show this screen at startup** check box at the bottom of the welcome screen. Uncheck this check box if you don't want the welcome screen to open automatically every time Elements is launched.

Fear not, though. Your old friend hasn't been banished to some great Adobe abyss, never to be seen from again. If you feel that you need access to the welcome screen anew, you can always easily open it back up by choosing **Window > Welcome**.

Photoshop Elements Interface

Menu Bar

File Edit Image Enhance Layer Select Filter View Window Help

As with pretty much every other program for your computer, Elements has a **menu bar** at the top of the screen. The menu bar is a series of options, all organized by topic. In Elements, the choices are File, Edit, Image, Enhance, Layer, Select, Filter, View, Window, and Help.

Many common and useful tasks in Elements are located inside these menus. For example, if you wanted to adjust the brightness or contrast of an image, you would click on **Enhance > Adjust Brightness/Contrast > Brightness/Contrast**. You will be using many options from the menu bar over the course of this book, so you'll get plenty of practice learning and understanding where everything is.

Toolbox

The **Toolbox**, as its name implies, is the box where all your tools are stored. From here you will select all the tools that you'll need to manipulate, select, modify, and work with your images. At the very bottom of the Toolbox is where you can select foreground and background colors for use in your image. You can also reposition the Toolbox (much like many of the other windows in Elements) anywhere you'd like on your screen. Simply drag it from its title bar to wherever you would like to move it.

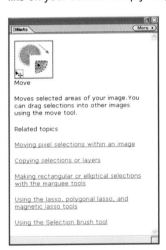

If you hover your mouse over one of the tools in the Toolbox, the Hints palette (if you have it open) will show you a brief hint, or a little information, about the tool your mouse is hovering over (a *very* useful feature). It's somewhat like those little help balloons that you might have seen before, but on steroids because the hint also gives you helpful links to other related topics!

Warning: Moving your mouse cursor off of a tool in the Toolbox will cause the Hints palette to go back to its default display. If you want to read more in the Hints palette about a tool you're hovering your mouse over in the Toolbox, click on the tool to select it. Then you can scroll through the Hints palette information and click on any available links.

To select a tool to use, simply click on it. The tool that you currently have selected will be highlighted in your Toolbox.

You'll also notice that certain tools in the Toolbox have a small, black triangle just below the lower-right corner of the tool. These tools have additional "hidden" tools. Contrary to the exciting and mysterious name, hidden tools are usually just tools that do similar things, but because of their separate capabilities have been broken off into their own tool. To access one of these hidden tools, simply click and hold on one of the tools that has a black triangle at its lower right, and you'll be presented with a small submenu of the hidden tools.

One other useful item, at the top of the Toolbox, is the Elements logo—a sunflower. Clicking on the sunflower will take you to Adobe Online, a central repository to download updates and add-ons for Elements.

You will learn more about the tools in the Toolbox in greater detail throughout the remainder of the chapters in this book. Rather than describe (in boring detail) what each tool does, I instead prefer to show you how the tools perform in the context of editing or creating a graphic.

Shortcuts Bar

The **shortcuts bar** is essentially a collection of buttons that gives you easy, one-click access to common commands. Everything that you can do in the shortcuts bar you can also accomplish via the menu bar, except it takes fewer clicks with the shortcuts bar, and common tasks are all nicely organized and sorted out in the open for you. One extremely useful feature of the shortcuts bar is the Help search field. Need help with something? Want to know what the Selection Brush is? Type in your question in the Help search field, click the **Search** button, and you're presented with a list of possible answers in a Search Results window. Clicking on one of those results opens your Web browser and displays a detailed answer to your question. How awesome is that?

Here is a breakdown of the buttons on the shortcuts bar and what they do:

Shortcuts Bar Buttons	
Button	**Description**
New	Opens the New Image dialog box, where you can specify settings to create a new image.
Open	Opens the Open dialog box, where you can choose an image to open.
Browse	Opens the File Browser, where you can browse through your computer for an image to open.
Import	Opens the Select Import Source dialog box, where you can choose a device (scanner, digital camera, and so on) to import images from.
Save	Saves changes you've made to your image. If you haven't yet saved your Elements image, clicking the Save button opens the Save As window where you can specify a location/name to save your image.
	continues on next page

Shortcuts Bar Buttons *continued*	
Button	**Description**
Save for Web	Opens the Save for Web window, where you can specify compression settings to save your image in a format suitable for e-mailing or posting to a Web site (GIF, JPEG, and so on).
Save as PDF	Opens the Save window, where you can choose a location/name to save your image as a PDF file.
Attach to E-mail	Can automatically save your image in a format suitable for sending over e-mail (JPEG); automatically launches your default e-mail client, and attaches your image to a new email.
Online Services	Connects to Adobe Online and opens the Online Services Assistant window, where you can download add-ons to Elements as well as connect to online providers such as photo printing companies and online photo sharing companies. Internet access is required for this feature.
Print	Opens the Print window, where you can specify settings to print your image.
Print Preview	Opens the Print Preview window, where you can preview how the image will look and where it will be placed on paper when it is printed.
Step Backward	Undoes the last thing you did to your image. You can keep undoing your changes by repeatedly clicking on the Step Backward button. The number of steps backward allowed is specified in your preferences (the default is 20 steps).
Step Forward	The opposite of the Step Backward button. If you've used the Step Backward button to undo changes, the Step Forward button will redo the changes. Essentially, the Step Backward and Step Forward buttons allow you to go forward and backward through the history of your image.
Quick Fix	Opens the Quick Fix window, where you can easily modify the brightness, color, focus, and rotation of your image.
Color Variations	Opens the Color Variations window, where you can modify—in steps—the color of your image.
Search field	Use this field to enter in a term or terms you want to search the help documentation for. Clicking on the Search button will then perform a search.
Help	Launches Microsoft Internet Explorer and opens the HTML-based help documentation for Elements.

As you can see, the shortcuts bar lives up to its name and has buttons to quickly and easily access many of the frequently used items in Elements. You will practice using many of the shortcut buttons in later chapters.

Palettes

Organized by topic, *palettes* are small, floating windows that give you options and feedback about your images. When you first start using Elements, you may be a little overwhelmed by the quantity of palettes and all of the different options that you're given for each one. After working with a few of the palettes in later exercises, you'll be amazed at how simple Adobe has made it for you. The next section breaks down the different pieces and options of a standard palette.

Palettes that you will mostly likely be working with the most are the File Browser, Hints, How To, Layers, Filters, Effects, and Info…heck, almost all of them! You can see a list of the available palettes in the Window menu on the menu bar.

You can reposition a palette on your workspace by dragging its title bar. You can also easily change the size of a palette by dragging at any corner of the palette (Windows only) or by dragging from the size box at the lower-right corner. One other fantastic interface feature is that palettes can be clumped together into a palette group. You can group palettes together by dragging a palette's tab onto another palette.

Grouping palettes allows you to customize how the palettes are laid out as well as enabling you to quickly and easily refer back to them. For now, leave your palettes in their default order until you have learned a little more about Elements. If you have already moved them around, you can reset their positions by choosing **Window > Reset Palette Locations**. Once you feel you have a good grasp on the program, *then* go back and reorder the palettes in whichever way you feel is best for your workflow. To ungroup a palette, simply do the reverse of grouping: drag a palette's tab away onto the workspace and it then becomes ungrouped.

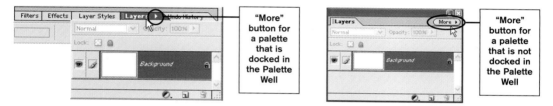

At the upper-right corner of each palette is a button labeled **More**. Clicking on this button will give you more options for that specific palette. Some (not all) palettes have their own preferences. You can access these palette preferences by clicking on the **More** button at the top of the palette and then choosing **Palette Options**.

Note: When a palette is in the Palette Well, the More button is replaced by a small, white triangle (visible only when you click on a palette tab in the Palette Well).

You will be dealing with various palettes and learning their different options throughout the exercises in later chapters.

The Palette Well

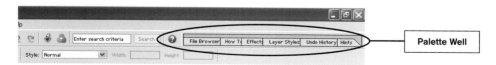

First introduced in Photoshop, the Palette Well was a great solution to the modern day problem of "Where do I put all these stinkin' palettes?!" Located (by default) to the right of the shortcuts bar, the Palette Well is essentially a place to store a few of your palettes that you want easy access to without cluttering up your workspace.

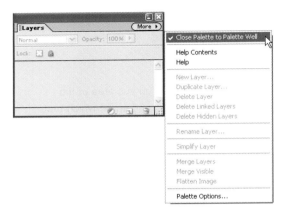

By clicking on the **More** button at the top right of a palette, you can choose the option **Close Palette to Palette Well**, which will make the palette appear in the Palette Well the next time you close that palette. Another way to add a palette to the Palette Well is to simply drag the palette (from its tab) onto the Palette Well.

Once a palette has been docked onto the Palette Well, click on its tab and it will open up to display its options. To remove a palette from the Palette Well, simply click on a palette tab to maximize it, then drag the tab off of the Palette Well. At this point in the book, you don't have much experience with the different palettes, so the practicality of the Palette Well may seem somewhat vague to you. But after you have used Elements for awhile, you will find that the Palette Well is a tremendous help in keeping your work environment organized. However, don't put any palettes in the Palette Well that you use often or refer to frequently because the content of docked palettes isn't continually visible (all you see is their tabs poking out of the Palette Well). I like to keep the File Browser, Undo History, Filters, and Effects palettes docked in the Palette Well. Other palettes such as Layers, Hints, and Info I keep out all the time because I use them often. However, in the screenshots in this book, you will see the Layers palette docked in the Palette Well. This was done simply to conserve space in my work environment while taking screenshots. For your own setup, I would still recommend leaving the Layers palette open and not docked to the Palette Well.

Options Bar

By default, the **options bar** is located right beneath the shortcuts bar. It's a unique area of the Elements interface—the options displayed in the options bar will change depending on which tool is currently selected.

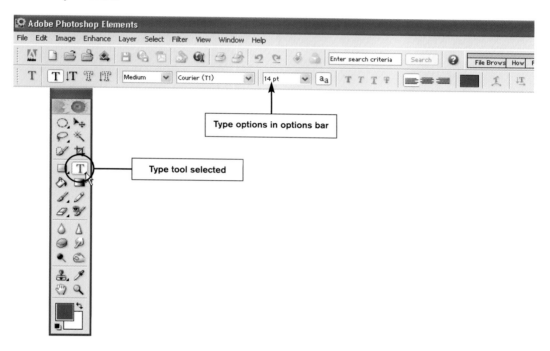

Type options in options bar

Type tool selected

Although some tools have very few options to choose from in the options bar (such as the Arrow tool and the Eyedropper tool), other tools have a large number of options (such as the Type tool and the Marquee tool, to name a few). The options bar is a very important part of the Elements interface. You will use it to modify how a few of your tools perform so that you can create certain effects or accomplish specific tasks. Again, rather than go over each option in the options bar (which would surely put you to sleep), I instead integrate learning about the options bar into the different exercises and examples that you will be building later in this book.

Now that you've had a brief tour of the Elements interface, next you're going to actually start opening and working with images. So batten down the hatches Matey, and shiver me timbers, and all that other good pirate stuff...here is where the fun begins. :-)

3.
Opening and Importing Images

| Supported Formats | Importing from a Scanner |
| Importing from a Digital Camera |
| Opening Images | File Browser | Place |
| Frame from Video | New Image | Image Modes |

chap_03

Photoshop Elements 2
H•O•T CD-ROM

This chapter walks you through the basic but fundamental steps of opening images, creating new images, and importing images from various sources. You'll learn how to use the File Browser, open scanned and digital camera images, create new images, place vector artwork into another file, grab a frame of video, and change image color modes. If that sounds like a mouthful of new skills, you'll gain confidence by following the exercises and getting a taste of hands-on experience using these features.

Supported Image Formats

As you begin to open and work with images in Elements, recognizing the different kinds of images that Elements can open is important. Images from different sources, such as your scanner, a Web page, or from an e-mail that someone sent you, will come in a variety of different formats. For example, most images on the Internet that look like photographs are probably saved in an image format called JPEG (also known as JPG). This is also a common image format that many digital cameras automatically store the photos you shoot as. However, if you were to scan an image on your desktop scanner, it would most likely be saved as a high-quality format such as TIFF, BMP, or PICT. For reference, here is a list of the different image formats that Elements can open:

Supported Image Formats	
Photoshop	PSD, PDD
BMP	BMP, RLE, DIB
CompuServe GIF	GIF
Photoshop EPS	EPS
EPS TIFF Preview	EPS
Filmstrip	FLM
JPEG	JPG, JPEG, JPE
Generic PDF	PDF, PDP, AI
Generic EPS	AI3, AI4, AI5, AI6, AI7, AI8, PS, EPS, AI
PCX	PCX
Photoshop PDF	PDF, PDP
Acrobat TouchUp Image	PDF, AI, PDP
Photo CD	PCD
PICT file	PCT, PICT
Pixar	PXR
PNG	PNG
Raw	RAW
Scitex CT	SCT
Targa	TGA, VDA, ICB, VST
TIFF	TIF, TIFF
Wireless bitmap	WBMP, WBM

I. ——————————Importing Images from a Scanner

Once you have connected your desktop scanner to your computer and correctly installed the software that came with it, scanning images and bringing them into Elements to edit is a breeze. If your scanner software installs either Photoshop Elements–compatible plug-in modules or TWAIN drivers (refer to your scanner's user manual or to the scanner manufacturer's Web site to see if it does, in fact, support these features), follow these steps:

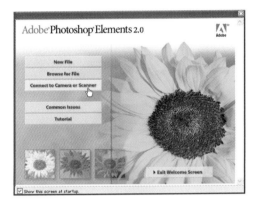

1. From the welcome screen, click on the **Connect to Camera or Scanner** button. This will open the **Select Import Source** dialog box.

2. If you've installed the software correctly, you should see the name of your scanner from the pull-down menu. In the screenshot above, I've selected my scanner, an **Epson Perfection 1650**.

3. Select your scanner name from the pull-down menu and click **OK**. This will launch your scanner software. From this point you can proceed with scanning your images by following the instructions that come with your scanner software.

Note: *These steps don't demonstrate how to scan images from your particular scanner because the process differs widely depending on the brand and model of scanner you are using.*

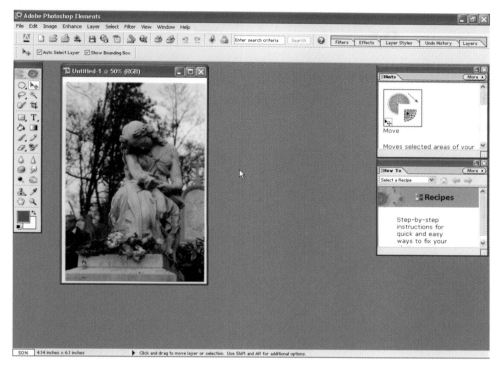

4. After you have scanned your photograph (in this case, a picture of Chopin's grave in Paris), it should appear in a new window within Elements. From here you can edit and modify it (as you'll learn in later chapters) to your heart's content!

The process of scanning a photograph and then opening that photograph in Elements is relatively simple. Most of the work is done by the actual scanner software that came with your scanner. Elements merely acts as a façade for your scanner software.

*Tip: Instead of clicking on the **Connect to Camera or Scanner** button on the welcome screen, you can also access your scanner by choosing **File > Import** and choosing your scanner name there. You should see the same list of input options that you get from the Select Input Source window that you access from the welcome screen.*

Note: If your scanner does not come with Photoshop Elements–compatible plug-ins or TWAIN scanner drivers, you will not see your scanner name listed from the File > Import menu. Instead, you will have to use the scanner software that came with your scanner to scan in your image. From the scanner software, simply save the scanned image as a TIFF, PICT, or BMP, and then open that image in Elements. From Elements, first resave your scanned image as a Photoshop file (PSD), then work with the image as you normally would.

2.————————**Importing Images from a Digital Camera**

The process of importing images from a digital camera is nearly identical to the process of importing images from a scanner. After you have correctly installed the camera software, you can follow these steps:

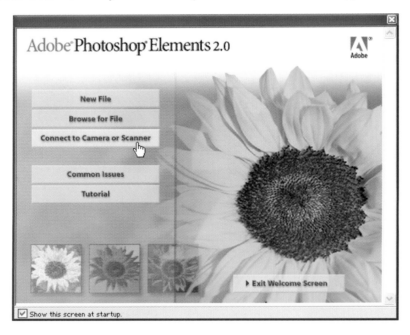

1. From the welcome screen, click on the **Connect to Camera or Scanner** button. If you don't have your welcome screen open, you can open it again by choosing **Window > Welcome**.

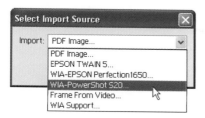

2. Click on the **Select Import Source** pull-down menu and choose your camera name. If you don't see your camera listed here, make sure that you have the camera drivers correctly installed (refer to your camera's user manual for driver installation instructions) and that you're using the latest version of those camera drivers (refer to the camera manufacturer's Web site for the latest drivers). In my case, I've selected my camera, a **Canon PowerShot S20**. Click **OK**.

At this point, Elements will launch the software that came with your digital camera (assuming you installed all the software correctly). Because the bundled software for digital cameras differs widely, these steps don't show this process. Refer to the manual that came with your digital camera for more information on retrieving images from the camera.

After you have selected and imported your image(s) from your digital camera, Elements automatically opens them. From there, you can save the images as Photoshop documents (PSD) and may modify/edit them.

Note: *Some digital cameras, when connected to your computer, mount themselves on your Desktop the same way a hard drive or CD-ROM does (you'll see a camera icon appear on your Desktop). In this case, you cannot access the camera images from the **Connect to Camera or Scanner** button in the welcome screen, nor from the **File > Import** menu. Instead you can use Elements' **File Browser** feature (which you'll learn about later in this chapter), or you can choose **File > Open** to navigate to and open the digital camera's images. Once you've opened the image(s) in Elements, you can save them as Adobe Photoshop (PSD) documents and can then modify/edit them as you would any Elements image.*

The trickiest part to the process of importing images from a digital camera or scanner is making sure that you install the camera or scanner software correctly. Once you've done that, the rest is a breeze.

—————————Opening Images

Showing you how to best use Photoshop Elements without showing you how to open an image would be like showing you how to drive a Ferrari and not giving you the keys. It would be like your parents raising you and teaching you everything there is to know in life, but never letting you leave the house. It would be like…well…you get the point. Opening an image is a very simple but fundamental piece in working with any program.

1. Copy the **chap_03** folder and files from the **H•O•T CD-ROM** to your hard drive.

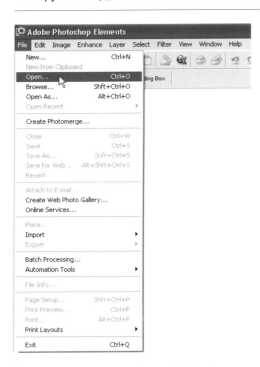

2. From the menu bar, choose **File > Open**.

*This brings up the **Open** dialog box. This window will look different depending on the operating system you're using (Windows XP, Windows 2000, Mac OS 9, Mac OS X, and so on), but the basic concept remains the same. Within the Open dialog box you can browse, locate, and open any file that is supported by Photoshop Elements (for a list of supported file formats, see the chart at the beginning of this chapter).*

3. From the **Open** dialog box, browse to where you copied the **chap_03** folder. Because I copied mine to the Desktop, I'm going to browse there.

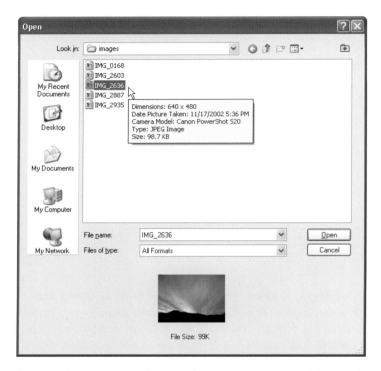

4. Open the **chap_03** folder, and then open the **images** folder. In the images folder, you should see five images. Click once on one of the images to see a small preview of the image. If you're using Windows XP, hovering your mouse over the image will also show you more information about that image, such as the dimensions, when the picture was taken, and so on. This same information is also available on other operating systems; it is just located elsewhere (I show you where in later chapters).

5. Double-click on **IMG_2636**. Elements opens the image.

6. Because you won't be needing this image again in this exercise, close it by choosing **File > Close**.

Double-clicking on an image from your hard drive doesn't always open that image in Elements. That particular file type (JPG, GIF, TIFF, and so on) might not be associated with Elements. Double-clicking on an image file might cause that image to open in a different program. In the Windows version of Elements, Adobe has added an easy way for you to change which image file types should be opened with Elements when they're double-clicked.

By choosing **Edit > File Association** *(a Windows-only feature...sorry fellow Macintosh users), you can pick and choose which file types should be opened with Elements when double-clicked.*

Putting checkmarks next to the different file types will instruct Windows to launch Elements when you double-click an image with one of those file types. Nifty!

Using the File Browser Palette

In the last exercise, you saw how to easily open an image using the File > Open command. In this exercise, you're going to look at a much more "feature-rich" way of opening images that gives you a lot of information about an image before you choose to open it—a very useful feature if you're dealing with large images that take a long time to open. First introduced in Photoshop, the File Browser is my preferred method for browsing and opening images. The File Browser allows you to not only browse and open images, but also move, rename, delete, and rotate images, as well as create new folders. It'll even provide you with a detailed description of the specifics of each image, such as the date the picture was taken, the shutter speed, F-stop settings, and a whole bunch of other information that you never knew existed (if your digital camera stores what's called "EXIF" data; if not, the File Browser will just display basic information about the image, such as file size, dimensions, and so on). Now if I can just get it to file my taxes for me as well…

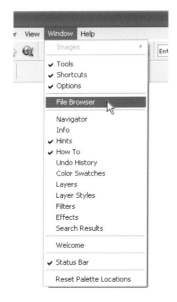

1. First make sure that you have the File Browser window open by choosing **Window > File Browser**.

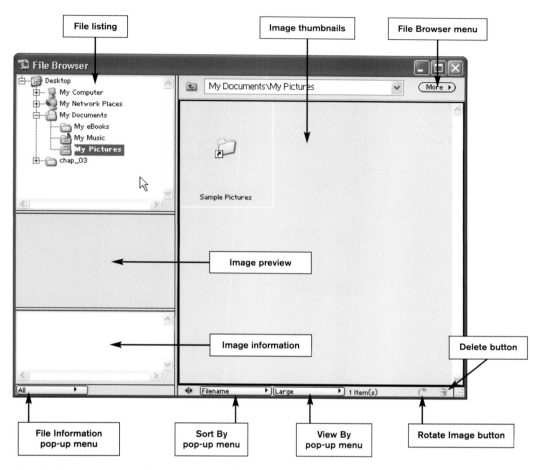

File listing

Image thumbnails

File Browser menu

Image preview

Image information

Delete button

File Information pop-up menu

Sort By pop-up menu

View By pop-up menu

Rotate Image button

*The File Browser window is broken up into four main parts. The file listing section is where you browse through your computer's hard drive. The image thumbnails section is where you see small thumbnails of the images and folders within the directory that is currently selected in the file listing section. The image preview section is where you can see a small preview of an image that you select in the image thumbnails section. Lastly, the image information section gives you various feedback and information about the image that is selected in the image thumbnails section. *whew**

2. In the file listing section, navigate to where you copied the chap_03 files and click on the **maximize view** button to the left of the **chap_03** folder (in the Mac File Browser window, the maximize and minimize icons are gray triangles instead of plus and minus signs). This will expand the folder and display the subfolders. Click on the **images** folder to display the contents of that directory. You should see five image thumbnails appear in the image thumbnails section. Single-click on one of the thumbnails.

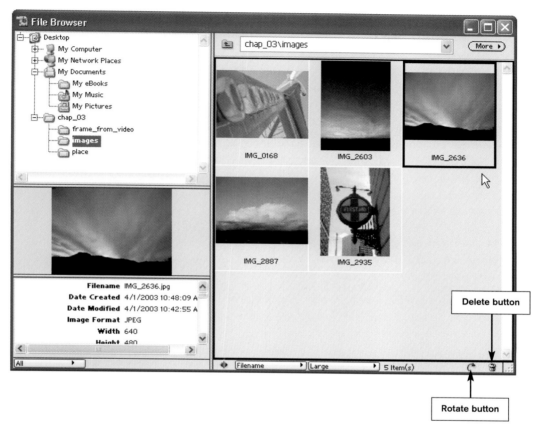

When you select an image from the image thumbnails section, you'll see a larger thumbnail appear in the image preview section and a detailed description appear in the image information section. If your camera stores EXIF data (see the manual that came with your camera), you'll see a very detailed description of the image including the exact time it was taken, the exposure time, the F-stop setting, and a whole bunch of other information that most digital cameras create automatically when you take a photo. How's that for being helpful?

3. Double-click on one of the image thumbnails to open the full-sized image. After you've opened the image, go ahead and close it again (by choosing **File > Close**) because you won't be needing it again in this exercise. I know, I know…opening and closing images is fun and all, but try to stay with me here. Focusss…focussss…

Note: As I mentioned in the introduction to this exercise, the File Browser can do much more than just browse for and open images. Once you have an image thumbnail selected, you can rotate it by clicking on the Rotate button, and you can delete it by clicking on the Delete button. By clicking on the File Browser menu button, you can see that there are many more options available, such as renaming the image (and even options for renaming multiple files at a time [batch renaming], creating new folders, and so on). I'm not going to be the one responsible for causing you to lapse into a coma by going over what each option does here, but you will get a chance to use quite a few of these File Browser features in later exercises.

4. Click on the **File Browser** menu button at the top right of the File Browser palette, and from the pop-up menu choose **Dock to Palette Well**. This docks the File Browser to the Palette Well, where you can easily access it by simply clicking on its tab.

*You will be using the File Browser quite a bit throughout the remainder of the exercises in this book, so no need to say goodbye. You'll! be working with it again soon enough. *sniffle**

5. ————————Place

Now that you've seen various ways of opening images, you'll learn one method of combining multiple documents together. In this simple exercise, you're going to use the Place feature of Elements to add a logo to a business card.

1. Using the File Browser, navigate to where you copied your chap_03 folder on your computer, open the **chap_03** folder, and single-click on the **place** folder within it. You should see two image files: **business_card_base** and **blot_logo**.

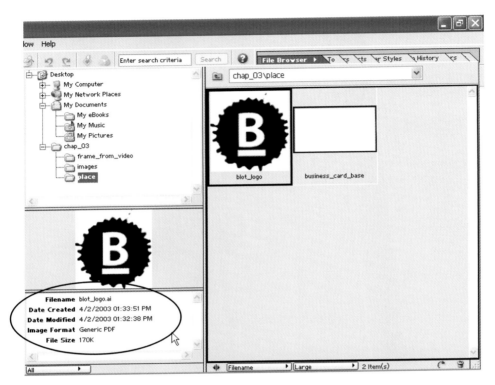

2. Single-click on the **blot_logo** image thumbnail. In the image preview section, you can see that the image is a logo for my illustration business, Blot Illustration. Also note that in the image information section (circled above) you can see that the Image Format is Generic PDF. You're going to use the Elements Place command to add this image file to the other image in the **place** folder, **business_card_base**.

The Place command will only allow you to place PDF, Adobe Illustrator, or EPS (Encapsulated PostScript) files into other images. You'll be learning more about PDF files in Chapter 12, "Elements and the Web." Now that you've seen what format the blot_logo image is in, you're going to open the business card and add the logo to it.

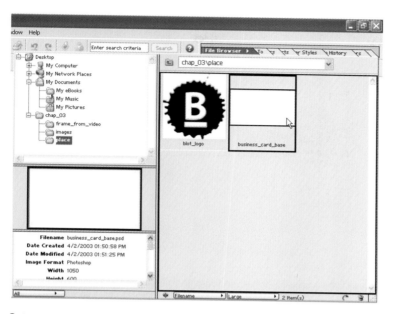

3. In the File Browser, double-click on the **business_card_base** image thumbnail. This will open the image in a new window in Elements.

4. Choose **File > Place**. This will open the **Place** window, which looks and functions much like the Open window you learned about earlier in this chapter. The difference with the Place window, however, is that now you're browsing for a file to place inside the image you currently have open, **business_card_base**.

Windows XP   *Macintosh OS X*

5. In the **Place** dialog box, navigate to the **chap_03** folder and into the **place** folder. You should see one file, **blot_logo**. Double-click on it.

Note: The Mac OS X Place window looks a little different than the Windows XP one (pictured above). I've also included a screenshot of the Macintosh Place window (also pictured above) for you Mac users out there…you know who you are. ;-)

This places the Blot Illustration logo right in the middle of the business card image.

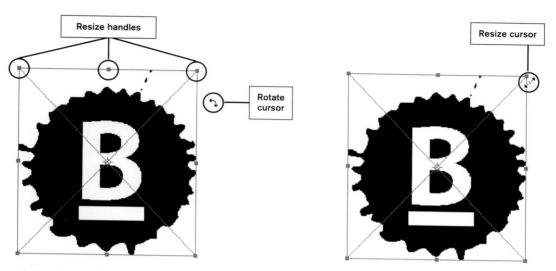

Notice the gray box around the outside of the logo with gray boxes on the corners and the middles of the box. These are called resize handles. Dragging the resize handles around will cause the logo to...well...resize! Also note that moving your mouse cursor over the resize handles causes your cursor icon to change to two opposite-facing arrows.

Tip: Resizing a placed graphic (such as the Blot Illustration logo) might cause the logo to be resized nonproportionally (meaning it might get squished or stretched). To resize a graphic proportionately as you drag its resize handles, hold down the **Shift** key while dragging. Also, if you hold the **Option** key (Mac) or **Alt** key (Windows) as you drag the resize handles, the graphic will resize from the center instead of from the bottom-left.

Moving your mouse cursor off to the sides or to the top or bottom of the graphic, you'll notice that your cursor changes again, this time to a Rotate icon. Dragging your mouse around will cause the placed logo to rotate.

Note: If you're more of a numbers person, you can also resize, rotate, and skew your placed graphic numerically from the options bar.

6. To increase the size of the logo a little, hold down the **Option+Shift** keys (Mac) or **Alt+Shift** keys (Windows) and then drag one of the corner resize handles up.

7. Once you're satisfied with the logo's size, you need to "commit place." I know that this sounds like a very serious thing to do (especially for you bachelors out there who shirk from the word "commit"), but all it means is simply that Elements needs to know when you're finished resizing the placed file. Up until this point the Blot Illustration logo is a vector graphic (see Chapter 7, "*Shapes and Layer Styles,*" for a full description of vector graphics and bitmap graphics). Once you commit place, however, Elements changes it from a vector graphic to a bitmap graphic. From that point on, you shouldn't resize the placed graphic to a larger size, because it will look distorted and unattractive. You can scale a bitmap graphic smaller and it will look fine, but if you scale it larger it will not. To commit place, simply press **Return** (Mac) or **Enter** (Windows). You can also click on the **Commit Place** button in your options bar.

Note: *The Place command is essentially designed to place a vector graphic (Adobe Illustrator, PDF, EPS) inside of another image document—in this case, a business card.*

*Before you click on the Commit Place button, some of you might be wondering what that **Anti-Alias** check box does. Leaving this check box checked will anti-alias your placed graphic (it will smooth the edges of the graphic) when you commit the place. Unchecking the Anti-Alias check box will alias the graphic (it won't smooth the edges of the graphic; instead it will be jagged) when you commit the place.*

8. Choose **File > Save As**. Name the file **business_card**, make sure that **Format** is set to **Photoshop**, and save it in the **chap_03** folder. You'll be using this business card again in later exercises. After you save the **business_card** file, close it by choosing **File > Close**.

*Note: Performing a Save As on a file will allow you to save your file as a different name and/or in a different location on your computer. That way you won't permanently overwrite the file that you originally opened (**business_card_base**).*

Congratulations! You just merged two separate image files together! That is the fundamental, rudimentary idea behind photo compositing, which you'll be learning about in Chapter 11, "Photo Manipulation."

Video Formats Supported by Elements 2.0

In the next exercise, you'll learn how to import a frame of video into Elements. Don't worry if you don't have any video on your hard drive to import; you'll find a sample movie to work with in the **chap_03** exercise folder. To import your own video files, here is a helpful chart listing the video formats that Photoshop Elements will accept on both Macs and Windows.

Accepted Video Formats		
	Macintosh	Windows
AVI		X
WMV		X
ASF		X
MPG	X	X
MPEG	X	X
M1V		X
MOV (QuickTime)	X	

6. _____Frame From Video

Frame From Video is one of the cool, new features of Elements 2.0. Simply, it allows you to grab a frame—or multiple frames—from a video file. Elements won't actually get the video off of your video camera—that you have to do yourself. But once you have your video saved in a format that Elements supports, you can use the Frame From Video feature to grab some still frames from it. Why the heck would you need this? Say you have some video clips—of the kids that you want the grandparents to see, or maybe some vacation footage that you want to show off to your friends—but you don't really want to wait 10 hours while you e-mail them a 50MB video file over your 56k modem. Instead you can just peruse through your movie file, grab some choice frames, and then e-mail them to whomever you'd like. The video camera also doubles nicely as a dual-purpose digital camera, but one that you can sort through and pick out the best pictures from. Granted, the resolution of a still picture taken from a video camera isn't usually digital camera–quality, but if you're just e-mailing a snapshot to some friends or posting pictures to a Web site for family to see, it really makes little difference.

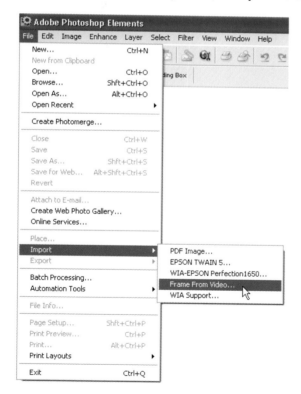

1. Choose **File > Import > Frame From Video.**

2. This will open the **Frame From Video** window. First you need to select the video that you want to grab a frame from. Click **Browse**.

3. The **Open** window will appear. Navigate to the **chap_03** folder and then into the **frame_from_video** folder. If you're running Windows, click on the file **eating_cake_win** and then click **Open**. On a Mac, click on the file **eating_cake_mac** and then click **Open**.

*Note: The file **eating_cake_win** is encoded as an AVI (**A**udio **V**ideo **I**nterleave) file whereas the **eating_cake_mac** is encoded as a QuickTime movie file.*

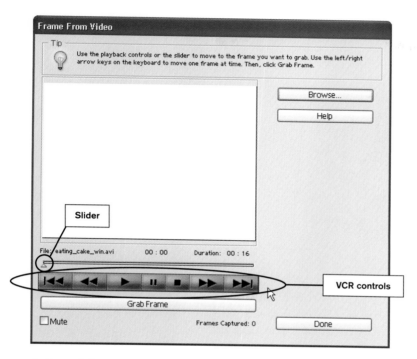

4. Now all that you need to do is pick the frame(s) you want to "grab." There are three methods from which to choose from when reviewing a video clip. You can use the VCR-type controls to play through the video and pause on the frame you want to grab. You can drag the slider back and forth until you've located the frame you want to keep. Or, you can use the left and right arrow keys on your keyboard to navigate through the video clip one frame at a time. Of course, you can also use all three of these methods in combination to find the exact frame that you want.

I use a combination of all three methods. I start with the VCR controls to find the general area of the video I want. Then I switch to the slider to get closer to my preferred frame. Lastly I switch to the ever-so-precise right and left arrows on my keyboard to browse through the video one frame at a time until I've located the exact frame I'm looking for.

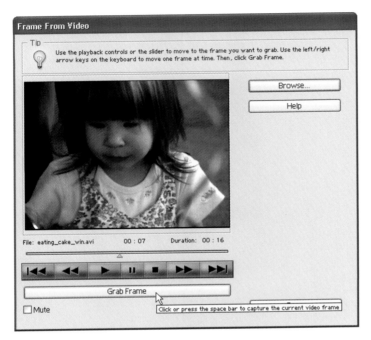

5. Once you've located the frame of the video you want to grab, click **Grab Frame**. You'll notice a slight pause, and then behind the Frame From Video window will appear the frame of video that you grabbed, but now in its own window! Awesome! In later chapters, you'll learn what you can do with those images, including manipulating them, putting them on a Web page, e-mailing them to friends and family, and so on.

6. You can continue browsing through the video and clicking **Grab Frame** each time you see a video frame that you like. Elements keeps a running tally of how many frames you've captured from this particular clip. When you're done, click **Done**.

7. You won't be needing these images again, so close them by choosing **File > Close**. If you are prompted to save your changes, click **No**.

For those of you that dabble in video, this is a great way to easily pull individual still images out of the video clip to edit, manipulate, or e-mail to friends and relatives.

7. ————————**Creating a New Image**

In this exercise, you will learn the process of creating a new image in Elements. Just like opening an image, creating a new, blank image is one of the fundamental need-to-knows.

1. Choose **File > New**.

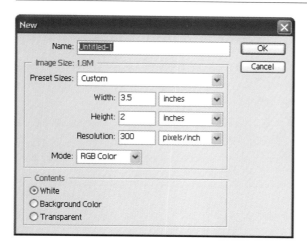

2. Change the settings to match what you see in the image above.

In the screenshot above, I'm creating a new image to design a business card in. It's 3.5 inches wide, 2 inches tall and, because it is going to be printed, is at a high resolution of 300 ppi. The table on the following page summarizes the options you can set when creating a new image.

New Image Options	
Option	**Description**
Name	Give your image a name here (optional). This name is used when saving your file. If you don't enter a name in here, Elements will prompt you for a name when you save the file.
Preset Sizes	Select, from a large list, preset image sizes for common uses such as **Letter**, **Legal**, **5 × 7**, and so on. Alternatively, you can set your own custom image size in the Width and Height fields.
Width and Height	Choose what your measurement unit is (**inches**, **pixels**, **mm**, and so on) and then enter in your dimensions in the Width and Height fields.
Resolution	You can see as you change the number in the Resolution field that it has no effect on the physical size of the image. The resolution determines how many pixels per inch your image contains (although clicking on the Resolution pull-down menu also lets you set the amount of pixels per centimeter). The higher the resolution is, the more detailed the image is when printed. If an image is going to be e-mailed or posted on a Web site, I would suggest setting the resolution to something low, like 72 ppi.
Mode	Allows you to set the mode for this image, such as **RGB Color** (RGB stands for **R**ed, **G**reen, **B**lue, by the way), **Grayscale**, or **Bitmap.** You'll learn about these image modes in more detail in the section that follows this exercise.
Background Layer	Choose what the initial layer contains, such as white, whatever the Background Color is set to in your Toolbox, or to just have it be transparent. (More on layers in Chapter 4, "*Layers*.")

3. Click **OK**. A new, blank Elements window is opened.

You will be creating (and opening) quite a few images during the course of this book, so you'll get plenty of experience with setting and understanding these new image options.

4. You won't be needing this blank image again, so close it by choosing **File > Close**.

What Are Image Modes?

When creating a new image (as you just saw in the last exercise), you have three choices for image modes: **RGB Color**, **Grayscale**, and **Bitmap**. What do these image modes mean and when should you choose one over another?

RGB Color is pretty self-explanatory. If you want to create a color image, you want to set your image mode to RGB Color. Elements—unbeknownst to you for the most part—divides your image up into three "channels:" red, green, and blue. RGB images, on the whole, are mostly used to be displayed onscreen, such as images sent via e-mail or posted onto a Web site. However, most common consumer inkjet printers also print RGB images quite well so don't worry about your images looking like a color disaster when they're printed.

Grayscale is another self-explanatory one. It's used when you want to create a black-and-white image. A grayscale image has no color information, so you'll only be able to work with black, white, and all of the grays in-between. Grayscale images are mostly used when working with black-and-white photography. After you've created a grayscale image, you can easily change it to an RGB color image if you'd like by simply choosing **Image > Mode > RGB Color**.

The last image mode option is Bitmap. An image that has a color mode of Bitmap is comprised of only black or white—no grays and no color. Bitmap color mode images are mostly used for line art (drawings). However, if you are going to edit an image that has an image mode of Bitmap, Elements requires that you change the image mode to something else first, such as grayscale or RGB color.

Working with Image Modes

In this exercise, you will learn to change the color mode of an image. You will open a color RGB image and convert it to Grayscale and Bitmap modes, observing how the image changes as you alter the image modes.

1. Open the **File Browser** and navigate to the **chap_03** folder and into the **images** folder. In there, locate the image **IMG_2935** (the first aid sign) and open it by double-clicking on it.

To give you an idea of the different color modes and what they look like, you're going to modify the color mode of this image.

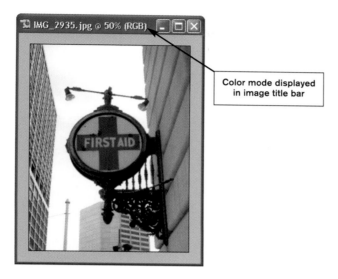

You can tell what the color mode is by looking at the image title bar.

2. Choose **Image > Mode > Grayscale**. You'll then be presented with a dialog box that's there just to make sure that you didn't click on that menu item by mistake. It says **Discard color information?**. And yes, you're purposely converting this image to grayscale, so click **OK**. Once you do that, presto! You now have a black-and-white image.

3. Now choose **Image > Mode > Bitmap**. You'll be presented with the **Bitmap** dialog box asking you what you want the resolution of the output image to be as well as what method of bitmap translation you want. Leave the resolution set to **180**, but change the method to **50% Threshold**. Click **OK**.

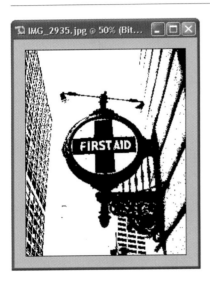

4. Neat-o! Now you have a stylized version of your image, somewhat akin to a photocopy. As I mentioned earlier, an image with an image mode of Bitmap can only have black or white—no grays and no color. So here is a translation of the original color image, but comprised of only two colors: black and white.

5. You won't be needing this image again, so after you're finished admiring your handiwork, close it by choosing **File > Close**.

You might have noticed under the Image > Mode pull-down menu another image mode called **Indexed Color**. *This mode is primarily used when saving an image as a GIF file, suitable for posting onto a Web page or e-mailing to someone. As such, I don't discuss the Indexed Color image mode until Chapter 12, "Elements and the Web."*

Now that you have some of the basics out of the way, in the next chapter you'll be learning all about layers—the fundamental building block needed to create complex images in Elements. Using multiple layers allows great freedom when creating an image because it enables you to easily combine, overlay, and mix images together to create a unique composition. I bet you're just itching to get started… so what are you waiting for? Read on!

4.
Layers

| What Are Layers? | Layer Basics |
| Non-Destructive Editing | Fill and Adjustment Layers |
| Blending Modes |

chap_04

Photoshop Elements 2
H•O•T CD-ROM

This chapter introduces you to the very important, powerful, and flexible feature known as layers. Layers offer much more control over editing your image. By putting different elements on different layers, you gain the ability to modify one part of your image without modifying any other part. Using layers also opens the door to being able to make changes and alterations to your images without those changes being permanent. By using fill and adjustment layers, you can easily change your entire image with the click of a button. Come one, come all, to the wonderful, feature-filled world of layers!

What Are Layers?

The greatest invention since those little plastic nibs that hold the ends of your shoelaces together is the advent of layers in digital imaging programs such as Photoshop and Elements. The name "layers," by itself, is pretty self-explanatory.

Using layers allows you to put different parts of your image on different, overlapping layers. You can think of layers as transparent sheets stacked one atop another. In the preceding image, Background layer is the bottom-most layer. Clouds layer is above the Background layer, and anything located on the Clouds layer will overlap anything on the Background layer. The Sunflower layer overlaps the Clouds layer, and so on and so forth. Pretty simple concept, eh? The power of layers is evident when you can create one image composition that is actually comprised of many different images, each on its own layer. By putting separate parts of your image on their own layers, you can easily manipulate them separately from the other parts of your image. As you'll see in later exercises, layers give you maximum control over your imagery. I highly encourage you to use them whenever possible.

I. —————————**Layer Basics—Part One**

1. Copy the **chap_04** folder and files from the **H•O•T CD-ROM** to your hard drive.

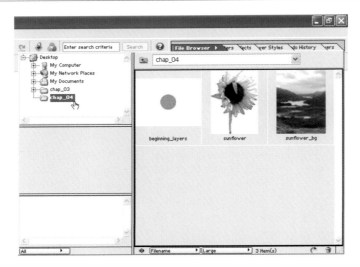

2. Open the **File Browser** window by choosing **Window > File Browser**, and navigate to where you copied your **chap_04** folder. (I copied mine to the Desktop to make it easy to find.) Double-click on the **beginning_layers** file to open it.

*Note: If you don't see your **chap_04** folder in the File Browser window, right-click (Windows) or Ctrl+click (Mac) anywhere on the file listing portion of the File Browser window. A pop-up menu appears (with one option) that says **Refresh**. Select that option to refresh the file listing, displaying your **chap_04** folder. Elements keeps a cache of the location of your files, and if you've added something (such as copying the **chap_04** folder off of the **H•O•T CD-ROM**) since the last time you used the File Browser, it might not display your new files. Using that Refresh option, however, forces Elements to update its cache.*

3. Once you've opened the **beginning_layers** image, open the **Layers** palette (click on its tab if you've docked it to the Palette Well, or choose **Window > Layers**).

See how this file has two layers, Layer 1 and Background? Whenever you create a new image, by default, Elements creates this background layer for you. (It does this because all images in Elements have to have at least one layer in them. In other words, you cannot have an image in Elements that has no layers in it. Images must have at least one layer.) Also notice the small lock icon to the right-hand side of the Background layer. This means that the layer is partially locked and (in this case) you cannot move it. In later exercises, you'll see how to alter that layer and why you would need or want to.

Note: *Notice that the Layer 1 thumbnail image has a blue circle in it that is surrounded by a gray and white checkered pattern? Whenever you see that pattern, it signifies a **transparent area**. This allows you to instantly see that the entire layer is transparent except for the blue circle. Of course, any part of the image that is transparent will allow you to see through to whatever is in the layer underneath.*

4. Double-click on the layer named **Layer 1**. This will highlight the layer name and allow you to name it something else. Type **blue circle** and press **Enter** (Windows) or **Return** (Mac) to rename the layer. Make sure the blue circle layer is selected by single-clicking on it in the Layers palette.

Note: *In Elements, when you want to modify a layer or edit the contents of a layer, you first need to make sure that layer is selected in the Layers palette (selected layers are highlighted in blue). That's easy enough to do. Just single-click on the layer you want to modify in your Layers palette, and you're good to go.*

5. Single-click on the **Opacity** pull-down menu, and a slider will pop up underneath it. By dragging the **Opacity** slider back and forth, you can modify the opacity (transparency) of everything that is in the blue circle layer (the layer you currently have selected). Drag the slider to **50%** and then release your mouse button.

Notice how the blue circle is now lighter than it was. That's because it is now 50 percent opaque, and you're partially seeing through to the white Background layer beneath it.

6. In your Layers palette, drag the **blue circle** layer onto the **New Layer** icon. This will duplicate the blue circle layer, place it above the original in the Layers palette, and automatically rename it **blue circle copy**. Easy!

Note: *This is only one way to duplicate a layer. As with most things in Elements, you can do the same thing many ways. This is my preferred method of duplicating a layer—it's quick, easy, and takes fewer mouse clicks than the other methods.*

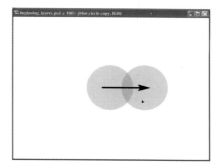

Move tool

7. With the **blue circle copy** layer selected, select the **Move** tool. Drag the blue circle on the document over to the right a little.

Notice how it's darker where the blue circles overlap? That's because you have two overlapping shapes that have their opacities set to 50% (the blue circle copy also has that same 50% opacity because...well...it's a copy). Where the two shapes overlap, they create a darker area. This is just one small example of how using layers can be helpful. By having each blue circle on separate layers, you can move, edit, and manipulate one circle without affecting the other.

What if you wanted to move both those blue circles at the same time? If you were to drag one circle around the image space, you'd quickly notice that even though you were thinking about moving both circles together (sorry...Elements doesn't read minds...yet), only one circle will actually move. There is a way to get the images on both of the layers to move at the same time.

Link icon

8. In the Layers palette, with the **blue circle copy** layer selected, click on the small box between the blue circle thumbnail image and the black eye. (Ohhh...that sounds rather nefarious, doesn't it? I'll talk more about that eye in the next exercise.) You'll see a little chain icon appear in that box. This means that the layer you have selected (**blue circle copy**) and the **blue circle** layer are now linked. Make sure your **Move** tool is still selected and drag one of the blue circles around in the image window. You'll notice that they now move together! When you want to unlink them, simply click on the link icon and they'll be unlinked. You can then move them around independently again.

9. When you are finished moving the circles around the image space, unlink them in the Layers palette by clicking on the chain icon to remove it.

You must be getting sick of those two blue circles by now. In the next step, you're going to change the color of one of them.

10. Single-click on the **blue circle copy** layer and then click on the **Lock Transparent Pixels** icon.

*When you lock the transparent pixels, you'll notice a small lock icon appear to the right of the **blue circle copy** layer. This lock signifies that you cannot edit the transparent parts of the **blue circle copy** layer. When modifying the color of this circle shape (as you're about to do), you'll want to make sure that you don't edit any other part of the image except the contents of the layer—in this case, a circle. Locking the transparent pixels does just that.*

Note: *As you can already see, you're working with the Layers palette quite a bit. If it is easier for you, you can undock the Layers palette so that it is always visible as you work with your images (instead of having to click on its tab in the Palette Well every time you want access to it). To undock the Layers palette, click on its tab in the Palette Well to open the Layers palette; then drag the Layers tab off of the Palette Well to a different location on your computer screen. This will make your Layers palette undock and become a free-floating palette that you can place wherever you'd like.*

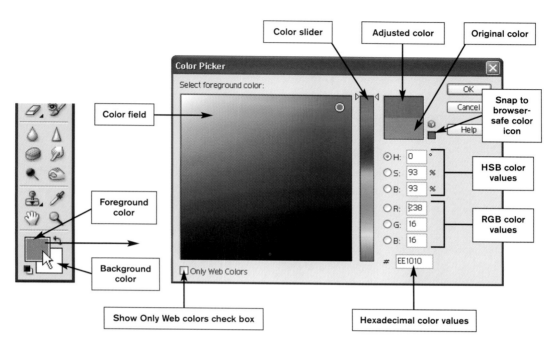

Color slider | Adjusted color | Original color

Color field

Foreground color

Background color

Snap to browser-safe color icon

HSB color values

RGB color values

Show Only Web colors check box

Hexadecimal color values

11. In your Toolbox, single-click on the **foreground color** swatch. The **Color Picker** window will open. From there, you can choose any color under the sun. (To pick a color, drag your mouse up and down the **Color slider** until you have found the color hue that you want. Then drag your mouse around the **Color field** until you've found a value and saturation that you like. For a more detailed explanation of the Color Picker, see Chapter 6, "*Painting and Colors.*") I selected a red color for this example. When you've found the color you want, click **OK**.

12. Choose **Edit > Fill**. This will open the **Fill** dialog box. From the **Use** pull-down menu, make sure **Foreground Color** is selected (you want to fill your object with the foreground color you chose). While you're here, make sure that the **Blending Mode** is set to **Normal** (you'll learn more about blending modes later in this chapter) and the **Opacity** is set to **100%**. Click **OK**.

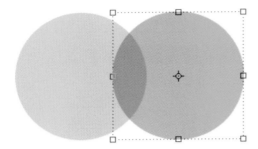

13. Presto! Your **blue circle copy** should now be filled with whatever color you chose. Yippee! This is a great technique for changing the color of artwork in a separate layer. You're done with this image and you won't need it again. Feel free to close the image or save it, print it out, and hang it up on your wall as your first masterpiece!! Bravisimo! ;-)

Note: After completing Step 11, if your whole image (instead of just the one blue circle) fills with the color you picked, go back and make sure you completed Step 10 correctly.

*Note: You'll notice that even though you filled one of the blue circles with a different, 100-percent opaque color, the circle still looks transparent. Why? If you remember back in Step 5, you changed the Opacity of the layer (which you duplicated to create the second circle) to 50%. Even though you're filling one of the circles with a 100-percent opaque color, the layer itself is still set to 50 percent opaque. This will cause everything in that layer to also be 50 percent opaque. To see what your circle (that you just changed the color of) looks like without the opacity change, drag the **Opacity** slider (as mentioned in Step 5) up to **100%**.*

There's an enormous amount of things you can do with layers. You'll get plenty of exposure to the layer features you have seen (as well as those you haven't) in later exercises. After working through this exercise, you should have a good understanding of layer basics and how best to select and manipulate them.

2. ———————Layer Basics—Part Two

Now that you've had a little experience working with layers in the context of simple circles, you're going to reinforce what you've learned. This time, however, you will be working with photographic imagery.

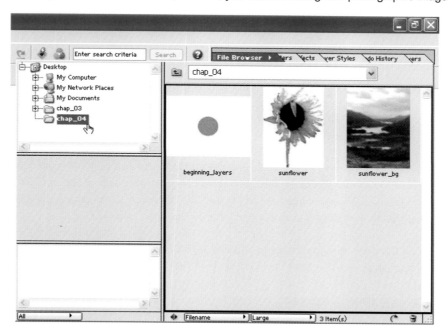

1. Open the **File Browser** window by choosing **Window > File Browser**, and navigate to where you copied your **chap_04** folder. Double-click the **sunflower_bg** file to open the image in Elements.

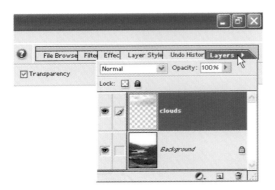

2. Open the **Layers** palette by choosing **Window > Layers**. Single-click on the top-most layer, **clouds**, to select it.

Note how the sunflower_bg image has two layers: Background and clouds. (You might need to expand the size of the Layers palette to see both layers.) Next you're going to add another image (and hence, another layer) to the sunflower_bg image. This technique demonstrates the essence of photo compositing: putting multiple images together to create one composition.

3. Open the **File Browser** again by choosing **Window > File Browser** and make sure you still have the **chap_04** folder selected. This time, double-click on the **sunflower** image to open it.

4. Open the **Layers** palette again by choosing **Window > Layers**. This time you'll notice that there are two layers in this image. The layer titled **sunflower** contains…well…a sunflower, and the **Background** layer is just filled with white.

5. Position your two open images, **sunflower_bg** and **sunflower**, so that you can simultaneously see both (as shown above). Make sure that the "active image" (the image you're currently working with) is the **sunflower** image. You can make it your active image by clicking anywhere on it.

6. Open the **Layers** palette and single-click on the **sunflower** layer to make sure it's selected.

Move tool

7. Select the Move tool, and drag the **sunflower** from the **sunflower** image over to the **sunflower_bg** image. When you let go of your mouse button, you'll see that the **sunflower** is now sitting on top of the **sunflower_bg** image!

8. Click on the **sunflower_bg** image to make it the active image, and open the **Layers** palette by choosing **Window > Layers**.

Where before the sunflower_bg image had two layers, it now has three layers. And Elements was smart enough to also name this new layer the same as it was in the sunflower image: **sunflower**. *By dragging one image (sunflower) into another (sunflower_bg), Elements automatically creates a new layer to hold that image.*

Note: *The reason I wanted you to first select the clouds layer way back in Step 2 was because when you dragged the sunflower over into the sunflower_bg document, Elements automatically created a new layer to hold that sunflower in the layer* above *the selected layer in your Layers palette. By selecting the clouds layer first, you ensured that the sunflower layer would be created above the clouds layer. Of course, you could have always reordered the layers by just dragging them up or down, but this saves you a little time.*

Tip: *You can temporarily turn off the visibility of a layer by clicking on the* **Layer Visibility** *icon (the small black eye to the left-hand side of the Layers palette) next to the layer that you want to hide or show. This is very useful if, when you're working with multiple layers, one layer is obscuring something that you need to see or edit in a layer underneath.*

Move tool

9. Select the **Move** tool in the Toolbox, and then drag the sunflower into place.

Notice the dotted line surrounding the sunflower with corner and side boxes along it? Elements automatically displays this bounding box around the outside of the image in the selected layer in your Layers palette (you must have the Move tool selected to see this bounding box). Identical to the corner and side resize handles you saw in Chapter 3, "Opening and Importing Images," these resize handles also allow you to easily rotate and scale the image in your current layer. This is one simple demonstration of the power of layers. You can easily scale or rotate the sunflower without altering the sunflower_bg image in the layer beneath it.

10. Choose **File > Save As** and name the file **sunflower_composite**. Make sure the **Format** is set to **Photoshop** and save it in the **chap_04** folder. You'll be utilizing this image again in later exercises.

Non-Destructive Editing

Imagine this. You decide to color your hair fluorescent pink late one evening after a night out with some friends. The next morning, after you've scared yourself silly in the bathroom mirror, you decide that you made a big mistake and you want your old hair back. Easy! Wiggle your nose and your hair returns back to its former (and much less pinkish) color. That would be nice now, wouldn't it? That obscure analogy summarizes the concept of non-destructive image editing in Elements. In many cases (note "many," not "all"), you can easily modify an image so that the changes you make are not permanent. Why make a permanent change if you don't need to? Image editing features such as (I know you don't know what these are yet, please bear with me) fill layers, adjustment layers, and the ability to group layers is your key to non-destructive image editing. When possible, you're going to use one of these methods to make changes to your images that do not permanently alter them. You can, however, easily turn off non-destructive editing with the click of a mouse. In the next two exercises, you're going to learn about ways to use non-destructive image editing to your advantage. Now where's that hair dye...

_____**Fill and Adjustment Layers**

In this exercise you're going to learn how to modify images non-destructively. To do this, you will be using two types of layers that you haven't seen yet: fill layers and adjustment layers. If you've worked with other image editing programs before and haven't seen this kind of feature, you'll shortly be wondering where it's been all your life.

1. Open the **File Browser** by choosing **Window > File Browser**, navigate to the **chap_04** folder, and double-click on **sunflower_composite** (the file you worked on earlier) to open it.

2. Open the **Layers** palette by choosing **Window > Layers**. Single-click on the **sunflower** layer to select it.

First you're going to add an adjustment layer to adjust the levels of the image. What are levels you say? **Levels** _are the highlights, midtones, and shadows that make up your image. This is also called the "tonal range"—throw that term out at a party to get a few ooohs and ahhhs, eh? "Ahh yes. Before I arrived at this party I was at home adjusting the tonal range of my photographic portfolio." Essentially, in layman's terms, it's the brightness/darkness of an image._

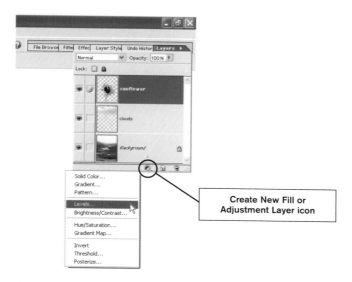

Create New Fill or
Adjustment Layer icon

3. With the **sunflower** layer selected, click and hold on the **Create New Fill or Adjustment Layer** icon. This will pop up a menu. From that menu, choose **Levels**.

You'll learn more about levels in Chapter 9, "Correcting Photos" (and the "proper" way to use levels), but in this example you're focusing more on adjustment and fill layers, not on levels.

Black slider   Gray slider   White slider

4. The **Levels** dialog box will appear. Drag your **Black**, **Gray**, and **White** sliders so that they match the screen shot above. The black input level (the left-most field) should be at **25**; the gray at **1.96** (or thereabouts); and the white at **244**. If you have your windows positioned so that you can see this dialog box and your sunflower_composite image at the same time, you'll notice the darks and lights in your image changing as you drag the sliders around. Once you've finished setting your black, gray, and white points, click **OK**.

Note: The Levels dialog box allows you to change the white, black, and gray values of an image. By dragging the White slider to the left, you increase the intensity of the image's highlights. Conversely, by dragging the Black slider to the right, you increase the intensity of the image's shadows. As you'll see in Chapter 9, "Correcting Photos," levels are superb at correcting the values of an image.

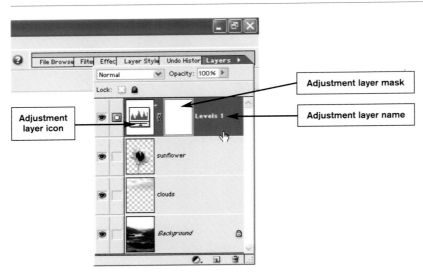

5. Open the **Layers** palette. You'll quickly notice that there is now a new layer above the sunflower layer titled **Levels 1**. This is your new adjustment layer (awww...isn't it cuuute!). To be specific, it's a levels adjustment layer because it's a layer that's adjusting the levels of your image.

Here's the nifty part...

*To see the before/after image, simply toggle the visibility on and off for your adjustment layer. To do that, just click on the **Layer Visibility** icon (the black eye) to the left of the **Levels 1** layer. Congratulations! You're now witness to the flexibility of working with an adjustment layer. In early versions of Photoshop, if you were to change the levels of an image as you just did, it would be a permanent change. Didn't like the levels change you made? Too bad...you were stuck with it. But thanks to adjustment layers, if you don't like the changes, you can simply alter the levels again, hide the layer, or even delete the adjustment layer completely. How awesome is that?*

*Note: To access the Levels dialog box for your adjustment layer, simply double-click on the **adjustment layer** icon and you'll be presented with the Levels dialog box again. If you want to delete the layer, just drag it to the **Trash** icon at the bottom of the Layers palette.*

*Now what if you like the levels changes you just made but you only want to apply those levels to the sunflower—not to everything else in the image? You're about to learn a brilliant way to do just that. It's called **grouping layers**.*

6. Open the **Layers** palette. Hold down your **Alt** key (Windows) or **Option** key (Mac) and move your mouse cursor so that it's between the **Levels 1** layer and the **sunflower** layer. You'll notice that your cursor will change to two overlapping circles. When you see that icon, click.

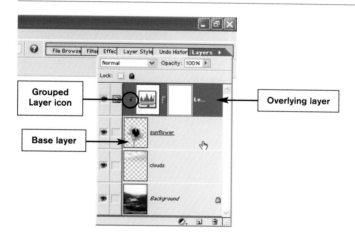

You'll quickly notice a few things have happened in the Layers palette. Most obvious is that the Levels 1 layer is now indented slightly and it has an icon next to it. This is the **Grouped Layer** icon, and it is telling you that now the Levels 1 layer is being applied only to the layer directly beneath it, the sunflower layer. The sunflower layer and the Levels 1 layer are now a layer group. The sunflower layer is called the **base layer** (the sunflower layer name is now underlined to signify that it is the base layer), and the Levels 1 layer is called the **overlying layer**. Regardless of the different names of the layer group, you've now told Elements to have that levels adjustment layer be applied only to the sunflower layer (yet another fantastic reason to use layers, and a great example of the power of adjustment layers). Looking beyond the Layers palette, look at your image. Now those levels you set earlier are no longer being applied to the whole image. They're being applied only to the sunflower.

Note: *To ungroup your layer grouping, simply reverse your steps. Hold down your **Alt** key (Windows) or **Option** key (Mac), move your mouse between the Levels 1 and sunflower layers, and click when you see your mouse cursor change to two overlapping circles. The layers will then become ungrouped. It's a snap!*

Now that you've seen an example of an adjustment layer, you'll learn about using a fill layer.

7. Drag the **Levels 1** adjustment layer to the **Delete Layer** icon (the Trash) at the bottom right of the Layers palette. This will, of course, delete your adjustment layer.

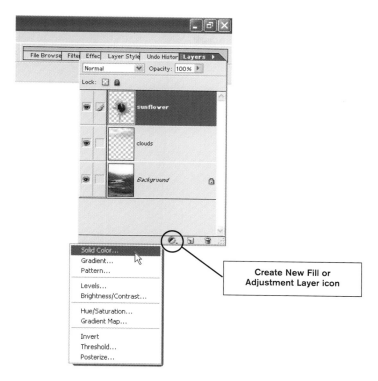

Create New Fill or
Adjustment Layer icon

8. In your Layers palette, once again, single-click on the **sunflower** layer to make sure it's selected. Then single-click on the **Create New Fill or Adjustment Layer** icon. From the pop-up menu that appears, choose **Solid Color**.

9. The **Color Picker** window will appear. Pick a color…any color. In this example, I chose a **bright yellow** color. When you've found the color you want, click **OK**.

Now don't get scared and run away when you see your image. It is now completely filled with the color you picked! But remember, this is just an adjustment layer. As you saw earlier, you can easily modify, turn on/off, and delete adjustment layers. Your image is still there…it's just underneath a blanket of color.

Next you're going to use a layer grouping to have your fill adjustment layer be applied to only the sunflower layer. Remember how to do that?

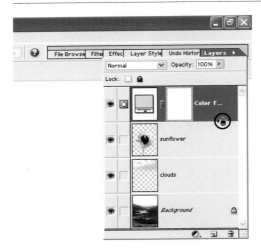

10. Open the **Layers** palette. Hold down your **Alt** key (Windows) or the **Option** key (Mac), move your mouse cursor so that it is positioned between the **Color Fill 1** layer and the **sunflower** layer, and click when your mouse cursor turns into two overlapping circles.

As you saw earlier in this exercise, this groups the two layers together. Again, all this essentially means is that now the color fill adjustment layer is being applied to only the sunflower layer instead of to the entire image.

Neat! The resulting image is a sunflower that is now completely covered by the color fill adjustment layer. Leave this image open—you'll be using it again in the next exercise.

Note: *To reiterate, the reason why only the flower fills with yellow is because in the sunflower layer, everything else is transparent except for the sunflower. You can easily see this by opening up the Layers palette, looking at the sunflower layer, and noticing how in the layer thumbnail image everything (except for the sunflower) is filled with that gray and white checkerboard pattern (which as I spoke about earlier, represents transparent areas).*

Although this exercise was done mostly to give you some hands-on experience with fill layers and grouping layers, the techniques covered are certainly applicable to working with your own digital images. For instance, you could use a fill layer in combination with layer grouping (as you did in this exercise) to silhouette an image in a layer, or you could also adjust the opacity of the color fill layer to give a color tint to the other layer(s) beneath it. There really are myriad effects that you can achieve using these techniques, and I encourage you to explore. You will gain more experience in later chapters, where you will be using more of both adjustment layers and layer grouping.

As I mentioned at the beginning of this exercise, the best thing about adjustment layers is that they're non-permanent. Once you have created an adjustment layer, it's very easy to go back and modify the settings or to just delete it completely—all without permanently altering the image in the slightest. You also learned the powerful feature of being able to group layers together so that one layer affects only the layer directly underneath it and not the entire image. You'll be gaining more experience with these techniques by using them again in later exercises.

What Are Layer Blending Modes?

In the upcoming exercise, you will gain hands-on experience using layer blending modes. Before you get started, the following chart shows the various blending modes, what they do, and what the result looks like using a sample image.

Layer Blending Modes		
Blending Mode	**Description**	**Preview**
Normal	Displays the layer normally without any changes.	
Dissolve	Same as Normal except the edges of the graphic are "randomly replaced," or scattered.	
Darken	Displays only the darker values of an image. The lighter values are replaced (made transparent).	
Multiply	Multiplies (hence the name) the colors of the layer image (called the "base color") with the colors of the layer images beneath (called the "blend color"). This always results in a darker color.	

continues on next page

Layer Blending Modes *continued*

Blending Mode	Description	Preview
Color Burn	Darkens the color of the layer image to be the same value as the layer images beneath.	
Linear Burn	Similar to Color Burn, but Linear Burn darkens the color of the layer image— by decreasing the brightness—to be the same as the layer images beneath.	
Lighten	Opposite of Darken. Displays only the lighter values of an image. The darker values are replaced (made transparent).	
Screen	Similar to Multiply, except Screen multiplies the *inverse* of the layer image colors with the colors in the layers underneath. This always results in a lighter color.	
Color Dodge	Similar to Color Burn, but instead of darkening the layer image, Color Dodge lightens it to be the same value as the layer images underneath.	

continues on next page

Layer Blending Modes *continued*

Blending Mode	Description	Preview
Linear Dodge	Similar to Linear Burn, but instead of darkening the layer image, Linear Dodge lightens it—by increasing the brightness—to be the same as the layer images underneath.	
Overlay	Overlay is a complex blending mode. It mixes the colors (using either a Multiply or Screen effect) of the layer image with the colors of the layer images beneath while preserving the highlights and shadows of the image.	
Soft Light	If a color in the layer image is lighter than 50 percent gray, it is lightened; if a color is darker than 50 percent gray, it is darkened.	
Hard Light	Similar to Soft Light, except if a color in the layer image is lighter than 50 percent gray, it is lightened—like if it were screened; if a color is darker than 50 percent gray, it is darkened—like if it were multiplied.	
Vivid Light	If a color in the image is lighter than 50 percent gray, it is lightened by decreasing the contrast; if a color is darker than 50 percent gray, it is darkened by increasing the contrast.	

continues on next page

Layer Blending Modes *continued*		
Blending Mode	**Description**	**Preview**
Linear Light	Similar to Vivid Light. If a color in the layer image is lighter than 50 percent gray, it is lightened by increasing the brightness; if a color is darker than 50 percent gray, it is darkened by decreasing the brightness.	
Pin Light	If a color in the image is lighter than 50 percent gray, the dark parts of the image are replaced (made transparent), and the light parts are unchanged. If the color is darker than 50 percent gray, the light parts of the image are replaced, and the dark parts are unchanged.	
Difference	Compares the color values of the layer image with the color values of the layer images underneath. Depending upon which color values have a greater brightness, Elements will either subtract that color in the layer image from the color in the layer images underneath or vice-versa. Essentially, you end up with a very unique image. ;-)	
Exclusion	Similar to Difference, but the end result is an effect that is lower in contrast.	
Hue	Keeps the luminance (the intensity of the brightness) and the saturation (how colorful or "pure" an image is) the same, but changes the layer image hue (shade of color) to be the same as the layer images underneath. Essentially, it keeps the brightness/darkness and the saturation of the layer image the same, but then changes the actual *colors* of the layer image to match that of the layer images underneath.	

continues on next page

Layer Blending Modes *continued*		
Blending Mode	**Description**	**Preview**
Saturation	Similar to Hue except the luminance and hue of the layer image remain the same while the saturation of the layer image is changed to match the saturation of the layer images beneath.	
Color	Similar to Hue and Saturation except the luminance of the layer image remains the same while the hue and saturation of the layer image is changed to match those of the layer images underneath. The Color blending mode is especially useful for colorizing black-and-white images.	
Luminosity	Similar to Hue, Saturation, and Color modes, except the hue and saturation of the layer image remains the same while the luminosity of the layer image changes to match that of the layer images underneath.	

Blending modes is, in essence, how one layer blends into the other layers underneath it. By default, every layer you create has its blending mode set to Normal. Although there are too many blending modes to cover in this one exercise, I'd still like to show you a few so that you can get an idea of what they're capable of. Blending modes is one of my personal favorite features in Elements that I use, without fail, very frequently in my illustrations. Using blending modes properly can go a long way toward giving your image a beautiful and unique look.

Note: Blending modes can also be assigned to certain tools such as Paintbrush, Pencil, Gradient, and Paint Bucket. That way, as you use the tools, you're working directly with a blending mode. This is very useful if you want to apply a blending mode to a specific brush stroke or area of your image but you don't want to apply that same blending mode to the graphics in an entire layer. You'll learn more about tool-specific blending modes in Chapter 6, "*Painting and Colors.*"

4. ——————Using Blending Modes

In this exercise you will learn how to use blending modes. Utilizing blending modes allows you to modify how the colors and values of an image in one layer are affected by the colors and values of images in other layers underneath it. Sound confusing? Complicated? It's actually quite easy, as you'll see.

1. First, make sure that the image you were working on in the last exercise, **sunflower_composite**, is back to the way it was since the last time you saved it. With the **sunflower_composite** image open, choose **File > Revert**. This will revert your image back to the way it was when you last saved it.

2. Open the **Layers** palette by choosing **Window > Layers**. Single-click on the top-most layer, **sunflower**, to select it.

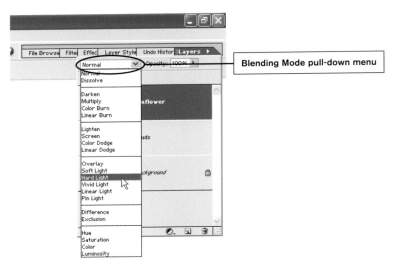

Blending Mode pull-down menu

3. Click on the **Blending Mode** pull-down menu and choose **Hard Light**.

before

after

As you can see in the before and after images, the sunflower (after having the Hard Light blending mode applied to it) now has a greater contrast (stronger light values and stronger dark values), and in places, you can even partially see through the sunflower to the layers underneath. Cool! Blending modes are especially useful when doing photo montages and photo compositing. As such, you'll get more experience using blending modes in later chapters.

4. Open the **Layers** palette again, make sure the **sunflower** layer is selected, and from the **Blending Modes** pull-down menu choose **Difference**. Holy psychedelic, Batman! The Difference blending mode is always good for a laugh or two.

5. When you're finished, close this image and don't save changes.

As you can see, you can achieve some very interesting and artistic effects by using blending modes. I encourage you to experiment with different blending modes when working with your images. Sometimes you can be pleasantly surprised with the results. :-)

In the next chapter, you'll be learning all about selecting. Selecting is an important part of image editing because it allows you to select specific portions of an image to work with or modify. In this chapter (Chapter 4), how do you think I got the sunflower to be in its own transparent layer? I selected it using various selection tools and removed it from its background (much like cutting an image out of a magazine). In the next chapter, you'll learn all the tools needed to accomplish such a task. Onward and upward!

5.

Selecting

| About Selections | Pre-Selecting Advice |
| Using Selection Tools |
| Adding and Subtracting from a Selection |
| Moving and Saving Selections | Building an Image |

chap_05

Photoshop Elements 2
H•O•T CD-ROM

Learning how to properly select different parts of your images is one of the need-to-know keystones in Elements. Selecting is the doorway that leads you to more exciting things such as image manipulation, color correction, and photo compositing. As a professional illustrator, I can safely say that when I'm working on an illustration, I spend at least half the amount of time selecting different parts of images before I begin drawing or editing. Whether you want to apply a filter or effect to a portion of your image or cut a part of your image out and paste it someplace else, selecting is the key to performing those tasks. So put on your thinking cap (geez, I hated it when the teacher used to say that) and off we go!

About Selections

Plain and simple, selections are what they sound like. You use various tools and methods to select a portion of your image so that you can apply filters or effects to parts of the image, or to simply extract from the rest of the image—akin to cutting an image out of a magazine. Why would you want to do this? Well, what if I had a picture of a flower, and I wanted to place that flower (*just* the flower) onto a different background (just like you did in the last chapter...not-so-coincidentally)? The only way to do that is by selecting the flower, extracting it from its background, and putting it against a different background. One day I imagine a voice-activated version of Elements that upon hearing me utter "cut out picture of flower" would proceed to extract the image of a flower from its background. In Elements 2, however, you still have to do it the "old-fashioned," manual way. Sure, I will show you other ways to make the process simpler and less time-consuming, but you'll find that selecting portions of your images is still a mostly manual and non-automated task that requires a good deal of time and dexterity. You will certainly be using selections in later chapters (especially Chapter 10, "*Retouching Photos*" and Chapter 11, "*Photo Manipulation*"), so this chapter is meant just as an introduction and overview of the various ways to select portions of an image. Later, you will learn what you can actually do with those selections.

The selection tools that you will be using in this chapter are all located towards the top of the Toolbox. They are the Marquee tools (Rectangular and Elliptical), the Lasso tools (Normal, Polygonal, and Magnetic), the Magic Wand tool, and the Selection Brush tool.

Pre-Selecting Advice

Keep in mind a few of the following details while you are scanning and photographing your images—they'll make a huge difference when you attempt to select portions of those images.

This picture is a scan I made of a live ladybug. I just found her, plopped her on my scanner bed, gently laid a sheet of paper over her, and held the edges down so she wouldn't move while I made the scan.

*Note: No ladybugs were harmed during the production of this book.

Now wouldn't it be nice if you could digitally "cut" the ladybug away from the paper background and "paste" it onto another image? How about...say...that composition you worked on in the last chapter where you placed an image of a sunflower against a landscape? In this chapter, I'll show you how to do exactly that.

When selecting part of an image, whether you want to take a particular part of it and put it into another image, or to just apply a filter or effect to it, you should first evaluate the subject matter. Does the object that you want to select have lots of straight edges? Does it have lots of curved lines? Is it a complex shape? Simple? What kind of background is the object against? A flat color? Textured? Evaluating your subject matter first will enable you to pick the best tool for the job. In this case, your subject matter (a ladybug), has lots of curved lines to its complex shape, but it's against a relatively flat background color.

If you are taking a photograph that you know you will later want to cut objects out of, shooting your subject matter against a flat background color will certainly be *extremely* beneficial. For example, you could use a piece of white or black cloth—you might have also heard the movie term "blue screen" or "green screen." When using special effects, filmmakers often shoot their subject matter against a bright blue or green cloth. This enables the special effects team to easily and digitally cut the subject matter away from the background, allowing them to then place their content seamlessly against any other background of their choosing. This is essentially what you will be doing in this chapter. As you'll see with this ladybug, having a flat color behind your image can save you a lot of time when trying to select it.

I.————————Using and Choosing Proper Selection Tools

In this exercise, you will learn about the various tools that select specific parts of an image. As I mentioned at the beginning of this chapter, learning how to select certain parts of your image is critical to image manipulation, application of filters and effects, and photo compositing. A bit of warning about this exercise—you're going to be learning about a lot of new tools! Normally, once you know what tools work best, you'll go right to the correct selection tool and won't need to use all the techniques you learn in this exercise. For learning purposes, however, you'll get to tinker with a lot of selection techniques to help you get to know the tools a little better. In this particular exercise, the process of getting there is more important than where you're going!

1. Copy the **chap_05** folder and files from the **H•O•T CD-ROM** to your hard drive.

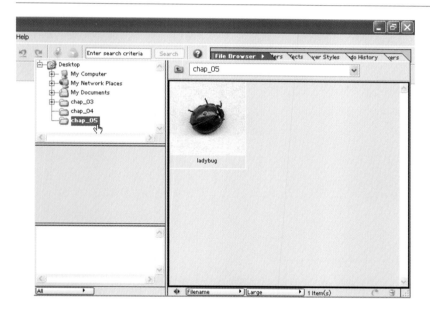

2. Open the **File Browser** by choosing **File > Browse**, and navigate to where you copied the **chap_05** files on your computer. Locate the file titled **ladybug** and double-click on it to open it.

As I mentioned in the last chapter, if you open the File Browser and you don't see the **chap_05** *folder, you may need to right-click (Windows) or Ctrl-click (Mac) on the file listing portion of the File Browser window and choose* **Refresh.**

Tip: When the File Browser window is open, you can also refresh the file listing by pressing **F5.**

Rectangular Marquee tool

3. It's time to take the Rectangular Marquee tool for a test drive. Click on it in your **Toolbox** to select it. If you have the Elliptical Marquee tool selected, switch back at this time to the Rectangular Marquee tool by clicking—and holding—on the **Elliptical Marquee** tool. When the hidden tools pop-up menu appears, select the **Rectangular Marquee** tool.

4. Position your cursor (which turns into a crosshairs icon) over the ladybug image. Then (not to sound like a bad infomercial) just click and drag to create a selection. When you release the mouse button, the selection is created and you'll see a dashed line that appears to animate. This is your selection, and that animation is called the "marching ants."

Congratulations! You have just created your first selection by using the Rectangular Marquee tool to select part of the ladybug image. At this point, you could add a filter or effect to just the portion of the ladybug image that you selected, or you could cut it out of this image and paste it into another. The Elliptical Marquee tool creates a selection (like you just did with the Rectangular Marquee tool), except, of course, it's elliptical (rounded). If your purpose is to select just the ladybug, the Marquee tools aren't really right for the job. The shape of the ladybug is too complex to correctly select with either of the Marquee tools. Why don't you try the Lasso tools next?

5. Because the selection you just made with the Marquee tool isn't quite the right one, get rid of that selection (called **deselecting**) before experimenting with the other selection tools. To deselect your selection, choose **Select > Deselect**. Because deselecting is such a common practice, you should learn its shortcut key: **Ctrl+D** (Windows) or **Cmd+D** (Mac).

Lasso tool

6. Select the **Lasso** tool by clicking on it in the Toolbox. When you move your mouse cursor over your image, notice how your cursor changes to the shape of…well…a lasso. (The bottom part of the lasso is the actual point from where you draw your selection, by the way.)

7. Drag your lasso icon around the outside of the ladybug to create your selection. Make sure to end up very near where you started dragging. When you've deftly drawn around the entire ladybug, release your mouse button and your selection is created. *Whew.* The Lasso tool requires great dexterity with the mouse, a steady hand, a smooth mousing surface, and very little caffeine. As I'm sure you can see from this example, the Lasso tool is a great way to create more "organic" selections (unlike the simple lines of the Rectangular and Elliptical Marquee tools), but it's not very good at creating precise lines around the edges of a shape. Adobe realizes this, and has given you a few more options with the two hidden Lasso tools: the **Polygonal Lasso** and **Magnetic Lasso** tools.

8. Deselect the selection that you just made with the Lasso tool by using the shortcut key **Ctrl+D** (Windows) or **Cmd+D** (Mac). Select the **Polygonal Lasso** tool by clicking and holding on the **Lasso** tool until the hidden tools pop-up menu appears. Then from the pop-up menu choose the **Polygonal Lasso** tool.

Note: *You can also access the hidden Lasso tools from the options bar. Just simply click on the standard Lasso tool in the Toolbox, and you'll see the additional Lasso tools (as well as a few options you'll see later) appear in the options bar.*

The Polygonal Lasso tool functions a bit differently than the standard Lasso tool. To create a selection with the Lasso tool, you dragged your mouse around the object (or the part of the image) that you wanted to select. With the Polygonal Lasso tool, you click from point to point around the image to create your selection. Every time you click your mouse with the Polygonal Lasso tool, it creates an anchor point. If you move your mouse elsewhere on the document you'll notice a line that extends away from the point that you clicked. Clicking again creates another anchor point, and so on and so forth.

9. At this point, go ahead and click with the **Polygonal Lasso** tool around the ladybug to create your selection. Once you've worked all the way around the ladybug, click on the point where you first started clicking (you'll notice that when you get close to the point where you started clicking, the Lasso tool cursor will change to have a small circle at its bottom right; when you see that cursor, clicking will create the selection).

The Polygonal Lasso tool requires less mouse dexterity than the standard Lasso tool, and you can create more precise selections with it to boot. While creating a selection with the Polygonal Lasso tool, you can temporarily have it behave as a standard lasso tool! To do that, simply hold down the Option key (Mac) or the Alt key (Windows). This will turn your polygonal lasso tool into a standard lasso tool (able to create a selection with a curved line) for as long as you hold the Option or Alt key down.

*Tip: When you're using the Polygonal Lasso tool, and you want to remove the last anchor point you created, simply press **Backspace** (Windows) or **Delete** (Mac). *Thanks to Lynda's husband, Bruce Heavin, for showing me that trick a few years ago.*

*Tip: You can also use your standard Lasso tool as a Polygonal Lasso tool. Without any selection currently active, and with the standard Lasso tool selected, hold down the **Alt** key (Windows) or **Option** key (Mac). Then, instead of dragging around your image with the Lasso tool, click around it like you would with the Polygonal Lasso tool. Fantastico—the standard Lasso tool is behaving just like the Polygonal Lasso tool does. When you've completed your selection, release the **Option** or **Alt** key and your selection is created.*

Magnetic Lasso tool

10. Deselect your selection by pressing **Ctrl+D** (Windows) or **Cmd+D** (Mac). In the options bar, click on the **Magnetic Lasso** tool icon to select it. When you do, you'll see some new options appear to the right side of the options bar.

The Magnetic Lasso tool sounds quite mysterious, doesn't it? Just like the other Lasso tools, the Magnetic Lasso tool allows you to make a selection. The difference between the Magnetic Lasso tool and the other Lasso tools, however, is quite dramatic. Whereas the Lasso and Polygonal Lasso tools are very manual, the Magnetic Lasso tool is more automatic. As you move your mouse around the image, the Magnetic Lasso tool constantly tries to find the edge of a shape and snaps your selection to fit it. Ohhhh. The Magnetic Lasso tool works best for selecting images against a high-contrast background. Here's an explanation of those new options that appear on the options bar:

Magnetic Lasso Tool Options	
Option	**Description**
Width	Specifies the area of edge detection the Magnetic Lasso tool uses to find edges of your shape. If an object you want to select has lots of other content around or near it, you probably are going to want to set Width to a low number.
Edge Contrast	Controls how sensitive the Magnetic Lasso tool is to detecting the edges of the part of the image you're trying to select. Enter a higher number to have the Magnetic Lasso tool select the parts of your image that have a high contrast. Conversely, entering a lower number lets the tool select parts of your image with areas of low contrast.
Frequency	Sets the rate at which the Magnetic Lasso tool lays down anchor points around the area that you're trying to select. Entering a higher value allows the Magnetic Lasso tool to add more anchor points around the image, thereby making the selection process go by faster.

For this example, leave the Width, Edge Contrast, and Frequency settings at their default. Width is 10 pixels, Edge Contrast is 10%, and Frequency is 57.

11. With the **Magnetic Lasso** tool, click on the edge of your shape (the ladybug, in this case) to create your initial anchor point. Then, without holding the mouse button down, move your mouse cursor around the edge of the ladybug until you're back to where you started from. You don't need to trace the edge exactly; you just need to trace near it.

That's the beauty (or one of them anyway) of the Magnetic Lasso tool. As you move your mouse around the edges of the ladybug, you'll notice it laying a selection line around the edges of the shape. Exactly where and how close it lays down the selection line is dependent on the settings you specified in the options bar (as discussed in Step 10). When you're near the selection's starting point, the Magnetic Lasso tool cursor will change to include a small circle at its lower right (just like the Polygonal Lasso tool, remember?). Single-clicking when you see that cursor icon will complete the selection (don't double-click—that will deselect your entire selection!).

Tip: The Magnetic Lasso tool is better when used on image edges with high contrast, so you will get better selection results if you increase the contrast of your source image first and then use your Magnetic Lasso tool to create the selection. You will be learning more about increasing the contrast of images in Chapter 9, "Correcting Photos."

Although the Lasso tools are a great way of manually creating complex selections, they are still very time consuming and require a steady hand. Next you're going to learn to use the Magic Wand tool to easily create selections with a simple click.

Magic Wand tool

12. Deselect the selection you made with the Magnetic Lasso tool by pressing **Ctrl+D** (Windows) or **Cmd+D** (Mac). Next, click on the **Magic Wand** tool to select it.

Magic Wand tool options

Once you've selected the Magic Wand tool, you'll notice a few new options in the options bar.

Magic Wand Tool Options	
Option	**Description**
Tolerance	This is the most important Magic Wand tool setting. A low Tolerance specifies that fewer colors will be considered similar to the one that you click on, whereas a higher Tolerance specifies that more colors will be considered similar. Essentially, the lower the tolerance, the fewer pixels will be selected around where you clicked; the higher the tolerance, the more pixels will be selected. For now, though, leave the Tolerance option set to the default 32.
Anti-aliased	When this box is checked, the edges of your selection will be smoothed (anti-aliased). In most cases, you will probably want to leave this checked.
Contiguous	When this box is checked, only the pixels that are directly contiguous (adjacent) to each other will be selected. Unchecking this check box will cause pixels with a similar color to the one you clicked on to be selected over the entire image.
Use All Layers	When this box is checked, the Magic Wand tool selects pixels that span all of the layers in your image.

13. Move your mouse cursor over onto the white area of the ladybug image and click.

Presto! Instant selection. Now isn't that a heck of a lot easier than using the manual Lasso tools? As you can see, however, the selection runs a little wide around the side of the ladybug that is in shadow. You can make the selection cinch up closer to the ladybug by setting the **Tolerance** *to a higher number, which means that the Magic Wand tool will consider more pixels similar to the one you clicked on.*

---

14. Deselect your selection by choosing **Select > Deselect**. With the Magic Wand tool still selected, set the **Tolerance** in the options bar to **125**. Lastly, move your mouse cursor over to the image and click on the white (paper) area of the ladybug image again.

Great! Now you've created a selection again, but this time you'll notice that the selection runs up much closer to the edge of the ladybug. You can see that in some parts of the ladybug, the selection actually runs into the ladybug itself, but that's easily corrected using the other selection tools, as you'll see in the next exercise.

Some of you might be saying, "Wait a second! I didn't select the ladybug, I selected the paper!" This is most certainly true. Because the ladybug is all different colors and values but the paper is generally one solid color (which is much easier to select with the Magic Wand tool), you selected the paper. To select the ladybug, you simply want to tell Elements to take your selection and invert it—so that everything currently selected is not, and everything not selected is. Capisce? This is a very easy thing to do in Elements.

15. Choose **Select > Inverse**. Now, instead of the paper being selected, the ladybug is. Magic!

From this example, I hope you can see how, in some cases, the Magic Wand tool can save you a lot of time when selecting an object. Where the Magic Wand tool fails, however, is when you want to select a portion of an image against a textured, patterned, or complex background. In that case, you need to bring out the big selection gun: the **Selection Brush***.*

The Selection Brush is a new and novel way to create selections in Elements—by just painting with the paintbrush. By specifying a few options and then "painting" with the Selection Brush on your image, you're actually defining a selection! After using the Selection Brush, you'll probably never go back to the Lasso tool again! Aren't you glad you learned it the hard way first?

Selection Brush tool

16. Deselect your selection once more by pressing **Ctrl+D** (Windows) or **Cmd+D** (Mac). In your Toolbox, click on the **Selection Brush** tool to select it.

Selection Brush presets | Brush Size slider | Selection Brush tool options

As with the other selection tools, when you select the Selection Brush tool you'll see some new options in the options bar.

Selection Brush Tool Options

Option	Description
Selection Brush presets	From the Selection Brush presets pull-down menu, you can choose the style of brush you want to use when defining your selection. You'll gain more experience with brushes in Chapter 6, "*Painting and Colors*." For now, just leave the brush set at its default which is a hard, round, 13-pixel-wide brush.
Size	Click on the little arrow to the right of the Size field. From the slider that pops up, you can specify a size for your Selection Brush. **Tip:** You can quickly change the size of your brush by pressing the] and [(bracket) keys to make your brush size larger and smaller, respectively, without the hassle of accessing the Size slider. How about that?! Using the keyboard to dynamically change the size of the Selection Brush is *very* useful—especially when moving from selecting large areas to smaller, more detailed areas. *With thanks again to Lynda's husband, Bruce, for showing me that trick so long ago.
Mode	This selects whether you want to paint with a selection or a mask. With the Mode set to **Selection**, where you paint with the paintbrush is what becomes your selection. With the Mode set to **Mask**, where you paint (by default) is covered in a 50 percent transparent red color. With the Mask feature, you're essentially painting the area of your image you want to mask out, or hide. After painting a mask, if you choose **Selection** from the pull-down menu, you'll see that everything but what you painted is selected. The advantage of using the Mask mode is that if you choose a different brush preset, you can actually see the different brush edges, such as hard, soft, and so on, as you're painting with them. When you're using the Selection mode brush, you can't see the different brush edges.
Hardness	The Hardness slider specifies how "hard" the edge of the brush is. A higher value denotes a hard-edged brush; a low value signifies a soft-edged brush. Again, you won't really see a difference while you're creating a selection with the mode set to Selection. You'll notice this while working with the mode set to Mask.
Overlay Opacity and Overlay Color	If you have your mode set to Mask, you can also set how opaque your mask color will be. By clicking on the Overlay Color box, you can also specify what color to use as well.

17. The default brush size of **13** is a little too small to work with for this image, so set your brush size to **30 px**. You can do this by either dragging the Brush Size slider or by typing **30** into the **Size** field and pressing **Enter** (Windows) or **Return** (Mac). Leave the **Mode** set to **Selection** and the **Hardness** set to **100%**.

18. Move your mouse cursor onto the image of the ladybug and drag your mouse around to start defining a selection. Simply, you're "painting" a selection onto the ladybug. I used the **30 px** brush to first draw around the outside edge of the ladybug (ignoring any small parts like legs) and then filled in the center area. Then, press **[** (left bracket key) until your brush size is **7 px**, which will give you a nice, small Selection Brush tool so that you can define the legs as well. As you paint with the Selection Brush, you're adding to the selection you already have. Don't worry about being a little messy and selecting small areas that are a little too far outside of your shape; I'm going to show you next how to remove (by painting) parts of the selection.

*Tip: If you really want to make sure your selection is just perfect, you can zoom closer into the lady-bug for more precise selecting. Normally, you can just select the Magnify tool in the Toolbox and then click on the area of the image you want to zoom into. But to prevent confusion that would be caused by flipping back and forth between the Magnify tool and the Selection Brush tool, use the keyboard shortcut instead. To zoom into your image, press **Ctrl + +** (that's the Ctrl key and the plus sign key on Windows), or **Cmd + +** (that's the Command key and the plus sign key on a Mac). You can keep pressing that keyboard shortcut to zoom closer into the image. Now that you're nice and close, you should be able to more easily select small areas of an image, such as the legs of the ladybug. When you're ready to zoom out, press **Ctrl + -** (Windows) or **Cmd + -** (Mac). Like the zoom-in keyboard shortcut, you can press it repeatedly to zoom further and further out of the image.*

19. Hold down the **Alt** key (Windows) or **Option** key (Mac) and drag the **Selection Brush** icon over the areas of the selection that hang too far outside of the ladybug shape. You'll notice that as you drag the Selection Brush over the selection, it'll actually remove that part of the selection.

Neat! By using this method, you can easily add and subtract from a selection until you have selected the exact part of the image you want.

20. Leave your ladybug image open with your selection still active—you will be using it again in the next exercise.

How Do I Add or Subtract from a Selection?

Subtracting from a selection works the same way with the Selection Brush as it does with all of the other selection tools. To subtract from a selection you already have, hold down the **Alt** key (Windows) or the **Option** key (Mac) while you're using your selection tool. Where the two selections overlap, that part of the selection gets deleted.

Adding to a selection with the other selection tools isn't as easy as it is with the Selection Brush tool. When using another selection tool *besides* the Selection Brush tool, hold down your **Shift** key while using the tool to add to any selection that you already have.

Selection options

When using the Marquee, Magic Wand, and Lasso tools, you can also specify—in the options bar for each tool—how the selection will interact with other selections (if any). The circled options above are **New Selection**, **Add to Selection**, **Subtract from Selection**, and **Intersect with Selection**, respectively.

Now that you've seen how to create selections using a wide variety of selection tools, in the next exercise you will learn how to move those selections around and how to save them for later use.

2.————————**Moving and Saving Selections**

In this exercise, you will learn how to move and save your selections (now that you've slaved long and hard over them to make sure that they're perfect). Saving a selection in particular is very useful because you can then recall that selection at any time you want for any other purpose. Anytime you have a complex selection that you would rather not spend the time to re-create, save it because you never know when you may need it again.

1. With the **ladybug** image from the previous exercise still open, select any of your selection tools *except* the Selection Brush tool. Position your selection tool cursor over the selection and drag it to a new location.

You can move the selection anywhere else in the image that you'd like. This is often very useful if your selection is off by a little bit—you can move it back into the correct location by simply dragging it. You can also use the arrow keys to nudge a selection in small increments.

Note: *Logic would suggest that you should use the Move tool if you want to move a selection, yes? What actually happens, though, is that Elements moves the part of the image you have selected, not the selection itself. If you need to move your selection, you must have a selection tool selected first.*

Step Backward button

2. Click on the **Step Backward** button in your shortcuts bar—and keep clicking on it if need be until your selection is back where it was, on top of the ladybug. You need it back in its original location because next you will learn how to save your selection.

3. Choose **Select > Save Selection**.

4. From the **Save Selection** dialog box, leave the **Selection** pull-down menu set to **New** (there aren't any other options to choose from at this point anyway), and in the **Name** field, type **Ladybug**. Click **OK**.

5. Now for the moment of truth…take a deep breath…and deselect your hard-earned ladybug selection by pressing **Ctrl+D** (Windows) or **Cmd+D** (Mac). Now you're going to resurrect it. Choose **Select > Load Selection**.

6. From the **Load Selection** dialog box that appears, leave the **Selection** pull-down menu set to **Ladybug** and click **OK**.

Yayy! Like the phoenix rising from the ashes, your selection is now back on the ladybug image in the exact same place. As I mentioned earlier, saving a selection is very useful when you've spent a lot of time making a selection and you don't want to lose it. It also allows you to save the selection for later use while you continue to work on other parts, or other layers, of your image.

7. Leave the ladybug image open and the selection active—you will be using it again in the next exercise.

In the next exercise, you will take what you've learned so far in this book to combine two images together in a simple photo composite.

Building an Image

In this exercise you're going to combine the ladybug image with another image that you worked on in Chapter 4, "*Layers*," called **sunflower_composite**.

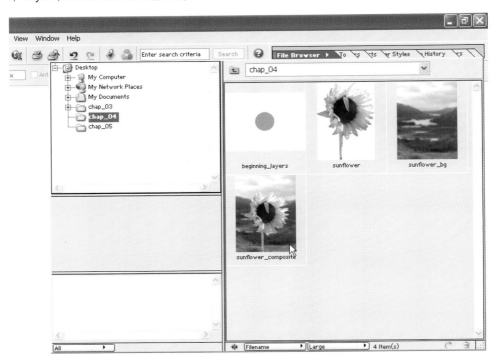

1. Open your File Browser by choosing **File > Browse** and navigate to the **chap_04** folder. In the **chap_04** folder should be **sunflower_composite**, the image you worked on and saved in Chapter 4. Double-click on it to open it.

2. At this point you should now have two images open in Elements. You should have the **ladybug** image open—with its selection still active—and the **sunflower_composite** image open. Position them next to each other so that you can see both at the same time.

3. Select the **Move** tool and drag the selected **ladybug** over onto the **sunflower_composite** image and release your mouse button.

In the sunflower_composite image, the ladybug that you dragged over may or may not be on top of the sunflower. It all depends on which layer you had selected in the sunflower_composite image when you dragged the ladybug onto it. You need to make sure that the ladybug is on top of the sunflower and that it's the proper size and orientation.

4. Make sure that your **sunflower_composite** image is the active image (click on its title bar) and open the **Layers** palette by choosing **Window > Layers**. If your ladybug layer (which is probably titled **Layer 1**) is below the **sunflower** layer, drag the ladybug layer so that it is above the **sunflower** layer.

The reason why you need to do that—of course—is because you want the ladybug to be positioned like it is sitting on top of the sunflower.

Next you're going to...holey baloobey! That's one giant ladybug that's about to swallow that sunflower whole! Run for the hills Bessie-Sue!

Voila! The ladybug is now in the sunflower image and is positioned on top of the sunflower! This is similar to the exercise in Chapter 4, "Layers," where you dragged the sunflower image onto a different background image, except this time you selected the ladybug yourself using selection tools, and effectively cut it out and moved it into another image! You should give yourself a huge pat on the back (not too hard now—I still need you around to read the rest of this book) because you've now learned the basics of photo compositing...and you've done it from scratch to boot! In the next steps, you're going to make that ladybug look like it's part of the whole sunflower image by decreasing its size, rotating it, and applying a blending mode.

5. While you have the Layers Palette open, rename your ladybug layer (by double-clicking on the layer name) to **ladybug**, of course.

6. Make sure the Move tool is still selected, hold down the **Alt** key (Windows) or the **Option** key (Mac) and the **Shift** key, and drag down one of the top corner resize handles (around the outside corner of the ladybug), thereby making the ladybug smaller. Holding down the **Alt** (Windows) or **Option** key (Mac) while you drag resizes the ladybug from its center (instead of from the bottom left). Holding down the **Shift** key while you drag resizes the ladybug proportionately. Once you have the ladybug at the size you want it, press **Enter** (Windows) or **Return** (Mac) to commit to the size transformation you just made.

7. Is that box around the ladybug image getting in your way? If so, you can temporarily hide it by making sure your Move tool is selected and then unchecking the **Show Bounding Box** check box in your options bar. Want the box back again so that you can easily resize/rotate the image? Just recheck the **Show Bounding Box** check box.

For now, uncheck the Show Bounding Box check box so you can easily see the blending mode you will be applying to the ladybug.

8. To best see the blending mode changes you will be making in the next step, make sure you are viewing your image at 100% by choosing **View > Actual Pixels**. If you're viewing your image at less than 100% (actual size), it will zoom in. If you're viewing your image at greater than 100%, it will zoom out.

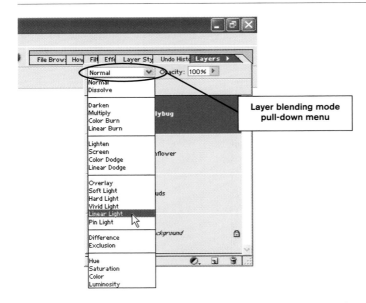

Layer blending mode
pull-down menu

9. Open the Layers Palette by choosing **Windows > Layers** and make sure the **ladybug** layer is selected. From the blending mode pull-down menu, choose **Linear Light** as the blending mode.

Linear Light (as you saw from the blending modes table toward the end of Chapter 4, "Layers") essentially makes the image on that layer more vivid. It brightens the lights and darkens the darks based on the values of the sunflower image that's behind it.

The end result! If you listen verrry quietly, you can almost hear her calling "coomme heere little aphid's aphid's...comme heeerre..." ;-)

Note: *If you see a small, white "halo" around the outside edge of the ladybug, it's there because you selected part of the ladybug's white background. To fix it, go back to the ladybug image and use the selection techniques you've learned thus far to reselect the ladybug and avoid selecting any of the white background. Then in the sunflower_composite image, throw away the old ladybug layer by dragging the layer to the Trash icon at the lower right of the Layers Palette, and then repeat Steps 3 through 9.*

10. So that you don't get confused later, place the checkmark back into the **Show Bounding Box** check box (you can do this by making sure the Move tool is selected and placing a check mark in the **Show Bounding Box** check box).

11. Save your **sunflower_composite** image by using the keyboard shortcut **Ctrl+S** (Windows) or **Cmd+S** (Mac). I recommend that you memorize this keyboard shortcut because saving is something you will do quite frequently.

12. Close the ladybug image, and if prompted to save your changes, click **No** (Windows) or **Don't Save** (Mac).

In this chapter you learned how to use the different selection tools. As you use those tools to select different parts of your own images, you'll gain more experience with understanding which selection tools work best for different types of images. You also learned the beginnings of photo compositing by cutting the ladybug out from its background, adding it to a completely different image, and making a few changes to make that ladybug look like it belongs in that photo. Photo compositing is kind of like applying makeup (well...uhhh...so I'm told)—when it's done correctly, you should never notice it. Good photo compositing shouldn't look like photo compositing at all. It should just look like one, cohesive image.

In the next chapter, you will be learning about painting, drawing, and colors. See you there!

6.

Painting and Colors

| Painting and Drawing | Erasing |
| Modifying Colors |

chap_06

Photoshop Elements 2
H·O·T CD-ROM

"I'm not an artist!" you might be saying to your-self. "I don't need to know about painting and colors." In this chapter, I'm not going to show you how to paint a pretty picture using the various drawing and painting tools in Elements. If you want to learn that, you should enroll at an art school or take evening art classes at your local community college. What I *am* going to demonstrate is how the painting and drawing tools work, and how to pick and swap around colors. In this chapter, you will focus more on the tools than how best to apply them. In later chapters, you will apply what you learned in this chapter towards more advanced exercises such as photo correction, retouching, and compositing. You don't need to be an artist to be able to understand the painting tools and color selection; you just need to follow along—and have fun for goodness sakes!

Painting and Drawing

In this exercise, you're going to learn the basics of the paintbrush, drawing, and gradient tools. As you read further in this book, you will build on some of what you learn in this exercise and chapter. Initially, in these first few exercises, you will be working only with the colors black and white (and the grays in-between), which will allow you to concentrate on the new tasks you're learning and will prevent you from getting sidetracked or confused by dealing with multiple colors. Later in this chapter, however, you will be introduced to the Color Picker and how to choose various colors.

1. Create a new image document by choosing **File > New**.

2. In the **New** dialog box, click on the **Preset Sizes** pull-down menu and, from the list of image presets, choose **640 x 480**. Make sure your resolution is **72 pixels/inch** and the **Mode** is **RGB Color**. Under **Contents**, make sure that the **White** radio button is selected. Click **OK**.

This will create an image for you that is 640 pixels wide by 480 pixels high, has a resolution of 72ppi, is color, and has a white background. Although the resolution of this image is low (72ppi), you will just be using it for learning purposes. If you wanted to print this image, you would set the resolution to something higher, like 300ppi.

Default Foreground and Background Colors button

3. To make sure that you're using the same colors as I am in this exercise, first set your foreground and background colors to their defaults. You can do this by clicking on the **Default Foreground and Background Colors** button, which is placed just down and to the left of the foreground and background color swatches in the Toolbox. Later in this chapter, I'll go more into detail about those foreground and background color swatches and on color itself.

4. Select the **Pencil** tool by single-clicking on its icon in the Toolbox.

| Brush presets | Brush size | Brush painting mode | Brush opacity |

5. One of the first things you should do before drawing with the Pencil tool is to set up the pencil options in the options bar.

Pencil Tool Options	
Option	**Description**
Brush presets	A pull-down menu where you can easily select a brush size and shape.
	Note: The Pencil tool draws with an "aliased" line, meaning that the edges of the line will be jagged (also called "stair-stepped") and not smooth. If you want the edges of your line to be smooth, use the Paintbrush tool, which has an "anti-aliased," smoothed edge. You'll learn more about the Paintbrush tool coming up next.
Brush size	A slider that allows you to choose what size your pencil (or paintbrush) draws with.
Brush painting mode	In Chapter 4, "*Layers*," you learned about layer blending modes. Layer blending modes allow you to control how an image in one layer blends into the images on other layers beneath it. Brush painting modes are very similar in that they control how what you draw or paint blends into the images on other layers (or the same layer) underneath them. For more information about blending modes, flip back to Chapter 4 and read the section "What Are Layer Blending Modes?".
Brush opacity	Also in Chapter 4, "*Layers*," you learned about layer opacity. Layer opacity allows you to change the opacity of your imagery on a layer-by-layer basis. Brush opacity is very similar, except instead of controlling the opacity of the layer, it controls *just* the opacity of what you're drawing or painting.
Auto Erase	With Auto Erase unchecked, your Pencil tool behaves just like if you were drawing on paper. If you draw over a line, it just draws on top of it. But with Auto Erase *checked*, if you draw on top of a line you've already drawn, it'll use your background color to draw over that line instead.

6. Click on the **Brush Presets** pull-down menu and choose the **hard round 5 pixels** brush. Leave the **Mode** set to **Normal**, the **Opacity** set to **100%**, and leave **Auto Erase** unchecked.

Note: The brush preset thumbnails will look a little different on a Mac. They have a tapered, pointed edge. The brushes and their effects are the same on both Mac and Windows—just the thumbnail images differ. By hovering your mouse over one of the brush presets, Elements will pop up a small yellow box that states the name of the brush preset.

Tip: So that you have maximum control over anything you draw, you should always create a new layer to draw on.

7. Open the **Layers** palette by choosing **Window > Layers** and click on the **Create a New Layer** icon. This will create a new layer (titled **Layer 1**) above the Background layer.

8. Move your mouse cursor onto your image document, and start drawing! Go crazy! And yes, this is a sketch of me *before* I've had my morning tea. Remember, if you make a mistake, you can always click the **Step Backward** button in the shortcuts bar, or press the undo keyboard shortcut, **Ctrl+Z** (Windows) or **Cmd+Z** (Mac).

By default, you can undo the last 20 things you did. You have no idea how many times I've wished that life had an undo button. I'm still waiting for Life version 2 to come out...ho-hum.

9. If you don't already have it open, open your **Layers** palette (by choosing **Window > Layers**). Rename **Layer 1** (which has your drawing on it) to **pencil drawing**. Remember, to rename a layer, simply double-click on the layer name in the Layers palette.

10. Create a new layer by clicking on the **Create a New Layer** icon. Next you're going to be painting with the Paintbrush tool, so this is the layer that the paintbrush drawing will go on.

11. Single-click on the **Paintbrush** tool icon in the Toolbox.

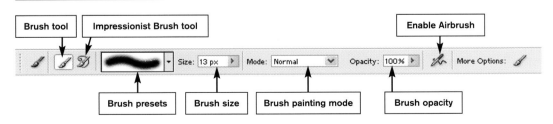

Just like the Pencil tool, before using the Paintbrush tool you should set the options for the Paintbrush tool in the options bar. As you'll notice, many of the options for the Paintbrush tool in the options bar are identical to the Pencil tool options. However, a few options are different:

Paintbrush Tool Options	
Option	**Description**
Brush tool and Impressionist Brush tool icons	Allow you to switch between the Brush tool and the Impressionist Brush tool. By simply selecting the Impressionist Brush tool and then "painting" with it over an image, it will make the part of the image that you paint on look like an impressionistic painting.
Enable Airbrush	Treats your paintbrush as an airbrush. The longer you hold your mouse button down on a spot, the darker and larger that spot will grow—simulating paint from the airbrush building up.
More Options	Gives you access and control over the brush dynamics such as brush shape, scattering, size, and color. By modifying the brush dynamics, you can get some really great, hand-drawn paintbrush styles.

12. From the **Brush Presets** pull-down menu, select the brush **soft round 35 pixels**. Set the **Mode** to **Normal**, the **Opacity** to **100%**, **Enable Airbrush** off (button not depressed), and make sure that the standard **Brush** tool is selected (on the far-left of the options bar) and not the Impressionist Brush.

13. Before you start painting, first make sure that you have the correct layer (**Layer 1**) selected in the Layers palette. Then, just like you did with the Pencil tool, start painting!

In this example, I've drawn a rather ominous but tiny rain cloud above my "self portrait." As you can clearly see in this example, the Pencil and Paintbrush tools draw very different lines—the Pencil tool draws a line with a hard edge, and the Paintbrush tool draws with a very soft edge. When picking a drawing tool for your own future use, you can simply choose which tool you want for the job at hand. Do you want a soft-edged or a hard-edged line?

You'll be using the Paintbrush tool many more times throughout this book, so you'll get plenty of experience using and working with it in later exercises. Next you're going to learn about the basics of the Gradient tool, which, of course, allows you to create gradients.

14. Open the **Layers** palette (if you closed it, you can open it again by choosing **Window > Layers**) and rename the layer (by double-clicking on the layer name) with your paintbrushed image on it to **paintbrush drawing**. Then create a new layer by clicking on the **Create a New Layer** button.

15. In the Layers palette, drag the new layer (titled **Layer 1**) down so that it's underneath the **pencil drawing** layer. The gradient that you are about to create is going to go in this new layer, but in this example the gradient needs to be *behind* the pencil and paintbrush layers.

16. Single-click the **Gradient** tool in the Toolbox to select it.

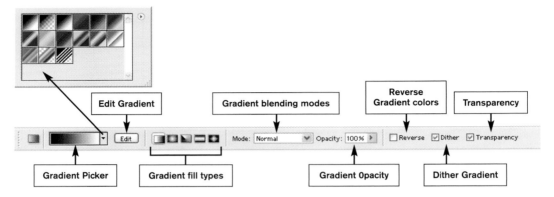

As with the other painting and drawing tools that you've seen thus far in this chapter, the Gradient tool has a variety of options that you can set. Here are descriptions of those features that differ from the Pencil and Paintbrush tools, which were described earlier:

Paintbrush Tool Options

Option	Description
Gradient Picker	Clicking on the small, black triangle to the right of the Gradient Picker will pop open a small window that gives you access to some prebuilt gradients. Single-clicking on a preset gradient will select it for your use.
Gradient fill types	Single-click on one of these five buttons to define the style of gradient you want. For your reference, here's a table outlining the different gradient fill types: **Linear Gradient** creates a gradient in a straight line starting with the foreground color and ending with the background color. **Radial Gradient** creates a gradient in a circle pattern with the foreground color in the middle and fading to the background color around the outside. **Angle Gradient** creates a gradient that sweeps around your starting point in a counterclockwise direction. **Reflected Gradient** is similar to the linear gradient except that the Reflected Gradient creates an opposite gradient that moves away from your starting point in the opposite direction. This mirror gradient effect gives the Reflected Gradient its name. **Diamond Gradient** creates a gradient in the shape of a diamond. Bling bling.

continues on next page

Paintbrush Tool Options *continued*	
Option	**Description**
Reverse Gradient colors	Fairly self-explanatory—it reverses your gradient colors. If your gradient went from black to white, clicking on the **Reverse** check box would change the gradient so it went from white to black.
Dither Gradient	This adds a little bit of "noise" (dithering) to your gradient. What the heck do you need this for? When working with smooth gradations (such as a gradient), you might notice something called "banding." Banding is where your supposedly smooth gradient appears to have "bands" in it, or areas where the gradient has clumped together. This is especially prevalent if your monitor is set to thousands of colors (instead of millions) or if you're exporting your image as a GIF (more on GIFs in Chapter 12, "*Elements and the Web*"). By checking the **Dither** check box, Elements will add a slight amount of dots (called "noise") to your dither, which will reduce the banding effect.
Transparency	There is a preset gradient in the Gradient Picker pull-down menu that fades from whatever your foreground color is to transparent. You can also design a gradient to have transparent colors in it. Leaving the **Transparency** check box checked will allow your gradient to have transparent colors in it. Unchecking the check box will disallow transparent colors in gradients.

17. With your **Gradient** tool still selected, in the options bar make sure that **Linear Gradient** is the currently selected gradient type, **Mode** is set to **Normal**, **Opacity** is at **50%**, **Reverse** is unchecked, **Dither** is checked, and **Transparency** is checked.

18. Before you create the gradient, first double-check that you have **Layer 1** selected (which you created in Steps 14 and 15). Move your mouse over onto your image document and position your cursor so that it's near the top of the image window. Then, simply drag down until the cursor is a few inches above the bottom of the image window. By dragging the mouse cursor, you're defining where the gradient starts and where it ends.

19. When you let go of your mouse button, you should see your gradient fill the background of your image. Yay! Now, in my example, thanks to the gray background and a dark rain cloud overhead, my self-portrait is ready to go. Happy days! (Note the sarcasm in my voice.)

20. Feel free to save your masterpiece, or just close it without saving the document. Either way, make sure your image is closed before continuing to the next exercise.

In this exercise you were introduced to the Pencil, Paintbrush, and Gradient tools. As you've seen, there are quite a few options that you can configure for each tool. Even though you will be gaining more experience with some of these tools in later chapters, I still highly encourage you to experiment and play around with the different tools and options. I can't begin to tell you how many times I've discovered a neat effect or something I didn't know about before just by experimenting.

2. _____**Erasing**

Now that you've learned the basics of painting and drawing, you should also learn how to erase those mistakes…er…I mean, those "creative errors." In this exercise you're going to learn about the Eraser tools: Eraser, Background Eraser, and the Magic Eraser.

1. Copy the **chap_06** files and folders from the **H·O·T CD-ROM** to your hard drive.

2. Open the **File Browser** by choosing **File > Browse**, and navigate to where you copied the **chap_06** files to on your computer. Locate the file titled **blot_logo_flat** inside the **chap_06** folder, and double-click on it to open it.

*As you can see, it's the Blot Illustration logo again. But you'll also notice only one layer, **Background**, when you open the Layers palette (by choosing **Window > Layers**). Now what if (in a real-world example), this is the file that "the client" has given you, along with instructions to take the logo and put it on their stationery and on their Web site. "Aww great," you say to yourself. "This logo is against a red background. Both the stationery and the Web site have white backgrounds! I need to find a way to get the logo off of the red background so I can integrate it into the stationery and the Web site." In this exercise, you are going to look into using the Eraser tool to erase the red background, leaving you with the logo against a transparent background—perfect for transplanting onto a Web site or stationery.*

3. The first thing you need to do is change the default **Background** layer into a normal layer. The **Background** layer, as mentioned previously, is a special type of layer in Elements, and you cannot edit it because it is locked. To change it into a normal layer, double-click on the layer. When the **New Layer** dialog box appears, simply click **OK**.

Now you'll notice in the Layers palette that the layer is no longer titled **Background**; instead it is titled **Layer 0**.

4. Single-click on the **Eraser** tool in the Toolbox to select it. As with other tools, you should learn about a few options (in the options bar) before continuing.

Eraser Tool Options	
Option	**Description**
Brush presets	The same as the Pencil and Paintbrush Brush presets, this pull-down menu allows you to select a brush shape and size to do your erasing with.
Brush size	This slider allows you to select, in pixels, the size of the brush that you will be using to do your erasing.
Erasing mode	From this pull-down menu, choose whether you want your Eraser tool to act like a brush (anti-aliased [smooth] edge), pencil (aliased [jagged] edge), or block (just a plain, non-resizable square).
Opacity	This slider allows you to determine at what opacity you will be erasing with. For example, if the Opacity slider is at 50%, whatever you are erasing will be 50% opaque.

5. In the options bar, make sure that the **Eraser** tool is selected, **Size** is set to **30 px** (pixels), **Mode** is set to **Brush**, and the **Opacity** is **100%**.

6. Move your mouse cursor over onto your image document; then drag your mouse around the logo, attempting to erase all of the red areas.

Although you can see that it is *in fact erasing the red, this would be a painstaking task to erase just the red areas while leaving the logo intact. The Eraser tool does a great job erasing parts of an image, but in this case, for this task, the regular Eraser tool isn't quite the right tool for the job.*

7. Repeatedly click on the **Step Backward** button in the shortcuts bar until you're back to the unaltered image. If you continue to click on the **Step Backward** button, but your image won't go all the way back to the way it was when you first opened it, it's probably because you made more than 20 alterations to the image (20 is, by default, how many steps backward you can go). So to get the image looking the way it did when you first started, choose **File > Revert**. The image will then revert back to the way it was when it was last saved.

*Note: If you press the **Step Backward** button too many times, or if you choose **File > Revert** to revert the image back to the way it was when it was last saved, you will have also undone the changing of the* Background *layer to a normal layer. Before you continue, make sure you open the Layers palette (**Window > Layers**) and check that your layer (the only layer) isn't titled **Background**. If it is, you'll simply need to repeat Step 3.*

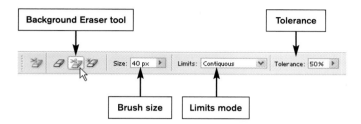

8. In the Toolbox, make sure you have the **Eraser** tool selected. Then in the options bar, single-click on the **Background Eraser** tool to select it.

Once you choose the Background Eraser tool, you need to set a few options (also in the options bar). The following chart explains what the possible options are, and the next step will instruct you how to best set your options for this particular image.

Background Eraser Tool Options	
Option	**Description**
Brush size	Same as the standard Eraser tool, this sets the size of the eraser brush.
Limits mode	**Contiguous** erases areas that are connected *only* to each other. **Discontiguous** erases the color you are sampling/erasing wherever it appears under the brush.
Tolerance	Similar to the Tolerance setting you saw with the Magic Wand tool in Chapter 5. The higher the tolerance percentage, the more colors will be considered similar to the one you're sampling and, therefore, more area will be erased. The lower the tolerance percentage, the fewer colors will be considered similar to the colors you're sampling, and fewer areas will be erased.

9. In the options bar, set **Size** to **40 px** (either by dragging the **Size** slider until it reaches **40**, or by typing **40** in the **Size** field and pressing **Enter** [Windows] or **Return** [Mac]). Set **Limits** to **Contiguous**. (The Limits mode is irrelevant in this case because the background you're erasing is one solid color. If the background was textured, however, you would most likely want to select **Discontiguous**). Set the **Tolerance** to **50%**.

10. Move your mouse over onto the image document, and start dragging your mouse cursor around the outside of the logo. As you drag the Background Eraser, always keep the crosshairs over the color(s) that you want to erase (in this case, the red). Like magic, you'll see the color being wiped away very cleanly all the way up to the edge of the black in the logo. Nifty! And yes, to make it easier to erase the small areas, you can zoom closer into the image if you'd like. Press the keyboard shortcut **Ctrl++** (that's the Ctrl key and the plus sign key on Windows) or **Cmd++** (Mac) to zoom into the image; **Ctrl+−** (Windows) or **Cmd+−** (Mac) will zoom out of the image.

*Note: While using the Background Eraser tool, if you still see a small fringe—or halo—around the outside edge of the logo, you can tell Elements to consider more colors similar to the red background color. In the options bar, simply increase the Tolerance percentage by dragging the **Tolerance** slider up. Then next time you use the Background Eraser tool, it should erase more of that halo away because it considers more colors to be similar, and thereby within its range to erase.*

11. Repeatedly click on the **Step Backward** button in the shortcuts bar (just like you did in Step 7) until your image is back to where the background is a solid red.

*Note: Again, if you press the **Step Backward** button too many times, or if you choose **File > Revert** to revert the image back to the way it was when it was last saved, you will have also undone the changing of the Background layer to a normal layer. Before you continue, make sure you open the Layers palette (**Window > Layers**) and check that your layer (the only layer) isn't titled **Background.** If it is, simply repeat Step 3.*

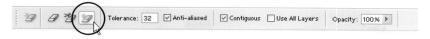

12. In the Toolbox, make sure you have the **Eraser** tool selected. Then in the options bar, single-click on the **Magic Eraser** tool to select it.

After you choose the Magic Eraser tool, you need to set a few options in the options bar. (These options are identical to the Magic Wand tool's options, by the way.) The following chart explains the possible options for this tool. In the following step, you'll be instructed how to set the proper settings for the image at hand.

Magic Eraser Tool Options	
Option	**Description**
Tolerance	The most important option is the Tolerance setting. A low Tolerance specifies that fewer colors will be considered similar to the one that you click on, whereas a higher Tolerance specifies that more colors will be considered similar. Essentially, the lower the tolerance, the fewer pixels will be erased around where you clicked; the higher the tolerance, the more pixels will be erased. For now, though, leave the **Tolerance** option set to the default **32**.
Anti-aliased	The Anti-aliased check box toggles whether or not you want the edges of what is erased to be smoothed (anti-aliased). In most cases, you will probably want to leave this check box checked.
Contiguous	The Contiguous check box sets whether or not you want only the pixels that are directly contiguous (adjacent) to each other to be erased. Unchecking this check box will cause pixels with a similar color to the one you clicked on to be erased over the entire image.
Use All Layers	The Use All Layers check box is fairly self-explanatory. Do you want to use the Magic Eraser tool to erase pixels that span all of the layers in your image or not?
Opacity	This slider allows you to determine at what opacity you will be erasing with. For example, if the Opacity slider is at 50%, whatever you are erasing will be 50% opaque.

13. For now, leave the Magic Eraser tool options at their defaults: **Tolerance** is **32**, **Anti-aliased** is checked, **Contiguous** is checked, **Use All Layers** is unchecked (it's irrelevant in our case because this image has only one layer anyway), and **Opacity** is **100%**. Move your mouse cursor onto the red part of the image, and single-click.

Holey bajoley! Some of you are probably saying (to whomever is within earshot) "That jerk! Why didn't he show me this way first*?!" Well...I have only my naturally sadistic nature to blame. Muahahaha.*

Actually, although in this case the Magic Eraser tool (now you see why it's called the "Magic" Eraser tool, eh?) made an extremely quick and easy job of removing that flat, red background, it doesn't work that great in all situations. The Magic Eraser tool works best in removing large areas of flat color. If the background you're trying to remove is textured or patterned in any way, your results won't be this good. Modifying your Tolerance settings is how you get the Magic Eraser tool to work better in different situations. But I'll be a monkey's uncle if that nifty Magic Eraser tool didn't do a bang-up job getting rid of that red background. Now that the logo is on its own layer, and everything else except the logo is transparent, you can easily add it to the stationery and the Web site as the client requested. Everyone's happy!

Note: The Magic Eraser tool, it seems, is truly magical. Remember how, back in Step 3, you changed the Background to a normal layer so that you could work with it? Well, the Magic Eraser tool will also do that for you as well! It slices; it dices; it cuts tomatoes, tin cans; it even...well...you get the point. If you are using the Magic Eraser to remove the background from your image, you don't need to convert the Background layer into a normal layer first because the Magic Eraser will also do that task for you as well.

14. Choose **File > Save As**. Name the file **blot_logo_layered**, and save it in the **chap_06** folder that you copied to your computer earlier. After you have saved the file, don't close it—you will be using it again in the next exercise.

3. ————————————**Modifying Colors**

Break out the champagne glasses 'cause it's time to work with some color, baby! In this exercise, you will learn how the Color Picker works, how to pick new colors, and how to apply those colors to your images. You should still have your image open from the last exercise. If you accidentally closed it, you can open it back up again. You should have saved it in your **chap_06** folder, and it should be titled **blot_logo_layered**. For now, leave the image open but move it off to the side of your screen or minimize it so that it's out of the way.

At the bottom of the Toolbox are two overlapping color swatches. By this point in the book, they might not be the default black and white, but their current color is irrelevant at the moment. The color swatch that's on the top is the **foreground color** swatch; the one behind it is the **background color** swatch. You can switch the foreground and background colors by clicking on the **Switch Colors** icon (or by pressing **X** on the keyboard), and you can always easily revert back to the default colors (black in the foreground and white in the background) by clicking the **Default Colors** icon, or by pressing **D** on your keyboard. Pretty simple, eh?

So what are the foreground and background colors used for? The foreground color is used by Elements in a variety of tasks, such as when you are painting with your paintbrush or pencil tools, and it is also used when you fill shapes, too. The background color is also used (among other things) to create fills such as gradient fills. Both the foreground and background colors are also used in some Elements filters.

Now why don't you take a look at picking colors? (This process is the same, by the way, when changing the background color as well.)

1. Single-click on the **foreground color** swatch. The Color Picker window will open. From here you can choose any color under the sun...and more.

Here is the process that you will generally want to follow when choosing a color from the Color Picker.

• *By clicking on one of the radio buttons, you can choose how you want to view and select your color, HSB (**H**ue, **S**aturation, or **B**rightness) or RGB (**R**ed, **G**reen, or **B**lue). If you click through the HSB and RGB radio buttons, you can see how both the Color slider and Color field changes—reflecting how you're choosing to select your color. Chances are you will be spending the majority of your time in the Color Picker viewing colors in the Hue mode. So for now, leave the **H** radio button selected.*

• *After you have selected Hue as your chosen color value, drag your mouse up and down the **Color** slider until you have found the color (hue) that you want.*

• *From the Color field, you can choose (based on the color you picked from the Color slider) the saturation and brightness of the color. By dragging your mouse left and right, you determine the saturation. By dragging your mouse up and down within the **Color** field, you determine the brightness.*

• *As you are locating a new color, you can easily compare your new color with the original color (the color that was already in your foreground color swatch) by looking at the Adjusted color and Original color swatches in the Color Picker window.*

• *If you are building graphics in Elements that will be posted on a Web site, you might want to check the* **Only Web Colors** *check box. On some older computer monitors that cannot display thousands or millions of colors, colors in images will shift slightly. (To exacerbate the problem, the shifted colors will differ on Mac and Windows computers.) To ensure that the colors the viewer is seeing are the same as the colors you pick, check the* **Only Web Colors** *check box. The Color Picker will then display only "browser-safe colors," that is, certain specific colors that do not shift on these older computer monitors. Check the Only Web Colors check box only if you are creating graphics for a Web page, and you need to ensure that the colors don't shift on these older computer monitors. Otherwise, leave this check box unchecked because it will limit the colors you can pick to 216 instead of millions+. If you are interested, you can read an excellent article about browser-safe colors at* **http://www.lynda.com/hex.html.**

• *If you are building graphics in Elements that will be posted on a Web site and you need to use a specific color (for instance, a color that is the same as the background color of a Web page), you can enter the hexadecimal equivalent of that color in the* **Hexadecimal** *color value field.*

• *Related to browser-safe colors is the* **Snap to Browser-Safe Color** *icon. As you are choosing a color, you might notice a small color swatch with a box icon above it appear next to the Original color swatch. Clicking on that small color swatch will snap whatever color you have currently picked to the closest browser-safe equivalent.*

2. For now, select a **red** color. I chose a semi-dark red that is (as I can see under the saturation and brightness fields) **82%** saturated and **62%** bright. Its **RGB** value is **158, 29, 29** (respectively). If you want to use the same color values as I'm using in this example, you can just type the values into the **HSB** and **RGB** fields in your Color Picker window. Click **OK**.

You'll now notice that in the Toolbox, the foreground color swatch is now the color you picked. I chose red, so my foreground color swatch is red. Now that you've picked the color you want and it's ready in the foreground color swatch to use, you need to find a place to use it! Here is where that logo you were working on in the last exercise comes back into play.

3. At the beginning of this exercise I asked that you move the **blot_logo_layered** image off to the side so that it wouldn't get in the way while you were learning about color. Now that you've learned to pick colors, you're going to apply the color you picked to the logo. Bring that logo image back into view so you can work with it some more. (If you've accidentally closed it, you can easily open it back up again by navigating to your **chap_06** folder and double-clicking on **blot_logo_layered**.)

The goal here is to change the color of the logo to the color that you picked (in my case, red). Every part of the logo that is black you will change over to your new color, but the white parts of the logo (the letters "B" and "I") will remain white.

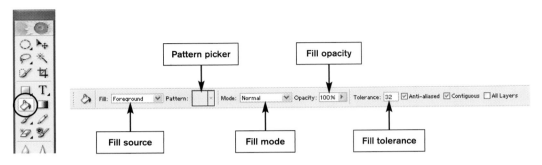

4. Start by selecting the **Paint Bucket** tool in the Toolbox.

As with many of the other tools, there are options you can set in the options bar. By now, you should also be starting to realize that many of the options you can modify are the same (or they set very similar things) across many of the tools. This is a good thing because you won't have to learn a bunch of new settings for each tool in the Toolbox. Thank goodness! Here is a breakdown of the Paint Bucket options you can set.

Paint Bucket Tool Options	
Option	**Description**
Fill source	From this pull-down menu, you can specify what you're filling with. Your two options are **Foreground** and **Pattern.** The Foreground option is pretty obvious—you can use the Paint Bucket tool to fill objects with whatever your foreground color is. Pattern allows you to fill with…yep—you made the obvious leap in logic—a pattern. If you select Pattern, you can choose a pattern to fill an object with. Which leads me to…
Pattern picker	From this pull-down menu, you can choose from a list of prebuilt patterns to fill your object with. You have choices ranging from **Wood** to **Bubbles**, and even **Tie Dye.**
Fill mode	The **Fill** mode allows you to specify how the color (and the value [the degree of lightness/darkness] of that color) you're filling with interacts with the other colors underneath it. For more information about blending modes (the same thing as Fill modes, essentially), refer back to Chapter 4, "*Layers.*"
	continues on next page

Paint Bucket Tool Options *continued*	
Option	**Description**
Fill opacity	From this slider you can specify how opaque of a color you are filling with.
Fill tolerance	Sets how similar a color must be (to the one you click on) for it to be filled with the Paint Bucket tool. The higher the number, the broader the range of colors are considered similar and the more area will be filled. The lower the number, the fewer the range of colors are considered similar and less area will be filled. In essence, when you use the Paint Bucket tool and you click on an object to fill it with your foreground color, if it doesn't fill enough of the object that you want to fill, *increase* the Tolerance and try again. If it fills too much of the object, *decrease* the Tolerance and try again.
Anti-aliased	Sets whether or not you want the edge of your fill to be smoothed (anti-aliased) or jagged (aliased). In most cases, you will want to leave the Anti-aliased check box checked.
Contiguous	Fill only the pixels that are contiguous (adjacent) to the pixel you click on with the Paint Bucket. By unchecking this check box, Elements will fill all similar colors ("similar" is defined by your Fill tolerance) over the *entire image.*
All Layers	Pretty straightforward. Do you want to use the Paint Bucket tool to fill shapes in only the layer that you currently have selected in the Layers palette or throughout all layers in your image document?

5. Make sure you have the **Paint Bucket** tool selected, and in the options bar—now that you've learned what all the options do—you need to set them up for this particular image. Set **Fill** to **Foreground, Mode** to **Normal, Opacity** to **100%,** and **Tolerance** to **32** (the default will do fine for this example). The **Anti-aliased** check box should be checked, the **Contiguous** check box should be unchecked (remember, you want to change the color of the black in the logo throughout the *entire* image), and **All Layers** should be unchecked as well (it's actually a moot point because this image document doesn't have any other layers).

6. Move your **Paint Bucket** cursor over onto the black area of the logo and single-click. If you've set up the options correctly, all the black areas of the logo should now be replaced with your chosen foreground color. Ohhh…ahhhh.

7. Save this image by pressing the keyboard shortcut **Ctrl+S** (Windows) or **Cmd+S** (Mac). Once the image has been saved, close it because you won't be needing it again in this chapter.

*Note: You can also use the menu item **Edit > Fill** to fill objects (with the foreground color). The Edit > Fill method, however, fills everything in a layer and doesn't give you the selective fill settings (based on a tolerance) like the Paint Bucket tool does. That is why you used the Paint Bucket tool for this particular example. But the Edit > Fill method is also a great and easy way to fill the contents of a layer. I'll talk a little more about using Edit > Fill in conjunction with the preserve transparency feature later in this chapter, and you will also get some experience using Edit > Fill in other chapters as well.*

*Also not to be overlooked in the arena of choosing and selecting colors is the Eyedropper tool. It's super simple to use. Just single-click on the **Eyedropper** tool in the Toolbox; then click on a part of an image that you want to take a color sample of. You also have one pull-down menu of options in the options bar. The pull-down menu allows you to specify if you want to take a color sample of the exact pixel color that you click on (**Point Sample**), or if you want to have Elements take an average color sample of the three pixels around that point or even five pixels around (**3 by 3 Average** and **5 by 5 Average**, respectively). The color that you pick will be inserted into your foreground color swatch. To have Elements take the color you pick and insert it into the background color swatch instead, hold down the **Alt** key (Windows) or **Option** key (Mac) when you click on an image with the Eyedropper tool.*

Note | Preserve Transparency

In the last exercise, you saw how to fill part of an image using the Paint Bucket tool. Another way to fill the contents of a layer, while at the same time preserving the transparent areas in a layer, is by using a feature called **preserve transparency**.

To enable the preserve transparency feature of a layer, select a layer in the Layers palette and click on the **Lock Transparency Pixels** button. This means that when you fill a particular layer with a color, Elements will preserve all the transparent areas of the layer and fill only those areas that *aren't* transparent.

By choosing **Edit > Fill** or by using the keyboard shortcut (**Alt+Backspace** [Windows] or **Option+Delete** [Mac]) to fill with the foreground color, the object will be filled with your chosen color. Thanks to the preserve transparency feature, only the contents of the layer (in this example, a ladybug) were filled. If the preserve transparency feature is turned off when you use **Edit > Fill**, the entire layer will be filled, transparent areas and all.

In this chapter you learned how to draw and paint using the Pencil, Paintbrush, and Gradient tools. You learned to use the different Eraser tools to erase portions and even entire swatches of an image based on tolerance settings. Lastly, you learned how to use the Color Picker to pick different colors and how to apply those colors to objects using the Paint Bucket tool. Wow-ee!

*In the next chapter you will be expanding on your drawing/painting/graphics creation skills by learning about Elements shapes and layer styles. *Warning* Fun and cool (oh yeah...and useful, too) stuff ahead!*

7.

Shapes and Layer Styles

| Bitmaps and Vectors | Creating Shapes |
| About Layer Styles | Layer Styles |

chap_07

Photoshop Elements 2
H•O•T CD-ROM

In this chapter you will learn about bitmap (raster) and vector graphics, and how Elements can work with both. You'll learn how to easily create vector shapes and then how to add a little spice to them by applying layer styles to those shapes. Layer styles are an exciting way to non-destructively add effects (such as bevels, drop shadows, glows, and so forth) to the graphics in layers. These layer styles can easily be turned on or off, or customized to your liking. So what are you waiting for? Oh right…you're waiting for me to stop babbling… ;-)

Bitmaps and Vectors

bitmap   *vector*

There are essentially two ways for graphics programs to create your graphics: bitmap (a.k.a. raster images) or vector. **Bitmap graphics** are constructed entirely of tiny squares of color (pixels). If the resolution (how many of those pixels there are per inch) is high enough, when you look at the image at its actual size you won't even see the pixels. Like a painting by Georges Seurat, the tiny points of color blend together to create a detailed image. **Vector images**, on the other hand, are created by lines and curves. These lines and curves combine to create your image.

Bitmap images are "resolution dependent," meaning that an image has a fixed number of pixels (you define how many when you create a new image). This is the primary reason why enlarging a bitmap graphic is discouraged. When you enlarge a bitmap graphic (called "resampling"), the graphics program (in this case, Elements) has to take an image that has a fixed number of pixels and find a way to make a larger image with *more* pixels. Elements does this in a process called *interpolation*, where it actually adds pixels to the image based on the color values of existing pixels. This always results in an image with lower quality. (You can't get something from nothing, eh?)

Vector images, on the other hand, are "resolution independent," meaning that vector images are *not* dependent on the resolution of an image and can be resized up or down without any loss in image quality. Here is a short list of pros and cons of bitmap and vector images.

Bitmap

Pros: Because you have complete control over every pixel that makes up an image, and because complex images can be created with those pixels, bitmap images are great for continuous-tone images (photographs). Working with a bitmap image, you can also easily add filters or effects to images to distort their appearances.

Cons: You can't increase the size of a bitmap image without losing image quality. Bitmap images also require more memory and hard drive space to work with than vector images. This is because Elements has to keep track of *every pixel* in a bitmap image, whereas with a vector image, Elements has to keep track of just the vector points that make up the lines and curves of a vector image.

Vector

Pros: You can easily increase or decrease the size of a vector image without any degradation in quality. They also require less memory and hard drive space than equivalent bitmap images.

Cons: You don't have the same level of control with a vector image as you do with a bitmap image. You can't add the same kind of specialized filters or effects to vector images that you can add to bitmap images. In vector editing programs, such as Adobe Illustrator, you *can* add some specialized effects to vector images, but not nearly the same type, variety, or quantity of effects available for bitmap images.

The reason why I bring up this discussion and a breakdown of bitmaps and vectors now (as some of you might be wondering) is because Elements uses vector graphics to create certain objects, such as type and shapes. As you'll see in this chapter, Elements can work simultaneously within one image using both bitmap and vector graphics.

I. ————————Creating Shapes

In this exercise, you're going to learn the basics of shapes in Elements. In the next exercise, you'll spice those shapes up a bit by adding layer styles to those shapes.

1. Copy the **chap_07** folder and files from the **H•O•T CD-ROM** to your hard drive.

2. Create a new image by choosing **File > New**. In the New dialog box, from the **Preset Sizes** pull-down menu, choose **640 x 480**. Make sure the **Mode** is **RGB Color** and under **Contents** that the **White** radio button is selected. Click **OK**. This will create a new, blank, 640 x 480 document at 72 ppi.

3. Open the file browser by choosing **Window > File Browser**. Within the file browser, navigate to the **chap_07** folder that you copied onto your computer in Step 1 and double-click on the **sunset** picture to open it.

In this exercise, you are going to add a little spice to a photograph by using shapes and layer styles. In the next chapter, you will also add a little bit of text to the image as well. In this hypothetical situation, you're going to email a photo to someone (or put it up on a Web site...more on both of those in Chapter 12, "Elements and the Web"), but you are going to add a little more visual interest to the photo first.

Now at this point you should have two images open: the blank 640 x 480 image that you created in Step 2 and the sunset picture that you just opened.

4. First make sure that you have the **Move** tool selected; then, with the images open so you can see both of them together, drag the **sunset** picture onto the blank, 640 x 480 image. After you've success- fully done this, you can close the **sunset** image document because you won't need it further.

5. Position the **sunset** image so that it's towards the top of the image space and roughly centered horizontally within the overall image space.

Next you are going to create a shape to go behind the sunset photograph—visually framing it.

6. Open the **Layers** palette by choosing **Window > Layers**. Select the **Background** layer by single-clicking on it.

7. In the Toolbox, single-click on the **Shape** tool.

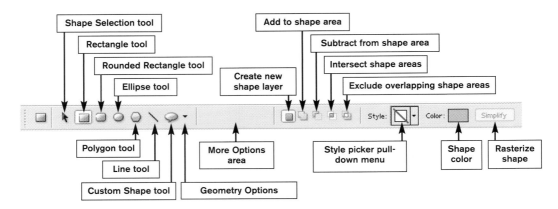

Once you click on the Shape tool, you're greeted with a variety of options in the options bar. Toward the left-hand side of the options bar, you can choose which shape you want to draw with. Your options are a rectangle, rounded rectangle (the corners are rounded), ellipse, polygon, line, or a custom shape. When you click on some of the aforementioned shapes in the options bar, you are given an option to set in the options area. For instance, when you click on the Rounded Rectangle tool, you can specify the corner radius for the curve, and when you click on the Custom Shape tool you can select, from a preset list, which shape to draw with. To the right of the Custom Shape tool is a small, downward-facing, black arrow. This is the Geometry Options button. Single-clicking on it will give you additional geometry options to set for each tool.

To the right of the More Options area is where you specify shape interaction. It's here where you control how you want the shapes to interact with each other when they are drawn. The following table outlines the options you're given and what they mean:

Shape Tool Options

Option	Description
Create new shape layer (default)	Creates a new, unique layer for each shape that you draw.
Add to shape area	Adds the shape you're drawing to the same shape layer that you currently have selected. If you don't have another shape layer selected, this option is grayed-out.
Subtract from shape area	Subtracts the shape you're drawing from any other shapes in your shapes layer, wherever they overlap.
Intersect shape areas	Shows only the areas where shapes intersect (overlap). All other areas will be removed.

continues on next page

Shape Tool Options *continued*

Option	Description
Exclude overlapping shape areas	The opposite of Intersect. Removes the area where shapes intersect and shows all other areas.
Style picker pull-down menu	As you'll see in the next exercise, the Style picker pull-down menu allows you to apply a layer style to the shape you're drawing.
Shape color	Where you can choose what color to make the shape you're drawing.
Rasterize shape button	To add a filter or effect to a shape, the shape must first be rasterized (converted from a vector to a bitmap). Clicking on this button will allow you to rasterize your vector shape in preparation to add a filter or effect.

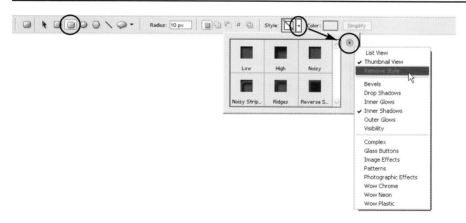

8. With the **Shape** tool selected, in the options bar single-click on the **Rounded Rectangle** tool. Leave the corner radius set to the default **10 px**. (If your corner radius is not set to 10, type **10** into the **Radius** field and press **Enter** [Windows] or **Return** [Mac].)

Note: If you used a layer style while playing around with Elements previously, a layer style might still be selected in the Style picker pull-down menu. Because you don't want the shape you're about to draw to automatically have a layer style applied to it, make sure you single-click on the Style picker pull-down menu. From the Style picker menu that appears, single-click on the additional layer styles pull-down menu button (a circle button with a right-facing triangle in it) and choose **Remove Style.** *If you already have a style selected, this will remove it.*

9. Single-click on the **shape** color swatch. In the Color Picker window that opens, choose any color you'd like. Click **OK**.

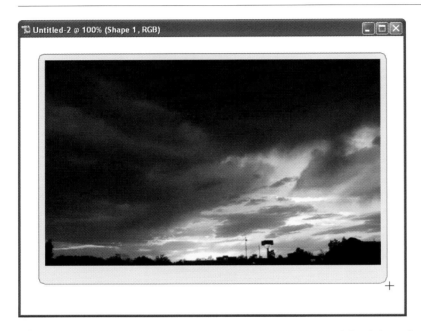

10. In the image document, drag from the top left down toward the right until you've created a shape around the sunset photograph. Give a little bit of room around the left, right, and top of the photograph, but a little extra room at the bottom.

Congratulations! You've just created a vector shape in Elements!

Note: Because this is a vector shape, you can easily scale it up or down with no loss in quality, as I described at the beginning of this chapter. Scaling up bitmaps is highly discouraged because it will slightly distort and blur the image. Vector shapes, on the other hand, can be scaled up or down without any degradation. So feel free to scale that shape around because it's a vector! Yeah, baby, yeah!

Next you're going to learn how to change the color of a vector shape. Changing the color of a shape, although very easy, is done quite differently than changing the color of objects.

11. Open the **Layers** palette by choosing **Window > Layers**. In the Layers palette, you'll see a layer titled **Shape 1**. Notice how it is underneath the layer with the sunset photo (**Layer 1**) and above the Background layer? The reason why it's in that particular place is because before you created the shape, back in Step 6, you first selected the Background layer. So when you drew out your shape, it was automatically added above the layer you had selected (just like when you create a new layer). This is precisely what you want because this shape is supposed to be *behind* the sunset photo. Aren't you smart! ;-)

12. Double-click on the **Shape 1** layer thumbnail. When the Color Picker window appears, enter **214** in the **R** (Red) field, **234** in the **G** (Green) field, and **237** in the **B** (Blue) field. (If you need help with the Color Picker, refer back to Chapter 6, "*Painting and Colors*.") This will give you a light turquoise color. Click **OK**.

Awesome! Now in the image document, the shape that you drew is the new color you just picked! Told ya it was easy! See, I'd never lead you astray…except there was that one time with the Magic Eraser tool… ;-)

13. Leave the image open–you will be using it in the next exercise.

At this point, I would encourage you to create a new blank image document (just like you did in Step 1) and experiment with the different shapes. In this exercise, you only gained experience with the rounded rectangle shape but, as was pointed out, there are other shapes that we didn't cover. However, the process of creating the other shapes is the same as the process of creating the rounded rectangle shape.

In the next exercise, you will learn how to apply a layer style to the shape that you just created. A layer style is a great and easy way to add a little flair to the dull, flat shape that is created by the Shape tool.

About Layer Styles

Layer styles are an easy way to add a complex effect to the contents of a layer. Elements gives you many different preset effects to choose from–ranging from simple drop shadows and bevels to more complex effects such as "cactus" and "molten gold." As you'll see in this next exercise, applying and modifying layer styles to the shape that you created in the last exercise is easier than pie…or is it "simpler than cake"? Well…you get the idea. ;-)

Simply put, layer styles go back to that term I introduced in Chapter 4, "*Layers*," called "non-destructive editing." What this means is that when you add a layer style to a layer, you're not permanently altering the graphics in that layer. Layer styles can easily be applied and removed from layers with a couple clicks of the mouse. So go crazy! Experiment! You can do so knowing that if you mess up, or if you don't like the changes you have made to your image using layer styles, you can always easily delete the effect, and you're back to your original, unaltered graphic. It just doesn't get any cooler than that…

2. ————————Layer Styles

In this exercise, you will learn how to add layer styles to the shapes that you created in the last exercise.

1. Open the **Layers** palette by choosing **Window > Layers** and single-click on the **Shape 1** layer to select it.

Note: If you already have the Move tool selected, you'll notice that when you select the Shape 1 layer, a bounding box (a dashed outline with boxes on the corners and sides) will appear around the shape in the image. This is how Elements tells you, visually, that the shape is selected. Now that it is selected, you can add a layer style to it.

2. Make sure that the **Move** tool is selected by single-clicking on it in the Toolbox.

Style Libraries
pull-down menu

3. Open the **Layer Styles** palette by choosing **Window > Layer Styles**. In the Layer Styles palette, single-click on the **Style Libraries** pull-down menu. From this pull-down menu, you can choose from a variety of different styles (effects) to add to your shape. Select **Inner Shadows**.

4. The Layer Styles palette will change to show you the different Inner Shadow effects you can apply to your shape. If you hover your mouse over one of the effects, a small tip will appear, telling you the full name of the effect. Single-click **Low**.

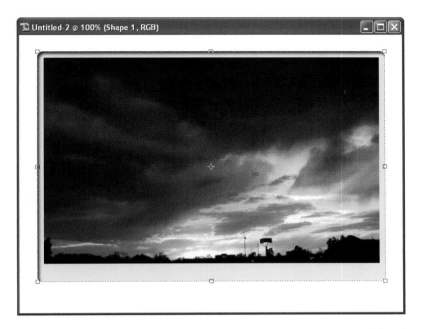

Wow! Instantly the shape behind the sunset picture now has a small, interior drop shadow. That was easy!

Next you're going to learn how to change the settings for that effect.

5. Open the **Layers** palette by choosing **Window > Layers** and double-click on the **Layer Styles** icon (it looks like an "**f**" inside a circle) on the **Shape 1** layer.

6. The **Style Settings** dialog box will open. From here, you can specify the settings for the particular style that you've applied to your shape. As you can see in this example, you can modify the **Shadow Distance.** (Unchecking the **Use Global Light** check box would enable you to modify the other settings, but all you want to modify right now is the Shadow Distance, anyway.) Drag the **Shadow Distance** slider down from the default of **5** to a more subtle **2**. If you prefer, you can also just type **2** in the Shadow Distance field. Notice that as you drag the slider around, you can see it change the effect in real time. Nifty!

7. Click **OK**.

Next you are going to draw another shape. This new shape will act as a backdrop where you can type a small description of the image.

8. Open the **Layers** palette by choosing **Window > Layers**. Single-click on the layer with the sunset picture on it, **Layer 1**.

9. Single-click on the **Rounded Rectangle** tool in the Toolbox to select it. Then, draw a long rectangle below the sunset picture, about as wide as the sunset image and about one-inch high.

Note: It's normal if this second shape is a different color than the first, larger shape you drew. When you draw a shape, Elements will color that shape with the current foreground color. In this case, however, because you're about to apply a layer style to the shape that will change the shape's color, it doesn't matter what color it is.

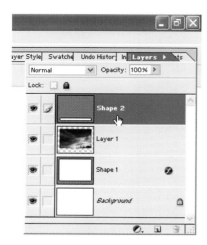

10. Checking to make sure you have the correct layer selected before you begin editing is a good practice to get into. First, open the **Layers** palette by choosing **Window > Layers**. Then, single-click on the **Shape 2** layer to double-check that it is selected.

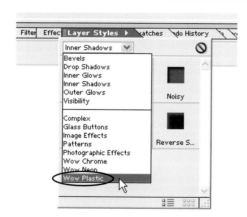

11. Single-click on the **Move** tool in the Toolbox to make sure it's selected, and then open the **Layer Styles** palette by choosing **Window > Layer Styles**. Click on the **Style Libraries** pull-down menu and choose the bottom-most option, **Wow Plastic**.

12. In the Layer Styles palette, single-click on **Wow-Plastic Gray**.

Nice! You just applied a layer style to the new shape. In the next chapter, you're going to add some text on top of that shape to give the image a short description.

13. Save the image by choosing **File > Save**. In the **File name** field, name the image **first_shape**, make sure the **Format** is set to **Photoshop**, and save the image in the **chap_07** folder.

14. After you have saved the image, leave it open because you will be using it again in the next chapter.

Note: *There are some very useful layer style options tucked away under **Layer > Layer Style** to be aware of. You can get access to **Style Settings** (which you already modified in Steps 5–7 by double-clicking on the Layer Styles icon on the shape layer); you can easily copy a layer style that you've added to a layer by choosing **Copy Layer Style**; and you can then apply that layer style to another layer by selecting the layer in the Layers palette that you want to apply the style to, and then choose **Paste Layer Style.** To remove a layer style, choose **Clear Layer Style**. If you want to temporarily hide the layer style you've added to a layer, simply choose **Hide All Effects**. (To show the layer style once you've hidden it, choose the **Layer > Layer Style** menu item again and select **Show All Effects** to make your layer style visible again.) Lastly, you can easily scale the layer style (independently from the graphics on that layer) by choosing **Scale Effects**.*

Tip: *If you really want to "push the envelope," you can apply a layer style on top of other layer styles. Normally, if you choose a different layer style to add to a layer, it removes the old layer style first and then applies the new one. But if you want to apply one (or more) layer style(s) on top of another, after you've applied one layer style, open the layer style picker pop-up menu again, and while holding down the Shift key, single-click on a different layer style. There you have it! Instead of having only one layer style per layer, you can now have multiple layer styles that overlap and affect each other. Be careful, though—you might go blind from some of the wacky (and extremely ugly) visual effects you can achieve using this method. ;-)*

In this chapter you learned how to create a simple shape and then how to apply and modify a layer style to that shape. Shapes and layer styles can also be used with great success to create snappy Web graphics or to easily add some nice effects to a postcard or flyer.

In the next chapter you will learn the ins and outs of working with type in Elements. You will also learn how to apply layer styles—like you learned in this chapter—to some text to give it a little more "umph" as well. I'll see you there!

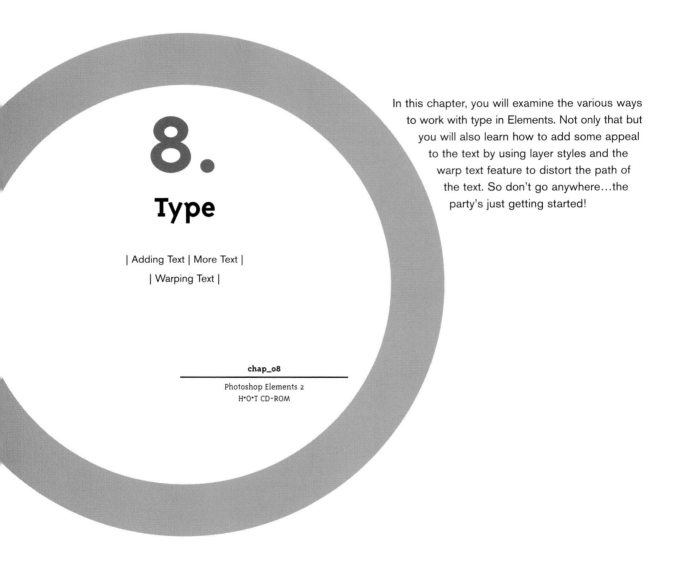

8.

Type

| Adding Text | More Text |
| Warping Text |

chap_08

Photoshop Elements 2
H•O•T CD-ROM

In this chapter, you will examine the various ways to work with type in Elements. Not only that but you will also learn how to add some appeal to the text by using layer styles and the warp text feature to distort the path of the text. So don't go anywhere…the party's just getting started!

I. _____Adding Text

In this exercise and the next, you will learn how to add type to an image document, and how to change various type settings such as font size/face, font color, font alignment, and so forth.

1. Make sure you have the image open that you were working on in the previous chapter, **first_shape**. If you accidentally closed it, you can open it back up—assuming you followed the steps in the previous chapter and saved the document—by opening the file browser (**Window > File Browser**), navigating to the **chap_07** folder, and double-clicking on the image **first_shape**.

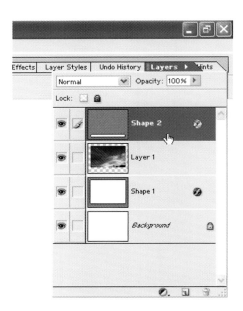

2. Open the **Layers** palette by choosing **Window > Layers**. Make sure that you have the top-most layer, **Shape 2**, selected by single-clicking on it.

3. Single-click on the **Type** tool in the Toolbox to select it.

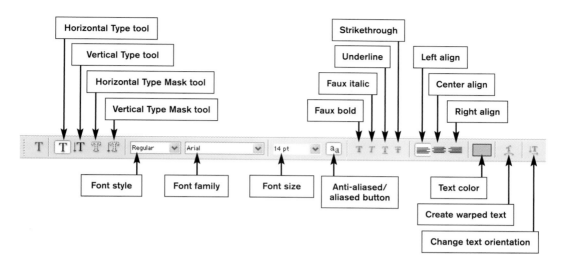

As with the other tools you have learned thus far in this book, the Type tool offers a variety of options in the options bar. Here is a chart describing what each items does.

Type Tool Options	
Option	**Description**
Horizontal Type tool	The default option. Allows you to create text along a horizontal (left-to-right) line.
Vertical Type tool	Selecting this option allows you to type text vertically (top to bottom).
Horizontal Type Mask tool	Same as the Horizontal Type tool, except the type becomes a mask (simply, a selection).
Vertical Type Mask tool	Same as the Horizontal Type Mask tool, except the type is vertical (top to bottom) instead of horizontal (left to right).
Font style	Based on whichever font is selected in the font family pull-down menu, the font style pull-down menu allows you to choose a style for the selected font (bold, italic, and so forth). **Note:** Some font families don't have any styles associated with them. If this happens to you, see (in this chart) faux bold and faux italic.

continues on next page

Type Tool Options *continued*	
Option	**Description**
Font family	From this pull-down menu, select the font family (font face) that you want to type with.
Font size	Choose what size you want the type to be. The size is rated in points (pt). For your reference, a 72-pt font is approximately one-inch high when added to an image that is 72 ppi. Increasing the resolution of an image will make the type look smaller because in a higher-resolution image, the pixels are closer together.
Anti-aliased button	Turns anti-aliasing on or off for your type. An anti-aliased type-face will have a smoothed edge, whereas an aliased typeface will have a jagged ("stair-stepped") edge.
Faux bold	If the chosen font family does not include a bold style, you can elect to have Elements make the font look bolded for you. Most, if not all, typographers and designers cringe at faux bold—and faux italic for that matter—because they distort the typeface in a manner that the original font designer didn't construct. Although I would recommend not using faux bold or faux italic—because many printers don't like/support font families that are using faux bold/italic—it will do in a pinch.
Faux italic	Same as faux bold, except italicized instead of bolded.
Underline	Underlines the text, <u>like this</u>.
Strikethrough	Puts a line through the text, ~~like this~~.
Left align	Aligns a block of text so that each line of type is aligned together on the left.
Center align	Aligns a block of text so that each line of type is aligned, centered, to the place where you originally clicked with the Type tool.
Right align	Aligns a block of text so that each line of type is aligned together on the right.
	continues on next page

Type Tool Options *continued*

Option	Description
Text color	Single-clicking on this color swatch will open the Color Picker window. From here, you can choose what color your type will be. **Note:** The foreground color swatch in the Toolbox and the text color swatch are interconnected. Changing one will change the other. So another way to change your text color would be to just change the foreground color swatch color in the Toolbox.
Create warped text	After typing some text in your image document (or by clicking with the Type tool in the image document window), you can click on the Create warped text button. This will open the Warp Text dialog box, where you can choose (from a preset list) different styles to warp your text (such as Arch, Bulge, Fisheye, and so forth).
Change text orientation	Clicking on this button will change the orientation (horizontal to vertical, or vertical to horizontal) of your selected text.

4. From the **font family** pull-down menu, choose a font. In this example, I've chosen the standard font: **Arial**. Also, if the font you selected has the proper font style, choose **Bold**.

Note: The fonts that you see in the font family pull-down menu are fonts that you currently have installed on your computer.

5. From the **font size** pull-down menu, choose **18 pt**. Make sure that the **Horizontal Type** tool is selected, **anti-aliased** is selected, and that the alignment is set to **left aligned**.

6. Now, you need to set the foreground and background colors to their defaults (**black** for foreground and **white** for background). You can do this by clicking the small **black/white color swatches** icon located at the bottom-left of the main foreground/background color swatches in the Toolbox. Because the text color pulls its color choice from the foreground color, this makes the text color black.

7. Then, simply single-click toward the left side of the gray bar that's underneath the picture. This creates an insertion point—the place where you will start typing your text.

You should see a blinking vertical line where you clicked. This is Element's way of telling you that it is ready for you to start entering text.

8. Type **Arizona Sunset**. As you type, you'll see the text appearing from left to right. This is much the same as working with type in a text editor, such as Microsoft Word.

9. When you're finished typing, click on the **Commit Edits** button in the options bar. This will make the blinking vertical line disappear, and now, if you'd like, you can select the **Move** tool from the Toolbox and drag the text around the document to reposition it wherever you'd like. Pretty straightforward, eh?

*Note: You can also commit the text changes by pressing **Enter** (on the keypad) for both Windows and Mac. Commit edits will also be performed automatically as soon as you select another tool, such as the Move tool.*

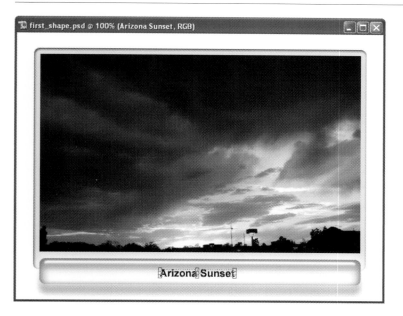

Note: As I mentioned in previous chapters, when you have the Move tool selected, the content in the currently selected layer will have a "bounding box" around the outside of it. This is how Elements shows you that you have content selected in the image. For more information about the bounding box, and what its uses are, refer to Chapter 3, "Opening and Importing Images" in the Place exercise.

*Tip: While you are typing your text, you can always quickly and easily reposition the text block without having to commit the changes first. While you're editing text, hold down the **Ctrl** key (Windows) or **Cmd** key (Mac). This will change your mouse cursor to the Move tool icon. Once you see the Move cursor, drag the text around the stage. When you have moved the text block to the correct location, simply release the **Ctrl** (Windows) or **Cmd** key (Mac) and you're back in text-editing mode. Yippee!*

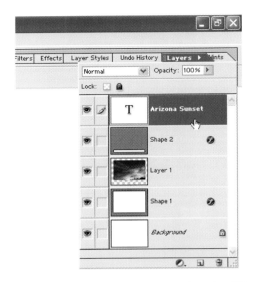

10. Open the **Layers** palette by choosing **Window > Layers**. Notice that there's now a new layer titled **Arizona Sunset**.

Where in the world did that come from? When you add text to a document, Elements will automatically create a new layer for you to hold that text. Very cool! Not only that but it will also automatically name that layer based on whatever text you are typing in. If you type in a paragraph of text, however, Elements will only display the first 30 characters of that text in the layer name. Ahhh...I remember back in the good ol' days when I had to create text layers and rename them all...manually! And I had to hike a mile...no, two miles...in the snow...just to get to my bus stop... ;-)

11. When you're done, save your changes and close the image.

More Text

In this exercise, you're going to learn more about editing and creating text in Elements. Because this exercise is for experimenting with the different text options, you're going to start by creating a blank document to give you a place to play.

1. Create a new document by pressing the keyboard shortcut **Ctrl+N** (Windows) or **Cmd+N** (Mac). In the **New** dialog box, choose **640 x 480** from the **Preset Sizes** pull-down menu. Make sure the **Mode** is **RGB Color** and select the **White** radio button. Click **OK**. This will create a new, blank, 640 x 480 document at 72 ppi.

2. Single-click on the **Type** tool in the Toolbox.

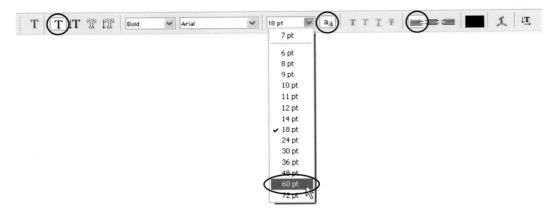

3. Before you start typing, you need to specify the font settings in the options bar. From the **font family** pull-down menu, choose a font. In this example, I've chosen the standard font **Arial**. Also, if the font you've selected has the proper font style, choose **Bold**. From the **font size** pull-down menu, choose **60 pt**. Make sure that the **Horizontal Type** tool and **anti-aliased** are selected, and that the alignment is set to **left aligned**.

4. Then, simply single-click toward the left-hand side of the image document and start typing! Type **ce n'est pas text**. After you have finished typing, click on the **Commit Edits** button in the options bar.

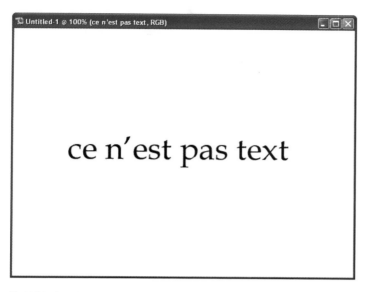

5. With the Type tool still selected, single-click on the **font family** pull-down menu again and choose a different font face. In this example, I chose **Book Antiqua**. Notice that the text in the image changes immediately!

As you can see, changing the font family of a block of text is quite simple. Just make sure you have the layer with the text on it selected in the Layers palette, make sure any of the Type tools are selected (Horizontal, Vertical, and so on), and then change the font from the font family pull-down menu in the options bar. The same technique applies, of course, to changing the font style, font size, text alignment, and color.

*Note: When you clicked with the Type tool, typed out some text, and clicked on the Commit Edits button, you created what is technically called a **type block** (because it's one "block" of text). Well, all of the text in a type block doesn't have to be all the same font family, size, or color. Different letters can be different font families, sizes, and colors.*

ce n'es

6. Make sure the **Type** tool is selected; then drag your mouse to select just the letter **c** in the first word.

Note: In Elements—and in other graphics programs—it's very easy to accidentally create a new text block when you actually meant to select some text in an existing text block. So be careful to click right on *the existing text. If you click too far away from a text block, Elements will think you are trying to create a new text block, and it will automatically create a new insertion point and text layer. I've seen beginner students wind up with multiple text layers with no text in them because they weren't clicking right on the text they were trying to edit and were inadvertently creating new text layers instead. Also, when editing the text in a layer, you don't have to have the layer selected first to be able to edit it. As long as you click with your Type tool right on the text block, Elements will automatically select the text layer for you. Nifty!*

Ce n'est

7. In the options bar, change the **font family**, **font style**, **font size**, and **text color** to something different. In this example, I chose **Arial**, **Bold**, **100 pt** (I typed **100** into the **font size** field), and **blue**. Because the letter **C** was the only letter in the type block that I had selected when I made those changes, it is the only letter that was modified.

As you can see, you have quite a bit of flexibility when working with type in Elements. But that's not all...

8. Single-click on the **Move** tool in the Toolbox. If you're currently editing text, this will commit the changes you've made.

9. Open the **Layer Styles** palette by choosing **Window > Layer Styles**. From the **style libraries** pull-down menu, choose **Bevels**. Then, single-click on the **Simple Sharp Outer** style.

Wow! With just one click from the Layer Styles palette, the text now looks like it is embossed on the page. Also note that the text is still editable. If you select the Type tool and click anywhere on the text, you'll notice that you can still edit and modify the text. If you add, remove, or change the text in the layer that you just added the layer style to, the layer style will automatically change as well to fit the edits you make to the text! That definitely rates a 10 on the coolness factor! :-)

10. Leave this image open—you will be using it again in the next exercise.

Next you're going to ratchet this whole text funny business up a notch. In the next exercise, you're going to distort the text—that still has a layer style applied to it—using the built-in warp text feature. So fasten your seat belts ladies and gentlemen, 'cause this ride is about to get a whoooole lot crazier! Actually... it's really straightforward and simple, but I'm trying to get you pumped up here...play along, would ya?

3. ————————**Warping Text**

In this exercise, you will learn how to distort the appearance of text using Element's built-in warped text feature.

1. Before you get started, make sure that you have the correct layer and tool selected. Open the Layers palette by choosing **Window > Layers**. Make sure that the "ce n'est pas text" layer is selected by single-clicking on it. Then single-click on the Type tool in the Toolbox to make sure that it is selected as well. When applying the warp text feature in this manner, you need to make sure that the layer that contains the text is selected and that the Type tool is selected.

2. Single-click on the **Create warped text** button in the options bar. This will open the **Warp Text** dialog box.

*Note: You can also warp text by selecting the layer containing the text you want to warp in the Layers palette and choosing **Layer > Type > Warp Text.***

3. In the **Warp Text** dialog box, from the **Style** pull-down menu, choose **Rise**.

As you can see from this pull-down menu, there are quite a few other warp text styles to choose from. I would recommend giving them a try (later) so you can get a good idea of what each one looks like.

*As soon as you choose **Rise** from the style pull-down menu, the text in the image document will immediately show you what that style looks like. Neat!*

Tip: *With the Warp text dialog box still open, move your mouse over the text in the image and drag to easily reposition the text. This allows you to change the position of the text in case the applied style makes it run off the edge of the image document.*

4. Leave the **Rise** style settings in the Warp Text dialog box set to their defaults. If you *were* to change the settings, however, the text in the image immediately updates to incorporate the setting changes. Click **OK**.

5. Single-click on the **Type** tool in the Toolbox, once again, to make sure you have it selected. Then move your mouse onto the image document, and drag to select just the letter **C** at the beginning of the phrase.

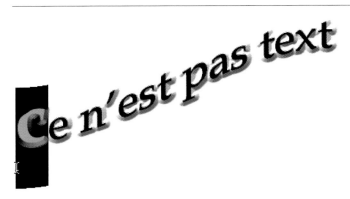

6. From the **font family** pull-down menu in the options bar, select the same font family that you chose for the rest of the phrase. In this example, I selected **Book Antiqua**–the same font family as the rest of the text in the phrase.

7. Single-click on the **Commit Edits** button in the options bar to commit the changes that you made to this text.

Ce n'est pas text

So, as you can see from this example, even after applying a layer style to this text, and even after warping the text, it is still editable. I remember quite clearly when I first saw this feature...I was blown away.

At this point, feel free to play around some more, using this text, with different warp text styles, different type settings, or even different layer styles. When you're finished experimenting, close the image and don't save the changes—you won't need this image again.

In this chapter, you learned how to add type to a document, how to apply a layer style to the text, and even how to warp it using the warp text feature. Although the text options in Elements are limited—by Adobe Photoshop standards—there is still a lot you can do with type in Elements.

In the next chapter, you will depart from the more "basic" features of Elements you have been learning thus far and will delve more into the photo correcting features that Elements provides. You will learn how to adjust the value and hue of your photographs, using various methods, to fix a poor image or to enhance its good qualities. There's lots of information to cover in the next chapter so make sure you take a bathroom break, grab a cup of tea, and meet me back here in 10 minutes, mmm k? I'm starting the timer......now! ;-)

9.
Correcting Photos

| Adjusting the Value of a Photo |
Bringing Out Details in Shadows	Correcting Overexposed Areas
Automatic Value Adjustments	Dodge and Burn
Color Adjustments	Automatic Color Adjustments
The Sponge Tool	Transforming Your Image

chap_09

Photoshop Elements 2
H•O•T CD-ROM

Just arriving back from a six-week vacation in Italy, Greece, China, Russia, and the Isle of Man, you can't wait to get those photos developed. After dropping them off at the photo developers, you return later to pick them up. Opening up the photo packages as you head back to your car, you stop dead in your tracks—some of the photos look horrible! Some are grayish because the contrast is all off, some have horrible color, and others are either under- or overexposed!! What'll you do? Throw them all away?! How can you when in that stack of horrible photos are hundreds of memories of Rome, Moscow, the Great Wall of China, and who could forget the fine city of Peel on the Isle of Man? *Sigh*

In this chapter, you will learn the skills to fix those photos. You will learn how to adjust the value (darkness/lightness) and color (hue) of photos by using a variety of different techniques—everything from one-click adjustments to using precise, manual methods. So grab the IV coffee drip and lock your office door because there's lots to cover in this chapter.

It Starts with the Source

If at all possible, you should try to make every attempt to take good photos. Sure, in this chapter, I will show you how to correct photos with bad contrast and color. In later chapters, I will even show you how to remove scratches, dust, and stains from photos. Elements can do a lot to a photo after it has been taken. But why spend hours trying to fix a photo when you could spend a couple minutes taking a few precautions to make sure you end up with a good photo? Although many digital cameras do a bang-up job of automatically correcting for different lighting and color situations, it's still a wise idea to make sure you are taking photographs under the best possible situations. Here is a short and simple list of tips for taking good photographs:

• Buy a tripod or monopod. This will stabilize the photos you take and will yield sharper photos. Tripods are essential if you are going to be taking photographs in low-light situations. A good brand to go with is Bogen (**http://www.bogenphoto.com**). Of course, for the budget-conscious, there's always the local WalMart or Target—I'm no tripod snob.

• Make sure you have proper lighting. Too much light and your photos could be overexposed—too much light in the image washes out all the detail; too little light and your image could be underexposed (too dark), of course. If you're shooting photos in low-light situations, a flash will help to illuminate the nearby area and give you instant sufficient light. Beware though, using a flash tends to overexpose anything that is too close to the flash itself.

• If you are using a film-based camera (nondigital), make sure that you have appropriate film speed for what you will be shooting. Film is rated by its sensitivity to light, called its ASA (or ISO) rating. The higher the ASA rating, the more sensitive the film is to light. So if you were taking photos of you and the family at the beach on a sunny day, 100 ASA film would work fine. On the other hand, if you were taking pictures on a cloudy day at dusk, you would need film with a higher ASA rating, like 400 or higher. A good all-purpose film is ASA 200. Be aware though, because higher ASA film can pick up low-light images better, they also have the unfortunate side effect of giving images a grainy or "soft" look.

Adjusting the Value of a Photo

In this exercise, you will learn to adjust the value (darkness/lightness) of a photograph by using a few different methods—each with its own strengths.

1. Copy the **chap_09** folder and files from the **H•O•T CD-ROM** to your hard drive.

2. Open the File Browser by choosing **Window > File Browser**. Navigate to where you copied the **chap_09** folder and single-click on it. In it, you should see six images. Double-click on the image **glass_sign** to open it.

*Note: If you don't see your **chap_09** folder in the File Browser window, right-click (Windows) or Ctrl+click (Mac) anywhere on the file listing portion of the File Browser window. A pop-up menu appears with one option that says **Refresh**. Select that option to refresh the file listing, displaying your **chap_09** folder. Elements keeps a cache of the location of your files, and if you've added something—such as copying the **chap_09** folder off of the **H•O•T CD-ROM**—since the last time you used the File Browser, it might not display your new files. Using the Refresh option, however, forces Elements to update its cache.*

As you can see, here is a good example of an image that needs its values adjusted. (No…it doesn't need to go to counseling…the other *kind of value adjusting.) One element that makes up good imagery is strong lights and darks. In this image, the darkest point is a dark gray color, and the lightest point is a light gray color. What this image is lacking is a black-point (some part of the image that is black) and a white-point (some part of the image that is white). You can achieve this by increasing the contrast of the image, which you can do in a few different ways.*

3. First, you are going to adjust the brightness/contrast of this image. Choose **Enhance > Adjust Brightness/Contrast > Brightness/Contrast**.

This menu command will open a rather unassuming dialog box. By dragging the Brightness slider up and down, you can increase or decrease the total amount of light in the image. This is essentially like adding white or black to your picture. Conversely, by dragging the Contrast slider up and down, you are either increasing or decreasing the intensity of the lights and darks in the image. The higher the contrast, the greater the intensity of the lights and darks in the image. The lower the contrast, the lesser the intensity of lights and darks. You can also adjust the values by entering a number in the fields above the sliders.

4. Because this image is a little dark, and its contrast is a little too low–see how the image looks a little faded?–you're going to increase both the brightness and contrast. Drag the **Brightness** slider (or type in this number in the **Brightness** field) up to **+8**. Then drag the **Contrast** slider up to **+52**. As long as you have the **Preview** check box checked, you should see these changes occur as you drag the sliders.

Note: The gamma value (the value of the middle tones of colors) that Mac and Windows computers use to display their graphics onscreen will differ. What this simply means is that Windows computers will display images a little darker than Mac computers will. A brightness adjustment of +8 and a contrast adjustment of +52 might look good on a Windows computer, but an image with those same settings will look a little too light on a Mac computer. The reason I'm mentioning this is because this exercise, and the accompanying screen shots, were done on a Windows XP system. As such, you may need to compensate the brightness and contrast settings if you are using a Mac. On a Mac, set the brightness to be the same (+8), but set the contrast to be +58. Keep this in mind as you work with the exercises throughout the remainder of this book. If you're using a Mac, you may need to slightly adjust any value changes in the exercises to compensate.

5. Once you have your brightness and contrast values set, click **OK**.

Now, doesn't that image look much better? Because you increased the contrast of the image, the lights and darks of the image are more intense. This gives the image some zest...some panache... a certain...je ne sais quoi...you get the idea. ;-)

*Next, you're going to adjust the values of the image again, but this time using a different method. Why do it again, you ask? Although the method you just learned (**Enhance > Adjust Brightness/Contrast > Brightness/Contrast**) works well, your options are fairly limited. In this next method, as you'll see, you have more options and control over adjusting the values of an image.*

6. Revert back to the unaltered, original image by choosing **File > Revert**. Your image should then revert back to its boring ol' self.

7. Choose **Enhance > Adjust Brightness/Contrast > Levels**.

The Levels dialog box will open. Don't worry about all those buttons and sliders—you're only going to focus on a few in this exercise.

8. Start by increasing the intensity of the highlights in the image. Drag the **white input level** slider toward the left. Technically, you're supposed to drag the white input level slider to the left until it reaches the point where the black histogram starts to rise. From an aesthetical point of view, however, I sometimes like to drag the white input level slider farther to the left, past that point. Sometimes I may want more a more intense highlight—it all depends on the image. For this image, drag the **white input level** slider until the **white input level** text box reads **210**.

Note: In case you're wondering what the numbers (0–255) correspond to, here it is. Each channel of color—Red, Green, and Blue in this case—can have 256 (0 also counts as a value) different shades of value intensity (brightness/darkness). By dragging the black, gray, and white input sliders back and forth, you're essentially specifying how intense you want the image's shadows, midtones, and highlights to be.

9. Drag the **black input level** slider until the **black input level** text box reads **69**.

Note: *Here are a few other items in the Levels dialog box you might find interesting:*

- *The **Channel** pull-down menu. From this pull-down menu, you can choose which channel's levels you want to modify. By default, you modify all three channels simultaneously (RGB). But by clicking on the pull-down menu, you can choose to modify either the Red, Green, or Blue channels—independently from the others. Simply select the channel from the pull-down menu, and drag the black, gray, and white sliders around to suit your needs. Why would you want to do this? Maybe you have a picture you took of a bunch of roses, and you want to modify the levels of just the red in the flowers. Simply select the Red channel and adjust the levels accordingly.*

- *The **black output level** and **white output level** sliders. By adjusting these sliders, you can effectively lighten the shadow range or darken the highlight range. By dragging the white output level slider to the left, you are essentially instructing Elements to lower the value of the highlight range in the image, which means the image will get darker overall. Alternatively, by dragging the black output level slider to the right, you are telling Elements to lighten the value of the shadow range of the image, which means the image will get lighter overall.*

10. Click **OK**.

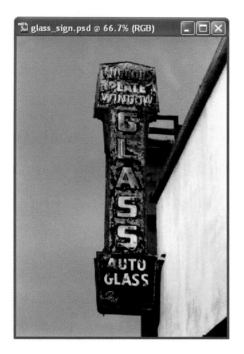

As you can see, the resulting corrected image is similar to what **Enhance > Adjust Brightness/ Contrast > Brightness/Contrast** yielded starting on Step 3. But when you use **Enhance > Adjust Brightness/Contrast > Levels**, you have much more control over the shadow, midpoint, and highlight tonal range (the lights and darks) of an image. You even have the option of adjusting the tonal range of each channel (Red, Green, or Blue) independently of one another! The more you work with adjusting the values of your images, the more I think you'll learn to appreciate the power that Levels gives you.

11. Close this image and don't save the changes. You'll be using this image again in an exercise later in this chapter, and you'll need to keep the original image as is—uncorrected.

MOVIE | **Bringing Out Details in Shadows**

Included on the **H•O•T CD-ROM** in the **movies** folder is a movie titled **shadow_details.mov**. In this movie, I demonstrate, using the file **fill_flash.psd** file in the **chap_09** folder on the **H•O•T CD-ROM**, how to lighten an image and to bring out details that are hidden in the shadows.

Note: Some operating systems, particularly Windows systems, hide the file extensions (.psd, .mov, and so forth) from you. So although I may reference a file titled **fill_flash.psd**, your computer may only display a file titled **fill_flash**. Rest assured that it is the same file.

You will open the **fill_flash.psd** file and use the **Enhance > Adjust Lighting > Fill Flash** command to bring detail into the shadowed area of the image. As you can see, the **fill_flash.psd** image foreground is heavily in shadow.

But by using the **Fill Flash** command, you can easily and quickly bring some detail into the shadowed areas of the image.

MOVIE | Correcting Overexposed Areas

Included on the **H•O•T CD-ROM** in the **movies** folder is a movie titled **overexposed.mov**. In this movie, I demonstrate, using the file **first_aid.psd** file in the **chap_09** folder on the **H•O•T CD-ROM**, how to correct overexposed (too bright) areas of a photograph and how to bring some more detail into those areas.

You will open the **first_aid.psd** file and use the **Enhance > Adjust Lighting > Adjust Backlighting** command to bring detail into and darken the overexposed areas of the image. Backlighting happens when the subject matter that is the focus of the picture—in this case, the First Aid sign—has a strong light source behind it. In this shot, the bright background gets washed out and loses detail.

The **Adjust Backlighting** command is designed to bring detail back into the overexposed places by darkening those areas. **Adjust Backlighting**, unfortunately, also has the tendency to lighten parts of the image you don't necessarily want lightened. To fix this, you will learn to use layers in combination with a layer blending mode to darken only the overexposed areas while leaving the other areas of the photograph relatively untouched.

2. ─────────────**Automatic Value Adjustments**

In a rush? Can't be bothered with correcting the value of your image by noodling with all of the sliders in the Levels dialog box? Then the automatic value adjustment commands may be just what you're looking for. In this exercise, you will learn how to use the **Auto Levels** and **Auto Contrast** commands to have Elements automatically correct the values of an image for you.

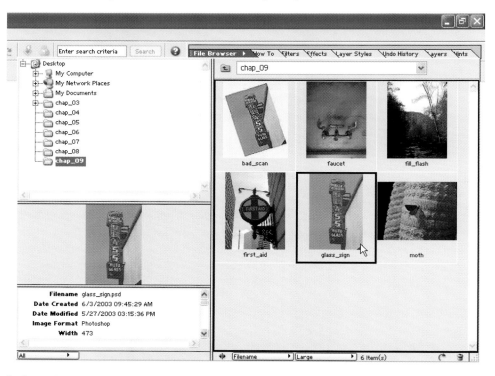

1. Open the **File Browser** by choosing **Window > File Browser**. Navigate to where you copied the **chap_09** folder and single-click on it. In the File Browser window, double-click on the file **glass_sign** to open it.

2. First, you're going to have Elements automatically guess what the best contrast settings are for this image. Choose **Enhance > Auto Contrast**.

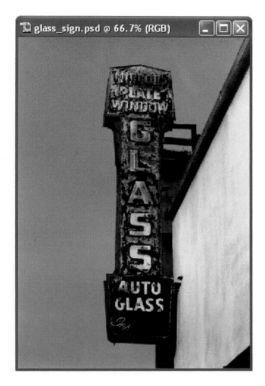

Presto! Now go take a break because that was hard work! Just kidding, of course. ;-) As you can see, Elements did a decent job automatically adjusting the contrast of the image. It takes the darkest parts of the image and sets them to black, and takes the lightest parts of the image and sets them to white. This obviously increases the contrast of the image. An image with strong contrast almost always is more engaging and interesting to look at than an image with weak contrast. Next, you're going to revert the image back to its original, uncorrected state, and check out the Auto Levels feature.

3. Revert back to the unaltered, original image by choosing **File > Revert**. Your image should then return to the way it was when you first opened it.

4. Choose **Enhance > Auto Levels**.

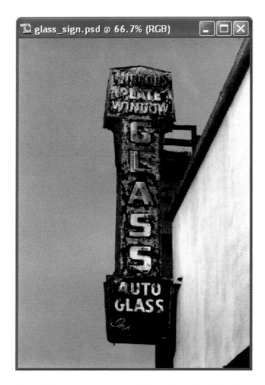

Great! As you can see, Auto Levels did a bang-up job correcting that ugly, grayish photo for you. Similar to Auto Contrast, Auto Levels sets the darkest parts of the image to black, and the lightest parts to white. At this point, some of you may be asking, "Geez…what's the difference? They both look the same to me!" The main difference between Auto Levels and Auto Contrast is that Auto Contrast adjusts the values in an image to all the channels (Red, Green, and Blue) simultaneously. Auto Levels, on the other hand, also adjusts the values of an image on each channel, but it does so one channel at a time. Because Auto Levels adjusts the channel values one at a time, it has the added side effect of possibly adding or removing color tints (where the image appears to have a subtle tint to it). You can see this if you compare the results of the Auto Contrast and Auto Levels images. The Auto Contrast image will have a slight greenish tinge to it that the Auto Levels image is lacking. This is because the Auto Levels feature automatically removed that green color tint by apply-ing value adjustments to each channel of the image, one at a time. Although this may sound like a good thing, Auto Levels might also inadvertently add a color tint to the image. If Auto Levels gives your image a slightly tinted color, undo Auto Levels and try applying Auto Contrast instead.

5. When you are finished with this image, close it and don't save any changes.

3. ——————Dodge and Burn Tools

With the adjustment techniques I've shown you thus far, the entire image is adjusted. But what if you wanted to lighten or darken only a specific part of your image—not the whole caboodle? One way is to use selections—as demonstrated in Chapter 5, "*Selecting*"—to select only part of an image, and then use the techniques you've learned so far to adjust just that area. Another method is to use two specific tools—the **Dodge** and **Burn** tools—to selectively lighten and darken (respectively) portions of an image. Because you have already learned how to use and make selections, in this exercise, you will learn how to adjust the value of specific parts of an image by using those two tools.

1. Open the **File Browser** by choosing **Window > File Browser**. Navigate to where you copied the **chap_09** folder and single-click on it. In the File Browser window, double-click on the **fill_flash** file to open it.

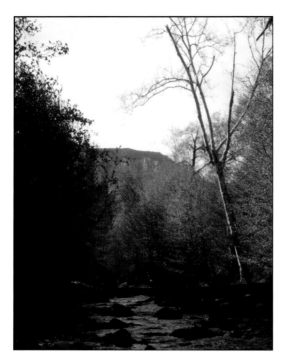

As you can see, the trees and rocks in the foreground/middleground are so dark that much of the detail has been lost. In the movie **shadow_details.mov** on the **H·O·T CD-ROM**, I demonstrate how to lighten this image by using the Fill Flash feature. The only problem with Fill Flash is that it lightens the entire image, not just the dark areas. Yes, you could use selections in combination with Fill Flash to lighten only certain areas of the image. In this case, however, why go through the hassle of making a decent selection and then utilizing Fill Flash when you can do it faster and easier with the Dodge and Burn tools?

2. Select the **Dodge** tool by single-clicking on it in the Toolbox.

As with most tools, there are a few options you will need to look over before you actually dig in and start using the tool. The following table describes those options and their meanings:

Dodge Tool Options	
Option	**Description**
Brush presets	From this pull-down menu, you can choose from a preset list of brush sizes and styles—everything from hard-edged brushes to soft-edged brushes, and a circular-shaped brush to a grass-shaped brush (and more). It's all inside this pull-down menu.
Brush size slider	Dragging this slider (or typing a value in the Size field) allows you to specify the size of the brush you will be using to lighten the image.
Tonal range	Choose which tonal range you want to lighten. Do you want to lighten the Midtones, Shadows, or Highlights in the image?
Exposure slider	Essentially, this is how much you want to lighten the image per stroke of the brush. Is it lightening the image too much for your liking when you drag the brush across the image? Lower the exposure percentage. Not lightening the image enough? Raise the exposure percentage. Nuf said. ;-)

3. From the **brush presets** pull-down menu, choose the **Soft Round 65 pixels** brush. (Remember, if you hover your mouse over one of the brush preset images, it will show you the name of that brush preset.) When you select that brush preset, the **Size** should automatically set itself to **65 px**. Also, set the **Range** to **Midtones** and the **Exposure** to **35%**. You may think that the tonal range should be set to Shadow (after all, you want to lighten the shadows), but in this case, you don't want to lighten just the shadows, but the midtones of the image as well.

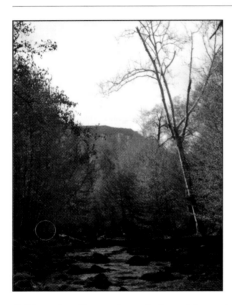

4. Then, just like you're painting with a paintbrush, drag the **Dodge** tool brush around the tree in the left middleground of the image to lighten it up.

Note: If you paint over the same area more than once, it will lighten even further. This is because the Exposure is set to 35%, so every time you paint with the Dodge tool over a previously painted area, it lightens an additional 35 percent. To make sure I'm lightening the image consistently, I usually make one pass with the Dodge tool over everything I want to lighten without letting go of the mouse button. I also try to make sure that I don't go over the same area more than once. Then I know that all of these areas should be lightened by 35 percent.

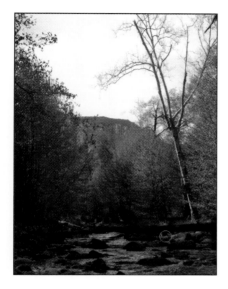

5. Press the **[** (left bracket) key on your keyboard about three times to reduce the size of the brush to **40 px**. Now drag over the smaller areas you want to lighten, such as the rocks in the stream foreground, the tree that's hanging over the stream, and so forth. Be careful that you don't go Dodge-tool crazy and lighten everything though! Remember, strong lights and darks makes for an interesting image. If you remove all of the strong darks with the Dodge tool, the image will become boring and dull to look at.

*Note: If you want to go one step further, feel free to set the **Range** to **Highlights** and drag over some of the highlights in the stream. This will bring some more light into the lower half of the image, increasing the overall contrast, and also helping to visually balance out the light area in the top half of the image.*

At the moment, the sky is somewhat of a white blob at the top of the image and could use a little darkening in places. You're going to use the Burn tool to give it a little dimension.

6. Single-click on the **Burn** tool in the Toolbox.

Just like the Dodge tool, the Burn tool also has options you can set in the options bar. I won't outline what each option does—the options are identical to those of the Dodge tool, except the Burn tool options apply to burning (darkening) the image, not dodging (lightening) it.

7. From the **brush presets** pull-down menu, choose **Soft Round 65 pixels**. Set the **Range** pull-down menu to **Midtones** and set **Exposure** to **75%**.

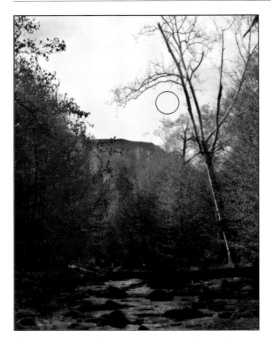

8. Drag around the sky to darken parts of it.

The Burn tool can't really do much with some parts of the sky where it is really bright (such as between the dead tree in the middle of the image and the green tress on the left). But at the top left of the image and around the branches of the dead tree, you'll notice that the Burn tool will darken the sky a little and will bring some detail back into those overexposed areas.

9. Close the image and don't save the changes.

From this exercise, I hope you learned how the manual tools, in some ways, can give you more control and yield better results than their menu counterparts, such as the Fill Flash command. In this case, the resulting adjusted image looks more balanced, and no details get lost in shadows.

Color Adjustments

Now that you have learned how to adjust the value of an image, it's time to look at adjusting the color of an image. In this exercise, you will learn a variety (variety? heck...a smorgasbord!) of different techniques to adjust the color of an image. You can do everything—change the saturation (how "bright" or "dull" a color is), remove colors, and even replace colors. When you get pictures developed from a film-based camera (that is, non digital), many different factors can determine how the colors in the photographs look. How old the film is, how clean (or dirty) the developing chemicals are at the photo lab, how well trained the staff is, and even the quality of the paper that the photos are printed on will all play a part in the quality of the photos. The techniques you will learn in this exercise—combined with what you learned earlier in this chapter—will enable you to bring home those sometimes poorly printed photographs and correct them so they look like they were printed by a professional. Of course, I can't help you if you took a picture with your thumb in the frame, or if you accidentally cropped off everyone's head.

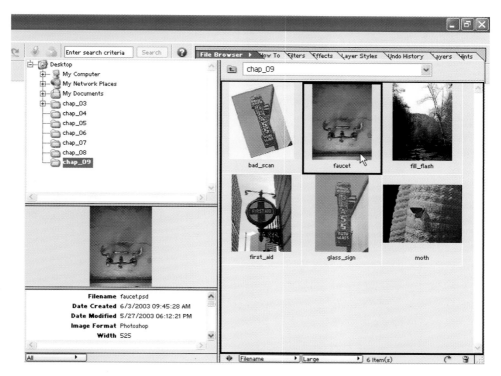

1. Open the **File Browser** by choosing **Window > File Browser**. Navigate to where you copied the **chap_09** folder and single-click on it. In the File Browser window, double-click on the file **faucet** to open it.

*Because you weren't "on location" when this photograph was taken, you can't tell that the actual scene didn't have a blue tint to it like this photograph does. The wall is actually supposed to be a semi-desaturated (dull) green color. My digital camera performed an automatic white balance when I shot this photo, which gave this image a blue tint. Using the **Color Cast** feature of Elements, however, you're going to remove that blue color tint.*

2. Choose **Enhance > Adjust Color > Color Cast**.

*The **Color Cast Correction** dialog box appears, and it kindly informs you that to correct a color cast (the blue tint in the **faucet** image), click around the area of the image that should be gray, white, or black. Pretty simple concept, eh? Don't click **OK** just yet.*

3. Leave the Color Cast Correction dialog box open and simply move your mouse over onto the image until your cursor turns into an **eyedropper**. Then, click on an area of the image. In this case, I clicked on a middle tone (gray value) area of the image.

*As if by magic (poof!), the blue color cast is gone! Now the image color looks great, and the wall is the color it should be—a desaturated green. One of the nice features of the **Color Cast** command is if you don't like the results you get the first time, you can continue to click with the eyedropper in different parts of the image until the color cast has been corrected to your liking. Nice!*

Note: *After clicking around with the eyedropper for awhile, if you feel you need to revert back to the original, uncorrected image so you can start over again, simply click on the **Reset** button in the Color Cast Correction dialog box. Your image will then reset to the way it was before you started making color cast changes.*

4. When you have the image looking the way you want it, click **OK** to accept the changes.

Next, you're going to learn how to adjust the overall hue and saturation (color and color intensity) of this image. This technique is very useful when you want to add a little extra color to dull images, or when you want to tint an image a certain color.

5. Choose **Enhance > Adjust Color > Hue/Saturation**.

*The **Hue/Saturation** dialog box will open. From here, you can adjust the **Hue** (color), **Saturation** (color intensity), and **Lightness** (similar to Brightness, which you saw earlier in this chapter when you learned the Brightness/Contrast feature) of an image. By dragging these sliders around, you can modify the entire image, or by choosing a color from the **Edit** pull-down menu, you can make adjustments to one specific color while leaving the other colors untouched. You can also check the **Colorize** check box to add a color tint to the image. By dragging the **Hue**, **Saturation**, and **Lightness** sliders back and forth, you can adjust the settings of that color tint.*

6. Experiment with the sliders by dragging them around and noticing the changes it makes to your image. You can always reset the image back to the way it was by dragging the sliders to the middle (0) point. Notice that the colors in the image change as you drag the **Hue** slider to the left and right. Now try dragging the **Saturation** slider. Notice that when you drag it to the left, the colors in the image start to fade until it is completely black and white. Dragging it to the right, on the other hand, increases the intensity of the colors. Lastly, try dragging the **Lightness** slider, which simply increases how light or dark the image is.

Next, you're going to use the Hue/Saturation feature to tint the image. This is a great effect to utilize when you want an image to look like a duotone because you are simply limiting the image's color palette to one hue.

7. Click on the **Colorize** check box. This instructs Elements to display the image using only one color—well, two colors if you count black, hence the name "duotone." Drag the **Hue** slider to determine the color you want to use to display the image. As I just discussed, you can also adjust the saturation and lightness of that color by dragging the **Saturation** and **Lightness** sliders. Remember, you can also type numbers into the **Hue**, **Saturation**, and **Lightness** fields if you happen to know the exact numbers you want to use. Set **Hue** to **160**, **Saturation** to **19**, and **Lightness** to **+5**. Click **OK**.

As you can see, this will tint the picture with a green hue. Cool!

But after presenting this image to the (hypothetical) client, he comes back with "Yeah. That's…nice. But try making the image black and white…let's see what that looks like." So back to the drawing board you go…muttering about clients who can't make up their minds. ;-) Luckily for you, converting an image to black and white is a snap.

8. Choose **Enhance > Adjust Color > Remove Color.**

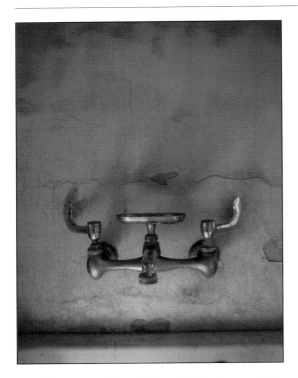

Voilà! Instant, no-fuss, black-and-white image. It doesn't get any easier than that.

Tip: Converting an image into black and white is a great way to look at just the values (the darks and lights) of an image without getting distracted by the hues (the colors). If you would rather not go through the process of converting an image to black and white, you can always use your built-in converter—your very own eyeballs! If you squint at an image, so that your eyes are barely open, you can quickly see the lights and darks in an image. I've said it before, and I'll say it again: One of the major keys to making an image look good is contrast. If you have strong lights and darks in an image—especially if they're right next to each other—the image will appear more interesting and dynamic. The preceding image looks a little washed out because it doesn't have strong lights and darks. Luckily, you've already learned how to adjust the values of an image by using Levels, so you know how to "fix" this image. :-)

9. Close this image and don't save the changes. You won't be needing this image again in this exercise.

5. ———————More Color Adjustments

In this exercise, you are going to replace the sky color with a different color by using the **Replace Color** feature in Elements.

> **1.** Open the **File Browser** by choosing **Window > File Browser**. Navigate to where you copied the **chap_09** folder and single-click on it. In the File Browser window, double-click on the file **glass_sign** to open it.

> **2.** Choose **Enhance > Adjust Color > Replace Color**.

> *This will open the **Replace Color** dialog box, which is broken up into two main sections.*
> ***Selection**, at the top, displays the color you have picked to replace, and **Transform**, at the*
> *bottom, is essentially the same as the Hue/Saturation dialog box.*

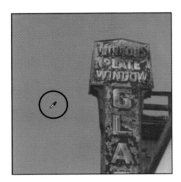

3. With the **Replace Color** dialog box still open, move your mouse over onto the **glass_sign** image. When your cursor passes over the image, it should turn into an **eyedropper** icon. Move your mouse onto the color you want to replace—in this example, the blue sky—and single-click.

*Now look at the Replace Color dialog box. You should see a small, black-and-white silhouette of the glass sign, which represents your image. Everything that is colored black won't be replaced, and everything that is colored white will be replaced. You can change the range of colors that Elements considers similar to the one you clicked on by dragging the **Fuzziness** slider to the left or right. Dragging it to the right tells Elements to consider more colors similar to the one you first clicked on. Dragging it to the left tells Elements to consider fewer colors similar. Your goal with the **Fuzziness** setting is finding the right balance between selecting the colors you want to replace versus those you want to leave alone.*

4. Drag the **Fuzziness** slider to **70**, or just type **70** in the **Fuzziness** field. As you can see in the black-and-white thumbnail image, this highlights the majority of the sky in white and leaves the rest of the image as black. Remember, when you select a new color, it will replace the parts of the image that are highlighted white, while leaving the highlighted black parts untouched. In the **Transform** section, choose a color to replace the blue sky with by setting the **Hue** to **+180**, the **Saturation** to **−45**, and the **Lightness** to **+60**. Click **OK**.

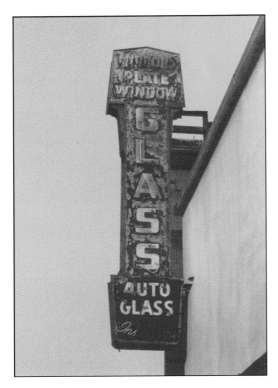

Neat! Now every place in the image that had a blue sky color has been replaced with the new color. All too easy...

Next, you're going to learn about a really easy and intuitive way to change the hue, saturation, and lightness of an image. Yes, you already learned how to do that using the Hue/Saturation dialog box, but this method does it a little differently, as you'll see. Using **Color Variations***, you are going to make the* **glass_sign** *image look somewhat like an old photograph by modifying the colors.*

5. Choose **Enhance > Adjust Color > Color Variations**.

This will open the **Color Variations** dialog box. As you can see, you have quite a few options. Luckily, Adobe has made it very intuitive to use. At the top of the window are two thumbnails of the **glass_sign** image. The one on the left is the Before image, and the one on the right is the After image. As you adjust the color of the image, you'll see the After image update to reflect the changes you're making. On the bottom half of the Color Variations window, you have some numbered options:

- **Step 1: Select area of image to adjust.** From here, you can choose whether to adjust the **Midtones**, **Shadows**, **Highlights**, or the **Saturation** of this image.

- **Step 2: Adjust Color Intensity.** By dragging the **Amount** slider to the left or right, you can decrease or increase (respectively) the amount that the color variations will be applied to the image. A low amount means that a color variation of **Lighten**, for example, will only lighten the image a little, whereas a high amount will lighten the image a lot.

- **Step 3: Use buttons below to adjust your image.** From here, all you need to do is click on the image that represents what you want to do to the image. If you want to darken it, click on the **Darken** graphic. Pretty straightforward, eh? You can also easily undo or redo the last color variation you applied, or even reset the image back to the way it was before you opened the Color Variations window by clicking on the self-explanatory buttons at the right side of the window.

6. Select the **Midtones** radio button and make sure the **Amount** slider is in the middle. Then, make the image look a little faded and yellowish. To do that, click on the **Decrease Blue** graphic three times and the **Decrease Red** graphic once.

This has the effect of making the image look like an old, yellowed photograph. The image is a little too saturated, though. In the next step, you will use Color Variations to lower the saturation of the image a little.

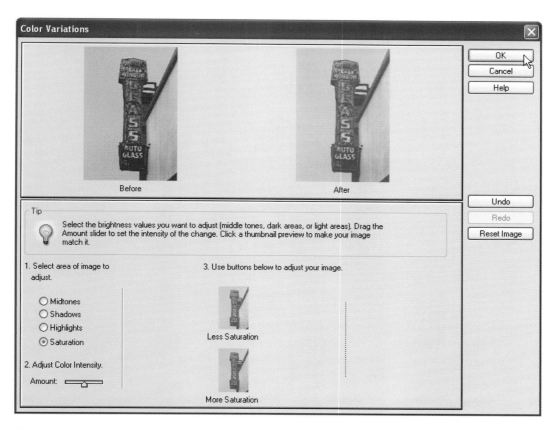

7. Click on the **Saturation** radio button. Then, Step 3 will change to display only two options: **Less Saturation** or **More Saturation**. Because you want to decrease the image saturation, click on the **Less Saturation** graphic once. You're all done! Click **OK**.

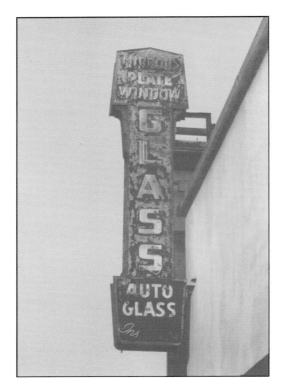

Now, thanks to Color Variations, the **glass_sign** image looks like a 30-year-old photograph pulled out of an old box in the attic.

Color Variations is also a great way to subtly modify the hue, saturation, and lightness of an image. It's similar to the Hue/Saturation window, but it is unique because it allows you to make these modifications piecemeal. This allows you to easily make small, incremental changes to your images in a step-by-step fashion.

---

8. Leave this image open—you will be using it in the next exercise.

In this exercise, you learned a variety of different ways to modify, remove, and replace colors in an image—each with its own strengths. In the remainder of the chapter, you will learn a few more methods to modify the colors in your images, as well as how to fix poorly scanned photographs.

---

6. —————————Automatic Color Adjustments

Now that you've seen some more "manual" ways of adjusting the color of an image in Elements, you're going to sit back and let Elements do the work for you.

1. Choose **File > Revert** to revert back to the previously saved version of **glass_sign**. If you accidentally closed the **glass_sign** image between this exercise and the last, you can reopen it again by opening the **File Browser** (**Window > File Browser**), navigating to the **chap_09** folder, and double-clicking on the file **glass_sign**.

2. Choose **Enhance > Auto Color Correction**.

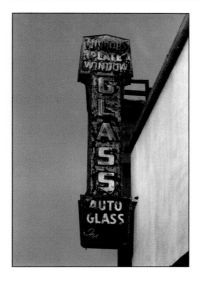

*As always, my sadistic nature shines through. I wait until after I've shown you all the "hard" ways before I show you the one-click, "easy" way. MUAHAHAHAHA!!! (cue evil cackle) ;-) The **Auto Color Correction** command, as its name implies, automatically adjusts the contrast and color of an image. It often is a little too aggressive for my taste, but it certainly wins a blue ribbon in doing a bang-up job in an extremely short amount of time with minimal effort. Modifying the color of images using the manual methods, as you have seen thus far in this chapter, have their obvious advantages, however. By using Levels in combination with the Hue/Saturation window, I have full and complete control over all of the values and hues in my image. Although Auto Color Correction does a great job, there's something to be said for manually tweaking your images to get the exact look you want.*

3. Close this image and don't save the changes.

7.————————**The Sponge Tool**

In Exercise 4 of this chapter, you learned how to change the saturation of an image using the Hue/ Saturation window. Unless you selected only a portion of the image first, changing the saturation affected the whole image. The **Sponge** tool, however, allows you to selectively modify the saturation of an image.

1. Open the **File Browser** by choosing **Window > File Browser**. Navigate to where you copied the **chap_09** folder and single-click on it. In the File Browser window, double-click on the **moth** file to open it.

In this exercise, you are going to bring attention to the moth by decreasing the saturation on everything but *the moth, and then slightly increasing the saturation on the moth itself.*

2. Single-click on the **Sponge** tool in the Toolbox. It looks like…well…a sponge.

The Sponge tool has a few options you can set before you begin working with it. Here is a break-down of the different options and what they mean:

Sponge Tool Options	
Option	**Description**
Brush presets	From this pull-down menu, you can choose from a list of preset brush sizes and styles to work with.
Brush size slider	This allows you to choose what size brush you want to use for the Sponge tool.
Sponge mode	Choose whether you want the Sponge tool to saturate or desaturate the image as you are painting with it.
Flow percentage slider	This allows you to set the rate at which the image's saturation changes. A low Flow percentage will change the saturation of the image more slowly than will a high Flow percentage. Set the Flow percentage to a low number for a subtle effect or to a high number for a more dramatic effect.

3. From the **brush presets** pull-down menu, choose a fairly large, **Soft Round 100 pixels** brush. Make sure the **Mode** is set to **Desaturate** and the **Flow** is set to **100%**. The first thing you are going to do is to desaturate the area around the moth.

4. Move your brush onto the moth image, and start dragging it around. Drag it over everything *except* the moth. Notice how I didn't desaturate the image right up to the moth. I gave myself a little bit of room. The 100-pixel round brush is just a little too big to get all the detailed areas.

5. Press the **[** (left bracket) key five times to reduce the size of the brush. Then, drag closer around the outside of the moth to desaturate any of the area that's left over. Remember, don't desaturate the moth itself.

6. Click on the **Mode** pull-down menu and choose **Saturate**. Now the Sponge brush will saturate (increase the color intensity) whatever it paints over instead of desaturating. Also, set **Flow** to **25%** so that the saturation effects are more subtle.

7. Drag around the moth—being careful not to stray outside the moth—to slightly increase the saturation.

before   *after*

By simply changing the saturation, you've given more interest and attention to the moth, which is what you want the focus of the image to be. You did this, quite easily, by using the Sponge tool to saturate and desaturate portions of the image. Great job!

8. Close this image and don't save the changes.

MOVIE | Transforming Your Image

Included on the **H•O•T CD-ROM** in the **movies** folder is a movie titled **transforming.mov**. In this movie, I demonstrate how to correct a poorly scanned image.

The **transforming.mov** movie opens the image **bad_scan.psd** in the **chap_09** folder on the **H•O•T CD-ROM**.

By using a command under the **Image** menu and the **Crop** tool, you will learn to straighten and crop the image.

In this chapter, you covered a huge amount of information. You learned how to take a poor photograph and improve its quality by adjusting its value and hue. As you saw, there were a variety of ways to go about adjusting those two simple things. Each method had its own strengths and weaknesses. Some were simple, and others required a little more work to master. As you work with more images, you'll learn which methods work best for you, and under which circumstances.

In the next chapter, you will delve into the image-editing universe of retouching photos. You will learn how to remove "red eye," wrinkles, and dust and scratches. You will also learn how to sharpen and blur photos to draw the viewer's interest to where you want it. There's a lot of new and exciting information coming your way. Now would probably be a good time to take that bathroom break you've been holding out on... ;-)

10.

Retouching Photos

| Removing "Red Eye" | Removing Wrinkles |
| Removing Dust, Scratches, and Imperfections |
| Sharpening a Photo | Blurring a Photo |
| Colorizing a Black-and-White Photo |

chap_10

Photoshop Elements 2
H·O·T CD-ROM

In the last chapter, you learned how to correct a photo that has bad value or color. In this chapter, it's all about the details. You will learn how to easily remove the annoying "red eye" (that makes your kind uncle Bob look like a homicidal maniac), how to subtly remove wrinkles from a face (better than botox injections—and less painful, too!), how to remove dust, scratches, and imperfections from a photo, how to sharpen/blur areas selectively, and how to colorize a black-and-white photo. So, as you can see, there are lots of new and really fun things to cover in this chapter. Read on, good friend, read on.

I. ———————Removing Red Eye

In this exercise, you will learn how to easily remove red eye from a photograph. The dreaded red eye is caused when light—from the flash on your camera, for instance—is reflected off of the back of someone's eye(s). Although many digital cameras do a good job at filtering out red eye, some photos with red eye will invariably slip through, especially if you take pictures with a standard film-based camera.

1. Copy the **chap_10** folder and files from the **H•O•T CD-ROM** to your hard drive.

2. Open the **File Browser** by choosing **Window > File Browser**. Navigate to the **chap_10** folder you copied onto your computer in Step 1, and double-click on the **red_eye** picture to open it.

*As you can see in the photograph, not only are her hands filthy, but she's got a bad case of the red eye. Luckily, it's easily corrected in Elements using the **Red Eye Brush** tool. The Red Eye Brush tool is essentially the Eyedropper tool and the Clone stamp tool, which you'll learn later in this chapter, mixed together into one tool…but in a very smart way. The Red Eye Brush tool allows you to quickly sample a color you want to replace in an image (the red pupils in the sample image) and replace it with a color of your choosing (in this case, you'll replace the red with black). Not only that, but the Red Eye Brush tool leaves the texture in the image intact while changing only the color. Pretty spiffy, eh?*

3. Single-click on the **Red Eye Brush** tool in the Toolbox.

And what would a tool be if there weren't some options to set? The following table outlines the options you're given and what they mean:

Red Eye Brush Tool Options	
Option	**Description**
Brush presets	Allows you to choose different brush sizes, styles, and shapes.
Brush size	Allows you to choose what size brush you want to use. When removing red eye, you optimally want the brush size to be a little larger than the pupil.
Current color	Displays the color that the Red Eye Brush tool is currently hovering over. You can use the feedback you get from the current color swatch to make sure you are targeting (for replacement) the exact color you want.
Replacement color	Here you set which color you want to use to replace the color you're sampling with the Red Eye Brush tool. The default replacement color is black—fitting for the pupil of the eye. However, you can choose whichever color you want for replacement. Click on the Replacement color swatch to get the Color Picker where you can choose any replacement color you'd like.
Default Colors button	Sets the Current and Replacement colors back to their defaults: red for the Current color and black for the Replacement color.
Sampling pull-down menu	Allows you to choose how the target color (the color you're choosing to replace) is chosen. **First Click** means that the first color you click on with the Red Eye Brush tool will be the targeted color that will be replaced. If you select Current Color, on the other hand, you can then click on the Current color swatch, and from the Color Picker, pick a specific target color you want replaced. In most cases, leave it set to First Click so you can easily sample the exact color you want to remove in an image.
Tolerance slider	Sets how similar a color in the image must be (to your Current color) for it to be replaced. The higher the number, the more similar colors will be replaced. The lower the number, the fewer similar colors will be replaced.

4. With the **Red Eye Brush** tool selected, you need to set a few of those options in the options bar before you start. Single-click on the **brush presets** pull-down menu, and choose the **Soft Round 13 pixels** brush. Click on the **Default Colors** button to set the **Current** and **Replacement** colors to their defaults (the **Current** color will change when you move the **Red Eye Brush** tool over the image), set **Sampling** to **First Click**, and set **Tolerance** to **30%**.

Note: The Tolerance setting is one of the more important settings for the Red Eye Brush tool because it determines how much of the target color (the red in the red eye) will be replaced as you drag the Red Eye Brush tool over the image. I'd recommend starting with the default **Tolerance** of **30%** to see if it removes enough of the red eye in your image. If the Red Eye Brush tool is not removing enough of the red at that Tolerance level, increase it a little and try again. Conversely, if you see some areas in the image that are being affected by the Red Eye Brush—such as the pink color of the eyelid or surrounding areas—try lowering the Tolerance so that the Red Eye Brush tool is removing only the red in the red eye.

5. Zoom into the image by using the keyboard shortcut **Ctrl++** (the Ctrl key and the plus sign key—on Windows) or **Cmd++** (the Cmd key and the plus sign key—on the Mac) three times. This will zoom you closer into the image at 400 percent. Alternatively, you can also select the **Zoom** tool (the magnifying glass) in the Toolbox and click repeatedly on the image to zoom into it.

6. Make sure you have the **Red Eye Brush** tool selected first. Then, position the tool over the pupil on one of her eyes so that the small plus sign in the middle of the tool icon (a circle) is over the red color. Next, simply drag—press and hold the mouse button while you drag—around the pupil of her eye, making sure to drag over all the areas that are red. The **Red Eye Brush** tool might miss a few spots initially—because of the **Tolerance** setting of **30%**, those left-out colors are out of range. To get rid of any left-over red areas, simply click on them with the crosshairs in the center of the **Red Eye Brush** tool.

7. Repeat this process for the other eye until all of the red eye has been removed.

8. When you're done, zoom out of the image, back to 100 percent. One easy way to do that is to simply double-click on the **Zoom** tool (magnifying glass icon) in the Toolbox.

before   *after*

9. Choose **File > Save As**. Save this image in the **chap_10** folder with a title of **no_red_eye**, and then close it.

So as you can see, removing the dreaded red eye with the Red Eye Brush tool is not only quick and easy, it also does an awesome job as well! As I mentioned earlier in this exercise, one of the nifty things about the Red Eye Brush tool is that it just replaces colors and won't modify the texture in an image. Because of this, anyone would be hard pressed to tell that the "after" image had ever been modified at all. Now…if they could only come out with a Finger Cleaning Brush tool…;-)

MOVIE | Removing Wrinkles

Included on the **H·O·T CD-ROM** in the **movies** folder is a movie titled **wrinkles.mov**. In this movie, I demonstrate how to remove wrinkles from a face in the **remove_wrinkles.psd** file in the **chap_10** folder on the **H·O·T CD-ROM**.

In the **wrinkles.mov** movie, you will first open the file **remove_wrinkles.psd**. This is a picture of someone who has a few wrinkles you can touch up.

Note: Removing wrinkles, using the method that I demonstrate in the movie, is not intended to make an 80-year-old man appear like he's in his 20s. (You'll need much more than Elements for that— instead do a search on Google for "Plastic Surgery.") This technique of covering up wrinkles is better suited for a face that has a few wrinkles around the eyes, mouth, or forehead that can be easily touched up without altering the overall appearance of the face. Wrinkles give a face character, so you need to be careful which ones to remove and how many. You'll learn this, over time, with practice.

You'll then use the Clone Stamp tool coupled with a blending mode to carefully, and subtly, cover up some of the wrinkles around the eyes. The end result should be like applying makeup—you shouldn't notice it.

2.———————Removing Dust, Scratches, and Imperfections

In this exercise, you will learn how to remove dust, scratches, and other imperfections from a photograph. This is the same method you would use, by the way, to fix up an old, torn, and stained family photo. In this case, we're going to use a photo—for learning purposes—that has a few imperfections and scratches, and could do with a color overhaul.

1. Open the **File Browser** by choosing **Window > File Browser**. In the File Browser, navigate to the **chap_10** folder you copied onto your computer earlier, and double-click on the **dust_and_scratches** file.

2. When the image opens, double-click on the **Zoom** tool (the magnifying glass icon) in the Toolbox. This sets the image so that you're viewing it at 100 percent its actual size. When adjusting the details of an image (as you're about to do), it's always best to work with the image when it's at 100 percent, or even closer, like 200 or 400 percent. It's just easier to see the details that way.

Tip: Hold down the spacebar on your keyboard to change whatever tool you're currently using into the Hand tool, which enables you to drag the image around. This is very helpful when you zoom close into an image but want to change the part of the image you're currently looking at. Keep in mind that you're not actually moving the image itself, you're just choosing what part of the image to look at in the image window. To return to whichever tool you were using, simply release the spacebar.

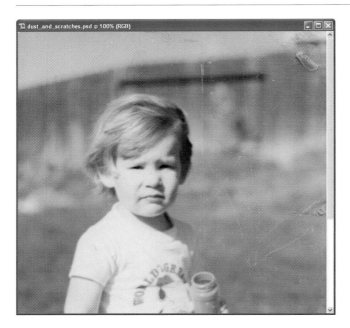

3. Use the **Hand** tool (remember, you can just hold down the spacebar to temporarily activate the Hand tool) or the scrollbars on the sides of the image window to position the image so that you can see the top-right corner of the image.

(And yes, as you can see by my t-shirt in this image, even at the age of three, I was already the "World's Greatest Baseball Player." I was the envy of all of the other three-year-olds on my block.) Notice how the top-right corner of the image is scratched and contains a few "lumps." In this exercise, you're going to use a few techniques and tools that will make it look like those imperfections were never there. You're even going to slightly adjust the saturation and levels in this image so that it looks like it was photographed yesterday!

First, you're going to get rid of those scratches…

4. Zoom out one tick by pressing **Ctrl+−** (Ctrl key and the minus [or hyphen] key on Windows) or the **Cmd+−** (Cmd key and the minus [or hyphen] key on the Mac) once. This will zoom the image out to 66.67 percent.

I know, I know, I just told you that it's best to edit images at 100 percent or greater. So why are you zooming out then? Because first you need to select the area that has the scratches on it. These scratches cover such a large part of the image that it's best to zoom out a little so you can see the whole area without having to scroll around. If you're one of those people who is blessed with a large monitor, you probably won't need to zoom out because you'll have plenty of monitor space (often called "screen real estate") to see the whole image, even while viewing it at 100 percent. For the rest of you, though, you'll need to zoom out once to see all of the area you want to select.

5. Select the **Lasso** tool by single-clicking on it in the Toolbox.

6. In the options bar, make sure that the standard **Lasso** tool is selected and not the **Polygonal** or **Magnetic Lasso** tool. Set **Feather** to **15 px**, which will make the edge of the selection—and whatever you do to the image in that selection—softer. Make sure that the **Anti-aliased** check box is checked.

7. Then, simply drag–press the mouse button down while you move the mouse–around the right side of the image, making sure to end back where you started drawing. Avoid the "lumps" on the middle right and top right of the image because you will deal with those in a different way. Also give yourself a little bit of room next to the boy (yes, I'm referring to myself in third person). You don't want the selection to be touching, or directly next to him.

*Note: At this point, some of you might be wondering "The selection that I made with my Lasso tool is very…rough. Isn't that going to make whatever I do to that part of the image look horrible?" Remember, waaay back in Step 6, when you added a **Feather** of **15 px** to the **Lasso** tool? What this will do (even though your selection looks jagged or rough) is make a nice, smooth transition between what is selected, and what isn't. That way, when you do anything to the image within that selection, you won't see a jagged or rough line where the image was selected. Instead, it will be a nice, smooth transition. This also relates to why I had you give a little bit of room between the boy and the area you were selecting. If you had made the selection too close to the boy, because the selection is feathered 15 pixels, the cleanup you perform on that selection might have crossed over a little and been partially applied to the boy as well.*

*Note: If you make a mistake while creating your selection, it's easy to clear what you've done and start over again. To do that, choose **Select > Deselect.** This will clear your selection, and you can start over again.*

8. After you finish your selection, choose **Filter > Noise > Dust & Scratches**.

This will open the **Dust & Scratches** dialog box. This filter works by changing pixels in the image that are different from those surrounding it—thereby concealing the dust and scratches on an image. From this window, you can set the **Radius** (how far the **Dust & Scratches** filter will search outside of your selection for dissimilar pixels), and the **Threshold** (how dissimilar a pixel must be from those surrounding it before it gets eliminated). I recommend starting off with both **Radius** and **Threshold** at their lowest settings. Then slowly start dragging up the **Radius** slider until the dust and scratches disappear. (You can see how the filter is working in the thumbnail image above the sliders.) Because increasing the **Radius** tends to blur the image, you can somewhat counteract the blurriness by slowly dragging up the **Threshold** slider. You're looking for the point right before the dust and scratches become visible.

Tip: You can easily see a before/after image by clicking on the thumbnail preview in the **Dust & Scratches** window. When you click and hold on the thumbnail image, it temporarily reverts back to the original. Releasing the mouse button changes the thumbnail image back to a preview of what it will look like with the current filter settings applied. You can also view different parts of the thumbnail image by dragging it around with your mouse.

9. Set the **Radius** to **4** and the **Threshold** to **2**. This seems to be the best overall setting for this particular image. Click **OK**.

10. Get rid of the current selection by choosing **Select > Deselect**.

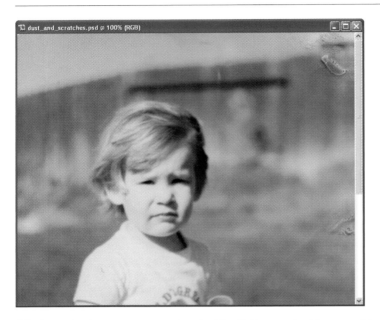

11. Zoom back to 100 percent by double-clicking on the **Zoom** tool in the Toolbox. Wow! It's hard to tell there were ever any scratches there. Because the **Dust & Scratches** filter slightly blurs the image when it removes dust and scratches, it is best used on images that are already slightly blurry, much like the background is in this sample image.

*In the next steps, you're going to learn how to get rid of those lumps on the right side of the image. To do that, you're going to learn how to use the totally awesome **Clone Stamp** tool, which, in its bare essence, allows you to take a sample of an image and paint with that sample someplace else on the image. This is great when you want to cover up parts of an image you don't like—such as the lumps in this image. You can simply sample part of the image and paint with that sample on top of the lumps, thereby covering them up.*

12. Single-click on the **Clone Stamp** tool in the Toolbox to select it.

There are, of course, some Clone Stamp tool options you should be aware of before continuing:

Clone Stamp Tool Options	
Option	**Description**
Clone Stamp tool	Selects the Clone Stamp tool. The Clone Stamp tool allows you to take a sample of a portion of your image, and uses that to paint with on other areas in the image.
Pattern Stamp tool	Selects the Pattern Stamp tool. The Pattern Stamp tool allows you to paint with a pattern you've selected from the Pattern Picker pop-up menu. (Try saying *that* fast 10 times.) The Pattern Picker pop-up menu will appear next to the Opacity slider when you select the Pattern Stamp tool.
Brush presets	Allows you to choose different brush sizes, styles, and shapes.
Size	Allows you to choose what size brush you want to use.
Mode	Allows you to choose what blending mode you want applied to the Clone Stamp or Pattern Stamp tool as you work with them. For more information on blending modes, refer to Chapter 4, "*Layers.*"
Opacity	Allows you to set the opacity the Clone Stamp and Pattern Stamp tools paint with.
Aligned	If checked, when you first sample part of the image, that sampling stays at that relative distance but will follow the Stamp tool around the image as you stop and resume painting. If unchecked, each time you stop and resume painting, the sampling point will go back to the original spot you sampled.
Use All Layers	If checked, when you sample a spot in your image with one of the Stamp tools, it will use all of your layers (much as if the layers were flattened into one) to take a sample from. If unchecked, when you sample a spot, it will sample only from the layer that is currently selected.

13. Select the **Clone Stamp** tool, and from the **brush presets** pull-down menu, choose the **Soft Round 45 pixels** brush. Set **Mode** to **Normal** and **Opacity** to **50%**. The **Aligned** check box should be checked, and **Use All Layers** should be unchecked.

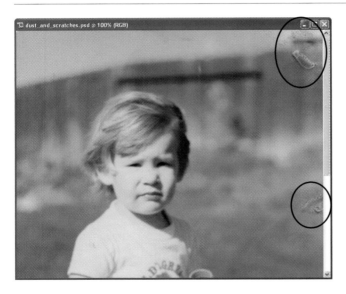

The first thing you need to do is look at the image and figure out which imperfections you want to get rid of. Then decide what other parts of the image you can borrow (sample) from to cover up those imperfections. Circled in the preceding screen shot are the two main imperfections—those "lumps" I was referring to earlier—you need to cover up. The top lump is sitting half on the sky and half on the fence (the brown shape in the background). The bottom lump is sitting on top of the grass in the middle ground. The bottom lump is easy to cover up—you can just sample some of the blurry grass to its left, and use that sample to cover up the lump. On the other hand, the top lump is a little more difficult because it sits half on, half off of two different backgrounds—sky and fence. But you should be able to easily sample a portion of the sky to the left of the top lump and use that to paint over the part of the lump sitting over the sky. Sampling part of the fence will allow you to paint over the other half of the lump that is over the fence background. It's a snap! Give it a try by starting with the easy, lower imperfection.

14. Move the **Clone Stamp** tool onto the image, and position it to the left of the bottom imperfection so that it's over the grass but not over the imperfection itself. Then, hold down the **Alt** key (Windows) or the **Option** key (Mac). When you do, you'll see the **Clone Stamp** tool icon (a circle) turn into a small circle with crosshairs in the middle. Those crosshairs represent where you are taking your image sample from. Once you see those crosshairs, make sure they're positioned over the correct spot and then click. After you've clicked, you can release the **Alt** or **Option** key.

Congratulations! You've successfully taken a sample of that image. Now, you need to use it.

15. Move the **Clone Stamp** tool (the circle) over onto the imperfection. Then, simply drag—press and hold the mouse button while you drag—over the imperfection.

As you do, you'll see it start to fade a little. As you drag the Clone Stamp tool around, you'll notice a little plus sign that follows your movements. That plus sign represents what part of the image is being sampled, and therefore what part of the image you're currently painting with. "How did it know to start there?" you ask? Back in Step 14, you Alt-clicked (Windows) or Option-clicked (Mac) on the area to the left of the imperfection. By doing that, you instructed Elements where you wanted to take the sample from. Now, as you drag the Clone Stamp tool around, that sampling point (represented by the plus sign) follows the Clone Stamp tool around. It continually samples the part of the image beneath the plus sign, and funnels that into the Clone Stamp brush you're painting over the imperfections with. If it sounds complicated at this point, I'm sure it will become clearer to you as you get more experience working with it.

Note: Make sure that the sampling point (the plus sign) never crosses over the imperfect area. If it does, you will be painting with that imperfection, and that's just plain counterproductive. If you're sampling point is getting too close to what you're trying to paint over, simply take a new sample (**Alt-click** or **Option-click**) of an area farther away from the imperfection and keep painting!

16. Because back in Step 13 you set the **Clone Stamp** tool **Opacity** to **50%**, you will need to make a few passes to completely cover up the imperfection. Drag over the imperfection until it's not fading any more, and then release the mouse button, take a new sample, and drag over the imperfection again. Repeat as many times as necessary. When you're done, it should look awesome! Anyone would be hard-pressed to tell that there was ever a big lump in that spot.

Next, you're going to repeat those steps for the top imperfection.

17. At the top of the image, with the **Clone Stamp** tool still selected, **Alt-click** (Windows) or **Option-click** (Mac) on part of the sky to the left of the imperfection. Then, just like you did in Steps 15 and 16, drag the **Clone Stamp** brush over the part of the imperfection that is atop the sky to paint over it.

Like magic it disappears! The first time I saw the Clone Stamp tool being used, I was amazed.

18. To get rid of the lump on the fence (kind of sounds like a bad horror movie title), first take a sample of another piece of the fence. (I chose to take a sample below the imperfection because the fence to the left has different patterns/values than the part of the fence that I want to paint over.) Then just drag the **Clone Stamp** brush around to paint over the imperfection. Again, you may need to retake the sample if the sample point strays too close to the imperfection, and you will need to paint over the imperfection a few times. This is because the **Clone Stamp** brush is set to **50% Opacity** (so that you can get some nice subtlety when cloning), which will require you to make a couple passes to fully cover the imperfection.

19. Zoom out one tick by pressing **Ctrl+–** (Ctrl key and the minus [or hyphen] key on Windows) or the **Cmd+–** (Cmd key and the minus key [or hyphen] on the Mac) once. This will zoom the image out to 66.67 percent. You should be able to see the whole image at this point. If you have a small monitor, you may need to zoom out once more to be able to see the image in its entirety.

The (nearly) finished image! It is now almost completely devoid of scratches and imperfections. For an old photo, it's starting to look almost new. But what image makeover would be complete without adjusting the levels and saturation of the image?

20. Open the **Layers** palette (**Window > Layers**) and add a **Hue/Saturation** adjustment layer by clicking on the **Adjustment Layer** icon (a circle that's half black, half white) and choosing **Hue/Saturation**. Increase the saturation of the colors in the image by dragging the **Saturation** slider until it reads **+20**. Click **OK**.

21. Open the **Layers** palette again (**Window > Layers**), and this time, add a **Levels** adjustment layer to the image by clicking on the **Adjustment Layer** icon and choosing **Levels**. In the **Levels** window, set the **black input level** (the left-most Input Levels field) to **8**, leave the **gray input level** (the middle Input Levels field) set to **1.00**, and change the **white input level** (the right-most Input Levels field) to **248**. Click **OK**.

before   after

As you can see in the before and after images, there is a huge improvement in the after image. Thanks to the Dust & Scratches filter, and thanks to the Clone Stamp tool, you've made short work of the dust, scratches, and imperfections that marred this image. You also utilized Hue/Saturation and Levels Adjustment layers to improve the hue and value of the finished image. Give yourself a big pat on the back because you covered a lot of material in this exercise and learned how to take an old photo and manipulate it until it looks like it was taken a few weeks ago instead of 25 years ago!

22. Choose **File > Save As**. Name this file **no_dust_or_scratches**, and save it in the **chap_10** folder. After the image has saved, close it.

—————————Sharpening a Photo

Don't you hate those photos that would be perfect if they weren't just a little blurry? In this exercise, you will learn how to fix those blurry photos by sharpening them. You will see not only how to sharpen an entire photo, but also how to use the Sharpen tool to sharpen specific areas of an image. Now don't expect to be able to take a super blurry photo—one that looks like it was taken on a foggy day, or in a car wash, or underwater—and expect to run it through Elements' Sharpen filter, and have it come out the other side all crispy sharp. The techniques you're about to learn are best used when sharpening a photo that is a little blurry. If it's *too* blurry, sharpening it is only going to make it look weird.

1. Open the **File Browser** by choosing **Window > File Browser**. Navigate to the **chap_10** folder, and double-click on the file **blurry_moth**.

*As you can see, this image is a little blurry. First, try sharpening the whole image by using a **Sharpen** filter.*

2. Choose **Filter > Sharpen > Unsharp Mask**.

"Why choose Unsharp Mask?" you ask? "What about the other sharpen filters that I saw under that menu?" you say? **Sharpen**, **Sharpen Edges**, *and* **Sharpen More** *will sharpen the image, but they don't give you options to set for* how much *to sharpen the image.* **Unsharp Mask***, however, allows you to specify various options when sharpening an image. This ultimately gives you more control over how much, or how little, to sharpen an image.*

The Unsharp Mask filter window has three fields/sliders:

- **Amount:** *A percentage of how much you want to increase the contrast of the pixels in the image. Adobe recommends setting the Amount slider to **150%** to **200%** for high-resolution (200ppi or higher) images you are going to print.*

- **Radius:** *The number of pixels to sharpen around edges. A low Radius sharpens only the pixels right near edges, whereas a high Radius sharpens a wider area around edges. Adobe recommends a Radius between **1** and **2** for high-resolution images you are going to print.*

- **Threshold:** *Sets how different a pixel must be from the other pixels surrounding it before it is considered an "edge pixel" and sharpened. A Threshold of 0, the default, sharpens all the pixels in the image. Essentially, the lower the threshold, the more pixels will be sharpened; the higher the threshold, the fewer pixels will be sharpened. To avoid reducing visual "noise" in the image, Adobe recommends setting the Threshold somewhere between **2** and **20**.*

*When I sharpen images, I usually start by setting the **Amount** to **100%** (it's a good starting spot), and then slowly increase the **Radius** amount until the image has the sharpness I want. If there's too much of an "edge" around shapes, I can fine-tune it with the **Threshold** slider.*

3. For this particular image, set the **Amount** to **150%**, the **Radius** to **1.4** pixels, and leave the **Threshold** set to **0** levels.

*Note: An easy way to see a quick preview of how the image looked before your current filter settings, and how it looks after the filter will be applied, is to simply click on the image thumbnail in the **Unsharp Mask** window. By holding the mouse button down on the image thumbnail, you can see how the image looked before any filter settings were applied to it. When you release the mouse button, you will see a preview of how the image will look (based on the current filter settings) after the filter has been applied.*

4. After you enter the Unsharp Mask settings, click **OK**.

before (detail)   after (detail)

As you can see in the before/after images, there's quite a big difference. The before image (although nice artistically because of its blurry, dreamlike quality) is quite blurry when compared to the sharpened after image.

But what if you didn't intend to sharpen the whole image? What if you like the blurry qualities of the before image, and you just want to make the moth itself sharper? At this point you would have two options. You can either use your various selection tools to first select the moth, and then apply a Sharpen filter to that selection, or you can use the Sharpen tool to selectively sharpen only the areas you want. You have already learned the skills necessary to select and sharpen images, so now you're going to learn how to sharpen areas of an image by using the Sharpen tool.

5. Choose **File > Save As**. Check the **As a Copy** check box, name the image **sharp_moth**, and click the **Save** button to save it in the **chap_10** folder.

The As a Copy check box tells Elements to save this image as…well…a copy. This allows you to save the current state of the image, while leaving the image you're currently working with alone. The reason you're doing this is because you want to continue to work with and modify this image, but in the next exercise you will work with the sharpened image—sharp_moth. If you look at the title bar of the image you're currently working with, you'll notice that it still has the same name, blurry_moth.

6. Revert to the saved, blurry version of this moth image by choosing **File > Revert**.

7. Single-click on the **Sharpen** tool in the Toolbox.

There are, of course, some options for the Sharpen tool. Here's what they all mean:

Sharpen Tool Options	
Option	**Description**
Brush presets	Allows you to choose different brush sizes, styles, and shapes.
Brush size	Allows you to choose what size brush you want to use.
Effect mode	From this pull-down menu, you can choose a blending mode to be applied to the areas you're sharpening. Note that only a few blending modes are available. This is because the Sharpen tool just sharpens images, and cannot affect the image in ways that would allow the use of the other blending modes. Most of the time, you will probably want to leave this set to **Normal.**
Sharpen strength	Specify the amount that you want to sharpen the image, 0% to 100%. The greater the percentage, the more it will sharpen the image.
Use All Layers	With this checked, the Sharpen tool will sharpen images that are in all of the layers in an image. With this option unchecked (the default), the Sharpen tool will only sharpen the image that is in the currently selected layer.

8. With the **Sharpen** tool selected, in the options bar, choose the **Soft Round 100 pixels** brush from the **brush presets** pull-down menu. Set the **Mode** to **Normal** and set **Strength** to **50%**. **Use All Layers** should be unchecked.

9. Move the **Sharpen** tool onto the image, and drag over the moth, as well as a little of the area around the moth—so that it doesn't appear as if the moth, while in focus, is floating on this unfocused background.

I find it helpful to "dab" when I use the Sharpen tool. I'll drag a small area with the tool, and then release the mouse button. Drag, release. Drag, release. That way I can make sure that I don't go too far and over-sharpen the image. You'll know when you have over-sharpened the image when you start to see some "noise" (small, multi-colored dots) being introduced into the image. Your goal is to sharpen the image to the point you want it, but not to sharpen it so much that you see noise. Dabbing helps to make sure that you don't overdo the sharpening. If you dab, and start to see noise appear, you can always undo the last command. At that point, you know the image is as sharp as it's going to get.

10. Close this image and don't save the changes.

In this exercise you saw how to sharpen the entire image using the Sharpen filter, and you saw how to sharpen specific areas of an image—while leaving the other areas untouched—by using the Sharpen tool. In the next exercise, you will switch from learning how to sharpen an image to learning how to blur an image.

4. ——————— Blurring a Photo

You've seen it in magazine pictures, and you've seen it in your own pictures (but probably due to an accident). Now it's time to learn how to blur your photos! *Cue echo machine* At this point, you're probably wondering why you are going to learn how to blur photos. "Sharpening a photo I can understand, but making a photo blurry?" you say. "Are you nuts?" Yes I am. But that doesn't have anything to do with blurring images! Blurring photographs can be used for a variety of purposes. The most common is to draw the viewer's eyes toward specific areas of the image by blurring areas that you want to draw their attention away from. The viewers eyes will inherently stray away from blurry areas and will be drawn towards areas of contrast and areas that are in focus.

1. Open the **File Browser** by choosing **Window > File Browser**. Navigate to the **chap_10** folder and double-click on the image **sharp_moth** to open it.

This is the image you applied the Sharpen filter to, and saved, in the preceding exercise. For the sake of this exercise, suppose you want to add that blurry, dream-like quality back to this moth image. Luckily for you, Elements not only sharpens, it blurs as well. (Elements is better than a Ginsu® knife, I tell ya!)

2. Choose **Filter > Blur > Gaussian Blur**, which enables you to add a nice, hazy blur to an image.

3. The Gaussian Blur filter is super straightforward. The **Radius** slider is the only setting you can modify. Essentially, the higher the **Radius**, the more the image is blurred. As you can see in the thumbnail preview, as you drag the slider farther to the right, it will eventually become an unintelligible, blurry mess. (That's what my computer screen looks like at 4:00 a.m.) For this example, however, you just want to blur the image a little, so drag the Radius slider to the right until it reads **1.5**. Click **OK**.

before (detail)

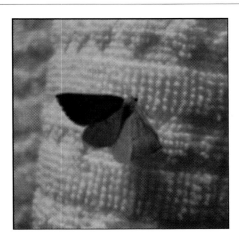

after (detail)

As you can clearly see in the before and after images, the Gaussian Blur filter certainly does its job. The after image now has that same blurry look back again—you've gone full circle. ;-)

Although the Gaussian Blur filter did a good job at blurring the entire image, sometimes you don't want the entire image blurred. Elements has a Blur tool that will allow you to selectively blur portions of the image. Because blurring an already blurred image won't do much good, you first need to revert this image back to its saved, sharp state.

4. Choose **File > Revert**.

5. Single-click on the **Blur** tool in the Toolbox.

In the options bar, there are options you can set. I won't go over them because they are the same as the options for the Sharpen tool (which I covered in the last exercise). Just keep in mind that these options refer to blurring *an image, not* sharpening *it.*

6. From the **brush presets** pull-down menu, choose **Soft Round 100 pixels**. Set the **Mode** to **Normal** and the **Strength** to **50%**, and make sure that **Use All Layers** is unchecked.

7. Move the **Blur** tool onto the image, and start dragging it around. The goal, in this example, is to blur everything but the moth and the area directly around it. You can blur some areas more than others by repeatedly dragging the **Blur** tool across the area multiple times. Be sure to release the mouse button after each pass. Releasing the mouse button, and then dragging over an area again, adds more blur to that part of the image.

When you're done, you have effectively brought the viewer's eye, and thereby the point of focus of the image, to the moth. Because everything is blurry except for the moth, the viewer's eye will continually be drawn back to that area. That's one practical reason to selectively use sharpening and blurring—it will allow you to draw attention to certain areas or objects in an image.

8. Close this image and don't save the changes. You won't need the image again in this chapter.

MOVIE | Colorizing a Black-and-White Photo

Included on the **H•O•T CD-ROM** in the **movies** folder is a movie titled **colorizing.mov**. In this movie, I demonstrate how to take a black-and-white image and colorize it using a combination of layers, blending modes, and the Paintbrush tool. You will learn how to do this using the **b&w_moth.psd** file included in the **chap_10** folder on the **H•O•T CD-ROM**.

In the **colorizing.mov** movie, you will start by opening a black-and-white image.

Then, by using layers, blending modes, and the Paintbrush tool, you will add color to selective portions of the image. This is a great and beautiful way to add some new life to an old image. You'll be surprised at how easy it is to colorize an old photo, and how simple it is to easily change the colors to anything you want.

In this chapter, you learned some very powerful and very important image-editing techniques. You learned how to remove the dreaded red eye, how to subtly remove wrinkles from a face, how to remove dust, scratches, and imperfections from an old(ish) picture, how to selectively sharpen and blur a photograph, and how to colorize a black-and-white image. You're on your way to creating your own "image restoration" business with just the techniques you learned in this chapter!

In the next chapter, you will learn the intricate ins and outs of photo manipulation. Everything from creating a panoramic photo using a series of stitched-together photographs, to photo compositing (creating one photo "composition" using a series of separate photos), to some fun and useful experimentation with the Smudge tool and Liquify filter. Turn the page...you can do it! :-)

11.

Photo Manipulation

| Photomerge | Photo Compositing |
| Smudge Tool | Liquify |

chap_11

Photoshop Elements 2
H•O•T CD-ROM

This is it. This is the chapter where you finally learn how to add giant hairy moles to a picture of your sister's face. This is where you learn how to make it look like her eyes are about to pop out of her head, and her nose is dripping down her face. This is where, sorry, I forgot where I was for a moment. Although you *could* do all those things with the skills you learn in this chapter (if you are so inclined), you will instead learn by using more practical examples. In this chapter, you will learn how to create a panoramic photo, how to take multiple photos and combine them together into one image composition, how to utilize the Smudge tool, and how to use the Liquify filter. This chapter is a mix of both serious and important learning material (photo compositing) as well as more fun and playful examples (Liquify). I'm ready. Are you?

I. —————————**Photomerge**

Ever gone on vacation to a scenic area, where you have a wide-open view and every direction you look is beautiful? A common thing to do under those circumstances is to whip out the camera and start taking pictures. You'll take a picture and turn a little, take another picture and turn a little, and so on and so forth. Then when you get the pictures developed (if you're using a film-based camera), you'll tape them all together to create a Frankenstein poster of images in a desperate attempt to recapture that moment. *Sigh.* Well now, using Elements, you can combine all those separate photos together to create one, seamless, panoramic photo. This feature is called **Photomerge**.

1. Copy the **chap_11** folder and files from the **H•O•T CD-ROM** to your hard drive.

2. Choose **File > Create Photomerge**. This will open the **Photomerge** window.

3. From here, you choose which files you want to merge together into a panoramic photo. Click **Browse**.

4. From the **Open** window, navigate to where you copied the **chap_11** folder, and open the folder **photomerge**. In that folder, you will see three images: **photomerge-1**, **photomerge-2**, and **photomerge-3**. These are the three photographs you will be merging. Single-click on **photomerge-1**, hold down the **Shift** key, and single-click on **photomerge-3**. This will select all three images. Click **Open**.

5. Now you'll see that Elements has placed the three images you want to merge together in the **Source Files** list. Click **OK**.

Then just sit back and watch Elements go crazy. All by itself, Elements will open the three images, shuffle them around, open the Photomerge window, and stitch the three photos together by making its best guess. That process right there is probably one of the more impressive features that Elements has. All you had to do was select the images you want to merge, and Elements goes and does the rest. Very, very cool!

Note: *Sometimes, Elements doesn't understand how to place one of the photos you've chosen in the panorama. If it can't automatically place all the images, it will kindly inform you that it "could not automatically arrange the images." Any images that Elements could not automatically place in the panorama are placed in the Lightbox area. All you'd need to do is drag them from the Lightbox to the work area, and position them in the panoramic photo.*

As you can see in the Photomerge window, Elements did a fantastic job of merging those three photos to create one panoramic shot.

6. Zoom into the panorama a little by selecting the **Zoom** tool (magnifying glass icon) in the Toolbox, moving your mouse onto the panorama, and clicking a couple times.

*Note: These three photos combine together to create a nice panoramic photo, but that's not always the case. Sometimes, when Elements tries to automatically place the images in the panorama, it might place them a little off from where you want them to be. To change the position of a photo in the panorama, simply select the Arrow tool in the Photomerge Toolbox and drag the image you want to reposition. You'll also notice that as you drag an image around, it becomes partially transparent. This is to help you to align the images together properly. If you need to, you can also rotate the image by selecting the Rotate tool and dragging the image to adjust its rotation. Easy! As you're attempting to reposition an image in the panorama, you will notice that it has a tendency to snap to the other images. The **Snap to Image** check box, on the right side of the Photomerge window, causes an image that is being repositioned to snap to the other images in the panorama. Uncheck the **Snap to Image** check box to turn off that feature.*

Notice the darkened, diagonal lines that extend toward the center of the image? Those darkened lines are where Elements is blending the images together. To get a smoother transition between the images, follow these steps:

7. Click on the **Advanced Blending** check box so that it's checked, and click on the **Preview** button.

Elements takes a few seconds to think about it, and then shows you the same panoramic photo. If you look closely, however, you'll notice that now those diagonal, darkened lines are much less notice- able. You can still see a little bit of that darkened area towards the top of the image, but most of that will be cropped out when you trim the image at the end of this exercise.

8. When you're done marveling at what an excellent job Elements does at blending those photos, click on the **Exit Preview** button.

Note: Under the Settings section, the **Perspective** *radio button will add—you guessed it—perspective to the image. This will change the position of the images in the panorama so they all point towards a vanishing point in the image. (By default, the vanishing point is the center-most image.) When you have* **Perspective** *selected, you can change which image is the default vanishing point by selecting the* **Vanishing Point** *tool in the Toolbox (underneath the* **Rotate** *tool) and then click on the image you want to be the vanishing point. The other images in the panorama will adjust themselves accordingly. This option is useful if you want the image to look as if it actually has perspective—that the panoramic photos all point towards a singular vanishing point. When using perspective, you can also check the* **Cylindrical Mapping** *check box to counteract the bending and warping that occurs when perspective is applied. I don't like the image distortion that occurs when perspective is applied to a panorama, so I usually don't turn it on.*

9. If you like the way the panoramic photo looks, and you don't need to do any adjusting, click **OK**.

Elements takes a few seconds to stitch all those photos together, and then voilà! As you can see, Elements does a fantastic job stitching those separate photos together to create one panoramic photo. You'll also notice, however, that some small transparent areas are visible at the top right and bottom left of the image. This is space left over from when Elements automatically repositioned some of the images to make sure that they all lined up. No worries, though, you can just crop them out.

10. Single-click on the **Crop** tool in the Toolbox to select it.

11. With the **Crop** tool, drag around the entire image. Then, by dragging the resize handles on the sides of the crop area (the animated, dashed line), resize the crop area so that the transparent areas (checkerboard pattern) at the top right and bottom left of the image are on the *outside* of the crop area.

Note: When trying to drag a side of the crop area close to the edge of an image, the crop area might snap to the edge of the image. This is really annoying if you are trying to crop off just a little bit around the outside of the image. Luckily, it's easy to turn off that snapping feature. Just choose **View > Snap to Grid** *to uncheck it. Then you should be able to easily drag the crop edge right next to the image edge without it snapping. Yay!*

12. Once you have the crop area where you want it, press **Enter** (Windows) or **Return** (Mac) to have Elements crop the image.

Now you're left with a beautiful panoramic photo. It's hard to tell that this photo actually started off as three separate photos!

13. Choose **File > Save** (or if you're feeling adventurous, use the keyboard shortcut to save the file: **Ctrl+S** [Windows] or **Cmd+S** [Mac]). Title this image **photomerged** and save it in the **photomerge** folder in the **chap_11** folder you copied onto your computer at the beginning of the exercise. After the image has finished saving, close it.

Here are some suggestions from Adobe to make sure the Photomerge feature will work the best it can with your images:

- *When you're taking photos of a scene, make sure to overlap the photos about 15 to 45 percent. In other words, don't take a picture, and then take the next picture where you think the last one got cut off—overlap the photos by about a third. Elements needs the pictures to overlap a little to give you the best results.*

- *As you're taking photographs of a scene you are going to turn into a panorama, make sure that you keep the camera level. Using a tripod makes that super simple.*

- *Stay in the same place as you take the photographs. Don't walk around when you're shooting the photos because if you do, parts of the image will shift and change perspective. This will make the final panorama look blurry, and you'll be able to more easily see the seams between the photographs.*

- *Don't zoom in or out between photographs. Pick whatever zoom level you want, but keep it the same as you take all the photographs for the panorama.*

- *Don't use any distortion lenses, such as Fisheye. Elements will have a harder time attempting to create a seamless panoramic photo if the image is distorted.*

- *Don't use the flash for one photo in the panorama and not for others. Try to keep the exposure for each photo the same. If the lighting is the same throughout all the photos in the panorama, you'll have better success with making the final image look seamless.*

Now get out there, snap away, and capture the moment!

 ## MOVIE | Photo Compositing

Included on the **H•O•T CD-ROM** in the **movies** folder is a movie titled **composite.mov**. In this movie, I demonstrate how to combine multiple photographs, using a variety of techniques, to create a singular image composition.

You will work with images provided for you on the CD-ROM. You will edit, combine, and modify them to create one image composition.

In the end, you're left with one, beautiful image composition.

2. —————————Smudge Tool

In this exercise, you will learn how to use the **Smudge** tool to add a little distortion to an image. Although I find the Smudge tool quite useful to distort and warp areas of my illustrations, it's also fun to just play around with.

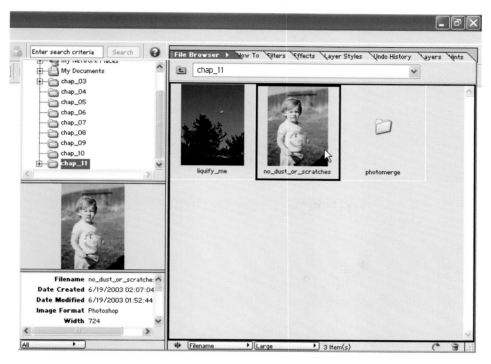

1. Open the **File Browser** by choosing **Window > File Browser**. Navigate to the **chap_11** folder and double-click on the file titled **no_dust_or_scratches** to open it.

2. Make sure you're viewing the image at 100 percent by double-clicking on the **Zoom** tool (the magnifying glass icon) in the Toolbox.

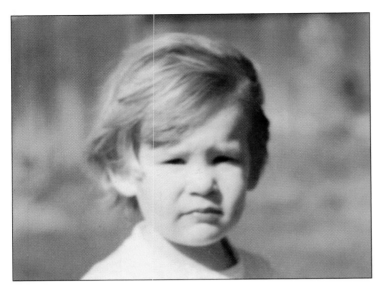

In this exercise, you're going to use the **Smudge** tool to make it look like this boy's hair is being blown around by the wind.

3. Single-click on the **Smudge** tool in the Toolbox.

The options (in the options bar) for the Smudge tool are pretty standard. The following table outlines the options and what they mean:

Smudge Tool Options	
Option	**Description**
Brush presets	Allows you to choose different brush sizes, styles, and shapes.
Brush size	Allows you to choose what size brush you want to use.
Effect mode	From this pull-down menu, you can choose a blending mode to be applied to the areas you're smudging. Note that only a few blending modes are available. This is because the Smudge tool smudges only images and cannot affect the image in ways that would allow the use of the other blending modes. Most of the time, you will probably want to leave this set to Normal.
Smudge strength	Specify the amount you want to smudge the image, from 0 to 100 percent. The greater the percentage, the more it will smudge the image.
Use All Layers	With this checked, the Smudge tool will affect parts of the image that are in all of the layers. With this option unchecked (the default), the Smudge tool will only affect the part of the image that is in the currently selected layer.
Finger Painting	With this check box unchecked (the default), the Smudge tool smudges the image using the color in the image you initially click on. If checked, the Smudge tool will smudge the image using the current foreground color.

4. Click on the **brush presets** pull-down menu, and choose the brush **Soft Round 17 pixels**. Set **Mode** to **Normal** and **Strength** to **50%**, and **Use All Layers** and **Finger Painting** should both be unchecked.

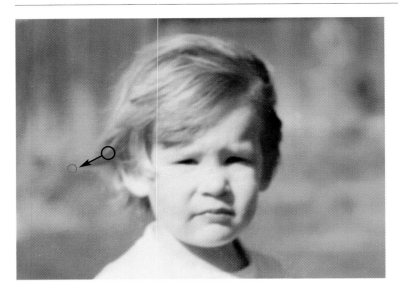

5. Move your cursor over the image, and then starting from on the hair, drag to the left. The effect is subtle, so you'll probably need to do it a few times before you start seeing results. Just make sure that after you've dragged the mouse a little to the left, release the mouse button, and then drag again from the hair, off to the left a little.

As you'll start to see, the Smudge tool smudges the pixels in the image! It's almost like the image is made of wet paint, and you're running your finger through it. So cool!

6. Continue doing this on different spots on the left side (your left side) of his head until it looks like the hair is being blown in the wind.

Tip: If you want to make it look more realistic, vary the size of the brush you're smudging with. Remember, it's really easy to change the size of the brush. Just press the [(left bracket) or] (right bracket) keys to decrease or increase, respectively, the size of the brush. That way, you'll make some thick smudges and some thin smudges, creating a more realistic effect. Neat!

This is just a small and subtle example of the Smudge tool. The Smudge tool, very simply, smudges pixels in an image. Think of the possibilities!

7. When you're finished smudging, close this image and don't save the changes.

3. ——————Liquify

Admittedly, Liquify is just fun to play around with. Liquify allows you to, for example, take a picture of your third-grade teacher who used to smack your hands with her ruler when you weren't paying attention, and turn her face into silly putty. You can stretch out her nose, make her eyes bug out, or give her gopher teeth. Ahhh—modern technology. In this exercise, you won't be doing anything so immature. (I mean, what kind of guy do you think I am?) But seriously, the Liquify filter can be used to create some really neat effects in your imagery. It's all up to you. Should you use it for good, or for…muah… muaaha…MUAHAHAH…evil? ;-)

1. Open the **File Browser** by choosing **Window > File Browser**. Then navigate to the **chap_11** folder and double-click on the **liquify_me** image.

*This will open up the **liquify_me** image. As you can see, it's a tranquil night scene with a crescent moon hovering in the sky. Using Liquify, however, you're going to add a little twist to this image.*

2. Choose **Filter > Distort > Liquify**.

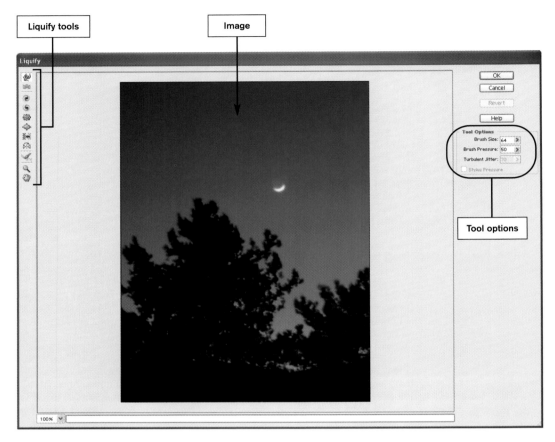

On the surface, the Liquify window is pretty harmless. But if you look closer at the Liquify tools, you'll notice that you have quite a variety of tools to choose from. From Turbulence, to Twirl, to Pucker, to Bloat, you can construct a wide variety of effects from this one, unassuming window. First, you're going to make the moon a little bigger.

3. Single-click on the **Bloat** tool in the Liquify Toolbox.

4. Set the **Brush Size** to **52** and the **Brush Pressure** to **50**.

5. Position the cursor so that the moon is in the middle of it. Then, hold the mouse button down until the moon has nearly filled the brush cursor.

Neat! You've just used the Bloat tool to increase the size of the moon. How's that for wielding ultimate power!! Next you're going to add a little something extra to give the moon a twist–quite literally.

6. Single-click on the **Twirl Clockwise** tool in the Liquify Toolbox.

7. Position the mouse cursor so that the moon is in the center, and then hold the mouse button down until the moon starts to twist around itself a little. The longer you hold the mouse button down, the more the moon will twist. Say—this image is starting to look a little like a Van Gogh painting! ;-)

That twist effect is so neat, why don't you apply a little of it to the tree branches to give them a stylized look.

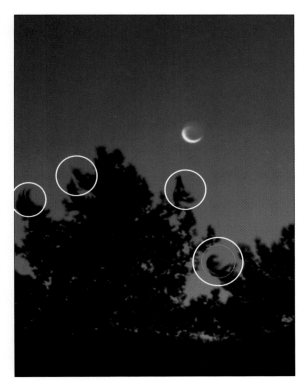

8. Just like you did with the moon, press and hold the mouse button on a few of the ends of the tree branches to make them twirl a bit, too.

Note: *You can also get some neat effects by moving the brush slightly while you hold down the mouse button. This will continue to twirl the image as you drag across it.*

9. Mix it up a little by single-clicking on the **Twirl Counter Clockwise** tool in the Liquify Toolbox.

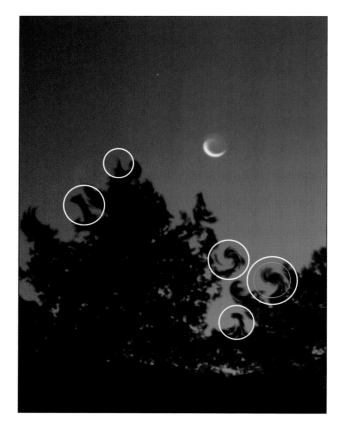

10. Just like what you did with the **Twirl Clockwise** tool, use the **Twirl Counter Clockwise** tool to twirl some of the branches in the opposite direction. Oooh–spooky.

11. When you're finished warping, twisting, bulging, and puckering the image, click **OK**.

There you have it. A spooky, stylized night scene—complete with a twisted, crescent moon.

12. Close this image and don't save the changes.

By playing around with the Liquify filter, you got a glimpse of how easy it was to use the Liquify tools to twist and bulge an image like it's clay. There are many other Liquify tools that weren't covered in this exercise, but they're all really straightforward and easy to use, so I encourage you to experiment with them at your leisure. I don't know about you, but I think the Liquify filter is a really fun and playful way to distort your pictures, and it gives you great freedom to manipulate images.

In the next chapter, you will be departing from learning how to adjust, correct, manipulate, and composite images, and instead will learn how Elements can work with the Web. You'll learn how to easily send your images via email, create an animated GIF (an animated image to put on a Web page), create a gallery of images to put up on the Internet, and create a PDF slideshow of images. The next chapter is one you definitely don't want to skip over.

12.

Elements and the Web

| Image Sizes, Resolutions, and the Web |
Attach to Email	Web Photo Gallery
Save for the Web	Creating an Animated GIF
What Is PDF?	PDF Slideshow

chap_12

Photoshop Elements 2
H•O•T CD-ROM

This chapter is a slight departure from the others that came before it. Rather than focus on adjusting the value or hue of your photographs, or on how to replace your date in your prom photo with a picture of someone else, you will instead learn how Elements can create content for Web and email delivery. Coming from an image-editing program, it may be somewhat surprising to you that Elements can easily (and I mean *easily*) attach photos to an email, create a Web photo gallery, create an animated GIF, and even assemble a PDF slideshow you can send to friends and family. By this point, you may be asking yourself, "Geez. What does this program *not* do? Can it do my dishes, take out the trash, and mow the lawn?" My answer would be yes, it can…err…I mean…not yet it can't. ;-)

Image Sizes, Resolutions, and the Web

Now that you are going to be learning how to put your images on a Web page, and how to email them to people, it's important that you revisit, and have a good understanding of, the topic of image size and image resolution.

When posting an image to a Web site, or emailing photos to someone, you should be aware of image size. A common error that beginners make when emailing photos to a friend, or when posting images on a Web site, is using an image that is much too large for the job at hand. In a hypothetical situation, you are going to email a photo of a flower to your mom for Mother's Day (awwww). So you go out to the garden with your digital camera, snap a photo, load it onto your computer, attach it to an email, and click Send. After waiting 10 minutes, and the image still hasn't finished uploading, you start to wonder what the problem is. So you cancel the email, open the image in Elements, and choose **Image > Resize > Image Size**. It's then that you see this:

From this **Image Size** window, you can see that the **Document Size** is 11.4 inches wide by 8.5 inches high, and the Resolution is 180 pixels/inch (ppi)! No wonder that image was taking a long time to send over an email; the file size (how much "space" it takes up on your hard drive) of the image must be huge! Essentially, the larger the image, the larger the file size, and the longer it will take to send and receive the picture on the Web or via email. Although there are no hard and fast rules for sizes and resolutions for specific purposes, here are my suggestions:

Image Size and Resolution Suggestions	
Target	**Image Size and Resolution setting**
Image to send via email to someone who will view it on her computer screen	640 pixels wide by 480 pixels tall (or thereabouts) 72 ppi
Image to send via email to someone who will view it on his computer screen *and* print it out	5 inches high by 7 inches wide (or thereabouts) 300 ppi
Image to post on a Web site	Whatever pixel dimensions you require 72 ppi
Image to give to a professional printer for printing.	Whatever size is required 300 to 350 ppi

When preparing an image that someone will only view on her computer screen (on a Web site, or sent via email), the pixel dimensions are what you want to pay close attention to. Whatever dimensions you have entered for the image under **Pixels Dimensions** will dictate how large (or small) the image will appear on the viewer's computer screen. Remember, the larger the image, the bigger the file size, and the longer it will take to upload or download from your computer.

On the other hand, when preparing an image for printing, you want to pay close attention not only to the document size (how many inches wide or high it is), but to the resolution as well. A standard photograph size is 4 inches high by 6 inches wide, or 5 inches high by 7 inches wide. And if you're going to print the image, you will want the **Resolution** around 300 to 350 ppi.

Fortunately, in many cases, you won't have to deal with resolution and image size. Elements knows that it can be a confusing topic, so in many cases it does much of the resizing work for you automatically. Whew!

I.————————Attach to Email

In this exercise, you'll learn the process of attaching a photo to an email so that it can be easily sent to whomever you'd like.

1. Copy the **chap_12** folder and files from the **H•O•T CD-ROM** to your hard drive.

2. Open the **File Browser** by choosing **Window > File Browser**. Navigate to where you copied the **chap_12** folder, and within that folder, double-click on the **sunflower_detail** image to open it. This is an image straight from my digital camera, and as yet has not been resized or optimized for Web or email delivery.

When the *sunflower_detail* image opens up, you can see that it's quite large. If you look at the title bar of the image, you'll also notice that it says **33.3%**. (If you have a large monitor, it might have a different value, such as **50%**.) As I've mentioned previously, this value symbolizes how far zoomed in or out you are to the image. This image is so large, that you're currently viewing it at only 33.3 percent of its actual size. But what is the actual size of this image?

3. Choose **Image > Resize > Image Size**.

*In the **Image Size** window, you can see that this image is 2048 pixels wide by 1536 pixels high, and its resolution is 180 ppi. Because you are just emailing this photo to a friend to look at, this image certainly doesn't need to be that large with that high of a resolution. Luckily, you don't have to worry about changing a thing. Elements is going to do it all automatically for you.*

4. Click **Cancel** to exit the Image Size window.

5. Single-click on the **Attach to E-mail** button in the shortcuts bar.

*Elements also recognizes that you probably don't want to email such a large photograph, so it offers to automatically convert the image to a smaller size for you. Of course, if your intent is to email this large image as is, you can just click on the **Send As Is** button. In this case, however, you definitely want Elements to resize the image to something more appropriate for email delivery.*

6. Single-click on the button **Auto Convert**.

At this point, you'll see Elements going crazy! Windows will start opening up, resizing, and closing. What Elements is actually doing is resizing your image and compressing it for you—all to get ready to send it via email.

Note: *Element's Attach to Email feature works with your default email program and your existing Internet connection. Unfortunately, it can't get you an Internet connection, install an email program, and send itself off with the click of a button. To use the Attach to Email feature, you need to have an active Internet account as well as an installed email program. (You should already be able to send/receive emails through it.) If you haven't yet set up your email program, your operating system (Windows, Mac, and so on) might prompt you to do so. Also, some email programs (especially the myriad fantastic email programs available for Mac OS X) aren't compatible with the Attach to Email feature. If your chosen email client isn't compatible, Elements will let you know. If your email client isn't compatible, and you really want to use the Attach to Email feature, you'll need to change your preferred email program to one that is compatible with Elements. Good choices would be Mail on Mac OS X and Outlook on Windows.*

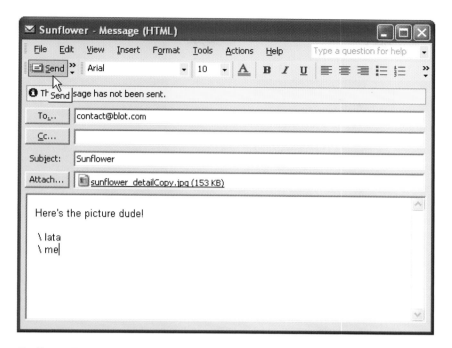

*So if your Internet connection is active, and your email program has been configured and set up, you should see a new email message open with your image already attached! All you have to do is enter the recipient's email address, add a subject line, type a message, and click **Send**. Was that super easy or what?! As long as you have Internet access and an email program, attaching an image to an email is only a couple clicks away.*

MOVIE | **Web Photo Gallery**

Included on the **H•O•T CD-ROM** in the **movies** folder is a movie titled **photo_gallery.mov**, which shows you how to take a folder of images (also provided on the **H•O•T CD-ROM**) and use Element's Web Photo Gallery feature to create an interactive photo gallery you can easily upload to the Web. Most ISPs (Internet Service Providers—the people that give you Internet access) give you a small amount of free Web space. Make use of that free Web space by putting your Web photo galleries there and then give the URL (http://www.mywebpage.com, for example) to family and friends. The Web Photo Gallery is a great feature to use when you have a lot of images you want to show friends and family, and you don't want to have to email the images to a whole bunch of people. With the Web Photo Gallery, you just build it, upload it, and pass out the URL to whomever you want to see the photos. (For more information about uploading your Web Photo Gallery, contact your ISP.)

In the **photo_gallery.mov** movie, you will start by choosing **File > Create Web Photo Gallery**. You will then tell Elements where the photos (included on the **H•O•T CD-ROM**) are located on your computer, specify where you want the finished Web photo gallery to go, and select a few different options such as how big to make the small, medium, and large images. Then, you just click **OK** and watch Elements do the rest.

continues on next page

MOVIE | Web Photo Gallery *continued*

Elements will then go through your images, process them, build an interactive Web page, and open it in Internet Explorer where you can scroll through your images and click on the thumbnails to see larger versions. One word: Wow. Actually, one more: Simple.

GIF or JPEG?

When an image gets compressed (as either a GIF or a JPEG), the compression program (in this case, Elements) actually removes data from the image to lower the file size. That way, when you send the photo via email or post it on a Web site, it can be sent and received faster. Depending on whether you choose GIF or JPEG, some information in the image will be removed in different ways. GIF removes visual information from your image in a way that favors large areas of flat color, whereas JPEG removes information in a way that is more friendly towards photographs (a.k.a. "continuous tone images"). Also note that whereas an image saved as a JPEG can be comprised of millions of colors, a GIF image can have only 256 colors at the most—yet another reason why JPEG is best if used to compress photographs, and GIF is best if used to compress flat color graphics.

2. _____Save for the Web

In this exercise, you will learn how to "manually" open an image (that you—in a hypothetical situation—imported from your digital camera or scanner), resize it, and compress it using Elements' Save for Web feature. Knowing this technique is very important if you plan to send your images via email or put them on a Web site. Before you do either of those things, you need to make sure you're saving your images at a proper size and compressing them properly for email or Web delivery. Why should you learn how to resize and optimize an image manually when Elements can do it for you in the click of a button? Good question. When you use the Attach to Email feature, Elements will optimize and resize the image without any input from you. But what if you want to save the image at a different size? What if you want to spend a little extra time trying to optimize the image as much as you possibly can so it uploads and downloads faster? Although the Attach to Email feature does a great job at quickly optimizing and resizing your image for email delivery, it gives you absolutely no control over how the image is either resized or optimized. What you will learn in this exercise will allow you to do both.

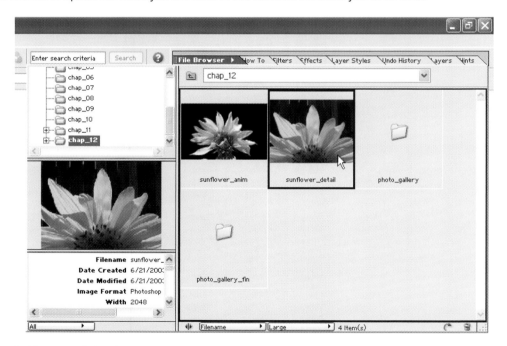

1. First, you obviously need to open the image. Open the **File Browser** by choosing **Window > File Browser**. Navigate to the **chap_12** folder, and within that folder, double-click on the **sunflower_detail** file (the same image you used in Exercise 1).

As you saw in the first exercise, this image is very large. It's 2048 pixels wide by 1536 pixels high (in this case, that's approximately 11.4 inches wide by 8.5 inches high) at 180 ppi. Because you just want to email this photo to a friend and post it to your Web site, it doesn't need to be nearly that large. A size that fits neatly onscreen would do much better. Not only is a large-sized image overkill, but it also makes for an image that takes up more room on your hard drive. (That is, it has a large file size.) The only time I would recommend emailing someone an image with large pixel dimensions is if the recipient wants to print it. Remember, you want a high-resolution (more pixels) image when you want to print. That way the printed image will have more detail and will look better.

2. Click on the **Save for Web** button in the options bar.

Now don't get scared and run away when you see this giant Save For Web dialog box with many different fields, buttons, and pull-down menus for you to click on. It's actually quite simple and straightforward. Here's a short description of what everything does:

Save for Web Options	
Option/Setting	**Description**
Save for Web toolbox	The **Hand** tool allows you to pan around the image in either the original image or compressed image window. This functions the same way as the hand in the Elements Toolbox. The **Zoom** tool (magnifying glass icon) allows you to zoom in and out of the image. (Hold down the **Alt** [Windows] or **Option** [Macintosh] key to zoom out.) Double-clicking on the **Zoom** tool will also zoom the image to 100%. The **Eyedropper** tool allows you to take a sample of color in the image, which is useful if you're creating a GIF image that you want to contain transparency.
Color Picker	Clicking on this color swatch will open the standard Color Picker you have seen in earlier exercises. From here, you can pick a color that will be used, for instance, when creating a GIF image.
Optimization settings	From this set of pull-down menus and options, you specify how you want to compress your image. Two main forms of image compression are used: JPEG and GIF. (You will also see PNG under one of the pull-down menus in the **Optimization** settings, but they are another matter entirely.) To put it very simply, use JPEG image compression if you are compressing a continuous tone image (a photograph), and use GIF image compression if you are compressing a flat-color image (such as text, a business logo, and so on).
Image Size information	Here you can view and change the size of your image. One thing you'll notice missing is the ppi of the image. When posting images on a Web page, the ppi of the image doesn't matter, only the pixel dimensions of the image does. Elements knows this, so it doesn't even bother displaying the ppi of the image in the Save For Web dialog box. It displays only the pixel dimensions.
Animation options	When creating an animated GIF (as is demonstrated in a movie on the **H•O•T CD-ROM**), you can specify various options as to how the animated GIF will perform.
Zoom menu	From this pull-down menu, you can choose how far to zoom in or out of the image.
Browser preview button	By clicking on this button, you can preview your image in a Web browser. (The default, as it is in many other places throughout Elements, is Internet Explorer.) You can change the preview browser by clicking on the pull-down menu to the right of the button, choosing **Other**, and then locating a different browser. This button is useful to see how your compressed image will look in a Web browser, but more importantly, it will allow you to preview an animated GIF while you're still working on it. Neato.

The first thing you should do is change the size of the image to something more appropriate for email/Web delivery.

3. In the **New Size** area, change the **Width** to **700**. Because the **Constrain Proportions** check box is checked (it is by default), changing the width will also automatically scale the height as well. It does this so your image doesn't scale out of proportion. Click **Apply**.

4. Click on the pull-down menu in the **Settings** area and choose **JPEG**.

Because this image you're optimizing (the sunflower) is a continuous-tone image (a photograph), a compression format of JPEG will work the best.

Compression method pull-down menu

Preset Optimization settings

JPEG Quality slider

Compression quality pull-down menu

When you select JPEG from the Compression method pull-down menu, you are given a few options to set:

JPEG Compression Options	
Option	**Description**
JPEG Quality slider	When compressing an image as a JPEG, this is probably the setting you will want to pay the most attention to. The higher the **Quality** value, the higher the quality of the image, but the larger the file size. (Remember, larger file sizes take longer to email or upload to a Web site.) A lower **Quality** value gives you a lower-quality image, but will also yield an image with a smaller file size.
Optimized check box	Leaving this check box checked will create an image with a smaller file size, but might not be compatible (viewable) with older computers.
Compression quality pull-down menu	If you don't want to bother with dragging the **Quality** slider around, click on this pull-down menu and select a preset quality from **Low** to **Maximum.**

continues on next page

JPEG Compression Options *continued*

Option	Description
Progressive check box	Checking this check box will enable the **Progressive** option, which means that your JPEG, when viewed in a Web browser, doesn't display all at once. The browser first displays the image at low quality, and then as the image is downloaded over the Internet to the viewer's computer, it draws in a successively higher quality image until the final image is displayed. Almost immediately, viewers see the "first pass," low-quality image, but from that they can get a sense of whether or not they want to hang around for the entire image to download. Leaving this check box unchecked will allow you to save the image as a standard JPEG, which will download the image to the viewer's computer, at the quality you specify, from top to bottom. Although it sounds neat, I recommend leaving the **Progressive** check box unchecked because **Progressive** JPEGs aren't supported by some Web browsers.
ICC Profile check box	ICC stands for International Color Consortium, which is essentially a group of companies who are attempting to standardize color management on the computer screen and in print. Clicking on this check box will embed the ICC color profile for your computer into the JPEG image. Theoretically, when a JPEG image with an embedded ICC color profile is viewed in someone's Web browser, the image will actually shift its color to compensate for the viewer's monitor color calibration. Translation? The image will change itself on the viewer's computer so the colors look the same as the ones you saw on your monitor. Because each computer monitor displays colors differently (even with the same image), **ICC Profile** is a great way to try to standardize how colors are displayed across different computer monitors. Unfortunately, not all Web browsers support JPEG images with embedded ICC Profiles, and not all computer users have taken the time to calibrate their monitors.
Matte color	JPEG images cannot have transparency in them. So if the image you are compressing contains transparent areas, Elements will need to make those transparent areas some opaque color. Whichever color you pick for the Matte color will be used to fill in any transparent areas in your image. Usually, if your image has any transparent areas, you would want to pick the same color that is going to be on the background of your Web page. That way the image will blend in better with the Web page itself.

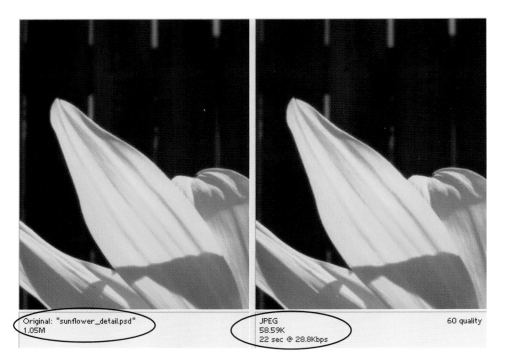

Original: "sunflower_detail.psd"
1.05M

JPEG
58.59K
22 sec @ 28.8Kbps

60 quality

Note: *As you are compressing an image and changing the compression settings, you can see how the compression you're applying is affecting the image. In the original and compressed image previews in the middle of the Save For Web dialog box, right underneath the images, Elements will show you what the original file size of the image is—in this case, 1.05 MB. (Hint: That's quite a large file size to be emailing to someone.) Many ISPs put a cap of 3 to 5 MB on each email. If you try to send an email with more than the allotted limit, the email will get bounced back to you and won't be delivered. You'll also see the file size of the compressed image—in this case, a measly 58.6 Kb. Elements will also tell you how long it will take for you to email this image (and also, how long it will take the recipient of your email to receive it) on a 28.8 Kbps modem. So as you are changing the compression settings for your image, keep your eye on the file size of your compressed image. The goal is to get the file size the smallest while still keeping the image looking decent.*

Original: "sunflower_detail.psd"
1.05M

JPEG   60 quality
58.59K
22 sec @ 28.8Kbps

5. Make sure the **Hand** tool is selected in the Save For Web dialog box Toolbox and drag the sunflower image around to get a better view of it. (It doesn't matter which image you drag from—they will drag together.)

By looking at different parts of the image, you can get a better idea what the image looks like with the selected compression. In this case, you can hardly tell the image has been compressed at all. Why don't you try a lower JPEG quality and see what that gives you?

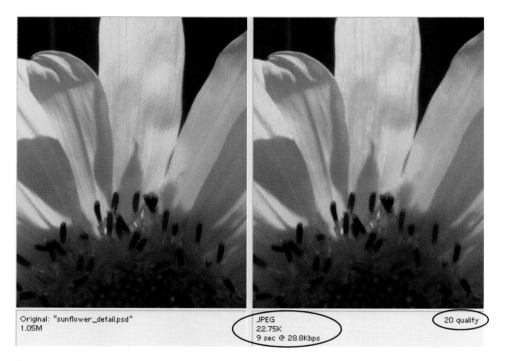

Original: "sunflower_detail.psd"
1.05M

JPEG
22.75K
9 sec @ 28.8Kbps

20 quality

6. Drag the JPEG **Quality** slider down to **20**, and then look at the optimized image again.

*At a compression quality of 20, you can clearly see heavy JPEG compression having an adverse affect on the quality of the image. Especially towards the center of the sunflower, you can see how the image is starting to get blurry and clumpy. This is even more evident at a lower quality, such as 10 or even 5. Yuck! But look at that file size!! It's a paltry 22.75 Kb. Elements also tells you that even on a slow 28.8 Kbps modem, this image will take only nine seconds to download. Zowee! The question that I always ask myself at this point is, "Is that file size worth that image quality?" In other words, yeah, the file size of the image is small, but is the loss in image quality worth having that smaller file size? To really answer that question, I'll usually raise the JPEG **Quality** slider until the image looks just good enough to where I'd consider it "acceptable." I'll then look at that file size, compare it to this low image quality file size, and then decide if the loss in image quality is worth the smaller file size.*

7. Set your JPEG **Quality** to **40**. After looking at the image at different quality settings, this middle value seems to be the best combination of image compression and small file size. Click **OK**.

8. The **Save Optimized As** dialog box appears. From here, you can choose what name to give this file and where to save it. Name the file **sunflower_compressed**, navigate to the **chap_12** folder you copied onto your computer at the beginning of this exercise, and click **Save**.

*Note: After you click Save, the compressed image will be saved into the **chap_12** folder. The Save Optimized As window will automatically close, the Save For Web window will also automatically close, and you'll then be back in the Elements interface with the original **sunflower_detail** image. Now remember, when you saved the optimized image, you performed a Save As. This means that the optimized image was saved without making any changes or modifications to the original image (which you see in front of you now).*

9. Close the image and don't save any changes.

*Note: If you are a Mac OS X user, and you like the idea of putting your images on a Web page, you might want to consider signing up for Apple's .mac service. .Mac (not to sound like an Apple adver-tisement or anything) gives you the ability to easily put your photos online for the world to see—plus many, many other nifty goodies. .Mac is integrated with iPhoto (Apple's photo organizing program), which allows you to easily take a collection of photos and put them on your own .mac Web site as a photo gallery, or you can also use the .mac Web space to take your own Elements-generated photo gallery or optimized images and put them online as well. For more information about this service, check out **http://www.mac.com.***

*Congratulations! You just took a large, medium resolution image and scaled it, optimized (compressed) it as a JPEG image, and saved it into your **chap_12** folder. Now if you wanted to attach it to an email, or upload it to your Web site, the image is all ready to go. You just need to follow the directions that came with your email program to attach the image to an email, or follow the directions your ISP gives on how to upload the image to your Web site.*

MOVIE | Creating an Animated GIF

In the **movies** folder of the **H•O•T CD-ROM** is a movie titled **anim_gif.mov**, which shows you how to take a layered Elements file and turn it into an animated GIF. An animated GIF (as I'm sure you've seen many, many times all over the Internet) is a single GIF image file that is actually composed of multiple images within it. When this image is displayed in a browser, it animates. It's a great, quick, and easy way to add a little bit of animation to your Web page(s).

You will start by opening the file **sunflower_anim** image from the **chap_12** folder. This file is actually just a standard Elements PSD file that is composed of a series of layers. On each layer, the image is a little different from the one before it.

continues on next page

MOVIE | **Creating an Animated GIF** *continued*

Then, by using the **Save For Web** dialog box, you will set up the compression options to create, optimize, and save an animated GIF.

What Is PDF?

(from the upcoming *Learning Adobe Acrobat 6 H•O•T* book by Garrick Chow):

Adobe Acrobat and the **P**ortable **D**ocument **F**ormat (PDF) were developed out of a need for a universal file format that could be opened on any computer, regardless of platform or operating system. The PDF format allows you to create exact copies of your documents for the purpose of electronic distribution. With Acrobat installed on your computer, you can create PDF files from any application that has a print function, and remain confident that your users will see the document exactly as you intended it to be viewed. PDF files preserve a document's layout, formatting, fonts, colors, and graphics and can be opened and accurately printed by anyone who has Acrobat or the free Adobe Reader installed on his or her computer.

3.———————PDF Slideshow

In the first exercise in this chapter, you saw how to open a photo and, by using the Attach to Email feature that Elements provides, easily attach a photo to an email. But what if you had a series of photos you wanted a friend to see, and what if you didn't want her to have to worry about how to open the photos, or even if they're in the right format? Along comes Elements 2 with the sparklin' new PDF Slideshow feature. Elements allows you to take a series of images and use those to create an interactive PDF slideshow. Because many computers and software come with Adobe Reader, you're nearly guaranteed that whomever you're sending your PDF slideshow to will already have the software installed to view it. In the off chance that the person you emailed the PDF slideshow to doesn't have Adobe Reader installed on her computer, she can always download it for free from Adobe's Web site.

1. Choose **File > Automation Tools > PDF Slideshow**.

2. This will open the **PDF Slideshow** dialog box. The first thing you need to do is tell Elements what images you want to put in the slideshow. Click on the **Browse** button.

3. In turn, this will open the **Open** dialog box. Navigate to the **chap_12** folder you copied onto your computer back in Exercise 1, and then into the **photo_gallery** folder. These images are the images you want to make into a PDF slideshow. Single-click on the top-most image, **gallery-01**, and then hold down the **Shift** key and click on the bottom-most image in the list, **gallery-11**. This will select all of the images in the **photo_gallery** folder. Click **Open**.

4. Back in the **PDF Slideshow** dialog box, click on the **Advanced** button.

5. From here, you can specify how the images will be compressed when they are built into the PDF Slideshow. Because they're photographs, JPEG will do just fine. But a **Quality** setting of 10 (the default) is a little too high in my opinion. Drag the slider down until the **Quality** is **6**. (You can always go back and change it later if you'd like by repeating this exercise.) Click **OK**.

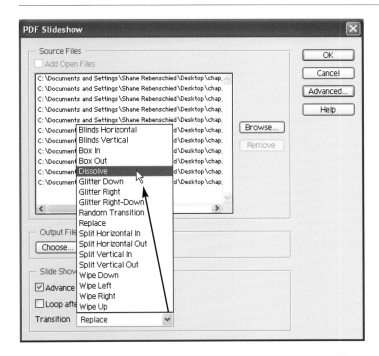

6. Click on the **Transition** pull-down menu, and from the transition options that appear, choose **Dissolve**. These different options all allow you to choose how you want the slideshow to transition between each slide. As you can see, there are quite a few to choose from.

7. Now that you have selected which images you want to make into a PDF slideshow, you've chosen how to compress those images, and you've specified how each slide will transition into one another (the **Advance Every ____ Seconds** is self-explanatory), you now need to tell Elements where to save the slideshow PDF. Click on the **Choose** button.

8. In the **Save** window that appears, navigate to the **chap_12** folder, name the file **my_slideshow**, and click **Save**. Now even though you clicked **Save**, the file hasn't actually been saved yet. Not until the next step, that is.

---

9. In the **PDF Slideshow** dialog box, click **OK**. Elements will then go to work, automatically opening and closing images as it creates your slideshow for you. Boy, this is *hard* work. *whew* ;-) When the construction of the slideshow is complete, Elements will open a window telling you that "PDF slideshow was successful." Just click **OK** to exit out of that message.

---

10. Minimize Elements (or hide it on the Mac), and open the **chap_12** folder where you have been saving all your work in this chapter. In there, you should see the PDF slideshow you just created, **my_slideshow**. However, sometimes on Mac OS X and in Windows XP, if you were to double-click on the slideshow PDF to open it, it would not open in Adobe Reader. Mac OS X prefers to open PDF files using its built-in Preview program, and Windows XP prefers to open PDF files using Windows Picture and Fax Viewer. To see the slideshow, you need to open it in Adobe Reader.

11. Right-click (Windows) or Ctrl-click (Mac) on the **my_slideshow** file, select **Open With**, and from there you should see an option to open the file with Acrobat Reader.

*After performing these steps, if you don't see the Acrobat Reader from this list, first make sure that you have it installed. There's a free Acrobat Reader installer on your Adobe Elements 2 CD-ROM and on the **H•O•T CD-ROM**. After you've installed Acrobat Reader, go back and perform this step again.*

Once the file opens in Acrobat Reader, you'll notice that the screen will fill with black, and the first slide will "dissolve" in. The slide will stay on the screen for five seconds (this is based on the setting in the PDF Slideshow dialog box), at which point it will dissolve into the next slide. It continues doing this until it reaches the end of the slideshow, where it stops. Very, very neat! You can also go back and forth through the slides in the slideshow by pressing the right arrow and left arrow keys. So as you can see, creating a PDF slideshow is a more stylish way of presenting a group of images than just sending someone a folder of images. If you know more about Adobe Acrobat (the professional version, not the free Acrobat Reader), at this point you could also add voiceover audio files, movies, music, and more PDF pages to make this a fully interactive presentation. Groovin' baby…groovin'.

Tip: *To exit out of the slideshow (because there is no "exit" or "quit" button), press the **Escape** key. This will exit you out of the slideshow and back into Acrobat Reader.*

In this chapter, you learned how Elements can create Web content—everything from easily sending images via email to creating an online, interactive Web photo gallery to creating an interactive PDF slideshow. Not only can Elements create these things for you, but it also does most of the work, leaving you to kick back, surf the Web, and check out prices on that new digital camera you've been dreaming about. ;-)

In the next chapter, you will learn how to print your images. Elements has a few cool features (of course it does!) when printing out a batch of images, including printing out a contact sheet and printing out a professional-style picture package. So go grab some ink and paper and warm up that printer because it's time to get down and dirty with printing in Elements!

13.
Printing

| Print Preview | Contact Sheet |
| Picture Package |

chap_13

Photoshop Elements 2
H•O•T CD-ROM

If you've followed the exercises in this book from the beginning (or from close to the beginning anyway), you should congratulate yourself. You've covered a large amount of information that will only begin to sink in if you continue to work with it and experiment with your own imagery. But something is strangely lacking. Ah-ha—printing! You haven't yet learned how to print your images. Printing your images is something that will vary widely from Mac to Windows, and from printer to printer. Each printer manufacturer develops their own, unique software to enable you to print out images. Some of that software is really good, and some of it is really bad. This chapter, however, will focus on the different print options that Elements provides you.

─────────────**Print Preview**

Have you ever printed an image, only to realize—after waiting 10 minutes for the high-quality printout on glossy paper to finish printing—that the image was too small? Too big? Not in the right place on the paper? In this exercise, you will learn about an Elements feature called Print Preview, which allows you to preview (imagine that!) your image document before you print it. Although I wouldn't recommend using the Print Preview feature to test how the color will look when it's printed (you, unfortunately, actually have to print the image to see that), you can still use it to test what the image size and position on the paper will be when it is printed.

1. Open the **File Browser** by choosing **Window > File Browser**. Navigate to the **chap_12** folder you copied onto your computer in Chapter 12, and double-click on the **sunflower_detail** image to open it.

2. After the image opens, click on the **Print Preview** button in the options bar.

As you can see in the Print Preview dialog box, you have quite a few options to choose from. You can also see that if you had just printed the image without previewing it first, the image would have run right off of the paper. This sunflower image has a "landscape" orientation, meaning that it is longer than it is wide. If it was the other way around—wider than it was long—the image would have a "portrait" orientation. So because this sunflower image is landscape, it would stand to reason that the paper should be rotated to be landscape as well. (By default, the printer will print out portrait unless you tell it otherwise.) The place to change the orientation to landscape or portrait is in Page Setup, which you will learn to access next.

3. On the right side of the Print Preview window, click on **Page Setup**.

4. Although this Page Setup window will look different depending on the brand/model of your printer and which operating system you're running, the essence is still the same. Change the **Orientation** from **Portrait** to **Landscape**. Click **OK**.

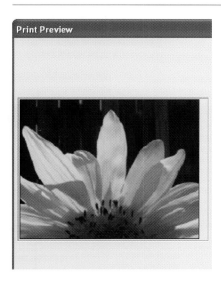

As you can see in the Print Preview thumbnail image, the image fits better once the printer has been told to print the image using landscape orientation instead of portrait. The image is still a little too big for this paper size, however.

5. Resize the image in the thumbnail image by moving your mouse over the top edge of the image. Your mouse cursor will then change to an up/down arrow. When you see that icon, drag your mouse down. As you drag your mouse, the image will resize! Remember, the white box in this thumbnail image represents a sheet of paper in your printer, and the image thumbnail represents your actual photograph, where it will be placed on the paper, and how large it will be. Resize the image so there's a little room around all four sides.

*Note: You can also scale the printed image's size by changing the scale percentage or the height and width values directly in the **Scaled Print Size** area of the Print Preview dialog box. By clicking on the **Scale to Fit Media** check box, you can also have Elements scale your image (I would only recommend checking this checkbox if your image is larger than the paper size, not smaller) to fit inside your paper dimensions.*

6. Under the **Position** section, uncheck the check box **Center Image**. Then, by dragging the image thumbnail, you can drag the image around the paper area, thereby changing where that image will be placed on paper when it is printed. Keep in mind, this is all done *before* any actual printing is done. Neat-o! If you want the image to snap back to the center of the paper area, recheck the **Center Image** check box.

*Note: By clicking on the **Show More Options** check box at the bottom of the Print Preview window, you can set some more options such as creating crop marks and color calibration. Due to their advanced nature, these topics aren't covered in this book.*

7. Once you've positioned the image thumbnail where you want it, click **OK**.

8. Then, all you have to do to print your image is click on the **Print** icon in the options bar. Your image will then print out just the way you specified in the Print Preview dialog box.

Print Preview is a fantastic way, as you just saw, to check your image before you print it. It enables you to make sure that when the image is actually printed, it gets printed at the correct size and location on paper. When you're first getting started in Elements, I highly suggest going through Print Preview first to make sure your image is set up correctly for printing.

9. Close the image and don't save the changes.

Note: *If you were to save the image, the modifications you've made to the print settings would be saved along with the image. So the next time you opened the image and printed it, it would have all the same customizations you specified.*

2. _____Contact Sheet

When I illustrate a book cover that requires a model, I contract out the photo shoot to a photographer in New York. A couple of days after the photo shoot, I receive the photos, copied onto a CD-ROM, with a couple of prints in the package as well. On the prints are small, thumbnail images of all of the photographs, with the name of the file printed underneath each image. This saves me a great deal of time because by looking at the printout, I can pick which photos I like. Then, I can just look at the file-name, and easily find that exact file on the CD-ROM; I don't have to open each file (or wait while the File Browser tries to preview 50 high-resolution images) to find the ones I want. In this exercise, you're going to learn to create that same printout. It's called a contact sheet, and it essentially allows you to take a batch of photos and print small thumbnails, each labeled with the filename of that photograph. This is *invaluable* if you have a collection of photographs on your computer, and you don't want to have to open each photo to find the exact one you're looking for. Printing a contact sheet, for example, is also a great way to visualize a series of photos you've backed up onto a CD-ROM.

1. Choose **File > Print Layouts > Contact Sheet**.

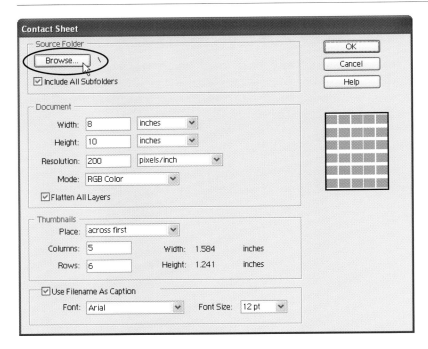

2. This will open the **Contact Sheet** dialog box, where you can specify myriad options for how the photos will be arranged when they're printed. First, choose the photos you want to make a contact sheet with by clicking **Browse** (or **Choose** on the Mac).

3. In the **Browse For Folder** dialog box, browse to the **chap_12** folder and maximize it by clicking on the small plus sign to the left of the **chap_12** folder. Then, single-click on **photo_gallery** to select it, and click **OK**. (See the following screen shot and accompanying text for the Mac steps.)

You've just picked a folder of images (the same folder of images you used in the Web Photo Gallery exercise in the last chapter) for Elements to create the contact sheet with.

Note: *On the Mac, the Browse For Folder dialog box is titled **Select image directory**, and it looks quite different from the Windows dialog box. On the Mac, browse to the same **chap_12** folder, single-click on the **photo_gallery** folder, and click **Choose**.*

4. The rest of the options are pretty self-explanatory. Under **Document**, set the **Width** and **Height** of the paper you're printing on, minus about half an inch for the margins (a standard, consumer printer can't print all the way to the edge of a piece of paper), as well as the **Resolution**. If you want to print the contact sheet in black and white, just select **Grayscale** from the **Mode** pull-down menu. For my printer (and the same settings might work for your printer as well), I chose a **Width** of **8 inches**, a **Height** of **10 inches**, and set the **Resolution** to **200 pixels/inch**. Leave **Mode** set to **RGB Color**, and leave the **Flatten All Layers** check box checked.

Note: The Contact Sheet feature is best if used to print out a folder of high- to medium-resolution images. In other words, your results aren't going to be very good if you instruct Elements to print out a contact sheet of a bunch of 72-ppi images. When printing, make sure the ppi of the image is around 200 or higher (preferably 300) for the best results.

5. Under **Thumbnails**, choose **across first** from the **Place** pull-down menu (which means that the images will be printed sequentially from left to right instead of top to bottom), set the **Columns** to **4**, and the **Rows** to **5**. The fewer columns and rows you have, the larger the thumbnails will be on the contact sheet. Conversely, the more columns and rows you have, the smaller the thumbnails will be.

6. Check the **Use Filename As Caption** check box, and choose a font from the **Font** pull-down menu and a font size from the **Font Size** pull-down menu. On the Mac, the font defaults to **Helvetica**; on Windows, the font defaults to **Arial**.

You'll notice that on the right side of the dialog box is a layout preview of the contact sheet. As you modify the settings in the Contact Sheet dialog box, this preview will update to reflect your changes. Sweet!

7. Click **OK**. Then just kick back, relax, and marvel at the beauty of this automated task. It's fun to watch as Elements opens each image in the folder you chose, resizes it, places it into a new document, and types the filename under each image. And you hardly had to lift a finger!

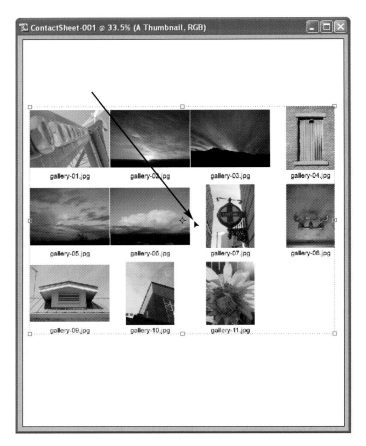

When Elements finishes, you're left with a sheet of thumbnail images that are all nicely labeled for you and ready to print out. Elements places this grouping of thumbnail images, by default, at the top left of this image. If you'd like, you can drag that thumbnail image grouping down toward the center of the image space.

*As you just witnessed, very little effort is involved to print out a contact sheet such as this. Just point Elements to a directory of images, set a few options, click **OK**, and off it goes! Again, this feature works great if you're backing up your photo collection to a CD-ROM. After you've burned the CD-ROM, just point the Contact Sheet feature at the CD-ROM, click **OK**, and presto! You have a nice, labeled printout of all the images on the CD-ROM.*

---

8. Feel free to print this image if you want. After you're finished with it, however, close the image and don't save the changes.

MOVIE | Picture Package

When I was in elementary school, they would have a photo shoot day, once a year. Every year they would line up the whole class, take a group photo, and then you would go to another room to get individual photos taken. About a month later, they would hand out manila envelopes with the photos inside. To save costs, the photo companies would place as many photos as they could on a single sheet of photo paper—some large, some small, some medium, and some "wallet sized." Most photography studios still do this. In the movie **picture_package.mov** on the **H•O•T CD-ROM**, I will show you how to use Elements' Picture Package feature to print out the same kind of image layout that professional photography studios use.

In the movie, you will use the Picture Package feature to have Elements automatically arrange a photo on a standard 8.5 x 11-inch sheet of paper. This is a great feature to utilize, for example, if you want to send out a picture to a large group of people. By using Picture Package, you don't have to worry about trying to squeeze as many pictures onto the page as possible (*whew*—try saying that fast 10 times!). Elements will do that for you.

In this chapter, you learned about some of the features that Elements provides to make printing images a little easier. The Print Preview feature is a great paper-saver because it allows you to catch mistakes by simulating a print before you actually click the Print button. The Contact Sheet and Picture Package features are also extremely valuable and useful—not to mention that their automation makes for some good entertainment for those days when there's nothing good on TV. ;-)

A.
Online Resources

H•O•T

Photoshop Elements 2

Thanks to the Internet, and to a few individuals with some spare time, there are some great online resources for Adobe Elements. Although some information and tutorials you find online will cover what you already learned in this book, others will magnify what you know and show you new ways of working in Elements. This appendix lists a few of the best resources for expanding your knowledge of Elements.

A Few Elements-Related Web Sites

Adobe

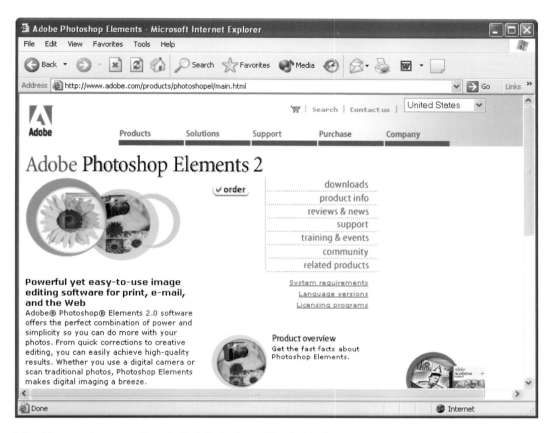

http://www.adobe.com/products/photoshopel/main.html

Jay Arraich's Photoshop Elements Tips

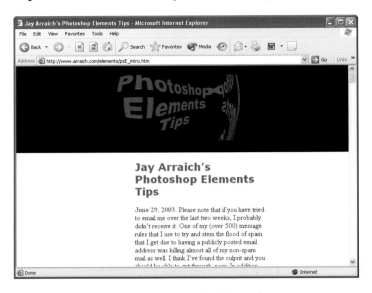

http://www.arraich.com/elements/psE_intro.htm

About.com Photoshop Elements Resources

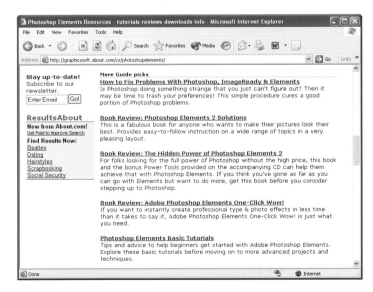

http://graphicssoft.about.com/cs/photoshopelements/

Stock Photo and Clip Art Sites

iStockPhoto.com

http://www.istockphoto.com

ClipArt.com

http://www.clipart.com

B.

Technical Support

H•O•T

Photoshop Elements 2

If you run into any problems while following the exercises in this book, there are a few places you can turn for help. This document will be maintained and expanded upon at this book's companion Web site:

http://www.lynda.com/products/ books/elm2hot/

Adobe Technical Support

http://www.adobe.com/support/

206-675-6258 (Mac) 206-675-6358 (Windows)

If you are having problems with Elements, please contact Adobe Technical Support at the number listed here. Adobe staff will be able to help you with such typical problems as these: the trial version has expired on your computer; the application crashes when you try and launch it; and so forth. Please note that lynda.com cannot help troubleshoot technical problems with Elements.

Peachpit Press

customer_service@peachpit.com

If your book has a defective CD-ROM, please contact the customer service department at this email address. We do not have extra CDs at lynda.com, so they must be requested directly from the publisher.

lynda.com

http://www.lynda.com/products/books/elm2hot/

elm2faq@lynda.com

We have created a companion Web site for this book, which can be found at **http://www.lynda.com/ products/books/elm2hot/**. Any errors in the book will be posted to the Web site, and it's always a good idea to check there for up-to-date information. We encourage and welcome your comments and error reports to **elm2faq@lynda.com**.

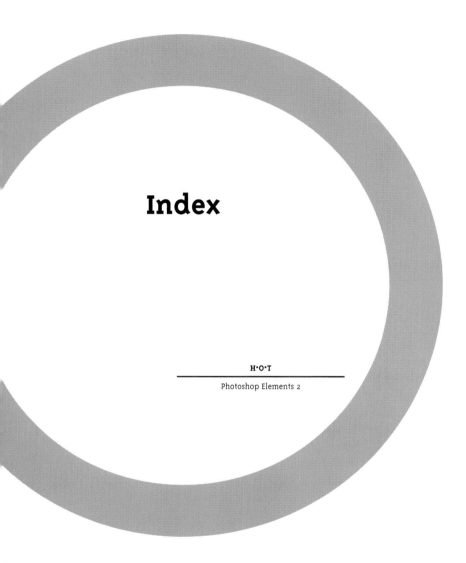

Index

H•O•T

Photoshop Elements 2

A

Acrobat, 304
Acrobat Reader, opening PDF slideshows with, 311
active images, 69
Add to shape area option (Shape tool), 150
adding
    palettes to Palette Well, 22
    to selections, 104
adjustment layers, 72
    deleting, 76
    Hue/Saturation, 240
    levels, 72-74, 241
    viewing/hiding, 74
adjustments. *See also* photo correction
    color adjustments, 201-202
      automatic adjustments, 215
      black-and-white images, 205-206
      Color Cast Correction dialog box, 202-203
      Color Variations dialog box, 210-214
      Hue/Saturation adjustment layer, 204-205, 240
      Levels adjustment layer, 241
      Replace Color dialog box, 207-210
    value adjustments, 184-185
      automatic adjustments, 192-194
      contrast, 185-186
      Dodge and Burn tools, 195-200
      Levels dialog box, 187-189
      overexposure, 191
      shadow details, 190
Adobe Acrobat, 304
Adobe Acrobat Reader, opening PDF slideshows with, 311
Adobe Online, 17
Adobe Photoshop Elements. *See* Photoshop Elements
Adobe Photoshop versus Photoshop Elements, 3-4
Advanced Blending option (Photomerge feature), 263
airbrushing, Enable Airbrush option (Paintbrush tool), 121
aligned option (Clone Stamp tool), 235
aligning text, 168
anchor points (selections), removing, 96
angle gradient fill type, 124
animated GIFs, 303-304
animation options (Save for Web dialog box), 294
Anti-aliased option
    Magic Eraser tool, 133
    Magic Wand tool, 98

Paint Bucket tool, 141
Type tool, 168
anti-aliasing images, 44
Apple .mac service, 302
associating file types with Photoshop Elements, 32-33
Attach to E-mail button (shortcuts bar), 19
attach to e-mail feature, 10, 19
attaching photographs to email, 285-289
Auto Contrast command versus Auto Levels command, 194
Auto Levels command versus Auto Contrast command, 194
automatic color adjustments (photo correction), 215
automatic startup of Welcome screen, disabling, 14
automatic value adjustments (photo correction), 192-194

B

background color, 136
    setting to default, 116, 136
Background Eraser tool, 131-132
Background layer, changing to normal layer, 128
backlighting, 191
Bitmap dialog box, 56
bitmap graphics, 145-146
    changing vector graphics to, 44
Bitmap image mode, 53
    converting RGB Color to, 54-57
black input level slider (Levels dialog box), 188
black output level slider (Levels dialog box), 188
black-and-white images
    colorizing, 256
    converting color images to, 54-57, 205-206
black-points, 185
blending modes, 85-87, 113
    for tools, 84
    list of, 80, 84
Bloat tool, 277
Blur tool, 253-255
blurring photos, 251-255
blurry photos, sharpening, 243-250
bounding box, showing/hiding, 111
brightness. *See* levels
brightness adjustments. *See* value adjustments
Browse button (shortcuts bar), 18
Browse for File button (Welcome screen), 13

Browse for Folder dialog box, 319
browser-safe colors in Color Picker, 138
brush presets
    Clone Stamp tool, 235
    Dodge tool, 197
    Eraser tool, 129
    Pencil tool, 117
    Red Eye Brush tool, 225
    Sharpen tool, 249
    Smudge tool, 271
    Sponge tool, 217
Brush size option
    Dodge tool, 197
    Red Eye Brush tool, 225
    Sharpen tool, 249
    Smudge tool, 271
    Sponge tool, 217
brushes
    Gradient tool, 123-126
    Impressionist Brush tool, 121
    Paintbrush tool, 120-122
    Pencil tool, 116-119
Burn tool, 195-200
button bar. *See* shortcuts bar

C

cameras. *See* digital cameras
capturing. *See* importing
Center align option (Type tool), 168
Channel pull-down menu (Levels dialog box), 188
choosing. *See* selecting
clips. *See* video
Clone Stamp tool, 234-240
closing images, 32
color adjustments (photo correction),
        201-202
    automatic adjustments, 215
    black-and-white images, 205-206
    Color Cast Correction dialog box, 202-203
    Color Variations dialog box, 210-214
    Hue/Saturation adjustment layer,
        204-205, 240
    Levels adjustment layer, 241
    Replace Color dialog box, 207-210
Color blending mode, 84
Color Burn blending mode, 81
Color Cast Correction dialog box, 202-203
Color Dodge blending mode, 81
color images, converting to black and white, 54-57,
        205-206
color modes. *See* image modes
Color Picker window, 137-139

changing colors, 65
fill layers, 77-78
Save for Web dialog box, 294
Color Variations button (shortcuts bar), 19
Color Variations dialog box, 210-214
colorizing black-and-white photos, 256
colors, 136
    background color, 136
        setting to default, 116, 136
    changing, 65-66
        Eyedropper tool, 142
        Fill command, 142
        Paint Bucket tool, 140-142
        Preserve Transparency feature, 143
    foreground color, 136
        setting to default, 116, 136
        swapping with background color, 136
    of text, 169
    Red Eye Brush tool, 225
    selecting. *See* Color Picker window
    Shape tool, 151
    of shapes, 159
        changing, 152-154
    and transparency, 66
Commit Edits button (Type tool), 171
Commit Place button (options bar), 44
commit place of images, 44
Common Issues button (Welcome
        screen), 14
composite images, creating, 108-113
compositing photos, 268
compression of images
    GIF versus JPEG, 291
    JPEG options, 296
    for PDF slideshows, 307
Connect to Camera or Scanner button (Welcome
        screen), 13, 26, 28
Contact Sheet dialog box, 318
contact sheets, printing, 318-322
Contiguous option
    Magic Eraser tool, 133
    Magic Wand tool, 98
    Paint Bucket tool, 141
contrast adjustments (photo correction), 185-186
converting color images to black and white, 54-57,
        205-206
copy, saving images as, 248
copying
    layer styles, 163
    layers, 62
correcting photos. *See* photo correction
Create new shape layer option (Shape
        tool), 150

Create warped text option (Type tool), 169
creating images, 51-52, 115
Crop tool, 265-266
Current color option (Red Eye Brush
        tool), 225
Custom Shape tool, 150

D

Darken blending mode, 80
darkness. *See* levels
darkness adjustments. *See* value
        adjustments
default Background layer, 61
Default Colors option (Red Eye Brush
        tool), 225
default foreground and background
        colors, 116, 136
default palette positions, resetting, 21
deleting. *See* removing
deselecting selections, 93
dialog tips, 6
Difference blending mode, 83, 87
digital cameras
        Connect to Camera or Scanner button
                (Welcome screen), 13
        importing images from, 28-29
disabling
        automatic startup of Welcome screen, 14
        Snap to Grid feature, 266
Dissolve blending mode, 80
distortion. *See also* warping
        Liquify filter, 274-281
        Smudge tool, 269-273
Dither Gradient option (Gradient tool), 125
Dodge tool, 195-200
double-clicking images, 32
downloading updates to Photoshop Elements, 11
drawing
        Eraser tools, 127-128
                Background Eraser, 131-132
                Eraser, 129-130
                Magic Eraser, 133-135
        Gradient tool, 123-126
        Impressionist Brush tool, 121
        Paintbrush tool, 120-122
        Pencil tool, 116-119
duotones, 205
duplicating. *See* copying
Dust & Scratches filter, 233-234
dust removal (photo retouching), 229-240

E

Edge Contrast option (Magnetic Lasso tool), 97
editing text, 173-176
Effect mode
        Sharpen tool, 249
        Smudge tool, 271
Elements. *See* Photoshop Elements
Elliptical Marquee tool, 92
email
        attach to e-mail feature, 10, 19
        attaching photographs to, 285-289
        image size and resolution, 283-284
        images for (Save for Web feature), 292-302
Enable Airbrush option (Paintbrush
        tool), 121
Eraser tools, 127-128
        Background Eraser, 131-132
        Eraser, 129-130
        Magic Eraser, 133-135
Erasing mode (Eraser tool), 129
error messages, 6
Exclusion blending mode, 83
Exit Welcome Screen button (Welcome screen), 14
Eyedropper tool, 142

F

Faux bold option (Type tool), 168
Faux italic option (Type tool), 168
File Association Manager dialog box, 33
file associations, changing, 32-33
File Browser palette, 13
        opening images, 34-38
        placing images, 39-45
        refreshing file listing, 60, 91, 184
file formats. *See* formats
file listing section (File Browser palette), 35
Fill command, changing colors in
                images, 142
Fill dialog box, 65
Fill Flash command, 190
fill layers, 72, 76-79
        selecting colors, 77-78
        and transparency, 79
Fill source option (Paint Bucket tool), 140
fill types (Gradient tool), 124
film speed, tips for taking photographs, 183
filters
        Dust & Scratches, 233-234
        Gaussian Blur, 252-253
        Liquify, 274-281
        Unsharp Mask, 244-247

Font family option (Type tool), 168
Font size option (Type tool), 168
fonts. *See* text
foreground color, 136
    changing colors, 65
    setting to default, 116, 136
    swapping with background color, 136
formats
    for images
        determining current format, 40
        list of, 25
    for video, list of, 46
Frame From Video feature, 8, 47-50
Frequency option (Magnetic Lasso tool), 97
Fuzziness slider (Replace Color dialog box), 209

G

gamma values on Windows versus Macintosh
        computers, 186
Gaussian Blur filter, 252-253
Geometry Options (Shape tool), 150
GIF image compression
    animated GIFs, 303-304
    versus JPEG, 291
Gradient Picker (Gradient tool), 124
Gradient tool, 123-126
graphical user interface. *See* interface
graphics. *See* images
Grayscale image mode, 53
    converting RGB Color to, 54-57
grouping
    layers, 74-75, 78
    palettes, 20-21
GUI (graphical user interface). *See* interface

H

Hand tool, 230
Hard Light blending mode, 82, 86
Hardness option (Selection Brush tool), 101
Height option (New dialog box), 52
help features
    Common Issues button (Welcome
            screen), 14
    Help search field (shortcuts bar), 7, 18-19
    Tutorial button (Welcome screen), 14
Help search field (shortcuts bar), 7, 18-19
Hexadecimal color value (Color Picker), 138
hidden tools, 17
hiding
    adjustment layers, 74
    bounding box, 111

layer styles, 163
layers, 70
highlights. *See* levels
Hints palette, 16
Horizontal Type Mask tool, 167
Horizontal Type tool, 167
How To window, 14
Hue blending mode, 83
Hue/Saturation adjustment layer,
        204-205, 240

I

ICC profile option (JPEG image
        compression), 297
image information section (File Browser palette),
        35, 40
image modes, 53
    Bitmap, 53
    changing, 54-57
    Grayscale, 53
    Indexed Color, 57
    RGB Color, 53
image preview section (File Browser palette), 35
Image Size window, 283, 287
    Save for Web dialog box, 294
image thumbnails section (File Browser palette),
        35-37
images. *See also* photographs
    active images, 69
    anti-aliasing, 44
    bitmap, 145-146
    blending modes, 113
    changing colors in
        Eyedropper tool, 142
        Fill command, 142
        Paint Bucket tool, 140-142
        Preserve Transparency feature, 143
    changing file associations for, 32-33
    closing, 32
    commit place, 44
    composite images, creating, 108-113
    compression
        GIF versus JPEG, 291
        JPEG options, 296
        for PDF slideshows, 307
    creating, 51-52, 115
    double-clicking, 32
    formats for
        determining current format, 40
        list of, 25
    image modes, 53
        Bitmap, 53

changing, 54-57
Grayscale, 53
Indexed Color, 57
RGB Color, 53
importing
from digital camera, 28-29
from scanner, 26-27
from video, 47-50
non-destructive editing, 71
opening, 30-33
with File Browser palette, 34-38
placing, 39-45
positioning for printing, 316
previewing in File Browser palette, 35
printing
contact sheets, 318-322
Picture Package feature, 323
Print Preview feature, 313-317
resizing, 43-44, 111
in layers, 71
for printing, 316
resolution, 5
setting, 115
for Web usage, 283-284
reverting to saved, 85, 130
rotating, 43
saving, 45
as copy, 248
Save for Web feature, 292-302
scaling for printing, 316
selecting parts of. See selections
size, 5
setting, 115
for Web usage, 283-284
text, 165-171
applying layer styles, 176-177
editing, 173-176
layers for, 172, 176
moving, 171
warping, 178-181
transforming, 221
vector, 145-146
viewing at 100%, 112
zooming, 102, 226
importing images
from digital camera, 28-29
from scanner, 26-27
from video, 47-50
Impressionist Brush tool, 121
Indexed Color image mode, 57
insertion points, 170

interface
menu bar, 15
options bar, 23
Palette Well, 21-22
palettes, 20
adding to Palette Well, 22
grouping, 20-21
More button, 21
moving, 20
opening from Palette Well, 22
preferences, 21
removing from Palette Well, 22
resetting positions of, 21
resizing, 20
ungrouping, 21
shortcuts bar, 18-19
Toolbox, 16-17
Adobe Online, 17
Hints palette, 16
Welcome screen, 13
Browse for File button, 13
Common Issues button, 14
Connect to Camera or Scanner button, 13, 26, 28
disabling automatic startup of, 14
Exit Welcome Screen button, 14
New File button, 13
opening, 14
Tutorial button, 14
interpolation, 145
Intersect shape areas option (Shape tool), 151
intersecting selections, 104
inverting selections, 100

J-K

JPEG image compression
options, 296
versus GIF, 291

L

landscape orientation, 314
Lasso tool, 93-94, 231
layer styles, 154
adding to shapes, 155-163
applying multiple, 163
applying to text, 176-177
copying, 163
hiding/viewing, 163

removing, 151, 163
scaling, 163
Layer Styles palette, 156-157
layers, 58-61, 67
  adjustment layers, 72
    deleting, 76
    Hue/Saturation, 240
    levels, 72-74, 241
    viewing/hiding, 74
  Background layer, changing to normal
    layer, 128
  blending modes, 85-87
    list of, 80, 84
    for tools, 84
  colors, changing, 65-66
  creating, 118
  default Background layer, 61
  deleting, 74
  duplicating, 62
  fill layers, 72, 76-79
    selecting colors, 77-78
    and transparency, 79
  grouping, 74-75, 78
  hiding, 70
  linking, 63
  locking transparent pixels, 64
  moving, 63, 69-70, 123
  non-destructive image editing, 71
  overlapping images on, 63
  Preserve Transparency feature, 143
  renaming, 61, 119
  resizing images in, 71
  selecting, 61, 69
  sorting, 70
  for text, 172
    accidentally creating, 176
  transparency, 61
    effect on colors, 66
    modifying, 62
  ungrouping, 76
  unlinking, 64
  viewing, 70
Layers palette. *See also* layers
  blending modes, 113
  creating composite images, 110
  opening, 61
  undocking, 64
Left align option (Type tool), 168
levels, 72-74
Levels adjustment layer, 241
Levels dialog box, 73-74
  value adjustments (photo correction),
    187-189
Lighten blending mode, 81

lighting
  backlighting, 191
  tips for taking photographs, 183
lightness adjustments. *See* value
    adjustments
Limits mode (Background Eraser tool), 131
Linear Burn blending mode, 81
Linear Dodge blending mode, 82
linear gradient fill type, 124
Linear Light blending mode, 83, 113
linking layers, 63
Liquify filter, 274-281
Load Selection dialog box, 107
locking transparent pixels in layers, 64
Luminosity blending mode, 84

M

Mac OS X, optimization for, 10
.mac service, 302
Macintosh computers, gamma values
    on, 186
Magic Eraser tool, 133-135
Magic Wand tool, 98-99
Magnetic Lasso tool, 96-98
manipulating photos. *See* photo
    manipulation
"marching ants" (selections), 92
Marquee tools, 92
masks, creating with Selection Brush
    tool, 101
menu bar, 15
merging
  image files. *See* placing images
  photographs. *See* Photomerge feature
midtones. *See* levels
mode option
  Clone Stamp tool, 235
  New dialog box, 52
  Selection Brush tool, 101
modes. *See* image modes
More button (palettes), 21
Move tool, 148, 171
  creating composite images, 109
moving
  layers, 63, 69-70, 123
  palettes, 20
  selections, 105-106
  text, 171
  windows, 16
multiple layer styles, applying, 163
multiple photographs, compositing, 268
Multiply blending mode, 80

N

Name option (New dialog box), 52
New button (shortcuts bar), 18
New dialog box, 51
new features in Photoshop Elements
    attach to e-mail feature, 10
    dialog tips, 6
    Frame From Video, 8
    help search field, 7
    optimization for Mac OS X and
        Windows XP, 10
    PDF slideshow feature, 9
    Quick Fix, 7
    Selection Brush, 8
    smart error messages, 6
New File button (Welcome screen), 13
non-destructive image editing, 71
Normal blending mode, 80

O

Online Services button (shortcuts bar), 19
Only Web Colors option (Color Picker), 138
opacity. *See also* transparency
    Clone Stamp tool, 235
    Pencil tool, 117
    Preserve Transparency feature, 143
Opacity option (layers), modifying, 62
Open button (shortcuts bar), 18
Open dialog box, 31
opening
    images, 30-33
        with File Browser palette, 34-38
    Layers Palette, 61
    palettes from Palette Well, 22
    PDF slideshows with Acrobat Reader, 311
    Welcome screen, 14
optimization
    JPEG image compression, 296
    for Mac OS X and Windows XP, 10
    Save for Web dialog box, 294
options bar, 23. *See also* preferences
ordering. *See* sorting
orientation of images, 314
overexposure (photo correction), 191
overlapping images on layers, 63
Overlay blending mode, 82
Overlay Color option (Selection Brush
    tool), 101
Overlay Opacity option (Selection Brush tool), 101

P

Page Setup window, 315
Paint Bucket tool, 140-142
Paintbrush tool, 120-122
painting mode (Pencil tool), 117
Palette Well, 21-22
palettes, 20
    adding to Palette Well, 22
    grouping, 20-21
    Hints, 16
    More button, 21
    moving, 20
    opening from Palette Well, 22
    Palette Well, 21-22
    preferences, 21
    removing from Palette Well, 22
    resetting positions of, 21
    resizing, 20
    ungrouping, 21
panoramic photos
    creating, 259-268
    repositioning, 262
Pattern Stamp tool, 235
PDF (Portable Document Format), 9, 304
PDF slideshow feature, 9, 305-311
Pencil tool, 116, 118-119
Perspective option (Photomerge
    feature), 264
photo correction, 182. *See also* photo
    manipulation; photo retouching
    color adjustments, 201-202
        automatic adjustments, 215
        black-and-white images, 205-206
        Color Cast Correction dialog box, 202-203
        Color Variations dialog box, 210-214
        Hue/Saturation adjustment layer, 204-205,
            240
        Levels adjustment layer, 241
        Replace Color dialog box, 207-210
    Sponge tool, 216-220
    value adjustments, 184-185
        automatic adjustments, 192-194
        contrast, 185-186
        Dodge and Burn tools, 195-200
        Levels dialog box, 187-189
        overexposure, 191
        shadow details, 190
photo manipulation, 258. *See also* photo
    correction; photo retouching
    compositing photos, 268
    Liquify filter, 274-281

panoramic photo creation, 259-268
Smudge tool, 269-273
photo retouching, 222. *See also* photo correction;
    photo manipulation
    blurring photos, 251-255
    colorizing black-and-white photos, 256
    dust and scratch removal, 229-240
    red eye removal, 223-227
    sharpening photos, 243-250
    wrinkle removal, 228
photographs. *See also* images; photo correction;
    photo manipulation; photo retouching
    attaching to email, 285-289
    contact sheets, printing, 318-322
    PDF Slideshow feature, 305-311
    Picture Package feature, 323
    tips for taking, 183
    Web Photo Gallery feature, 290-291
Photomerge feature, 259-268
Photoshop versus Photoshop
    Elements, 3-4
Photoshop Elements
    interface. *See* interface
    new features
        attach to e-mail feature, 10
        dialog tips, 6
        Frame From Video, 8
        help search field, 7
        optimization for Mac OS X and Windows XP,
            10
        PDF slideshow feature, 9
        Quick Fix, 7
        Selection Brush, 8
        smart error messages, 6
    overview, 3
    updates to, 11
    versus Photoshop, 3-4
Picture Package feature, 323
pictures. *See* images; photographs
Pin Light blending mode, 83
pixels, 5
    bitmap versus vector images, 145
Place dialog box, 41-42
placing images, 39-45
Polygonal Lasso tool, 94-96
Portable Document Format (PDF), 9, 304
portrait orientation, 314
positioning images for printing, 316
preferences. *See also* options bar
    creating new images, 51
    palettes, 21
preparing for selections, 90

Preserve Transparency feature, changing colors in
    images, 143
Preset Sizes option (New dialog box), 52
presets (Selection Brush tool), 101
previewing images (File Browser
    palette), 35
Print button (shortcuts bar), 19
Print Preview feature, 19, 313-317
printing images
    contact sheets, 318-322
    Picture Package feature, 323
    Print Preview feature, 19, 313-317
proportionally resizing images, 43

Q

Quality slider (JPEG image
    compression), 296
Quick Fix feature, 7, 19

R

radial gradient fill type, 124
raster images. *See* bitmap images
Rectangular Marquee tool, 92
Red Eye Brush tool, 224-227
red eye removal (photo retouching),
    223-227
reflected gradient fill type, 124
refreshing File Browser palette file listing, 60, 91,
    184
removing
    adjustment layers, 76
    anchor points (selections), 96
    dust and scratches (photo retouching),
        229-240
    layer styles, 151, 163
    layers, 74
    palettes from Palette Well, 22
    red eye (photo retouching), 223-227
    selection parts, 103
    wrinkles (photo retouching), 228
renaming layers, 61, 119
reordering. *See* sorting
Replace Color dialog box, 207-210
Replacement color option (Red Eye Brush tool),
    225
repositioning panoramic photos, 262. *See also*
    moving
resampling bitmap images, 145
resizing
    images, 43-44, 111

in layers, 71
for printing, 316
palettes, 20
resolution
bitmap versus vector images, 145
of images, 5
setting, 115
for Web usage, 283-284
Resolution option (New dialog box), 52
retouching photos. *See* photo retouching
Reverse Gradient colors option (Gradient tool), 125
reverting to saved images, 85, 130
reviewing video clips, 49
RGB Color image mode, 53
converting to Grayscale or Bitmap, 54-57
rotating images, 43
Rounded Rectangle tool, 151

S

Sampling pull-down menu (Red Eye Brush tool), 225
saturation (Sponge tool), 216-220. *See also* Hue/Saturation adjustment layer
Saturation blending mode, 84
Save as PDF button (shortcuts bar), 19
Save for Web feature, 19, 292-302
Save Optimized As dialog box, 302
Save Selection dialog box, 106
saved images, reverting to, 85, 130
saving
images, 45
as copy, 248
Save for Web feature, 19, 292-302
selections, 105-107
scaling
images for printing, 316
layer styles, 163
scanned images, transforming, 221
scanners
Connect to Camera or Scanner button (Welcome screen), 13
importing images from, 26-27
scratch removal (photo retouching), 229-240
Screen blending mode, 81
Search button (shortcuts bar), 19
Select Input Source dialog box, 13, 26, 29
selecting. *See also* selections
colors. *See* Color Picker window
layers, 61, 69
shapes, 155
tools, 17

Selection Brush tool, 8, 100, 102-103
selection tools, 89, 91
Elliptical Marquee tool, 92
Lasso tool, 93-94
Magic Wand tool, 98-99
Magnetic Lasso tool, 96-98
Polygonal Lasso tool, 94-96
Rectangular Marquee tool, 92
Selection Brush tool, 8, 100, 102-103
selections, 89. *See also* selecting
adding to, 104
choosing tools for, 91-103
deselecting, 93
intersecting, 104
inverting, 100
Lasso tool, 231
moving, 105-106
preparing for, 90
saving, 105-107
subtracting from, 103
transitions between, 232
shadow adjustments (photo correction), 190
shadows. *See* levels
Shape color option (Shape tool), 151
Shape tool, 149-152
shapes, 147-149
adding layer styles to, 155-163
colors, 159
changing, 152-154
selecting, 155
Shape tool, 149-152
Sharpen strength option (Sharpen tool), 249
Sharpen tool, 247-250
sharpening photos, 243-250
shortcuts bar, 18-19
showing. *See* viewing
size
Background Eraser tool, 131
Clone Stamp tool, 235
Eraser tool, 129
of images, 5
for Web usage, 283-284
setting, 115
Pencil tool, 117
Selection Brush tool, 101
sizing. *See* resizing
slideshows, PDF slideshow feature, 9, 305-311
smart error messages, 6
Smudge strength option (Smudge tool), 271
Smudge tool, 269-273

Snap to Browser-Safe Color option (Color Picker), 138
Snap to Grid feature, disabling, 266
Soft Light blending mode, 82
sorting layers, 70
sponge mode option (Sponge tool), 217
Sponge tool, 216-220
startup, disabling Welcome screen at, 14
Step Backward button (shortcuts bar), 19
Step Forward button (shortcuts bar), 19
Strikethrough option (Type tool), 168
Style picker option (Shape tool), 151
styles. *See* layer styles
Subtract from shape area option (Shape tool), 150
subtracting from selections, 103
supported formats. *See* formats
swapping foreground and background color swatches, 136
Switch Colors option (Toolbox), 136
switching to Hand tool, 230

T

text
    adding to images, 165-171
    aligning, 168
    applying layer styles, 176-177
    colors of, 169
    editing, 173-176
    layers for, 172
        accidentally creating, 176
    moving, 171
    warping, 169, 178-181
Text color option (Type tool), 169
thumbnails
    image thumbnails section (File Browser palette), 35-37
    of photographs, printing on contact sheets, 318-322
tint adjustments. *See* color adjustments
Tolerance option
    Magic Eraser tool, 133
    Magic Wand tool, 98
    Paint Bucket tool, 141
tonal range option (Dodge tool), 197. *See also* levels
tool tips. *See* Hints palette
Toolbox, 16-17
    Adobe Online, 17
    background color swatch, 136
    Bloat tool, 277
    Blur tool, 253-255

brushes
    Gradient tool, 123-126
    Impressionist Brush tool, 121
    Paintbrush tool, 120-122
    Pencil tool, 116, 118-119
Burn tool, 195-200
Clone Stamp tool, 234-240
Crop tool, 265-266
Dodge tool, 195-200
Eraser tools, 127-128
    Background Eraser, 131-132
    Eraser, 129-130
    Magic Eraser, 133-135
Eyedropper tool, 142
foreground color swatch, 136
    changing, 65
    setting to default, 136
    swapping with background color swatch, 136
Hand tool, 230
Hints palette, 16
Lasso tool, 231
Move tool, 148, 171
    creating composite images, 109
Paint Bucket tool, 140-142
Pattern Stamp tool, 235
Red Eye Brush tool, 224-227
selection tools, 89-91
    Elliptical Marquee tool, 92
    Lasso tool, 93-94
    Magic Wand tool, 98-99
    Magnetic Lasso tool, 96-98
    Polygonal Lasso tool, 94-96
    Rectangular Marquee tool, 92
    Selection Brush tool, 8, 100, 102-103
Shape tool, 149-152
Sharpen tool, 247-250
Smudge tool, 269-273
Sponge tool, 216-220
Twirl Clockwise tool, 278-279
Twirl Counter Clockwise tool, 279-280
Type tool, 166-171. *See also* text
tools
    blending modes for, 84
    hidden tools, 17
    options bar, 23
    selecting, 17
transforming images, 221
transitions
    between selections, 232
    for PDF slideshows, 307
transparency in layers, 61. *See also* opacity

effect on colors, 66
and fill layers, 79
locking transparent pixels, 64
modifying, 62
overlapping images on, 63
Transparency option (Gradient tool), 125
tripods, tips for taking photographs, 183
Tutorial button (Welcome screen), 14
Twirl Clockwise tool, 278-279
Twirl Counter Clockwise tool, 279-280
type blocks, 175
Type tool, 166-171. *See also* text
typefaces. *See* text

U

Underline option (Type tool), 168
undocking Layers palette, 64
undoing changes, reverting to saved images, 130
ungrouping
    layers, 76
    palettes, 21
unlinking layers, 64
Unsharp Mask filter, 244-247
updates to Photoshop Elements, 11
Use All Layers option
    Magic Eraser tool, 133
    Magic Wand tool, 98
    Smudge tool, 271
user interface. *See* interface

V

value adjustments (photo correction),
    184-185
    automatic adjustments, 192-194
    contrast, 185-186
    Dodge and Burn tools, 195-200
    Levels dialog box, 187-189
    overexposure, 191
    shadow details, 190
vector graphics, 145-146. *See also* shapes
    changing to bitmap graphics, 44
Vertical Type Mask tool, 167
Vertical Type tool, 167
video
    formats for, 46
    importing images from, 47-50
    reviewing clips, 49

viewing
    adjustment layers, 74
    bounding box, 111
    images
        at 100%, 112
        zooming, 102
    layer styles, 163
    layers, 70
visibility of layers, changing, 70
    adjustment layers, 74
Vivid Light blending mode, 82

W

Warp Text dialog box, 178
warping text, 169, 178-181
Web colors in Color Picker, 138
Web Photo Gallery feature, 290-291
Web sites
    animated GIFs, 303-304
    image size and resolution, 283-284
    images for (Save for Web feature), 292-302
Welcome screen, 13
    Browse for File button, 13
    Common Issues button, 14
    Connect to Camera or Scanner button, 13, 26,
        28
    disabling automatic startup of, 14
    Exit Welcome Screen button, 14
    New File button, 13
    opening, 14
    Tutorial button, 14
white input level slider (Levels dialog
    box), 187
white output level slider (Levels dialog box), 188
white-points, 185
Width option
    Magnetic Lasso tool, 97
    New dialog box, 52
windows, moving, 16. *See also* palettes
Windows computers, gamma values on, 186
Windows XP, optimization for, 10
wrinkle removal (photo retouching), 228

X-Y-Z

Zoom menu (Save for Web dialog box), 294
zooming images, 102, 226

A-Z OF
THE HUMAN BODY

A-Z OF THE HUMAN

An illustrated guide to the world's most amazing machine

THE READER'S DIGEST ASSOCIATION LIMITED
LONDON AND NEW YORK

BODY

A-Z OF THE HUMAN BODY

Consultant Editor for the UK Edition:
   James Cox, M.B., B.S., D.R.C.O.G., M.R.C.G.P.
   General Practitioner, Caldbeck, Cumbria
   Examiner, Royal College of
   General Practitioners

Editor: Alma E. Guinness
Art Editor: Robert M. Grant
Associate Editor: Suzanne E. Weiss
Research Editor: Shirley A. Miller
Art Associates: Perri DeFino,
   Larissa Lawrynenko

Picture Editor: Robert J. Woodward

Contributors
Writers: Virginia Adams, Hal Bowser, Walter Fox,
   Nancy Gross, Mary MacEwen, Jean McKeon,
   Wendy Murphy, Sara Stein

Picture Researchers: Natalie Goldstein,
   Leora Kahn Kravitz

Researcher: Timothy Guzley

Indexer: James M. Beran

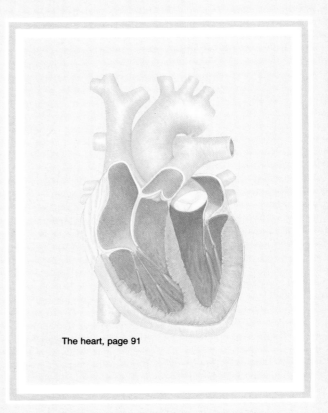

The heart, page 91

First Edition Copyright © 1987
The Reader's Digest Association Limited, 25 Berkeley Square,
London W1X 6AB

Copyright © 1987, Reader's Digest Association Far East Limited
Philippines Copyright © 1987, Reader's Digest Association Far East Ltd

Published as ABC'S OF THE HUMAN BODY by
The Reader's Digest Association, Inc., Pleasantville, New York

Printed and bound by Jarrold and Sons Ltd, Norwich

CONSULTANTS

Farrington Daniels, Jr., M.D., M.P.H.
*Professor Emeritus of Medicine and
Public Health, former Head of
Dermatological Division
Cornell University Medical College*

Lloyd R. Dropkin, M.D.
*Assistant Professor of Otolaryngology
Cornell University Medical College*

Jonathan K. Fears, M.D.
*Division of Allergy and Immunology
Department of Medicine
Cornell University Medical College*

Anna-Riitta Fuchs, Dr. Sc.
*Associate Professor of Reproductive
Biology
Cornell University Medical College*

Roger L. Greif, M.D.
*Professor Emeritus of Physiology
and Biophysics
Cornell University Medical College*

John H. Healey, M.D.
*Assistant Professor of Orthopaedic
Surgery
The Hospital for Special Surgery
Cornell University Medical College*

M.-H. Heinemann, M.D.
*Assistant Professor of Ophthalmology
Cornell University Medical College*

Michael Jacewicz, M.D.
*Louis and Gertrude Feil Fellow in
Medical Cerebrovascular Research
Cornell University Medical College*

W. Peter McCabe, M.D.
*Clinical Assistant Professor of
Surgery (Plastic)
Wayne State University School of
Medicine*

R. Ernest Sosa, M.D.
*Assistant Professor of Surgery
(Urology)
Cornell University Medical College*

Thomas A. Wilson, M.S., D.D.S.
*Associate Professor of Prosthetic
Dentistry
Columbia University School of
Dental and Oral Surgery*

David Zakim, M.D.
*Vincent Astor Distinguished
Professor of Medicine
Cornell University Medical College
Director, Digestive Diseases
The New York Hospital*

FOR COMMISSIONED ART

Bruce Ian Bogart, Ph.D.
*Associate Professor of Cell Biology
and Anatomy
New York University School of
Medicine*

About This Book . . .

A-Z OF THE HUMAN BODY is intended to inform and entertain readers of all ages with explanations of the miracles and mysteries, the foibles and frailties, of the human body. When you come right down to it, the most incredible creation in the universe is *you*—with your fantastic senses and strengths, your ingenious defence systems, and mental capabilities so great you can never use them to the fullest. Your body is a structural masterpiece more amazing than science fiction.

In question-and-answer format, in an easy-to-read, informal style, and based on consultation with distinguished experts, this book answers questions you have wondered about all of your life. Twelve chapters take you on a fantastic voyage of discovery. We hope you will browse through the table of contents, where every question is listed. As you thumb through the book, note the entertaining, illustrated features (including Did You Know . . . ?, The Story Behind the Words, Early Theories, and Folklore of the Body). A comprehensive index has been provided for ready reference. A-Z OF THE HUMAN BODY provides the answers to everything you've ever wanted to know about your body in a way you won't soon forget.

—The Editors

TABLE OF CONTENTS

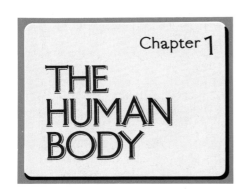

Chapter 1

THE HUMAN BODY

Is laughter good for your health?.. 20
What keeps you healthy?......... 20
Why do some people have more
    energy than others? 20
Which is more important, heredity
    or environment?............... 21
Are you programmed to die at
    a certain age? 21
If the genes control aging, why
    bother about good
    health habits? 21

How the Body Is Organized
What is the human body
    made of?..................... 22
What are the most basic units
    of the body? 22
What do tissues do?............. 22
How do organs relate to body
    systems?..................... 22

Feeling Well or Ill
What does being healthy really
    mean? 24
What happens when your body's
    control mechanisms
    break down? 24
What is hypochondria?.......... 24
Are psychosomatic disorders real,
    or only imaginary? 25
What is Münchhausen's
    syndrome?................... 25

Our Basic Building Blocks
What are the smallest living units
    in the body? 26
What are the main parts
    of a cell?.................... 26
How long do cells live? 26
Where does the cell get its
    energy?..................... 27
What is the internal environment
    of the body? 27

Discovering the Invisible World
What causes disease? 28
What are germs?................ 28
Are viruses the same as germs? .. 29
Can adults get "childhood
    diseases"? 29
Has science wiped out any
    diseases? 29

The Body Under Attack
What are the main kinds
    of disease?................... 30
Do parasites usually kill their
    victims?..................... 30
Are infectious and contagious
    diseases the same thing? 31
What is the difference between an
    acute and a chronic disease? ... 31

The Enemy Within
Are all tumours cancer? 32
What are the main types of
    cancer? 32
What causes cancer? 32
How is cancer treated?.......... 33

The Geography of Disease
What do world explorers and
    traders have in common? 34
Why are tropical diseases difficult
    to eradicate?................. 34
What are snail fever and
    sleeping sickness?............ 34
Why do you so often get diarrhoea
    when you travel? 35
Do you need a lot of injections
    before you travel abroad? 35

Are people healthier in advanced
    societies than primitive
    ones?....................... 35

Of Doctors and Dosages
How does a doctor determine the
    right dosage of medicine?...... 36
Do medicines ever backfire?...... 36
Are gullible people the only ones
    who respond to placebos? 36
War: The Crucible of Medical
    Practice 37

The Rules of Heredity
How does the cell nucleus relate
    to chromosomes
    and genes?................... 38
Why do children tend to look
    like their parents? 38
How do children get genes from
    their parents? 38
Are all genes equally powerful? ... 39
Why don't all brothers and
    sisters look more alike
    than they do?................ 39
What do identical twins reveal
    about heredity? 39

Symptoms and Syndromes
Are genetic defects rare? 40
How many different disorders
    can be passed on by
    abnormal genes? 40
What happens if a person has
    the wrong number of
    chromosomes?................ 40
Which sex is more vulnerable to
    genetic disease?.............. 40

**Orchestrating Our
Development**
How do cells "know" what
    to do?....................... 42
How do genes work? 42
What is genetic engineering? 43

High-Tech Science
Can human beings be cloned?.... 44
Are new diseases really new? 44
What will the body be like
    tomorrow?................... 44
What medical breakthroughs
    are ahead? 45

Thermography, page 24

6

Chapter 2

THE BRAIN & NERVOUS SYSTEM

What does the brain do? 46
Are the mind and the brain the
    same thing? 46
Is the brain a computer? 47
What is an idiot savant? 47

The Most Complex Organ in the Body

What does the brain look like? 48
What are the main parts of the
    nervous system? 48
What do the different parts of
    the brain do? 48
What is the blood-brain barrier? ... 48
How long can the brain go
    without oxygen? 48

The Amazing Network of Nerves

How do messages get around
    in the brain? 50
What happens if nerves are
    damaged or destroyed? 50
Why are nerve cells in the
    brain so remarkable? 50
What does being nervous have
    to do with nerves? 51
Why does your leg jerk when the
    doctor taps your knee? 51
How do messages travel from one
    cell to another? 51

How the Brain Works

How can scientists find out which
    parts of the brain do what? 52
Are the two halves of your brain
    equal in language ability? 52
Can a person have normal eyes
    and still be unable to see? 52
Can one part of the brain take over
    the function of another? 53

Hormones and Hemispheres

Are men's and women's brains
    alike? 54
Are there any behavioural sex
    differences? 54
What is the evidence that males
    are more aggressive than
    females? 54
Are disorders influenced by sex? .. 55
Can both sides of your brain
    recognize faces? 55

Scanning the Brain for Signals

Can an X-ray see inside
    the brain? 56
What can CAT, PET, and MRI scans
    see that X-rays can't? 56
Will scanners be able to read your
    mind some day? 56
What are brain waves? 57
When is a person considered
    "brain dead"? 57

To Sleep: Perchance to Dream. . . .

What is the purpose of sleep? 58
Does everyone need eight hours
    of sleep a night? 58
What does prolonged lack of sleep
    do to people? 58
Why do you dream? 59
Are people who dream in
    colour rare? 59
What causes insomnia? 59
What is the opposite of
    insomnia? 59

Awareness of the World

Can you think without words? 60
What part of your brain learns? ... 60
Do you notice most of what
    happens around you? 60
Why does practice make perfect? .. 60
Are babies capable of depth
    perception? 61

How We Store Our Experiences

Why do you forget a telephone
    number right after
    looking it up? 62
Why do the elderly remember the
    past but not the present? 62
Why don't you remember the time
    when you were a baby? 62
What causes amnesia? 63

Phineas Gage, page 69

Can you remember better if you're
    hypnotized? 63
Why can smells evoke powerful
    memories? 63
What is a déjà vu experience? 63

Measuring Human Intelligence

What is intelligence? 64
Is intelligence inherited? 64
What do tests and teasers
    show? 64
Is intelligence one ability,
    or several? 65
Can you raise your IQ? 65

The Power of Moods and Emotions

How close are laughter
    and tears? 66
Can your emotions make
    you ill? 66
When is depression a sign of
    mental illness? 66
What causes anger to reach
    dangerous levels? 66
Insanity: From Chains to
    Tranquilizers 67

Injury and Aftermath

Can alcohol harm your brain? 68
Are your thoughts and emotions
    independent of
    each other? 68
Do all your nerves feel pain? 69

*How many kinds of pain
are there?* 69

What is your pain threshold? 69

Coping With Pain

Can stress relieve pain? 70

*What is the difference between
local and general
anaesthesia?* 70

*Is acupuncture witchcraft
or science?* 70

*Are you aware of anything while
you're under a general
anaesthetic?* 71

What are pain clinics? 71

Disorders of the Brain

*Is a headache a pain in
the brain?* 72

*What are the symptoms of a
brain tumour?* 72

What is Alzheimer's disease? 72

*How is schizophrenia
manifested?* 72

*How do we know the right brain is
more emotional than the left?* ... 73

Insanity, page 67

Chapter 3

THE ENDOCRINE SYSTEM

What are hormones? 74

What causes jet lag? 74

*Why do some athletes take
steroids?* 75

*Does eating a lot of sugar cause
diabetes?* 75

*Why do people like to frighten
themselves?* 75

The Mysterious Organs

*How did the endocrine system
get its name?* 76

*How many hormones does
your body make?* 76

*Why is a hormone molecule
like a key?* 76

*What prevents a healthy gland
from secreting too much
hormone?* 76

*What kinds of things do hormones
do for you?* 77

The Master Glands

*How do your brain and your body
"talk" to each other?* 78

*Why is the pituitary sometimes
called the master gland?* 78

What causes giantism? 78

*What is the difference between
a dwarf and a midget?* 78

*Giants, Dwarfs, and Variations
in Growth* 79

The Influence of Hormones
on Growth

*When does the human body begin
to produce sex hormones?* 80

*Why do adolescents grow
so fast?* 80

*Do adults need growth
hormone?* 80

*Do men produce any female
hormones?* 80

*What makes a boy's voice
deepen?* 81

*How do male hormones affect
normal women?* 81

Sex and the Life Cycle

*Do boys and girls mature earlier
than they used to?* 82

*Is adolescence bound to be
stormy?* 82

*Do hormone levels affect
your sex life?* 82

*What happens when you're in
the mood for love?* 83

*Can an active sex life keep you
feeling young?* 83

How We Respond to Fear
and Stress

What do the adrenal glands do? .. 84

*Why does your heart pound when
you're frightened?* 84

*What does your endocrine system
do when you're under stress?* ... 85

*Are there any medical uses for
adrenaline?* 85

*Can prolonged glucocorticoid
treatment do you any harm?* ... 85

Energy Control, Sugar
Balance

*What does the thyroid gland have
to do with energy?* 86

What causes goitre? 86

*How can some people eat and
eat and never gain weight?* 86

*Does the pancreas secrete more
than one hormone?* 87

What is diabetes mellitus? 87

Fear, page 84

Chapter 4

THE HEART & CIRCULATORY SYSTEM

Is the heart on the left side?...... 88
What makes bruises "black
  and blue"?................... 88
Does the heart ever rest?........ 88
How does emotional stress
  affect the heart?.............. 89
Can people be cold-blooded?..... 89
Where is the body's thermostat?.. 89
Why are hats important in
  cold weather?................. 89

Your Heart: The Double Pump
How complicated is your heart?.. 90
What makes the heart beat?...... 90
What can be done if the heart's
  natural pacemaker is faulty?... 90
What causes heart murmurs?..... 91

The Circulatory Network
What is the function of arteries?... 92
How do veins differ from arteries? 92
What does your pulse indicate?... 93
How much blood does the
  heart pump?.................. 93
What do the kidneys do?......... 93

An Army of Specialists
What is blood made of?.......... 94
Why is blood red?............... 94
What do red cells do?........... 94
Are white blood cells really
  white?....................... 95
What makes blood clot?......... 95
How does altitude affect the
  composition of blood?......... 95

Blood Groups and Transfusions
Why do blood types matter?...... 96
What are the main blood types?.. 96
What is the Rh factor?........... 96
What gets counted in a
  blood count?.................. 97
Can you give yourself a blood
  transfusion?.................. 97
Can blood type prove paternity?.. 97

Repairing Cuts and Bruises
How does the body control
  bleeding?.................... 98
When bleeding doesn't stop,
  what can be done?............ 99
How and when does
  healing begin?............... 99
What causes pus to form?........ 99
Why do some people heal more
  quickly than others?.......... 99

The Mysteries of Immunity
How does the body defend itself
  against disease?.............. 100
What if the body cannot fight off
  the agents of disease?........ 100
How do vaccines work?......... 100
When are antitoxins and gamma
  globulin used?............... 100
What happens when the immune
  system breaks down?........ 101

Monitoring the Heart
How is blood pressure
  measured?................... 102
What is normal blood pressure?. 102
What are the dangers of high
  blood pressure?.............. 102
Does high blood pressure run
  in families?.................. 103
Does salt have any effect on
  blood pressure?.............. 103
What happens when blood
  pressure falls too low?........ 103
What does an electrocardiogram
  show about your heart?....... 103

When Things Go Wrong
Which is the most common
  heart disorder?.............. 104
What happens to the heart in
  coronary artery disease?...... 104
What are other risk factors in
  coronary artery disease?...... 104
Does cholesterol really matter?.. 104
Does a heart attack always
  mean invalidism
  or death?.................... 105

Blood and Circulatory Disorders
What causes varicose veins?..... 106
What is phlebitis?.............. 106
What is a stroke?.............. 106
Who is most likely to suffer
  a stroke?.................... 106
Can stroke victims ever be
  normal again?............... 107
What is gangrene?............. 107
What is the kissing disease?..... 107

Heart, page 91

Deficiencies of the Blood
What is anaemia?.............. 108
Can X-rays produce
  anaemia?.................... 108
Are some people more
  vulnerable to anaemia
  than others?................. 108
Can anyone get haemophilia?... 108
Haemophilia: A Blood Disease
  That Influenced History....... 109

The Little-Known Lymphatic System
What is the lymphatic
  system?..................... 110
Why do we need lymph
  nodes?...................... 110
What does the spleen do?....... 110
What is a lymphoma?........... 110
What is Hodgkin's disease?...... 111

Chapter 5

THE RESPIRATORY SYSTEM

What is breathing? 112
What happens when you are
  "out of breath"? 112
What causes snoring, and can
  it be cured? 112
Why do you yawn? 113
What is passive smoking? 113
Can vitamin C reduce
  susceptibility to colds? 113

The Breath of Life
How do the lungs work? 114
What determines how much
  you breathe? 114
What is the diaphragm? 114
What happens when you
  hiccup? 114
Is it ever dangerous to breathe
  pure oxygen? 114

Taking Your Measure
How much air can your lungs
  hold? 116

Corsets, page 117

Why does the doctor tap your
  chest? 116
What does "palpation" indicate
  about your chest and lungs? . . 116
What is a stethoscope? 116
What does a bronchoscope do? . . 116
How often should you have
  a chest X-ray? 116
What are pulmonary function
  tests? 117

Sneezes, Wheezes, and Coughs
What is a sneeze? 118
What causes coughing? 118
Can cough medicines help? 118
What is a common cold? 119
Why does a cold start with a
  runny nose? 119
Why do you get more colds
  in winter? 119
Can you get a cold from
  wet feet? 119

Our Shared Miseries
How do viruses cause a cold? . . . 120
Are some people more vulnerable
  to colds than others? 120
Is influenza just a bad version
  of the common cold? 120
Influenza: The Elusive Enemy 121

Disorders and Diseases of the Lung
What is bronchitis? 122
What causes asthma? 122
Why is lung cancer on the rise? . . 123
Has tuberculosis ceased to be a
  health hazard? 123

Respiratory Emergencies
What is hyperventilation? 124
What causes a lung to collapse? . 124
What is emphysema, and can
  it be cured? 124
What should you do if someone
  chokes? 124
How does artificial respiration
  work? 125

Hazards in the Environment
What is mountain sickness? 126
How does the weather affect
  breathing? 126
Which air pollutants are most
  hazardous to health? 126
Can your house be dangerous? . . 126
What jobs can put your lungs
  at high risk? 127

Report on Smoking
Why is smoking bad for you? 128
What substances in smoke
  cause cancer? 128
Are some kinds of smoking more
  dangerous than others? 129
Are there extra hazards to
  smoking during pregnancy? . . . 129
Is it ever too late to stop
  smoking? 129

Allergens, page 122

Chapter 6
THE SKIN

What does skin do? 130
Why are some people
    more ticklish
    than others? 130
What causes clammy hands
    and cold sweats? 130
What happens when you blush? . . 131
Why are people different
    colours? 131
What is so special about
    red hair? 131

Skin: Our Remarkable Armour
Why do we tend to think
    that skin is a simple
    structure? 132
How does skin grow? 132
What good are goose pimples? . . 132
Why do we sweat? 132
Is sweating a lot good
    for you? 132
How deep is "skin deep"? 133

The Ecology of Skin
Is human skin ever really
    clean? 134
Are germs on the skin
    harmful? 134
Can skin micro-organisms do
    us any good? 134
Do infants have skin bacteria
    like the rest of us? 135

Can insects and other creatures
    live on human skin? 135

The Skin You Are Born With
Why do some people have
    freckles? 136
What causes albinism? 136
What are birthmarks? 136
When are moles dangerous? 136
Are your fingerprints of any
    practical use to you? 136
Can footprints be used as
    a means of identification? 137

The Sensitivity of the Human Skin
How important is the sense
    of touch? 138
What happens when you touch
    something? 138
What causes itching? 138
How sensitive are your lips? 139
Why do lips chap? 139
How do you tell hot from cold? . . 139
Why do extreme cold and extreme
    heat often feel the same? 139

Your Skin at Risk
Can you protect yourself from
    insect bites and stings? 140
What should you do if you are
    stung? 140
How should a tick be removed? . 140
Can toads cause warts? 140
Why do you look like a prune
    after a bath? 141
Can clothing harm your skin? . . . 141
Why do you get calluses
    and corns? 141
How does an abrasion heal? 141

From Sunburn to Frostbite
What causes sunburn? 142
Why does sunburned skin redden
    and peel before it tans? 142
Can you sunburn when it's
    cold out? 142
How can cold weather be harmful
    to the skin? 142
Why is frostbite dangerous? 142
What is the best first aid for
    burns? 143
Can skin be grown in a
    test tube? 143

Common Skin Problems
What is the commonest skin
    disorder? 144
Can acne be cured? 144

What's the difference between a
    boil and a carbuncle? 144
How did athlete's foot get
    its name? 144
What is the mystery of
    psoriasis? 145
What can be done about
    psoriasis? 145
Are all skin cancers equally
    dangerous? 145

Repairing Damage, Taking Tucks
Why does the skin lose resilience
    and wrinkle when you age? . . . 146
How are face lifts done? 146
Can exercise or massage or
    anything rejuvenate
    aging skin? 147
Why do people undergo plastic
    surgery? 147
Why is surgery on the nose
    inadvisable for very
    young people? 147
Does a reconstructed breast look
    normal? 147

Healing and Hazards
Can surgeons do anything about
    wrinkles and scars? 148
Why do some injuries
    leave scars? 148
What are keloid scars, and how
    do they develop? 148
Can tattoos be removed? 148
The Human Skin as a Canvas 149

How and Where Hair Grows
Does hair serve a useful
    function? 150
Is your hair alive, or dead? 150
If my hair isn't alive, why does
    it keep getting longer? 150
Can your hair actually stand
    on end? 151
How many kinds of hair
    are there? 151

Cosmetics, page 149

Hair, page 155

Why is hair thick, coarse,
or fine? 151
What causes dandruff? 151

Hair: Too Little, Too Much
What is baldness?.............. 152
Why do more men than women
go bald? 152
Can baldness be cured?........ 152
Can your hair fall out
overnight? 152
What causes excessive
hairiness? 153
Can you get rid of unsightly
hair?....................... 153

Making Changes in Your Hair
Can your hair turn white
overnight? 154
What turns hair grey? 154
How does dyeing work? 154
Is it safe to dye your hair? 155
Can swimming hurt
your hair?................... 155

Your Telltale Nails
Are your nails dead or alive? 156
How do hair, fingernails, and
toenails compare? 156
Do people's nails really keep
growing after death?.......... 156
What makes fingernails brittle? .. 156
What do your nails reveal about
your health? 157
What is a hangnail? 157
What causes ingrowing
toenails? 157

Chapter 7
THE BONES & MUSCLES

What do engineers think of the
human body? 158
How old are your bones? 158
Does a baby have as many bones
as an adult? 159
Can heavy drinking injure
your bones?.................. 159
How do you learn to walk?...... 159
What does "muscle-bound"
actually mean? 159

The Framework of the Body
What do bones do? 160
What goes on inside living
bones?...................... 160
Can you feel pain in your
bones?...................... 160
How can you tell male and
female skeletons apart?....... 160
Can your bones endanger
your body in
any way? 160

The Secret of Muscular Action
Why is your body like the mast
of an old-time sailing
vessel?...................... 162
How many kinds of muscle are
there?....................... 163
What does the inside of a muscle
look like? 163
How do muscles work? 163
What makes the heart muscle
so tough? 163

Degrees of Flexibility
How do joints work?........... 164
What makes joints operate
smoothly? 164
Which joint is most
vulnerable?.................. 164
Are all your joints movable?..... 164
What is a ball-and-socket joint? .. 164
What makes your joints
crack? 164
What does it mean if a person
is double-jointed? 165

The Casing for the Brain
Why are infants born soft-
headed? 166
What is the function of
the skull? 166
What happens when you hit
your head?................... 167
When is a fractured skull a
serious matter?............... 167
Can "heading" a soccer ball
cause brain damage? 167

What's Behind Your Smile
How many muscles are there
in the face? 168
Is there a universal language
of expression?............... 168
What is the temporomandibular
(TMJ) disorder? 169

The Development of Teeth
What are your teeth made of? 170
Why are baby teeth important? .. 170
How do your teeth grow? 170
Why are wisdom teeth so often
troublesome? 171
Why are straight teeth and a good
bite important to health?...... 171
Is it worthwhile for adults to
straighten their teeth? 171
Why do teeth become
discoloured? 171
What can you do if you lose
a tooth?..................... 171

The Spine: Supple or Stiff
How is the spine organized? 172
How important is good posture?. 172
Why are backaches so
common? 172
Are people ever born with
giraffe-like necks? 172

Joints, page 165

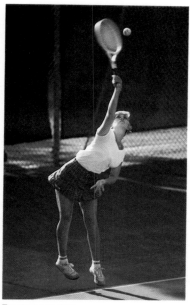

Tennis, page 174

*What makes a person
hunchback?* 173
*What is the key to good
posture?* 173

Straight From the Shoulder
*How do the arms and shoulders
work?* 174
*Is frozen shoulder a cold-weather
affliction?* 174
*What happens when you
dislocate your shoulder?* 174
*Why is a blow to your funny
bone no laughing matter?* 175
What is tennis elbow? 175
*What is the difference between
tendons and
ligaments?* 175

The Dexterous Human Hand
*What makes your hands so
flexible?* 176
*Is a mallet finger a serious
sports injury?* 176
Why is a painful wrist serious? . . 176
What's in a name? 176
*Is it harmful to crack your
knuckles?* 177
What is "trigger finger"? 177
What is Colles' fracture? 177

The Long, Strong Bones
and Muscles
*How do hip, thigh, and knee
relate to one another?* 178

What is "housemaid's knee"? 178
What is a locking knee? 178
*Can you tell a dead man's
height from a single
skeletal bone?* 178
Feet as a Target of Fashion 179

The Springs on Which You Move
*What is the common job of the
foot, ankle, and calf?* 180
What is your Achilles' heel? 180
What is club foot? 180
What causes flat feet? 180
Are bunions hereditary? 181
How does the foot work? 181

Wear and Tear on the Body
Is bed rest ever hazardous? 182
Why do bones lose calcium? 182
*What is the biggest threat to
your joints?* 182
*What happens when osteoarthritis
strikes?* 182
*How do doctors replace hips
and knees?* 183

Strains, Sprains, and Fractures
How do injuries differ? 184
How does a broken bone heal? . . 184
*Do all bones heal at the
same rate?* 184
What is the value of traction? 184
*Can sports be harmful for
children?* 184
*Why does a sprained ankle
hurt so much?* 184
*What happens when you get a
"whiplash" injury?* 185

Keeping Fit Through Exercise
*What are the benefits of regular
exercise?* 186
*Should you be able to bend over
and touch your toes?* 186
*Should you always warm
up before exercise?* 187
What is your strongest muscle? . . 187
*Why do weight lifters often
have pot bellies?* 187
*What does your centre of
gravity have to do
with posture?* 187

Chapter 8
THE EYE

*Are you right-eyed or
left-eyed?* 188
*Why do people have different
eye colours?* 188
What are floaters? 188
*Can too much reading weaken
your eyesight?* 189
Why do eyes get bloodshot? 189
*Is make-up ever a cause of eye
inflammation?* 189
*Does it hurt your eyes to cross
them intentionally?* 189

The Workings of the Eye
*How does the eye compare
with a camera?* 190
*What happens when light enters
the eye?* 190
*What can an eye doctor tell by
looking into your eyes?* 190
*What are the different eye
specialities?* 190
*Why does the doctor use drops
when examining
your eyes?* 190
*What do your pupils reveal
about you?* 191

When the Tears Flow
Where do tears come from? 192
Why do you blink your eyes? 192
*How many kinds of tears
are there?* 192
Is crying good for you? 192
*Why do you sometimes cry
when you laugh?* 192
*Can a speck in the eye be
dangerous?* 192
The Evolution of Spectacles 193

Bringing the World Into Focus
What is normal vision? 194
*What are the most common
visual defects?* 194
*How do spectacles correct
your vision?* 194
*Can the wrong spectacles ruin
your eyes?* 194
*What kinds of contact lenses are
available?* 195

13

Glasses, page 193

Are contacts better than
  glasses? 195
Can contacts harm the eyes?..... 195
Do sunglasses really do
  any good? 195
Why do older people need
  glasses for close work? 195

Everyday Optical Illusions
Do you see everything
  upside down? 196
How do you see in 3-D? 196
How do people with "cross-eyes"
  or "wall-eyes" see
  the world? 197
Is depth perception possible
  with only one eye? 197
How do movies move?......... 197
Can a batsman really keep his
  eye on the ball? 197

Visual Tricks and Treats
Can your brain draw the wrong
  conclusion? 198
Why do some optical illusions
  seem to flip back
  and forth?................... 198
Are optical illusions of any
  practical importance? 198
How can we "see" more than is
  actually visible? 199

The Amazing World of Colour
How does the eye see colour?... 200
Is your sky as blue as mine? 200
Does colour affect our moods?... 200
What colours do babies prefer?... 201
Why do you sometimes see
  light even after you
  close your eyes? 201

Limitations of Vision
Why is colour blindness usually
  a misnomer? 202
Can colour blindness be
  corrected?................... 202
How do your eyes adapt to
  darkness and bright light?..... 202
What causes night blindness?.... 202
Can blindness be prevented? 202
Are the other senses of the blind
  especially acute? 203
Does alcohol affect eyesight?.... 203

Eye Problems and Remedies
What causes cataracts?......... 204
Can the results of cataract
  surgery be predicted?........ 204
How is glaucoma treated
  today? 204
How are detached retinas
  reattached? 204
How does the world look when
  vision is impaired?........... 205
What is corneal grafting? 205

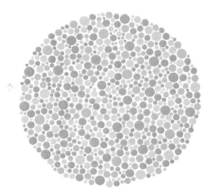

Colour blindness, page 202

Chapter 9
THE EAR, NOSE, & THROAT

Why are the ear, nose, and throat
  related medically? 206
Can you test your own
  hearing? 206
Do you hear your voice as
  others hear it?............... 206
Does one sex have a keener
  sense of smell than
  the other?.................. 207
Can your sense of smell
  wear out? 207
Why do some people get motion
  sickness? 207

The Ear: A Marvel of Miniaturization
How is the ear constructed?..... 208
What is the function of the
  external ear? 208
How does the middle ear
  work?...................... 209
What does the inner ear do?..... 209

The Sounds Around Us
What is sound? 210
What are the main characteristics
  of sound? 210
Can we hear all possible
  sounds?.................... 211
How does having two ears affect
  your hearing? 211
Can blind people see with
  their ears? 211

Degrees of Hearing Loss
How is hearing tested?......... 212
What causes deafness?......... 212
Can music damage your ears? .. 212
Are some people more sensitive
  to noise than others? 213
What is tone deafness? 213
Can noise impair your efficiency
  or your general health? 213
Which sense is more important,
  sight or hearing? 213

Ear Problems and Remedies

What is the most common cause
   of earaches? 214

Is ringing in the ears cause
   for concern? 214

What can you do if you're hard
   of hearing? 214

Hearing Aids: Capturing
   Sound Waves 215

Keeping Your Balance

How do you keep your balance? 216

What is Ménière's disease? 216

Why do your ears pop when
   you fly? 217

Does one-sided hearing loss mean
   anything special? 217

The "Air Conditioner" of the Body

What does your nose do
   for you? 218

What does the interior of the
   nose look like? 218

How does the nose filter air? 218

Why is it better to breathe through
   your nose than your mouth? . . . 219

Is there a right way to blow
   your nose? 219

Why are some drugs administered
   through the nose? 219

What is the effect of a deviated
   septum? 219

How does the plastic surgeon
   change the shape of the nose? . 219

The Smell-Taste Connection

What is smell? 220

Where is your sense of smell
   located? 220

Why is it difficult to taste food
   when you have a cold? 221

Are there primary odours
   comparable to primary colours? 221

How many smells can
   you smell? 221

Hyssop, page 223

Four Sets of Sinus Cavities

Where are the sinuses, and
   what do they do? 222

How do you recognize sinusitis,
   and what is the treatment? 222

What is allergic rhinitis? 222

Is there any cure for
   hay fever? 223

What are adenoids? 223

The Switch From Breathing to Swallowing

How is the throat constructed? . . 224

What keeps food from entering
   your windpipe? 224

Why does a tongue depressor
   make you gag? 224

What does the little flap at the
   back of the throat do? 224

What happens when you get a
   "lump in the throat"? 225

What does it mean to be
   tongue-tied? 225

Can choking be prevented? 225

Miseries of the Nose and Throat

What is postnasal drip? 226

Are nasal decongestants ever
   dangerous? 226

What are nasal polyps, and are
   they harmful? 226

Why do people get nosebleeds? . . 226

Is a sore throat a disease? 227

What is streptococcal sore throat
   and is it dangerous? 227

Does everyone have an
   Adam's apple? 227

The Wonderful Human Voice

What is speech, and how do we
   learn to communicate with it? . . 228

How do we speak? 228

Why does the voice change in
   adolescence? 229

What causes laryngitis? 229

How do you whisper? 229

What do opera singers and
   babies have in common? 229

Overcoming Speech and Hearing Problems

What causes speech disorders? . . 230

Why do some people stutter? 230

Can anything be done for
   deaf-mutes? 230

How do you know if an infant
   can't hear? 231

If you lose your larynx, do you
   lose the ability to speak? 231

Chapter 10
THE DIGESTIVE SYSTEM

What makes you hungry? 232

Why do you feel thirsty? 232

Why does your stomach
   rumble? 233

Does it matter when you eat
   your biggest meal of
   the day? 233

Can mouthwash cure
   bad breath? 233

Does brushing your teeth affect
   your sense of taste? 233

Do you need extra protein when
   you engage in sports? 233

Is sugar bad for you? 233

The Food Journey

What happens when you eat? . . . 234

What does the mouth do? 234

Why is saliva important? 234

Where does your saliva
   come from? 234

What prompts salivation? 234

How does your food get down
   to your stomach? 235

How long does it take food to go
   through the digestive tract? . . . 235

How You Taste Your Food

What does your tongue do? 236

What does a healthy tongue
   look like? 236

How do you taste food? 236

What are the primary tastes? 236

Can every taste bud sense
   every taste? 237

Do particular foods taste the
   same to everyone? 237

Is the sense of taste sharper in
   infancy or in adulthood? 237

Care of Teeth and Gums

Why do your teeth decay? 238

What causes a toothache? 238

Can tooth decay be prevented? . . 238

How do fluorides work? 238

Are fluorides dangerous? 239

15

Stomach, page 240

What if a toothache goes away
on its own? 239
Can a dead tooth be saved? 239
What is the major dental problem
of middle age? 239
What can you do about gum
disease? 239

Filling Your Stomach

Why is it important to chew your
food thoroughly? 240
What happens when you
swallow? 240
Does swallowing depend
on gravity? 240
Is "heartburn" a misnomer? 241
Why are hiatus hernias often
misdiagnosed? 241
What is the commonest
misconception about
the stomach? 241
What does your stomach do
to food? 241
What causes an upset
stomach? 241

What the Stomach Really Does

How long does food stay in
the stomach? 242
Why doesn't the stomach digest
itself? 242
How much food will the
stomach hold? 242
What do gastric juices do? 242
What happens when you
vomit? 242
The Paradox of Salt 243

The Liver: A Chemical Factory

Is it true that the liver does 500
different things? 244

What is the role of the liver in
digestion? 245
Is drinking the only cause
of cirrhosis of the liver? 245
What is so remarkable about
liver cells? 245
How much does the liver filter
in a year? 245
How does the liver maintain
the blood sugar level? 245

The Gallbladder and the Pancreas

Why does liver disease turn
you yellow? 246
Is there more than one kind of
viral hepatitis? 246
Where is the gallbladder, and
what does it do? 247
Can you live without your
gallbladder? 247
What does the pancreas do? 247
How does the pancreas promote
digestion? 247
Can the pancreas digest itself? .. 247

Where Absorption Takes Place

How large is the small
intestine? 248
What happens to food in the
small intestine? 248
How are nutrients absorbed
into the body? 248
Are all intestinal movements
alike? 249
Why are some foods more
quickly digested
than others? 249
Do the bacteria in your digestive
tract hurt you? 249
Does the appendix serve a
purpose? 249

The End of the Journey

Is the large intestine really
large? 250
How does the large intestine fit
into the body? 250
What are faeces made of? 250
How can you prevent wind? 250
What causes the odour of faeces
and flatus? 251
Does constipation matter? 251
What causes diarrhoea? 251

Fuelling the Body

What is a Calorie? 252
What foods should you eat daily
for proper nutrition? 252
What is your acceptable weight? . 252

How much protein do
you need? 253
What is "high-quality" protein? .. 253
How much fat should you eat? .. 253
If children choose their food,
will they eat what is
good for them? 253

Pluses and Minuses of Food

What is fibre, and why is it
good for you? 254
Can you consume too
much fibre? 254
Do you need vitamin
supplements? 254
Are vitamin megadoses helpful
or harmful? 254
Are the additives in foods
dangerous? 255
Is caffeine harmless? 255
Can food really poison you? 255

Eating: Too Much, Too Little

Do diets really work? 256
Is exercise effective against fat? .. 256
Is there any sensible way to
lose weight? 256
When does loss of appetite
become dangerous? 256
What is bulimia? 257

Henry VIII, page 254

Chapter 11

THE URINARY & REPRODUCTIVE SYSTEMS

What is the most surprising characteristic of urine? 258

How does what you consume affect your need to urinate? 258

When is it especially important to drink plenty of fluids? 258

Why does nervousness sometimes produce an urge to urinate? 258

Why does the colour of urine vary? . 259

Do the kidneys have anything to do with hangovers? 259

Are over-the-counter medications harmful to the kidneys? 259

At what age do children learn to control their bladders? 259

Is there any connection between diet, weight, and reproduction? 259

What is the menopause? 259

Is there such a thing as "male menopause"? 259

Maintaining Your Fluid Balance

How does your body respond to thirst? 260

What is the role of the kidneys? . . 260

How do the kidneys function? . . . 260

How does an artificial kidney work? 260

Are kidney transplants usually successful? 261

Where are your kidneys, and what do they do? 261

The Composition of Urine

What is urine made of? 262

How is urine eliminated? 262

What stimulates urination? 262

Do you eliminate the same amount of fluid that you take in? 263

What causes an increase or a decrease in the volume of urine? 263

How do the male and female urinary systems differ? 263

Urinary Problems and Remedies

Why is it important to treat minor urinary tract infections? 264

Why do some children wet their beds? 264

What are kidney stones? 264

Is surgery always necessary to relieve kidney stones? 264

How can kidney stones be prevented? 265

The Male Reproductive System

What is the structure of the testicles? 266

Why does the scrotum lie outside the abdomen? 266

What are the main parts of the male reproductive system? 266

What leads to an erection of the penis? 267

What happens during ejaculation? 267

Is the prostate gland related to sexual performance? 267

Why is the prostate so often a source of trouble for older men? 267

Does surgery for an enlarged prostate affect sexual functioning? 267

Why do doctors examine the rectum to detect an enlarged prostate? 267

What is the reason for circumcision? 267

The Production of Sperm

How are sperm produced? 268

How many sperm does the male release in each ejaculation? 268

What is semen for? 268

Do semen and urine ever mix? . . 268

Are nocturnal emissions normal? 269

Is self-examination of the testicles necessary? 269

Do all testicular masses represent tumours? 269

Who is at greatest risk to develop a tumour of the testis? 269

Why is mumps dangerous for men? 269

Causes of Impotence

Do many men suffer from sexual impotence? 270

What are the most frequent causes of chronic impotence? 270

Can drugs make a man impotent? 270

How do doctors find out what causes impotence? 270

Can premature ejaculation be prevented? 270

Is sexual intercourse safe after a heart attack? 270

Can a vasectomy cause impotence? 270

The Female Reproductive System

What are the principal parts of the female reproductive system? 272

What are the major functions of the ovaries? 272

How many eggs do the ovaries contain? 272

What is the structure of the uterus? 272

How does ovulation come about? 272

What is the function of the vagina? 273

What is the vulva? 273

The Functioning of the Uterus

Why are regular cervical smears advisable? 274

What is a D and C? 274

Why are fibroids removed? 274

What is removed in a hysterectomy? 274

Sperm, page 268

What is the psychological effect
  of a hysterectomy? 274
Is premenstrual discomfort all in
  your mind? 275

Understanding the Female Body
What is the structure of
  the breast? 276
What if you find a lump in
  your breast? 276
What is cystic breast disease? ... 277
Does the size of the breast affect
  its nurturing capacity? 277
What happens when a woman
  experiences sexual arousal? ... 277
Why is the female orgasm
  important? 277
Can frigidity be cured? 277

Sexually Transmitted Diseases
What diseases are sexually
  transmitted? 278
Which sexually transmitted disease
  often causes sterility? 278
Is it easy to tell if you have
  chlamydia? 279
Are all herpes viruses sexually
  transmitted? 279
Can genital herpes be
  prevented? 279
Can you contract venereal disease
  by using public toilets? 279

The Changing Nature of VD
What is pelvic inflammatory
  disease? 280
What are the characteristics and
  dangers of syphilis? 280
Can syphilis be inherited? 281
Why is gonorrhoea sometimes
  difficult to detect? 281
How does gonorrhoea spread? .. 281
Why is early treatment of
  gonorrhoea important? 281
Who is most likely to
  catch AIDS? 281
Is there any chance of soon
  finding a cure or a
  vaccine for AIDS? 281

The Timing of Fertility
How many days a month is a
  woman fertile? 282
What is the role of female
  hormones in fertilization? 282
How does age affect fertility? 282
How long does it take sperm
  to mature? 282
Can a woman become pregnant
  while breast feeding? 282

Marriage: The Ceremonies Vary,
  but the Meaning Is the Same ... 283

Dealing With Infertility
How can a tubal infection prevent
  pregnancy? 284
When are fertility drugs
  effective? 284
What are the two major causes
  of female infertility? 284
What is the most frequent cause
  of male infertility? 284
What other factors affect
  male fertility? 284
What is an ectopic pregnancy? ... 285
When is artificial insemination
  useful? 285
How does test-tube conception
  circumvent infertility? 285

Methods of Contraception
What are the main methods of
  contraception? 286
How do barrier methods of
  contraception work? 286
Is the IUD safe? 287
How does the Pill prevent
  pregnancy? 287
Is the Pill safe for everyone? 287
Is sterilization by tubal ligation
  reversible? 287

Wedding rings, page 283

How is the expected birth date
  figured out? 288
What is the difference between
  an embryo and a foetus? 288
Is delayed parenthood risky
  for the foetus? 288
What if pregnancy lasts longer
  than nine months? 289
Is there such a thing as a
  "nesting" instinct? 289
What is "witches' milk"? 289
Can the baby sense its mother's
  emotions? 289
Can anything be done about
  morning sickness? 289

When Conception Takes Place
How soon can pregnancy be
  detected? 290
How is a pregnancy test done? .. 290
Why doesn't the mother have
  periods during pregnancy? 290
How does a baby begin? 290
How does a fertilized egg get
  into the uterus? 290
What determines a baby's sex? ... 291

The Early Stages of Pregnancy
What is the job of the placenta? .. 292
How is the umbilical cord
  formed? 293
Where does the fluid in the
  amniotic sac come from? 293
Is spontaneous abortion common
  after the first trimester? 293

Protecting the Unborn
How important is good nutrition? 294
Does a mother's intake of alcohol
  affect her baby? 294
Is it safe to take drugs during
  pregnancy? 294
How long should a woman
  continue with her job
  during pregnancy? 294
Could intercourse hurt the
  growing baby? 295

How much of a woman's weight
  gain is the baby itself? 295
How does a woman's body
  change during pregnancy? 295
Does having a baby spoil a
  woman's figure? 295

How the Baby Grows
What does the unborn baby look
  like one month after
  conception? 296
How does the baby spend
  its day? 296
Does the foetus sleep? 296
How is development
  completed? 297
How soon does the baby
  grow hair? 297
When can a foetus live on
  its own? 297

The Mother-Child Relationship
When does the mother first feel
  her baby's movements? 298
Why do babies kick the most
  when the mother
  lies down? 298
Can babies see and hear inside
  the womb? 298
When does excretion
  first occur? 298
Do babies learn before birth? 298
Can a mother find out about
  her baby's temperament
  before birth? 299
What are the odds that a
  pregnant woman will
  bear a boy? 299
When is the sex of the baby
  apparent? 299
How does the baby change in
  the last three months? 299

The Phenomenon of Twins
Why are twins often born
  early? 300
How do twins come about? 300
What are Siamese twins? 300
Why do fertility drugs cause
  multiple births? 300
The Marvel of Multiple Births..... 301

**The Different Ways of
Giving Birth**
When should a woman choose a
  birthing method? 302
What is the difference between a
  midwife and a doctor? 302
Can a woman choose to have her
  baby delivered at home? 302

Swaddling, page 311

Does natural childbirth ensure
  painless delivery? 302
What can go wrong in the
  last months? 303
Why are so many babies
  delivered by Caesarean section
  these days? 303
Can a mother give birth
  normally after she's had
  a Caesarean? 303

Potential Problems of Pregnancy
What does "spotting" mean during
  pregnancy? 304
What causes miscarriage? 304
Is amniocentesis safe? 304
Can you find out your baby's sex
  before it is born? 305
Does the umbilical cord
  ever tangle? 305
What is "false" labour? 305

The Onset of Labour
What makes the uterus
  contract? 306
What are the signs that labour is
  beginning? 306
How long does labour last? 306
Is there a natural way to
  shorten labour? 306
Is there a danger of "dry labour"
  if the sac of water
  breaks early? 307

The Miracle of Birth
Is labour always painful? 308
Why are most babies born
  headfirst? 308
Why is a breech birth more
  difficult than a normal one? ... 309
Can forceps injure the baby? 309

After the Baby Is Born
Is it easy for the newborn baby
  to breathe? 310

Does a newborn cry because
  the experience of birth
  is painful? 310
Does the baby feel anything
  when its umbilical
  cord is cut? 310
How much blood does the
  mother lose during
  childbirth? 311

The Best Food for the Infant
When can a baby first suckle? ... 312
Can a small-breasted woman
  make enough milk for
  her baby? 312
How much milk is enough? 312
Why do most newborns lose
  weight? 312
How does breast milk differ
  from cow's milk? 312
Are nutritional advantages the
  only reason for
  breast feeding? 312
Are there many women who can't
  breast feed their babies? 313
Should breast feeding be
  supplemented with bottles? ... 313
How long do babies usually
  sleep? 313

A Growing Awareness
Are there tests to tell if the
  baby is normal? 314
What can parents do to prevent
  cot death? 314
Is all crying alike? 314
Are babies genetically
  programmed to smile? 315
What makes babies smile? 315

Milestones of Development
What do babies know, and when
  do they know it? 316
What determines growth? 316
How does a child grow? 316
When do most babies learn
  to walk? 316
Is it a bad sign if your baby
  walks later than the
  average child? 317

Index 318

**Credits and
Acknowledgments**.......... 334

Chapter 1

THE HUMAN BODY

Our oldest, closest personal possession is the body in which we live. Yet who has not been amazed to discover how it works, how it develops and reproduces itself?

How the Body Is Organized	22
Feeling Well or Ill	24
Our Basic Building Blocks	26
Discovering the Invisible World	28
The Body Under Attack	30
The Enemy Within	32
The Geography of Disease	34
Of Doctors and Dosages	36
War: The Crucible of Medical Practice	37
The Rules of Heredity	38
Symptoms and Syndromes	40
Orchestrating Our Development	42
High-Tech Science	44

Is laughter good for your health?

As soon as you give way to laughter, electrical impulses are triggered by nerves in your brain, which set off chemical reactions there and in other parts of the body. Your endocrine (glandular) system orders your brain to secrete its natural tranquilizers and painkillers, which ease anxiety and relieve pain. Other substances released in the wake of laughter aid digestion, while others make the arteries contract and relax, improving blood flow and possibly alleviating high blood pressure. To say laughter is the *best* remedy for what ails you is going too far, but if you call it *good* medicine instead, few doctors will disagree with you.

What keeps you healthy?

Inside the body, everything stays about the same. Your temperature stands at 37° C (98.6° F) or so either in the Antarctic or in the Tropics. The concentration of sugar in your blood normally does not vary widely, whether you're on a diet or given to gorging on ice cream. This constancy of the internal environment, maintained in the face of external change, is called homoeostasis. The term comes from the Greek words meaning "staying the same." Without homoeostasis, human beings would be buffeted by change, and faced with the confining—and impossible—task of trying to find a constant environment.

What makes homoeostasis possible? It is the operation of regulatory mechanisms that monitor conditions inside the body. When the internal balance is challenged, the body reacts. Responses that range from shivering to sweating help to restore normal conditions and keep the body in equilibrium with the outer world.

Why do some people have more energy than others?

There are people whose supply of energy seems inexhaustible, who regularly accomplish more in a day than

Beyond the polite laughter of social occasions, there's the real laugh: the irresistible, contagious, overwhelming laughter that strains your muscles, brings tears to your eyes, and leaves you gasping for breath. As a workout for the whole body and a distraction from care, hearty laughter is unbeatable.

most of us achieve in a month. Often, such people seem to stay younger longer than others. In most cases, it is difficult to pinpoint the reason for their tirelessness. Their exceptional energy may be inherited. Or perhaps they are simply bursting with good health and a zest for life.

It may be more useful to ask why some people are always tired. Persistent lethargy can have a physical cause, ranging from mild thyroid deficiency to arthritis, diabetes, or cancer. Sometimes fatigue is caused by a hidden depression, and can be alleviated by therapy. Fatigue can also be a side effect of certain medications. For the commonplace kind of fatigue, vitamin pills and tranquilizers are rarely good medicine. Often, it is something that can easily be remedied, such as poor eating habits. Other drains on energy include dwelling on worries, boredom, and, oddly enough, too little activity. Yes, too little, not too much activity.

Which is more important, heredity or environment?

The debate over the relative importance of nature and nurture, of heredity and environment, is centuries old. If undesirable traits are determined by heredity, there is not much anyone can do to improve human health or performance. Nowadays, most scientists avoid the debate. They say instead that heredity determines potential capacities, and it sets limits. A child who is born retarded cannot grow up to be a Nobel prizewinner.

But scientists emphasize that *both* heredity and environment are important, that how a person turns out depends on a complex interaction between the two. An analogy may make the point clearer. It takes moisture and cold to make snow; you cannot say that the moisture has twice as much influence as the cold in producing the snow—or half—both elements are essential.

Are you programmed to die at a certain age?

A few years ago, newspapers ran stories about remote places in the world where people lived to be 150. On investigation, these reports did not hold up. Although survival to 115 has been documented, few live beyond 90. This suggests that human beings may be programmed to age and die at some point and that the genes (structures in cells that govern inheritance) may carry instructions to stop working after a time. Scientists have found that in the laboratory cells stop reproducing after they have replicated themselves a certain number of times, and that the quality of the cells gradually deteriorates.

But, you may ask, hasn't modern science managed to lengthen human life and thus shown that environment, not heredity, determines how long you live? Not really. In truth, the usual upper limit of about 90 has remained constant throughout history. Medical advances have increased *average life expectancy*, but they have not increased the *maximum life span*. That is, babies born today have a better chance than babies born years ago of living beyond infancy and of surviving accidents and infections, but they are no more likely than they ever were to live past the age of 90.

If the genes control aging, why bother about good health habits?

A person can have the hereditary potential to live to old age, but accident, illness, or some other environmental factor can prevent realization of this potential. You may shorten your life if you smoke, fail to control high blood pressure, and eat in such a way as to increase the amount of cholesterol in your blood. You may enhance your chances of a longer life if you keep your weight down, get enough exercise, and establish other good health habits. Very likely you *can* exert a measure of control over the actual length of your life. As one expert wrote, to some extent, you "can choose not to age rapidly."

21

How the Body Is Organized

What is the human body made of?

In a way, the body seems almost unimpressive. The 20-odd commonplace elements that compose it are all present in the earth's dry dust, and every one of them is found today in scores of ordinary objects. But in the body, they are combined in so many different ways that a human being is actually made up of thousands upon thousands of complex chemical compounds. The main substance, accounting for 70 to 85 percent of the body, is nothing more unusual than water. But many of the other compounds in the body do not exist at all in the non-living world.

After water, the most abundant substances in the body are proteins, making up 10 to 20 percent of the whole. Then come inorganic salts (combinations of metals with nonmetals), lipids (mainly fats), carbohydrates (sugar), and the wondrous nucleic acids. There are two nucleic acids: DNA, which contains the master plans for building the body; and RNA, which enables the body to follow those plans.

Most remarkable of all is the fact that the body is not just a static jumble of chemicals but a dynamic, highly organized, marvellously integrated, *living* organism. It constructs itself. It grows, acts and reacts, regulates its own activities, and keeps its parts in fairly good repair. And besides all that, it reproduces and so ensures the continuity of human life.

What are the most basic units of the body?

In the human body, there are four organizational levels. The smallest living units are the cells, some 75 to 100 million million of them falling into more than 100 different types. Similar cells, along with the non-living material, called matrix, in which they are embedded, are grouped to form tissues, each kind designed to carry out a specific function. Related tissues are joined together into organs adapted to perform particular tasks. Last come the body's systems, groups of organs responsible for a series of interrelated functions. The body as a whole has been described as a community of cells, a social order in which each of 75 million million individuals has some assigned place to occupy, or role to play.

What do tissues do?

Single cells do not function in isolation but in groups that form tissues. The human body contains four primary kinds of tissues: connective, epithelial, muscle, and nerve. These specialized structural materials perform so many different functions that only advanced textbooks list them all.

Connective tissue is the most abundant of the four. As its name suggests, it generally binds and supports other tissues. But certain varieties of it store fat, eat bacteria, produce blood cells, and produce antibodies against disease. You may be surprised to learn that both blood and bones are sometimes classified as connective tissues, though they are occasionally considered organs.

Sheets of epithelial tissue line body cavities and cover and protect the surface of the body. In the small intestine, epithelial tissue absorbs nutrients from food. In the glands, it secretes digestive enzymes, hormones, mucus, perspiration, and saliva.

The special function of muscle tissue is to contract, and thus move body parts. The skeletal muscles are under voluntary control: you consciously decide to play the piano or run around the block. Visceral muscles in the stomach and cardiac muscles in the heart work automatically: you cannot command them to move food or to make the heart pump.

By conducting electrochemical impulses, nerve tissue receives signals from the outside world and from inside the body and sends messages to and from all body parts. Many of the cells in nerve tissue look very different from other cells; they can be as much as 2 metres (6.5 feet) long.

How do organs relate to body systems?

The word *organ* brings to mind such structures as the heart, liver, or stomach. But an eye, an arm, or a leg is an organ, too, and so, some say, is every separate bone in your body. In general, an organ can be defined as a collection of related tissues that performs some definite function.

The lungs are wonderfully adapted for extracting oxygen from the air, but it is only in combination with the nasal passages, pharynx, larynx, tra-

Original photograph   Retouched, two right sides   Retouched, two left sides

The two sides of the body are symmetrical, but not perfectly so, as these pictures illustrate. To see how symmetrical your own face is, find a front-facing photo; then hold a pocket mirror at right angles to the picture. Adjust to find a normal proportion of nose and chin; then try the other side.

The Interplay of Ten Systems

In most instances, the organs that make up a system are related in some obvious way; you can guess which ones go together. But there are a few surprises. For example: occasionally, the same organ belongs to more than one system. The ovaries and testes clearly belong to the reproductive system, but since one of their functions is to produce hormones, they are also components of the endocrine system. Body systems do not operate independently; they exert important effects on each other. For example, when you exercise hard, your muscular system needs extra oxygen, so your respiratory system works harder than usual in order to supply it.

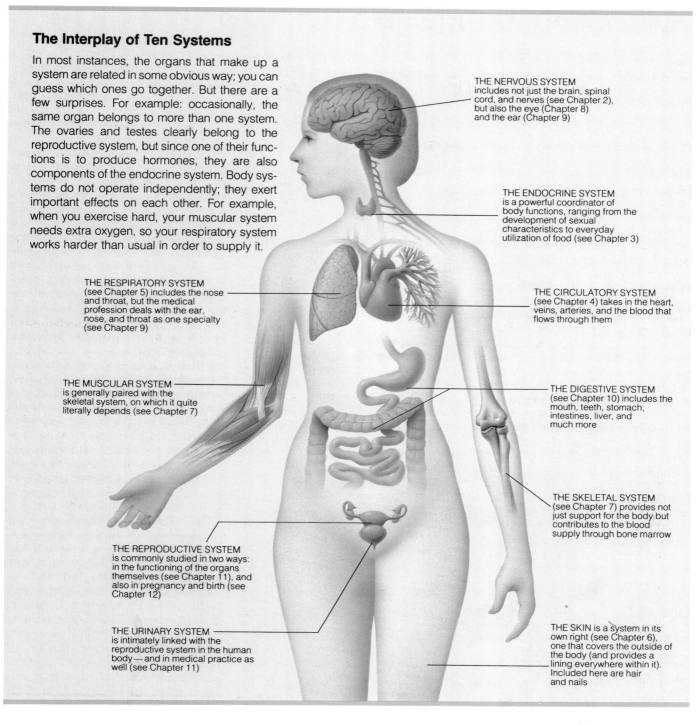

THE NERVOUS SYSTEM includes not just the brain, spinal cord, and nerves (see Chapter 2), but also the eye (Chapter 8) and the ear (Chapter 9)

THE ENDOCRINE SYSTEM is a powerful coordinator of body functions, ranging from the development of sexual characteristics to everyday utilization of food (see Chapter 3)

THE CIRCULATORY SYSTEM (see Chapter 4) takes in the heart, veins, arteries, and the blood that flows through them

THE RESPIRATORY SYSTEM (see Chapter 5) includes the nose and throat, but the medical profession deals with the ear, nose, and throat as one specialty (see Chapter 9)

THE DIGESTIVE SYSTEM (see Chapter 10) includes the mouth, teeth, stomach, intestines, liver, and much more

THE MUSCULAR SYSTEM is generally paired with the skeletal system, on which it quite literally depends (see Chapter 7)

THE SKELETAL SYSTEM (see Chapter 7) provides not just support for the body but contributes to the blood supply through bone marrow

THE REPRODUCTIVE SYSTEM is commonly studied in two ways: in the functioning of the organs themselves (see Chapter 11), and also in pregnancy and birth (see Chapter 12)

THE URINARY SYSTEM is intimately linked with the reproductive system in the human body—and in medical practice as well (see Chapter 11)

THE SKIN is a system in its own right (see Chapter 6), one that covers the outside of the body (and provides a lining everywhere within it). Included here are hair and nails

chea, and bronchi that they can function. The lungs and the air-transporting structures together make up the respiratory system. Similarly, each of the nine other systems in the body is made up of several organs. Each organ is designed to perform part of some specialized task needed to keep the human body as a whole functioning well. The organs in a system work as a team to accomplish that task.

Just as the organs in a single system need each other, so the body's ten organ systems are also interdependent. Your respiratory system needs the circulatory system to distribute oxygen-laden blood and to deliver "used" blood filled with carbon dioxide for disposal by the lungs. Even with a respiratory system in good condition, you cannot live unless your circulatory system—and all your other organ groups—also work reasonably well. Moreover, when something happens in one of your systems, that event usually has repercussions elsewhere. If your nervous system brings you bad news while you're eating, your digestive system is unlikely to function as well as usual.

Feeling Well or Ill

What does being healthy really mean?

Sometimes even a simple word can be defined in several different ways, as you will see if you look up *health* in the dictionary. If you wanted to decide on a meaning that seemed right to you, you could begin by tracing the word to its Anglo-Saxon root, which means the state of being "whole."

You could also consider the definition by the World Health Organization: "Health is a state of complete physical, mental, and social well-being and not merely the absence of disease or infirmity." Another approach is to define health in terms of measurable values, to say that you are healthy if your temperature, blood pressure, and the like are all normal. The problem with that is biological variability: what is normal for someone else may be abnormal for you.

To many medical theorists, the best definition is relative. To them, health means one thing for a librarian who works quietly all day, while it means something else for a construction worker. In other words, to be healthy, you don't have to measure up to any absolute standards. You just have to be able to meet the demands of your particular life style.

What happens when your body's control mechanisms break down?

Sometimes the symptoms of illness are so dramatic—high fever, vomiting, loss of consciousness—there's no doubt your body is reacting violently to some kind of internal emergency. At other times, illness is less obvious. Your doctor may order lab tests to see if there is a departure from the normal range. An example: an abnormally high level of sugar in your urine sometimes means that your body has lost the ability to regulate blood sugar, thus indicating that you may have diabetes. Generally, homeostatic, or regulatory, processes are apt to break down when you're sick.

Some control mechanisms work poorly in newborns, who have just emerged from an environment so protected that self-regulation was largely unnecessary. The mechanisms soon develop, but meanwhile, a change of just a few degrees in room temperature may alter the baby's body temperature significantly. Cold is dangerous for the elderly, too; age brings a falling off in the efficiency of all self-regulatory mechanisms.

What is hypochondria?

Early in their training, young doctors-to-be occasionally become temporarily afflicted with hypochondria, an exaggerated concern about one's health in a person who is in fact healthy. Hypochondria is an ancient medical term for feeling downcast and apprehensive. Learning for the first time about some terrible disease, medical students may fear that they themselves may be ill, and they may imagine that they detect symptoms of the disease in themselves.

But a really serious case of hypochondria (now defined as a morbid preoccupation with bodily processes and disease, with many physical complaints) is a neurotic reaction that reflects some underlying anxiety or emotional difficulty. When preoccupation with health begins to exclude other interests, it may be wise to consider professional counselling.

Thermography: A Diagnostic Tool

The human body always gives off heat. During World War II, that fact was the basis for the snooperscope, a device used after dark to detect unseen enemies. After the war, an offshoot of the snooperscope began to be used in thermography, a technique for converting heat emanations into "heat maps" and using them to diagnose certain ailments. Paired parts of the body, such as shoulders and arms or hips and legs, usually emit the same amount of heat. If maps of comparable areas are dissimilar, something may be amiss.

On thermal maps, made by a heat-sensitive camera, the warmest areas on a hand and on a child's body appear light green. The coolest ones are dark green.

But try to distinguish between normal concern and excessive anxiety. It is natural, and useful, to notice symptoms in yourself and to consult a doctor about them. Unless you're a hypochondriac, a medical examination that discloses no disease reassures you; you are relieved to know that nothing is wrong. But hypochondriacs usually cannot accept reassurance. They believe that the doctor must have overlooked some grave illness, or that he is deceiving them to spare them the shattering truth. Occasionally, hypochondriacs do believe the doctor for a short time. But then the conviction that they are ill reappears, centring sometimes on the originally feared illness and sometimes on a new one.

Are psychosomatic disorders real, or only imaginary?

The Greek words *psyche* and *soma* mean, respectively, "mind" and "body," and a psychosomatic disorder is one in which the mind influences the body. More specifically, it is a *real* physical ailment caused partly or entirely by unconscious emotional conflicts or other psychological factors. Doctors do not yet fully understand how emotions can impair the functioning of body organs, but it is certain that they can do so. Unlike a hypochondriac, whose illness is imaginary, a person with a psychosomatic illness is physically sick. Often, a psychosomatic ailment can be cured by treating the psychological problem that lies at the root of it.

Such disorders as ulcers, headaches, and heart palpitations are often (but not invariably) psychosomatic. That list is far from all-inclusive; many doctors today believe that most physical illnesses, including perhaps even cancer, are influenced to some degree by psychological factors.

Psychosomatic medicine, dealing with the relationship of mind and body, is a new field, but the idea is not new. It has long been recognized that a person's health can be seriously undermined by deep sorrow or prolonged stress.

Münchhausen's syndrome is a disorder in which illness is faked. Baron Münchhausen (left), a colourful German character, told tall tales, one of which is illustrated (above).

What is Münchhausen's syndrome?

If you are like most human beings, you fear going to the hospital, and you would much rather be well than sick. But there are people who want nothing so much as to be ordered into a hospital, and they go to elaborate lengths to make doctors think they are very ill. These people will feign severe illness of a dramatic and emergency nature and may mutilate themselves and interfere with diagnostic procedures. They may have been hospitalized many times, seen innumerable doctors, and even been operated upon. Their motives are not understood. They may take insulin to lower their blood sugar, spit up blood from a rubber container held in the mouth, or inject themselves with faeces to produce an abscess. Psychiatrists call this behaviour pattern Münchhausen's syndrome, or factitious illness.

Factitious means sham, and people with Münchhausen's syndrome are fakers and liars. They also induce illness in themselves. They are not to be confused with hypochondriacs,

who genuinely believe they are sick. Nor are they malingerers, who also fake illness, but with a clear purpose: to escape some obligation. The striking thing in Münchhausen's syndrome is the lack of any clear motive. It has been theorized that Münchhausenites are not so much masochists in search of suffering as unhappy human beings engaged in a desperate quest for sympathy. But it has also been suggested that the patients' motives are hostile, that they take advantage of doctors to revenge themselves, indirectly, on people who disappointed them early in life. Münchhausenites are often people who have had lifelong difficulties in establishing close ties to others, and many of them have experienced deprivation and brutality.

Don R. Lipsitt, a psychiatrist with a particular interest in this disorder, has estimated that in the United States alone, as many as 4,000 people a year, most of them men in their 20s and 30s, "devote their energies to fooling medical practitioners." One patient, he says, got himself admitted to hospitals 400 times in 25 years.

Our Basic Building Blocks

What are the smallest living units in the body?

Although subatomic particles are the tiniest units in the human body, they lack four capacities that distinguish the living from the non-living. Scientists define living units as able to do these things: react to stimuli, transform nutrients into energy, grow, and reproduce. Thus cells are the smallest living body components.

Except for the human egg, which can be seen with the naked eye as about the size of a dot, cells are microscopic. Most cells are measured in micrometres. Although a nerve cell may be a metre (3 feet) long, and a muscle cell may measure 25 millimetres (1 inch), single cells are so fine as to be invisible.

Some cells look like columns, some like cubes, some like spheres. Red blood cells resemble saucers; nerve cells look like threads; cheek cells suggest flat paving stones.

Cells also vary in life span. Cells in the lining of the intestine die after a day and a half, white blood cells after 13 days, red blood cells after 120 days. Meanwhile, nerve cells can live for 100 years.

Although all cells have the capacity to produce, store, and utilize energy, different cells perform additional, highly specialized functions. Heart cells obviously play a different role than do liver cells. In other words, there is a division of labour in the body; the technical term for this capacity of the cells to become more specialized is cell differentiation.

What are the main parts of a cell?

Whatever their special function, most cells have about the same components. Each has a membrane that encloses the cell, a nucleus that serves as the control centre, and a mass of cytoplasm where most of the cell's work is done.

The membrane, thinner than a cobweb and semi-permeable, is more than an envelope. In a way, it is like a guard posted at a factory gate. The membrane has special physical and chemical properties that allow it to recognize and interact with other cells and to "decide" what may leave or enter the cell. Somehow, the membrane signals "stop" at the approach of unwanted materials. Normal cells obey the signal; cancer cells also obey, but to a lesser degree and in a more uncontrolled manner. It may be that defects in the cell membrane have something to do with the spread of cancer, a possibility that researchers are investigating.

At the heart of the cell is the nucleus, which directs the chemical reactions that go on in the cell and is something like the chief engineer in a factory. The nucleus of every cell contains a complete set of the body's genes. If the cell nucleus is removed in the laboratory, the cell loses its ability to reproduce, and though in other respects it may function normally for a while, it eventually dies.

The living matter outside the nucleus, called the cytoplasm, is a watery gel crowded with specialized structures, or organelles, that resemble the departments in a factory. They manufacture, modify, store, and transport proteins, and also dispose of cellular wastes.

How long do cells live?

Many cells, including those that compose the skin and the blood, have a short life span and divide to replenish themselves about every 10 to 30 hours. Certain muscle cells reproduce themselves only once every few years. Others reproduce only under special circumstances. For example,

Early Theories: THE INFLUENCE OF STARS AND "HUMOURS"

In seeking answers to the mysteries of the human body and its many functions and malfunctions, the sages of medieval times had to fall back on ancient lore. One source of knowledge was astrology, the belief that the heavenly bodies influenced the lives of individuals. Here, on a page from a 14th-century manuscript prepared for a French prince, the Duc de Berry, the 12 signs of the zodiac are assigned to

various parts of the body. In those days, astrology ranked as a science, a facet of astronomy. Wisdom of the times also stressed the theory that man's health and temperament were affected by fluids called "humours." As described by the Greek physician, Hippocrates, these were blood, phlegm, black bile, and yellow bile. If the humours were in balance, a person felt well; if they were out of balance, then pain and disease would result.

This painting is from a world famous manuscript, *Les Très Riches Heures*, a "book of hours," created in the Middle Ages.

The Cell: A Walled City

Your body is made up of millions of millions of cells, the basic units of life. Each one reacts to stimuli, transforms nutrients into energy, grows, and reproduces. Inside every cell, specialized substructures called organelles carry on a ceaseless round of chemical activities, making the cell comparable to a city that never sleeps. At the wall-like membrane enclosing the cell, protein molecules are stationed like sentries to permit the import of some chemicals and the export of others. At the heart of the cell, the powerful nucleus, which contains the genes, governs the whole vibrant cell-city.

CELL MEMBRANE protects the cell, acts as a filter

CYTOPLASM is a watery gel in which cell structures are suspended

THE NUCLEUS is the central government of the cell

NUCLEOLUS is prominent in cells that export proteins

CHROMOSOMES carry the cell's hereditary information

GOLGI COMPLEX is where proteins made within the cell are packaged for export

RIBOSOMES. Proteins are assembled on ribosomes for use inside the cell

SMOOTH ENDOPLASMIC RETICULUM (ER) is a network of channels for moving substances within the cell

MICROVILLI are fingerlike projections on the surface of the cell that increase surface area, hence the cell's ability to absorb

LYSOSOMES are bags of digestive juices that break down nutrients and unwanted parts of the cell

MITOCHONDRIA are powerhouses that produce energy to keep the cell going

ROUGH ENDOPLASMIC RETICULUM is where proteins are assembled for export

LIPID (fat) droplets within cell

---

if seven eighths of the liver is surgically removed, the process of cell division, or mitosis, begins in the remaining cells and continues until the organ has regained its full size. The most specialized cells in the body are not capable of mitosis. Among these are certain cells of the nervous system, including the brain. If, after a certain age, injury or disease damages nerve cells, they cannot reproduce themselves and are gone for ever.

Where does the cell get its energy?

As electricity powers a factory, so a chemical compound called ATP (for adenosine triphosphate) runs a large proportion of your body and every cell in it. Without ATP, you couldn't move or even think; all the body processes that keep you alive would cease.

Each of the cells produces ATP from the food you eat. The actual work of generation goes on mainly in the tiny structures of the cytoplasm called mitochondria, the cell's power plants.

The cells store very little ATP; at any moment, your whole body contains no more than 90 millilitres (3 fluid ounces) of this energy-rich substance. The cells make ATP as it is needed. If you're a very active person, your cells may produce your weight of ATP every day. Suppose ATP could be drained from your body and crystallized: from 3,500 Calories of food, your cells could make a mound of white powder measuring 0.1 cubic metres (3 cubic feet). Now suppose the chemical energy in the powder could be converted into electrical energy: there would be enough of it to power 1,500 100-watt light bulbs for a full minute.

What is the internal environment of the body?

The external environment is a familiar concept. But since the mid-19th century, physiologists have also been speaking of an internal environment, an idea that is much less understood. Thousands of living crea-

tures have no internal environment; most live in the sea. Land animals and human beings, by contrast, do have an internal environment—and curiously, it is much like seawater.

Your internal environment consists of extracellular fluid, or ECF, so named because it exists outside the cells. One third of the fluid in your body is ECF. (The other two thirds is inside the cells and is called intracellular fluid, or ICF.) There are several kinds of ECF, including blood plasma (the liquid part of the blood, as distinct from the solids suspended in it), eye fluids, and cerebrospinal and digestive fluids.

Extracellular fluid is constantly in motion everywhere in the body. All your cells are bathed in it, and physiologists are accustomed to saying that the cells live in it, in somewhat the same way that sea creatures live in the ocean. Your cells can function and grow in this internal environment, provided it contains the right amounts of amino acids, fats, glucose, electrolytes or salts, and oxygen.

Discovering the Invisible World

The Modest Beginnings of the Science of Microscopy

One day in 1674, in the Dutch city of Delft, Anton van Leeuwenhoek took material from between his teeth and looked at it through a microscope he had made. "I then saw, with great wonder . . . many very little living animalcules, very prettily a-moving." Of course, they were bacteria, and Leeuwenhoek was the first person ever to see them, though he did not realize that some of them can cause disease. When he reported his sensational findings to the Royal Society in England, an important organization of scientists, some members refused to believe him at first. But eventually, the society elected him to membership. His later studies made him world famous and brought him such visitors as the queen of England and the tsar of Russia.

Microscope made by van Leeuwenhoek and the bacteria he sketched

Once a shopkeeper, later a civil servant, Anton van Leeuwenhoek ground lenses as a hobby and used them to study the nature of tiny objects.

Today's scanning electron microscope, combined with a flash X-ray source of high intensity, produces an amazing image of an intact (living) blood platelet.

What causes disease?

The ancients had a ready answer for that question. Disease, they were sure, was the work of demons, sorcerers, or other evildoers. Hippocrates, the Greek physician who lived from 460 to 370 B.C., was the first to argue that the causes of illness are not supernatural but earthly. He introduced the idea of fluid "humours."

For hundreds of years, there was little dissent from Hippocrates' idea, not even when microbes were first discovered by Anton van Leeuwenhoek in the 17th century. In fact, another 200 years passed before the work of Louis Pasteur, and others, led to the germ theory of infectious disease. Now every schoolchild knows that infectious diseases are caused by micro-organisms of some sort: bacteria, viruses, or other tiny living beings that invade the human body.

What are germs?

If bacteria cause infection or disease, they are commonly called germs. Bacteria are one-celled living organisms, generally only a few thousandths of a millimetre across, that take several shapes: rodlike (bacillus), spherical (coccus), and spiral (spirochete). They are everywhere—in the water and soil and inside other living organisms, including human beings; they can even flourish in airless environments. Bacteria are not necessarily harmful. Some types are necessary for the growth and production of food by plants.

Disease-bearing bacteria produce poisons called toxins, against some of which science has developed antitoxins. The discovery that certain bacteria destroy others led to the development of antibiotics. Among the diseases caused by bacteria are cholera, pneumonia, tuberculosis, some venereal diseases, and staphylococcus and streptococcus infections.

You can pick up bacterial diseases from infected human beings or insects, from contaminated objects, or from tainted food or water. A cut or an abrasion that is not cleansed can give entry to bacteria. One of the most feared bacterial diseases is botulism, which comes from improperly preserved food. As soon as you open a can of tainted food, the botulism bacteria die; air kills them. But the deadly exotoxin they released into the food while they were growing in the airless environment of the can remains potent—so potent that a fraction of a gram of it can kill millions of people.

Are viruses the same as germs?

Viruses are more primitive and much smaller than bacteria; they occupy the border area between living and non-living things. They show no lifelike activity unless they are introduced into a living cell. Unlike bacteria, viruses are very difficult to grow in the laboratory on simple nutrient substances.

Once inside a cell, a virus can control the processes that occur within the cell, including the process of reproducing itself. By changing the cell's chemistry, viruses cause the cell to produce toxins. Viruses (and bacteria) also act as antigens—that is, they stimulate the cell to form antibodies to fight viral disease.

Specific viruses are responsible for a host of diseases; among them, the common cold, influenza, AIDS, shingles, mumps, measles, chicken pox, smallpox, rabies, and poliomyelitis. Antibiotics cannot kill viruses of any kind. However, many viral diseases— for example, smallpox, rubella (German measles), and polio—can be prevented by vaccination.

Certain viruses have been proved to cause cancer in laboratory animals. There is suggestive evidence that certain types of cancer, such as leukaemia, may be caused by viruses. This does not mean, however, that cancer is contagious.

Can adults get "childhood diseases"?

Infection is no respecter of age. No matter how old you are, your years alone cannot protect you from chick-

MONSTER SOUP commonly called THAMES WATER, being a correct representation of that precious stuff dated out to us !!!

In the 1820s, sewage floated in the River Thames, yet London entrepreneurs sold the water for drinking. No one knew that polluted water causes disease, but many, like the woman in this satiric etching, recoiled intuitively from the "monsters"—bacteria—in water seen under a microscope.

enpox, measles, mumps, or whooping cough. Then why are they called childhood diseases? Because they used to attack mainly children. But that is no longer the case.

A generation or two ago, the childhood diseases were common; most children got them. When they did, their bodies developed antibodies against the illnesses, conferring lifelong immunity to further attacks. Nowadays, however, vaccination has made it more unusual for children to develop measles and whooping cough.

Most childhood diseases are more serious in older children and adults. While a small child with mumps may be only off-colour with swollen cheeks and a slight fever, a man with the same infection could develop inflammation of the testicles and become permanently infertile.

Chickenpox does not usually make a child very ill. However, the chickenpox or "zoster" virus can remain in the body for many years, only to re-emerge later in life as painful shingles. Instead of the rash affecting the whole body, as in chickenpox, shingles appears over an area of skin supplied by one nerve.

Has science wiped out any diseases?

Beginning at least as early as the Middle Ages, smallpox had a devastating effect on the people and nations of the world. Millions of smallpox victims died, millions were blinded, and millions more were disfigured for life. Vaccination, which was first widely practised in the 19th century, soon brought smallpox under control in most of the Western world. But in 1948, when the World Health Organization undertook a global drive to eradicate the disease, 10 million cases were reported in Africa, Southeast Asia, Indonesia, and Brazil.

The last case of naturally occurring smallpox in the world was reported in Somalia on October 26, 1977. Finally, on May 8, 1980, WHO decided that it was safe to announce: "The world and all its people have won freedom from smallpox . . . an unprecedented achievement in public health."

Scientists believe that the reason it has been possible to wipe out smallpox is that human beings were apparently the only reservoirs of the disease. Nevertheless, there is ongoing, worldwide surveillance by health authorities to be certain this ancient enemy has indeed been conquered.

The Body Under Attack

What are the main kinds of disease?

Human beings are subject to thousands of diseases. There are several ways of classifying these ailments. One is to divide them into categories according to their causes. Under that system, there are 11 principal types of disease: (1) bacterial disease, including such diverse ailments as rheumatic fever, typhoid, tuberculosis, cholera, and food poisoning; (2) viral disease, which includes polio, rubella, flu, and the common cold; (3) parasitic disease, including fungal infections, worms, and protozoa such as the amoebas that cause amoebic dysentery. These diseases are all caused by external agents.

Mainly a consequence of poverty is (4) nutritional disease, ranging from vitamin deficiency to kwashiorkor, a protein deficiency that causes a wasting of the body, catastrophically undermining the health of infants.

Diseases in which the attack comes from within include (5) neoplastic disorders, chiefly tumours and cancer; (6) autoimmune disease that results from a breakdown of the body's ability to recognize its own cells, as in the case of rheumatoid arthritis; (7) endocrine disease, in which the endocrine glands work imperfectly, failing to produce the right hormones in the necessary proportions, as in diabetes; (8) genetic disease, inherited at conception and including disorders such as Down's syndrome (a form of retardation) and sickle cell anaemia; (9) degenerative disease, such as loss of hearing and vision, a common consequence of aging.

Diseases caused by (10) chemical or physical injury include poisoning, burns, falls, and other accidents; (11) iatrogenic disease is caused by medical treatment. This is sometimes accidental; more often it is a trade-off: a powerful drug may cause temporary illness, but does so while curing or alleviating a more serious condition. A further cause of disease is abuse of drugs and alcohol.

Do parasites usually kill their victims?

A parasite is an organism that lives on or in another organism, depriving it of nourishment, or poisoning or devouring its tissues. Parasites range from microscopic protozoans that cause malaria to a tapeworm that may be several metres (yards) long.

Parasitic diseases are often spread by insect and animal vectors, or carriers. Malaria comes from the sting of an infected anopheles mosquito. In certain countries tapeworms can be acquired by eating undercooked pork or beef.

Some parasitic diseases are minor,

Agents of Human Disease and Distress

Modern medicine is no match for the microbe. A single bacterium can multiply to 250,000 bacteria in just a few hours. The body's own resistance to disease is the first line of defence, and good sanitation helps. When disease does strike, antibiotics can hasten recovery. But for the foreseeable future, we can all expect to play host to bacterial—and viral—diseases from time to time. However, there *are* diseases that can be brought under control to a far greater extent than at present. Among them are the nutritional disorders common in underdeveloped countries, and the obesity that is the blight of many industrial nations. Paradoxically, technological achievements have created a new class of health hazards—effective insecticides are sometimes dangerous to human beings. Industrial production brings with it a dismaying amount of debris. We have a responsibility to protect the environment, and ourselves, from pollution.

Staphylococcus bacteria are a very common cause of boils and a type of food poisoning.

In some countries bats and dogs may be infected with rabies virus, which can be transmitted by the bite of the infected animal. Unless treatment is prompt, the virus travels to the brain and causes feelings of terror and rage, then paralysis, and death. The British Isles are free of rabies.

Anthrax (left), a bacterial disease of cattle, can be transmitted to humans.

like the fungus infection athlete's foot; others are serious, even lethal. (Malaria is the greatest single killer in the world.) However, most parasites do not kill. If they did, they themselves would die off, and the disease would disappear. Instead, parasite and host usually live together in what has been described as a truce. When people are well nourished and healthy, their bodies can withstand the damage that parasites cause. Where nutrition and health are poor, parasitic diseases are dangerous.

Are infectious and contagious diseases the same thing?

Many people use the words *infectious* and *contagious* interchangeably, but it is not correct to do so. The more inclusive of the two terms is *infectious;* it applies to all diseases that can be transmitted, whether by infected animals or people or by contaminated food, water, or objects. *Contagious* is a narrow term referring only to diseases that spread directly from person to person. Both infectious and contagious diseases are caused by micro-organisms, or, to use the more popular word, *germs.* Diseases that are not caused by such living agents—multiple sclerosis, for one—cannot be transmitted.

Bubonic plague, the Black Death that killed one third of the European population in the 14th century, was predominantly an infectious but not, strictly, a contagious disease; people got it when they were bitten by fleas infected with plague bacteria from the rats on which they were parasites (though person-to-person transmission can also occur, as in pneumonic plague). Rabies is another infectious disease. A rabid person poses no danger to the people around him; you can get rabies only from the bite of an infected dog, bat, or other animal. By contrast, influenza is both infectious, because it spreads, and contagious, because the way it spreads is by airborne droplets containing the virus that are picked up by another person.

What is the difference between an acute and a chronic disease?

Acute indigestion and acute appendicitis are familiar terms. Acute ailments develop suddenly, with severe and sometimes disabling symptoms. The indigestion subsides; the victim of appendicitis is rushed off to the hospital for emergency surgery. *Chronos* is Greek for "time," and chronic diseases—arthritis, for instance, or atherosclerosis—persist for years. Certain other diseases, like malaria, are described as recurrent because symptom-free periods alternate with periods of illness.

Asbestos (shown magnified) was once valued as a fireproof insulating material. Now we know it can cause lung cancer.

Malnutrition, which is mainly due to lack of protein, afflicts 1,500 million people. It harms children most, retarding growth and increasing susceptibility to infection.

Fly ash, with its curious spheres-within-spheres, is spewed from smokestacks. This common air pollutant is a mere 0.1 millimetres (0.004 inches) across, small enough to be inhaled with every breath, in cities and industrial areas.

The Enemy Within

Are all tumours cancer?

Every tumour is a neoplasm, a new, abnormal growth of tissue that serves no physiological purpose in the body. There are two main kinds of neoplasms: benign and malignant, or cancerous. The main difference between them is that benign tumours grow slowly, forming sharply demarcated masses, that do not invade vital structures. Malignant tumours, which may grow slowly or quickly, spread both by the invasion of adjacent organs and by metastasis. This means that cancer cells break off from the original tumour, get into the bloodstream or lymphatic system, and are carried to distant parts of the body.

Cancer develops when something goes wrong with the controls that regulate cell growth, causing cells to begin multiplying in a poorly con-trolled fashion. The bad thing about cancer cells is not just rapid growth, but the fact that they do not stop multiplying. Cancer cells keep proliferating, increasing in number endlessly. And while normal cells "recognize" neighbouring cells and stop multiplying when they come in contact with them, cancer cells do not.

Malignant cells are abnormal in size, shape, and functioning. Very often they resemble embryonic cells. In fact, what happens as cancer develops is in some ways the opposite of what happens when an embryo, with its simple, all-purpose cells, grows into a human being, with specialized cells in different organs. Cancer cells, apparently, undergo a regressive process known as dedifferentiation: instead of remaining specialized, like the cells from which they formed, they get simpler.

What are the main types of cancer?

Specialists who study tumours are called oncologists, from the Greek word *onkos*, meaning "mass." They have discovered hundreds of kinds of malignant tumours; that is why they so often say that cancer is not just one disease but many. All cancers fall into one of three main types. Carcinomas are malignancies that arise in epithelial, or surface, tissues, in the glands, the lining of organs, and the skin. Sarcomas develop in such connective tissues as bone, cartilage, and muscle. Leukaemias are malignancies of the blood and lymphatic system.

What causes cancer?

The basic cause of malignant tumours is unknown. However, it is widely believed that cancer usually develops because of an inherited susceptibility, or predisposition, to the disease. Then, too, some precipitating factor, such as a virus and/or a prolonged exposure to tobacco smoke, may trigger the cancer.

Although some cancers, such as a rare malignancy of the eye (retinoblastoma) and breast cancer are more common in certain families, cancer itself is not inherited; the fact that any of your relatives had it does not mean that you are fated to get it. Nor does exposure to a known cancer-promoting agent doom you to cancer. A carcinogen probably promotes malignancy only if it causes certain chemical changes inside a human cell—and sometimes not even then.

So far, scientists have identified about two dozen chemicals that can cause cancer in human beings under some conditions. The list, which gets longer as research continues, includes substances found in industrial wastes, car exhausts, pesticides, building materials, and processed foods. Radiation—from the sun, from X-rays, and from atomic weapons—is also associated with cancer. So are viruses, which have been linked with certain types of leukaemia and cancer of the cervix of the

The Use and Abuse of Drugs

A number of drugs have a legitimate and at times a vital place in medicine. Morphine is irreplaceable as a painkiller. Marijuana is valuable in the treatment of glaucoma, an eye disease that can cause blindness, and it can also relieve the nausea and vomiting that accompany cancer chemotherapy. But when drug use becomes drug abuse, the consequences—physical or psychological dependence, illness, accidents, or even death—can be devastating. Of course, the non-medical use of psychoactive drugs (those that affect the mind) is by no means new. Such substances have always been used in the hope of easing tension or of experiencing euphoria. In ancient Greece, cake and sweets containing opium (from which heroin and morphine are derived) were freely sold on the streets. What is new in modern society is the frequent use of more than one drug at a time: of alcohol, for instance, along with tranquilizers, cocaine, barbiturates, or heroin. In one study, heavy marijuana smokers were found to be heavy drinkers, too. Unfortunately, it is not widely understood that drugs "potentiate" each other: when two of them are taken together, their effects become much more powerful. A person who drives after drinking alcohol and smoking marijuana, for example, is more dangerous to himself and to others than is someone who has simply been drinking.

Marijuana comes from the *Cannabis sativa* plant, which grows wild in most parts of the world. The plant contains potent drugs that have mind-altering properties when smoked.

womb. In some malignancies, especially those of the breast and prostate, hormones may be among the causal factors. Other cancers, including those of the mouth and lip, sometimes develop after a long period of irritation from ill-fitting dentures or hot pipe stems.

How is cancer treated?

The standard cancer treatments are surgery, radiation, and chemotherapy. One recent advance in surgery is the laser beam, which can be sharply focused to avoid damaging normal cells. Another new technique is cryosurgery, which uses extreme cold as a kind of knife. This bloodless surgery reduces the risk of spreading cancer through the bloodstream.

Cancer would be easier to treat and cure if cells could not detach themselves from the original tumour and spread to distant sites. Metastatic cancer—cancer that has spread— usually goes beyond the reach of the surgeon's knife.

One of the paradoxes of cancer is that radiation can not only induce it but also cure it. Technicians administer radiation both by machine and in needles or capsules of radioactive material implanted in the tumour.

Chemotherapy is the use of a combination of chemicals to destroy cancer cells. Among the newer drugs are anti-metabolites, which resemble cell nutrients but actually interfere with nutrition in the cells. New antibiotics have been developed that are so powerful that they are not used in treating infections; they actually interfere with the synthesis of DNA, and so prevent reproduction of the tumour cell. In the past, researchers relied largely on trial and error to find cancer drugs. Nowadays, computers are sometimes used to predict the effectiveness of many drugs in a short time. Exciting new developments are "monoclonal antibodies," and interferon—human defence chemicals created in the laboratory, then injected. This and other methods appear promising, but their effectiveness remains to be proved.

The Hôtel-Dieu, a Paris hospital, about 1500, shows two patients in one bed, a custom with lethal consequences. In foreground, nuns sew the dead into shrouds.

The Hospital in History

In 1793, the French Revolutionary Government ordered that every hospital patient be assigned a bed to himself. That decree says a lot about the difference between hospitals then and now. Though hospitals in India in the third century B.C. emphasized cleanliness, kindness to patients, and diet therapy, many other early hospitals were little more than almshouses. Most early Western institutions for the sick were founded by churches, and care was given by religious orders. For centuries, people who could afford care at home shunned hospitals because they were likely to be overcrowded and dirty, with high mortality rates. Not until the turn of the 20th century was the hospital widely regarded as a place where a sick person could hope to recover.

Surgical procedures in modern hospitals now include the reattachment of severed limbs. This is made possible by microsurgery (note microscope at eye level).

The Geography of Disease

Millions of people in 70 tropical countries are afflicted with snail fever, or schistosomiasis. The disease is caused by the worms shown here (the threadlike one is female, the broader one, male) and spread by infected snails in contaminated water. Fibrous tissue develops around worm eggs laid in the human body and prevents organs from functioning normally.

What do world explorers and traders have in common?

The human body tends to become resistant to familiar germs; unfamiliar ones are much more dangerous. Thus living in geographic isolation, without meeting any new people or encountering any new germs, has always had something to recommend it. So it is that early explorers and traders both contributed to the spread of diseases from one part of the globe to another.

In the 14th century, traders from Genoa, Italy, visited the Orient and returned to Europe with furs, silks—and the bubonic plague. Then, in the 18th century, Captain James Cook, the British explorer, reached Hawaii bearing microbes that the hitherto healthy islanders had never before encountered. The result was the death of thousands of Hawaiians from such diseases as measles, influenza, and tuberculosis. In 1778, the year of Cook's first visit, Hawaii had a population of approximately 300,000. Little more than 80 years later, that number had dropped to fewer than 37,000. Something comparable, although on a lesser scale, happened at the beginning of the 20th century, when white explorers disturbed the isolation of the Inuits, or Eskimos, and brought with them the germs of measles, tuberculosis, and other illnesses. In one particular Inuit community of 99 villagers, 98 died of measles.

Why are tropical diseases difficult to eradicate?

The developing nations, including Africa, Southeast Asia, and much of India, southern China, and the Middle East, lie mainly in the Tropics, the hot regions on either side of the equator. Flies, worms, and other pests that cause or transmit disease thrive in these areas, spreading parasitic disease. Poor sanitation and nutrition also contribute to the prevalence of disease. Of the 1,500 million people who live in the Tropics, 1,000 million suffer from one or more tropical diseases. These diseases are hard to get rid of, and just as hard for people to avoid in the course of daily life. Drugs to treat parasite-borne diseases tend to be expensive, or to have dangerous side effects. Moreover, much of the threatened population is poor, ill-nourished, and particularly vulnerable to diseases of all kinds.

What are snail fever and sleeping sickness?

One of the worst parasitic diseases is snail fever, or schistosomiasis (also called bilharziasis), which has apparently afflicted mankind for 40 centuries. Now the most common ailment in the world after malaria, snail fever goes through a complicated cycle. Larvae of the worms that cause it enter the human body when people drink contaminated water or when they bathe, swim, or work in it. In the bloodstream, the larvae mature into worms, multiply, and deposit from 300 to 3,000 eggs a day. Some of the eggs get trapped in the tissues, causing painful and sometimes fatal damage to one or more organs. Other eggs are expelled with the faeces and urine and eventually make their way to irrigation ditches, ponds, rice paddies, and rivers. Initially, the eggs hatch into larvae that infect snails, where they live for a while and continue to develop. Not until the larvae emerge from the snails can they live in human beings. The particular tragedy of snail fever is that progress—the development of a new and much-needed irrigation system, for example—may bring more disease. A parasitologist has said that, "the burden of the disease may cancel out the overall benefits of any agricultural advance a new water project brings."

Another disabling parasitic disease is sleeping sickness, spread by infected tsetse flies. When the flies bite, parasites enter the bloodstream and breed there, destroying blood cells, causing anaemia, and occasionally inflammation of the heart. It then moves into the nervous system. Damage to the brain and spinal cord leads to lethargy and, in some cases, death.

Why do you so often get diarrhoea when you travel?

Traveller's diarrhoea has nothing to do with fatigue or jet lag, or even with eating unfamiliar foods, assuming they are properly prepared. The main cause is usually the common bacterium *Escherichia coli*. That infectious micro-organism is normally found in everyone's intestinal tract, and it usually causes no trouble, because the body becomes accustomed to it. But *E. coli* exists in several forms, and if you encounter an unfamiliar variant, as you may in a strange country, it may, or may not, make you sick.

Prevention can be as simple as watching your diet and using bottled water. The best general advice is the old adage: if you can't peel it, boil it, or cook it, forget it.

Most cases of diarrhoea cure themselves in a few days. If you do feel seriously ill, or the symptoms persist, you should seek medical help. In any case, you must guard against dehydration—using bottled fluids.

Do you need a lot of injections before you travel abroad?

Preparations for travel depend on where you're going—consult your doctor or travel agent. Meanwhile, here are a few points that may be of use. *Cholera:* If you're going to an undeveloped country where vaccination is advised but not required, get the vaccination. *Malaria:* You run a definite risk of contracting it in Africa, Asia, Central America, and northern South America, but there are effective preventive drugs. Consult your travel agent or doctor for up-to-date advice. *Poliomyelitis:* The virus that causes it is still around; vaccination may be desirable. *Typhoid:* Before you travel abroad, vaccination may be a good idea.

Are people healthier in advanced societies than primitive ones?

When 17th-century explorers returned home, they often wrote impressionistic descriptions of the healthy savages they had encountered. These may sound too good to be true, but they are basically valid. About 0.1 percent of the world's people lead isolated lives in primitive societies—and these people, it appears, may be among the healthiest anywhere. The most unhealthy are those whose societies are in transition. These are the people living in developing nations where they have lost the benefits of the simple life and have not yet profited from the advances made in the developed countries.

The Tribulations of Transitional Societies

A few years ago, anthropologists, biologists, and physicians studied several simple societies where people lived isolated from the modern world but enjoyed vigorous good health and lived long, apparently satisfying lives. The Aborigines of Australia, for instance, following a nomadic way of life in the desert, were found to be as healthy as British workers or Swedish executives. A tribe of blacks, the Mabaans of Africa, and a group of Brazilian jungle tribes, known as the Xinguano Indians, were generally free of cancer, high blood pressure, tooth decay, and other ailments that plague civilized societies.

This member of the Mabaan tribe in the Sudan, striding along and enjoying her pipe, is 80 years old and in rugged good health—like many people in simple, isolated societies.

A scene in a developing nation dramatizes the plight of slum dwellers. Their health is poor because they benefit little from medical advances that help the rich.

Of Doctors and Dosages

How does a doctor determine the right dosage of medicine?

Until the 1920s, many available drugs did little good—but at least most of them were safe. Today, most drugs are effective—but a lot are dangerously potent. Prescribing the right dose has become crucial; if the dose is too small, it won't cure the patient; if it's too big, it may do damage.

Doctors look for guidance to reports put out by the government bodies that regulate drugs. Publications such as the *British National Formulary* and *British Pharmacopoeia* sometimes suggest precise doses. But because the same quantity of a drug may have different effects on different patients, they now sometimes list the "usual dosage range." In writing a prescription, the doctor takes into account that range and the particular patient's age, weight and general condition.

Drug manufacturers suggest optimum dosages only after many tests and complex calculations. Researchers determine the median effective dose, the amount that causes a certain desired reaction in half of the subjects tested; the median toxic dose, the quantity that leads to undesirable side effects in half of the subjects.

After all that, prescribing the right dose still isn't easy. One example: the amount of digitalis required to produce beneficial effects on the heart is only a little less than the amount that causes digitalis poisoning.

Do medicines ever backfire?

Not long after antibiotics came into use, medical practitioners found that these wonder drugs were creating new strains of drug-resistant bacteria. When an antibiotic was used against a particular kind of harmful bacteria, some of these micro-organisms were so hardy they did not succumb, but multiplied, transmitting to their descendants their ability to withstand the antibiotic.

Also, when antibiotics kill some harmful micro-organisms, they sometimes clear the way for others to make trouble. If you have a streptococcus infection, penicillin will most likely wipe out all or most of the strep germs, but it won't touch most of the staphylococcus germs that are also likely to be present in your body. Facing reduced competition for nutrients, the staph germs may proliferate wildly and cause a new infection.

In addition, antibiotics attack indiscriminately, often killing not only harmful bacteria but also useful ones that normally keep certain other micro-organisms at bay. If you are taking penicillin, the drug may wipe out both the germ that made you sick and the germ that stops the growth of the fungus *Candida albicans.* Cured of your original illness, you may find you have a mouth and throat infection caused by candida.

Are gullible people the only ones who respond to placebos?

Chemically inactive substances, called placebos, can often relieve pain. They can also produce measurable changes in body temperature, blood pressure, and even in the chemical composition of the blood. You wouldn't think that such sugar pills could help suffering patients. But studies have proved that people sometimes respond to such pills as if they were powerful drugs.

Doctors used to think that placebos affected only people who are unusually suggestible, but studies do not support that idea. Perhaps you assume that placebos work only if the patient believes the placebo is really a potent drug. But in a study at Johns Hopkins Medical School in Baltimore, patients suffering from anxiety were frankly told they were getting a placebo—and yet most improved anyway. The explanation may have something to do with a patient's trust in an obviously caring doctor. According to Dr. Herbert Benson of Harvard Medical School, a good relationship between doctor and patient "is the real basis for the placebo effect."

THE STORY BEHIND THE WORDS...

A chip off the old block usually means a son who is strikingly like his father in looks or personality or both, as if the child had been chipped from the same block of wood or stone as the parent. The common presumption is that the resemblance is inherited. In fact, genes exert a direct influence only on physical traits, such as eye colour and height; personality cannot be inherited. However, there is evidence that the genes do play some role in a few psychological characteristics, among them intelligence, aggressiveness, and shyness. In general, the kind of person you are depends on both heredity and environment, not on either alone.

Cancer was named more than 2,000 years ago by a physician who performed some of the first operations ever done to remove cancerous breasts. When he observed how wedges of malignant cells could cut into healthy tissues, he was reminded of crab claws, and he called malignancies *karkinoma,* which is the Greek word for "crab."

Doctor, from the Latin verb *docere,* "to teach," originally carried no medical connotation; it was simply a title of respect bestowed on learned persons not only in medicine but in other fields as well.

Charlatan is linked with the Italian verb *ciarlare,* "to chatter," while *quack* comes from an old Dutch word, *kwakzalver,* a travelling peddler who touts useless remedies at country fairs. *Kwakzalver,* in turn, can be traced to verbs meaning "to quack" and "to apply salve." Thus a charlatan or quack is a fast talker, a spieler whose volubility is intended to hide both ignorance and chicanery.

War: The Crucible of Medical Practice

One of the ironies of war is that it has often served as a laboratory for medical research and innovation. From the carnage of the battlefield have come scientific advances responsible for the saving of countless lives in peacetime. In all wars before the 20th century, more people died of disease than of wounds. Finally, during the American Civil War of the 1860s, the link between dirt and disease began to be apparent, and civilians soon benefited from this awareness. World War I is notable for advances in plastic surgery that came about because of the terrible facial wounds inflicted in that conflict, while World War II spurred large-scale production of penicillin and insecticides.

"**He who would learn surgery** should join an army and follow it." So the Greek physician Hippocrates advised some 2,500 years ago.

A wounded soldier is lifted onto a chariot in this detail from an Etruscan urn, made in ancient Italy. The same urn also depicts Achilles, the legendary Greek warrior, who was said to be skilled in the art of healing.

During World War II, transfusions of plasma (blood minus red and white cells) eliminated the need for matching blood types and thus ensured fast treatment of men who would otherwise have died of shock.

The use of helicopters, now widespread for the emergency transportation of civilian patients, owes a great deal to the Korean War, in which evacuation by air was first practised on a large scale.

The Rules of Heredity

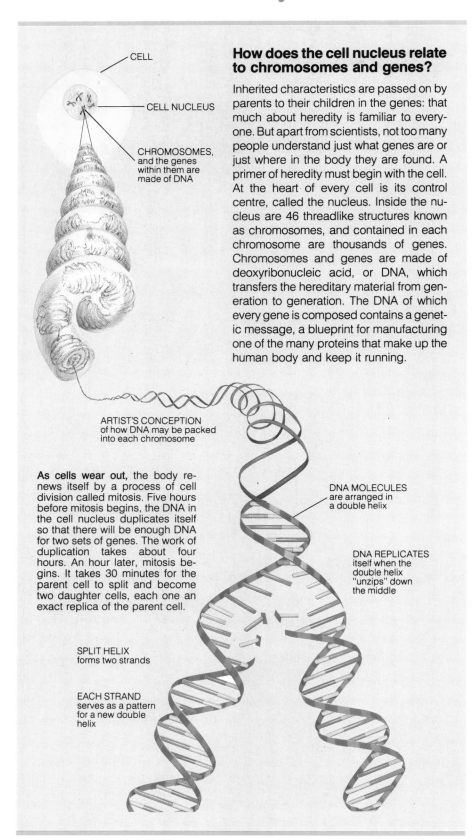

CELL

CELL NUCLEUS

CHROMOSOMES,
and the genes
within them are
made of DNA

ARTIST'S CONCEPTION
of how DNA may be packed
into each chromosome

As cells wear out, the body re-
news itself by a process of cell
division called mitosis. Five hours
before mitosis begins, the DNA in
the cell nucleus duplicates itself
so that there will be enough DNA
for two sets of genes. The work of
duplication takes about four
hours. An hour later, mitosis begins. It takes 30 minutes for the
parent cell to split and become
two daughter cells, each one an
exact replica of the parent cell.

SPLIT HELIX
forms two strands

EACH STRAND
serves as a pattern
for a new double
helix

DNA MOLECULES
are arranged in
a double helix

DNA REPLICATES
itself when the
double helix
"unzips" down
the middle

How does the cell nucleus relate to chromosomes and genes?

Inherited characteristics are passed on by
parents to their children in the genes: that
much about heredity is familiar to everyone. But apart from scientists, not too many
people understand just what genes are or
just where in the body they are found. A
primer of heredity must begin with the cell.
At the heart of every cell is its control
centre, called the nucleus. Inside the nucleus are 46 threadlike structures known
as chromosomes, and contained in each
chromosome are thousands of genes.
Chromosomes and genes are made of
deoxyribonucleic acid, or DNA, which
transfers the hereditary material from generation to generation. The DNA of which
every gene is composed contains a genetic message, a blueprint for manufacturing
one of the many proteins that make up the
human body and keep it running.

Why do children tend to look like their parents?

It was not until the 20th century
that scientists could explain *why*
children so often resemble their parents. The reason they do is that parents pass on to their offspring living
particles, called genes, containing
coded instructions specifying many
of a person's characteristics.

Though there is still much to be
learned about genes, we know that
they are parts of threadlike structures called chromosomes, which can
be found in the nucleus of every human cell. Genes and chromosomes
are made of deoxyribonucleic acid,
abbreviated to DNA. Every human
cell is thought to contain nearly 2
metres (6 feet) of DNA, which adds up
to 27,000 million kilometres (17,000
million miles) in the whole body. One
scientist has described DNA as an
"exquisitely thin filament," so light
that a thread of it running all the way
from the earth to the sun would
weigh only 0.5 grams (0.02 ounces).

How do children get genes from their parents?

The process of inheritance—the
transfer of genes from one generation
to the next—begins in the man's testes and the woman's ovaries. There,
germ cells become reproductive cells:
sperm in men, ova in women. Parents
transmit their genes to their children
in these reproductive cells.

Like all other human cells except
sperm and ova, germ cells contain 46
chromosomes. In the course of becoming a sperm or an ovum, a germ
cell divides by a special process, called
meiosis, that halves the number of
chromosomes. A sperm, or an ovum,
contains 23 chromosomes, half the
normal human complement. When a
sperm penetrates an ovum, the newly created embryo gets 46 chromosomes, half from each parent. Passed
on with the chromosomes are, of
course, all the genes they contain.
Fertilization is thus the principal
event that determines a person's biological inheritance.

Are all genes equally powerful?

Consider this: you can inherit a gene for a particular characteristic without showing any outward sign that your cells carry that gene. For instance, you may have a gene for fair hair, but your own hair may be dark. This is because some genes are more likely than others to exert an effect on a person.

Genes come in pairs; everyone has two genes for each characteristic governed by heredity. There are two kinds of genes, dominants and recessives. If one gene of a pair is a dominant and one is a recessive, the dominant will exert its effect, overriding the potential influence of the other, recessive gene. A recessive can exert its influence only if the two genes of a pair are both recessives.

In other words, if you inherit a recessive gene for a trait from *both* parents, your body will show that trait. If you inherit a recessive gene from only *one* parent, you may never know you carry the gene.

Here is an example. Brown hair is governed by a dominant gene; label it B. Fair hair is controlled by a recessive gene; label it b. (Geneticists use capital letters for dominant genes, small letters for recessive ones.) If you have brown hair, either you inherited a B gene, for brown hair, from both parents, or you inherited one B gene from one parent and one b gene, for fair hair, from the other. If you have fair hair, you can be sure that you inherited two b genes, one from your mother and one from your father.

In a similar situation, it is possible for two brown-eyed parents to have a blue-eyed child. The explanation is that in each parent, the gene-pair governing eye colour includes a dominant gene for brown eyes and a recessive gene for blue eyes. Since dominant genes override recessive ones, the parents have brown eyes. But both of them are carriers of blueness, and apparently both passed on their recessive genes for blue eyes. With no dominant gene for brown eyes to override them, the recessives wielded their influence and made the child's eyes blue.

Tim and Greg Hildebrandt are identical twins whose painting style is identical, too. They take turns on the same job and jointly painted the poster for the movie *Star Wars*.

What do identical twins reveal about heredity?

Even when brought up in different families, identical twins often show remarkable resemblances. In some cases, similarities may be due to chance or to the fact that the twins grew up in similar households and met while growing up. Yet many resemblances almost surely demonstrate the power of heredity. Identical twins' gestures can be strikingly alike; both members of a pair may have a firm handshake, or tap their fingers for emphasis. They may have the same psychological difficulties, and often prove astonishingly alike in artistic or athletic interests. In a study of identical twins separated at birth, each of one separated-twin pair had won a boxing championship. In another pair, both were singers, and had played the same kinds of theatrical roles.

Why don't all brothers and sisters look more alike than they do?

Except for identical twins, brothers and sisters do not share precisely the same heredity. They would if each child inherited *all* of both parents' genes. But each inherits only *half* of each parent's genes. For any child that half is a different combination of the parental genes, a chance selection of the heritable characteristics of both parents.

This situation comes about because of what happens at two points: when germ cells form and when fertilization occurs. When germ cells divide to become sperm or ova, the chromosomes are pulled apart, and sections of two chromosomes, made up of genes, may change places. Such shifts lead to new gene combinations in the sperm and ova.

In theory, a man can make 8 million genetically different sperm. Because a healthy man releases between 140 and 400 million sperm during each ejaculation, obviously some of the sperm are genetically identical to one another. However, a woman also has the potential to produce more than 8 million genetically different ova. When a child is conceived, which sperm fertilizes which ovum is a matter of chance. Statistically, then, one mother and father have the capacity to produce a staggering 64 million genetically different offspring. In actuality, this is not the case because a woman produces a total of only 200,000 to 400,000 ova in her lifetime, only a few hundred of which ripen in the ovaries, and still fewer of which are fertilized.

Symptoms and Syndromes

Are genetic defects rare?

The thought is sobering but true: every one of us has a statistical chance of transmitting a serious genetic disorder to the next generation. The reason is that each of us is thought to have approximately five to eight "bad" recessive genes that carry genetic abnormalities. If you happened to marry someone with one of the same recessive genes, you might well have a child with a genetic defect. Of all babies born alive today, an estimated 0.7 percent suffer from some inherited abnormality.

How many different disorders can be passed on by abnormal genes?

Scientists have so far identified more than 1,800 diseases that are transmitted by defective genes. Of these, about 1,000 are passed on by dominant genes, the kind so powerful that if they are present in a person's cells, they always exert their effect. A baby cannot be born with a dominant-gene defect unless at least one of its parents either has the same abnormality or is destined to develop it sooner or later; some genetic defects cause no symptoms until later life, so people can pass on those disorders before they know that they themselves are afflicted. One such ailment is Huntington's chorea, which caused the mental deterioration and eventual death of the folk singer Woody Guthrie.

If only one parent suffers from a dominant-gene defect, each child has a 50-50 chance of inheriting it. Of four children, the statistical probability is that two will have the disorder and two will be normal. If both parents are victims, each child has a 75 percent chance of inheriting it. Of four children, only one can be expected to be normal.

Another 800 disorders are passed on by recessive genes, the kind that are less powerful than dominants. Usually, the parents do not suffer from the disease, but both are carriers of it; their bodies contain not only the abnormal recessive gene but a normal dominant that overrides the defective recessive. You cannot suffer from a recessive-gene defect unless you inherit the abnormal gene from both parents. A common disease called phenylketonuria is inherited in that way. Often called PKU, it causes extreme mental retardation unless properly diagnosed and treated.

What happens if a person has the wrong number of chromosomes?

Most genetic disorders are caused by a single abnormal dominant gene or by a pair of identical abnormal recessive genes. But a few inherited disorders are the result of abnormalities in the larger structures of heredity, the chromosomes, which are made up of genes.

During the process of cell division, one or more chromosomes may get damaged, or the number of chromosomes may change, leading, in the next generation, to a person with more or fewer than the normal complement of 46. Many babies with chromosome defects are stillborn; others live but are mentally retarded and physically malformed.

One of the commonest chromosomal disorders is Down's syndrome, which causes both severe mental retardation and numerous physical abnormalities. Down's babies have 47 chromosomes, and it is possible, but not certain, that their abnormalities are caused by excess enzymes produced by the thousands of genes in the extra chromosome.

Which sex is more vulnerable to genetic disease?

When it comes to most inherited ailments (such as sickle cell anaemia), sex is largely irrelevant. Sex-linked disorders are those that are inherited along with the sex chromosomes that determine gender. Unlike the other genetic abnormalities, sex-linked disorders occur much more often in men than in women.

A man's vulnerability to sex-linked abnormalities comes from two facts. First, the X chromosome carries far more genes than the Y, including the

---

DID YOU KNOW...?

- **Fevers are caused by pyrogens,** which result from the breakdown of protein and other molecules. It is believed that pyrogens upset the body's thermostat. The result is that the body's heat-producing and heat-conserving mechanisms come into play, but as the temperature rises from 37° C to perhaps 40° C (99° F to 104° F), the patient feels a chill. No one is certain exactly what happens during a fever. Disease organisms may not multiply rapidly at high temperatures. Fevers can usually be brought down with paracetamol. But new studies suggest that perhaps a not-too-high fever should be allowed to run its course.

- **If aspirin were discovered today,** it would probably be a prescription drug, not an over-the-counter medication. Aspirin, which is the most widely and casually used drug in the world, is both more dangerous and more useful than you think. In children with chickenpox, aspirin has been linked to the disease Reye's syndrome. It is now recommended that it should not be given to children under 12. In adults, it has been linked with irritation of the intestinal tract. On the positive side, this willow-derived drug relieves aches and pains and reduces fever.

- **Sighs are not emitted just by the weary** or by yearning lovers; they are often a product of tension. First the person takes in a deep, long-drawn breath, then lets it out quickly, forcefully, and audibly. Frequently, the person is unaware of the depth or frequency of the sighs.

- **An epidemic is an outbreak** of a communicable disease that affects large numbers of people in one area at the same time. An unusually widespread epidemic, such as the Spanish influenza of 1918, is known as a pandemic. A disease may also be endemic—occurring persistently in a certain region.

Heredity and the House of Hapsburg

Among the most important ruling dynasties in Europe from the 15th to the 20th centuries was that of the Hapsburgs, or Habsburgs. Their name derives from their family seat, Habichtsburg, Hawk's Castle. Their characteristic look—a prominent jaw and lower lip—results from their genes. Early in the dynasty's history, when nothing was known about the laws of heredity, people must have wondered about that recurrent look. Now we know more about its causes. The Hapsburgs extended their influence in Austria, Germany, Hungary, Spain, and other nations not only by war but through marriage and intermarriage with other powerful families. Chronic inbreeding exaggerated the somewhat odd appearance of many Hapsburgs. It also aggravated their more serious genetic weaknesses and was responsible for the ultimate extinction of the male Hapsburg line.

Frederick III (1415–1493) was the first ruling Hapsburg to manifest the famous Hapsburg look, which he supposedly inherited from his mother.

Generations of inbreeding magnified the effects of family heredity. By the time of Philip IV of Spain (1605–1665), the dynasty was past its heyday.

The son of Frederick III was Maximilian I (1459–1519), shown, at far left, with his family. No one could miss the striking resemblance of his children; they are unmistakably products of the Hapsburg genes.

recessive genes for the commonest sex-linked disorders, colour blindness and haemophilia. Second, women have two X chromosomes, while men have only one X, along with one Y.

The son of a woman who is a carrier of colour blindness or haemophilia has a 50-50 chance of inheriting either of her two X chromosomes, the X with a dominant gene for normal vision (or normal blood clotting) or the X with the recessive gene for one abnormality or the other. If he inherits the recessive gene, he is certain to be a victim of the abnormality it carries, because he has no second X chromosome that might include a normal, dominant gene to override the abnormal recessive. By contrast, a girl who inherits her mother's abnormal recessive may nevertheless escape the abnormality, because her second X, which she gets from her father, may carry a normal dominant gene.

Of course, there are a few colour-blind women, and there are also a small number of women who suffer from haemophilia. In those rare cases, the women inherited a defective gene on each of their X chromosomes.

Orchestrating Our Development

How do cells "know" what to do?

In biology, perhaps even more than in other sciences, much is still theory and not necessarily fact. One of the things that biologists would most like to figure out is how cells differentiate— that is, how some cells become heart cells, others liver cells, others brain cells, and so on. So far, scientists can only guess at the answer.

What makes the mystery greater is the fact that every one of your cells contains all of the genes you inherited from your parents. This means that each cell has a complete set of blueprints for creating every structure in your body and for performing every bodily function. A liver cell, for instance, "knows" how to be a blood cell, but it doesn't use that knowledge—and a good thing, too. If all the genes in a cell were active, they would be working at cross purposes, and the result would be utter confusion. But apparently most genes in a given cell are quiescent, leaving just a few to form a particular kind of cell and to keep it working at whatever are its own special tasks.

What initiates the selection process? Perhaps a chemical compound within the cell turns off most of the genes, allowing only a few active ones to tell the cell what to do. Or perhaps something activates certain genes, but not others. If that is the case, you could think of the genes in a cell as if they were the keyboard of a typewriter or a musical instrument. And you could think of the "something" that activates particular genes as a typist, or musician, who strikes certain keys to form words or create melodies.

How do genes work?

So far, scientists have identified more than 1,500 traits that are controlled by single genes: about 750 traits determined by dominant genes and another 800 produced by recessive ones. Single-gene dominant traits include nearsightedness, normal hearing, and polydactylism (extra fingers and toes). Single-gene recessive traits include normal vision, congenital deafness, and the normal number of digits.

But there is not always a simple cause and effect relationship between one gene and one trait. In fact, most human characteristics are controlled by polygenes—that is, by several genes working together to produce their effect. One such trait is height, which is governed by polygenes that

Explorer Ponce de León "finds" the mythical fountain of youth.

In Search of an Elixir of Life

The wish for eternal youth seems itself eternal. Ancient Hindus believed in a fountain that could bring back the prime of life. Many modern men and women imagine they can stay young by following some special regimen of diet and exercise or by submitting themselves to injections of mysterious substances. Sadly, there is no elixir of life. Few people live beyond 90, and heredity seems to decree an outside limit of 115. Survival beyond that age has not been documented.

This venerable Soviet citizen has attained the age of 113.

direct hormone production, bone formation, and other bodily processes.

Your genes keep working as long as you live. They control the reproduction of your stomach lining and of all other cells that keep replacing themselves. They "tell" all parts of the body—from nose to toes—when to stop growing.

What is genetic engineering?

Although scientists can trace each of hundreds of disorders to a defect in one particular gene, they usually do not understand just how that abnormal gene acts to create and perpetuate the abnormality. That is one reason that only a few genetic diseases can be treated.

Some day it may become possible to change the hereditary characteristics of human beings. That statement may sound a bit like science fiction. But reputable biologists believe that eventually they may be able to substitute normal genes for defective ones and thus cure sickle cell anaemia, haemophilia, and other types of hereditary disease. Genes have already been synthesized in the laboratory, and the manipulation of the processes of heredity and reproduction in lower organisms is already possible on a small scale.

The foundation for genetic engineering was laid a few years ago with the discovery of enzymes that can split apart the molecules of DNA, which is the fundamental hereditary material of human beings and of most animals and plants. By means of gene splicing, or recombinant DNA technology, scientists can now combine DNA from rabbits and frogs with DNA from bacteria. These "remodelled" bacteria follow the genetic instructions contained in the DNA from higher organisms.

Bacteria altered in this way have been made to produce insulin and human growth hormone in small quantities, and it is hoped that the same technique will some day lead to the production of large quantities of many medically important substances at low cost.

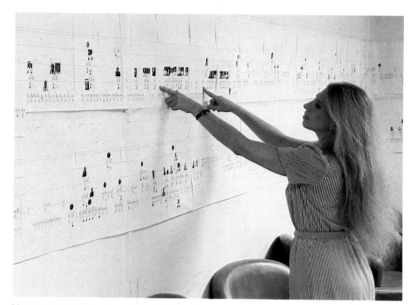

Nancy Wexler helped compile this family tree showing the incidence of Huntington's chorea in 3,000 people over eight generations.

A Genetic Detective Story

One of the most terrible things about Huntington's chorea, a degenerative, fatal brain disorder, is that its symptoms usually do not appear until midlife. This means that victims often have children (who stand a 50-50 chance of inheriting the affliction) before the parents know that they themselves carry the disease in their genes. Recently, scientists have been tracking down cases of Huntington's chorea in a group of interrelated Venezuelan families and trying to figure out the patterns of inheritance. The researchers have been using their findings to develop a diagnostic test that would let members of vulnerable families know their fate early. Painful as that knowledge might be, it would give carriers a chance to forgo childbearing if they wanted to. An experimental test has been devised for individuals who have ten relatives available for study. One of the test developers, Nancy Wexler, may fall victim to Huntington's but cannot use the test because she has too few relatives for a comparison.

The twisted hand of this patient, photographed in a Venezuelan clinic, is just one sign of Huntington's. The symptoms of the disease include jerky movements of the body, emotional disturbance, and progressive mental deterioration.

High-Tech Science

To study high-mortality diseases for which there is no cure, scientists work in centres called "hot labs." Lethal viruses, many from Africa, are isolated in sealed cabinets, where workers can reach them by putting their arms into long-sleeved gloves attached to the chamber. Other precautions include protective clothing and twice-daily chemical showers.

Can human beings be cloned?

In 1978, a science writer caused a stir by publishing a book purporting to tell the story of a rich man who with the help of scientists cloned a baby—that is, created an exact genetic copy of himself from just one of his own cells. In 1981, a judge ruled the book a hoax. In fact, the cloning of human beings is impossible now and may remain so for ever.

Cloning of plants, however, has been practicable, and practised, ever since ancient times. Growing a plant from a cutting is cloning. Scientists have cloned carrots, taking one carrot cell and growing it in coconut milk until it became a carrot like the one from which the cell came. Frogs and mice have also been cloned.

Human beings are more complicated. To clone one, you would have to remove the nucleus (the part with the genes) from a woman's ovum; take one cell from a donor and remove its nucleus; insert the donated nucleus into the ovum, implant the ovum in a woman's uterus, and wait for it to become a baby.

One difficulty is that mature human cells seem to lose the full genetic potential they had when they were part of an early embryo. A skin cell, for example, cannot become a blood or bone or brain cell, so how could it become a person? And then, people are the product of environment as well as heredity. A cloned infant would have the same genes as the person who donated the initial cell, but it could not grow up to be a carbon copy of the donor because, as one scientist explains, "You cannot reproduce the environment of the donor. It is already past."

Are new diseases really new?

In recent years, stories about Legionnaires' disease, toxic shock syndrome, and AIDS (acquired immune deficiency syndrome) have made headlines as new diseases. But it may be more accurate to describe these infections as *newly recognized* rather than new. With any unfamiliar disease, there is always the possibility that the disorder existed before it came to prominence, but was rare, and passed unnoticed until something happened to make it common.

What will the body be like tomorrow?

Writers of science fiction speculate that man will become increasingly intelligent in centuries to come, developing a larger brain in a smaller body. Some believe that wisdom teeth will disappear, and perhaps the appendix as well. Futurologists often predict a general loss of hair—on the body and on the head. And some look forward to a day when scientists could deliberately improve the human body in certain ways, perhaps enabling people to subsist on very little food or get by on only two hours' sleep a night. Very few scientists believe that any of this is likely.

Going by the past, predictions of a much-changed human body in the future don't hold up. From Egyptian, Peruvian, and other mummies, we know that human beings of the past suffered from the very same diseases that challenge medical science today: tooth decay and atherosclerosis, malaria and mumps, epilepsy and cancer, to name only a few. "Human disease has not essentially changed since earliest time," concludes the medical historian Arturo Castiglione.

The unchanging nature of human anatomy and physiology is the main obstacle in the way of establishing colonies in space. Yet scientists are already making plans for a permanently manned orbiting space station and for a settlement on the moon, where people would live for months at a time. Their task is to invent technology and design equipment that will take account of bodily characteristics in space. For instance, as soon as a space surgeon made an abdominal incision, the patient's intestines would rise up, so new operating techniques must be devised.

What medical breakthroughs are ahead?

All the exciting medical achievements of today—ranging from the transplanting of a liver to the reattachment of a severed limb—suggest even more spectacular advances in the future. Scientists have developed an artificial arm that uses muscle impulses in the shoulder to power an artificial hand—one capable of doing many tasks that a real hand can do. In the future, the paralyzed may walk, with the help of miniaturized and perhaps implanted computers.

Two of the most promising areas of science to watch are immunology (how the body defends itself) and genetics. The most impressive advance in immunology is the development of monoclonal antibodies. Each of these chemicals, which are made by the immune system, selectively targets one disease and can be used to diagnose and treat it. Also, vaccines may someday protect us from arthritis, herpes, and even some cancer. Drugs such as cyclosporine are making organ transplants more successful without completely suppressing the body's defences and so putting the patient at risk of infection.

Genetic engineering is currently being used to make bacteria synthesize pure human hormones such as insulin and growth hormone. In the future, genetic manipulation may allow doctors to replace the defective

genes responsible for such diseases as sickle cell anaemia and thalassaemia with normal ones.

From time to time, the press hails the discovery of some "miracle" substance that will supposedly halt the aging process or cure cancer or some other dread disease. Thymosine, for example, was heralded as a key to "living for 150 years." There is so much hope and urgency behind these

announcements that they are all the more disappointing when they fail to live up to their billing. Nevertheless, many fundamental discoveries come out of seemingly unproductive efforts, and while claims for thymosine, interferon, tumour necrosis factor, and the like may have been overstated, these substances may ultimately be a part of some future therapy, a piece of the puzzle.

Mummies Reveal Their Ancient Secrets

A space-age machine has proved its worth in diagnosing not only 20th-century ills but those from antiquity. Looking for data that could shed light on disease today, scientists are using sophisticated X-ray devices called CAT scanners to examine mummies and bodies preserved by chance in peat bogs and perpetual ice. One Egyptian mummy showed signs of six diseases, including hardening of the arteries and silicosis (probably caused by desert sands). In many Peruvian mummies and in a single Chinese specimen, there was evidence of atherosclerosis, parasitic diseases, and tuberculosis. One radiologist's summary of the findings: "Diseases are pretty much the same down through the ages."

Gilded case (right) holds the remains of Ankhper-hor, an Egyptian who lived before 600 B.C. The image on the screen shows the mummy in the scanner (top). Unlike autopsies, scanners leave mummies and their cases intact.

Chapter 2

THE BRAIN & NERVOUS SYSTEM

The more we learn about the brain, the more wonderful it seems: incredibly intricate, vigilant, responsive, powerful —the home of the human spirit.

The Most Complex Organ in the Body	48
The Amazing Network of Nerves	50
How the Brain Works	52
Hormones and Hemispheres	54
Scanning the Brain for Signals	56
To Sleep: Perchance to Dream. . . .	58
Awareness of the World	60
How We Store Our Experiences	62
Measuring Human Intelligence	64
The Power of Moods and Emotions	66
Insanity: From Chains to Tranquilizers	67
Injury and Aftermath	68
Coping With Pain	70
Disorders of the Brain	72

What does the brain do?

Language and abstract thought, judgment and planning, advanced reasoning and learning: all of these would be impossible without the highly developed human brain. But the brain is much, much more than the centre of intellectual activity. You need your brain to breathe, to metabolize food, and even to excrete wastes. The brain regulates and coordinates all the voluntary and involuntary moves you make, all the sensory impressions you receive, all the emotions you feel. Without your brain, you could not appreciate a painting or a poem, a symphony or a scenic vista. To your brain you owe your consciousness of yourself and the world around you, your unconscious life, your creativity, your personality.

In short, your brain is what makes you human. The Greek physician Hippocrates recognized as much in the fifth century B.C., when he observed what happened to people with head wounds. "From the brain and from the brain only," he said, "arise our pleasures, joys, laughter, and jests as well as our sorrows, pains, griefs, and fears."

Are the mind and the brain the same thing?

"Mind, in essence, is all the things the brain does," according to a prominent neurologist. Most but not all neuroscientists now share this view. Of course, experts acknowledge that we do not yet understand everything about what we think of as "mind." But they tend to believe that science will eventually unravel the mysteries; everything that goes on in the mind appears to be the result of specific electrochemical events in the brain— even though scientists do not yet know what all those events are.

On the other hand, a neurobiologist has said that the word *mind* is so "fuzzy at the edges" that it falls outside the realm of science. That is, "mind" suggests something too elusive and ethereal to be pinned down, and some issues, including the mind-brain question, are really philosophical rather than scientific. As such, they may be unresolvable.

Is the brain a computer?

To begin with, computers depend on instructions that tell them to do first this, and then that, and then this (so-called linear sequential programs). The brain needs nothing comparable. The closest thing to a program in the brain (and it's not very close) is the capacity to direct our attention first to one thought, sensation, or action, and then to another. While a computer processes information a single step at a time, the brain, with its millions of millions of cross-linked neural connections, processes information along millions of multi-directional pathways simultaneously. Both a computer and a brain are equipped with electricity-powered mechanisms for storing, retrieving, and processing information. Does all this make the brain a computer? In this limited sense, yes.

But the brain is much more than a computer. No computer can decide that it is bored or wasting its talents and should embark on a new way of life. The computer cannot drastically alter its own program; before it sets out in a new direction, a person with a brain must reprogram it.

More important still, a computer cannot relax, or daydream, or laugh. It cannot become inspired or creative. It cannot experience consciousness or perceive meaning. It cannot fall in love. Once more, then: is the brain a computer? In a word, no.

What is an idiot savant?

Idiot savants can perform remarkable mental feats, but in most respects they are retarded. More often than not, their feats are mathematical, entailing lightning-fast calculations or recognition, and incredible extensions of pattern. Idiot savants may be able to figure out the cube root of a six-digit number in six seconds, or go to a play and tell you how many

steps the actors took; or rattle off long passages, read to them just once, in an unfamiliar language. One set of identical twins with IQ's between 60 and 70 could not do simple arithmetic, but they could say in seconds which dates fell on Sunday in some year many centuries ago, or what day of the week it would be on any date thousands of years in the future. A 10-year-old idiot savant multiplied 365,365,365,365,365,365 by itself; and in just one minute came up with the correct answer: 133,491,850,208, 566,925,016,658,299,941,583,225.

While performing a mental feat, a savant's concentration is fierce, but not necessarily quiet. As the 10-year-old's neuron computer whirred away in his head, he "flew around the room like a top," an observer tells us. He also "pulled his pantaloons over the tops of his boots, bit his hands, rolled his eyes in his sockets, sometimes smiling and talking, and then seeming to be in agony." When asked how they perform their prodigies, idiot savants report only, "It's in my head." No one has yet found a better answer.

Without tutoring, sculptor Alonzo Clemens has created innumerable beautiful animals such as the horses at left. What's amazing is the fact that Clemens (shown here with his mother) has an IQ of about 40. Even among the rare breed of retarded-but-brilliant people called "savants," Clemens is unusual; few have ever shown artistic ability.

The Most Complex Organ in the Body

Looking like a root system, motor nerves twine through muscle fibres, and terminate in clusters that are called motor end plates. It is here that the nervous system triggers muscle contractions, by means of chemical messengers.

What does the brain look like?

If you are an Agatha Christie fan, you will remember the words of her fictional detective, Hercule Poirot: "Let us exercise our little grey cells!" Indeed, much of the human brain does look grey, or as one description has it, like "day-old slush." But underneath the grey matter, which is composed of the bodies of thousands of millions of nerve cells, lies white matter, which is made up of thin nerve fibres projecting like tails from the cells.

What are the main parts of the nervous system?

The nervous system controls all of your activities: the functioning of your internal organs, your movements, your perceptions, even your thoughts and emotions. The main parts of this network are the *central nervous system*, which includes the brain and the spinal cord, and the *peripheral nervous system*, which includes the somatic and the autonomic systems.

The somatic system includes the sensory nerves that keep the body in touch with the outside world, along with the nerves that govern bodily responses to that world. The autonomic system controls the internal environment. It governs breathing, heart rate, and other physiological activities, and also such physical responses to emotion as sweating palms that often accompany fear.

What do the different parts of the brain do?

Compared to the brain, the other organs of the human body could almost be called simple. They are not as important as the brain, either, at least in the sense that they don't really serve to set man apart from the animals. For the brain is the centre of human consciousness—and of the subconscious, too.

The brain is composed of three principal divisions: the cerebrum, the cerebellum, and the brain stem. If intelligence, learning, and judgment could be said to reside anywhere in the brain, it would be in the two halves, or hemispheres, of the *cerebrum*. You can get some idea of the cerebrum's importance from the fact that it fills the entire upper part of your skull. The *cerebellum* (Latin for

"little cerebrum") is only one-eighth the size of the cerebrum. Its main functions: to maintain equilibrium and to coordinate muscular activities. The *brain stem*, sometimes referred to as the lower brain, includes such structures as the thalamus and hypothalamus, which regulate hunger, thirst, sleep, and sexual behaviour; the midbrain and pons, whose task is to transfer impulses from one part of the brain to another; and the medulla, which governs breathing, blood pressure, the beating of the heart, and other vital functions.

What is the blood-brain barrier?

Your brain requires a controlled, consistent environment. If it were exposed to fluctuating quantities of the chemicals that it needs, or to substances that are foreign to it, it would function abnormally, perhaps with drastic consequences. Because your bloodstream transports a number of potentially brain-damaging substances throughout the body, you would expect the brain to suffer from their effects. In fact, the brain is different from all other organs in that it has a special protective system, called the blood-brain barrier. Because of it, chemicals that are composed of large molecules cannot generally pass from the blood into the brain as they do into other organs.

How so? In most parts of the body, the smallest blood vessels are porous. But the cells of such vessels in the brain are joined to each other with tight junctions; adjacent cells are almost fused together. Nevertheless, substances with small molecules, including oxygen, alcohol, and most anaesthetics, can cross the barrier easily. That is how your brain gets the oxygen it needs. It is also why you can get drunk or be anaesthetized.

How long can the brain go without oxygen?

A child falls into an icy lake, is pulled out apparently dead after 40 minutes or more—and is then re-

The Parts of the Brain—And Their Functions

The brain weighs about 1.5 kilograms (3 pounds), is rather larger than a grapefruit, and in consistency resembles an undercooked custard or a ripe avocado. The main part of it, the dome-shaped cerebrum, brings to mind an oversized, shelled walnut. The surface of the cerebrum, the cerebral cortex, is where most of the brain's information is stored. There are four lobes that cover the brain like a hood: the frontal, temporal, parietal, and occipital lobes. There is little more to be seen on the outside than the peach-sized cerebellum at the back, and the brain stem connecting brain and spinal cord.

PREMOTOR CORTEX controls muscular coordination, such as swinging the arms while walking

SUPPLEMENTARY MOTOR AREA

MOTOR CORTEX controls the voluntary muscles

FRONTAL EYE FIELD

SOMATOSENSORY CORTEX receives and analyses sensory impulses coming from all parts of the body

PREFRONTAL AREA is concerned with intellectual activities

FRONTAL LOBE

PARIETAL LOBE

VISUAL CENTRE lies at the back of the brain. In one part, visual impressions are received, and in another, they are interpreted

TEMPORAL LOBE

OCCIPITAL LOBE

BROCA'S AREA (only on the left side of the brain) controls the muscles that are involved in speech

AUDITORY CENTRE

BRAIN STEM

CEREBELLUM

THE BRAIN receives information via one set of nerves and issues instructions for action via another set

SPINAL CORD is protected by the bony vertebral column. At intervals, the nerves branch out

NERVES penetrate every part of the body

SOMATOSENSORY CORTEX

MOTOR CORTEX

FISSURE

Viewing the brain from above, you can see that the longitudinal fissure of the cortex runs from front to back, dividing the brain into right and left hemispheres. Fissures also run from side to side. The motor and somatosensory cortices form bands across the top of the brain.

vived, with little or no damage to the brain. Until a few years ago, it was axiomatic that brain cells begin to die after they have been without oxygen for only four minutes. Now, from a succession of previously unexplained survivals, doctors realize that the brain doesn't die as fast as they had thought; it just idles, as one neurosurgeon has put it.

What saves some apparent victims of drowning is the mammalian diving reflex, found in both human beings and in sea animals. When the face is immersed in cold water, the cold stimulates a reflex reaction in which metabolism slows, so that the brain and other vital organs need less oxygen than usual. (Indeed, dropping body temperature is used in some

forms of neurosurgery and cardiac surgery because cold reduces metabolism.) In addition, blood is redistributed from the arms and legs to the brain and the other organs most in need of the life-giving oxygen it contains. The reflex doesn't work when the face is no longer immersed, so rescuscitation efforts must begin as soon as the victim is out of the water.

The Amazing Network of Nerves

How do messages get around in the brain?

When one part of the brain sends a message to another, it uses two kinds of power, electrical and chemical. Electricity moves the message from one end of a long nerve cell to another. But how does the message get from one cell to another? That is more complicated, because the cells are not directly linked; there is a gap, or synapse, between one cell and another.

Alvin Silverstein, author of a widely used physiology textbook, employs a metaphor that clarifies what happens. He suggests thinking of the synapse as a river that cuts two sections of a railway track in two. When a train gets to the river via the tracks on one side of it, it crosses the water by ferry and rolls right onto the second section of track to continue its journey. Similarly, a message in the brain is "ferried" across the synapse by a chemical called a neurotransmitter, which pours out of the end of the cell just as the message approaches the synapse. The electrical power that has brought the message so far now shuts down, and the neurotransmitter takes the message aboard and moves it across the channel to the next cell along the route. Then the electricity comes on again, and the whole process is repeated until the message reaches its destination.

It takes a message—more technically, a nervous impulse—from one one-thousandth to three one-thousandths of a second to make the chemical crossing. That is slower than electrical transmission (if you drink a cup of coffee, the caffeine in it speeds things up). Different parts of the brain manufacture different neurotransmitters—some 30 in all.

What happens if nerve cells are damaged or destroyed?

All the nerve cells you ever have are present at birth; once a nerve cell dies, it cannot be replaced. However, the stock of nerve cells is so large that—barring catastrophic injury—an individual will have more than enough to last a lifetime. Though the cell body cannot be replaced, some

Why are nerve cells in the brain so remarkable?

An individual brain cell may be connected to as many as 10,000 other brain cells—perhaps more. These illustrations do not attempt to represent the actual number of cell-to-cell connections because the density of the filaments would be so great as to obscure the picture.

Nerve cell. The individual nerve cell receives information from other nerve cells, then "decides" whether or not to pass the message along. The decision depends on the amount of electrical charge that is built up on the cell surface.

Dendrites. These fine, branching filaments, which give the cell its octopus-like appearance, receive messages from other nerve cells.

Axon. The axon is a slender extension of the nerve cell. This cable is a one-way conduit from one nerve cell to the axon terminal. Each nerve cell has a single axon, but the axon may have many branches.

Axon terminal. This is the point where the electrical charge sent from a nerve cell is changed into a chemical signal. See a representation of this on the facing page.

Synapse. A site of contact where cell-to-cell chemical communication takes place.

Site of transfer. The surface membranes of nerve cells are sensitive to certain signals.

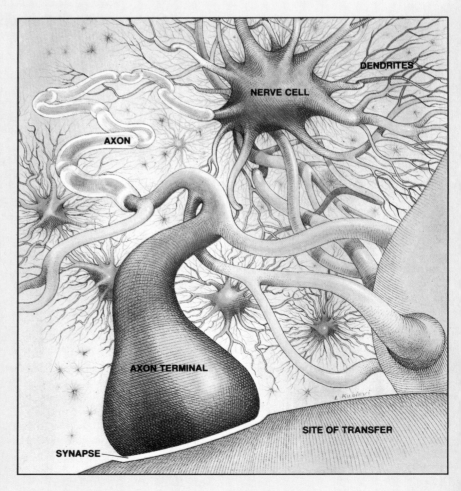

50

extensions can regenerate after injury. This explains how it is possible for reattached limbs to regain some of their function.

What does being nervous have to do with nerves?

Nervousness feels as if it arises from the pit of the stomach, but nerves are really the source. Let's say the dentist has just told you he'll have to extract a tooth. Before common sense can inform you there's nothing to fear, the sounds of his words have stimulated your brain.

Instantly, your mind focuses on your tooth. Deeper in the brain where "mindless" thoughts occur, neurons interpret the event as danger. Before you have even closed your mouth to check with your tongue that the tooth is still in place, signals have been sent out to your adrenal gland to release adrenaline into the bloodstream. Adrenaline has effects throughout the body—the rapid heartbeat, the butterflies, and the sinking sensation you feel as nervousness.

Unfortunately, once released, the hormone remains active for some minutes, even if the dentist says you can keep your tooth after all. In fact, the nervous system doesn't need a real, outside stimulus for the panic button to be pushed. As far as it is concerned, a thought is as good as a deed. Nervous thoughts alone can make you nervous, and once your brain recognizes the symptoms, it figures there must be something to be nervous about!

Why does your leg jerk when the doctor taps your knee?

Built-in short circuits in the spinal cord process signals without waiting for the brain to have its say. The knee jerk is one such reflex. Hitting the tendon at the knee pulls at the muscle to which it is attached, stretching it. When the stretch signal is received at the spinal cord, a signal is sent to the muscle to contract. If there is no knee jerk, or if it is incomplete, there may be something wrong with connections to the spinal cord.

How do messages travel from one cell to another?

Electrical messages are turned into chemical signals at the point where a sending cell meets a receiving one. But, amazingly, the two do not touch. Instead, communication is across a gap, which is called the synaptic cleft. Molecules complete the transmission of the signal.

Axon. All nerve cells (neurons) have an axon and one or many axon terminals.

Synaptic cleft. This infinitesimal space, about 40 thousandths of a millimetre (millionth of an inch), is where chemical signals are transmitted from nerve cell to nerve cell.

Axon terminal. In this cutaway drawing, a stylized representation of a complex chemical event, you see a number of tiny sacs. These contain molecules (represented as green balls) that actually carry the messages, drifting across the synaptic cleft.

Receptors. The sensitive surface of the membrane is uniquely attuned to certain molecules, the neurotransmitters.

Neurotransmitters. These molecules that match the molecules in the receptor in much the same way as a lock and key are uniquely suited to one another.

AXON

AXON TERMINAL

SYNAPTIC CLEFT

RECEPTORS

NEUROTRANSMITTERS

How the Brain Works

How can scientists find out which parts of the brain do what?

Just about everyone knows that different parts of the brain are specialized to perform different functions. Yet how can anyone know that, since there is no way to observe a living brain directly? Over the years, scientists have devised increasingly sophisticated ways of exploring the geography of the brain, and they have succeeded in mapping it in considerable detail.

One early method was to do autopsies on people who suffered from speech difficulties, paralysis, or other types of neurological problems as a result of strokes, head wounds, or birth injuries. When autopsy showed a tumour or some other abnormality in one part of the brain, it was presumed that that part was responsible for the function in question. That was how scientists pinpointed both Broca's area and Wernicke's area, two identifiable spots in the brain that control different aspects of speech.

Another source of information is split-brain research, in which scientists study the effect of severing the corpus callosum, a bundle of 50 million nerve fibres that connects the two halves of the brain. (The operation is a rare one, done to treat intractable epilepsy.) By observing the performance of split-brain patients on certain laboratory tests, researchers have learned about the distinctive characteristics of the right and left hemispheres of the brain.

Both of these methods of mapping the brain can be criticized because the people studied were not normal; what was learned about their brains might not apply to everyone. Today, researchers use scanners to study the brains of normal, living subjects. These instruments can measure the blood flow in the brain and translate the measurements into pictures of the brain on a screen. When a person talks, or moves his hand, or sings, a different part of the screen lights up.

Are the two halves of your brain equal in language ability?

Recent studies indicate that people who sustain damage to the right hemisphere of the brain often lose the ability to understand jokes, figures of speech, and subtle shades of meaning. The inference is that the right half of the brain plays some role in language. Nevertheless, research demonstrates that language is mainly a function of the left hemisphere; a massive stroke that devastates the left half of the brain leaves its victim without the ability to speak or comprehend spoken language. It destroys the ability to calculate, too, for mathematics is the left hemisphere's second major speciality. The specialities of the right hemisphere are spatial perception, music and the other arts, and creativity.

However, the fact that each half of your brain is especially good at dealing with particular subjects is not the most important thing. The crucial difference between the two hemispheres is that each has its own style of thinking. The left brain tends to be rational, logical, and analytic. It is very good at dealing with symbols and at grasping such broad concepts as honour or truth. The right brain is generally emotional, intuitive, and holistic, but it requires the language capacities of the left hemisphere in order to function. To the right brain, specific objects and events are more meaningful than abstract ideas.

Can a person have normal eyes and still be unable to see?

You do not see with your eyes alone, but rather with your eyes and brain together. The eyes pick up impressions from the outside world and send messages about that world to the brain for interpretation. Full vision requires not only the brain's principal vision centre, the primary visual cortex in the occipital lobes at the back of the head, but also many other places in the brain specialized to make sense of visual data.

If your primary visual cortex were

Early Theories: READING THE SKULL

Feel the bumps on a person's skull and thus read his character: so Franz Joseph Gall, a Viennese doctor, and his flamboyant disciples counselled in the 1800s. The father of the pseudo-science of phrenology, Gall held that the brain was made up of 30-odd "organs," each responsible for a single trait. Phrenology swept Europe and the United States, spawning phrenological societies, books, pamphlets, and sideshows. The craze

attracted Edgar Allan Poe, Karl Marx, and Queen Victoria, who got a phrenologist to palpate the royal children's cranial knobs. "Phrenologist after phrenologist may die," one fanatic proclaimed, "but phrenology can never perish." But perish it did, under the onslaught of reason and ridicule. Of course, the shape of the skull does not reflect the structure of the brain. But the phrenologists were on the right track with their idea of brain localization. Indeed, you might almost call them the forerunners of today's scientific brain mappers.

Nineteenth-century scientists and fairground showmen alike promoted the idea that different brain areas do different things. In principle, at least, they were right.

Specialization in the Brain

The two halves of the brain, the hemispheres, are not only different in size, but each has a slightly different shape and different roles. First of all, the right hemisphere controls the left side of the body and vice versa. Communication between hemispheres takes place via dense bundles of nerve fibres called the corpus callosum. Apparently, each hemisphere has its own particular talents. In most people, the left brain seems to be good at language, mathematics, and logical thinking. The right is important in spatial perception, art and music appreciation, creativity, and intuitive thinking. Why this specialization? No one is sure, but in any case, it lets you do many things at the same time.

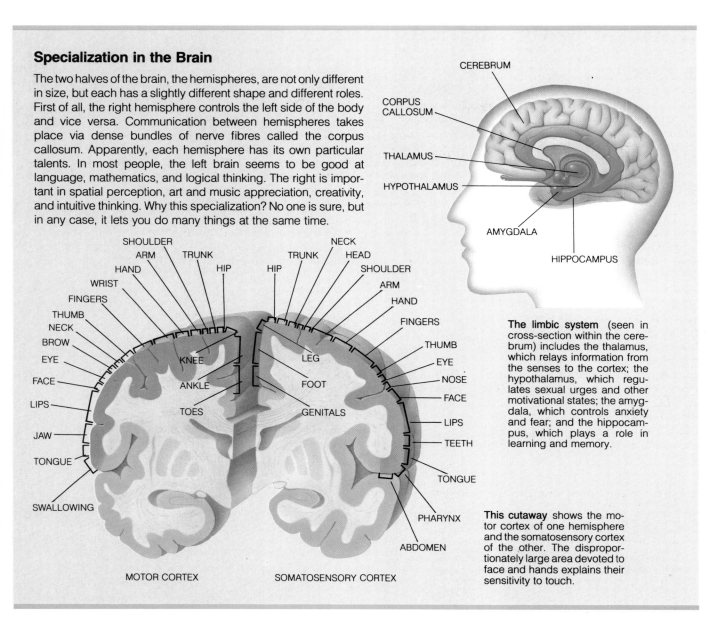

CEREBRUM

CORPUS CALLOSUM

THALAMUS

HYPOTHALAMUS

AMYGDALA

HIPPOCAMPUS

SHOULDER
ARM
TRUNK
HAND
HIP
WRIST
FINGERS
THUMB
NECK
BROW
EYE
FACE
LIPS
JAW
TONGUE
SWALLOWING

NECK
TRUNK
HEAD
HIP
SHOULDER
ARM
HAND
FINGERS
THUMB
EYE
NOSE
FACE
LIPS
TEETH
TONGUE
PHARYNX
ABDOMEN

KNEE
ANKLE
TOES

LEG
FOOT
GENITALS

MOTOR CORTEX

SOMATOSENSORY CORTEX

The limbic system (seen in cross-section within the cerebrum) includes the thalamus, which relays information from the senses to the cortex; the hypothalamus, which regulates sexual urges and other motivational states; the amygdala, which controls anxiety and fear; and the hippocampus, which plays a role in learning and memory.

This cutaway shows the motor cortex of one hemisphere and the somatosensory cortex of the other. The disproportionately large area devoted to face and hands explains their sensitivity to touch.

entirely removed or destroyed, you would be blind, at least as far as you were consciously aware—even though there was nothing wrong with your eyes. Nevertheless, tests would show that you were still reacting, without being aware of it, to certain visual signals from your eyes. For instance, you would continue to turn your eyes or your head in response to changes in the brightness of light. If certain parts of the visual areas in the brain were destroyed, you might have trouble with some but not all aspects of vision. Depending on which parts were affected, you might be unable to judge the size, shape, or purpose of objects.

To turn the situation around, suppose that your brain was normal while your eyes were blind, or were simply closed. And suppose electrical stimulation were applied to the visual areas of your brain. What happened would vary with the part of the brain that was stimulated. You might see flashes of light, colours, stars—or even a familiar scene from some earlier period in your life.

Can one part of the brain take over the function of another?

Full recovery from a stroke is rare, even though one of the brain's two hemispheres remains entirely undamaged. By the time that a person reaches adulthood, each half of his brain has become adept at certain tasks and has developed a characteristic style of functioning. In short, the two halves of the brain are so specialized that it is difficult or impossible for the intact hemisphere to take over the other hemisphere's lost functions. However, if damage to the brain occurs in infancy or early childhood, recovery is more likely to occur. A stroke that has damaged the left hemisphere (which usually governs speech) in a child of six may not prevent the eventual development of normal language abilities.

Hormones and Hemispheres

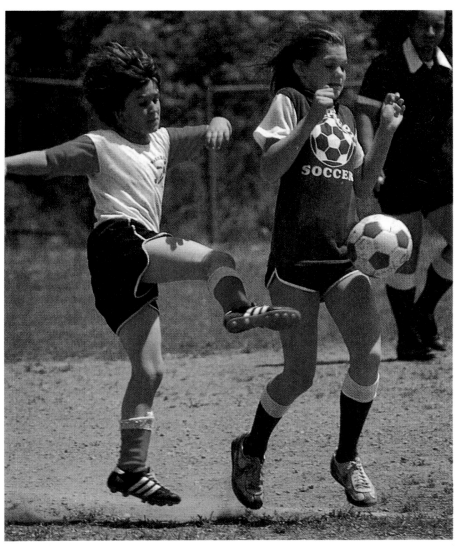

The moment of truth—when the ball comes straight at you. In this mixed soccer game of 10- to 12-year-olds, the boy advances, the girl withdraws. Not only sex, but age and cultural values influence performance.

Are men's and women's brains alike?

Since there are well-established differences between the sexes in a small number of abilities and characteristics and in susceptibility to a few disorders, it would be surprising if there were no parallel anatomical differences in the brain. As a matter of fact, a few researchers believe they have demonstrated dissimilarities in men's and women's brains. Most others, however, say that no one has yet offered convincing proof—possibly because neuroscientists rarely get to

examine living human brains. But scientists strongly suspect the differences are there, and they think they know what produced them. Presumably, male and female hormones that circulate in the foetus either masculinize or feminize not only the developing genitals but the brain as well.

Are there any behavioural sex differences?

Studying human behaviour is not like studying chemistry. It is difficult to measure behaviour—that is, to

assign mathematical values to it— and almost impossible to be objective about it; two researchers may interpret the same behaviour in different ways. Thus the first thing to be said about sex differences (apart from the anatomical ones) is that nothing has been proved as absolute fact.

Nevertheless, scientists generally agree that the reality of four sex differences has been fairly well established: boys are more aggressive than girls; they are better at mathematics; they are superior in visual-spatial ability, which includes such skills as reading maps and figuring out mazes; girls are better than boys at verbal tasks, which includes understanding difficult material and speaking fluently. Scientists who accept the existence of these differences often cite as their source a classic study of sex differences by two psychologists, Eleanor E. Maccoby and Carol N. Jacklin, who reached their conclusions after analysing more than 2,000 studies by many different researchers.

There is considerable evidence that two of the differences, those in aggression and in mathematics, have a biological basis: they are probably determined in part by the genes. But in all behavioural sex differences, learning and other environmental factors are thought to play an important role; if boys and girls were brought up in exactly the same way, they would probably be more alike.

But remember: the evidence for the four differences is based on statistical averages. It is not true that *all* boys are better at maths than *all* girls; *some* girls are better at it than *most* boys. In the same way, some boys outdo most girls in verbal ability.

What is the evidence that males are more aggressive than females?

Sometimes it happens that popular opinion is right. A survey of 67 studies shows that males are really more aggressive than females, both physically and verbally. In those studies, researchers made 94 comparisons of aggressive behaviour in children and found statistically meaningful differences between the sexes in 57 of the comparisons. In all but five instances, it was the boys who were more aggressive than the girls.

As to the question of whether or not aggressiveness is based on biology— on physiological differences between the sexes rather than on learning— some scientists consider the evidence now available to be inconclusive. However, there are a number of scientists who are convinced that aggression can be traced to the male hormone testosterone. In one especially provocative study of male juvenile delinquents, the most aggressive ones were those with the highest levels of testosterone in their bodies.

In addition, there is corroborative evidence from anthropology, showing that killing—whether it be in war or in daily life—occurs in thousands of different cultures and that the people who do the killing are chiefly men. If a sex difference is universal among human beings even though they grow up in very different cultures, there is a good chance that the difference comes not from the way people are brought up but from biological factors which are presumably the same in every society.

Are disorders influenced by sex?

Left-handedness, a trait shared by Charlie Chaplin, Michelangelo, Jack the Ripper, and an estimated 10 percent of the general population, is of course not a disorder. But it is more common in males than in females, and oddly enough, it is often associated with certain disorders that are also more frequently found in males than in females. One of these is dyslexia, the reading disability that makes some highly intelligent people read "saw" as "was" and "oil" as "710." Other disorders more likely to occur in males are stuttering and autism (extreme emotional withdrawal).

Many scientists believe that these difficulties, and left-handedness, too, must stem from physical structures in the brain, but as yet no brain-behaviour links have been established.

Can both sides of your brain recognize faces?

Brain lateralization—the specialization of each hemisphere for certain functions—is not an either-or proposition. Sometimes both halves of the brain can accomplish the same task, though each may do so under special circumstances. There are indications that novices use the right brain for certain tasks while experts accomplish the same tasks with the left. The average person uses his right brain to recognize melodies; a professional musician uses his left brain for that purpose. Similarly, while the ability to identify people by a quick look at their facial features has long been recognized as a speciality of the right hemisphere, studies suggest that you recognize a familiar face with your left hemisphere.

Incidentally, inability to recognize faces, called prosopagnosia, is a rare but striking disorder. Most of the victim's mental and visual abilities remain intact. If he looks at a person, he can usually describe the features he sees. But if he looks at his wife or children, he may not recognize them at all. It is not that he doesn't remember the identity of these well-known people. Rather, damage to a very small part of his brain has destroyed the link in his mind between face and identity. Yet if he hears his wife and children speak, he knows at once who they are.

Music and the Mind: The Role of the Right Brain

When a professional musician suffers a stroke that damages the right hemisphere of his brain, his musical ability is often impaired; when the damage is to the left hemisphere, such impairment is less frequently reported. That distinction is not the only evidence of the right brain's important role in music. Stroke victims with damage to the left hemisphere, which controls speech, often lose much of their ability to speak words—while retaining the capacity to sing them. One such patient was described in 1745: "He can sing certain hymns, which he had learned before he became ill, as...distinctly as any healthy person....Yet this man...cannot say a single word except 'yes.' "

The right brain is the domain of music appreciation and other musical abilities.

Scanning the Brain for Signals

CAT stands for *computerized axial tomography. These scanners X-ray the brain in cross-section. Computer screens then display "slices" of the brain viewed from any desired angle. (To get a picture of this, think of a hard-boiled egg sliced lengthwise or crosswise.)*

Can an X-ray see inside the brain?

Standard X-ray equipment will produce a clear picture of the skull, but not of the brain itself. Nevertheless, an expert can often infer information about the brain from an X-ray image of its bony framework. If, for example, the image shows erosion on the inner side of the skull, this may indicate a brain tumour, since a growth can actually wear away bone. Or if the X-ray shows the line of a skull fracture just above the place where an artery lies on the surface of the brain, there is reason to suspect bleeding inside the brain, because a fracture often rips the blood vessel open.

What can CAT, PET, and MRI scans see that X-rays can't?

With the help of computers, machines called scanners use X-rays, radioactivity, radio waves and magnetism to produce detailed pictures of the brain. Some scanners not only reveal anatomical structures but also show those structures in action. With scanners, doctors can pinpoint the size, shape, and position of a tumour or the particular spot in the brain that is responsible for epileptic seizures. Scanners are valuable not only in diagnosis and treatment but also in research. When it comes to detailed mapping of the brain—figuring out which parts do what—scanners are just about indispensable.

Will scanners be able to read your mind some day?

You don't have to worry; mind-reading scanners are almost certainly beyond the realm of possibility. It is true, however, that the most recently developed scanners can reveal quite a bit about what is going on in your brain when you think. But the human brain is such a versatile organ that it can use various neuronal path-

A Window Into the Workings of the Human Brain

PET (positron-emission tomography) scanners are sensitive to a harmless radioactive tracer substance given to a patient in a brain nutrient such as glucose. The tracer serves as a visible marker; attached to the invisible nutrient, it allows an observer to follow the progress of the nutrient through the brain and to see whether or not cells metabolize it to make energy. How can an observer "see" the tracer? The tracer emits positrons (bits of antimatter) that collide with electrons (ordinary matter) in the brain and produce bursts of energy that the scanner records. The intensity of the bursts varies with the amount of chemical activity in the brain. Certain disease states produce characteristic PET scans.

Normal brain pattern in PET scan.

Schizophrenia is markedly different.

Dementia, too, is identifiable in a scan.

ways to think (or to do anything else for that matter), and it therefore seems highly unlikely that a specific pattern of brain activity would always indicate the same thought in all human beings.

However, the idea of a spy-catching scanner isn't so far-fetched. Using a PET scanner, the Danish scientist Niels Lassen has demonstrated that when a person hears his own language spoken, his cerebral cortex generates certain "recognition patterns." The sound of a language he cannot understand doesn't activate those patterns.

What are brain waves?

In 1929, when the German psychiatrist Hans Berger said he had recorded electrical activity in the brain, other scientists didn't believe him. Then in 1932, the British electrophysiologist Edgar Adrian won a Nobel prize for his demonstration of such activity. These days, no one doubts that the brain, like the heart, is continuously generating electrical currents. The ones that pulse through your brain cells are weaker than those in your heart, but they can be picked up by a machine called an electroencephalograph, or EEG, which records changes in voltage (electrical pressure) and frequency (number of pulses per second) on a moving graph. Today, the EEG and an advanced version of it known as BEAM (brain electrical activity mapping) are used to study the brain and to diagnose brain disorders.

Brain waves are a mixture of two to four commonly seen patterns based on frequency. *Alpha* waves are recorded when you are in a state of relaxed awareness. When you are fully alert, your brain gives off *beta* waves. *Delta* waves occur when you are sleeping deeply or lying anaesthetized on an operating table; they are also characteristic of severe brain damage. Lastly, *theta* waves are of an intermediate frequency between delta and alpha and often provide the background pattern with which delta or beta are intermixed.

MRI (magnetic resonance imaging) scanners record radio signals given off by brain tissues while a person lies in a powerful magnetic field and is bombarded with radio waves. A computer converts the signals into pictures.

When is a person considered "brain dead"?

Perhaps the most fundamental—and controversial—question facing doctors, lawyers, philosophers, theologians, and ordinary men and women is how to define death, how to decide when a person has died. For centuries, it was accepted that death comes when the heart stops and breathing ceases. Then it was discovered that the heart and lungs could be restarted, and that machines could keep them going long after the usual signs of life had ceased.

It was about that time that the concept of brain death developed. In oversimplified terms, this means that a person is dead if his brain is dead. But authorities do not agree on what brain death means. Some say the brain is dead if only the cerebral cortex, the thinking part of the brain, has stopped functioning; others argue that the brain stem, which governs lower processes, must also cease to function before the brain can be considered dead.

To confirm death in potential donors for transplant operations, the British Medical Royal Colleges have laid down a series of criteria for brain death. Repeated testing must confirm, for example, that the patient does not respond in any way to touching the corneas of his eyes, squirting ice-cold water into his ears, or passing a suction tube down his trachea towards his lungs. When disconnected from his ventilator (life-support machine) he must show no sign of attempting to breathe on his own and the doctor must be certain that the patient is not sedated by drugs or suffering from hypothermia.

There is a difference between a person who is "brain dead" and one who is "vegetative." (The term *vegetative* was never meant to be pejorative, but to describe that the brain stem's "vegetative functions" were spared damage.) The former seldom survives for long despite intensive care. The latter, however, still has an intact brain stem that can regulate vital body functions and so can survive for many years.

To Sleep: Perchance to Dream....

What is the purpose of sleep?

On average, human beings spend a third of their lives in sleep, yet scientists do not yet know precisely what sleep accomplishes. It is presumed to serve some restorative function, but just how sleep refreshes us is unclear.

Whatever the function of sleep, the need for it is compelling. If you don't believe that, try to stay awake for 48 hours. Chances are that you can't do it—not unless you're especially anxious or excited, or perhaps are taking part in a sleep deprivation experiment in which researchers wake you up promptly every time you drop off.

One thing is sure: sleep is not a passive state. Electroencephalography, the study of electrical impulses from the cerebral cortex, shows that your brain is anything but inactive while you're asleep.

Does everyone need eight hours of sleep a night?

People need enough sleep to make them wake refreshed. That may mean no more than three hours a night for a very few human beings, five or six hours for a good many people, seven or eight for most of us, and in some cases as many as nine or more. When you were an infant, you undoubtedly needed 16 or 18 hours of sleep. As you get older, you'll require less sleep than you do now, however much or little that happens to be.

What does prolonged lack of sleep do to people?

Sleep-deprivation experiments reveal that when human beings are compelled to stay awake, they begin to function less capably than usual after only 24 hours. After about ten sleepless days, they have trouble carrying out mental and physical tasks, and their judgment and memory deteriorate. If they're kept awake long enough, they may hallucinate and show other signs of mental illness. Enforced sleeplessness also tends to break down willpower and to make people less vigilant and more suggestible. That is why sleep deprivation has often been imposed by unscrupulous police officers trying to extract

What Happens When You Sleep and Dream

There are two principal kinds of sleep, and you normally move from one to the other at 90-minute intervals throughout the night. When you first go to bed, you fall into slow-wave sleep, so named from the fact that brain waves slow down. You gradually drift into a quiet state in which both your temperature and pulse rate drop. This sleep is largely dreamless. Then, approximately 90 minutes after you fall asleep, your blood pressure, pulse, and respiration become irregular. Your ears are tuned for hearing, and your eyes dart back and forth, as if you were watching a movie. In fact, you are dreaming. This is REM (for rapid eye movement) sleep, which is also known as paradoxical sleep because it is unlike the popular idea of sleep as a quiet state. Your brain is as active as when you're awake, and your brain waves resemble those emitted in the daytime. In a normal night, you spend approximately 25 percent of the time in paradoxical sleep.

While you sleep, your brain keeps pulsing with electrical activity.

Brain waves of a person awake

Brain waves in light sleep

Pattern of waves in deep sleep

Brain waves of a person dreaming

By attaching electrodes to a sleeper's head, scientists can record brain waves during different stages of sleep.

confessions, by military interrogators hoping to gain information from wartime prisoners, and by political brainwashers seeking to win converts to their way of thinking.

Why do you dream?

Even if you have never remembered a dream in your life, you would probably do so if a sleep researcher woke you from REM sleep in a laboratory. Some experts estimate that 84 out of 100 people so awakened report a dream in progress. Other authorities say that everyone dreams every night.

In any case, people seem to have a strong need to dream, and it is possible that dreams are important to mental health. If a sleep researcher deprives you of dream sleep for a night by waking you every time you fall into the REM state, you'll feel tired and irritable the next day, even if you have been allowed eight hours of NREM (non-rapid-eye-movement) sleep. And the first chance you get to sleep undisturbed, you'll dream more or less continuously, as though you had a dream quota to meet.

But why should dreaming be essential to well-being? One theory is that dreaming is the brain's way of making sense of the day's events and discarding useless information. Freud's idea, by contrast, was that dreams let people express forbidden wishes in disguised form. Although the neurologist Richard M. Restak by no means accepts all of Freud's theories, he believes that some dreams can give us "creative insight" into the mind, our own and other people's. "Who," Restak asks, "hasn't experienced a prophetic dream, achieved an important insight about another person in a dream, or suddenly discovered a solution to a confusing daytime dilemma in a dream?"

Are people who dream in colour rare?

Even if you believe you dream only in black and white, you could be wrong. Reports of dreams in colour

Nightmares, frightening dreams remembered in detail, occur during dreaming sleep. They are not the same as night terrors, attacks of extreme panic that wake the victim from non-dreaming sleep.

are much more common when sleep researchers awaken people from their REM sleep and ask them for an immediate account of a dream than when the researchers wait until morning to ask their questions. For that reason, some scientists believe that we all dream in colour, even though many of us have forgotten that aspect of our dreams by morning.

What causes insomnia?

Traffic, noisy neighbours, and battered old mattresses are frequently blamed, but among the commonest reasons for insomnia are anxiety and depression. In one study, 70 percent of the people who had trouble sleeping suffered from emotional difficulties. Physical ailments, especially if they cause breathlessness, fever, or pain, can also make it difficult to sleep, and so can the drugs used to treat asthma, high blood pressure, and other diseases. Abuse of common drugs that affect the brain is a factor in many cases of insomnia. In others, the trouble may come from working the night shift, going to bed and getting up at irregular hours, or napping in the daytime.

In the long run, sleeping pills, especially barbiturates, are apt to make insomnia worse rather than

better. There are no pills that foster normal sleep. Some pills abolish the deepest stages of NREM sleep. And most suppress much-needed REM sleep, the kind during which most dreams occur.

What is the opposite of insomnia?

Pity the poor narcoleptic. He is likely to fall asleep at the height of a lively party, in the midst of a conversation with the boss, while driving a car, or even when he's making love to his wife. He suffers from narcolepsy, a disorder in which the victim is subject to sudden, uncontrollable attacks of sleep lasting anywhere from 5 to 20 minutes. While the insomniac cannot fall asleep at night, the narcoleptic cannot stay awake in the daytime. Narcoleptics may have other symptoms, too. They sometimes lose muscle tone suddenly and fall down, and in the few moments between waking and sleeping, they may hallucinate or experience brief paralysis.

The cause of most narcolepsy is not understood, but it seems to have something to do with an inability to inhibit REM, or dreaming, sleep. Most people must sleep for 90 minutes or so before falling into the REM state, but narcoleptics enter it almost as soon as they go to sleep.

Awareness of the World

White-bearded Ivan Pavlov (right) with dog that salivated when a bell rang.

Classical Conditioning: The Simplest Kind of Learning

One basic form of learning takes place outside awareness. In this process, called classical conditioning, the brain learns to associate two hitherto unconnected things. Pavlov, the Russian physiologist, found that if a bell regularly rings just before meat is given to a dog, the animal associates the sound of the bell with the mouth-watering meat and soon salivates at the sound alone. A similar process may explain how we acquire certain preferences. For example, we can be conditioned to like a particular kind of music because we unconsciously associate it with pleasant experiences.

Can you think without words?

In 1865, the German chemist Friedrich Kekulé von Stradonitz spent many hours trying to figure out the molecular structure of benzene, a major scientific mystery at that time. He had a daydream of a snake biting its tail, and from that image he evolved his theory of the so-called benzene ring, an arrangement of atoms linked together in a closed loop. In short, he solved a problem not by thinking about it in words but by contemplating a non-verbal, visual image. In much the same way, Albert Einstein once wrote that he frequently thought not in words but in "more or less clear images" that he manipulated in his mind.

Of course, you don't have to be an Einstein to think without language. You are thinking visually whenever you see something—a familiar view, a loved person, a distant city—in your mind's eye.

Psychological studies show that many people can use visual thinking to accomplish certain tasks. Consider this experiment. Subjects were shown a picture of a car and asked to form a mental picture of it. Once the picture was taken away, they were told to focus their mental gaze on either the front or the back end of the car. Next they were instructed to report whether or not the car had a bonnet ornament. When the subjects were concentrating on the front end of the car, they answered the question quickly. When they were "looking at" the back end, they needed more time to reply: apparently they were scanning their mental image from back to front exactly as if a real car stood before their eyes.

What part of your brain learns?

Most specialists agree that every memory is probably stored repeatedly in different parts of the brain; there is no one centre for learning. Support for this theory comes from studies of people who have lost brain tissue through injury or disease. In such cases, some details of memory may be lost, yet most of what was once learned can still be remembered.

Do you notice most of what happens around you?

Every second, your brain receives countless messages from all parts of your body and the world around you. Usually, you pay almost no attention to any of these perceptual signals. Occasionally, when you are in an unfamiliar or a threatening situation, you will be very alert to such signals.

Most of the time, your attention is highly selective. It's a rare occasion when you think about the sensations created by body processes or by the contact of clothing with your skin. Reading an absorbing novel, or concentrating on a difficult task at work, you don't even hear the blaring radio in the next room or the joking and laughter of fellow workers who have nothing to do at the moment. Overall, the brain ignores more than 99 percent of the messages it receives, and with good reason: most are insignificant, or irrelevant to whatever interests you at the moment.

Why does practice make perfect?

When you repeat something—a phrase at the piano, a tennis stroke, a list of foreign words—it is as if the repetition wore a groove in your brain. Don't take the analogy literally; there's no real groove in the brain. But repetition seems to cause anatomical and chemical changes that fix learned material in your memory and give you easy access to it.

No one is sure what those changes are. It is possible that parts of the neurons where memories are stored grow in size or number. There is also evidence that repeated stimulation of the neurons increases their output of memory-enhancing proteins. And there are indications that these and other changes strengthen the connections between neurons and facilitate the transmission of impulses along certain nerve pathways.

One important point to remember: practice makes for perfect performance only if what you practise is really what you want to remember. If you keep playing one wrong note in the musical phrase, if you keep pronouncing foreign words incorrectly, you will learn your mistakes, and you will find it very difficult to unlearn them subsequently. So be sure you have it right (whatever "it" may be) before you begin repeating it over and over to engrave it on your brain.

Are babies capable of depth perception?

Psychologist Eleanor Gibson had a scare when she visited the Grand Canyon with her psychologist husband and their daughter many years ago. The two-year-old child moved close to the edge of the canyon, and her mother snatched her back anxiously. She wasn't in the least reassured by her husband's insistence that a two-year-old's depth perception is as good as an adult's.

Years later, Dr. Gibson and Dr. Richard Walk conducted the now-famous "visual cliff experiment" to check her husband's assertion. The equipment they devised to create the illusion of a deep chasm is still pictured in textbooks. It was a glass-topped, split-level table with protective sides so an infant set down on the top of it couldn't fall off. Right under the glass on the "shallow" end was a surface with a bold chessboard design. The same design appeared on the floor one metre (40 inches) below

the glass on the "deep" side. The effect was as if the tabletop ended in the middle to create a sharp drop, and the presumption was that if a baby could perceive depth, he or she wouldn't want to venture out onto the glass over the "deep" end, through which the checkered surface could be seen far beneath. To grasp the idea, imagine a sheet of glass over a deep canyon and ask yourself if you'd care to move out onto it, no matter how strong, when you could see the canyon bottom so far below.

In the Gibson-Walk study, 36 babies, from 6½ to 14 months old, were placed, one by one, on the solid-looking "shallow" half of the table while their mothers stood at the "deep" end and urged the babies to come to them. Only three infants dared to crawl over the edge of the "cliff." Some cried because they couldn't reach their mothers, some patted the glass as if to check its solidity, but they backed away nonetheless. The inference: the babies could, indeed, perceive depth.

The Visual Cliff: Judging a Baby's Depth Perception

Most babies can recognize a cliff, yet they don't always heed danger and shouldn't be left alone at a brink. In the study pictured, the baby was safe; the apparent drop was covered with strong glass. Most babies backed away from the illusory cliff. But a few put their weight on the glass, though they clearly did not intend to; depth perception develops faster than physical coordination.

Special apparatus gives an illusion of a sharp drop-off at the baby's left.

How We Store Our Experiences

Why do you forget a telephone number right after looking it up?

There are two kinds of memory, short-term and long-term. Short-term memory holds only 5 to 7 items at a time and lasts a maximum of 60 seconds or so. Long-term memory persists for minutes or years, and its capacity almost defies belief. By one estimate, your brain can store 100 million million bits of information, compared to a thousand million for a computer. Don't let the word *store* confuse you. You don't have anything comparable to a library in your brain; there's no single centre where your memories are filed away. Remembering—one of the most important activities of the human brain—is a function of many parts of the brain, not of any one structure.

To last, a memory has to be consolidated in the brain, a process that requires rehearsal (repetition or study) and usually classification (assignment to a category of related items). Consolidation moves a fact from short-term to long-term storage and is believed to result in a memory trace: an actual alteration in the structure of the brain. A telephone number, unless it's one you call repeatedly, won't make its way into long-term memory. If you get an engaged tone, you'll have to look up the number again, because there's no memory trace of it in your brain.

Our Amazing Capacity to Remember Visual Images

Know the face, but can't remember the name? If this experience sounds familiar, there's a good reason: most people have an ability to remember things they've seen that far surpasses their capacity to recall "linguistic" information—words, numbers, and so on. Indeed, where visual perceptions are concerned, the average person has almost total recall, a fact that leads scientists to believe the brain has separate systems for storing pictorial and linguistic memories. Experiments show that visual images are taken in and preserved directly, while words and other linguistic symbols have to be decoded, sorted, and recoded by the brain. This complex process apparently does not accommodate as much information—which is why there may be scientific truth in the old adage that a picture is worth a thousand words.

In a landmark visual-memory experiment, volunteers were shown 2,560 photographs, one every 10 seconds, followed by 280 pairs of photos projected side-by-side. In each pair was one picture that had already been shown, and another that was similar but not previously seen. When the subjects were asked to identify which one in each pair they had seen before, 85 to 95 percent of their choices were correct.

Why do the elderly remember the past but not the present?

Reminiscing at the age of 91, an actor complained that he had no idea what he had done five weeks before. Yet he hadn't forgotten the role he had played in Shakespeare's *Henry VIII* when he was only 12 or 13. He could still deliver his principal speech, though he had "never looked at it from that day to this."

Several factors contribute to that pattern in the elderly. The ability to acquire new memories often declines in old age, partly because of physical and chemical changes in the brain, partly because, with advancing years, preoccupations change and interest in the present may fall off. At the same time, long-ago memories may sharpen if they have had years to consolidate, leaving indelible memory traces in the brain. This may be especially true if they have been recalled repeatedly over the years because of their special emotional significance.

Why don't you remember the time when you were a baby?

According to one theory, you don't remember much about your early years because at that time you lacked language in which to encode experiences in memory. Another view suggests that in babyhood, your brain structures had not yet developed the capacity to remember. Several researchers have advanced a more complex version of this hypothesis. They believe that the brain may have two kinds of memory circuits, one for retaining explicit facts, like names and faces, and another for preserving less conscious learning, including physical and mental skills. The circuitry for recording specific facts, the researchers say, does not mature in time to capture a child's earliest experiences.

What causes amnesia?

When you think of amnesia, you probably have in mind the kind of memory disturbance screenwriters love. After an emotional shock, the hero forgets his entire past and has no idea who he is—a situation that leads, in the cinema, at least, to wonderfully dramatic complications. In that kind of forgetting, which is rare in real life, the amnesiac forgets for psychological reasons; it is simply too painful to remember who he is.

Most amnesia is caused by physical damage to the brain. It can be either retrograde, in which the victim cannot remember the events that preceded injury, or anterograde, in which memory for events that occurred after the injury is impaired.

The most frequent cause of retrograde amnesia is a jarring blow to the head. The main effect, usually, is that the victim cannot remember what happened in the last hour or so before the blow, because the injured brain never had time to move those recent events from short-term memory into long-term storage.

A common cause of anterograde amnesia, in which a person cannot establish long-term memories of new events, is damage to the hippocampus, a part of the brain deep in the temporal lobes that is vital to memory. In this kind of amnesia, memory of the past remains reasonably intact, and the person may perform well on an intelligence test. Yet normal life is impossible, because each day dawns with no recollection of the day before. The victim cannot keep track of the

Hypnotism was once regarded as a parlour game, as this woman demonstrates. In this induced, sleep-like state, a person is susceptible to suggestion. Some claim hypnosis enhances memory; others say it distorts facts.

simplest events in his life. If he has moved since his injury, he does not know where he lives. He reads the same magazine articles over and over, because he does not remember that he has read them before.

Can you remember better if you're hypnotized?

Hypnosis may help to lift amnesia due to overwhelming emotional trauma, the sort a driver might experience after a crash in which his passengers died. Apart from such cases, though, psychologist John Brown of Bristol University says, there is "no reliable evidence that you can remember under hypnosis what you can't remember normally."

Why can smells evoke powerful memories?

Of all your senses, smell is closest to the hippocampus, one of the brain structures responsible for establishing memories. Smell is also the sense most directly connected to the limbic system, the brain's emotional centre. All your other senses must travel a long, roundabout route to get to the

memory and emotional circuits in the brain. Thus the geography of the brain has a lot to do with the fact that a familiar odour can stir vivid memories from long ago, even from very early childhood, and with them the poignant mix of happiness and longing we call nostalgia.

What is a déjà vu experience?

Déjà vu (French for "already seen") describes those odd moments when it seems as if you were living through an event for the second time. It probably stems from the physiology of the brain. One theory is that in storing an event in memory, a single area of the brain lags behind other parts for an instant. The sense of familiarity is created when that one spot catches up to the rest, processing what other parts have already recorded.

A second hypothesis is that occasionally a particular event in the present activates memory traces of a past experience that has some real or imagined link to the present. If, for example, you longed as a child to visit some romantic, far-off city and pored over pictures of it, your first real visit in adulthood might well give you a sense of déjà vu.

Measuring Human Intelligence

What do tests and teasers show?

In addition to tests that measure achievement—what you have learned—there are tests that measure aptitudes. These generally focus on your ability to solve problems in maths, language, logic, and spatial relations. Tests are often criticized because they do not measure other important qualities such as social skills. But tests are here to stay, and some are fun:

6	2	4
2	?	0
4	0	4

1. **A rule of arithmetic** applies across and down: two numbers in line produce a third. What's the missing number?

2. **Scrambled letters.** A woman arrived home and found a note from her husband. It had been accidentally torn into four pieces, each with four letters on it. The pieces are shown above. What did the message say?

3. **Novel items.** In each row, mark every card that is like the first card in the row. In this kind of test, which does not depend on learned information, the untaught individual has as good a chance of succeeding as an educated person.

4. **Space perception.** Which of the four patterns would result when the box is unfolded? (Clue: note that all three patterns can be seen in one perspective.)

1. The answer is 2. In each vertical and horizontal row, the second number is subtracted from the first.

2. Message reads "WILL COME HOME SOON".

W	C	L	E
O	O	M	E
S	H	M	N

3. First row: B, C, F. Second row: A, C, E.

4. The D answer is the correct one.

What is intelligence?

Though most of us think we recognize intelligence when we encounter it, we might have trouble explaining what it is. As a matter of fact, psychologists have never arrived at a definition that suits all of them. Many are content to say that intelligence is what intelligence tests measure, and while some of these psychologists are just being facetious, others consider that definition more useful than the customary vague formulations.

Of the latter, two are both familiar and typical. In 1905, the French psychologist Alfred Binet, who developed the intelligence test as it is known today, said that "the essential activities of intelligence" are "to judge well, to comprehend well, to reason well." And in 1958, the American psychologist Alfred Wechsler, who devised the widely used Wechsler Adult Intelligence Scale, defined intelligence as "the aggregate or global capacity of the individual to act purposefully, to think rationally, and to deal effectively with his environment."

Is intelligence inherited?

Like all human traits, intelligence is a product of both environment and genes. There is no single gene for intelligence; presumably, a number of genes contribute to it, though no specific ones have been identified. The evidence that heredity plays a major part in intelligence comes from studies showing that the more closely related people are, the more alike their IQ's. Identical twins, who share the same genes, are usually more alike in IQ than other siblings, who share only some of their genes.

One of the major controversies in psychology is the exact importance of heredity. Using complex statistical procedures, some psychologists have concluded that heredity accounts for only 25 percent of the difference in IQ between any two groups of people. Other psychologists say the figure is 80 percent, and you can find someone who cites almost any one of the percentages in between.

Whatever the precise figure for heredity, virtually all authorities agree that environment is also an important determinant of intelligence. People who grow up in the same household, whether or not they are related, are much more alike in IQ than people raised apart. One French study compared two sets of children born to the same group of unskilled workers. In one set, brought up by their mothers, the average IQ was 95; in the other, abandoned by their mothers before the age of six months and adopted by middle-class families, the average was 109. Many other studies also show correlations between IQ and socio-economic status; the higher the one, the higher the other.

Is intelligence one ability, or several?

Underlying nearly all definitions of intelligence is the idea that its essence is a fundamental brightness, or capacity to learn, that has nothing to do with training. Today most psychologists think of intelligence as a group of related abilities, including not only reasoning ability but creativity, insight, perseverance, flexibility, and the speed with which the brain processes information.

Many of the hundreds of intelligence tests now in use reflect the view of intelligence as multifaceted. Some measure just three components of intelligence: verbal, numerical, and reasoning abilities. Others measure such factors as memory span, verbal fluency, spatial perception, and the ability to classify, generalize, and reason by analogy.

Can you raise your IQ?

After the age of seven or so, a person's IQ tends to stay about the same for the rest of his life. There are exceptions. Some studies show changes, attributable at least partly to motivation and other emotional factors, of more than 15 points.

Scientifically sound studies of deliberate efforts to raise IQ are very

rare, and the question of whether or not such efforts can succeed is much disputed because of the acknowledged role of heredity in the determination of intelligence. One scientist who does not believe that IQ is fixed is Stephen Jay Gould. Biologists, he says, know that "heritable" does not mean "inevitable." He elaborates, "Genes do not make specific bits and

pieces of a body; they code for a range of forms under an array of environmental conditions. Moreover, even when a trait has been built and set, environmental intervention may still modify inherited defects. The claim that IQ is so many per cent 'heritable' does not conflict with the belief that enriched education can increase what we call 'intelligence.'"

Genius Under the Microscope

After the death of Albert Einstein in 1955, the body of the great theoretical physicist was cremated—all except his brain. That had been removed, at his request, for study, and scientists have been hoping to find in it some physiological basis for his superb intelligence. In 1985, a researcher announced that Einstein's brain had more glial cells than most brains. But glial cells do not produce thoughts, and they proliferate, like scar tissue, in old age, so they probably do not explain Einstein's creativity.

Even a powerful lens does not seem to reveal the nature of intelligence. Says one pathologist of Einstein's brain: "It looks just like anybody else's."

The Power of Moods and Emotions

How close are laughter and tears?

People often become misty-eyed at weddings, family reunions, or even after a hearty laugh. At other times, people will grin and bear it when they hear unpleasant news.

Although crying and laughing represent two extremes of emotional expression, they involve many of the same brain circuits and muscles. How do we know this? Some patients suffering from brain damage, often to the frontal lobes, lose voluntary control over emotional expression. For these unfortunate patients, social customs and inhibitions acquired over a lifetime can no longer restrain their feelings. Greeting an acquaintance may cause unusual weeping, and a simple joke may cause loud and prolonged laughter. In extreme cases, crying changes into laughter, and vice versa, for no apparent reason, and the patient cannot express any intermediate emotion. Imagine the dismay, when a grieving widow, overcome with emotion, began laughing uncontrollably at her husband's funeral. What do these people actually feel, when caught up in a fit of crying or laughter? The widow felt sad, when asked about her laughter. At other times, a trivial remark may bring on an emotional outburst without any bearing on the patient's true inner feelings.

Can your emotions make you ill?

Statistics show that the incidence of illness and death in people whose spouses have died is higher than in the general population. The reason, some scientists believe, is that when a person is under great stress, the brain impairs the ability of the immune system to fight off illness. Studies have already demonstrated a link between the brain and the immune system in animals, and recent research is beginning to suggest a similar connection in human beings.

When is depression a sign of mental illness?

Feeling sad or frightened is a normal response to stress. The depression people suffer when someone they love dies lets them withdraw from the outside world for a time while they rebuild their inner lives. Anxiety heightens the response to crises and fosters the strength of purpose and single-mindedness needed to cope with an illness, a lost job, or a shaky marriage. In all such cases, the mind's perception of reality is accurate, the emotional response appropriate, and the mood, however painful, is conducive to eventual recovery.

Depression and anxiety are abnormal whenever they do not reflect the way things really are, do not lead anywhere, and fail to go away no matter what good things happen. Disproportionate gloom or worry warrants medical attention.

What causes anger to reach dangerous levels?

Violence is often linked either to a tumour or to some other abnormality in the brain. There is some evidence that aggression is sometimes related to a deficiency in the amount of neurotransmitter serotonin produced by the brain. And the drug PCP, popularly called angel dust, is known to cause changes in the brain that can lead to rage, self-mutilation, and violent murder.

None of this means that all violence stems from brain abnormalities; given the level of aggression in the world, we can hardly imagine that all of it comes from brain dysfunction. As a matter of fact, under ordinary circumstances, the cerebral cortex, the thinking part of the brain, usually curbs the direct expression of people's aggressive impulses. A large body of research suggests that environmental causes—in particular, television and movie violence—play a significant role in violence. Efforts to discover hereditary tendencies to violent behaviour have not produced persuasive evidence.

THE STORY BEHIND THE WORDS...

Somnambulism, or sleepwalking, stems from Somnus, the Roman god of sleep, and is one of many English words derived from classical mythology. Somnambulism combines *somnus,* "sleep," and *ambulare,* "to walk." Related words include *somniloquy,* which means talking in one's sleep and blends *somnus* with *loqui; somniferous,* "inducing sleep"; *somnolent,* "feeling sleepy"; and *insomnia,* "without sleep."

Hypnosis is derived from the name of the Greek god of sleep, Hypnos, and is sometimes defined as "a sleep-like condition." According to legend, Hypnos inhabited a dark cave. There, lulled by the waters of Lethe, the river of forgetfulness that ran through the cave, he slept on a soft couch. *Lethargy,* which means drowsiness or sluggishness, stems from Lethe.

Sleeping like a log suggests total immobility, and many people claim they never moved from sleeping to waking. In fact, laboratory studies prove that everyone tosses and turns throughout the night. It's a good thing they do; complete immobility would be very bad for the circulation.

Trance is derived from the Latin *transire,* which means to die, or, literally, "to go across." A trance is an abnormal mental condition, a dissociation of consciousness like that caused by a blow to the head. In some cultures, a trance state is deliberately induced by drugs, special breathing exercises, fasting, drumming and dancing, or other rites.

Genius is extraordinary mental capacity, often reflected in great creative achievement in the arts or sciences. While environmental factors, such as health and upbringing, influence the development of innate ability, the potential for genius is inherited. The words *genius* and *genes* stem from the same Greek root, *gignesthai,* which means to be born.

Insanity: From Chains to Tranquilizers

In his attitude towards mental illness, the Spanish reformer Juan Luis Vives was ahead of his time. "One ought to feel compassion for so great a disaster to the health of the human mind," he wrote in 1525. For centuries before and after that date, the prevailing view was quite different. Among North American Indians and in some parts of the Orient, madness was sometimes regarded as a divine visitation to be tolerated. But mental derangement was much more commonly seen as the result of possession by demons or as punishment for moral depravity, and victims were imprisoned, chained, tortured, or burned alive. Until the 19th century, mental patients were often publicly exhibited for a fee. Not until the 1950s did scientists find drugs that would alleviate the symptoms of mental disorder.

Funnel identifies a quack surgeon (above) operating on a 16th-century mental patient. A victim of madness (below) is treated in a whirling chair.

Ancient superstition held that moonlight causes lunacy (from Luna, Roman goddess of the moon). Mentally ill or moonstruck women (above) dance in a town square of the 1600s.

When Philippe Pinel, a doctor, unshackled mental patients in 18th-century Paris asylums (left), his superior asked, "Are you not yourself mad to free these beasts?" But Pinel was convinced that kindness could have "the most favourable effect on the insane."

Injury and Aftermath

Can alcohol harm your brain?

Every time you drink, it has been alleged, you kill 100,000 brain cells. The allegation is untrue. In fact, there is no evidence that moderate drinking damages the brain. But many people drink immoderately. Those people have reason to fear that their excess drinking will damage both their livers and their brains.

The diet of alcoholics is often deficient in B-complex vitamins, a lack that eventually causes destruction of brain cells. Years of alcoholism can lead to Korsakoff's syndrome, a mental disorder in which the brain cannot establish new memories and in which some victims confabulate, or fill in memory gaps with "recollections" of events that never happened. Alcoholism can also lead to degeneration of the cerebellum, the part of the brain that governs balance and posture; to polyneuropathy, meaning nerve damage, with eventual loss of sensation and strength; and to Wernicke's disease, characterized by paralysis of eye movement, a stumbling walk, and mental deterioration.

Are your thoughts and emotions independent of each other?

It was a miracle Phineas Gage did not die. On September 13, 1848, while he was blasting rock on a Vermont railroad line, exploding gunpowder drove a tamping iron into his face under the left eye. The force of the explosion sent the rod up through his brain and out through his shattered skull at about the place where hair and forehead meet. Astonishingly, Gage made a complete physical recovery and lived for another dozen years.

Psychologically, however, he was a changed man: "no longer Gage," people said. Once emotionally well balanced, he became obstinate, capricious, impatient of anything that went against his wishes, and given to outbursts of profanity.

It was the frontal lobes of Gage's brain that were destroyed, a part of the brain about which neuroscientists had previously known little. The Gage case gave brain specialists the first clear evidence they had ever had that thoughts and emotions are closely related, and that they are so because of actual physical connections between the limbic system (the principal emotional centre in the brain) and other brain structures.

From this case and later studies, it now appears that the frontal lobes enable us to control our emotions. Damage to the lobes and destruction of their links to the limbic system bring about chemical and electrical

Of Crickets, Flutes, and Other Fearful Things

One of the oddest cases described by the ancient Greek physician Hippocrates was that of Nicanor: at banquets, the music of flutes filled him with terror. That kind of irrational fear—of anything you can name, from crickets to flowers—is called a phobia, after the Greek god Phobos, noted for provoking fear in his enemies. Phobias are common mental disorders, and disabling, too, because phobics will do anything to avoid the object of their panic: walk up 15 flights of stairs for fear of lifts, or stay indoors for years just to avoid open spaces. Simple measures, such as relaxation techniques to counter anxiety, can cure as many as 85 percent of all phobics.

Phobias are named after the Greek or Latin of what is feared. Gephyrophobia: fear of bridges.

Acrophobia: heights	Anthropophobia: people	Claustrophobia: closed spaces	Nyctophobia: darkness
Aerophobia: flying	Aquaphobia: water	Cynophobia: dogs	Ochlophobia: crows
Agoraphobia: open spaces	Arachnophobia: spiders	Herpetophobia: reptiles	Ornithophobia: birds
Ailurophobia: cats	Astraphobia: lightning	Mikrophobia: germs	Thanatophobia: death
Amaxophobia: vehicles, driving	Brontophobia: thunder	Murophobia: mice	Xenophobia: strangers

changes in many parts of the brain, and thus alter the way people experience and express their emotions.

Do all your nerves feel pain?

Nerves are not generalists but specialists. That is, no nerve can do everything; particular kinds of nerves are designed to carry out certain functions. One such function, an important one because it lets you know that something is wrong with your body, is sensitivity to pain. The special nerve endings that pick up pain signals are called pain receptors, and there are millions of them. They are of three different types, each of which responds to a different sort of tissue damage: that caused by mechanical stress, such as a cut or blow; by heat; or by certain chemicals.

Pain receptors of all three types are widely distributed in the outer layers of the skin and in such internal tissues as muscles, tendons, joints, and parts of the skull. Deep in the body, pain receptors are fewer, but you can still feel pain from within.

How many kinds of pain are there?

Cramping, throbbing, nauseating, sharp: those are just a few of the adjectives sufferers have used to describe the kind of pain they were feeling. But some physiologists say that pain generally falls into one of three categories: pricking, burning, or aching. Other physiologists speak of just two kinds of pain. What they call "first pain" is described as quick, sharp, and easy to localize: you know just where you hurt. "Second pain," they say, is diffuse, nagging, and particularly hard to bear. When you experience second pain, you may have a hard time telling just where it originates; nearly always, however, it comes from deep inside the body.

First pain is transmitted to the spinal cord and then to the brain by so-called fast fibres that move signals along at the rate of 6 to 30 metres (20 to 100 feet) a second. Second pain is transmitted by "slow fibres," along

The death mask and skull of Phineas Gage suggest the terrible brain damage caused by a rod driven through his head. The accident destroyed his personality, yet he survived for 12 years and even worked for a while.

which signals move at only 0.5 to 2 metres (1.5 to 6 feet) a second to the spinal cord. In the brain, all pain signals reach the thalamus first; that structure makes you aware that signals from a few scattered pain receptors in an internal organ can add up to some of the worst pain a person can experience.

What is your pain threshold?

A stubbed toe that sends your bare-footed friend hopping and howling may make you do nothing more than rub your toe for a moment and then walk on. There are two possible reasons for the difference between you and your friend: either your pain threshold is higher, or your tolerance for pain is greater.

Your pain threshold is the least intense stimulus (the least forceful blow, say, or the briefest contact with the dentist's drill) that feels painful to you. Laboratory studies of such diverse groups as Eskimos, Indians, and Caucasians suggest that most people have roughly the same pain threshold. With a heat lamp used to

raise the temperature of the skin gradually, most people first report sensations of pain when their skin reaches 45° C (113° F). (Not surprisingly, that is the temperature at which heat begins to damage body tissues.) Practically everyone reports feeling pain before the temperature rises to 47° C (116.6° F).

However, people differ in their reactions to pain. What seems intolerable to one person may not bother another, even though both feel pain. And while pain causes anguish, depression, nausea, and tears in some people, others exhibit no such effects. Tolerance for pain may vary with circumstances and psychological state, even in the same person. If you should stub your toe while running from a fierce dog or an armed robber, it probably wouldn't hurt at all. In hospitals, medical personnel have discovered that preoperative psychological preparation seems to reduce postoperative pain: patients who are told in advance how much pain to expect and just how they are likely to feel for how long generally need fewer painkillers after surgery than do unprepared patients.

Coping With Pain

Can stress relieve pain?

In the 1850s, the Scottish explorer David Livingstone described his feelings when a lion attacked him: "He caught my shoulder as he sprang, and we both came to the ground. ...Growling horribly close to my ear, he shook me as a terrier does a rat. The shock...caused a sort of dreaminess in which there was no sense of pain nor feeling of terror."

Livingstone's reaction was not unlike that of soldiers observed a century later during World War II. At Anzio beachhead in Italy, field surgeons marvelled at the apparent fortitude of the many badly wounded men, among them a youth, his arm shattered, who talked calmly to doctors and gave no sign that he was in pain or mental distress. At first, doctors theorized that such soldiers seemed oblivious to pain simply because they were glad to be alive. But many years—and scientific experiments—later, pain specialists came to recognize that Livingstone and the young soldier at Anzio were experiencing what is now called stress-induced analgesia: pain relief that results from extreme stress.

The explanation for this phenomenon is that the brain at times manufactures its own opiates. These pain relievers and mood elevators are of two types, called endorphins and enkephalins. Both kinds are similar to morphine—but much more powerful. Why, then, is pain one of the major problems in medicine? Because in most cases the body's natural narcotics do not obliterate pain; they seem to produce their most dramatic effects only under conditions of extreme stress.

What is the difference between local and general anaesthesia?

Hundreds of years ago, Arab doctors hit on the idea of anaesthetizing a patient's arm by packing it in snow. And in many parts of the world, before chemical anaesthetics were developed, wartime surgeons numbed a surgical patient's limb by pressing on a nearby nerve. (You know the effect if you have ever lain in one position so long that an arm "goes to sleep.") These techniques are early versions of local anaesthesia, which means loss of sensation in one part of the body without any loss of consciousness.

Today, doctors use a variety of methods to bring about local anaesthesia, but the most common way is to inject one of a number of chemicals close to the area to be operated on. Local anaesthetics work by blocking the transmission of pain impulses so that they cannot reach the brain; the brain itself is unaffected.

General anaesthetics, by contrast, put much of the nervous system out of action, obliterating consciousness and preventing the brain from perceiving pain. General anaesthetics can be gases, which the patient inhales, or liquids, which are injected. There are three stages of general anaesthe-

---

Is acupuncture witchcraft or science?

For at least 2,500 years, Chinese practitioners have been inserting needles into the human body at certain designated points and twirling them to bring relief from illness and pain. A series of pathways (called meridians) crisscross the body, each named after a particular internal organ. Of the 360 or so strategic points, most are far from the area they are believed to influence. For example, to relieve menstrual pains, a needle is inserted into point Liver 8 (located inside the knee). This technique, called acupuncture, was traditionally said to work

by bringing about a balance of certain "life forces." Among Western doctors, attitudes towards acupuncture range from outright scorn to acceptance by a minority. Scientists dismiss the mystical explanations, but some think that a number of the benefits are real. The preliminary research seems to show that puncturing the body with needles can cause the release of endorphins, the body's natural painkillers. In 1986 a British Medical Association report concluded that there is a scientific basis for claims that acupuncture is effective as a means of relieving pain for a small proportion of patients. The American Medical Association says the technique is as yet unproved, but it allows credit for the courses in acupuncture taught at several reputable medical schools. At the global level, the World Health Organization recognizes acupuncture as a treatment for several conditions, including sciatica, osteoarthritis, and ulcers.

Acupuncture points are carefully noted along the meridians on this 19th-century Japanese papier-mâché figure. In their adaptation of the Chinese methodology, the Japanese identified 660 points.

PRESCRIPTION FOR SCOLDING WIVES.

London Pub.ed by T. McLean, 26, Haymarket. Jan 1. 1830.

"Laughing gas," or nitrous oxide, discovered in 1772 by English scientist Joseph Priestley, was once regarded as a novelty. In this 1830 print, it is used to induce euphoria. Use of gas to prevent pain was not tried until the 1840s.

sia: the analgesic stage, a dreamlike period; the excitation stage, when the patient is unconscious but restless; and the tolerance stage, when major surgery is performed.

Are you aware of anything while you're under a general anaesthetic?

Until recently, just about everyone assumed that an anaesthetized, unconscious patient had no idea of what was going on while he was in the operating room. That is no longer a safe assumption. Henry Bennett, a psychologist at the University of California Medical School, and other researchers, have now discovered that unconscious patients can hear. As a result, Bennett has warned that careless remarks in the operating room—a doctor's comment that surgery is not going well, for instance—might distress a patient or hamper his recovery. But there are also indications that an appropriate suggestion could help an unconscious patient.

What is the evidence? In one study,

a tape played in the operating room asked patients to indicate that they had heard the recorded message by touching their ears during an interview that would take place after the operation. Later, the patients did just that, though they did not consciously remember hearing the tape. In another study, patients undergoing back surgery were told while they were unconscious that they would have no trouble urinating afterwards (sometimes a problem)—and they did not.

What are pain clinics?

You may be miserable when you're in acute pain, but at least you know it won't last forever, and your doctor is usually successful in treating both the pain and its underlying cause. Chronic pain (which can affect any part of the body) is different. Its origin is uncertain; it persists for months or even years despite efforts to relieve it; and its physical and emotional effects disrupt the lives of millions of sufferers and their families. To ease the

desperate plight of these people, pain clinics have been opened throughout the world.

The best clinics, often affiliated with hospitals and research institutions, use the services of a dozen or more specialists, including neurologists, radiotherapists, physiotherapists, and psychiatrists. Although clinic doctors frequently prescribe pain-relieving drugs, the emphasis is on other kinds of treatment, because many patients (with the unintentional help of doctors) have compounded their physical and psychological troubles by taking too many drugs in the past. Among the techniques the pain specialists use are hypnosis, relaxation, and psychotherapy. They may also prescribe TENS, the usual abbreviation for through-the-skin electrical nerve stimulation. This treatment makes use of battery-powered generators taped to the painful area and controlled by the patient. A related method is brain stimulation through electrodes implanted in the brain and activated by the patient with a handheld transmitter.

Disorders of the Brain

Is a headache a pain in the brain?

In order to understand headaches, you have to understand two phenomena. One is the brain's insensitivity to pain; brain tissue rarely hurts, not even when a surgeon's knife cuts into it. The other is referred pain, pain that arises in one part of the body but feels as if it came from another part.

Headaches are referred pain. The surface of your head hurts, but the tissues that are actually causing your pain are somewhere else. They may be inside the skull or outside it, and are usually stretched nerve endings in the walls of dilated blood vessels. You can get a headache from general fatigue or from emotional stress; from consuming too much caffeine or from suddenly giving it up; and from a host of other causes. It is reassuring to know that in most cases, a headache is not a sign of serious illness.

What are the symptoms of a brain tumour?

If you have a throbbing headache, the first thing you may think of is a brain tumour—yet that is ordinarily one of the last things you need worry about. Much more common early symptoms of a growth in the brain are dizzy spells, weakness in an arm or a leg, an uncertain gait, slurred speech, or loss of vision or hearing. But persistent headaches in someone who has rarely suffered from them in the past are suspect, especially if they get worse when the person lies down, or if they come on first thing in the morning and then go away. As a tumour grows, frequent headaches are likely. Mental deterioration becomes apparent only in advanced stages.

When a growth is in the brain, the distinction between benign and malignant tumours is less meaningful than usual, because there is no room in the skull for any growth to expand harmlessly; even a benign tumour can eventually compress and damage the brain tissue. Surgical treatment is complicated by the fact that in order to reach a growth, brain tissue may have to be destroyed; much depends on just where in the brain the tumour lies. In other cases, even partial removal, or radiation treatment, or both, can bring years of normal life.

What is Alzheimer's disease?

Alzheimer's disease is a disorder of the brain's neurotransmitters, the chemicals that enable the brain to send and receive messages. Victims sooner or later come to forget everything, including how to cook, drive, tell time, even tie their shoelaces. Ultimately, the disease leads to coma and death. In Britain, it affects about 6 percent of those over 65. This means that while there are millions of victims, most people will never be affected. Alzheimer's is not a result of the normal aging process, and it can strike people in their 40s and 50s.

How is schizophrenia manifested?

"I may be a 'Blue Baby' but 'Social Baby' not, but yet a blue heart baby could be in the Blue Book published before the war." Written by a schizophrenic, this is typical of the bizarre disturbances of thought, emotion, and perception that characterize schizophrenia, the most common of the serious psychiatric disorders.

The untreated schizophrenic lives in a fantasy world. He may suffer from hallucinations, or false perceptions; he may hear non-existent voices. The schizophrenic may also suffer from delusions, or false ideas, perhaps claiming to be some long-dead historical figure, or voicing the belief that someone is persecuting him. In one kind of schizophrenia, a patient may hold a single position—a squatting posture, say, or a dramatic, statue-like pose—for hours at a time. The emotional reactions of schizophrenics tend to be inappropriate; patients may be terrified, or enraged, by a seemingly trivial event, or may show indifference to a tragic one.

Schizophrenia has afflicted all societies in all ages. As to its cause, there is little agreement, but many specialists believe that the disorder results from an inherited predisposition triggered by environmental stress. Many studies suggest that there are abnormalities, not fully understood as yet, in the way the brains of schizophrenics manufacture neurotransmitters.

DID YOU KNOW...?

- **Meditation is a relaxing form of concentration.** You take a comfortable position in quiet surroundings and focus on a word that has no emotional meaning for you. By silently repeating the word to yourself (or focusing on an image), you exclude all other thoughts. Thus you gain relief from stress.

- **Daydreams are reveries,** moments of fantasy, and have nothing to do with real dreams. We all daydream from time to time, especially while riding in trains or listening to lectures. Many creative people are avowed daydreamers; inspiration may come while the brain is "idling." But it is easy to overdo these pleasant moments of wish fulfilment, and for some, daydreams are an unhealthy escape from reality. A study of old people has found that daydreams decrease with age.

- **Even when you sleep,** your brain consumes 20 percent of the oxygen that your body takes in. Waking or sleeping, the brain is always functioning. Thus it never rests — and doesn't need to.

- **By one estimate,** we use about 15 percent of our brain capacity. The evidence for this is indirect. For one thing, there are thousands of millions of cells in the brain. For another, there are cases of people who have lost brain tissue and have made remarkable recoveries. Thus there must be reserve cells in the brain.

- **Researchers are working on the possibility** of transplanting healthy brain tissue into diseased brains. The brain is what doctors call a "privileged site"; it is less likely than other organs to reject transplanted tissue. One of the diseases for which such transplants might prove effective is Parkinson's disease.

After a Stroke, New Roles for Some Brain Cells

Brain cells that have been destroyed by a stroke do not regenerate. Nevertheless, some stroke victims eventually regain many of their lost abilities. Such remarkable recoveries generally occur because functions once performed by stroke-damaged parts of the brain are taken over by other parts. Brain cells are surprisingly plastic; they can often learn new roles, even though it may take them quite a while to do so. A series of self-portraits by the German artist Anton Räderscheidt provides a dramatic example of recovery after a stroke. His cerebral accident seriously damaged the part of the brain responsible for visual attention, that is, for determining what a person notices. People with damage in that area tend to ignore the left half of their visual world, even though they can still see it perfectly well. When Räderscheidt did a self-portrait soon after suffering his stroke, he paid no attention at all to half his face. But as his recovery progressed, his view of himself expanded.

Anton Räderscheidt as a well man.

Painted two months after the stroke, this self-portrait omits half of his face.

Räderscheidt's next self-portrait was done three and a half months after the stroke.

In the third self-portrait, the artist's view of himself was more nearly complete.

The final portrait, filling the canvas, was painted nine months after the stroke.

How do we know the right brain is more emotional than the left?

Some stroke victims dismiss their paralysis as unimportant, and are mistakenly judged to be stoics; others actually deny their disability. Interestingly, both the seeming stoics and the outright deniers are all suffering from left-side paralysis, which means that their stroke damaged the right side of the brain. Their emotionally inappropriate reaction comes from this damage and suggests that the right brain is more concerned with emotion than the left. That idea is reinforced by the fact that victims of right-side paralysis—with a damaged left hemisphere—are likely to show signs of depression.

The emotional behaviour of stroke victims is only one of many indications that there is a connection between emotion and the right hemisphere. In one study, researchers showed films of mutilating surgery to subjects wearing special contact lenses that blocked sight on one side or the other. When the films were viewed from the left side (interpreted exclusively by the right brain), the subjects reported being much more upset than when the films were seen on the right side (by the left brain). The right brain's more emotional response was confirmed by measurements of the heart rate, which fluctuated most when the right brain was the viewer.

73

Chapter 3

THE ENDOCRINE SYSTEM

In dire emergencies, energy surges within us like a jolt of electricity. It is only at such times of toe-curling fear and stress that we are aware of the effects of endocrine hormones. More often, their potent influence on body functions is far too subtle for us to perceive.

The Mysterious Organs	76
The Master Glands	78
Giants, Dwarfs, and Variations in Growth	79
The Influence of Hormones on Growth	80
Sex and the Life Cycle	82
How We Respond to Fear and Stress	84
Energy Control, Sugar Balance	86

What are hormones?

If someone asked you to name the body's two major control systems, you could certainly come up with at least half the answer: the nervous system. But it wouldn't be surprising if you didn't know the second half: the endocrine system. Many people have scarcely heard of the small, oddly shaped glands in widely separated regions of the body that make up most of the endocrine system. The nervous and endocrine systems interact, and both are vitally important to your physical and mental health because, together, they coordinate most body functions.

Both the systems are great communications networks. The nervous system transmits its messages by means of electrochemical impulses, which travel quickly to the muscles and glands. The endocrine system employs chemical messengers called hormones, which move through the bloodstream, and can reach every cell in the body. Their effect can be rapid or delayed.

Hormones help maintain a constant environment inside the body, adjusting the amount of salt and water in your tissues, sugar in your blood, and salt in your sweat to suit the particular conditions around you. Hormones produce both long-term changes, such as a child's growth and sexual maturation, and rhythmic ones, such as the menstrual cycle. They trigger swift, dramatic responses in the body whenever illness or injury strikes or your brain perceives danger. And they have a lot to do with such powerful emotions as fear and anger, joy and despair.

What causes jet lag?

If you have travelled anywhere distant enough to take you out of your customary time zone, you know the symptoms of jet lag: fatigue, insomnia, and a sluggish, out-of-sorts feeling. The reason for these effects is that major changes in your schedule of waking, eating, and sleeping put your external life at odds with your internal body cycles. These circadian rhythms, as they are called, are essentially biological clocks, or pacemakers, that govern regular fluctuations in alertness, sleepiness, temperature, metabolism, and other body functions. Body clocks get important cues from the natural shifts in daylight and darkness, but once set, they tend to keep running more or less independently of outside cues.

Can you do anything about jet lag? Some doctors suggest that if your trip lasts only a day or two, your best bet is to try to work, eat, and sleep by your hometown clock. On longer trips, you will probably feel better sooner if you begin living by local time at once so that your internal clocks will reset themselves as quickly as possible.

Incidentally, the term *circadian*—Latin for "about a day"—was chosen to describe body rhythms because many cycles are approximately 24 hours in length; however, some cycles repeat themselves at intervals of hours or weeks. All such cycles are apparently regulated by a kind of master clock in the hypothalamus.

Ignoring circadian rhythms can be more than just uncomfortable. Changes from day to night shift may reduce productivity and have been blamed for accidents, especially if schedules change weekly instead of at longer intervals. And studies show that certain drugs, including some used to slow blood clotting or to treat cancer, are more effective when taken at certain times of the day.

Why do some athletes take steroids?

"Winning isn't everything," a famous football coach once said. "It's the only thing." Plenty of sports enthusiasts agree. In recent years, increasing numbers of young athletes have been risking their health and even their lives by taking anabolic steroids in the hope of gaining an edge over their competitors. The irony of it is that while the risks are real, the benefits may very well be illusory.

The anabolic steroids that some athletes take to build up muscle and

Why do people like to frighten themselves? *During a roller coaster ride, the sensation of racing headlong towards a precipitous fall turns on the body's "get ready for danger" hormones, from the adrenal gland. But even as the heart thumps with fear, the knowledge that no harm will come stimulates the brain to feel relief. A fright is transformed into a thrill.*

enhance aggressiveness are synthetic variants of testosterone, which is the hormone responsible for the development of secondary sex characteristics and the increase of muscle mass in male adolescents. Doctors will sometimes prescribe anabolic steroids to speed healing after surgery or to counter bone thinning in elderly women. The bodies of such patients are deficient in natural steroids, and the synthetics can help. But the bodies of athletes already secrete normal amounts of steroids, and some doctors say that there is no evidence to prove that supplements improve performance.

However, there is one thing that is not in doubt: taken in large quantities over long periods of time, anabolic steroids can have very grave side effects. They can stunt growth. They can damage the liver, perhaps even causing cancer. They are linked to strokes and heart disease. They sometimes stop the natural production of testosterone, resulting in atrophied testicles and infertility. In women, they can disrupt the menstrual cycle and may lead to masculine-looking muscles, a deep voice, excessive facial hair, and baldness.

Does eating a lot of sugar cause diabetes?

Children who gorge on sweets are more likely to develop tooth decay than diabetes. Nevertheless, there is at least the possibility—neither proved nor disproved as yet—that excess sugar may precipitate diabetes in people genetically predisposed to that disease.

The evidence of a link between sugar consumption and the onset of diabetes is conflicting. Laboratory rats with an inherited tendency to diabetes are more likely to develop it on a high-sugar diet than on a sugar-free one. Residents of Yemen, where diabetes is rare and the diet is low in sugar, frequently become both diabetic and obese if they emigrate to Israel, where sugar consumption is high. Yet some populations eat large quantities of sugar without becoming either overweight or diabetic. In any case, it is possible to be thin and diabetic, or fat and non-diabetic; 40 to 50 percent of people who are obese show no signs of the disease. Those who have already been diagnosed as diabetic must generally avoid sweets and sugared soft drinks.

The Mysterious Organs

How did the endocrine system get its name?

The glands in your body fall into two main groups, exocrine and endocrine. Both words are derived from the Greek: *exo* means "outside" and *endo*, "inside." Exocrine glands secrete their products into ducts, or channels, that carry them either to the outside of the body or into body cavities. Examples are the salivary glands and the sweat glands. Endocrine glands empty their products—hormones—inside the body. They have no ducts; instead, their secretions flow directly into the bloodstream. They are also known by two alternate names: the ductless glands and the glands of internal secretion. Among others, they include the pituitary, the thyroid, the adrenals, and the testes.

You have one gland that performs both exocrine and endocrine functions: the pancreas, which has been described as two unrelated organs in one. Most parts of the pancreas put out exocrine secretions that are carried by duct to the intestine, where they promote digestion. But scattered throughout the pancreas are the islets of Langerhans, microscopic groups of endocrine cells that manufacture insulin and other hormones. The number of these endocrine islands has been estimated at from 200,000 to 1,800,000.

How many hormones does your body make?

Not so long ago, scientists believed that there were about 40 hormones. Today, they count 100 or more, and tomorrow, the total may be even higher, because researchers keep finding new ones. It is already known that the digestive system manufactures at least five hormones. The ovaries secrete half a dozen different oestrogens, the pituitary and the hypothalamus together produce some 16 hormones of various types, and the adrenals at least 30 steroid hormones.

Why is a hormone molecule like a key?

Since blood travels to every part of the body, you might suppose that all the hormones in the bloodstream would affect all body tissues, but they don't. Each hormone can transmit its message only to certain target cells that have special receptors capable of recognizing that particular hormone. In a way, hormone molecules are similar to keys made so they fit some locks but not others, and receptors are like locks shaped to admit only certain keys. For instance, oxytocin, which causes the uterus to contract in childbirth, exerts no effect on most body tissues. But some hormone "keys" fit receptor "locks" in many different kinds of tissue; those hormones exert widespread effects.

The word *hormone* was coined from the Greek word for "excite" in 1905, but we now know that hormones can inhibit as well as stimulate body processes. Specifically, hormones act by turning off, or on, the genes for a special function, or by slowing down, or speeding up, the rate at which target cells perform their normal functions. Some hormones produce short-lived effects within seconds of their release; others act more slowly and create long-lasting effects.

What prevents a healthy gland from secreting too much hormone?

The amount of each hormone circulating in your blood is usually just about the quantity you need at that particular moment, because hormone production rises or falls as your requirements change. How is this possible? The answer lies in "feedback mechanisms," which regulate hormone production by feeding information about the body's current needs to the endocrine glands.

In a negative feedback system, the presence in your blood of an abnormally large amount of a hormone or other substance inhibits production of that hormone. For example, when large quantities of calcium are circu-

Early Theories: THE PINEAL GLAND AND THE HUMAN SOUL

To the French philosopher René Descartes, the pineal gland was the place where mind and body meet; to many early thinkers, it was nothing less than the seat of the soul. Shaped like a pinecone, this tiny structure remains largely a mystery. But today, scientists agree that it serves as a kind of internal clock. Though buried in darkness, it responds indirectly to light: messages about how bright or dark it is in the outside world are relayed to the gland from the eyes. As daylight fades to darkness, the pineal switches on and begins to secrete a hormone called melatonin. As day dawns, melatonin production stops. Thus in winter, when nights are long, melatonin production is high; in summer, when nights are short, production is low. Could it be that the pineal is the source of seasonal mood changes? Perhaps this gland accounts for spring fever as the days lengthen.

This woodcut, from a 1686 work by Descartes, illustrates his belief in a link between the eyes and the pineal gland.

lating in your bloodstream, their presence causes the parathyroid glands to secrete less parathyroid hormone. Large amounts of certain other hormones in the blood slow or stop their own secretion for a while.

In a positive feedback system, the presence of a hormone stimulates, instead of inhibiting, hormone production. Small amounts of oestrogen in the blood are needed to stimulate a hormone, which, in turn, allows ovulation (production of an egg) to occur.

What kinds of things do hormones do for you?

Scientists have isolated some hormones without discovering the specific part they play in keeping your internal environment constant. But it is clear that hormones are amazingly diverse in function. Here are just a few examples.

Growth hormone, or somatotrophin, secreted by the pituitary gland, is responsible (often via other hormones) for the development of the bones, muscles, and other organs.

The hormones manufactured in the adrenals have a host of functions to perform—among them, hormones help keep blood pressure normal and make it easier to cope with stress.

Glucagon, produced by the pancreas, raises the level of sugar in the blood when it gets low. This is a vital function for several reasons, including the fact that if you don't eat for some time, your brain is threatened by a shortage of an essential nutrient, the form of sugar called glucose.

Parathormone, produced by the parathyroid glands (which are embedded in the thyroid gland), raises the blood-calcium level by inhibiting the excretion of calcium from the body, promoting its absorption from the digestive tract, and fostering its release from the bones. That last function may sound odd. But an adult's body contains about 1 kilogram (2 pounds) of calcium, 99 percent of it in the bones, the rest in the bloodstream. And calcium is important not only for bones and teeth but also for such processes as nerve func-

The Control Centres of the Body's Processes

Various functions and rhythms of the human body are controlled by hormones, which might be defined as chemical messengers. Most of these hormones are produced by the major endocrine glands, shown here. But several other organs also manufacture hormones: the stomach, liver, intestines, kidneys, and heart all contain groups of hormone-secreting cells.

HYPOTHALAMUS controls pituitary secretions, body temperature, also hunger, thirst, and sex drives

PITUITARY GLAND controls bone growth and regulates activity in the other endocrine glands

PINEAL GLAND is believed to be the body's internal clock

THYROID GLAND controls rate of fuel use in the body and body development. PARATHYROIDS (embedded in the thyroid) control the level of calcium in the blood

THYMUS controls the production of a type of infection-fighting white blood cell in children (no known function in adults)

ADRENAL GLANDS control salt and water balance in the body and help prepare the body for emergencies

PANCREAS controls the level of sugar in the blood

OVARIES in females control sexual development and the production of eggs

TESTES in males control sexual development and the production of sperm

tion, muscle contraction, blood clotting, and glandular secretion. When you don't get enough calcium in your diet, the body takes it from your bones. When there is too little calcium in the bones, they can fracture spontaneously. Too much calcium in the blood leads to the formation of kidney stones and the weakening of muscle tone, while too little causes

twitching, spasms, convulsions, and even death.

A final example: vasopressin from the pituitary helps the body conserve water (and it may also have something to do with memory and learning). The reason beer, whisky, and the like increase the frequency of urination is that alcohol slows the secretion of vasopressin.

The Master Glands

The Hypothalamus-Pituitary Connection

The pituitary gland was once believed to be the principal controlling gland of the body. We now know that the hypothalamus is an essential link between the brain and the pituitary. In reality, the endocrine system is an intricate "feedback" system, in which hormones release or suppress other hormones, controlling the way the body works. For example, the hypothalamus releases hormones stored in the posterior pituitary—among them, oxytocin, vital in childbirth and nursing, and vasopressin, the water-regulating hormone; it also releases "turn on" hormones from the anterior pituitary, which stimulates secretions by other endocrine glands.

The pituitary, which is controlled by the hypothalamus, has two distinct parts, the anterior and posterior lobes. Each one releases different hormones.

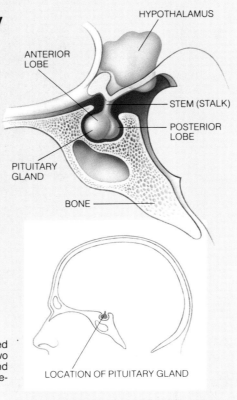

HYPOTHALAMUS

ANTERIOR LOBE

STEM (STALK)

POSTERIOR LOBE

PITUITARY GLAND

BONE

LOCATION OF PITUITARY GLAND

How do your brain and your body "talk" to each other?

The hypothalamus is just a tiny cluster of cells in the brain, and it was only in the late 1960s that scientists fully recognized its importance. The hypothalamus, it seems, monitors information about body states, and it is also the main coordinator of activities in the nervous system with those in the endocrine system. Thus it can be considered an intermediary between brain and body, the mechanism by which they "talk" to each other.

Messages that travel to or from the brain go through the hypothalamus. That organ "knows about" sensations that you are aware of, such as a beautiful sunset, a painful bee sting, or a delicious smell. It also possesses information about things outside of your awareness, such as the level of circulating hormones and the concentration of nutrients in the body.

The hypothalamus replies to state-of-the-body messages partly through the pituitary gland, an endocrine organ suspended just beneath it. Sometimes the hypothalamus communicates with the pituitary by means of nerve impulses and sometimes via hormones that the hypothalamus secretes. In response to demands from the hypothalamus, the pituitary produces hormones of its own, which circulate in the blood to a variety of body tissues, including many of the endocrine glands. In many instances, the information circuit is completed when news of physiological adjustments brought about by hormones feeds back to the hypothalamus.

Important as that organ is, some communication between brain and body also goes on independently. In an emergency, the sympathetic nervous system directly stimulates the adrenal glands to secrete adrenaline and noradrenaline, and it also discharges similar substances at its nerve endings.

Why is the pituitary sometimes called the master gland?

The pituitary gland, which lies in the centre of the skull, right behind the bridge of the nose, is no bigger than a pea, yet it has been called "the conductor of the endocrine orchestra." There is no doubt that the pituitary is a crucial link between the nervous system and the endocrine system, that it releases many different hormones, and that it affects such crucial processes as growth, metabolism, sexual development, and reproduction. Yet it does not exert its profound effects alone. The real master of the endocrine system is the hypothalamus, and the pituitary is subservient to it.

What causes giantism?

Giantism (correctly called gigantism) stems from an excess of growth hormone that is due to a tumour of the pituitary gland. Pituitary giants tend to be sexually underdeveloped, and, if untreated, they generally die in early adulthood. The reason is that their tumour grows until it destroys the pituitary, thus depriving the body of hormones that control sexual maturation and other vital body processes.

What is the difference between a dwarf and a midget?

Doctors use the term *dwarf* to designate anyone of abnormally short stature. The bodies of some dwarfs are well-proportioned, and many are sexually and intellectually normal. But in most people's minds, the word *dwarf* suggests disproportion, deformity, and mental abnormality, and for that reason many prefer the term *midget* for miniature adults who are normal in everything except height. All midgets are dwarfs, but only some dwarfs are midgets. Dwarfism can be inherited or acquired, and its causes are many. Most midgets are pituitary dwarfs of one type: their short stature results from an undersecretion of growth hormone by the pituitary.

Giants, Dwarfs, and Variations in Growth

Gigantism becomes apparent in adolescence, when the growing points of the bones (epiphyses) continue to grow after they should have stopped. Tall basketball players aren't giants: they are simply tall. Midgets are usually normal in size and weight at birth; growth hormone does not seem to be essential to growth in the womb. After birth, midgets tend to grow half as fast as normal children, often continuing to grow into their 20s, and eventually reaching a height of 1.2 metres (4 feet) or more. On the other hand, Pygmies, who may not be more than 1.4 metres (4 feet 8 inches) tall, are perfectly normal.

Rose Clare, a 940-millimetre (37-inch) midget, dressed elegantly and carried herself with dignity.

The outer-space being, E.T. the Extra-Terrestrial, in the film of that name, was "played" chiefly by an elaborate piece of machinery, but in some scenes, a dwarf played the role.

The 2.5-metre (8-foot 5-inch) giant Robert Wadlow is seen here having a fitting for a suit. No ready-made bargains for him!

Basketball player Manute Bol's height — 2.3 metres (7 feet 6 inches) — is a normal, inherited trait. He is a member of the Sudanese Dinka tribe, one of the tallest peoples in the world.

The Influence of Hormones on Growth

When does the human body begin to produce sex hormones?

The secretion of oestrogens and androgens begins just weeks after conception, and sexual differentiation begins then, too. Androgens stimulate the development of penis and scrotum out of primitive foetal tissue that has the potential of becoming either male or female. If many fewer androgens are present, female reproductive structures emerge from the primitive tissue. Oddly enough, though foetal testes that secrete androgens are essential to the development of a male, functioning foetal ovaries do not seem to be required for female development.

Sex hormones before birth may affect more than the genitals. Today, many brain specialists believe that sex hormones also masculinize or feminize the foetal brain, perhaps contributing thereby to later behavioural differences between men and women.

The production of sex hormones, stimulated in foetal life by placental hormones, falls off drastically after birth. It appears that a child's gonads are capable of producing hormones but that its hypothalamus probably does not yet secrete the releasing hormone needed to make the pituitary produce gonad-stimulating hormones, and nobody knows why. Only at puberty do the girl's ovaries begin to release large quantities of oestrogens and the boy's testicles, large quantities of androgens.

Why do adolescents grow so fast?

Infancy ranks first as the period of fastest growth, but adolescence is a close second. Boys shoot up at an average rate of 100 millimetres (4 inches) a year, girls at an average rate of 85 millimetres (3¼ inches) in the period of rapid growth. This ordinarily starts at about 10½ years for girls and finishes at about 14. It usually occurs one to two years later for boys.

The different parts of the adolescent's body grow at different rates. Head, hands, and feet reach adult

Red spots in this scintigram (a kind of scanning photo), mark growing areas at the ends of normal child's bones. Before puberty, growth depends mainly on somatotrophin; later, mainly on sex hormones.

size soonest and are therefore disproportionately large for a while. The legs grow faster than the torso and then stop, while the torso continues to grow. That is why "gangling adolescent" is such an apt phrase, and it is also the reason teenagers stop growing out of trousers before they stop outgrowing jackets.

Rapid growth in adolescence owes more to the sex hormones than to somatotrophin, or growth hormone. At this stage of life, the production of androgens in the adrenals of both sexes, and in the testes of boys increases strikingly. So does production of oestrogen in the ovaries.

Do adults need growth hormone?

Some years ago, physiologists believed that the body stopped producing growth hormone after adolescence. Now they know better. Even after people reach their full height, their pituitary glands continue to secrete growth hormone at almost the same rate as in childhood and early youth. At all ages, production rises and falls in response to circumstances; it goes up, for example, when a person fasts, exercises, falls asleep, or undergoes surgery.

During adulthood, a deficiency of growth hormone does not lead to any clearly identifiable effects, which suggests that the hormone may not be essential to adults. Remember that growth hormone does more than make young bodies grow; it also influences metabolism by promoting the manufacture of protein by the body, the use of stored fat for energy, and the use of the body's carbohydrate stores. While adults don't need the hormone to grow, they may benefit from its general metabolic effects.

Do men produce any female hormones?

When scientists first began studying sex hormones years ago, they took for granted that the differences between men and women were absolute: that men produced one set of hormones and women a different set.

It soon became evident that both males and females actually produce the same sex hormones. What makes the sexes different from each other is the proportion of masculinizing and feminizing hormones each one has. In men, the effect of androgens, secreted in large amounts, overrides that of oestrogens, produced in small amounts. In women, the influence of oestrogens is greater than that of androgens. By the time all this was discovered, androgens had already been designated "male hormones" and oestrogens, "female hormones." At least in popular usage, the labels have stuck, even though they are not precisely correct.

The adrenals of both men and women produce very small amounts of oestrogen and somewhat larger quantities of androgens. In women, androgens are also manufactured by the ovaries. In men, the testes secrete not only androgens but also tiny quantities of progesterone, the hormone that prepares women's bodies for pregnancy. The testes secrete oestrogen, too: one-fifth the amount produced by a non-pregnant woman. Interestingly, in both men and women, oestrogens are derived in part from the male hormone testosterone.

What makes a boy's voice deepen?

In the 17th and 18th centuries, the most famous singers of church and operatic music were male sopranos and altos. These were the castrati:

males castrated in boyhood to preserve the vocal range of prepuberty. This practice began in the 16th century, when women singers were barred from church and stage, and was widespread by the 18th century, when a majority of male opera singers were castrati. The great power of their voices was partly due to their lung capacity and to their physical bulk.

The story of the castrati highlights the influence of the male hormone testosterone during puberty. For it is testosterone that brings about the deepening of a boy's voice, mainly through the enlargement of the larynx and the doubling in length of the vocal cords. The pitch of the voice drops by about an octave, sometimes abruptly and sometimes gradually. In most cases the change becomes noticeable at just about the time that the penis is nearing its full adult size.

How do male hormones affect normal women?

Though small amounts of oestrogen can be found in the blood and urine of men, especially during adolescence and old age, the function of that hormone in men's bodies is unclear. Nor is it apparent why men produce progesterone and prolactin, the hormones of pregnancy and lactation.

The role of androgens in women is better understood. These male hormones exert their principal effects on women during puberty. They stimulate the growth of underarm and pubic hair, influence the development of the clitoris, and are also partly responsible for the general spurt in growth. In addition, androgens cause a barely noticeable deepening of girls' voices, and if a girl suffers from acne, she can blame it on androgens.

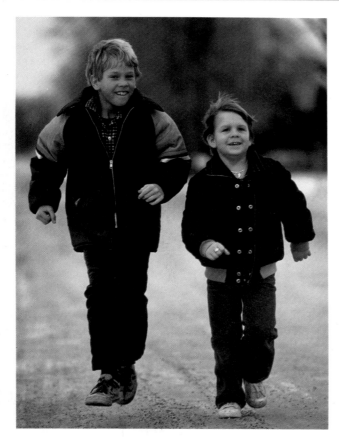

Growth-Hormone Deficiency

When a child is short for his age, it may be because he has inherited genes for short stature, but it can also be a sign that something is wrong. Possibilities include blood or liver disease, malnutrition, emotional deprivation, or insufficient production of growth hormone by the pituitary gland. One way doctors can determine whether short stature is normal, or a cause for concern, is to chart a child's growth rate. Between the ages of 3 and 9, the average youngster grows about 50 millimetres (2 inches) every year. Much slower growth is "a red flag," one specialist says, and signals the need for careful medical study. Injected growth hormone produces growth in some cases.

Each X-ray shows the hand of a child of five. The smaller hand, with shorter bones, reveals insufficient growth hormone.

At the age of ten, a hormone-deficient boy (right) is shorter than a nine-year-old (left). Treatment with growth hormone has produced some increase in height.

Sex and the Life Cycle

Early and Late Development in Males and Females

Sexual maturation brings with it not only development of the sex organs, but generally a deepening of the voice and broadening of the shoulders in males, and a broadening of the hips in females. Sex hormones speed up the rate of tissue formation by increasing the amount of protein that cells manufacture. Within a few years, late maturers catch up with their age groups.

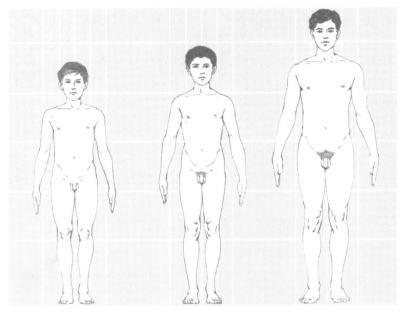

Boys in one study varied greatly in development, but all were 14¾ years old.

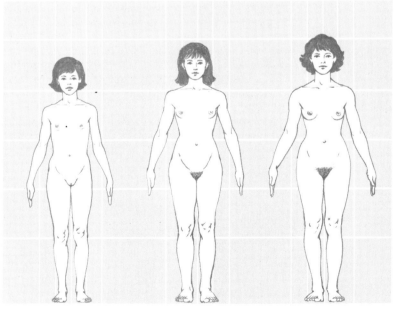

Girls in the same study exhibited comparable differences at 12¾ years of age.

Do boys and girls mature earlier than they used to?

The trend towards earlier menarche, or first menstruation, is found mainly in affluent societies, probably because good nutrition is among the most important determinants of sexual maturity. There is no objective measure of the sexual maturity of boys comparable to menarche, yet it is reasonable to presume that if girls are maturing earlier than they once did, boys are, too.

The trend has not proceeded without interruption. During the Industrial Revolution in the early 19th century, the trend was halted for a while. The trend then continued downwards. Now it has apparently come to a stop in Western societies, where there has been no drop in age at menarche, at least in the middle classes, for the past three decades.

Is adolescence bound to be stormy?

To the Greek philosopher Aristotle, adolescents were "passionate, irascible, and apt to be carried away by their impulses." Over and over again since then, psychologists, psychiatrists, and parents have accepted that notion. It is not hard to see why, given the changes of puberty and the need to adjust sexually, to achieve independence, and to prepare for a job.

Recently, some psychologists have come to realize that disturbed young people are not typical of all adolescents. Studies of adolescent boys and girls have found that by adolescence, most of them had already adopted their parents' standards and had gone a long way towards independence. In short, adolescence does not necessarily mean rebellion, upheaval, or psychological disaster.

Do hormone levels affect your sex life?

In human beings, sexual activity is widely considered to be influenced more by psychological than by physiological factors. Some authorities say that once men and women have developed a satisfying pattern of sexual activity, their sex lives can continue normally even if age or illness causes a decline in hormone production. According to this particular school of thought, decreased sexual interest and, in men, reduced potency are generally the result of such emotional difficulties as depression, guilt, and marital conflict.

But although the causes of impotence and lack of libido are usually psychological, in a few instances a man's sex life may be adversely affected by a deficiency of testosterone, a hormone produced primarily by the testes, or by an excess of another hormone, prolactin, secreted by the pituitary gland. In these men, normal sexual function can be restored by injections of testosterone or by some other treatment.

Oddly enough, there are indications that testosterone plays a role in the sexual behaviour of women as well as of men. A woman's adrenal glands secrete a small percentage of the amount of testosterone produced by a man's testes and adrenals together. If a woman has had surgery on her adrenals, her sex drive may subsequently be reduced; however, injections of testosterone can restore it. But oestrogen, the principal hormone secreted by the ovaries, does not seem to increase a woman's interest in sex or to affect the intensity of her orgasm in any way.

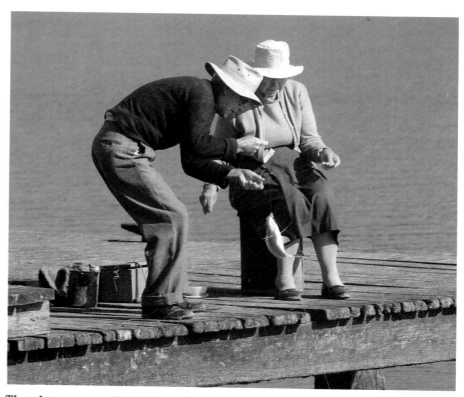

The pleasures and delights of youth need not be abandoned with old age, and the sense that life is very much worth living will be sustained by continuing to enjoy sexual intimacy into the later years.

What happens when you're in the mood for love?

Many people assume that sexual activity is accompanied by high levels of sex hormone production, but moment-to-moment roles for androgens or oestrogens during intercourse are not fully understood.

The menopause leaves a woman with not much more oestrogen than the tiny amount secreted by her adrenal glands, yet her sexual interest is usually undiminished. Indeed, many women report increased enjoyment of intercourse after the menopause,

probably because they don't have to worry about pregnancy any longer.

In men, an abnormally low level of testosterone is often associated with lack of interest in sex, and the administration of that hormone in such cases may heighten the sex drive.

Can an active sex life keep you feeling young?

There is a joke that defines old age as the time of life when a man flirts with girls but has forgotten why. Depending on your point of view, that is funny, or cruel. In either case, the attitude it reflects—a belief that sex in old age is either impossible or inappropriate—can constitute a self-fulfilling prophecy. Without consciously intending to, people who hold this belief may make it come true for themselves as they grow into middle age and beyond.

Age does bring physical changes that can alter sexual experience. Most older women find that vaginal lubrication decreases, but they learn that they can rely on artificial lubricants.

Men need more time to achieve an erection, but they discover that they can maintain it longer.

It is undoubtedly true that frequency of intercourse declines with age. Kinsey and his colleagues reported an average weekly frequency for married couples of 1.8 times at the age of 50 and of .7 at 70. Older men are generally more active sexually than women of the same age. One study found 70 percent of men sexually active at the age of 70 and 50 percent at 75; another found 70 percent of women active at the age of 60 and 50 percent at 65. The older people for whom sex remains important are usually those who were most active sexually in their younger years.

According to Masters and Johnson, men and women can function sexually into their 80s. The requisites, the two researchers say, are regular sexual activity, good physical health, an emotionally healthy attitude towards getting older, and an interesting and interested partner. If these requirements are met, many older people can look forward to enjoying sex throughout their lives.

How We Respond to Fear and Stress

What do the adrenal glands do?

Anyone who is familiar with a picture of Napoleon wearing his cocked hat already knows the shape of the adrenals. As the emperor's military headgear rested on his head, so each of your adrenals is perched, like a miniature hat, on each of your kidneys. (*Adrenal* is derived from the Latin words for "near" and "kidney.") These endocrine glands are only approximately 25 to 50 millimetres (1 to 2 inches) long, and they weigh only a few grams each. In spite of their size,

they secrete more than three dozen hormones.

The adrenal gland has two parts so different from each other that "the" adrenal is really a pair of glands, one inside the other. The cortex, or outer layer, which is yellow, takes its instructions about when and what to secrete mainly from the pituitary hormone ACTH, or adrenocorticotrophic hormone. The medulla, or inner part of the adrenal, is reddish brown in colour and responds to direct orders from the nervous system.

The hormones secreted by the cor-

tex are very much alike in chemical structure and are called steroids. There are three principal types: mineralocorticoids, whose main task is to control the balance of sodium and potassium in the body; glucocorticoids, which, among other things, raise the level of sugar in the blood; and sex hormones.

The adrenal medulla secretes only two hormones, adrenaline and noradrenaline. As the chemicals responsible for some of the reactions to fear and anger, they are sometimes characterized as emergency hormones.

Why does your heart pound when you're frightened?

Adrenaline, the substance also known as epinephrine, is often called the emergency hormone. The adrenal glands, which play a key role in the body's alarm system, secrete adrenaline when danger threatens, and it is one reason your heart beats wildly when you're afraid. For adrenaline is a powerful heart stimulant—so powerful that in cases of cardiac arrest, it is sometimes injected to start the heart beating again. A related compound, noradrenaline, is also released by nerve endings on the heart itself, which speeds up the heart when danger threatens. In the face of physical or psychological stress, the body prepares to fight the enemy or to flee to safety; this is the "fight-or-flight" response described in every introductory psychology course. Signalled by the nervous system, the adrenals pour both adrenaline and noradrenaline, (also called norepinephrine) into the bloodstream. These hormones dilate the coronary arteries so that the heart pumps faster, and constrict certain blood vessels so that blood pressure rises. Within seconds, the body changes.

HYPOTHALAMUS stimulates action

PITUITARY releases hormones

ADRENAL GLANDS release hormones

HEART CONTRACTS more strongly, beats faster

BLOOD PRESSURE rises

BLOOD SUGAR increases

BLOOD VESSELS on surface of skin contract (if injury occurs, bleeding is lessened)

HAIR SHAFT stands erect

PUPILS DILATE, sharpening vision

BREATHING TUBES open wider for deeper breathing

DIGESTION slows down

PERSPIRATION increases, keeping body cool

MUSCLES receive more blood, readying the body for vigorous action

A snarling guard dog strikes terror in the human heart. The immediate reaction is a marshalling of physical capabilities for defence.

What does your endocrine system do when you're under stress?

Undergoing an operation, or getting the news that you need one; coming home to find an armed burglar in the cellar, or worrying about unpaid bills; taking an exam, or waiting for a job interview; engaging in a furious quarrel, or sitting helpless in a long traffic jam—there is no end to the list of physical and mental events that make special demands on your body.

The endocrine system responds to stress quickly. The adrenal medulla releases adrenaline and noradrenaline, which make the heart beat faster and let the lungs take in more air. The hypothalamus secretes CRH, or corticotrophin-releasing hormone. CRH causes the pituitary to secrete a burst of ACTH, or adrenocorticotrophic hormone. ACTH stimulates the adrenal cortex to pour glucocorticoid hormones into the bloodstream.

The most important of these hormones is cortisol, also known as hydrocortisone. Stress may cause the adrenals to secrete 20 times the usual amount of cortisol, and this prepares the body to deal with trouble by mobilizing supplies. It pulls amino acids out of storage in muscles and other tissues, helps move them into the liver, and there speeds their conversion into much-needed glucose. It also releases fatty acids from fat tissues. It is still not clear how these changes help you handle stress.

Hormones are essential for dealing with illness or injury, for fleeing from an animal in the jungle, or for engaging in hand-to-hand combat with an enemy. But many of the stresses of civilized life do not call for a physical response, and the indiscriminate release of hormones that are not really needed may have adverse consequences for health.

Are there any medical uses for adrenaline?

Snakes may seem more alarming than bees, hornets, or wasps, but in some parts of the world, insect bites

kill twice as many people as snake bites every year. The cause of such deaths is usually an allergic reaction that strikes within minutes. People who have ever had a severe, general body reaction to insect stings may be dangerously allergic, and their doctors may advise them to carry emergency kits containing adrenaline that they can inject into themselves. The hormone opens the airways, stimulates the heart, and maintains blood pressure.

Adrenaline preparations are also sometimes called for in cardiac emergencies. If the heart has stopped beating completely, it is sometimes possible to start it beating once more by giving an injection of adrenaline.

Can prolonged glucocorticoid treatment do you any harm?

The usefulness of glucocorticoids (which includes cortisone) as drugs depends on their power to reduce inflammation and suppress the immune system—effects that appear only when the hormones are taken in

much larger amounts than the body normally produces. However, large amounts, especially over a long time, are likely to cause undesirable side effects. Among the least alarming, medically if not cosmetically, are unusual fat deposits and a "moon face." More serious are such complications as osteoporosis, or weakening of the bones, peptic ulcers, diabetes, high blood pressure, and slow wound healing. The suppressed immune system invites infections that may go undetected, because the absence of inflammation may mean there is less pain or fever to warn of danger. Another potential hazard is mental disturbance, which can range from mild euphoria to actual psychosis.

None of this necessarily means you should forego the benefits of glucocorticoid treatment. The most serious side effects can be prevented by taking the smallest possible doses for the shortest possible time, and today, most doctors are conservative in prescribing the drugs. Moreover, experts have discovered that even high doses can be fairly safe if taken on alternate days, a schedule that is sometimes highly effective against symptoms.

Energy Control, Sugar Balance

What does the thyroid gland have to do with energy?

Shaped like a butterfly and usually weighing about 20 grams (¾ ounce), your thyroid gland lies at the front of your neck just below the Adam's apple, one wing on each side of the windpipe. Its most important function is to secrete two hormones that play a crucial part in setting your metabolic rate, the speed with which the body transforms nutrients into energy. If that rate is slightly below normal, you may experience nothing worse than minor lassitude. A rate slightly above normal may produce some nervousness. If the metabolic rate is markedly increased, the results can be weight loss, nervousness, a sense of being warm, and flagrant emotional disturbance. If the metabolic rate is markedly decreased, a slowing of bodily functions will result.

The two energy-regulating hormones are thyroxine and triiodothyronine. Of the body's total supply of triiodothyronine, only 20 percent is made in the thyroid; the rest is made from thyroxine in other body tissues.

Before the concentration of thyroid hormones could be measured accurately in blood samples, one way doctors could find out how well the thyroid was functioning was to determine the basal metabolic rate, or the amount of oxygen required to maintain basic functions. The rate can drop as low as 40 percent below normal if the thyroid gland is not working at all; it can rise to 60 to 100 percent above normal if the thyroid is releasing excess hormones. However, even if your thyroid stopped working entirely, your metabolism might not slow down for some time, because the thyroid stores enough hormones to last one to three months.

What causes goitre?

When the body does not get enough iodine, the thyroid gland has trouble synthesizing its hormones. The result is often a goitre, an enlargement of the thyroid. There are parts of the world where iodine is so scarce that the sight of a neck without a goitre is rare. The swelling, which can be bigger than a cricket ball, occurs when the iodine-deprived gland produces too little thyroid hormone to stop the secretion of excess thyroid-stimulating hormone (TSH) from the pituitary gland. Sometimes, a much-enlarged gland produces enough hormones to meet the body's needs.

How can some people eat and eat and never gain weight?

If you have trouble keeping your weight down, you may envy those who seem to eat all the time without putting on weight. Many are physically active and burn up Calories. But others may suffer from hyperthyroidism, a disorder that results from an excess of thyroid hormones.

The unneeded hormones stimulate appetite and speed up metabolism so much that the body burns up enor-

आयोडिनको सूई लिनु होस

गलगाँडबाट बच्न

Nepalese poster shows a woman with goitre, urging victims to seek treatment.

The Vital Role of Iodine in the Diet

Every adult needs one ten thousandth part of a gram of iodine a day; without it, the thyroid gland cannot do its job. Food usually fills this quota, because iodine occurs in most soils and is taken up by plants. But in some parts of the world, the soil contains little or no iodine. To compensate, developed nations add iodine to table salt. In many poorer countries, where iodized salt may not be readily available, thyroid deficiency is common, and as a result, many children suffer from mental and physical retardation. In some less-affluent nations, the remedy for iodine deficiency is mass inoculation with iodized oil. This oil settles in body fat and releases iodine over a period of about five years.

Energy as well as emotional balance may rely on the normal functioning of the thyroid gland.

STRADDLING the windpipe, the thyroid lies at the front of the throat.

Two energy-regulating hormones are secreted by the thyroid gland.

mous quantities of food. Weight loss may be extreme. Victims are restless, hyperactive, and so keyed up that they cannot sleep, which means they feel worn out all the time. Sweating, inability to tolerate heat, hand tremors, heart palpitations, and muscular weakness are frequent symptoms.

One treatment for hyperthyroidism is to destroy the gland with radioactive iodine, after which the patient gets the necessary hormones by taking medication. So far, this has proved to be a safe procedure. Alternative treatments are drugs that decrease thyroid activity or surgery to remove part of the gland.

Does the pancreas secrete more than one hormone?

In a way, the pancreas is two organs. As a digestive organ, it secretes enzymes that help break food down into chemicals the body can use. As an endocrine organ, it puts out at least two hormones that regulate the metabolism of carbohydrates, plus other hormones with other functions. Most people have heard of only one pancreatic hormone that regulates blood sugar, insulin, but there is a second one, glucagon.

Insulin and glucagon are put out by groups of cells in the pancreas called the islets of Langerhans. After a meal, when the level of sugar in your blood rises, the pancreas secretes insulin. That hormone reduces the amount of sugar in the blood, partly by helping to move it through cell walls and into the cells themselves. When the level of blood sugar drops below that needed by the brain and other tissues, the pancreas secretes glucagon. That hormone increases the amount of sugar in the blood by mobilizing supplies of it from the liver.

What is diabetes mellitus?

Diabetes mellitus is a pancreatic disorder that is a major cause of illness, disability, and death. Its two main symptoms are loss of weight and excess urine production. The dis-

Insulin: A Treatment but Not a Cure

In 1922, when insulin was first used to treat diabetes, dying children rapidly regained their health, and many people mistakenly assumed that an almost miraculous cure had at long last been discovered. It is true that insulin injections enable diabetics whose bodies secrete insufficient insulin to live for decades with a disease that once made early death a certainty. Nevertheless, the daily injections are by no means a cure. They can supply the missing hormone, but they cannot induce the pancreas to secrete its own insulin, nor can they replace the capacity of a normal pancreas to regulate the hormone supply according to the body's changing needs.

A diabetic punctures the finger to secure a blood sample.

A patient prepares to test the sugar level of the blood.

An elderly diabetic injects herself with the required amount of the hormone insulin.

ease is also characterized by extreme hunger and thirst. Diabetes mellitus is a disorder of carbohydrate metabolism that occurs because the body either secretes too little insulin or is incapable of using the insulin that it does secrete.

There are two main types of the disease. In Type I diabetes, which is also called insulin-dependent or juvenile-onset diabetes, the pancreas produces little insulin, possibly because a virus or the patient's own immune system attacks the insulin-producing cells. This type usually strikes in childhood, appears suddenly, and is the more serious of the two kinds. In Type II diabetes, also known as non-

insulin-dependent or maturity-onset diabetes, the pancreas may produce normal amounts of insulin, but for some reason the body cannot use it to metabolize carbohydrates.

The two types have in common the fact that much of the sugar in the body cannot get into the cells and so accumulates in the blood and is excreted in the urine. One eventual result of uncontrolled diabetes, especially Type I, may be a disturbance of fat metabolism. This abnormality can lead to coma and death, and over a long period may be responsible for the complications of diabetes: premature atherosclerosis, strokes, kidney disease, and eye damage.

Chapter 4

THE HEART & CIRCULATORY SYSTEM

The secret of the heart's action lies in a patch of specialized tissue that produces an electric current. This natural pacemaker causes the muscular contractions that send your blood coursing through your body.

Your Heart: The Double Pump	90
The Circulatory Network	92
An Army of Specialists	94
Blood Groups and Transfusions	96
Repairing Cuts and Bruises	98
The Mysteries of Immunity	100
Monitoring the Heart	102
When Things Go Wrong	104
Blood and Circulatory Disorders	106
Deficiencies of the Blood	108
Haemophilia: The Blood Disease That Influenced History	109
The Little-Known Lymphatic System	110

Is the heart on the left side?

Mistaken ideas about the human body die hard, but there is often a simple reason for their persistence. Take the widely held belief that the human heart is on the left side of the body. It is not. Imagine a vertical line drawn through the precise centre of the chest. Normally, the heart is a bit off centre: a little more of it is on the left of the line than on the right of it.

Inside the chest, the heart lies diagonally, with its broad upper part to the right and its narrow end, or apex, tapering toward the left. The heartbeat is felt at the apex, which probably explains the common misunderstanding about the heart's location.

And one more thing: you shouldn't rely on St. Valentine's Day greeting cards for an accurate idea of the heart's shape. In fact, the heart looks something like a pear.

What makes bruises "black and blue"?

When tiny blood vessels, or capillaries, are ruptured, blood seeps into tissues, and red cells break. Haemoglobin, the principal pigment in red cells, turns blue when oxygen is removed. Tissues quickly use up oxygen, and it is not resupplied because the blood vessels have been broken. A bruise generally looks even bluer if the overlying tissue is pink.

As the red blood cells degenerate and are reabsorbed, a bruise disappears—usually in about 14 days. The breakdown products of haemoglobin are responsible for the yellowish colour of the bruise. The pigment is eventually removed by white blood cells.

Does the heart ever rest?

Many questions, on many subjects, can correctly be answered either yes or no, depending on how one defines words and interprets events. If you say that the heart never rests, you are right. And if you say that it rests a great deal, you are also right.

Some experts who have written

about the heart emphasize that under normal circumstances, the heart never ceases to beat, that as long as life lasts, it continues to contract and relax, contract and relax, over and over again. From this one may infer that the heart does not rest.

But other experts interpret the relaxation part of the cycle as a period of rest—this is time for the heart to fill. One respected textbook, for instance, says that "the heart rests for...a fraction of a second between beats." Another book, by the physician Howard B. Sprague, asserts that "in a lifetime of 70 years, the heart rests about 40 years." Indeed, Dr. Sprague adds, "it rests even when it is working its hardest, and gives an excellent lesson in the value of pacing exertion."

How does emotional stress affect the heart?

In the face of danger, tension, or conflict, adrenaline pours into your bloodstream, elevating blood pressure, narrowing blood vessels, and causing your heart to race. Doctors cite these physiological changes as evidence for their belief that emotional stress can harm the heart, since it is known that raised blood pressure and rapid heartbeat may have a harmful effect on your body.

Can people be cold-blooded?

Cruel or unfeeling human beings are commonly described as being cold-blooded. The term conveys a vivid, psychologically accurate impression, but it is not literally correct; no living person has cold blood.

Human beings are naturally warm-blooded, meaning that their primary source of heat is within them: the heat is created by their natural body processes. Birds and other mammals also share this characteristic, but all other animals are really cold-blooded—their body temperature is the same as their surroundings.

This distinction has very important practical consequences. Warm-blooded, well-insulated creatures can operate at full efficiency under a variety of weather conditions, while cold-blooded creatures—snakes, lizards, insects, and so on—function imperfectly or not at all unless the weather happens to be just right.

Where is the body's thermostat?

In spite of all the external temperature changes they experience in an average day, most people maintain a fairly consistent internal body temperature of about 37° C (98.6° F), the temperature at which body processes

Winter clothes *conserve the body's heat by trapping layers of warm air. To keep warm, wear substantial headgear; to cool off, doff your hat.*

work best. This miracle is accomplished with the help of a biological thermostat in the brain.

Near the base of the brain, a structure called the hypothalamus monitors the temperature of the blood flowing through it and triggers changes in the diameter of blood vessels. Suppose that the internal temperature rises above normal, which can happen if the weather or room temperature is very hot, if a person is exercising hard or has a fever, or simply because digestion and other normal body processes are producing a lot of heat. In that case, blood vessels to the skin expand or dilate. The volume of blood moving through them therefore increases and carries the heat to the surface, where it dissipates. If, on the other hand, the internal temperature falls, the skin blood vessels will shrink or constrict, reducing blood flow to the surface of the body and thus conserving heat.

In some operations on the heart or on the blood vessels, surgeons frequently lower a patient's body temperature artificially. The purpose is to reduce the need for circulating blood through the body's organs while surgery is in progress.

Why are hats important in cold weather?

On cold days, the circulatory system sometimes fails to deliver enough blood to reach the extremities. As a result, toes, fingers, nose, and ears may become pale or turn blue.

Both your brain and your extremities need heat in cold weather. When there isn't enough heat to go around, the circulatory system is adjusted so that the brain gets blood at the expense of less important tissue; even when nose and ears are suffering severely from the cold, the brain is kept at near normal temperature. Without a hat, an enormous amount of heat may be lost through the top of your head. So the old-fashioned advice to wear a hat to warm your toes is well-founded. With the brain adequately warmed, the body can spare some heat for frigid fingers and toes.

Your Heart: The Double Pump

How complicated is your heart?

Most people think of the heart as a single, unified organ, but actually it consists of two pumps, each with two chambers. The right side of the heart receives blood partly depleted of oxygen from the body's outlying areas and pumps it into the lungs, where it is replenished with life-giving oxygen. The left side receives this oxygenated blood from the lungs and sends it to the rest of the body.

The left and right portions of the heart are basically similar, although the left is somewhat more muscular than the right because it has more work to do: pumping blood at higher pressure to the most distant parts of the body. The blood pressure in the nearby lungs is much lower than in the arms. Each side of the heart has a thin-walled upper chamber called an atrium, a kind of holding chamber or receiving room in which incoming blood is collected. And each has a ventricle, a larger, more muscular, thicker-walled lower chamber, where most of the actual work of pumping is done.

Both the left and right sides of the heart are supplied with large veins and arteries. One-way valves pass blood from upper chamber to ventricle and from ventricle to artery. A septum, or dividing wall, separates the two pumps so that their contents do not mix.

The entire heart is quite neatly packaged in a loose sack, the pericardium, that keeps the beating heart from rubbing against the chest wall. The heart itself has three layers of specialized tissue. The outer one is the epicardium, a thin, shiny membrane. Next comes the thick heart muscle, the myocardium, which performs the main work of the heart. Finally, there is another smooth, shiny membrane, the endocardium, which lines the cavities of the heart. All of these tissues are nourished almost entirely by a supply of oxygen-rich blood from the coronary arteries—so-called because to early anatomists, they seemed to rest atop the heart like a crown.

What makes the heart beat?

The beat of your heart is produced by a tissue with special properties in the right upper chamber, or atrium. This centre acts as a natural electrical pacemaker. The pacemaker—a kind of spark plug—fires an electrical impulse that causes the muscle fibres of both upper chambers to contract. The contraction forces blood both forwards into the ventricle and backwards where it causes pulsation of vessels. Just milliseconds after the pacemaker fires, its electrical charge reaches a second piece of specialized tissue, which is made of slow-conducting muscle cells. This centre relays the charge after only a tenth of a second or so. The charge then excites the muscles of the ventricles, which then squeeze the blood in the heart, increasing its pressure. This is the force that closes the valves between atria and ventricles and opens the valves of the blood vessels going to the lungs (right ventricle) and rest of the body (left ventricle).

When the contraction ends, the pressure is higher in the circulation to the lungs than in the right ventricle, and higher in the arteries than it is in the left ventricle. This closes the valves, preventing backflow. The heart's "lub-dub" sounds are related to muscle and valve movement.

What can be done if the heart's natural pacemaker is faulty?

When the natural pacemaker fails to transmit impulses regularly, several kinds of medicines can be effective. The doctor will try to find out what kind of rhythm disorder is present and prescribe the appropriate drug—usually after he has seen an electrocardiogram that tells him about your heart's electrical activity.

In some cases, a surgeon can implant an artificial pacemaker. The typical device, complete with a battery, is usually inserted under local anaesthesia near the shoulder, and it is attached to the heart by a wire. The pacemaker can also be worn externally. Its main feature is an electrode that emits an electrical impulse at timed intervals to speed up an abnormally slow heart or make an erratic heart beat at an even rhythm. Now used by many people all over the world, pacemakers permit their wearers to lead essentially normal lives.

DID YOU KNOW...?

- **Your blood vessels,** if laid end to end, would—according to one estimate—encircle the globe twice over.

- **Pins and needles,** the sensation of prickling or tingling in the hands, legs, or feet, is caused by impaired blood circulation.

- **Certain behavioural traits** may indicate a greater risk of heart disease. The Type-A, or coronary-prone, personality, some experts believe, is excessively competitive, restless, time-conscious, and short-tempered. Type-B personalities, on the other hand, are relaxed and low-keyed. In several studies, researchers have found Type-A people more prone to heart disease than Type-B people of the same age and sex who work at the same kinds of jobs. Behaviour modification can help Type A's to reduce risk.

- **Men have more blood** in their circulatory systems than women. Men also have more red blood cells than women.

- **The commonest blood group** is O, accounting for about 46 percent of the world's population. However, in some areas, other blood groups predominate—in Norway, for example, type A is the most prevalent.

- **Nightmares** can seem so real, your heart pounds with fear. In one particular study, the dreamer's heart rate went to 150 beats a minute.

What causes heart murmurs?

Doctors call certain sounds heard with a stethoscope heart murmurs. But they may also be roars, or screeches, or soft, blowing sounds. Usually, they are just the noises the blood makes as it rushes through the parts of the heart; most can safely be ignored; only rarely are murmurs signs of serious heart trouble.

In some cases, however, murmurs indicate malfunctioning valves. If a valve does not close properly, it allows some of the blood to leak back into the chamber, and the leak becomes audible through a stethoscope.

Many heart murmurs that are due to disease occur because of changes in the mitral valve, the one between the left upper and lower chamber. Sometimes a baby is born with a malfunctioning valve; in other cases, the cause is rheumatic fever, formerly a frequent childhood disease. Fortunately, many valve abnormalities can be corrected by surgery.

Following a Single Red Corpuscle Through a Full Cycle

A red blood cell that has lost some of its oxygen (and is said to be "deoxygenated") returns to the heart, entering either through the superior vena cava (1) or the inferior vena cava (1). These veins lead into the right atrium (2). The red blood cell passes through the tricuspid valve (3) into the right ventricle (4). It is then pumped through the pulmonary valve (5) into the pulmonary artery (6) to the lungs. There the cell gives off carbon dioxide and picks up oxygen. The corpuscle returns to the heart via a pulmonary vein (7), enters the left atrium (8), passes through the mitral valve (9) and into the left ventricle (10). There it is pumped through the aortic valve (11) into the aorta (12) and out to the body.

Blood in. When heart relaxes, blood flows into all four chambers.

Blood out. When heart contracts, blood is forced through arteries.

The Circulatory Network

What is the function of arteries?

Arteries make up a major part of our blood circulatory system and contain, at any given moment, 15 percent of the blood supply. The pulmonary artery takes blood containing decreased amounts of oxygen (and increased amounts of carbon dioxide) to the lungs, where the process reverses. The other arteries carry newly oxygenated blood from the heart to every part of the body. Connections between pairs of arteries usually ensure continued blood supply, even when one has been damaged.

Every time the blood-filled ventricles of the heart contract, they pump blood under pressure into two great arteries, the pulmonary artery and the aorta. Shaped like the handle of a cane, the aorta goes up from the left ventricle and then down in front of the spine, bearing its vital burden of fresh blood. On the way, it branches out in smaller and smaller arteries.

Healthy arteries have thick, muscular walls to accommodate the pressure of the blood moving through them. They are elastic: as large volumes of blood surge through them with every heartbeat, they stretch, and as the blood moves on, they become smaller again. If an artery is cut, blood comes out in rhythmic spurts because of the alternate expansion and contraction of the blood vessels accompanying the beat of the heart.

How do veins differ from arteries?

Veins complement arteries; each is of no use without the other. Beginning at their smallest branchings, called venules, they transport blood, laden with waste products collected throughout the body and partly depleted of oxygen, back to the heart.

Though their distribution parallels that of the arteries, veins are more numerous and hold more of the body's blood (some 70 percent) at any one moment. Venous blood is under fairly low pressure, and veins are thinner-walled and hold more blood than arteries. This lower pressure accounts for the way a vein bleeds when cut: venous flow is steady, even, and less difficult to stop than is blood spurting from a cut artery.

In the veins, blood is forced to move against gravity much of the time. Indeed, you might expect most of your blood to run down and collect in the lower part of your body. To help keep the flow towards the heart, many veins are equipped with one-way valves. In addition, the action of the diaphragm and muscles in the arms and legs exert a massaging effect that helps to move blood back to the heart.

A micrograph of muscle tissue reveals capillaries carrying red blood cells. These channels are where veins and arteries connect. It is in this liquid world—and nowhere else—that the transfer between blood and tissue occurs. Nutrients from arterial blood enter each cell, and waste products diffuse out into the capillary.

The purpose of all this pumping and movement is to exchange oxygen and other nutrients for waste products. The transfer takes place across microscopic, one-cell-thick vessels called capillaries that connect the tiny muscular branches of arteries called arterioles, with tiny veins called venules. The capillaries allow nutrients, oxygen, and fluids to pass into tissue and also collect carbon dioxide waste materials and fluids for return to the veins and lymph system. The capillaries are where the important functions of the circulation take place: exchange of material between circulation and cells.

What does your pulse indicate?

The pulse felt in your wrist, or at the site of a major artery, is a pressure wave transmitted through the arterial system as each heartbeat injects blood into it. In the healthy heart of an adult at rest, 72 beats per minute is often cited as average, but the normal range is between 60 and 100.

Physical exertion can elevate the pulse to a maximum of about 220 minus a person's age. But a pulse this high could not be sustained; the rate might drop roughly 75 percent of the maximum during continued exertion, or to 135 at age 40.

Hormones, medications, fever, exercise, and emotional disturbance often cause a temporary rise in heart rate, but usually without any serious effect on the heart's performance. Where the heart rate is consistently higher or lower than normal, however, a physician should investigate to be sure there is no underlying disease. But note: those who exercise a lot *always* have a low pulse rate at rest—because their hearts have become very efficient through exercise.

How much blood does the heart pump?

Your heart weighs only 280 to 310 grams (10 to 11 ounces), and it's not much bigger than a clenched fist. The amount of work it accomplishes is

The Kidneys: Where the Blood Is Cleansed

The kidneys are paired organs that play an essential role in the circulatory system, removing waste products from the blood, while they also regulate the body's fluid and salt content. These small organs process and cleanse the total volume of blood in your body every 50 minutes. About 1800 litres (400 gallons) of blood are pumped to the kidneys per day. Though they account for less than .5 percent of your weight, they contain more than 2 million nephrons, microscopic filters, and tubes, which, if connected, would extend for almost 80 kilometres (50 miles). The kidneys are essential to life. If they fail, their work must be done by a dialysis machine.

ARTERIOLES carry blood to the nephrons, or filter loops

RENAL ARTERY carries blood into the kidney

RENAL VEIN brings the filtered blood back, returns it to circulation

URETER carries urine from the kidney to the bladder

CORTEX is where nephrons are located

therefore remarkable. The volume of blood pumped per heartbeat (by both ventricles) varies from person to person, but the average for an adult is 150 millilitres (5 fluid ounces) per beat. At a rough estimate of 73 beats per minute for an adult (105,120 beats per day), this works out to nearly 16,000 litres (3,500 gallons) of blood pumped every day through the body's 95,000 kilometres (60,000 miles) of blood vessels.

What do the kidneys do?

Often called the master chemists of the body, the kidneys function as combined excretory and regulatory organs—they excrete water *and* they conserve it. They eliminate, via urine, any potentially damaging substances from the breakdown of foods before they reach toxic levels. They return water, glucose, salt, potassium, and other vital substances to the blood in just the right proportions to keep the body's internal environment stable

despite variations in climate, diet, and other external conditions.

The kidneys are a pair of bean-shaped organs, about the size of a child's fist, just above the waistline at the back of the abdominal cavity. Their work begins when blood enters them through the renal arteries. Each artery divides into smaller and smaller branches until it ends in a microscopic structure called a nephron. Part of each nephron is a filter, and there are about a million of them in each kidney.

Inside the nephron, harmful substances are separated from useful ones. Wastes are shunted to a funnel-shaped cavity called the renal pelvis. From there they go to the ureter, a duct that leads to the bladder. Most of the filtrate—the fluid that has passed through the filter portion of the nephron—is reabsorbed into the capillaries and veins, bearing its balanced burden of useful chemicals. About 180 litres (40 gallons) of filtrate are processed daily, of which only 1.5 litres (2.5 pints) is disposed of as urine.

An Army of Specialists

What is blood made of?

A single drop of blood contains more than 250 *million* separate blood cells floating in a straw-coloured fluid called plasma. Blood cells constitute about 40 percent of the total volume of blood, which, in a mature adult of average size, amounts to between 3.5 and 5 litres (6 and 8.5 pints), roughly 7 percent of body weight.

You have three types of blood cells, each of which performs a different function. Red blood cells, or erythrocytes, transport oxygen and carbon dioxide; white blood cells, or leucocytes, defend the body against disease and other hostile intrusions; and your platelets, or thrombocytes, are key elements in blood clotting.

Plasma, which makes up about 55 percent of the blood, is over 90 percent water. Yet plasma contains thousands of different substances, including proteins, glucose, salts, vitamins, hormones, antibodies, and wastes—almost everything the body uses. Thanks to plasma, blood flows freely and distributes materials to all parts of the body that need them for nourishment and protection.

Why is blood red?

Interestingly enough, if you look at a tiny smear of blood under a microscope, it doesn't look red at all, but yellowish. The red colour shows only when great masses of cells are seen together. It comes from haemoglobin, an iron-containing red pigment that is the main component of red cells. The redness of any blood sample varies according to the amount of oxygen it is carrying. Oxygen-laden arterial blood is bright scarlet. As oxygen is removed, venous blood becomes a darker, bluish purple.

What do red cells do?

One of the most important properties of haemoglobin is its unique ability to combine loosely with oxygen when the two substances come together. That happens in the lungs, where each passing haemoglobin molecule picks up as many as four oxygen molecules and carries them via the bloodstream to the body's tissues. Red blood cells also are important in the transport of carbon dioxide, the gas that is produced by the breakdown of nutrients.

The red blood cells are small, thin, and disk-shaped, with depressions on both sides. They are by far the most numerous of the solid elements in the bloodstream. At any given time, the body contains perhaps 25 million million of them, enough, if spread out, to cover four tennis courts. The red blood cells work extraordinarily hard, circuiting the system some 300,000 times before they finally wear out and disintegrate after a life of about 120 days. Replacements are made, at a rate of 3 million new cells every second, in the bone marrow; there they are taken up by the capillary network and sent on their way through the bloodstream.

Birth of red blood cell takes 6 days. Here, cell is shown over a 3-day period, twisting into its final form. Cell lives about 120 days.

Red and White Cells Have Different Roles

Red blood cells function as supply troops, delivering oxygen to cells and carrying out carbon dioxide wastes, while white blood cells, called leucocytes, defend against attack, destroying invaders and clearing away the debris. Five types of leucocytes are strategically deployed in the body: 1) neutrophils spearhead the fight at the site of an injury, engulfing bacteria and foreign particles; 2) eosinophils combat certain allergic reactions and detoxify foreign substances; 3) basophils release anticoagulants and constrict and dilate blood vessels to heal inflammation; 4) lymphocytes battle disease microbes and accumulate at cancerous lesions; 5) monocytes swell up to become macrophages, able to swallow large particles whole.

Largest white blood cell, a macrophage, advances on bacteria.

Are white blood cells really white?

The body's defenders—the soldiers that fight bacteria and other enemies—are the so-called white cells. Their name, like that of the red cells, is somewhat misleading: they actually look not white but colourless.

While there is only one kind of red cell, white blood cells come in many varieties, each type capable of fighting the body's battles in a different way. One kind, for instance, destroys dead cells. Other kinds produce antibodies against viruses, detoxify foreign substances, or literally eat up and digest bacteria.

The life span of white cells varies, depending on the challenges they encounter as they travel through the bloodstream to the sites where they are needed. Despite their essential role in keeping the body alive and well, white cells are few compared with the red cells, numbering only 1 for every 700 red cells. The white cells are manufactured in several places. Some are made in the bone marrow; others originate in the lymph nodes, the spleen, the thymus, the tonsils, and other parts of the lymph system.

What makes blood clot?

At times of sudden danger, when a blood vessel has been cut or damaged and blood is escaping, platelets come swiftly to the rescue—and die in the process. Platelets stick to the edges of a wound, secrete a substance that summons other platelets to take part in the life-saving mission, clump together, and, if the wound is minor, close it with a platelet plug. If the wound is really bad, the platelets set off a series of chemical reactions that cause a clot to form and seal the hole.

The body has more platelets (15 million in each drop of blood) than white cells, but fewer than red ones. They are formed in the bone marrow. And they get their name from their shape: under a microscope, they look like round or oval plates. Platelets have a life span of five to eight days.

How does altitude affect the composition of blood?

As the many people who go mountain climbing know quite well, the higher the altitude they reach the lower the level of oxygen available to them. The human body has fairly fixed oxygen requirements, and in this situation, a built-in form of adaptation comes into play.

When oxygen is in short supply, the kidneys, which monitor blood as it flows through them, step up their production of a hormone called erythropoietin. (The liver produces this hormone as well.) When the hormone reaches the bone marrow, the manufacture of red blood cells is accelerated. If people remain for several weeks at an altitude of 4,250 metres (14,000 feet) or higher, the production of red blood cells in their bodies may rise as much as 30 to 40 percent. The greater the number of red blood cells produced, the more oxygen will ultimately reach its destination in body tissues.

The macrophage devours the colony of bacteria very rapidly.

These protectors cruise through the bloodstream until needed.

Blood Groups and Transfusions

Why do blood types matter?

When Europeans first experimented with blood transfusions in the 17th century, so many patients died that the procedure was outlawed in England, France, and Italy. It is said that the Incas in South America began transfusing blood much earlier, and that far fewer deaths resulted. If so, the reason, not understood at the time, may have been that nearly all of the Incas belonged to the same blood type, while the Europeans, like most groups of people, belonged to different—and incompatible—types. Today, blood transfusion is safe only because blood samples from donor and recipient are tested to ensure that no dangerous transfusion reaction can occur from the mixing of incompatible blood.

Blood types, which are inherited, were first discovered in 1900 by an Austrian, Karl Landsteiner, who won a Nobel Prize for his work on this life-saving medical advance. Since that time, other systems of classification have been devised, but Landsteiner's is still the most important one.

What are the main blood types?

In the ABO system, human blood is classifed into four types: A, B, AB, and O. If your blood type is A, your red blood cells carry a protein called antigen A and your plasma, a protein called antibody b. (An antigen is a substance that stimulates the body to produce an antibody.) If you are type B, your blood contains antigen B and antibody a. Blood type AB carries both antigens but no antibody, while type O blood has neither of the antigens but both of the antibodies.

These categories are important in transfusion because certain antigens and antibodies are hostile to each other and adhere in clumps that can cause fatal blood-vessel blockages.

Generally, people with type A blood can safely receive blood from A's and O's, while type B recipients are safe with blood from B's and O's. People whose blood is type AB are known as universal recipients, because their blood is compatible with types AB, A, B, and O. Type O people, on the other hand, are safe only with blood from type O donors, but they are themselves so-called universal donors, because they can give blood to anyone, provided that other blood groups, such as the Rh factor, are compatible.

What is the Rh factor?

The two most familiar antigens, A and B, are not the only ones to be found in human blood. Another antigen, which is known as the Rh factor, is contained in the red cells of more

Where Red Blood Cells Are Formed

The bone marrow has been termed the "blood factory" of the body, especially for red blood cells and platelets. Athough all bone cavities contain marrow, it is only certain bones in adults that have active, blood-producing, red marrow. These include the spongy parts of long bones such as the femur, and the flat bones of the ribs, breastbone, vertebrae, and skull.

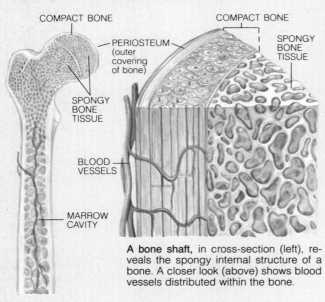

COMPACT BONE
COMPACT BONE
PERIOSTEUM (outer covering of bone)
SPONGY BONE TISSUE
SPONGY BONE TISSUE
BLOOD VESSELS
MARROW CAVITY

A bone shaft, in cross-section (left), reveals the spongy internal structure of a bone. A closer look (above) shows blood vessels distributed within the bone.

About 3 million red blood cells are produced by an adult per second. The intricate bone marrow structure shown in this micrograph is the site of blood production. It is here, too, that some of the iron from worn-out red cells is recycled in new red-cell production.

than 85 percent of the population of the world. This component becomes important when an Rh negative woman (a woman without Rh in her blood) conceives a child by an Rh positive man (a man whose blood contains Rh). Such cases may pose a threat to the unborn child.

The danger comes from two possibilities: that the mother's blood may contain antibodies hostile to the Rh factor and that these antibodies may cross the placenta and attack the foetus if it is Rh positive. As a result, the child may develop jaundice, or may even be born dead.

How does the mother acquire those destructive antibodies? She may get them through blood transfusion. It is also possible that her body will develop them if the blood of her foetus seeps into her own bloodstream during childbirth or miscarriage.

The first pregnancy poses little risk, because it takes time for the antibodies to build up. But once the mother's blood has become sensitized, Rh incompatibility may be a problem in the next pregnancy. To forestall the danger, doctors can administer a recently developed anti-Rh antibody to Rh negative mothers after each of their pregnancies so that their blood will not create antibodies hostile to Rh positive blood. Another modern technique is the exchange blood transfusion, in which all of a foetus's blood is replaced.

What gets counted in a blood count?

In a routine count the blood's basic components—red cells, haemoglobin, white cells, and platelets—are enumerated from a small sample of whole blood. Each number or percentage is then compared against a standard to check for deficiency or excess.

A more detailed blood count breaks down the relative numbers of the six specialized kinds of white cells. Abnormalities may indicate allergic reaction, infection, or blood disease.

A blood test begins with a fresh blood sample, which is diluted with distilled water and salts so that the

Transfusing blood directly from donor to recipient was risky before the discovery of blood types. Until 1900, no one knew shared blood must match.

concentrated cells separate. A known volume of the diluted sample is spread evenly over a grid under a glass cover, and the number of each kind of cell is counted under a microscope. In this way, a haematologist arrives at a number—the person's count for a particular type of cell. Today, electronic scanners can perform this task.

Can you give yourself a blood transfusion?

Blood transfusion has saved millions of lives, being the major method used by surgeons to treat shock caused by loss of blood from the circulation. Transfusions, however, are not without their dangers. They can transmit a disease from the person who gives the blood to the one who receives it, and if the blood of donor and recipient are not matched properly to be sure they are compatible, transfusions can cause troublesome and even fatal reactions.

The best way to guard against these potential hazards is for a patient to give blood to himself. Of course, this protective measure is impossible in emergency-surgery situations; it can be used only when a patient knows weeks or months in advance that he faces an operation. In that case, the patient goes to the hospital at intervals before the operation and allows

technicians to take 430 millilitres (15 fluid ounces) of blood at a time until several litres have been drawn. The hospital then stores the blood until it is required.

Can blood type prove paternity?

Heredity determines the blood type of every individual. A child inherits two blood-type genes, one from each parent, and cannot belong to any blood type unless at least one of his parents carries a gene for that type. Dissimilar blood types in two people may thus constitute evidence that they cannot be parent and child. Accordingly, blood types are often cited in paternity suits or in the case of a possible switch of two newborns in the hospital.

But even when a child and an alleged father have the same blood type, this proves only that the adult *could* be the child's father, not that he *is* the father: theoretically, countless other males with the same blood type could have fathered the child.

To take a simple example: suppose a child has type A blood and its mother type O. If the supposed father also belongs to type O, he cannot possibly be the father, because he has no gene for blood type A to pass on to his offspring. But if the alleged father belongs to type A, then the child could, indeed, be his.

Repairing Cuts and Bruises

How does the body control bleeding?

Whenever a blood vessel is damaged, its precious liquid pours out: in great rhythmic spurts from an artery, in a slow but steady stream from a vein, in smaller amounts from a capillary. If the spillage, technically termed a haemorrhage, continues, the volume of blood circulating in the body will drop enough to lower blood pressure drastically. Shock leading to possible

cardiac arrest and death can follow. In the case of smaller wounds, two safety mechanisms are activated as soon as haemorrhaging begins, which rapidly help to decrease bleeding.

The first mechanism is the formation of a blood clot. Clotting, a very complex process, begins when platelets in the spilled blood flow over the jagged edges of torn tissue. The contact stimulates the platelets to burst open. They then release protein substances, called blood platelet factors,

that initiate a series of chemical reactions. Ultimately, the plasma protein fibrinogen is converted to its solid form, fibrin. Fibrin strands form a tangle of threads over the wound. As blood flows through the threads, red and white corpuscles and platelets are trapped and bleeding ceases.

At the same time, the second safety mechanism serves to reduce the volume of blood flow locally. This happens when substances are released at the wound that cause the muscles in

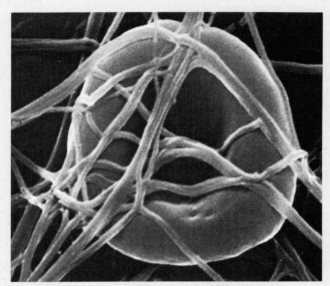

A **red blood cell** is trapped in a network of fibrin strands.

How a Skin Wound Heals Itself

Without platelets, you would repeatedly face the possibility of death, because you would lose great quantities of blood whenever you were injured. Immediately after a cut or tear in your skin occurs, your platelets clump together to plug the gap and discharge a substance that retards loss of blood. Fibrin strands then develop from a protein in the blood, and they rapidly weave the blood-clot structure. These strands cleave to the injured tissue, and confine platelets and blood cells within their network, thus strengthening it. Not long after the clot is formed, it constricts or shrinks, squeezing out watery plasma and drawing the sides of the wound together. The clot stems the flow of blood, fills the wound, and provides a framework for building new tissue. As the injury heals, the coagulated material firms up into a dry, hard scab on the surface of the wound, protecting the work going on underneath. There skin cells multiply, forming new tissue to fill in the break; white blood cells defend against infection and clean up damage; and blood flows into the area through new capillaries formed to nourish the new cells.

EPIDERMIS is broken

CLOT fills the wound

EPITHELIAL CELLS begin to migrate

WHITE BLOOD CELLS enter area of wound

BROKEN VENULE

Wound is filled with blood, dead cells, debris. Clotting components act to cover it.

SCAB forms as clot dries

EPITHELIAL CELLS cover the wound

FIBRIN STRANDS

FIBROBLASTS travel along fibrin strands

WHITE BLOOD CELLS remove debris

Repair work and regrowth go on beneath scab, as white blood cells digest debris.

SCAB

EPITHELIAL CELLS proliferate

NEW COLLAGEN tissue forms

NEW BLOOD VESSELS

Forming new tissue, epithelial cells, fibroblasts, collagen, capillaries fill in wound.

the blood vessels to squeeze shut. In cases where the bleeding is very extensive, and there is also low blood pressure, the substances send signals to the brain that cause a reduction in blood flow.

When bleeding doesn't stop, what can be done?

Sometimes injuries are so severe that they overwhelm normal protective mechanisms. There are some people—haemophiliacs, for example—who bleed more easily than other people. If necessary, they can be given transfusions of Factor VIII, their missing clotting factor, to stop the bleeding.

When, for whatever reason, bleeding continues beyond the normal few minutes or when it is abnormally heavy, medical help should be called, and the patient must receive emergency first aid treatment in the meantime. Apply firm pressure to the wound and elevate the bleeding part above the level of the heart if possible.

If the patient's blood pressure drops precipitously, the physician will administer fluid through an intravenous drip. Because the body is producing new blood all the time, a blood substitute may be as effective as a transfusion.

How and when does healing begin?

After *any* flow of blood, the mechanisms of healing take over as soon as bleeding stops. Knowing why the uncomfortable sensations occur may help you endure them.

The essential first step in that process is inflammation, with its redness, heat, swelling, and pain. The redness and heat of inflammation occur because blood vessels in the area become abnormally enlarged, flooding the damaged tissue with fresh blood. Capillary walls become thinner, and water from the blood plasma seeps through into the surrounding tissues, causing swelling. Pain devel-

THE STORY BEHIND THE WORDS...

Blue blood, which refers to a person born into a socially prominent or noble family, had its origin in Spain. Fair-skinned, pure-blooded Castilians, descended from a long line of artistocrats, maintained that their blood was blue to distinguish themselves from the more darkly complexioned Spaniards they ruled, whose ancestry was mixed with the Moors. In actuality, their veins were simply more pronounced because their skin was light.

Artery, a vessel that carries blood from the heart to the body, stems from a Greek word, *arteria,* which means "wind pipe." In examining the dead, the ancient Greeks noted that the arteries were empty and thus came to believe that the arteries were pipes or channels for circulating the air.

In cold blood means taking a deliberate action, based on reason, while being hot-blooded means being swayed by emotion. These words probably originated from an old belief in blood as the governor of emotional life.

Blood brothers are men who have forged an alliance through the ritual exchange of blood. In some societies, the mingling of blood establishes a bond as strong as kinship although it risks spreading disease.

Devil's pinches is a folk name to explain black and blue marks on the skin of a person who bruises easily. When such a person could not recall the incident that caused the blood vessels to break, the bruise was blamed on Satan.

ops when the swollen tissues put pressure on sensitive nerves, and the nerves send pain signals to the brain.

When the flow of blood slows, white blood cells called leucocytes enter the inflamed tissue. They clean up the debris left by the injury and kill bacteria that enter the wound through the ruptured skin. The leucocytes also release chemicals that attract other white cells to the injured area.

Once inflammation subsides, the constructive phases of healing begin. In some cases, this means the regeneration of identical new cells to replace those that were lost; in others, scar tissue forms to take the place of tissue that cannot regenerate.

What causes pus to form?

When an infection results from an injury, millions of white blood cells are drawn to the damaged area to combat bacteria. Pus is the yellowish, semi-solid mixture of those cells, as well as bacterial and other debris. In most situations, pus rises to the surface of the skin and discharges naturally under pressure.

Why do some people heal more quickly than others?

Just as no two people are born with identical fingerprints, so no two people's natural defence and repair systems are precisely the same. Each of us is born with a unique set of biological potentials, including clotting tendencies and the capacity for tissue regeneration, that influence the rate of healing.

As people age, healing takes longer. But age is not the only factor that influences healing. In ways that medical researchers are only beginning to understand, the general health of a person can also promote, or slow down, the healing process. Nutrition, and even emotional and environmental stress, are important, too. Lastly, some people are simply more prudent in caring for injuries than others: they use medications precisely as called for, and they keep their wounds clean and well-aired. Healing needs a certain degree of cooperation from the victim if it is to proceed smoothly and quickly. But cooperation does not entirely explain it; healing is always a small miracle.

The Mysteries of Immunity

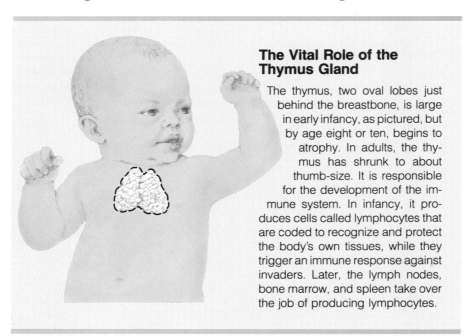

The Vital Role of the Thymus Gland

The thymus, two oval lobes just behind the breastbone, is large in early infancy, as pictured, but by age eight or ten, begins to atrophy. In adults, the thymus has shrunk to about thumb-size. It is responsible for the development of the immune system. In infancy, it produces cells called lymphocytes that are coded to recognize and protect the body's own tissues, while they trigger an immune response against invaders. Later, the lymph nodes, bone marrow, and spleen take over the job of producing lymphocytes.

How does the body defend itself against disease?

The body has very impressive armaments to ward off disease, ranging from the skin, which acts as a barrier to infection, to acids in the stomach that kill bacteria, to mucus in the respiratory and urogenital tracts that carry off alien particles. But the most intricate—and until modern times—most mysterious defences are those to be found in your blood and lymph nodes. Scavenger white blood cells and certain substances called antibodies in the blood are the warriors of your immune system, capable of destroying harmful invaders. The mechanisms of immunity are remarkably complex, and some scientists believe that an understanding and manipulation of antibodies and other substances in the blood will eventually revolutionize medical care.

Almost everyone is born with an intact but undeveloped immune system, which matures shortly after birth. During this maturation period, the infant's immunity is supplemented by factors acquired from the mother's blood and milk. Human beings are also naturally immune to many diseases that afflict animals. How efficiently your immune system works depends to some extent on heredity, but eating and working habits also have an influence on it.

What if the body cannot fight off the agents of disease?

There are many diseases for which the body does not develop immunity. Each person becomes resistant to a disease through acquired immunity. The hard way to acquire immunity is to get the disease. Every micro-organism carries with it a specific antigen, which the body perceives as foreign. In response, the blood and the lymphatic system begin to manufacture antibodies, proteins that can neutralize the effects of a specific antigen.

If the body's resistance is strong enough, the antibodies gradually overwhelm the invaders, and the disease subsides. From that time on, in the case of certain infections, the normal body is immune to attack by that particular disease.

How do vaccines work?

Another way to gain active immunity is through artificial immunization by vaccination. This involves giving injections of vaccines that are developed from the cultures of disease-causing organisms that have been rendered harmless, or nearly so, in the laboratory. Whatever form the vaccine takes, it stimulates the body to produce its own antibodies and thus to acquire immunity. In some instances, the organism is killed by heat, formaldehyde, or ultraviolet light before the vaccine is prepared; the vaccines against whooping cough and typhoid fever are prepared this way. Many vaccines, however, must be made from live organisms if they are to give effective immunity. To make them safe, the organisms are first weakened, or attenuated, with chemicals or by some other means. An example of this type is the Sabin oral polio vaccine. A third group of vaccines, which includes the ones against smallpox and tuberculosis, are derived from the live antigens of related but milder diseases.

When are antitoxins and gamma globulin used?

Some bacterial infections, chiefly tetanus, botulism, and gas gangrene, cause disease by dumping poisons into the bloodstream. Both antitoxins and gamma globulin may be used to combat their effects.

Antitoxins are developed by injecting small amounts of bacteria into laboratory animals. Antibodies are taken from animal blood and purified before being injected into human beings. They confer immediate but short-lived immunity, lasting perhaps no more than six weeks. Booster shots of the same antitoxin may be given if the danger of disease recurs.

Unlike antitoxins, gamma globulin is derived from the blood of a human donor who has previously contracted a specific disease and developed antibodies against it. Gamma globulin is sometimes given to individuals exposed to a serious disease against which they have not been vaccinated. It is administered most commonly following exposure to hepatitis A or B virus, but is often effective in preventing tetanus and measles as well.

What happens when the immune system breaks down?

Failure of the immune system can be very serious. One form of *congenital immune deficiency* results when the unborn infant's bone marrow cannot produce the specialized white blood cells essential to the immune system. Immunologically helpless against all infections, the child usually dies shortly after birth from infections that it is unable to fight.

Acquired immune deficiency syndrome, or A.I.D.S., develops in healthy people after infection by a virus that destroys specific white blood cells. They succumb to various diseases, most notably cancer of the immune system and infections.

Autoimmunity is the condition in which the body's immune system mistakes its own cells for foreign antigens. It then produces antibodies that attack and destroy healthy body tissue. There is strong evidence that rheumatoid arthritis, multiple sclerosis, and a form of hyperthyroidism may all be traceable to an abnormality of the immune system.

Triggering Immune Responses by Vaccination

Vaccination has a long history, beginning ages ago with the Chinese, who inhaled a powder made from smallpox victims' tissue, and the Greeks and Turks, who scraped healthy people with living smallpox germs. The latter was tried in England in the early 1700s, but it was not until 1796 that English physician Edward Jenner found a safe use of the concept. He noted that people who contracted mild cowpox were immune to smallpox, so he infected a patient with cowpox, hoping to protect him from smallpox. He succeeded, thus developing the first safe vaccination method in the Western world.

The use of cowpox vaccine in the 1800s worked but excited controversy and ridicule.

Edward Jenner showed his faith in vaccination by injecting his own son with cowpox, therefore immunizing the child against smallpox.

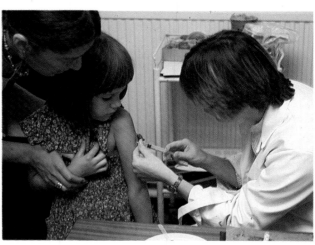

Young children receive most vaccines by injection. An exception is the polio vaccine which is given in the form of drops.

Monitoring the Heart

How is blood pressure measured?

Blood pressure—the force exerted by the blood against the arterial walls—is what keeps your blood circulating. So long as it stays within certain limits, the pressure puts no undue strain on the arteries. But both long-term high blood pressure (hypertension) and very low pressure (hypotension) can be health hazards or signs of underlying problems.

Your doctor measures your blood pressure during two phases in the heart's cycle. The doctor first measures "systolic" pressure—the peak pressure exerted on arterial walls when the left ventricle of the heart contracts in the process of pumping out blood. Secondly, the doctor checks "diastolic" pressure, the reduced pressure felt just before the next beat, when the heart is relaxed and blood is flowing into it. The two readings that result are recorded on your blood-pressure chart as a fraction, the systolic over the diastolic.

The tester wraps a soft, inflatable cuff around the individual's upper arm attached to a device measuring pressure (called a sphygmomanometer) and pumps air into the cuff until its pressure against the arm is sufficient to stop the flow of blood in the main artery. Then, listening with a stethoscope held over the artery just below the cuff, the tester releases air gradually until he hears the pulse resume. At this moment the pressure of the air in the cuff is slightly less than that of the blood in the artery, and the reading that shows up on the gauge is the systolic pressure. The tester then releases still more air, stopping as soon as no more sounds can be heard. The reading on the dial is the diastolic pressure.

What is normal blood pressure?

With blood pressure readings, as with most measures of health, the word *normal* has no single meaning that applies to everyone. However, the average blood pressure readings for young adults in good physical shape is 115 to 120 over 75 to 80. Newborns have a systolic pressure between 20 and 60, and the number rises progressively through the decades.

Normal blood pressure depends on such factors as the vigour of the heart pump, the tightness of the valve closures, the elasticity of the arterial walls, and the amount and consistency of the blood. Other factors that influence blood pressure are digestion, smoking, weight, and emotions.

What are the dangers of high blood pressure?

Severe high blood pressure can cause strokes or heart attacks; even slight elevations, if chronic, can reduce life expectancy. One possible result of long-term high blood pressure is an aneurysm, in which a weak spot in an arterial wall balloons out. In an extreme case, an aneurysm can be life threatening, especially if one on a major artery bursts, releasing a massive amount of blood into surrounding tissue and causing blood pressure throughout the system to drop so fast that death results.

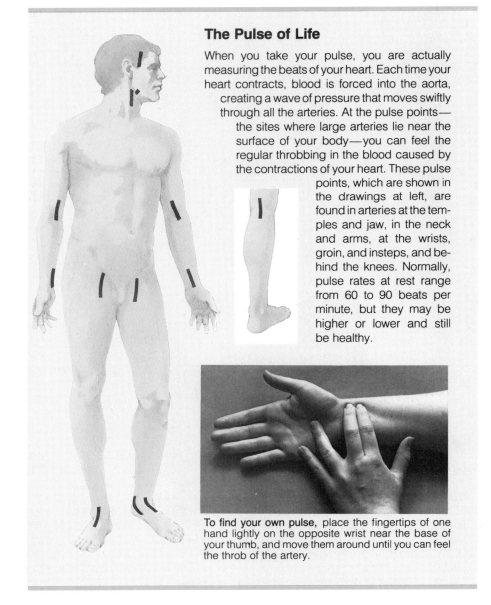

The Pulse of Life

When you take your pulse, you are actually measuring the beats of your heart. Each time your heart contracts, blood is forced into the aorta, creating a wave of pressure that moves swiftly through all the arteries. At the pulse points— the sites where large arteries lie near the surface of your body—you can feel the regular throbbing in the blood caused by the contractions of your heart. These pulse points, which are shown in the drawings at left, are found in arteries at the temples and jaw, in the neck and arms, at the wrists, groin, and insteps, and behind the knees. Normally, pulse rates at rest range from 60 to 90 beats per minute, but they may be higher or lower and still be healthy.

To find your own pulse, place the fingertips of one hand lightly on the opposite wrist near the base of your thumb, and move them around until you can feel the throb of the artery.

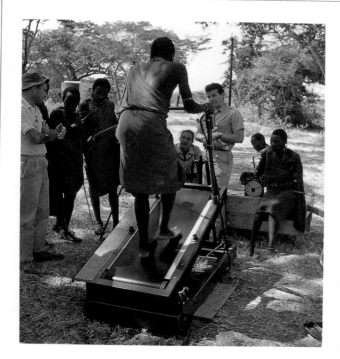

Special Tests That May Reveal Cardiovascular Disease

The treadmill test is important because some abnormalities in the heart's electrical activity show up only when the heart muscle is pumping hard. In this test, the subject paces on a motorized treadmill while an electrocardiogram monitors his heart. Another diagnostic technique is the coronary arteriograph, or angiogram, in which a thin plastic tube, or catheter, is inserted into a blood vessel and pushed through to the heart. The tube delivers a dye to the heart, and X-rays record the progress of the dye in the blood, producing a precise reading of congenital defects, heart leaks, arterial blockages, and valve malfunctions. Sometimes nuclear scanning is used instead, to provide the same information without the need for a catheter. In this case, radioactive thallium is injected into the blood and traced by camera. A computer then converts the data into an image of the beating heart on a screen. Still another technique, the echocardiogram, uses methods rather like underwater sonar also to project an image of the heart on a screen.

The heart of a Masai warrior shows great strength in a treadmill test. Researchers ascribe this to his active life style.

Does high blood pressure run in families?

One type of high blood pressure, called "essential hypertension," does seem to be hereditary. Doctors don't know what causes it, but some families are more prone to it than others. It accounts for most cases of high blood pressure. Usually it does not appear before middle age, and it can be controlled with diet, drugs, and a weight-loss programme.

Another kind of high blood pressure, "secondary hypertension," does not appear to be genetic. It develops as a consequence of some other disorder—kidney disease and heart disease, for example. Occasionally, it results from the use of birth-control pills. Once the underlying problem has been identified and treatment has begun, blood pressure usually returns to normal.

Does salt have any effect on blood pressure?

Salt is essential to life; its role in regulating the amount of water retained in the tissues is crucial. But it is all too easy to get too much of a good thing. Although the body needs only a minuscule quantity of salt every day, most people consume far more, year in and year out. Research has shown that wherever salty foods are a mainstay of the diet, blood pressure levels tend to be higher.

People with elevated blood pressure are advised to reduce their salt intake sharply. Salt is present not only in foods but also in antacids and laxatives, as well as in carbonated drinks. Even after scrupulous efforts to avoid salt, one may still take in more than the body needs because even natural, raw foods, to which no salt has been added, frequently contain substantial amounts of sodium chloride.

What happens when blood pressure falls too low?

Blood pressure that is lower than average, or chronic hypotension, is seldom cause for alarm. It causes few problems except, perhaps, transient episodes of dizziness or faintness. A condition called postural hypotension may occur when a person gets up abruptly. In a few seconds, however, stability is recovered.

Tall, lean people tend to have hypotension, because the pressure exerted by the heart pump is more likely to be dissipated by the time blood reaches the head than in the case of shorter people. (Tall people also have a greater tendency to faint.)

What does an electrocardiogram show about your heart?

To most of us an electrocardiogram is a very mystifying document. But to a doctor, those squiggles and scrawls recording the electrical impulses set off by the heart mean something—the peaks and dips, their shape and length, and irregularities in the pattern they make tell a lot about the heart and circulatory system.

Useful as the electrocradiogram (ECG) has proved to be in diagnosing heart disease, recording tissue injury and deterioration, it is nonetheless a poor predictor of future heart problems in a healthy person. Many people have suffered serious heart attacks just days or weeks after an electrocardiogram showed an apparently normal heart.

When Things Go Wrong

Which is the most common heart disorder?

Because diseases of the heart and blood vessels are the leading cause of death and disability in industrialized countries, these diseases have been called, collectively, the "black plague" of our time. There are many reasons for the breakdown of the cardiovascular system. The most common one is coronary artery disease, or deterioration of the coronary arteries, two blood vessels that branch off the aorta to nourish the heart muscle with fresh blood. In the Western world, coronary artery disease accounts for nearly a third of all deaths.

What happens to the heart in coronary artery disease?

Most of the heart gets the blood it needs through the two coronary arteries. If one of these arteries is blocked, part of the heart may die for lack of blood. A heart attack, or myo-cardial infarction, is the outward sign of this tissue death. Most infarctions occur in people 40 to 60 years old, but children as young as 5 have been known to have heart attacks.

Coronary artery disease is almost always traceable to a condition called atherosclerosis, in which fatty deposits, or atheromas, attach themselves to the inner lining of an artery. Though the condition has become the bane of prosperous, modern societies, it did not originate in the 20th century; signs of it have been found in ancient Egyptian mummies.

In atherosclerosis, arteries that were once smooth and elastic become rough, inflexible, and smaller than before. As they narrow, the volume of blood they can transport is progressively reduced. As a mass of atheroma grows, it may turn into a hard, chalky plaque that further inhibits blood flow, and further scars the arterial wall. The resulting pinch points in a vessel become natural sites for the formation of blood clots. In coronary thrombosis, a stationary blood clot formed in a coronary artery shuts off the flow of blood entirely. In coronary embolism, the blockage is caused by a clot that moves through the bloodstream and becomes lodged in an already narrowed coronary artery.

What are other risk factors in coronary artery disease?

Topping the list of unavoidable factors linked to coronary artery disease is heredity. If both your parents had atherosclerosis, your risk of developing it is greater than that of most other people. Age is another factor: detectable symptoms of coronary artery disease are uncommon before the age of 50, but they are increasingly prevalent thereafter.

Female sex hormones seem to offer some protection from coronary artery disease; women rarely develop it before the menopause, but after 60 are almost as susceptible to it as men.

Smoking a pack or more of cigarettes each day is estimated to at least double an individual's chances of coronary disease. Chronic high blood pressure, diabetes, obesity, emotional stress, and lack of exercise also raise the probability of developing atherosclerosis. By evaluating your own health habits and by changing them if necessary, you stand a good chance of protecting yourself against this epidemic disease.

Does cholesterol really matter?

Cholesterol is one of several fatty compounds that are found in human blood and tissue. Manufactured in the liver, it is essential for producing new cells and certain hormones. It is also taken into the body in food; meat, butter, milk, cheese, and eggs all contain cholesterol.

Doctors have noted that victims of heart disease tend to have abnormally high levels of cholesterol in their blood. And scientists believe that atherosclerosis begins when high blood levels of cholesterol penetrate the smooth lining of the arteries, forming small deposits there. The process,

Early Theories: BLEEDING AS A REMEDY

For hundreds of years, draining blood was the remedy for ailments as diverse as amnesia, deafness, and stroke. It was theorized that in disease blood stagnated in certain parts of the body and that letting blood out revitalized patients. In practice, these "cures" often bled patients white, weakening them and sometimes killing them. The techniques included applying leeches, cutting open a blood vessel, using suction cups to form blood blisters. In the 1860s, bleeding was discredited, but now doctors are reinvestigating blood letting. In certain microsurgery, leeches have removed excess blood from tissue that would otherwise clot and impede repair. And some disorders are caused by over-thick blood—in one technique, blood is drawn and replaced with plasma, to dilute it.

In medieval times, blood letting was accomplished by barber-surgeons, who frequently would cut open a vein at the site of the disorder.

gradual if the arteries are otherwise healthy, is believed to proceed much faster if a person has high blood pressure, and if he or she smokes.

Not everyone whose diet is rich in cholesterol develops atherosclerosis, however, perhaps because individuals vary in the way they process the substance. Everyone's body contains more than a dozen proteins that attach themselves to cholesterol. One is LDL (low-density lipoprotein), which is believed to collect cholesterol and deposit it in the cells. Another is HDL (high-density lipoprotein), which is thought to pick up excess cholesterol and help the body eliminate it. Those with lots of HDLs seem to have fewer heart attacks than others.

Although there is still much to be learned about the role of cholesterol and of LDL and HDL, most doctors believe that an individual can reduce the risk of heart disease by cutting down on those foods that are high in animal fats. This should retard the build-up of fatty deposits in the coronary arteries, and some doctors believe it may even cause already-formed atheromas to shrink.

Does a heart attack always mean invalidism or death?

No doubt about it: a heart attack is a terrifying experience. But the fact is that two out of three people survive the first heart attack. If death occurs, it is usually within two hours. The odds for a person who lives for a day are favourable, and after three weeks, long-term survival is probable. If you sustain a coronary thrombosis and live ten years, life expectancy is the same as that of a person who has never had an attack.

Just like a broken bone, a damaged heart heals. The healing process is helped by a programme of progressive exercise, particularly walking. People who were used to exercising and engaging in sports before their attack can expect to return gradually to their favourite activities. And after about two or three months (sometimes sooner), most people can go back to their old jobs.

How Arteries Become Clogged

Atherosclerosis begins with injuries to the lining of the arteries. The cause may be high blood pressure, high cholesterol levels, cigarette smoking, or other factors. Once an area has been damaged, lipids from the blood, including cholesterol, accumulate, building up a thick, fatty patch that is called plaque.

BLOOD LIPIDS

CELLS LINING ARTERY

Two types of blood cells contribute to the build-up of plaque: macrophages, which are large white blood cells, and platelets, the small blood cells that assist in the coagulation of blood. The macrophages fill up with cholesterol, which accumulates between the macrophages as well, leading to narrowed arteries.

PLATELETS

CELLS LINING ARTERY

Plaque narrows the artery. This narrowing hinders the flow of blood. A clot may detach itself from the site and move towards the heart or into a small artery, blocking it. An obstruction inside the coronary artery causes angina or heart attack. Blockage in an artery leading to the brain brings on stroke.

FIBROUS CAP

FATTY CORE

... and a New Method to Clear Them

This new medical tool for treating atherosclerosis, a clearer of clogged arteries, is an experimental device, which was inspired by the film *Star Wars* and invented by a cardiologist. Attached to a catheter, the laserscope is carefully inserted by the surgeon into the damaged artery, where it aims its beam on the fatty build-up that is obstructing circulation of blood. The beam vaporizes the fat. Just before the laser is fired, a balloon behind it inflates to stop the blood flow momentarily, thereby clearing a path for the beam and preventing damage to blood cells.

CATHETER TIP

Laserscope has three channels: one is a conduit for the laser beam; the second is for optical fibres that permit viewing of the artery; the third is for a vacuum device that is designed to sweep up particles left behind after the firing.

Blood and Circulatory Disorders

What causes varicose veins?

Veins keep blood flowing in a slow, steady stream towards the heart, and many are equipped with valves to prevent blood from pooling or moving backwards. But sometimes valves are defective or become damaged, and too much blood stays too long in one place. The result may be veins knotted and swollen to four or five times normal size (varicose). Haemorrhoids are one example of such veins, but most often they develop in legs, because when the body is upright, blood in the legs must flow uphill, against gravity. Poor circulation leaves skin near such veins undernourished, sometimes causing eczema or ulcerations, and occasionally these fragile veins may burst and bleed. People most vulnerable to varicose veins are those who have inherited weak valves; those whose jobs require hours of standing; pregnant women; the obese; the chronically constipated. Treatment ranges from wearing elastic hose to surgery.

NORMAL VEIN   ABNORMAL VEIN

Valve of healthy vein (left) opens and closes, halting blood's backward flow. Impaired valve (right) causes blood to pool.

LOWER LEGS are especially vulnerable to varicose veins

Varicose vein. As the blood backs up, the veins become distended and frequently painful.

What is phlebitis?

Varicose veins occasionally lead to a serious condition known as phlebitis, an inflammation of a vein usually in the leg. Phlebitis may also occur as an aftereffect of surgery. It is potentially quite dangerous because it is associated with the formation of a *thrombus*, or clot, in the vein. If the clot becomes detached from the wall of the vein, it is then called an embolus, and it may make its way through the circulatory system and become lodged in the pulmonary arteries, thus shutting off blood flow to a part of the lungs.

Phlebitis sometimes occurs during post-operative bed rest, childbirth, or on other occasions of inactivity. Though often dark in appearance, the condition was once known as "milk leg" because of the occasional whiteness of the affected leg.

What is a stroke?

Apoplexy, stroke, and cerebrovascular accident are all terms used to describe sudden mishaps that affect the supply of blood to the brain. The damage occurs when a blood vessel in the brain ruptures and bleeds into brain tissue, or when an artery leading to the brain is blocked by a blood clot, an air bubble, or some other abnormal particle. Deprived of oxygen, the affected brain cells either stop functioning temporarily or, if the oxygen cut-off is prolonged, actually die. As a result, the function of parts of the body controlled by those particular brain cells is impaired.

Strokes vary widely in severity, depending on how long oxygen is cut off and on what part of the brain is damaged. A brief episode of reduced blood flow, known as a transient ischaemic attack (TIA), is marked by such symptoms as slurred speech, weakness in hand or foot, blurred or double vision, all of which disappear within a few hours. Somewhat more serious is a "small stroke," which may produce a sudden, sharp headache, blackout, or some permanent, but often barely detectable, dysfunction.

More severe strokes sometimes result in a marked loss of memory or alertness, persistent unsteadiness on the feet, disturbing changes in emotional behaviour, and paralysis on one or both sides of the body, depending on which part of the brain is affected. If a stroke damages the brain centre that governs the respiratory system, death is quite likely. In Great Britain, strokes are the third most common cause of death, after heart disease and cancer.

Who is most likely to suffer a stroke?

High blood pressure is often called the "silent killer," because it rarely gives its victims any warning of the damage it's inflicting on the blood vessels. That damage can ultimately prove fatal. Indeed, 80 percent of the people who suffer strokes have a history of high blood pressure.

But victims of hypertension are not the only ones vulnerable to stroke. Overweight people, those with a genetic predisposition to hardening of the arteries, and certain victims of diabetes are also considered to be stroke candidates. Among men who are heavy smokers, nearly three times as many strokes occur as among nonsmokers. Birth-control pills seem to increase the risk of stroke, especially in women who also smoke, are obese, or suffer from raised blood pressure. Anyone who has undergone one or more transient stroke-like episodes is a high risk; four out of five people in

Never squeeze a pimple or pluck nasal hairs in the facial area called the "dangerous triangle," shown above. Infection can spread to the veins in the skull at the back of the eyes. Because these veins are small and surrounded by bone, they are easily blocked by infected clots.

this group will probably have a full-fledged stroke within five years unless preventive measures are taken. In some instances, medications designed to relax smooth muscles or reduce the likelihood of blood clots may be prescribed as part of a prevention plan. Also helpful are measures to control high blood pressure and hardening of the arteries. And since stress has sometimes been linked to stroke, it is a good idea to learn how to deal with emotional pressures.

Can stroke victims ever be normal again?

The popular actress Patricia Neal and the famous scientist Louis Pasteur have something in common. Both suffered massive strokes, both made heroic efforts to overcome the severe physical disabilities that resulted, and both eventually returned to phenomenally productive careers. Pasteur did remain partially paralysed, but Neal achieved something approaching full recovery.

Years ago, little was done for people who suffered a stroke. Nowadays, rehabilitation efforts begin early, sometimes on the very day a stroke happens. As a result, approximately 30 percent of stroke victims recover fully. Another 15 percent of them remain entirely incapacitated, while 55 percent have some lasting handicaps, although many of these people can still lead satisfying lives. Specialists who work with stroke victims say that the outcome depends not only on the extent of the original damage and on the skill of rehabilitation experts, but also on the victim's own determination to get better.

What is gangrene?

Gangrene is not the name of a disease; it is a term that means "dead flesh." Its extremely unpleasant nature is suggested by its derivation: the word is related to a Greek word that means "gnaw."

In gangrene, a section of body tissue dies and decays as the result of an infection or a diminished blood supply. Severe frostbite, which can destroy the circulatory network in the hands or feet, is one of the prime causes of gangrene. Arteriosclerosis, severe burns, uncontrolled diabetes,

persistent infection, a crushing injury, or an embolism can also lead to it. Unfortunately, amputation is sometimes necessary to prevent the spread of gangrene.

What is the kissing disease?

Glandular fever (also called infectious mononucleosis) is a persistent but seldom dangerous viral infection common among young people aged 15 to 25. Folklore has it that the virus is transmitted by kissing, a notion that could have some truth in it, since the virus can be found in saliva.

Its earliest symptoms are frequently mistaken for flu—fever, headache, sore throat, and general exhaustion. Within a day or two, the lymph nodes in the neck and sometimes in the armpits and groin may swell as the disease progresses. The spleen and the liver may also become enlarged, and a skin rash may develop. A blood test usually shows a marked rise in the number of unusual white blood cells and other abnormalities. Since it is of viral origin, glandular fever does not respond to antibiotics. The patient recovers in 3 to 12 weeks, though unusual fatigue sometimes persists for as long as a year.

Folklore of the Body: SEARCHING FOR HEART REMEDIES

The ridiculousness of many folk remedies (for example, a hare's right front foot to cure rheumatism) tends to obscure the validity of some of these early ventures into pharmacology. Eating powdered dried foxglove leaves had long been known to relieve "dropsy," the swelling of body tissue now known as oedema. In this case, modern medicine has proved the folk remedy to be right. Digitalis, the drug used to treat congestive heart failure, is made from foxglove leaves. Digitalis acts on the heart muscle, increasing its power to contract while slowing it down. Only a doctor can prescribe the proper dose of digitalis, since too much of this drug can be very harmful, even fatal.

Foxglove *(Digitalis purpurea)* is a purple-flowered garden plant; its leaves are the source of digitalis.

Deficiencies of the Blood

What is anaemia?

Any professor of medicine will tell you that anaemia is not a specific disease; it describes a state of affairs. That is, anaemia—a deficiency in the number of red blood cells or in the amount of haemoglobin they contain—is simply a sign of one of several underlying problems. Some of these are common and easily treated; others are rare and sometimes fatal.

Whatever its cause, anaemia may make the body function poorly because it does not get enough oxygen from the blood. People who are anaemic often feel weak, tired, run down, breathless, and sometimes faint after exercise, or in severe cases, at rest.

Anaemia can take a variety of forms. Iron-deficiency anaemia, in which the body cannot manufacture enough of the oxygen-bearing, iron-containing blood protein, haemoglobin, is the commonest kind of anaemia; treatment includes iron supplements. Folic-acid deficiency, usually the result of inadequacies of diet or the body's inability to absorb folic acid, can also cause anaemia; it is readily treated with folic-acid supplements. Pernicious anaemia, which is caused by the inability of the intestine to absorb vitamin B_{12} because of the failure of the stomach to produce an essential enzyme called the intrinsic factor, is

more serious; treatment for this condition involves the periodic injection of vitamin B_{12}.

Can X-rays produce anaemia?

Heavy or repeated exposure to X-rays, radioactive substances, microwaves, and other high-energy emissions can produce a condition known as aplastic anaemia. After such exposure, the bone marrow may produce fewer red and white blood cells. The deficiency of red cells causes the classic symptoms of anaemia, while the reduced number of white cells increases the risk of infection.

Aplastic anaemia may also develop from other causes such as exposure to benzene, arsenic, gold compounds, and other toxic chemicals. In some cases, drugs taken for other disorders lead to aplastic anaemia, and your doctor may try to reduce the dosage or substitute another drug.

Are some people more vulnerable to anaemia than others?

Sickle cell anaemia occurs most frequently in people of African descent, while Cooley's anaemia is almost entirely confined to those of Mediterranean descent. Both types of anaemia

are caused by a genetic mutation that produces no symptoms unless a person has inherited the mutant gene from *both* parents. At present, there is treatment but no cure for sickle cell anaemia. The only means of prevention is genetic counselling.

Victims of Cooley's anaemia not only produce abnormally small quantities of haemoglobin, but their red cells are uncommonly thin and fragile. The prognosis for children born with the disorder is poor, although periodic blood transfusions can prolong life.

Can anyone get haemophilia?

Most people need not worry about haemophilia. This hereditary disease, whose victims can bleed to death from a seemingly minor injury because their blood does not clot properly, afflicts only 1 male out of 10,000; and almost no females. Nearly all those who suffer from it are men because haemophilia is the result of a defective gene attached to the X chromosome, one of two chromosomes that determine sex. Men have only one X chromosome, and if that one carries a defective clotting gene, they are certain to have haemophilia. Women, however, have two X chromosomes; a defective clotting gene on one of them is usually counterbalanced by a normal gene on the other. Thus women suffer from haemophilia only if they inherit two defective genes, one from each parent.

Most haemophiliacs used to die in infancy. Now, however, they are likely to live to adulthood—and thus to marry and pass on their haemophilia gene. How is this possible? Because scientists can now obtain the purified missing clotting factor from the blood of normal donors and inject it into haemophiliacs.

This development does not always mean that victims of the disease can lead normal lives. They may require many injections of clotting factor every year, at a cost of thousands of pounds. They also face special hazards when they need surgery or dental care. And they must sometimes restrict their activities to avoid injury.

Normal red cells (left) are disc shaped. In sickle cell anaemia, the red cells are shaped like sickles (right). Their oxygen-carrying capacity is reduced, and they tend to clump, preventing oxygen from reaching parts of the body.

Haemophilia: A Blood Disease That Influenced History

When Queen Victoria and her family were painted in 1887, no one knew that genetic misfortune lay ahead for some royal offspring.

Queen Victoria transmitted haemophilia to many of her descendants. Through royal marriage, the disease has afflicted much of Europe's royalty. Of Victoria's nine children, one son had haemophilia, and two daughters carried the disease. Seven of the queen's many grandchildren inherited this genetic defect. After the four haemophiliac grandsons died, haemophilia lived on in the genes of three of the granddaughters: one married the king of Spain and bore three haemophiliac royal sons; another wed a Prussian prince and carried the disease to Germany; and the third, Alexandra, married Tsar Nicholas II of Russia and transmitted haemophilia to their son Alexis. The distress that the disorder caused the imperial family played a part in Russian history. Alexandra fell increasingly under the spell of the enigmatic peasant Rasputin because of his uncanny power to heal, temporarily, their only son. Rasputin's influence with the tsarina, and through her, with the tsar, contributed to the downfall of the Romanovs and to the success of Russia's Revolution.

Rasputin, mad monk and charismatic healer, attained power by treating the tsar's haemophiliac son. Rasputin's influence at court alienated many and aided in sealing the Romanovs' doom.

The Romanov children: Alexis, the haemophiliac heir to the Russian throne, and his sisters, the four grand duchesses. Alexis's affliction was already evident six weeks after his birth, when he began bleeding from the navel.

The Little-Known Lymphatic System

What is the lymphatic system?

Most of us have barely heard of the lymphatic system, yet without it, we would not live. Closely related to the cardiovascular system, the lymphatic system has several major functions. It is important among the body's defence mechanisms, filtering out disease-causing organisms, manufacturing white blood cells, as well as generating antibodies. The lymphatic system is also important in the distribution of fluid and nutrients all over the body because it drains off excess fluids and protein (left behind by the capillary circulation) so that the tissues do not swell.

The fluid that circulates in the system is called lymph. Derived from blood plasma, but clearer and more watery, lymph seeps through the capillary walls to fill tissue spaces. Besides lymph, the system includes lymphatic capillaries and larger vessels; lymph nodes, or glands; the spleen; the tonsils; and the thymus.

The lymphatic capillaries are open-ended, one-way vessels that are scattered throughout the body. Their job is to collect surplus fluid and transport it to two terminal vessels. One is the thoracic duct, the lymphatic system's main trunk, which lies along the spine, and enters a large vein on the left, close to the heart. The other is the right lymphatic duct, which enters a vein on the right side.

Unlike blood, which has the pumping of the heart to move it along, lymph flows without the assistance of any pump. Continuous pressure to move is exerted as new tissue fluid drains into the spaces between the cells, pushing the fluid already there. The contraction and the expansion of nearby arteries and muscles also exert a forward pressure on lymph. Lastly, the process of breathing creates a partial vacuum in the thoracic duct. This partial vacuum causes both venous blood and lymph to flow upwards and return to the bloodstream from which it came.

Why do we need lymph nodes?

Very tiny, oval, capsule-like structures—more than 100 of them—are strung along the lymph capillaries. These are the lymph nodes, or glands. Generally, they are thinly scattered, but in a few parts of the body—principally in the neck, groin, and armpits—they gather together in large numbers. Within each node is a series of fibrous traps through which lymph flows. The node acts as a barrier to the spread of infection, filtering out and destroying micro-organisms and toxins.

Lymph nodes can become enlarged and painful in response to infections; these are the swollen glands that develop in conjunction with inflammation of the ear or throat. The swelling indicates that the nodes are working overtime. Swelling that persists longer than two weeks without any identifiable cause should be investigated by a physician.

What does the spleen do?

The spleen is the largest body of lymphoid tissue. About the size of the heart and located on the left side just behind the stomach, it is a spongy mass capable of holding as much as one litre (1.75 pints) of blood. It carries out the same filtering activity as the lymph nodes, and produces white blood cells (lymphocytes) as well.

In addition, the spleen removes old and worn red cells from the blood, returning iron to the blood for reuse in manufacturing haemoglobin and breaking down the remainder of the molecules for disposal as waste products. The spleen also stores extra blood for release when shortages occur—a surge of blood may be needed when the oxygen in the circulation is depleted. In response to this need, the spleen contracts, thus squeezing virtually its entire reserve of nutrient-rich blood into the general supply.

What is a lymphoma?

Malignant tumours in lymphatic tissue are called lymphomas. Though the causes of lymphomas are not yet known, there is increasing evidence that several of them are of an infectious, viral origin.

An early sign of a lymphoma may be a lymph node or gland that is persistently enlarged and painless. Blood tests are usually followed by a biopsy. If these indicate the presence of a lymphoma, treatment generally begins right away to prevent the growth from spreading. As in many other forms of cancer, surgery, radiation, and chemotherapy may be required. Fortunately, though all lymphomas

The Versatile, Fragile Spleen

In its multiple functions (producing blood cells, filtering the blood, destroying old blood cells, and serving as a reserve blood supply), the spleen is undoubtedly a valuable organ. But when the spleen itself is injured, it generally cannot be repaired. One frequently hears, following a bad motor accident, that a victim of the crash has had his ruptured spleen removed surgically. This is because the spleen is so soft and spongy, and its covering is so thin, that it cannot be stitched up. It is removed to prevent loss of blood, and the patient never misses it.

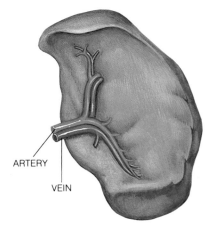

ARTERY

VEIN

The spleen sits behind the stomach.

The System of Fluids Inside the Tissues, Outside the Bloodstream

All the soft tissue of the body is bathed in a watery fluid that is called lymph. This second circulatory system is important in cleansing body fluids; lymph nodes filter out bacteria and also (along with the spleen) produce disease-fighting lymphocytes. But the lymphatic system has other functions as well. It is important in the digestion of fats, as well as the transport of nutrients and wastes. This is the system that preserves the fluid balance throughout the body. After an injury, the affected tissue generally swells. It is the lymphatic system that removes most of the excess fluid, and then puts it back into circulation. Unlike blood that is pumped by the heart, lymph has no pump. Large lymphatic vessels, however, do have valves that prevent back-flow. Lymph is moved by the pressure of breathing, muscular movements, and pressure from adjacent blood vessels.

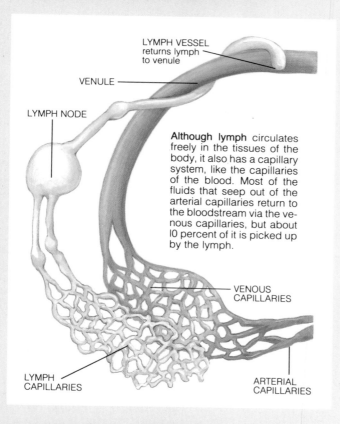

LYMPH VESSEL returns lymph to venule

VENULE

LYMPH NODE

Although lymph circulates freely in the tissues of the body, it also has a capillary system, like the capillaries of the blood. Most of the fluids that seep out of the arterial capillaries return to the bloodstream via the venous capillaries, but about 10 percent of it is picked up by the lymph.

VENOUS CAPILLARIES

LYMPH CAPILLARIES

ARTERIAL CAPILLARIES

RIGHT LYMPH DUCT enters right subclavian vein

THORACIC DUCT enters left subclavian vein or internal jugular vein

LARGE LYMPH DUCTS follow and feed into certain veins

SUPERFICIAL LYMPHATIC vessels are sketched here. In actuality, they are present wherever there are blood vessels

LYMPH NODES are abundant in the neck, under the jaw, under the arms (axillary glands), in the region of the liver, the intestines, and the groin

are potentially life threatening, the possibility of cure is much greater than it used to be.

What is Hodgkin's disease?

Only a few years ago, a diagnosis of Hodgkin's disease (a kind of lymphoma) was a sentence of death. No more. True, just 25 percent of those whose disease is detected in an advanced stage can count on cure. But when Hodgkin's is found and treated early with radiation and, sometimes, cancer-suppressing drugs, the long-term recovery rate rises to 90 percent.

The typical victim of Hodgkin's disease is either an adult aged 15 to 35, or a person over 50. In adults, the disease is twice as prevalent among males as females. It usually reveals itself in enlarged lymph nodes in the neck and gradually spreads throughout the lymphatic system, including the spleen. If left unchecked, the enlarged glands can eventually impair vital functions. Pressure on adjacent organs and nerve endings can result in dysfunction or paralysis.

Chapter 5

THE RESPIRATORY SYSTEM

We think of respiration as being the job of the lungs—with help from the nose and the mouth. The lungs do collect and exchange gases (using blood cells as their couriers), but actually, every living cell in the body is involved in respiration.

The Breath of Life   114

Taking Your Measure   116

Sneezes, Wheezes, and Coughs   118

Our Shared Miseries   120

Influenza: The Elusive Enemy   121

Disorders and Diseases of the Lung   122

Respiratory Emergencies   124

Hazards in the Environment   126

Report on Smoking   128

What is breathing?

Every day we breathe in and out nearly 19 cubic metres (670 cubic feet) of air. This accomplishes two things. Firstly, it supplies the body with oxygen, needed to burn food and release energy. Secondly, it expels carbon dioxide, a waste product of life processes. Oxygen, a gas that makes up approximately 20 percent of fresh air, is drawn into the lungs when you inhale. The exhaled air carries out excess carbon dioxide.

Though breathing is normally involuntary, you can consciously modify it—within limits. For instance, you can deliberately take big gulps of air before diving under water. You can also stop breathing voluntarily, but not for long; the involuntary reflexes forcing you to breathe are so strong that it is impossible to commit suicide by holding your breath.

What happens when you are "out of breath"?

During violent exercise, your muscles may use up oxygen faster than your fast-pumping heart and lungs can replace it. Nature provides for this emergency by permitting the muscles to incur a short-term oxygen debt. Until the debt is repaid, you are in a sense "out of breath," and you may continue to gasp for some minutes after extreme exertion.

What causes snoring, and can it be cured?

The buzzing, rattling, wheezing noise called snoring is not a serious physical problem in itself, but it has often been a cause of marital discord. It is also to blame for countless bad jokes—and for the invention of some 200 gadgets designed to cure it. Snoring accompanies the sleep of one in seven adults, typically people who breathe through the mouth. The villain is the uvula, a pendant of flesh at the back of the mouth which vibrates as your breathing goes across it.

Most individuals who snore sleep

with their mouths open because their throat or nasal passages are partly obstructed. Specific causes include nasal congestion, enlarged tonsils or adenoids, a nasal polyp, a deviated septum, loose dentures, or sleeping on the back, which lets the tongue fall back and partially close the windpipe.

Sewing a cotton reel on to the back of your nightclothes, one cure for snoring that dates back at least a couple of centuries, may discourage sleeping on the back, but it doesn't necessarily solve the problem because people who sleep on their sides can also snore. Losing weight is sometimes helpful, since obesity can cause nasal congestion. Heavily salted foods can have the same result, so you should try to avoid eating them just before bedtime. The best remedy, however, may be earplugs—worn by the snorer's spouse.

Why do you yawn?

If you see people yawning as they come out of the cinema, don't assume it was a terrible film. Contrary to popular opinion, yawning is not necessarily a sign of boredom. If you yawn, it simply indicates that you need more oxygen, and it is nothing but a reflex that forces oxygen into your lungs.

The body's oxygen supply is depleted after a long period of shallow breathing, which commonly occurs when you are tired, under stress, or have been sitting still for a long time. Yawning is not a sign of illness or abnormality. Oddly enough, yawning rarely occurs during serious mental or physical illness.

What is passive smoking?

In recent years, smokers and their opponents have exchanged numerous sharp words over smoking in public places. There is now plenty of evidence that smoking can harm not only smokers themselves but also the abstainers around them. As yet, doctors do not know how often so-called passive smoking causes lung cancer in non-smokers. However, in a study of 2,000 non-smokers, researchers turned up some interesting differences when they compared people who had little contact with smokers with those who regularly breathed the "secondhand" smoke of others. In almost every case, the exposed non-smokers showed some lung impairment, and after chronic exposure to heavy smokers, non-smokers exhibited reduced breathing capacity.

Can vitamin C reduce susceptibility to colds?

The idea that vitamin C can ward off colds and reduce their severity has been popular since the early 1970s. The theory's chief advocate, Dr. Linus Pauling, a Nobel chemist, claims that if you take 1,000 to 2,000 milligrams of vitamin C daily—and additional doses of 4,000 to 10,000 milligrams when a cold strikes—you will have fewer, milder, and shorter colds. His evidence includes the results of some experimental testing.

However, many specialists in upper respiratory infections have not found any definite indication that vitamin C substantially reduces the frequency or the severity of colds. Also taking large doses of vitamin C may have undesirable side effects.

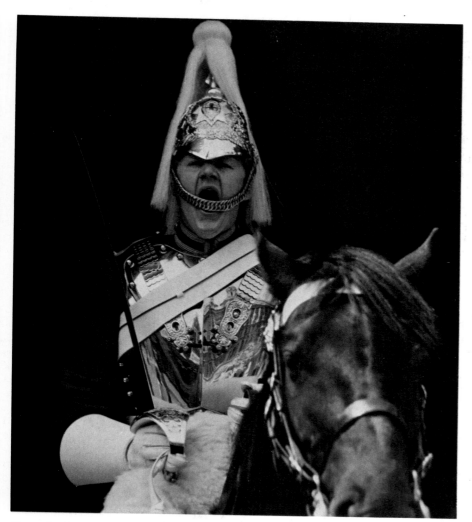

Everybody yawns —*even this mounted guardsman on duty in Whitehall, seat of Britain's government. Yawns oxygenate blood by expanding and aerating the tiny lung sacs called alveoli, and by expelling carbon dioxide.*

The Breath of Life

How do the lungs work?

Air is drawn through the pharynx, the larynx, and the trachea. This air enters and leaves each lung through a single main tube that branches from the trachea and is called the primary bronchus. Each bronchus branches profusely within its lung, carrying air through smaller and smaller passages known as bronchioles and the smaller alveolar ducts. Finally, the smallest branches terminate in air sacs called alveoli, which are laced with a dense network of the tiny blood vessels called capillaries. The walls of both alveoli and capillaries are so thin that gases can easily pass through them. It is here, in the body's 300 million alveoli, that the lungs perform their function—the exchange of oxygen and carbon dioxide.

When you inhale, the air, one-fifth of which is oxygen, enters the air sacs, and the oxygen enters the blood in the capillaries. Some of the entering oxygen is dissolved in the blood, but most of it combines chemically with haemoglobin, and is carried by it to the tissues. When the capillary blood reaches the body regions that need it, it releases oxygen. At the same time, the blood picks up the carbon dioxide produced by cells, and returns it to the alveoli to be exhaled.

What determines how much you breathe?

The rate and depth of respiration vary, depending on how quickly the body uses up oxygen and how fast it accumulates carbon dioxide. This usually depends on activity level. The respiratory centre in the brain sends out impulses that drive the respiratory muscles. Other parts of the nervous system monitor the level of carbon dioxide in the blood, and if it rises by even a minute amount, signal the respiratory centre. The centre immediately modifies the rate and depth of respiration so that the carbon dioxide level returns to normal. The system for regulating oxygen levels is less sensitive to small changes.

When you are engaged in a quiet pastime, you breathe about 15 times a minute. In each breath, perhaps 500 cubic centimetres (30 cubic inches) of air moves in and out of the lungs—no more than 12 percent of a healthy young adult's maximum single breath. In a strenuous activity, your breathing rate may double, and the amount of air taken into your lungs per breath may increase more than five times. By breathing deeper and faster, you use your lungs' reserve capacities.

What is the diaphragm?

The lungs are enclosed in a kind of cage in which the ribs form the sides and the diaphragm, an upwardly arching sheet of muscle, forms the floor. When you take a breath, the diaphragm is drawn downwards until it becomes flat. At the same time, the muscles that surround the ribs contract, lifting them up like the hoops of a hoop skirt. In this way, the chest cavity becomes deeper and wider, and its air capacity increases.

Is it ever dangerous to breathe pure oxygen?

Surprising as it may seem, too much oxygen is actually poisonous. Doctors do sometimes give 100 percent oxygen in certain health emergencies, such as severe lung disease. However, that is nearly five times the normal concentration of oxygen in the air. Continuous breathing of 100 percent oxygen for an extended period of time can cause accumulation of fluid in the lungs, collapse of the air sacs, convulsions, and, in premature infants, even blindness. Much lower oxygen concentrations are used for prolonged treatment in hospitals and in home equipment to treat asthmatics, victims of heart attacks, and patients recovering from lung surgery.

Exhausted football player inhales oxygen. This practice is widespread in the U.S., but opinons differ as to its value.

What happens when you hiccup?

A hiccup is a two-part phenomenon. First, the diaphragm contracts involuntarily because the nerves that control it have become irritated by eating too fast, or for some other reason. Then, as air is inhaled, the space between the vocal cords at the back of the throat snaps shut with a characteristic clicking sound.

There are many remedies for hiccups. Some people drink a glass of water without pausing for air. Others hold their breath until the hiccups stop. These techniques may restore the normal rhythm of the twitching diaphragm by reducing the oxygen supply and increasing the carbon dioxide level. Other "cures" attempt to trick the nervous system with diversionary tactics, such as tickling the nose to induce sneezing or pulling the tongue. If hiccups persist in spite of all efforts to stop them, medical attention should be sought.

Deep Chambers of the Respiratory System

The lungs are a pair of not-quite-identical, cone-shaped organs that lie within the chest cavity. They are protected by ribs, spine, breastbone, and respiratory muscles. Between the lungs lie the trachea and the heart. Not shown on this cutaway drawing is the oesophagus, which also lies between the lungs, but behind the trachea. (The oesophagus leads from the pharynx to the stomach.) A layer of moist membranes called the pleura covers the lungs, and another pleural layer covers the inside of the chest cavity. These lubricating surfaces allow the lungs to inflate and deflate smoothly, without sticking to one another. The diaphragm, which forms the floor of the chest cavity (and the roof of the abdominal cavity), is a continuous structure. The diaphragm has a few openings—where the oesophagus connects to the stomach and for blood vessels.

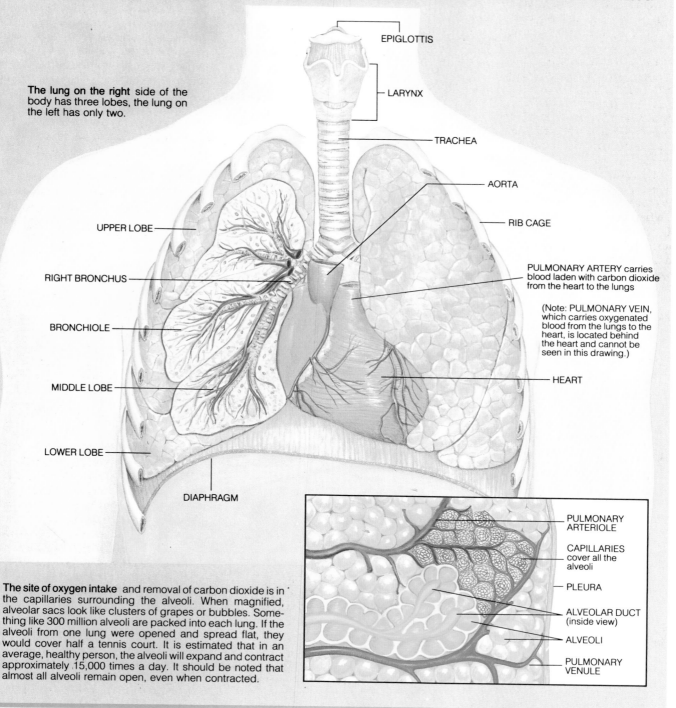

The lung on the right side of the body has three lobes, the lung on the left has only two.

EPIGLOTTIS

LARYNX

TRACHEA

AORTA

RIB CAGE

PULMONARY ARTERY carries blood laden with carbon dioxide from the heart to the lungs

(Note: PULMONARY VEIN, which carries oxygenated blood from the lungs to the heart, is located behind the heart and cannot be seen in this drawing.)

HEART

UPPER LOBE

RIGHT BRONCHUS

BRONCHIOLE

MIDDLE LOBE

LOWER LOBE

DIAPHRAGM

PULMONARY ARTERIOLE

CAPILLARIES cover all the alveoli

PLEURA

ALVEOLAR DUCT (inside view)

ALVEOLI

PULMONARY VENULE

The site of oxygen intake and removal of carbon dioxide is in the capillaries surrounding the alveoli. When magnified, alveolar sacs look like clusters of grapes or bubbles. Something like 300 million alveoli are packed into each lung. If the alveoli from one lung were opened and spread flat, they would cover half a tennis court. It is estimated that in an average, healthy person, the alveoli will expand and contract approximately 15,000 times a day. It should be noted that almost all alveoli remain open, even when contracted.

Taking Your Measure

How much air can your lungs hold?

For an average adult male, breathing normally, the amount of air in the chest is about 2,500 cubic centimetres (150 cubic inches). The term tidal volume is given to the amount of air that flows in and out of the lungs with each breath: about one-fifth of that. There is some air left in the lungs after exhalation.

LUNGS AT REST. Note position of diaphragm

—DIAPHRAGM

DEEP BREATH. The rib cage expands and the diaphragm lowers, which can more than double the volume of air in the lungs

—DIAPHRAGM

EXHALING TO THE MAXIMUM. The rib cage is forced down, the diaphragm rises

—DIAPHRAGM

Why does the doctor tap your chest?

Examining a patient's chest is a lot like beating a drum or trying to locate a stud in a wall. Using a technique called "percussion," the doctor places his fingers on your skin and taps them with fingers of the other hand. He repeats the tapping several times as he moves methodically around the upper torso, listening carefully to the subtly different sounds the tapping makes. To his trained ear, the nature of the sound reveals much about the organs in the chest cavity.

Healthy, air-filled lungs resonate or sound hollow. A lung with enlarged air sacs due to the disease called emphysema also resounds, but the resonance is greater than normal. By contrast, when tapped, a lung partially filled with fluid, or one that has collapsed, produces a dull sound.

What does "palpation" indicate about your chest and lungs?

Examination by touch, called palpation, may begin when the doctor places his hands symmetrically on both sides of the chest. He then will ask you to breathe deeply in order to set your chest in motion. If your lungs and thorax are in healthy working order, he should feel equal movement on the two sides.

The doctor may also ask you to say "ninety nine," a test term chosen for its resonating sound. Normally, the vibrations of the vocal cords are transmitted into the lungs and from there to the surface of the chest, where the doctor feels them through his fingers. Changes in transmission may be a sign of chest disease.

What is a stethoscope?

If you know how to interpret them, many noises inside the chest can reveal a lot about a person's physical condition. Several diseases produce characteristic, identifying sounds.

In order to hear these sounds, a physician uses a simple sound con-ductor called a stethoscope. (This instrument is also quite useful for listening to other parts of the body.)

In the examination that is known as "auscultation," the doctor places the sound-gathering end of the instrument against your chest and listens through the attached earpieces. What he hears is the air you breathe as it moves through your respiratory system. There is a rushing sound over the larger airways and a gentle whiff over the smaller ones in the normal individual. The stethoscope picks up abnormalities as distinctly different sounds consisting of crackles, squeaks, or an increase or a decrease in the normal sounds.

What does a bronchoscope do?

This thin, flexible tube, with fibre-optic light source and viewer allows the doctor to see the body's dark air passages all the way down to the small tubes that lead to the lungs; areas of irritation, growths, or blockages become visible. The patient is given a local anaesthetic, and the instrument is inserted through the nose or mouth. A suction device, bronchial brushes, and small forceps make it possible for the physician to remove foreign objects or to withdraw samples of tissue. A separate channel delivers medication to the precise site where it is needed. Admirably versatile, the bronchoscope thus performs a number of functions that once were possible only through surgery.

How often should you have a chest X-ray?

Chest X-rays were once part of a regular physical examination, but today, doctors order far fewer routine X-rays than they used to, the precise frequency depending on the reason for the examination. The reason for the change in policy is that X-ray examinations expose patients to radiation. Although the doses are very low, doctors now believe that risks may outweigh benefits except in certain situations—for instance, cardi-

Wasp-waisted women of the Victorian era swooned frequently. The cry would go up, "Cut her laces!" Allowed sufficient air, the woman would come to.

The Breathless Fashions of Yesteryear

The women of ancient Greece and Rome wore a three-part corset of linen wrappings, restraining the figure much as a full-body corset does today. The female waistline has been relocated upwards and downwards over the centuries, with varying degrees of discomfort. But this fashion did not become a real health hazard until whalebone corsets came into widespread use in the late 19th and early 20th centuries, with even more constriction.

The harm that corsets did to vital organs was recognized at the time. Compare the normal figure, left, with right.

LUNGS constricted

LIVER squeezed inhibiting function

STOMACH dislocated

SMALL INTESTINES and BOWELS squeezed

BLADDER compressed

ac conditions and to monitor heavy smokers and people whose occupations put them at risk of lung cancer.

In most other cases, X-ray photography is now used mainly to give doctors more information about an already-diagnosed disease or injury, or to check on the results of surgery. For purely diagnostic purposes, pulmonary function tests and other tests are often simpler, less expensive, and more informative, and they have replaced routine X-rays.

What are pulmonary function tests?

There is one thing most people don't have to worry about—being able to breathe in enough air. You have an enormous "respiratory re-serve"—that is, you can breathe in much more air than you need at rest, and your breathing increases with exercise. Even when a lung is removed, patients may not feel short of breath, unless they are exercising.

When people do complain of chronic shortness of breath at rest or during mild exercise or when lung disease is suspected, a physician may prescribe pulmonary function tests. These tests measure the respiratory capacities of your lungs against the mean capacities of healthy people of the same sex and age.

One test measures "tidal volume," the amount of air—about 500 cubic centimetres (30 cubic inches)—that moves in and out of the lungs with each breathing cycle of a resting subject.

Another test measures "maximal breathing capacity," the considerably larger volumes of air that you can move when you force yourself to inhale or exhale deeply. The normal range is about 0.125 to 0.17 cubic metres (4.5 to 6 cubic feet) per minute in healthy young male adults and about 0.1 to 0.14 cubic metres (3.5 to 5 cubic feet) in healthy young females. Since even healthy people tend to lose some lung elasticity over the years, reductions of 20 percent by age 60 and of 40 percent by age 75 are considered normal. Confinement to bed for several days reduces breathing capacity; regular exercise increases it.

Pulmonary function tests are performed with a spirometer, which collects and measures the air and records the findings on a graph. Some physicians have such equipment in their surgery; others refer patients to a hospital or specialized clinic.

Sneezes, Wheezes, and Coughs

Measurement of sneezers in action indicate that the expelled air may reach a speed of 160 kilometres (100 miles) or more an hour. In ancient times, people believed that the soul fled the body during a sneeze, and that devils would invade the body unless someone cried out, "God bless you!"

What is a sneeze?

Sneezes are frequently triggered off by dust, pollen, or other types of irritant particles that settle on the sensitive mucous membranes in the nose. Richly supplied with nerves, these membranes react by sending signals to the respiratory centre that is located at the base of the brain. Almost immediately, the signals are sent to the muscles involved in breathing, causing the subject first to inhale, and then to close the airways and use respiratory muscles to squeeze the chest. When the air in the lungs is under high enough pressure, the airways suddenly open, expelling the irritant from the nose and mouth. The result is a sneeze, a primitive defence mechanism by which the body tries to expel an irritant from its pathways. The air in the lungs virtually explodes upwards and outwards, carrying everything in its path.

The mucus-laden air exits primarily from the mouth, but it can also come from the nose. Each sneeze may contain as many as 5,000 droplets, and unless a hand or a handkerchief intervenes, some of this material, which may be infectious, can travel as far as 4 metres (13 feet).

What causes coughing?

Coughing is very similar to sneezing except that the irritating substances are located in the lower parts of the respiratory system—the larynx, the trachea, the bronchi.

Doctors tend to take coughs seriously when they last more than two weeks. Violent coughing may damage the vocal cords, bronchi, or lungs. It can also break ribs and strain abdominal muscles so severely as to cause some of them to tear away or rupture. At the very least, coughing disturbs sleep. Chronic coughing is sometimes a symptom of an underlying disorder, such as sinusitis, asthma, allergies, tuberculosis, emphysema, or lung cancer.

Can cough medicines help?

If you should have a dry, or so-called unproductive, cough—that is, one in which the irritant keeps triggering off the cough reflex without clearing the airway—a cough suppressant can be helpful. The most effective chemical agent is codeine, but because it is a narcotic that may cause dependency as well as other undesirable side effects, it is used only in very small amounts in over-the-counter medications, and physicians are usually conservative when they prescribe drugs containing codeine for any prolonged period. Somewhat less powerful is the non-narcotic suppressant called dextromethorphan.

Medications classed as "expectorants," available in both over-the-counter and prescription forms, are intended to encourage "productive" coughs: those that bring up fluid from the lungs. The manufacturers of expectorants say that these agents liquefy nasal mucus and thus help to clear it from the airways. However, some pharmacologists would dispute that claim, saying that many expectorant cough medicines are ineffective and that the rest carry a variety of health risks.

Sucking hard sweets, drinking lots of liquids, and keeping the air moist with a humidifier normally makes coughers more comfortable. But under no circumstances should you attempt to treat a prolonged cough on your own; see your doctor to determine its cause.

What is a common cold?

Surprisingly enough, the ever-unpopular and always-with-us affliction known as the common cold is not a single specific disease. Similar symptoms may be caused by some 200 different viruses.

Physicians define a cold as a rapidly developing infection that is localized in the upper respiratory passages and leads to nasal congestion or stuffiness, runny nose, and sometimes throat irritation. If you start counting from the moment the first symptoms appear to the time when cold-related congestion finally clears away, the typical cold lasts about seven days. But there is considerable variability from person to person and also from virus to virus.

Why does a cold start with a runny nose?

In fact, it doesn't. By the time your nose begins to run, your cold is already between one and four days old. Cold viruses produce no symptoms when they first enter the system; the real beginning of a cold therefore passes unnoticed.

What's happening when your nose runs is that the mucous membrane that lines it has stepped up its production of fluid in response to the viral attackers. Inflammation, which causes the tiny nasal blood vessels to swell and the passages to become congested, is also part of the defensive system of your body, however unwelcome the side effects of its protective efforts.

Why do you get more colds in winter?

The cold-producing viruses are not necessarily more active or more numerous in winter than at other seasons; the body is just more receptive to them then. Cooped up indoors during the colder months, people are constantly exposed at short range to the sources of infection. Equally important, winter air—especially indoors—tends to be exceptionally dry. Breathed into the respiratory system, dry air severely inhibits the mucous membrane's ability to resist infection. Consequently, a cold virus that would be vigorously resisted by the body in springtime may meet much less opposition in winter.

Can you get a cold from wet feet?

So far as specialists in the common cold can determine, there is no direct connection between contracting a cold and getting your feet wet, walking in the rain, or sitting around in a draught. Some years ago, researchers in Great Britain ran an elaborate experiment designed to discover the effect of chilling and physical misery on a group of volunteers. Dividing the subjects into three groups, the researchers inoculated one set with cold viruses and had them stand around in the cold for half an hour wearing wet swimsuits. A second group was exposed to the same physical discomfort but not inoculated. A third group was inoculated with cold virus but left dry and comfortable. In due course, the first and third groups succumbed to the sniffles at just about the same rate, while the soggy-suited second group, which had not been inoculated, stayed healthy.

Folklore of the Body: FEED A COLD, STARVE A FEVER

You should really feed both because any kind of infection uses up energy, and food furnishes the energy. The saying had its origins in the ancient belief concerning the humours—the supposed four fluids within the body (blood, phlegm, choler or yellow bile, and melancholy or black bile). Fever was once thought to be caused by excess of blood, the fiery hot humour. Depriving it of fuel (that is to say, food) would put the fire out. Correspondingly, stoking the body with food would counter the effects of the cold humour which was phlegm. The unending search for specific remedies for the miseries of colds, fevers, sore throats, and coughs has produced some fairly far-fetched concoctions—boiled

snails in barley water, for example. In Russian folk medicine, rubbing the chest with pork fat was thought to be quite efficacious, while in some parts of the United States, the skin and fur of a black cat was wrapped around the neck to try to do away with sore throats. These days, over-the-counter preparations are available to relieve some of the symptoms of a cold, but probably the best thing anyone can do is rest, keep warm, drink plenty of liquids, and eat light, easily digestible meals.

Traditionally, a cold sufferer has bundled up, soaked his feet in hot tubs, and sipped whatever concoction was in fashion. But no remedy is really able to shorten the duration of these afflictions.

Our Shared Miseries

How do viruses cause a cold?

In some ways, viruses are notably unimpressive enemies, and it seems surprising that they can cause so much misery.

As compared with bacteria, which are another principal cause of human disease, viruses are perhaps a hundred times smaller—averaging 3 millionths of a millimetre (ten millionths of an inch) in diameter. They are also far more primitive in their structure than bacteria. Viruses cannot reproduce outside a cell, an ability that they would seem to need in order to spread disease. Nevertheless, viruses do have a capability that makes up for some of their limitations: they can penetrate a body cell and live off its substance.

Fortunately, the body is not altogether helpless in a viral attack. The respiratory tract is visited by cold viruses quite frequently, but it succumbs to them only now and then. Nasal hairs, microscopic filaments on cells called cilia, and mucus are all actively engaged in keeping viruses from attaching themselves to cells.

Each species of virus is particular about the kind of cell it victimizes. Common cold viruses, for example, can attach themselves only to the mucous membrane that lines the respiratory tract. They get there mainly through the nostrils.

While it is possible to become infected as the result of someone sneezing in your face, you are far more likely to "catch a cold" from the surfaces you touch, particularly by touching someone who is in the early stages of a cold.

Are some people more vulnerable to colds than others?

It's a fact that as people get older, they tend to have fewer colds. The chief reason is that age seems to confer an increasing degree of immunity to common cold viruses, but it is also likely that older people wash their hands more often and are more careful about what they touch.

An otherwise healthy infant typically gets 6 to 12 colds and other respiratory infections in its first year of life. The frequency drops gradually until, by the teens, the youngster probably gets no more than two to three colds per year. That frequency continues, or even declines, until the individual becomes the parent of a young child. Then, close contact with youngsters who are themselves repeatedly infected may overwhelm a parent's immune defences. Mothers, especially, tend to share many of their younger children's colds.

Some studies of susceptibility to colds suggest that economic factors may also influence the frequency with which a person becomes infected. Families at the bottom end of the income scale suffer approximately one-third more colds than those at the top, perhaps because their diet is less nutritious and their living quarters more cramped.

There is also some evidence suggesting that stress may precipitate the common cold—just as it can other illnesses. While the reasons are not clearly established, specialists theorize that people frequently respond to stress by smoking or drinking to excess or by becoming overtired, all of which may impair the immune defences of the body.

Is influenza just a bad version of the common cold?

If your nose is stuffed up and your throat sore, you may not know (or even care) whether you have a flu or a cold; both ailments make you feel miserable in much the same way. But influenza and colds are caused by different viruses. And flu has some symptoms of its own, ranging from headache, chills, eye soreness, and widespread muscle ache to crushing fatigue and fever of 40 °C (104 °F) or higher.

Flu is considered a potentially dangerous infection for the very young, the elderly, and those made infirm by chronic heart or lung disease. Some doctors recommend yearly immunization against the most active flu strains for these three groups.

DID YOU KNOW...?

- **At one time** people believed that the main reason for breathing was to cool the blood, and also to provide for the voice.

- **Some native peoples of the Andes Mountains** of South America have adapted to the thin atmosphere of its high altitudes—only 0.5 kilograms per square centimetre (7 pounds per square inch) as compared with about twice as much at sea level—by developing oversized lungs.

- **The word "influenza"** is derived from the word *influence*—presumably an evil influence from the stars or some other source that brought pestilence.

- **Bouquets and plants** don't have to be taken out of a sickroom at night. True, plants do use oxygen when they are not in sunlight, but the amount they use is insignificant. A better reason for removal is that they can play host to insects, and the water in which flowers are placed can be a breeding ground for germs.

- **The stethoscope was invented** by Dr. Rene Läennec, a French physician of the late 18th and early 19th centuries. He had a patient with a heart condition, and found that he could not hear chest sounds. Läennec rolled paper tightly into a tube, put one end to her chest, the other to his ear, and heard perfectly. Later stethoscopes added earpieces, rubber tubing, and a chest piece, but the principle is exactly the same.

- **The average person breathes** some 400,000 cubic metres (14 million cubic feet) of air in an average lifetime.

Influenza: The Elusive Enemy

The annual immunization of people in "at risk" groups is recognition of the fact that influenza is a recurring threat. The trouble is, it is difficult to predict which of the many kinds of flu virus will sweep the globe in the coming winter. Type-A influenza virus has a pattern of returning every two to three years, Type-B influenza occurs in cycles of about four to five years. The immunity you get from having one type of influenza virus and forming specific antibodies to fight it is not effective against another type of influenza. Four major strains—A, B, C, and D viruses—have numerous sub-strains, which exhibit a tendency to mutate. That is, they can change significantly, to the detriment of their human hosts. Those at greatest risk are the very young, who have not had influenza before, and the elderly and infirm whose general resistance is low. The famous Asian flu epidemic of 1957 was just one strain of the Type-A virus.

Bristling with spikes, like explosive floating naval mines, these influenza-A viruses, magnified 200,000 times, are set to attack.

Landing on a lung cell, (above) an A-virus burrows its way deep inside, releases its genes and takes over, causing the cell to manufacture a great number of A-virus genes. Finally, the new viruses break out, ready to invade other cells.

Gauze masks proved useless during the 1918 influenza epidemic, which killed an estimated 20 million people worldwide.

121

Disorders and Diseases of the Lung

What is bronchitis?

In its acute, short-term form, bronchitis—an inflammation of the mucous membrane that lines the conducting airways—is usually not itself a disease but a complication of other diseases, such as the common cold, influenza, sinus infection, or measles. Sometimes it is caused by a bacterial infection. The typical symptoms of bronchitis are a cough, which brings up phlegm, mild fever, and general malaise. In otherwise healthy people, an attack usually subsides within ten days, or sooner if it is treated with antibiotics. In the elderly and the very young, however, it may be complicated by pneumonia and should be watched carefully.

Chronic bronchitis is a serious health problem. It can cause permanent damage to the respiratory system, including inflammation, thickening, and loss of elasticity in the walls of the conducting air passages. There may be partial obstruction with an excess of sticky mucus, and the lungs may be less able to transfer oxygen to the blood. Chronic bronchitis may also be a symptom of a preexisting lung disease.

A person is considered to have chronic bronchitis if bronchial symptoms last at least three months and recur in two or more consecutive years. More men than women suffer from the disease, which is more prevalent in urban than in rural areas. Heavy smoking and poor air quality are contributing factors.

What causes asthma?

Probably everyone knows someone who has had to give up a pet cat or dog because of an allergic reaction to animal hairs. Such a reaction can take several forms, including bronchial asthma. Animal hairs, however, are not the only foreign substances that can cause asthma; others are plant pollen, dust, feathers, and certain chemicals and foods. Typically, an attack occurs when the sufferer inhales the offending substance, called an allergen, and the hypersensitive muscles embedded in the smaller bronchi go into intense spasm. Virtual strangulation can occur as the air passages close down to pinhole size, and full recovery may take days.

Asthma cannot be cured, but it can usually be controlled by a combination of therapies once the substance or substances that trigger off attacks have been identified. In some instances, a drug taken regularly by inhaler, or by mouth, will help to prevent attacks. When an acute attack occurs, certain drugs that dilate the

Airborne Allergens

Asthma and hay fever, or allergic rhinitis, are unpleasant problems which are our bodies' abnormal reactions to substances that are known as allergens. Among these allergens are pollen, household dust, flecks of sloughed-off animal skin, and down-filled pillows. When these airborne irritants are breathed in by hypersensitive people, the immune system of their bodies reacts by pouring out "protective" histamines that cause wheezing, itching, sneezing, and other symptoms.

The tendency to develop an allergy is inherited, and up to 10 percent of the population suffers from one or more of them. The best and most obvious treatment for an allergy is to avoid the offending substance. But if that is not possible, specialists can now isolate allergens with skin tests and prescribe anti-allergy drugs to ease the symptoms. Some drugs, taken regularly, have the effect of "damping down" the body's allergic response to irritating allergens. Others, such as antihistamines, taken when symptoms appear, reduce the output of symptom-producing chemicals.

When a tiny dust mite (here greatly magnified) is inhaled, it can cause symptoms of allergy.

Pollen grains from timothy grass (left) make life unpleasant for victims of hay fever.

bronchi are helpful. In extreme cases hospitalization and a mechanical respirator may be required.

Asthma usually makes its first appearance during childhood. Fortunately, many of its victims outgrow their sensitivity by the time they reach adulthood. In some people, psychological factors can play a role in the severity of attacks, but all cases of asthma begin with a physical predisposition to hypersensitivity.

Why is lung cancer on the rise?

Once upon a time—that is, long before cigarette smoking became so popular, and air pollution was such a serious problem—lung cancer was a rare disease. However, now, at a time when the mortality rates for most kinds of cancers are declining, the number of deaths from lung cancer (technically called bronchogenic carcinoma) is rising. The dramatic increase in the number of women smokers is part of the explanation: lung cancer was for many years restricted almost entirely to men, among whom it accounted for approximately 30 percent of all cancer deaths. But as more women have become smokers—and heavy smokers at that—the frequency of lung cancer among them has risen steadily.

The worldwide decline in air quality as a result of industrial and urban growth has led to greater exposure to toxic materials via air pollution. The proportion of your lungs directly exposed to the environment is greater than any other part of the body—the inner surface of the lungs is 40 times larger than your skin. When you consider these facts, you can easily understand why the lungs are so sensitive to air quality.

Has tuberculosis ceased to be a health hazard?

Years ago, tuberculosis was known as consumption because, almost inevitably, it progressively "consumed," or wasted, the body. Thanks to immunization and the introduction of effective drug therapy in the 1950s, TB is no longer the common, deadly disease it once was. It still causes over 300 deaths each year in Britain, chiefly among elderly people who did not have the benefit of immunization.

The cause of TB is the bacillus called *Mycobacterium tuberculosis*. After establishing themselves in a vulnerable lung, the bacteria create cavities and cause the formation of scar tissue. Symptoms include persistent coughing, fatigue, blood in the sputum, loss of weight, or loss of appetite. Treatment for TB is usually drug therapy.

Windborne pollen from trees causes sneezing, tears, and runny noses.

Cats shed fur and skin that trigger allergies.

Respiratory Emergencies

What is hyperventilation?

One of the most frightening experiences anyone can have is an attack of "air hunger," a panicky feeling of suffocation that leads to deep, rapid breathing. The technical term for this experience is hyperventilation, sometimes called overbreathing.

Oddly enough, although victims of overbreathing feel short of breath and breathe more deeply and rapidly to get more air into their lungs, their real difficulty is that they are taking in *too much* air. Instead of making them feel better, their unusual breathing pattern makes things worse, because it removes too much carbon dioxide from the blood. We tend to think of oxygen as "good" and of carbon dioxide as "bad." In fact, the body needs only a certain amount of oxygen, and it is normal for some carbon dioxide to remain in the body.

Within minutes of the start of hyperventilation, the disturbance in the acidity of the blood due to loss of carbon dioxide produces lightheadedness, dizziness, sweating, rapid heartbeat, and tingling or numbness in hands and feet. Fainting sometimes occurs. (Hyperventilation may even be mistaken for a heart attack.)

Fortunately there is an easy way to end an attack. The right balance of oxygen and carbon dioxide in the blood can be restored by having the victim breathe into a paper bag for a few minutes. As some of the exhaled carbon dioxide is returned to the lungs from the bag, breathing returns to normal. If the victim faints, breathing may stop temporarily but will start again when enough carbon dioxide is produced by the body.

What causes a lung to collapse?

A collapsed lung, or atelectasis, is an emergency condition that sometimes occurs in infants right after birth because the lungs fail to expand properly. Adults may also experience a collapsed lung because of a chest injury, a foreign object in the windpipe, an obstruction of a bronchus (airway) by a mucus plug, or a tumour.

One form of lung collapse is known as pneumothorax. Normally, a very slight vacuum between the two layers of tissue surrounding the lung keeps it inflated. In pneumothorax, air gets into the space between these two layers, breaks the vacuum, and air deflates the lung, crowding it and preventing it from expanding. In almost all instances, with prompt medical treatment, the lung returns to normal breathing function.

What is emphysema, and can it be cured?

In emphysema, a serious lung condition, the air sacs, or alveoli, enlarge or overdistend, losing their elasticity and part of their blood supply. The disease interferes with the exchange of oxygen and carbon dioxide in the bloodstream. It is commonest among middle-aged and older men, those who suffer from bronchitis or asthma or live in air-polluted areas, and heavy smokers. Symptoms of emphysema include shortness of breath, wheezing, bluish skin (cyanosis), and a chronic, sometimes painful cough that produces thick, sticky sputum.

The damage caused by emphysema is irreversible, but if the victim stops smoking or moves to a place where air pollution is minimal, the progress of the disease can be halted. Unfortunately, those who suffer from emphysema are prone to secondary respiratory infections and to heart disease.

What should you do if someone chokes?

When food or some other foreign body gets stuck in the windpipe, permanent brain damage or death from asphyxiation can occur in the space of four minutes.

There are three things you can do to save someone who is choking. One is to compress the victim's thoracic cavity from below so that the air in the lungs is forced out of the windpipe, blowing the obstruction before it (see box at right).

A second possibility is to give the victim several blows between the shoulder blades with the heel of your hand. Preferably the victim should be lying on his side, with the head lower

Normal lung tissue (left) contrasts sharply with an emphysema victim's lung tissue (right) in these photomicrographs. Alveoli in the diseased lung have stretched, so less oxygen can penetrate their walls and enter the bloodstream.

than the chest; otherwise, the blows could drive the air-obstructing object further down instead of upwards.

In most cases of choking, the air passage is not completely blocked; if a person breathes quietly, he may be able to get enough air to sustain life for more than four minutes. So, if neither of these measures works, try to calm the victim's panic, and urge him to breathe slowly while you get him to a hospital.

One other thing: do not mistake choking for a heart attack. Someone having a heart attack can usually speak; one who is choking cannot.

How does artificial respiration work?

Several methods have been developed to restart breathing when it has stopped because of accident, asphyxiation, strangulation, heart stoppage, drug overdose, or electric shock. Artificial respiration keeps the body supplied with vital oxygen until the victim begins breathing naturally or can be put on a mechanical respirator.

Mouth-to-mouth resuscitation is the best known and most widely used method of artificial respiration. The rescuer stretches the victim out on his back, lifts his neck so that his head is tilted back as far as possible, and then breathes into his mouth at the rate of 15 times per minute for adults (20 times per minute for children), blowing hard enough each time to raise the chest as in normal breathing. It is important that the victim's nose should be pinched closed during the procedure to prevent air from escaping and to ensure that air is forced into the lungs.

Sometimes spontaneous breathing resumes after as many as three hours of seemingly fruitless effort. This is the reason why rescue professionals are trained to continue their highly demanding efforts as long as there is even the slightest hope of the victim responding positively.

Mechanical artificial respiration is administered with the aid of machinery that does the work of the body's own air exchange system.

Rescue of a Choking Victim

Quick, decisive action is needed when a person starts to choke due to something stuck in the throat, blocking the airway. The victim will not be able to call for help—he will only be able to gesture. The torso must be compressed sharply so that air in the lungs will explode out through the victim's trachea, dislodging the object. If you choke when on your own—or others don't know what to do—position yourself over a hardback chair or any firm object, and thrust your abdomen quickly and repeatedly against it until the obstruction is cleared.

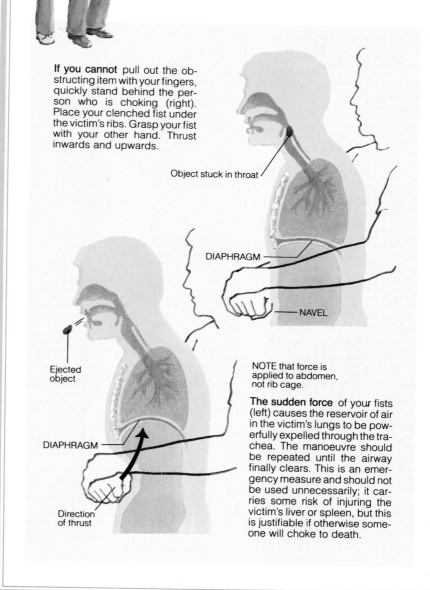

If you cannot pull out the obstructing item with your fingers, quickly stand behind the person who is choking (right). Place your clenched fist under the victim's ribs. Grasp your fist with your other hand. Thrust inwards and upwards.

Object stuck in throat

DIAPHRAGM

NAVEL

Ejected object

DIAPHRAGM

Direction of thrust

NOTE that force is applied to abdomen, not rib cage.

The sudden force of your fists (left) causes the reservoir of air in the victim's lungs to be powerfully expelled through the trachea. The manoeuvre should be repeated until the airway finally clears. This is an emergency measure and should not be used unnecessarily; it carries some risk of injuring the victim's liver or spleen, but this is justifiable if otherwise someone will choke to death.

Hazards in the Environment

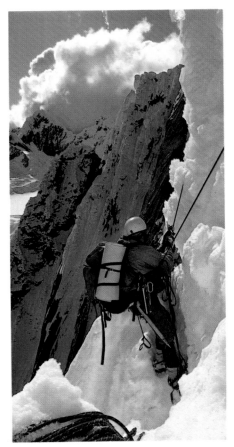

At high altitudes mountain climbers run the risk of hypoxia, an oxygen deficiency that can produce mental fatigue and drowsiness. The remedy is to carry a tank of oxygen.

What is mountain sickness?

Sherpas, the famed mountain people of Nepal (as well as famed mountaineers), can survive for many hours at altitudes as high as 8,000 metres (26,000 feet), where there is very little oxygen. The average dweller at sea level may begin to experience mountain sickness—the result of too little oxygen in the blood—at much lower altitudes, perhaps at about 2,500 metres (8,250 feet); for some the effects begin at lower altitudes. Even Sherpas need acclimatization to very high altitudes.

Most people live between sea level and 2,000 metres (6,500 feet) in altitude. As the altitude increases, the available oxygen decreases, but the differences among most cities are not great enough to cause discomfort in most healthy people travelling from a low- to a high-altitude city.

When altitude change is sudden and extreme, physical and psychological signs of mountain sickness begin to appear. The symptoms include dizziness, weakness, headache, shortness of breath, poor judgment, and either depression or, in some cases, an unnatural elation.

Mountain sickness can also occur in high-flying aeroplanes if cabin pressure is lost; that is why planes are equipped with oxygen masks. In the mountains, symptoms usually disappear by themselves in a few days as the body makes adjustments to decreases in available oxygen. After some time additional red blood cells are made to transport the limited amount of oxygen available. Drugs can also be used to combat mountain sickness. (The reason the Sherpas can survive better at high altitudes is that their bodies have been accustomed from birth to low oxygen levels, but they also must adjust to the *very* small amount of available oxygen at very great heights.)

How does the weather affect breathing?

In 1952, a London fog killed some 4,000 people—but this is certainly an extreme example of weather as a respiratory hazard.

People naturally vary widely in their susceptibility to the effects of air pollution, but research shows that certain weather conditions make breathing more difficult, and in some instances more dangerous, for just about everyone.

The most publicized of these conditions is temperature inversion. Usually, the temperature of the air drops as elevation increases. This situation can be reversed under certain atmospheric conditions. The temperature inversion that results can pose very serious health hazards to populations throughout the world.

When temperature inversion occurs, the warmer upper-air temperatures act as a lid to hold at ground level fog and pollutants that would otherwise dissipate. After a few days of exposure to such conditions, people whose vigour is marginal—such as newborn infants and the infirm elderly, and asthmatics—often suffer ill effects and even death.

Which air pollutants are most hazardous to health?

One thing is certain: clean air is definitely a rarity, not only in cities but, increasingly, in places located far from metropolitan centres. Government authorities have been raising standards for air quality, but progress is slow. Tests taken of urban air reveal such toxic substances as lead, copper, zinc, sulphur dioxide, and carbon monoxide.

While some pollutants are more toxic than others, the total quantity of pollutants to which people are exposed generally matters more than any particular substance. Consider the fact that near certain urban industrial complexes, more than 1 metric tonne of pollutants descend daily on each square kilometre (2.5 tons on each square mile). And surprisingly, even high-flying aeroplanes lower the quality of the air; a jet liner dumps an estimated 2 metric tonnes of carbon monoxide into the atmosphere in a six-hour flight, say across the Atlantic.

Can your house be dangerous?

Exposure to air pollution may be ten times greater inside your home than outdoors, according to an American survey. In a study of the air in 40 average households, it found such hazardous pollutants as formaldehyde, carbon monoxide, carbon dioxide, sulphur dioxide, asbestos, plastics, solvents, pesticides, chloroform, benzene, and smoke. Potential medical problems associated with inhaling some of these substances over a long period include allergic reactions, cancer, and birth defects.

Indoor air pollution has increased significantly with the changes in building materials and construction methods, and also with the growing use of house-cleaning and beauty-care products. Contributors to pollution include aerosols, unvented kerosene heaters, and even emissions from recently dry-cleaned fabrics.

Aggravating the problem are tightly built, super-insulated houses. So little fresh air enters some houses and so little stale air escapes that indoor pollutants accumulate and sometimes can reach health-threatening levels. Many medical authorities now recommend that people living in well-sealed houses install controlled ventilation systems that can monitor and upgrade indoor air.

What jobs can put your lungs at high risk?

The link between respiratory diseases and certain occupations is just about as old as civilization. When people work year after year in dusty, unventilated shops, mines, and factories, and breathe in high concentrations of one or more foreign substances, many cases of lung disease are inevitable. All of these diseases cause discomfort, varying degrees of disability, and sometimes death.

Three basic kinds of agents that can cause occupational lung diseases have been identified: organic dusts, including moulds, animal proteins, and plant dusts; inorganic dusts, including heavy metal particles; and airborne chemicals. Exposed to these agents, smokers are apparently at higher risk than the average worker.

Among the various diseases of the respiratory system triggered off by organic dusts are farmer's lung, which attacks farm workers who handle hay; brown lung, which is associated with the milling of cotton and other fibres; and mushroom worker's lung from mushroom spores.

Some occupational lung diseases due to inorganic dusts include silicosis, from quartz dust, sand, stone dust, and silicon; black-lung disease, caused by coal dust; and berylliosis, from the beryllium used in making fluorescent lamps.

Also implicated is asbestos, which when processed, yields a fine dust that obstructs the airways and scars the lungs. The resulting disease, asbestosis, makes breathing difficult and hampers the body's efforts to take in oxygen and get rid of carbon dioxide. Miners, factory workers, and construction workers are most at risk, but people in buildings in which asbestos has been used may also be exposed to excessive levels of it.

Job-related chemical offenders include the solvents used in paints and substances used in pesticides.

If you suspect you have a job-related lung problem, you should discuss it with your doctor. If you cannot change your working conditions, you may have to find a new job.

At approximately 10 metres (33 feet), the pressure is about twice the pressure the human body is used to.

The Dangers of the Deep

The reason that diving is hazardous to the novice is that the pressure of the air breathed increases in proportion to the increase in water pressure on descent. Scuba (self-contained underwater breathing apparatus) gear permits the continual equalization of the air with the water pressure. This equipment has freed divers from the heavy pressurized suits and the air lines to the surface, but it demands new knowledge and additional training. Spending too long at even a relatively shallow depth of water can result in headaches, dizziness, vomiting, pains in the joints, and other serious consequences. If the diver panics and holds his breath upon ascent, the pressurized air can rupture delicate lung tissue, forcing air into the bloodstream. Rising quickly to the brain, it can cause unconsciousness and death. The only treatment is prompt recompression. Bends, a serious consequence of too long a submersion at too great a depth, is the result of nitrogen bubbles in the tissue and the blood.

The deeper you go and the longer you stay down, the greater the danger of your getting the bends.

Report on Smoking

Smoking: A New World Invention

When Columbus landed in the New World in 1492, he and his men were astonished to find the native Indians smoking rolled-up tobacco leaves, the forerunners of present-day cigars. In the 16th century, Sir Walter Raleigh set London on its ear by puffing away on an elaborate pipe that he brought back from America. Soon tobacco smoking spread to Europe, and the craze was on. Doctors, noting its soothing effects, prescribed tobacco for all sorts of ailments, including lockjaw. In time, the craze was taken up by America's new settlers. Cigars, called "stogies" because the hard-bitten drivers of Conestoga wagons liked them, were especially popular. By the late 1800s, cigarettes, which were really tiny cigars wrapped in paper, were a major industry, with millions of millions being sold each year.

The sacred pipe (above) was an object of veneration for almost all American Indian tribes. It was used for relaxation and in all ceremonies.

The swashbuckling English adventurer Walter Raleigh created a sensation by introducing smoking to England. When a servant saw him puffing away on his pipe, his face wreathed in smoke, he panicked, and tried to put out the "fire" by dousing Raleigh with a mug of ale.

Why is smoking bad for you?

Bad breath, a chronic hacker's cough, emphysema, heart disease, cancer—all these, and more, can be blamed at least partly on smoking.

The smoke of burning tobacco contains many irritants and poisonous gases. First among them is carbon monoxide, the substance also found in the deadly fumes of motor car exhaust. What makes carbon monoxide dangerous is its extraordinary ability to combine with haemoglobin, the substance in the blood that carries life-giving oxygen to tissues. Carbon monoxide wins out over oxygen, so that heavy smokers deprive themselves of up to 10 percent of the oxygen-carrying capacity of the blood.

Lack of oxygen leads to a number of harmful changes in the way the body functions. For one thing, the heart must pump faster to supply oxygen. Smoking also constricts the blood vessels in the fingers and toes, causing poor circulation. Compared to a non-smoker, the average smoker has more than twice the chance of experiencing a heart attack. In addition, women who smoke *and* use oral contraceptives are 20 times more likely to develop heart disease than non-smokers. There may be other, still unknown changes in the smoker's blood chemistry.

What substances in smoke cause cancer?

Sticky black or brown substances not unlike the stuff used on highways, tobacco tars are the chief carcinogens in smoke. They collect on the sensitive tissues of the respiratory system, irritate them, and after a few years cause such disorders as chronic bronchitis and cancer.

Cigarette smoking can lead to cancer in many parts of the body, but not surprisingly, most of the damage it does is to the lungs. Lung cancer is now the most common form of cancer in the Western world. Men who have smoked heavily for 20 years or more are 20 times as susceptible to it as non-smokers. Women, in whom lung cancer was once rare, are now increasingly subject to the disease as they join the ranks of heavy smokers.

Are some kinds of smoking more dangerous than others?

Most cigarette smokers would like to believe they can protect themselves from cancer just by using a holder, or by switching to filter-tips, cigars, or a pipe. Unfortunately, they can't.

But not all kinds of smoking are alike. It is fairly well established that the dangers of smoking are directly related to the amounts of tar, nicotine, and carbon monoxide absorbed into the system. Cigarette smokers usually inhale smoke directly into the respiratory tract and lungs; pipe and cigar smokers do not. Thus, cigarettes are far more likely to be associated with lung cancer and heart disease than are pipes or cigars. But pipe and cigar smokers have their own worries. Lung cancer occurs more often among them than among non-smokers, and cancer of the lips, mouth, larynx, and oesophagus are considerably more common in pipe and cigar smokers.

As far as choosing between filter-tipped, regular, high-tar, high-nicotine and low-tar, or low-nicotine cigarettes, a smoker is theoretically better off with a filter-tipped brand that promises the least of everything bad. In practice, however, the "switcher" does not necessarily reduce his risks this way, because people accustomed to high concentrations of tar and nicotine compensate, when they switch, for the mildness of filter-tips by smoking more cigarettes and by inhaling more deeply. Those who take up cigarette holders often end up smoking more of each cigarette.

Are there extra hazards to smoking during pregnancy?

Because mother and foetus are so closely linked, the dangers of smoking predate birth. Studies show that pregnant women who smoke 15 to 20 cigarettes a day are twice as likely to miscarry as non-smoking mothers. Infants of mothers who smoke weigh less than do children of non-smokers. The probable explanation is oxygen deficiency, which afflicts not only the mother (because she inhales the carbon monoxide in cigarette smoke) but the developing infant, too.

In the weeks following birth, smokers' infants have a mortality rate nearly 30 percent higher than that of non-smokers' babies. Nursing babies take in small amounts of nicotine with breast milk. Later, they are more prone to respiratory infections and have a higher incidence of pneumonia than the rest of the population.

Is it ever too late to stop smoking?

All the destructive processes smoking generates seem, in the main, to halt once you have stubbed out your last cigarette. After you stop smoking, your chances of developing a smoking-associated disease diminish year by year.

In one recent large-scale study, researchers found that ten years after stopping smoking, ex-smokers had less than half the risk of developing lung cancer of those who continued to smoke. For men and women who had smoked for less than 20 years before giving up, the risk of developing lung cancer after ten years without cigarettes was no greater than that of non-smokers.

Some of the benefits of giving up smoking appear immediately—for instance there is more oxygen and less carbon monoxide in the bloodstream.

Scores of techniques for quitting—acupuncture, hypnosis, yoga, and so on—have been proposed, and all of them have helped some people. But the essential factor is clearly the individual's own determination to quit.

When the Movies Promoted Smoking

Smoking really took off when it became all but synonymous with glamour, maturity, sophistication, and sex appeal. Many a movie love scene featured slow drags on cigarettes and lingering close-ups as hazy smoke drifted across the lovers' faces. The movies also perpetuated other smoking clichés. Strong, silent Western heroes "rolled their own." Successful executives kept big cigars clenched in their teeth. Awed by such role models, generations of filmgoers embraced the notion that smoking proved you were grown-up. Smoking ran into rough going, however, in the 1960s when cigarettes began to be widely branded as a health hazard. Later there were moves in many Western countries to control tobacco advertising on television and in other media.

The high point of smoking in films came in *Now, Voyager* when Paul Henreid lit two cigarettes and gave one to Bette Davis.

129

Chapter 6

THE SKIN

It is surprising to think of skin as an organ, on a par with liver or lungs, but so it is—the largest organ of all. Skin protects the body, provides information by touch, and even synthesizes vitamin D.

Skin: Our Remarkable Armour	132
The Ecology of Skin	134
The Skin You Are Born With	136
The Sensitivity of Human Skin	138
Your Skin at Risk	140
From Sunburn to Frostbite	142
Common Skin Problems	144
Repairing Damage, Taking Tucks	146
Healing and Hazards	148
The Human Skin as a Canvas	149
How and Where Hair Grows	150
Hair: Too Little, Too Much	152
Making Changes in Your Hair	154
Your Telltale Nails	156

What does skin do?

As a protective mantle, your skin is phenomenal. It is waterproof; it helps regulate body temperature; it intercepts and destroys harmful bacteria; it grows hairs; it excretes liquids and salts; and by its keen sensitivity to touch, it enables you to make contact with the world around you.

That is not all. The skin also absorbs ultraviolet rays from the sun, and uses them to convert chemicals into vitamin D, which the body needs for proper utilization of calcium.

Your body "suit" weighs from 2.5 to 4.5 kilograms (6 to 10 pounds), and if it were spread out flat, it would cover an area of about 2 square metres (2.5 square yards).

Why are some people more ticklish than others?

One of the odd things about tickling is that you can't do it to yourself. Another is the ambivalence of the psychological response to tickling. The first reaction to it is usually pleasure, but sometimes the pleasure becomes tinged with anxiety. The familiar expression "tickled to death" reflects something of the mingled fear and delight that tickling evokes.

Although the phenomenon of tickling is not well understood, it has been suggested that tickling (gentle movement with the fingertips) excites certain small, fine nerve endings just beneath the surface of the skin, especially on the palms and soles.

The response to being tickled is involuntary, though a person can sometimes control it by concentrating very hard. The first and most obvious reaction is laughter. In addition, the pulse quickens, the blood pressure rises, and the body becomes keyed up and alert.

What causes clammy hands and cold sweats?

Damp hands and drenching sweats are products of the emotions, fever, or exercise. Sweaty palms are often associated with anxiety and tension, while cold sweats are generally caused by an exceptionally strong emotion: fear bordering on panic.

What happens when you blush?

As far as anyone knows, human beings are the only living creatures who blush. Possibly this is because they are the only ones capable of feeling the self-consciousness, embarrassment, or shame that so often gives rise to blushing.

Emotions of this kind are easily recognized, but surprisingly, there is no agreement among scientists as to exactly what happens to cause blushing. Tiny blood vessels that supply the skin widen, and more blood than usual flows through them, suffusing the skin—usually the face, neck, and upper chest—with colour.

Your awareness of the intense colour in your face adds to your emotional discomfort. In fact, you may have wondered if you could keep yourself from blushing just by exerting your will power. Don't even bother trying. Blushing is an entirely involuntary reaction; if you are embarrassed, there is absolutely nothing you can do to control it.

Why are people different colours?

Everyone—the blondest Scandinavian and the darkest African included—has approximately the same number of pigment-manufacturing cells as everyone else. So skin colour has nothing at all to do with how many of these cells a person has but rather with the way the cells function in different people.

Specifically, variations that occur among races and among individuals of the same race come from the amount of brown pigment, known as melanin, present in the skin. The pigment cells, or melanocytes, of dark-complexioned people, whatever their race, produce more of this substance than do the pigment cells of people with fair complexions.

Skin colour can serve a utilitarian purpose. This is because melanin absorbs ultraviolet light, which is harmful in excess but valuable in moderation. In Africa and other very sunny places, dark skin offers protection from too much ultraviolet light, and therefore has survival value. In Scandinavia and in other parts of the world where there is less ultraviolet light, fair skin lets people get the sunlight they need for the formation of vitamin D in the body.

What is so special about red hair?

"Rutilism" has a forbidding sound, but it is only the scientific term for redheadedness; it comes from the Latin word for "red." Apart from its striking appearance, red hair is unusual because it gets its colour in an odd way. Most hair colours come from greater or lesser amounts of the pigment melanin: lots of melanin produces black hair, while people with very little of it have fair hair. But "pure" redheads have a gene that makes them produce the special reddish pigment that gives their hair its startling hue.

Sometimes the red pigment cannot compete with the melanin that everyone's body produces. In such cases, a high level of melanin in the hair dilutes the red tones, allowing only intriguing tints of reddish-brown auburn to show through. If the redheaded gene occurs in a fair person, the result is strawberry-blond hair.

For some unknown reason, red hair occurs more frequently in some countries than in others. In northern Germany, for instance, under 1 percent of the population is redheaded, while in some parts of Scotland, the figure is 11 percent. Wherever it occurs, red hair is definitely eye-catching; however, it carries some drawbacks with it. Redheads sunburn easily, and their skin is also hypersensitive to many medications.

Skin colour is determined by a pigment called melanin; dark-skinned people have more of this substance than others. Pink-complexioned people have so little melanin that blood colour shows through; albinos lack melanin.

Skin: Our Remarkable Armour

Why do we tend to think that skin is a simple structure?

Most of us really don't know what skin is. We judge it by the visible surface of our bodies, which certainly looks uncomplicated. In fact, that surface is merely the topmost layer of a complex, deep-reaching system that differs from place to place in the body. Seen in cross-section, the skin has two main levels, the dermis and the epidermis. The dermis is the lower thick foundation layer containing blood vessels that supply nutrients to the upper layer, sweat glands, hair roots, and nerves.

One authority surveying parts of the body found that in certain places a small area of whole skin no bigger than a ten pence coin contained vast numbers of blood vessels, approximately 65 hairs, 100 oil glands, 650 sweat glands, uncounted nerves, and 1,500 assorted nerve receptors.

How does skin grow?

On top of the dermis (which in Greek means "skin") is the epidermis ("upon the skin"). The lower cells of the epidermis continually produce new cells that thrust up into, and gradually become, the horny layer. As they rise, these cells flatten out, grow hard, and begin dying. The epidermis, unlike the dermis, lacks blood vessels. The life-support system for this layer is a kind of seepage of nutrients from below. Because it has no blood vessels or nerves, the horny layer feels no pain. When you sew, you may have noticed that you occasionally pierce the skin without causing pain or bleeding.

What good are goose pimples?

To tell the truth, not much. Most often, they develop in cold weather as part of the body's effort to keep its internal temperature within the normal range. Stimulated by the outside air, the cold receptors in the skin send signals to a part of the brain called the hypothalamus; it, in turn, sends signals to small, specialized blood vessels, which are found in great numbers throughout the skin. The signals also go to tiny muscles, which contract, raising body hairs and producing goose pimples.

Why do we sweat?

Scattered throughout the dermis are millions of minute glands that manufacture sweat and transfer it to the surface of the skin. There are two types of sweat glands, the eccrine and the apocrine, which respond to different stimuli.

The eccrine glands, found throughout the human skin, produce the greatest amount of sweat. Both the body surface temperature and the emotions stimulate them into action. The apocrine glands—found primarily in the armpits, the nipples, and the genital area—are present at birth but do not become fully active until puberty. They are responsive to strong emotions, ranging from fear and anger to sexual excitement.

In themselves, apocrine and eccrine sweats have no unpleasant odour. But when they reach the skin surface, both kinds—apocrine sweat especially—can acquire an offensive smell from the action of bacteria that thrive on moist, warm surfaces.

Is sweating a lot good for you?

About a tumblerful of water is lost through the skin every day. Because you are not aware of it, this is called "insensible" perspiration, which does not originate in the sweat glands but results from diffusion through the horny layer.

When the temperature rises, or when you do strenuous work, real sweating begins. From the skin's millions of pores, the watery secretions now emerge on your skin in visible drops. Soon the sweat pours off in rivulets. Under these conditions it is possible to sweat away more than 10 litres (2 gallons) of fluid in 24 hours.

If such heavy sweating goes on for a long time, it may be harmful. If the sweat does not evaporate as fast as it forms, you lose its cooling effect. Furthermore, heavy sweating depletes the body's supply of vital salts. And since sweating makes you thirsty, you are more likely to drink large quantities of fresh water, thus further diluting your salt reserves.

DID YOU KNOW...?

- **Queen Elizabeth I** relied on a white powder of ground alabaster or starch to embellish her face. Elizabethan ladies followed her lead, and they covered their faces with a glaze of egg white as a form of make-up protection.

- **Short haircuts for women** didn't become commonplace until World War I, when women began working in factories to help in the war effort. Their luxuriant tresses, combs, and hairpins had a way of catching in the machinery, so for safety and convenience, they cropped their hair.

- **So tough and durable is human skin** that when a 2,000-year-old Egyptian mummy was fingerprinted, the ridges were found to be perfectly preserved.

- **Cold cream was invented by the Greeks** who used a mixture of olive oil, beeswax, water, and rose petals. It is the evaporation of water, which has a cooling effect, that gave cold cream its name. Today's products are highly refined and have extra ingredients, but the basic formula hasn't changed.

- **Ringworm is not caused by worms.** It is a highly contagious, very itchy fungus infection, tinea, that is spread on the body by scratching.

- **Hair grows faster in summer** than in winter, just as your nails do. But frequent haircuts do not speed growth; it just *seems* that way.

How deep is "skin deep"?

Skin thickness varies tremendously—it is thinnest on the eyelids, thickest on the palms of the hands and the soles of the feet. But on average, the epidermis, or topmost layer of skin, is only about 0.1 millimetres (1 two-hundred-and-fiftieth of an inch) thick. Beneath the epidermis lies the dermis, which is about four times thicker than the epidermis.

The outermost layer of the epidermis, called the horny layer, is made up of skin in its last stages—flattened, insensitive, and just about ready to flake off. The other layers of the epidermis are alive, receiving nourishment by a process called diffusion.

The dermis, which gives the skin its nutrition, sturdiness, and resilience, is composed primarily of collagen, a fibrous protein, among the strongest substances in the human body. Another component is elastin, also a protein, which—as its name implies—has the ability to stretch and then snap back.

Like the epidermis, the dermis is layered. The upper, or papillary, layer is made up of small mounds rich in blood vessels and nerve endings. The lower, or reticular, layer, a thick mesh of connective fibres, is attached at its base to the subcutaneous tissue, which is not considered part of the skin. The connective tissue and fat of the subcutaneous layer protect inner body structures.

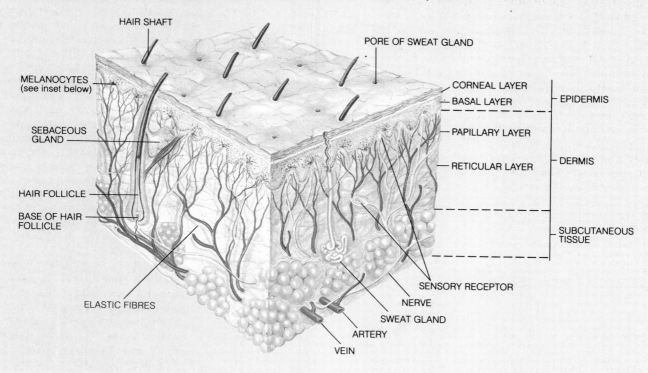

CORNEAL or HORNY LAYER, where cells become flattened and eventually slough off.

PRICKLE CELLS carry melanin granules (dark spots) upward from melanocytes.

MELANOCYTE (oddly enough, also called a clear cell) is shown among the basal cells, to which it transfers melanin granules.

Section of skin, stained to show shape of melanocyte.

Melanin that gives colour to skin is made by specialized cells called melanocytes, which are located in the basal layer of the epidermis (see above). The function of melanin pigment is to protect cells by absorbing ultraviolet rays. As melanin granules are formed, they travel through slender extensions of the melanocyte, and are literally injected into other epidermal cells, mainly basal cells. These cells divide and move up to form the prickle-cell layer, then the corneal or horny layer.

Melanocyte, amid basal cells, has few pigment granules.

With sunburn, melanin granules increase in number, move outward.

The Ecology of Skin

Is human skin ever really clean?

Getting out of the tub or the shower, you may feel wonderfully refreshed, but, in fact, you are not very clean—by strict, technical standards, that is. Of course, washing with soap and water removes the dust and soot of the day, some of the oily secretions of the body, and many micro-organisms. But it leaves behind thousands of millions of bacteria, yeasts, and fungi—full-time residents on the human skin that cannot be dispossessed, no matter how vigorously you scrub.

The micro-organisms to which you play host are particularly abundant where there are plenty of nutrients to sustain them. These nutrients are the products of the apocrine sweat glands and the sebaceous glands, which secrete an oily substance called sebum. The face, neck, armpits, and genital area have the highest bacteria count; an average man may have as many as 2.5 million per square centimetre (16 million per square inch) in his armpit. By contrast, the trunk and upper arms have the lowest bacteria count, because these parts of the body are not well supplied with apocrine or sebaceous glands. Certain kinds of micro-organisms concentrate in particular areas: fungi do well in the moist environment provided by the feet and groin, while the oily skin of the nose, ears, and scalp is especially hospitable to yeasts.

Are germs on the skin harmful?

The bacteria called *Staphylococcus aureus* are formidable foes of man. If they gain entrance to the bloodstream, they can cause ailments that range in severity from pimples and boils to serious—and even fatal—infections. Yet oddly enough, they do no damage as long as they remain only on the surface of the skin. Indeed, the vast majority of skin organisms are quite harmless.

For instance, the group of bacteria known as *Corynebacterium acnes*, normally found deep in the hair follicles, is harmless most of the time. However, during adolescence, when the sebaceous glands become particularly active, these bacteria can proliferate, causing that bane of the teen years, acne.

Similarly, the fungi that thrive on the soles of the feet and the skin between the toes usually cause no problems. But if the skin is broken, and particularly if the feet perspire excessively, these fungi invade the skin and cause athlete's foot.

Can skin micro-organisms do us any good?

The idea of things living on your skin may *sound* unpleasant, but as a matter of fact, scientists believe that most of these micro-organisms actually protect you from disease-causing organisms. These enemies are always present and ready to attack. Because

The Vital Importance of Clean Hands

A young obstetric assistant, Ignaz Semmelweis, serving at the Vienna Lying-In Hospital in the 1840's, was one of the first to recognize that disease organisms could be carried on the hands. Two clinics within the hospital, one for medical students, the other for midwives, were plagued by childbirth fever, but the mortality rate was much higher in the medical clinic. This disease afflicted maternity patients, who suffered high fever, rapid pulse, pain, and death. It was not until one of Semmelweis's colleagues died of an infection resembling childbirth fever that he saw the cause: the medical students performed autopsies, the midwives did not. Students were carrying infection from dissections to the maternity patients. Semmelweis devised an antiseptic to use before attending the patients. Although he reduced death from fever, it was not till years later that antisepsis was accepted.

Once reviled for his theory of antisepsis, Semmelweis is now honoured as a pioneer. His washstand and basin (right) are museum pieces.

the skin is already teeming with inhabitants, they may compete with each other, and this may be a form of protection. Other organisms take a more active role in fending off skin-surface enemies. One group of bacteria converts the sebum on which they feed into fatty acids that inhibit the growth of harmful organisms.

Do infants have skin bacteria like the rest of us?

The skin of babies delivered by Caesarean section is sterile at birth, but it begins to pick up micro-organisms immediately. The skin of babies born in the usual way acquires skin bacteria even earlier, during the very process of birth; bacteria are always present in the mother's birth canal, and some of them inevitably rub off on the infant. Some micro-organisms are transferred to an infant's skin by the simple act of touching or holding it. Others are present in the air—carried on the tiny flakes of dead skin that all of us regularly shed.

Can insects and other creatures live on human skin?

The skin sometimes plays host to microscopic parasites, in particular, the scabies mite. Only the female is attracted to human skin: it burrows in under the surface where it lays its eggs. These hatch in three or four days and make themselves known to their host a few weeks thereafter, in an itchy, allergic reaction.

Lice, which also feed on human blood via a suction tube like that of the mosquitoes, infest certain parts of the body. Those that spread typhus are the so-called body lice. Crab and head lice, less dangerous, both prefer the hairy parts, crab lice concentrating in the genital area and the armpits and head lice in the scalp. The eggs, or nits, of head lice can be seen on individual hairs. Unlike the scales of dandruff, the nits cannot be brushed off. Occasionally an individual louse can be seen with the naked eye.

A close-up of a human sweat gland makes clear why ordinary washing does not rid the body of germs. The skin's many pits are perfect hiding places for microbes, such as the bacteria (stained green) on the walls of the pore.

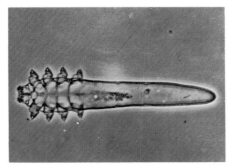

Skin dwellers may include the temporary, unwelcome kind like the louse at left. Lice bite and suck blood, and also carry disease. Usually harmless, but permanent inhabitants, such as the mite (above), live in your hair follicles.

The Skin You Are Born With

The tendency to freckle is inherited. Freckles manifest themselves, if at all, before the age of six; after the age of 20, most people don't get new ones.

Why do some people have freckles?

Although anyone can develop the tiny spots of pigment called freckles, they are most common among the fair skinned. Freckles do no harm, and some people even find them attractive. The tendency to develop freckles is apparently controlled, at least to some extent, by heredity.

Ordinarily, sunlight increases the production of melanin, the pigment that gives colour to the skin and protects it from the damage sunlight can do. In the fair, however, the pigment cells in the skin respond unevenly, if at all, to the sun's rays. The result is that the skin does not readily tan; instead, the pigment that is produced when the sun strikes the skin appears in an irregular pattern of little brown spots. Between the spots, the skin is likely to burn.

What causes albinism?

In a few people, the skin, hair, and eyes lack any colour of their own. These people are called albinos, from the Latin word *albus*, which means "white." Their skin may look faintly pink, because the underlying blood vessels show through, and their eyes may appear distinctly pink.

Albinism affects people of all races and occurs about once in 20,000 births. It is hereditary and comes from a complete absence of the pigment melanin, the substance that usually gives colour to the skin, hair, and eyes. Melanin is the end product of a complex set of chemical reactions; it cannot form without the help of an enzyme called tyrosinase. The bodies of albinos do not produce this enzyme, with the result that they do not produce melanin either.

What are birthmarks?

Birthmarks are abnormal distributions of blood vessels or pigment cells. When small strawberry marks appear on infants' faces a few weeks after birth, parents usually react with considerable but unnecessary dismay. True, these birthmarks—that is what they are called even though they are not visible when the baby is born—do get bigger for six months or so. But usually they disappear by the time a child is ready for school.

Port-wine stains are another matter. For one thing, they can disfigure as much as half the face. Until recently, the only solution to the problem was special make-up. Now, however, lasers are being used in some cases.

Both strawberry marks and port-wine stains are made up of abnormal collections of capillaries, the smallest of your blood vessels. Strawberry marks are gradually obscured as the child grows larger; port-wine stains are too large and too dense in structure to be obscured.

When are moles dangerous?

Moles, like freckles, are concentrations of melanin. Unlike freckles, however, they generally appear singly, rather than in clusters.

There is another difference between freckles and moles. In freckles, the melanin is deposited in the outer layer of skin, the epidermis. In moles, it is sometimes deposited in the underlying layer, the dermis, in which case it is known as an intradermal naevus. Alternatively, it may occur at the junction of the epidermis and the dermis; in that event, it is called a junctional naevus (Latin for "a mark on the body"). Intradermal moles are usually elevated above the surface of the skin, and hair frequently grows from them. Junctional naevi are more likely to be flat and very dark in colour.

Intradermal moles are not usually dangerous but should be seen by your doctor. Most junctional naevi are also benign, but a few are precursors of malignant melanomas. If you have a mole that changes visibly either in size or in colour, or suddenly begins to bleed, you should see a doctor.

Are your fingerprints of any practical use to you?

Everyone knows that fingerprints, made from skin ridges, are vital to the police for identifying criminals. They have been widely used for that purpose ever since the Galton-Henry system of fingerprint classification was introduced to Scotland Yard in 1901.

Less well known is the fact that the epidermal ridges and grooves, from which fingerprints are made, serve a useful purpose in our lives. They give roughness to the surface of the skin, providing you with traction when you pick things up, and they are essential for appreciation of what is touched.

Can footprints be used as a means of identification?

In some countries, the U.S. for example, hospitals take the footprints of newborn babies in case there is a mix-up over their identity. For identification purposes, footprints are not as reliable as fingerprints—but any ridged area of the

hand or foot would do. When dealing with a squirming baby and messy ink pads, it is much easier to make a clear impression of just two feet than of ten tiny fingers. With adults, fingerprints are easiest to take, and it happens that the patterns of arches, loops, or whorls on fingers lend themselves to classification.

Fingerprints: No Two Alike

The patterns of ridges and grooves on the fingertips of identical twins are similar—but never the same. Indeed, everyone's fingerprints are different from everyone else's. Your prints remain the same all your life; unless the bottom layer of the epidermis is destroyed, the skin that grows back after even a serious injury shows the same pattern it did when you were born. Thus fingerprints provide a foolproof way to identify everyone: amnesiacs who have forgotten their own names, accident victims whose faces have become unrecognizable, and, of course, criminals.

A ridge pattern may occur on any finger. Two of the pattern names, radial and ulnar, refer to the loops in relation to bones in the arm, the radius and the ulna. (The radius is on the thumb side.)

Creases in the palm are of interest to science; the simian fold (not shown here) is a sign of Down's syndrome.

Micrographs of skin from other parts of the body show patterns very different from the ridges found on the hands and the feet.

Skin pattern on an ear lobe.

Surface of skin on lower lip.

The Sensitivity of the Human Skin

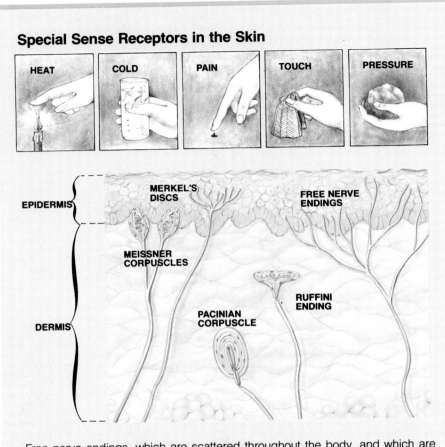

Special Sense Receptors in the Skin

HEAT   COLD   PAIN   TOUCH   PRESSURE

EPIDERMIS

MERKEL'S DISCS

FREE NERVE ENDINGS

MEISSNER CORPUSCLES

RUFFINI ENDING

PACINIAN CORPUSCLE

DERMIS

Free nerve endings, which are scattered throughout the body, and which are grouped around the bases of hairs, can register pain and pressure. Other, larger, specialized receptors are also present (see above). These occur in clusters, the more numerous, the more sensitive the area. The tips of the fingers have many such receptors, the shoulders have few. They report on the sensations of heat, cold, touch, and pressure. No single sensation is easily isolated—since feelings of touch, temperature, and perhaps pressure or pain tend to occur together.

How important is the sense of touch?

Unless babies are caressed, cuddled, and carried around in someone's loving arms, their physical and emotional growth slows down, and sometimes they die.

Before World War I, visitors to a certain children's hospital in Germany often noticed an old woman walking the wards with a puny-looking baby on her hip. "When we have done everything we can medically for a baby, and it is still not doing well," the hospital director explained, "we turn it over to Old Anna, and she is always successful." More recently, a U.S. study showed that premature infants who got only routine hospital care gained weight more slowly, cried more often, and were less active than other premature infants who were regularly held and stroked by nurses.

Obviously, then, the sense of touch is vitally important. And not just to babies. In adulthood, too, touching and being touched by other people can contribute a great deal to emotional well-being.

Moreover, receptors are a major source of information about the world and give warning of danger— if your skin could not react to pain, you could be seriously burned before you realized that you should move away from a hot stove. You can live without sight, hearing, taste, and smell—but not without the sense of touch, pain, heat, and cold.

You can get some idea of how important touch is from the number of times references to it crop up in everyday language. We speak of people, *thick-skinned* themselves, who *rub others the wrong way* and make *cutting* remarks that hurt *thin-skinned* or *touchy* acquaintances. We may or may not admire a person who is a *soft touch*. We think and talk a great deal of our *feelings* for others, and, invariably, we value the *human touch*. Given all this, you will not be surprised to learn that touch is probably one of the first of the human senses to develop.

What happens when you touch something?

If a large insect crawls on you, you can usually tell where it is, even with your eyes closed. The reason is that whenever something touches you, or vice versa, a whole battery of sensory mechanisms go into action.

The secret of this great sensitivity lies in bodily "structures" that respond to touch. One such structure is hair. Each hair is like a little antenna: touch it and you signal a bundle of nerves deep in the hair's follicle.

Areas of your body that have no hair nevertheless have their own kinds of alarm systems. Your lips, nipples, and external sex organs are densely supplied with extremely sensitive receptors, which are especially responsive to light stroking. Deep within the skin are other receptors that record continuing pressures on the skin surface. Finally, there are special receptors that enable us to sense vibrations, heat, and cold.

What causes itching?

Almost anything can cause this annoying sensation in the skin. Insects, allergies, fabrics, infections, emotional upset, even some medications—any or all of these, plus a host of other things, can produce itching.

Still, although itching can have an almost infinite number of causes, the reason it develops remains the same. Certain small fibres in the top portion of the skin are moved by a gentle, local stimulus, producing itching. The movement of these nerve endings is transmitted to the nervous system. Scratching the itch can either remove the stimulus or cause pain, which neutralizes the itching sensation in the spinal cord.

How sensitive are your lips?

Every mother knows that she can check her baby's temperature by feeling the child's forehead, since the body's internal temperature is reflected on the skin. The method is not as accurate as a thermometer, but it may help to tell if a fever is present. To get the best possible reading, however, use your lips rather than the palm of your hand. Although temperature receptors are present in every part of the body, there are relatively few in the hands (and the skin on the palms is thicker than the skin on most other parts of the body), whereas there are a large number in the lips.

Why do lips chap?

There is no mistaking the signs of chapping: painful slits and cracks that are very slow to heal. Not only the lips but also the whole face, the hands, and sometimes the heels and other body parts may be affected.

The basic cause of chapping is a drying out of the uppermost layer of the skin. Precipitating factors include soaps and detergents, dry indoor air, and exposure to cold, windy weather. Prevention and cure call for the same measures. Outdoors, it is a good idea to protect the face with a muffler. Indoors, the air can be moistened. You should gently pat—not vigorously rub—your skin to dry it after washing, and use emollient creams or lotions liberally and regularly to soften and moisturize the skin.

How do you tell hot from cold?

There are specialized nerve endings and structures located in the skin that are sensitive to temperature: some skin receptors are sensitive to warmth, and others are sensitive to cold. The warmer the temperature, the more frequently do the warm receptors fire; the colder it is, the more frequently the cold receptors fire. In this way, the brain senses the intensity of heat or cold.

Both warm and cold receptors have the ability to adapt—as everyone knows from personal experience. If you have ever stepped into a steaming hot bath or dived into an icy cold lake, the temperature may at first seem uncomfortable, perhaps even shocking. But in only a short time, your discomfort generally disappears.

Why do extreme cold and extreme heat often feel the same?

In addition to the temperature receptors it contains, the skin also has pain receptors that are responsive to temperature. But these receptors are stimulated only by extreme cold and extreme heat, and the brain experiences the two sensations in the same way. Some extremes of temperature, therefore, stimulate both the temperature and pain receptors, and you feel both heat—or cold—as pain.

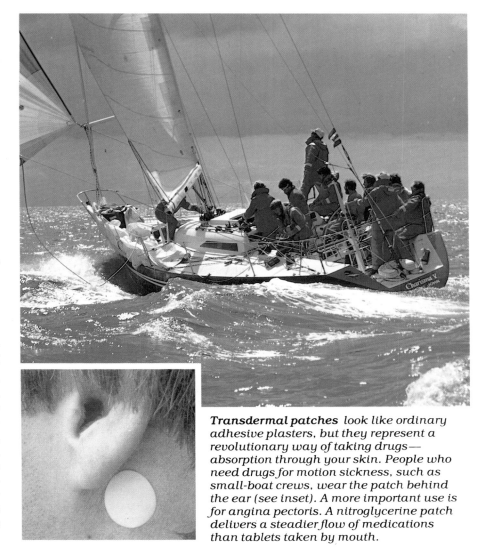

Transdermal patches look like ordinary adhesive plasters, but they represent a revolutionary way of taking drugs— absorption through your skin. People who need drugs for motion sickness, such as small-boat crews, wear the patch behind the ear (see inset). A more important use is for angina pectoris. A nitroglycerine patch delivers a steadier flow of medications than tablets taken by mouth.

Your Skin at Risk

Hazards of the Outdoors

The discomfort caused by lightly brushing your hand against a stinging nettle can seem out of all proportion to the action, but the whole plant bristles with fine hairs. On being touched, the tip of each hair breaks off and releases acid which causes a painful rash on the skin. The best first aid is bicarbonate of soda or weak ammonia. There are many plants that can produce a rash on contact (a condition known as contact dermatitis or contact eczema): primulas, ivy, greater celandines, stonecrops and chrysanthemums, for example. The best defence is to give them a wide berth or wear gloves when gardening.

STINGING NETTLE
(Urtica dioica)

Wasps are usually most troublesome in late summer when fruit is ripe.

A **browsing bee** may be at work within the petals of a flower, so look carefully before you pick.

Can you protect yourself from insect bites and stings?

The risk of being bitten by a bee or wasp is lowest in the spring when these insects are just starting to build their colonies and highest in summer and autumn when a single bee colony may have as many as 2,000 or 3,000 individuals. Their principal food source is flowers, so gardens and fields of wildflowers are the places where you are most likely to be attacked.

Because bees and wasps are attracted to bright colours, the safest kind of clothing to wear for outdoors is khaki. This fabric is not only pale in colour but tightly woven, which presents a barrier to the insect's sting.

It's also wise to avoid using perfume, scented lotion, or hair spray because their fragrances will attract stinging and biting insects. When using an insect repellent, be sure to read the instructions on the label as to how much and how often to apply it.

What should you do if you are stung?

If you are stung by a wasp or hornet, flick the insect away, then apply ice cubes to the sting site. If a bee leaves its sting in your skin, gently scrape it off with a blade or fingernail, and wash with soap and water. Apply ice wrapped in cloth to decrease absorption of venom. If a sting victim's face begins to swell, if there is shortness of breath, or some other sign of distress, get medical help immediately. People with a known severe allergy should carry an emergency kit.

How should a tick be removed?

These small blood-sucking creatures abound in heather and bracken. When a tick bites, its body becomes engorged with blood. One is tempted to pull the tick off at once, but because its head is embedded in the skin, it is important to make the tick "back out." An application of paraffin will close its breathing pores, and it should loosen its grip within 30 minutes. If it cannot be removed, medical advice should be sought urgently.

Can toads cause warts?

All kinds of old wives' tales surround these benign tumours; that they are caused by toads is one of them. Also, it used to be said that they could be cured by witchcraft, or by some miraculous potion. In fact, some warts tend to vanish by themselves as mysteriously as they came, and no doubt they have often done so just after some magic remedy was applied—which probably explains why folk tales persist.

The worst thing to do to a wart is to try to cut it out yourself. Besides endangering yourself by use of unsterilized instruments, you may reinfect yourself with the virus that caused your wart and start a whole new crop of them. There are over-the-counter preparations that may prove effective. For warts on the soles of the feet, medical attention is needed.

Why do you look like a prune after a bath?

A long, luxurious bath may be relaxing, but it temporarily undermines one of the skin's chief attributes: its capacity, under normal circumstances, to be waterproof. If skin were not waterproof, you would become waterlogged every time you went swimming or took a bath. The substance that keeps this from happening is keratin, a protein manufactured by special cells in the epidermis. Keratin acts as a protective barrier not only against moisture but against bacteria and many irritants.

During bathing, the top or horny layer of skin absorbs water and swells up, so that by the time you step out of the tub, your skin is full of the wrinkles and creases that give it that prune-like look. In time, the water evaporates from the cells, the skin regains its customary shape, and the wrinkles disappear.

Can clothing harm your skin?

Many people have a contact allergy to certain substances—wool and fur, for example. Less well known are contact allergies to leather. Leather jackets or sandals may unexpectedly cause violent rashes to break out. This is especially true if the substance used for tanning (the process

that turns animal hide into tough leather) is one taken from plants of the family that includes poison ivy. Leather hatbands, for instance, can cause a number of scaly eruptions.

Such reactions are not always produced by chemicals or fabrics. When clothing is too tight, excessive heat and moisture can build up, producing rashes or heightening a pre-existing allergic condition. Artificial elastics used in stretch pants and underwear can also cause rashes.

Why do you get calluses and corns?

Calluses, which are built-up pads of thickened skin, develop as a response to pressure and abrasion. When you wear shoes that are too tight or that rub—in the heel, for

instance—a callus will form. And calluses commonly form on the hands as a result of manual labour.

Corns differ from calluses in that they occur mostly on toes and take a conical shape. As the corn develops, increased pressure causes it to dig into the sensitive lower layers of the skin, which often results in excruciating pain. There are two types of corns: the hard ones that form on the outer surface of the foot and the soft corns that form between the toes.

To prevent the formation of calluses and corns, wear shoes that fit properly. Use of a pumice stone or file, particularly after bathing, can reduce the thickness of a callus. Corns, however, may require the help of a chiropodist to remove. You can avoid recurrence of corns and calluses by protecting the skin (usually on a toe joint) with small spongy pads.

How Does an Abrasion Heal?

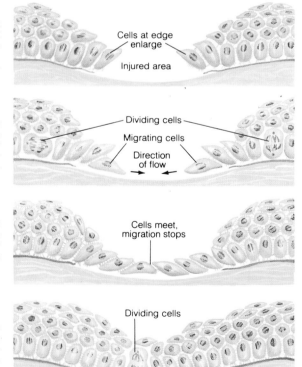

After an injury, perhaps a scrape, the cells adjacent to the wound break contact with the cells below. They then begin to enlarge and to move.

The altered cells begin to flow, migrating across the wound. Meanwhile, other basal cells multiply very rapidly, to supply the necessary replacements.

Flowing as a sheet from all sides of the wound, the migrating cells eventually meet. When these cells finally cover the wound, the migration stops.

The abrasion will continue to heal itself through the multiplying of epithelial cells. As cell division proceeds, the skin's normal thickness is restored.

141

From Sunburn to Frostbite

What causes sunburn?

Among the many kinds of light rays emitted by the sun are the invisible ultraviolet rays that have a shorter wavelength than visible light. Ultraviolet has some beneficial effects on the body, helping it, for example, to produce vitamin D. But too much ultraviolet ages the skin prematurely, causes sunburn, and even increases the risk of skin cancer. Fortunately, the body has a built-in defence against these dangers in the form of melanin, the pigment that gives the skin its colour. As ultraviolet passes through melanin, it is absorbed.

Why does sunburned skin redden and peel before it tans?

The ultraviolet rays that cause sunburn damage epidermal cells, which release substances that dilate blood vessels. In severe cases, deeper cells are involved, so that blisters may develop. Cell destruction is the process responsible for the peeling that follows redness. When skin cells are destroyed in large numbers, the body immediately sets to work to repair the damage by speeding up its production of new cells. It manufactures so many that they crowd one another to the surface, forcing the burned cells to peel off. And because the damage also stimulates the melanin-producing cells to multiply more rapidly than usual, more pigment is available for the new cells to pick up as they journey to the surface. This extra melanin gives the skin its tan.

Although lotions can screen out ultraviolet rays and so help protect against sunburn, it is still important to limit your time in the sun and to take it in small doses. It is also important, especially if you are fair-skinned, to cut down your exposure to ultraviolet radiation by sunbathing only in the early morning or late afternoon. At these times, the sun's rays are not direct, and much of the ultraviolet is filtered out.

One more thing: remember that you can sunburn even if you're not sitting in the sun. Ultraviolet rays can

Sunburned skin, orange-stained in this cross-section, shows top layer ready to slough off. Orange cell (right, centre) shows ultraviolet damage.

penetrate clouds. And they can be reflected from expanses of sea and sand and so reach you even if you think you have sheltered yourself completely with a big beach umbrella.

Can you sunburn when it's cold out?

Summer is not the only season for sunburn. You're just as likely to burn on the coldest day of winter as on the hottest summer day, just as vulnerable amidst snowcapped mountains as on the beach at sea level. How so? Because it's not the heat of the sun that burns but the ultraviolet light that streams from it at all seasons. And snow can reflect those burning rays and increase the danger from them just as well as sand can.

How can cold weather be harmful to the skin?

To be healthy, your skin must be kept moist. In cold weather, dry outside air can draw the normal protec-

tive moisture from the skin, leaving it chapped, scaly, and rough—even, in some cases, badly cracked. Soap and hot water can also damage the skin in cold weather. Soap removes fats and oils. To lessen the damage, take fewer baths, and in cold weather, use tepid, rather than hot, water for bathing. Creams and lotions that contain oil can also be helpful in protecting the skin from dryness; they work because the oil film prevents the natural moisture from evaporating.

Why is frostbite dangerous?

When the skin is frostbitten, it is literally frozen, and the blood vessels in the affected area—most commonly, the fingers, the toes, the ear lobes, and the cheeks or other exposed areas of the face—completely shut down. This loss of circulation threatens the very life of the tissue involved because if the blood flow is not restored in time, the tissue will die and become gangrenous.

This danger is compounded by the fact that frostbite sometimes goes unrecognized until it is too late. Frostbite is insidious, often creeping up with little or no warning. The victim may at first feel some pain and tingling, but once the body part is frozen, all sensation is lost.

The severity of any case of frostbite depends both on the degree of the cold and on the length of time the victim is exposed to it. In mild cases, only epidermal tissue is involved; with colder temperatures and longer exposure, the chill creeps deeper into the dermis and the tissue below; in the worst cases, it can extend as far down as the bone.

In extreme situations, amputation may provide the only cure. But when frostbite is less severe, it responds well to far less dramatic treatment. Moist heat, in the form of a hot bath, with the water about 40° C (104° F), will thaw out the frozen tissue. Rapid rather than slow rewarming is the goal. Test the water temperature with an unfrozen part of the skin before plunging in. Rubbing frostbitten skin with snow is harmful folklore.

What is the best first aid for burns?

Don't bother about butter or creams; they won't help. *Do* hold the burned part under cold running water, or use clean cloths wrung out in cold water. If a large area of the body has been burned, seek medical help immediately. The cold-water treatment is absolutely essential for burns from corrosive chemicals, which should be washed away (using running water if possible). In that case, the treatment should continue for 5 to 15 minutes or more before you stop to call a doctor.

If possible, remove jewellery from the affected area; burned skin swells, and it will be very difficult to remove it later. In general, the experts advise minimal first aid for burns. Doctors at a leading teaching hospital sum up their recommendations in these words, "the less the better."

Can skin be grown in a test tube?

The best skin graft for a bad burn comes from the patient's own body. But sometimes there isn't enough undamaged skin left for grafting. Doctors must then use substitutes.

Pigskin is enough like human skin so it can be used for temporary grafting, and skin banks exist to store skin from cadavers. But these are only temporary expedients, because the body rejects them as foreign.

In the past few years, researchers have developed a better permanent graft: small pieces of the patient's skin grown in the laboratory. The process requires only tiny bits of skin from the victim's body. These are ground up, mixed with substances that promote cell growth, and then allowed to proliferate in test tubes.

Skin produced this way lacks the dermis, and researchers do not yet know whether that really matters. However, the new method was used with apparent success to save the lives of two children who had burns over 97 percent of their bodies. In all, the doctors were able to grow nearly 1 square metre (about 1 square yard) of skin for each patient.

Degrees of Burn, Methods of Treatment

The severity of a burn corresponds to the depth of the skin that is damaged. A partial-thickness burn may damage only the outer layer, the epidermis, or may penetrate deeper into the dermis. Capillaries may be damaged and plasma may escape to produce blistering, but there are enough skin cells remaining for healing to occur without skin grafting. In full-thickness burns the whole depth of skin is damaged. Because all the nerve endings are destroyed, it may be less painful than a partial-thickness burn, but skin grafting may be necessary.

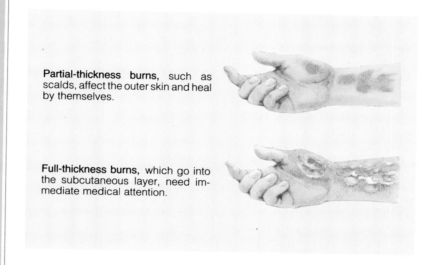

Partial-thickness burns, such as scalds, affect the outer skin and heal by themselves.

Full-thickness burns, which go into the subcutaneous layer, need immediate medical attention.

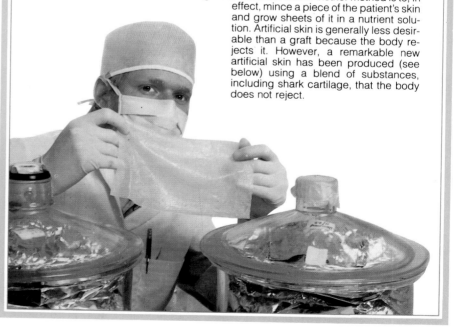

Skin grafts may be necessary in full-thickness burns because exposed subcutaneous tissue cannot heal fast enough to protect the body from infection and from loss of fluids. If the burn is not too extensive, there may be enough skin available from an undamaged part of the body to use as a graft. The piece does not have to be as big as the damaged area; it can be enlarged by a variety of techniques. One is to take skin from a donor site and cut it in a filigree to cover the burn. Another method is to, in effect, mince a piece of the patient's skin and grow sheets of it in a nutrient solution. Artificial skin is generally less desirable than a graft because the body rejects it. However, a remarkable new artificial skin has been produced (see below) using a blend of substances, including shark cartilage, that the body does not reject.

Common Skin Problems

How Acne Develops

Opening of the hair follicle has sebaceous glands at its base. At puberty, the output of sebum increases.

Whitehead forms when too much sebum collects, distends the channel, and clogs the opening of the pore.

Blackheads are often thought to be pockets of dirt. Actually, the dark colour is melanin, produced by the skin.

Acne or pimple forms when the hair follicle walls rupture. Squeezing a pimple tends to spread the infection.

What is the commonest skin disorder?

Nature is unkind to teenagers. Just when good looks become a major concern and attraction to the opposite sex a constant preoccupation, acne is likely to strike. Acne is not only cruel but common—the commonest of all skin disorders, in fact. The outbreaks are generally worse in boys than in girls, because the main cause of acne is an upsurge in the production of male hormones. Males, of course, secrete these in large quantities, but females secrete them too, although in much smaller amounts. Certain normal skin bacteria, which are present in both sexes, are also thought to contribute to acne by turning skin oils into irritating chemicals.

Normally, the sebaceous glands in the skin produce an oily substance called sebum that wells up through the hair follicles and benefits the skin by lubricating it. But during adolescence, male hormones stimulate the secretion of too much sebum, which often plugs up the follicles. The result is acne: whiteheads, blackheads, inflammation, and pimples, mainly on the face, neck, and shoulders. In the worst cases, large, painful cysts and abscesses also develop.

Can acne be cured?

Mistakenly believing that acne comes from dirt, many victims of the disorder go in for vigorous soap-and-water scrubbing of their faces several times a day. Chances are they are only making things worse.

There is no complete cure for acne but time. Nevertheless, much can be done to keep it under control until adolescence is over. Gentle face washing, especially when the skin feels oily, is a good idea. So is exposure to sunlight in moderation. Teenagers will be happy to learn that they need not give up chocolate, colas, or their favourite "junk" foods. Doctors once believed that these cause acne, but the evidence now is that they don't.

However, there are a few things to avoid: harsh soaps; face creams and moisturizers that may block hair follicles and trap sebum; and, perhaps surprisingly, headbands, turtleneck sweaters, and other tight clothing that may also trap sebum. If simple measures are not enough, you should see a doctor.

What's the difference between a boil and a carbuncle?

Once upon a time, carbuncles could kill. Nowadays, penicillin and other antibiotics can usually get rid of them in fairly short order. But the curability of carbuncles makes them no less painful while they last.

A carbuncle is either a giant boil or several boils linked by tunnels in the skin and involving several hair follicles. The cause is a staphylococcus infection that produces a kind of abscess filled with pus. Boils are likely to appear in the armpit or on the face, neck, back, or buttocks. As they grow larger, they hurt, because they press on nerves under the skin.

The simplest treatment is to apply a hot wet cloth for several minutes at regular intervals. This relieves pain and makes the boil come to a head sooner; when it does, it bursts and then heals quickly. A carbuncle, however, may have to be lanced by the doctor so it can drain properly.

The best defence against boils and carbuncles is general cleanliness and robust good health. Although most people develop a boil or two at some time in their lives, frequent recurrences are often traceable to poor hygiene, inadequate nutrition, or, occasionally, to diabetes.

How did athlete's foot get its name?

It's easy to pick up athlete's foot from the damp floors of locker rooms and the wet walkways around swimming pools. Nevertheless, there is no significant connection between this common fungus infection and sports. Anyone—athletic or not—can pick it up almost anywhere.

Tinea pedis—the technical term

for athlete's foot—is a strain of fungus that attacks the skin between and under the toes, causing itching, cracking, peeling, and occasionally blisters. The fungus thrives on moisture; people who keep their feet dry seldom have athlete's foot.

To prevent occurrences of athlete's foot—and also to treat it—make sure that your shoes permit air to circulate so that moisture cannot become trapped inside them. Your socks should be made of cotton or some other natural fibre that will absorb perspiration. After you bathe, you should always take care to dry your feet thoroughly (especially between the toes), and apply a fungus-killing powder, cream, or lotion.

What is the mystery of psoriasis?

There is not much good to say about psoriasis, as those who suffer from it know all too well. But a few facts about the disorder offer some comfort. Unless you are very young or very old, it cannot affect general health. It cannot spread from one person to another. And it often goes away entirely for years at a time. Of 5,600 patients in one study, 39 percent reported that they had experienced a remission lasting from 1 to 54 years. Moreover, 29 percent said that their symptoms had vanished without treatment of any kind.

The disease is mysterious, not only because its course is unpredictable but also because its cause is not understood. Heredity plays a role. Sometimes the symptoms first appear after an injury to the skin; sometimes they develop after a person has undergone some particularly stressful event.

In any case, the disorder is a sign that the skin cells are multiplying too rapidly to be shed in the usual way. Raised red patches, often coloured by white scales, appear—most often on the knees, elbows, and lower back.

What can be done about psoriasis?

Treatment helps virtually all psoriasis patients, at least temporarily. Sunbathing or an ultraviolet lamp are often recommended, along with ointments made from coal tar. In stubborn cases, doctors may prescribe steroids, though side effects can be serious. Many victims have found that they can help themselves by noticing what conditions seem to make their symptoms worse, and then regulating their lives accordingly.

Are all skin cancers equally dangerous?

The two most common forms of skin cancer are basal cell carcinoma, which attacks the cells in the innermost layer of the epidermis, and squamous cell carcinoma, which arises from other epidermal cells. These are also the two most curable of all malignancies; the vast majority of cases respond favourably to treatment.

The outlook is much less favourable for the third—and, fortunately, rarest—form of skin cancer. Malignant melanoma, a disorder of the cells that produce melanin, must be caught and treated early if chances of survival are to be good. These are dangerous because they have a tendency to spread to other parts of the body.

Despite the differences among them, the non-melanoma cancers have some things in common. They are most likely to develop on those parts of the body that receive the most sun, and they tend to occur in light-skinned people who sunburn easily.

Folklore of the Body: SAVING SALVES AND OINTMENTS

Back in the days when medical science was in its infancy and few people had any knowledge of how the body works, quack remedies abounded. When a particular nostrum was tried and the patient got well, the medicine got the credit—though the patient might have recovered without it. Remedies were often outlandish: ashes of snakeskin for wounds, seeds of nettles for dog bites, and a live spider encased in butter for jaundice. Folk medicine was a mixture of need, experimentation, and hope. When a medicine show came to town, customers were eager to buy the potions that would cure all. One patent medicine, Kennedy's Medical Discovery, promised to cure "scrofula, erysipelas, scald head, salt rheum, lepra, scurvy, pimples, ulcers, canker, and every disease of the skin of whatever name or nature." Magic played a part in folk medicine. Imps and demons were believed to inflict pain, and rituals and spells were invented to counteract them. Such gullibility seems incredible today, but not all early medicine was wide of the mark. Amazonian Indians discovered that the cinchona plant, the source of quinine, can help suppress malaria attacks, and quite a few narcotics were identified.

The heyday of patent medicines was the 19th century, when people pursued cures zestfully. Medicines such as Pratt's (right) were recommended for use by both man and beast.

Repairing Damage, Taking Tucks

The Natural Cleavage Lines of the Skin

The collagen in the lower, or reticular, layer of the dermis is arranged in bundles of fibres; these bundles form a pattern of natural creases in the skin. Called Langer's lines, these patterns vary in direction, as shown below. Even the most skilfully performed surgery leaves scars, but some are much less noticeable than others. This is because, whenever possible, the surgeon cuts into the body along a natural line, and the scar looks like just another crease.

Langer's lines (named after Carl Langer von Edenberg, the Austrian scientist who first identified them) are of significance in plastic surgery on every part of the body.

Why does the skin lose resilience and wrinkle when you age?

Skin aging is the result of changes in a substance called collagen, which makes up 30 percent of the body's protein. Collagen is the major constituent of the dermis, the middle layer of the skin, and of connective tissue as well; bones, cartilage, and tendons all contain considerable collagen. As collagen ages, it loses water through a process that is known as polymerization: its molecules link together in long chains, thus robbing it of much of its flexibility and give.

The lack of resilience in aging skin fosters wrinkling, but there are other factors that are even more significant. With age comes a loss of fat in the subcutaneous tissue, the layer that lies directly beneath the skin and acts as a cushion for the internal organs. As fat disappears from this layer, the skin loses some of its supporting structure, begins to sag, and buckles into folds and creases. To picture what happens, think of how pre-diet clothes look on people who have lost a lot of weight.

Another factor that contributes to the formation of wrinkles is the loss of moisture from the skin. Children's tissues contain proportionately more water than do those of adults; age slows down the activity of the sebaceous glands and the sweat glands, which supply the skin with oil and

How Are Face Lifts Done?

A face lift should really be called a skin lift. The surgeon cuts into the skin on each side of the face, beginning at the centre of the hairline and running just in front of the ear. The cut continues around and behind the ear to the scalp. The surgeon then separates the facial skin from the subcutaneous tissue all the way down to the chin, where fatty deposits are trimmed away from the jowl and neck. If the neck has come to have a ropy look, which sometimes happens as a result of aging, the doctor may make some modifications in the small muscle that is to blame. Next, the surgeon pulls the skin to the back of the face and smooths it to fit over its foundation. Finally, excess skin is snipped off, and each flap is sewn to the scalp.

Cleavage lines located on the head guide the surgeon.

First incision, as shown, is well above the hairline.

with water. As you age, your skin becomes increasingly dry, and that condition highlights, and deepens, laughter and frown lines.

Can exercise or massage or anything rejuvenate aging skin?

It is possible to slow down the effects of aging on the skin, but rejuvenation is definitely out of the question. Exercise and massage are good for toning the muscles, but the wrinkles and loss of resilience that are marks of aging skin are not reversed by exercising.

Short of cosmetic surgery, the most effective way to improve temporarily the appearance of aging skin is to make regular use of some kind of skin emollient. But no preparation can restore permanently the moisture that age takes from the skin.

External conditions can hasten the aging process. The more you expose yourself to the ultraviolet rays of the sun, the more rapidly your skin ages. According to many medical authorities, sun is far more damaging to the skin than is the aging process itself.

If you don't believe it, take a look at the parts of your body normally covered with clothes. The skin on the parts of your trunk that are covered by a swimsuit are far smoother and more youthful in appearance than the parts you expose to sun.

Why do people undergo plastic surgery?

Plastic surgery frequently has nothing to do with vanity. Some individuals are disfigured by accident, disease, or birth defects, so that they must have surgery if they are to lead normal lives.

The importance of reconstructive surgery became evident after World War I, when many soldiers were badly disfigured by land mines and other explosive devices. But the battlefield is not the only place such injuries can occur. Victims of road accidents often need reconstructive surgery, as do people who have undergone certain kinds of surgery for cancer. And skin grafting has become standard treatment for disfigured burn victims. Among the birth defects that can now be successfully repaired by advanced surgical techniques are webbed or extra fingers, cleft palates, and genital abnormalities.

Why is surgery on the nose inadvisable for very young people?

Adolescents are often dissatisfied with the size and shape of their noses. But rhinoplasty—cosmetic surgery to reshape the nose—should not be performed until the nasal bones have stopped growing and the nose has taken on its final shape.

Ordinarily, this means that the youngster should be at least 15 or 16 years old when the operation is done. However, for some, full growth may not be until the late teens.

Does a reconstructed breast look normal?

Recent technical advances in breast surgery have been paralleled by revolutionary changes in people's attitudes towards reconstruction. At one time considered vain, the operation is now generally recognized to be of vital psychological importance to some breast cancer patients. The result: breast reconstruction after surgery for cancer can now be performed under the N.H.S.

Of course, surgeons cannot duplicate the breast that was removed. Although the patient's own skin and muscle are used in the rebuilding process, the breast contour, or shape, is created with an implant of silicone jelly or saline solution enclosed in a plastic sac. The new breast is usually rounder, flatter, and firmer than the natural one.

In a booklet prepared for prospective patients, one hospital sums up the situation frankly by saying, "a reconstructed breast is not a normal breast." Nevertheless, most patients do look entirely natural in a brassiere, a swimsuit, or a low-cut dress.

Loosened skin is then drawn upward from the neck.

Trimmed and stitched, the skin heals in a few weeks.

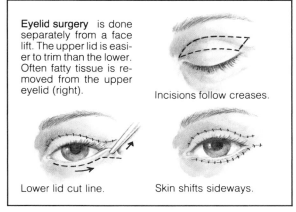

Eyelid surgery is done separately from a face lift. The upper lid is easier to trim than the lower. Often fatty tissue is removed from the upper eyelid (right).

Incisions follow creases.

Lower lid cut line.

Skin shifts sideways.

Healing and Hazards

Can surgeons do anything about wrinkles and scars?

The quest for smooth skin is hardly new. Some 3,500 years ago, Egyptian women rubbed their faces with an abrasive mixture that contained bits of alabaster bound together with milk and honey. Today, cosmetic surgeons employ a variety of techniques to repair skin. One, called dermabrasion, is a process in which the upper layers of the skin are literally sanded off. Although dermabrasion cannot remove the pits or any of the other deep scars of acne, it can make them less conspicuous, and it also helps to smooth out fine lines and wrinkles.

In removing the outer layers of the skin, dermabrasion also removes much of its pigment. The process may therefore affect the colour of the complexion, even after new skin has grown. This is especially true for blacks and others with dark skin.

Another technique is the chemical skin peel. For many years, physicians have used chemicals to burn off warts and other harmless skin growths. The procedure, technically known as chemosurgery, can also be used to burn away small wrinkles, especially those around the mouth and eyes.

For the patient, the process, and its effects, are similar to those in dermabrasion. Like dermabrasion, skin peels carry with them the danger that the treated complexion will never regain its previous colour. Some dermatologists recommend them only for fair-skinned people, for whom the procedure seems to work best.

Why do some injuries leave scars?

Injuries that affect only the epidermis leave no scars when they heal. But those that penetrate through this outer layer into the dermis sometimes leave scar tissue behind. The dermis is composed largely of collagen. When damage extends deep enough to affect the dermis, its collagen-producing cells speed up their activity, so that the destroyed tissue can be replaced. If the new material is formed in large enough quantity, it will be forced to rise above the dermis, into the outer layer of the skin, where it will show itself in the altered texture and appearance that we call a scar.

What are keloid scars, and how do they develop?

In its effort to repair the damage caused by injury, the body sometimes produces more new tissue than necessary. This tissue forms scars that may be raised slightly at first. Most soon level off, but some, so-called keloids, do not. They remain elevated, shiny, and smooth compared with the surrounding tissue. Moreover, they often cover an area somewhat larger than the one affected by the injury. Keloids are commoner in olive-complexioned and black people, and their development is usually associated with severe injury.

Created by a runaway production of collagen to heal the injury, keloids can be irritating during the healing process. They can also be unattractive, but they are harmless. It seldom does any good to remove them surgically since they usually grow back. In their early stages, however, they can be successfully treated with hydrocortisone, and later they may respond to treatment with X-rays.

Can tattoos be removed?

Because the pigment that is used in tattooing is always injected very deeply into the skin, it is difficult to remove without leaving an obvious scar. For small tattoos, surgical techniques have recently been developed that leave far less unsightly scars than dermabrasion, which was once a popular method of removal.

So far, the most common forms of treatment for larger tattoos are the procedures known as superficial dermabrasion and salabrasion. In superficial dermabrasion, only a very thin layer of skin is sanded off, to produce first irritation and then inflammation of the skin. Salabrasion—rubbing the tattooed area with ordinary table salt until it becomes irritated—works in much the same way. But although this technique sounds simple, it should be performed only by a qualified physician. Nowadays, many plastic surgeons prefer a method of surgical "shaving" that fills the tattooed area with a skin graft. This applies particularly to the dramatic, artistically complicated tattoos, which involve implantation of pigment deep into the skin.

The laser may also be used to remove tattoos. This powerful beam of light, aimed at the tattoo, simply vaporizes the pigment particles. But no method has yet been discovered to guarantee that scars will not remain and that infection will not set in.

THE STORY BEHIND THE WORDS...

To get under your skin, which means to irritate, probably refers to the intense itching caused by infestations such as scabies. The mite burrows into the skin and releases enzymes that let it feed on blood, causing its host to experience a maddening itch.

To split hairs means to quibble, to be ridiculously picky. When the expression came into use, it was impossible to split a hair, but today's laboratory equipment make hair-splitting easy—literally.

Hangnails, referring to torn, painful strips of skin around the nail, received their name by accident. The Anglo-Saxon word *agnail* described corns—*ang* ("painful"), *naegl* ("nail")—perhaps because a corn resembles a nail in the skin. In time, an "h" was added, to make hangnail. By what logic a corn on the foot became a bit of torn skin on the finger, no one knows.

The Human Skin as a Canvas

Resilient, washable, and convenient, human skin is—from all evidence—irresistible as an object of decoration. The purpose is frequently to embellish, but may also be to protect (in Iran, tattoos were used to ward off evil spirits), to express rank (in Polynesian facial designs), to distinguish different castes, to announce marital status, to express mourning, to frighten enemies, to represent the spirits of the gods. Most decoration is painted on, often at ritual times and in prescribed ways, using natural pigments and dyes. But some adornment requires considerable stamina on the part of the recipient, as in the case of tattooing. A design is drawn on the body, dye is applied, and the colour is forced into the skin by needles or special instruments. Another form of decoration that requires endurance—and probably considerable peer pressure--is scarification. Incisions are made in the skin, encouraging the development of a scar. Once prevalent in Africa and the Pacific, this practice is on the wane.

The eye make-up on this Egyptian painting may have had practical origins—kohl or malachite smudges around the eyes protect them from the glare of the sun. But by the time this sketch was done, more than 3,000 years ago, the intention of the eye make-up, in its elegant delineation, was clearly decorative.

This New Guinea chieftain, wearing blue paint, asserts his claim to leadership by means of body decoration and other forms of display.

Among the Japanese, tattooing is a fine art, called *irezumi*. It is considered a form of clothing; a full bodysuit generally takes more than a year to complete and may cost thousands of dollars.

How and Where Hair Grows

Does hair serve a useful function?

A visiting Martian, noticing the elaborate coiffures worn by many earth women, might conclude that hair plays a crucial role in human affairs. And so it does, though not as a Martian might suppose. Beautiful hair is undoubtedly an asset in romantic attraction. But flamboyant hairdos have a way of obscuring the real utility of hair. If you are struck on the head, your hair serves to cushion the blow. And when hot sun beats down on your head, your hair offers insulation and helps to screen out its harmful ultraviolet rays.

Your body hair acts as a sensitive antenna, registering the slightest touch on your skin. This reflex is strikingly evident when an insect brushes against an eyelash; your eye instantly blinks shut. Tiny hairs in your ears and nostrils intercept and filter out gritty dust particles floating about in the air. Even the eyebrows perform a useful function, serving as miniature sweat bands that soak up and shunt off to one side perspiration that might otherwise drip down into your eyes.

Though these hair functions are an aid to survival, people who lack some or all of these body hairs—through illness or accident—can generally manage to find suitable substitutes in hats, sweat bands, and the like.

Is your hair alive, or dead?

Despite advertisements that promise glowing, "alive" hair if you use certain products, your hair is in fact quite dead, and cannot be revived by lotions. What we call hair is actually an outgrowth of skin. It grows out of structures called follicles, of which the body has some 5 million—100,000 are found in the scalp alone. By the time a hair emerges into view from its follicle-cocoon deep beneath the skin, it is long since dead: its cells are no longer capable of dividing to produce new hair. Every day, during the process of combing and brushing, from 50 to 100 hairs break off. Although the hair is dead, it remains elastic; wet hair can be stretched up to 60 percent more than its normal length, and will then snap back.

If my hair isn't alive, why does it keep getting longer?

Barbers make their living from the fact that human hair grows 12 to 15 centimetres (5 or 6 inches) a year. This does not mean that the hair they cut is alive. Deep within the follicles, new hair cells are constantly being formed. As the new cells squeeze their way upward, they push the older, already dead cells up above the surface of your skin.

That process goes on for two to six years, and then the hair's root rests and stops producing new cells (15 percent of the roots are in the resting

The Structure of a Growing Hair

CORTEX
CUTICLE
MEDULLA
HAIR SHAFT
HAIR SHEATH
FOLLICLE BULB
ARRECTOR PILI MUSCLE
SEBACEOUS GLAND
MELANOCYTES give colour to hair

The only parts of the body's surface that do not have hair are the palms of the hands, the soles of the feet, and the lips. Some hairs are so fine that you hardly notice them—as, for example, the hairs on your stomach or on the undersides of your arm. But all hair, regardless of location or texture, arises from the same kind of structure. The individual strand grows from a follicle that is supplied with nutrients at its bulblike base, the papilla. Active growth of the hair is only within the bulb. Attached to the hair follicle is a tiny muscle called the arrector pili muscle, which can make the hair stand up. Two or more sebaceous glands open into the follicle; the oily sebum makes hair pliant.

SEBACEOUS GLAND
EPIDERMIS
CLUB HAIR
NEW HAIR

A hair lives for several years. The follicle rests for months, then produces another hair.

Micrograph of skin shows a growing hair (left) and a resting follicle (upper right).

phase at any one time). About three months later, the hair root becomes detached from the base of the follicle, and eventually a comb or brush pulls the hair out. After recuperating for another three months, the follicle grows another hair. Some roots are active far beyond the normal period, and hair sometimes grows to a length of one metre (3 feet) or more.

Can your hair actually stand on end?

An angry, frightened cat with all its fur erect is a startling apparition. The closest thing in human beings is the phenomenon of goose flesh. When goose flesh appears, the hair on your arms or legs, or both, stands on end. Goose flesh is caused by extreme cold or fright: stimulated by either of these, a muscle called the arrector pili (Latin for "erector of hair") tugs at a hair follicle, making it and its hair stand straight up. At the same time, the follicle raises on your skin a tiny mound of flesh (commonly called a goose pimple), and you experience a prickly feeling as hundreds of follicles "erect." Rumours to the contrary, there is no proof that scalp hair will stand on end for any length of time.

How many kinds of hair are there?

Long before birth—just three or four months after conception—hair appears on the human body. This kind of hair, called lanugo, covers the whole foetus until about a month before birth, when it generally disappears. Next comes a second coat of lanugo, which is lost in the third or fourth month after birth.

A different kind of hair, vellus, grows, and persists throughout life. Fine, soft, and downy, vellus is often nearly invisible. Yet it covers the body everywhere except for a few places such as the soles of the feet and the palms of the hands. Interestingly, even someone who has gone bald still has fine vellus growing on his scalp.

Your most conspicuous hair is the thick, strong, so-called terminal hair

Hair Often Changes Over the Years

Touched by the rays of the sun, a child's hair often seems almost iridescent, quite different in texture from adult hair. The onset of puberty, orchestrated by hormones, changes the whole body. Both sexes develop hair in the pubic area and in the armpits. The influence of hormones on hair is far more pronounced among males than among females. Most dramatic is the development of a coarse beard. Hair follicles in the face (present at birth) are stimulated, transforming the appearance from boy to man.

The boy's hair (a coppery colour as his father's once was) will probably darken with time.

that grows on your scalp and makes up your eyebrows, eyelashes, and, if you are a man, your beard.

Why is hair thick, coarse, or fine?

Hair texture—its coarseness or fineness—depends on two things: the diameter and shape of the hair's follicle; and the proportion of hard-shell cuticle in the hair's make-up.

If the hair and its follicle are small in diameter, the hair will be "fine"— for instance, it will stream out easily in the breeze. Whether hair is straight or curly depends on how the cells in the papillae grow. An even growth pattern in the follicle produces straight hair, an uneven pattern produces curly or wavy hair.

The differences between coarse and fine hair also have a physiochemical basis: all hairs have a tough, shell-like casing (the cuticle) and a soft, fibrous inner cortex. In coarse hair, the cuticle makes up 10 percent of the volume and the cortex 90 percent. In fine hair, the proportion is 40 percent cuticle and 60 percent cortex.

Both "fine" and "thick" heads of hair have about the same number of

hairs, though fair people tend to have more than dark people. When an individual's hair begins falling out because of either age or disease, it is said to be thinning out. This expression refers to the number of hairs, not to their diameter.

What causes dandruff?

Dandruff—or scalp flaking—has its normal and its abnormal aspects. Your scalp usually sheds skin quite rapidly. For most people, regular shampooing prevents a build-up of dandruff. However, for others, the condition persists. The exact cause of dandruff is not known, but some theories about it are false. One is that if facial soap gets into your hair, it can create dandruff. Hearsay also incorrectly implicates hair spray.

However, there is a kind of dandruff that can be treated medically. If the scalp is chronically inflamed, it will shed an abnormal amount of dead skin. This is known as seborrhoeic dermatitis and requires a doctor's attention; in all likelihood he will prescribe a medicated shampoo that will slow down cell division.

Hair: Too Little, Too Much

Male-Pattern Baldness

If a man's forebears were bald, chances are he will inherit the trait. Folk remedies—including scalp massage, exotic liniments, and vitamins—can do nothing to reverse the pattern, or even slow it down. In some men, the balding process slows after the hairline has receded, in others, when the crown has thinned out. Balding does not always go to the fringe stage.

Full head of hair

Receding at temples

Thinning of crown

Pronounced bald spot

Balding at back of head

Fringe at sides and back

What is baldness?

Many young men who have already begun to lose their hair may consider this a pointless question; they are too unhappy over their thinning hair to care much about what causes it. For although baldness is not a physical disability, some men find it depressing because they think it detracts from their appearance.

The medical name for baldness is alopecia. It seems to be connected with the male hormones called androgens. Androgens seem to "turn off" the centre in a hair's root bulb that makes it generate new hair cells. Sooner or later, it happens to almost all men: their scalp follicles stop generating thick "terminal" hairs and instead grow soft, fine vellus hair.

Usually, alopecia appears as male-pattern baldness with a slowly receding hairline. A different type of baldness not due to androgens is called alopecia areata. In this condition—with here and there a single area going bald—the hair may grow back.

The action of androgens, however, is not the only reason for baldness. Burns, infections, and too-vigorous brushing or combing are among the other causes of temporary and permanent baldness.

Why do more men than women go bald?

To begin with, baldness in women may be somewhat more common than most of us know. Men generally scorn wigs, so you usually know it if a man is bald. Women, by contrast, find baldness much more embarrassing than men do and are more likely to wear a hairpiece to conceal it.

Still, it is true that baldness strikes more men than women. The main reason is that baldness is precipitated by the male sex hormones (androgens) of which women's bodies produce fewer than men's.

When women do become bald, it is less noticeable. Instead of falling out in clumps and leaving areas of the scalp entirely bare, their hair thins out everywhere, but usually without completely exposing any part of the scalp. When this happens before a woman reaches 40, it is abnormal. If it happens later, especially after the onset of menopause, it is a normal result of the aging process.

Severe stress and childbirth can also result in temporary baldness. And in both men and women, some diseases (such as psoriasis) and medications (such as cancer chemotherapy) can cause temporary hair loss.

Can baldness be cured?

Obviously, one of the surest ways to get rich quick would be to discover a cure for baldness. Just as obviously, that's not easy to do, since no one has yet done it.

The simplest solution to baldness is a wig. A tedious but more effective approach is the "punch graft," or living-hair transplant, taken from the back of the scalp. The hair at the "recipient site" does grow, and baldness does not recur. (About 250 plugs would be needed to cover a normal receding hairline.)

For men, there is yet another possibility, more theoretical than practical: counteracting the hair-killing properties of the male hormones (androgens) by taking large doses of female hormones (oestrogens). Unfortunately, this drastic measure not only makes hair grow but also feminizes the male patient.

Can your hair fall out overnight?

Drastic reducing diets can be dangerous not only to your health in general but to your hair in particular. If pursued for any length of time, a diet that contains too little protein or too few Calories will lead to hair loss. When normal eating habits are resumed, the hair grows back. In certain illnesses—cancer, thyroid deficiencies, and sometimes diabetes—the hair gets very thin. In such cases the body loses only the normal quota of hairs every day (from 50 to 100), but it cannot replace them rapidly enough to keep up with the loss.

What causes excessive hairiness?

Generally, people of Mediterranean background are hairier than Scandinavians and Africans; the latter are hairier than American Indians or people of Chinese descent. Variations in hairiness are normal. Seldom is excessive hairiness so extreme as to be considered abnormal. In these few, very special cases, excessive hairy growth may be traceable to genetic factors, steroid drugs, glandular irregularities, or menopause.

Can you get rid of unsightly hair?

Visible hair on a woman's upper lip or on other parts of the face often seems to her to suggest a lack of femininity. In general, excessive hairiness, or hirsutism, is more upsetting to women than to men. The condition can be dealt with in three ways: by masking the hairiness with cosmetics, by removing it temporarily with a razor or depilatories, or by undergoing electrolysis to kill the hair follicle permanently.

High and Mighty Hairstyles

In ancient Egypt, wigs were serious business. The head was shaved, for cleanliness, and presumably for coolness, and wigs were worn as protection from the sun and as a sign of status. In later cultures, wigs were worn mainly by women. Then, in 1624, Louis XIII of France launched the era of the bigwig—by wearing one. The fashion held sway in Europe and its colonies until the American and French Revolutions swept away such symbols of rank. But hair continues to be expressive of ideas—a full head of hair is considered a sign of youth and vigour. Thus wigs, falls, and hair transplants are likely to be with us into the 21st century—and beyond.

The Duke of Marlborough, ancestor of Winston Churchill, wore a lavish wig of cascading curls as an expression of his importance.

Since the 18th century, British judges and barristers have worn wigs in court as a badge of office. Today, the wigs are nylon.

Transplanted plugs of hair from the back of the head are set into a bald patch (left). The new hair is sparse, but permanent (right).

Making Changes in Your Hair

Can your hair turn white overnight?

The great range of human hair colour, from black to platinum blond, depends on a pigment that is called melanin. The more melanin your hair has, the darker it is. The precise colour is genetically determined. Hair colour may change somewhat over the years. For instance, youngsters often have blondish hair that gets dark as they grow older. With advancing age, the production of melanin by hair follicles tends to slow down. Eventually, new hairs may get no melanin at all, so they grow out white.

Probably everybody has heard stories about people whose hair supposedly turned white overnight as a result of a particularly terrifying experience. One familiar example from history is Marie Antoinette, the wife of the French king Louis XVI: it is said that Marie Antoinette's hair lost all its colour the night before she was executed in the French Revolution.

Neither that story nor any similar one has ever been substantiated. However, some diseases—diffuse alopecia, for one—can make all of a person's pigmented hair fall out overnight, while the white hairs, previously intermixed with dark ones, remain unaffected. This gives the false impression that the victim's hair has suddenly turned white.

What turns hair grey?

First of all, what you may call grey hair is actually hair with varying degrees of dilution of pigment—ranging from normal to white in colour. Most people have a sprinkling of "grey" by their mid-thirties. And it is not uncommon to see people who have become prematurely grey as early as their teens.

But what makes hair white? That is, what causes the body's production of the natural hair-colouring agent melanin to shut down as you grow older? Even the specialists are not sure. It has been shown, however, that trapped inside the central shaft of a white hair are hundreds of microscopic air bubbles. (The shaft normally carries the hair's supply of melanin.) When light strikes dark hair, it is partly absorbed; when it strikes white hair, it is brilliantly reflected and refracted. That accounts for the bright, silvery highlights in white hair. Some animal experiments suggest that a diet lacking in certain vitamins produces a greying effect.

How does dyeing work?

There are three basic kinds of hair dye. *Temporary* dyes simply coat the surface of the hair; they cannot pene-

Two Perspectives on Hair

Viewed under a polarized light microscope (on this page) and under a scanning electron microscope (facing page), the effects of various hair treatments can be seen with startling clarity. The normal proportions of the three layers within each hair are shown below, with the middle layer, or cortex, making up the bulk of the strand. Compare this with the strand of hair in the picture to the right of it. As a result of chemical treatments and mechanical stress, the shaft is compressed and ruptured. Although hair is dead, it is remarkably resilient; a strand of hair is stronger than a strand of steel of the same size. Various treatments—dictated by fashion—often play havoc with hair structure, damaging its texture and dulling its sheen. However, as long as the follicles remain healthy, replacement hair is always on the way.

Fractured hair shows effect of rubber bands and tight plaits.

Normal hair showing three layers: inner medulla, cortex, and cuticle.

Bleaching, dyeing, and permanent waving distort hair, break cuticle.

trate the hair's outer shell, or cuticle, because their molecules are too large to "fit between the cracks." Such hair dyes wash away just as soon as the hair is shampooed.

Semi-permanent dyes have smaller molecules that can penetrate the hair somewhat. For this reason they can usually withstand at least five shampooings before the colour begins to fade noticeably.

By far the most effective and most popular hair dyes are *permanent*, "oxidation" dyes. They combine three liquids. One carries the primary colour; the second is the familiar hydrogen peroxide; the third is a "coupler" that unites the two. All three liquids are made up of extremely small molecules that readily penetrate to the centre of the hair—its cortex. There they come together to form large molecules that are trapped in the cortex and so cannot be washed away when the hair is shampooed. Many oxida-

tion dyes come in compartmented aerosol cans that mix the three components as they are sprayed onto the hair. Because they last so long, such dyes are the wrong choice for someone who likes to experiment with different colours several times a year.

No matter how effective any dye is to begin with, the scalp soon pushes up more hair of the original colour; even the best dye job must be repeated after three or four weeks.

Is it safe to dye your hair?

People have been changing the colour of their hair for at least 3,000 years. Today many people, especially women, dye their hair on a regular basis, and the manufacturing of dye has become standardized to a great extent. Both dye makers and, in some countries, consumer agencies make a great point of warning customers to

follow the manufacturers' instructions to the letter. Since many dyes contain potentially dangerous chemicals—among them substances that are highly irritating to the skin and the eyes—it pays to follow this advice scrupulously.

Can swimming hurt your hair?

Despite old wives' tales to the contrary, pure water is not at all harmful to your hair. But the water in chlorinated swimming pools is another matter. Scientists have found that chlorine can soften the hair's protective outer shell, its scaly cuticle. Under an electron microscope, the cuticle can be seen to have melted or worn away. It takes only ten hours of exposure to do the damage; so the answer for pool swimmers is to wear a watertight cap or to wash their hair when they come out of the water.

Normal cuticle lies flat. Ordinary combing doesn't ruffle the cells on the cuticle.

Curling irons, if used too hot or too long, can cause blisters. Hair actually melts.

Hair lacquer coats and thickens the shaft. The dried coating links and stiffens hair.

Back-combing, or teasing, goes against the cuticle grain, lifting and tearing the cells.

Bleached and back-combed, the shaft is seriously damaged, resulting in a dull look.

Dry shampoo, which lifts dirt from hair, also leaves a residue of particles (stained green).

Your Telltale Nails

How Fingernails Grow

On average, it takes about three to six months for a nail to grow from its base to its top. The direction of growth is guided by the small flap of skin that curves around the base of the nail. Provided the root of the nail is not destroyed, injury to a nail tends to accelerate its growth, until it has recovered. Eating gelatin does not influence the rate of growth or the strength of nails; a more effective way to protect them is to wear rubber or plastic gloves when washing dishes or clothes.

ROOT or MATRIX where nail cells are produced (see inset below)

CUTICLE (the technical name is EPONYCHIUM)

NAIL PLATE

FINGER BONE

An injury to the matrix may produce a harmless bump or blemish on the nail. The cuticle is important in protecting the growing area of the nail. Therefore, the cuticle should be treated gently—either it should be left alone or pushed down with a cuticle stick.

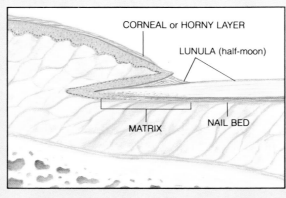

CORNEAL or HORNY LAYER

LUNULA (half-moon)

MATRIX   NAIL BED

Are your nails dead or alive?

Your nails are tough—they serve as armour plating for the sensitive tips of your fingers and toes—but they are quite lifeless. What makes the nails such effective shields for vulnerable body areas is the material they're made of, a protein called keratin that gives the nails their rugged character. If you walk a trail barefoot and suddenly stub your toe against a log, your shock-resistant, nerveless toenails spare you at least some of the pain you would otherwise feel.

Your fingernails serve still other functions. They come in handy for delicate tasks, such as pulling apart a knotted shoelace. And although fingernails themselves lack nerves, they make excellent "antennae," because they are embedded in sensitive tissue that picks up even the slightest impact when the nail touches an object.

The visible part of a nail, called the body, or nail plate, is only 0.5 millimetres (0.02 inches) thick. It grows out of the root, or matrix, which is hidden beneath the nail at its base. Also at the base, there is a whitish crescent called the lunula (Latin for "little moon"), which may or may not be visible. The area underlying the entire nail is called the nail bed.

How do hair, fingernails, and toenails compare?

In one respect, your nails and hair are alike: both are a modified form of skin tissue stiffened by keratin. As for the differences between them, most are obvious, but one is not readily apparent: while the growth of individual hairs is interrupted every few years by a so-called "resting state," your nails never stop growing.

But nails grow much more slowly than hair. Ordinarily, your fingernails grow about 4 centimetres (1.5 inches) a year, your toenails only one-third or one-half that length in the same period, and your hair, a full 12.5 centimetres (5 inches) or more.

Although nails grow continuously, they grow faster at some times than at others. Nail growth is quickest in your twenties and thirties and slowest in infancy and old age. Warm weather and pregnancy accelerate growth; malnutrition and starvation slow it down sharply.

Finally, if you happen to be right-handed, your right thumbnail most likely grows faster than your left; the reverse holds true for left-handers. The difference may be due to the greater activity of the dominant hand or greater blood flow.

Do people's nails really keep growing after death?

This durable old wives' tale isn't true, but it's easy to understand how it started. The skin on a dead person's fingers shrivels slightly, and often pulls back from the base of the nail, which makes the nail *look* a little longer than it did just before death.

What makes fingernails brittle?

Brittle, cracked fingernails are a source of distress—especially among women who spend considerable time and money on manicures and hand care. The principal, rather prosaic, cause of the disorder seems to be ordinary tap water. Nails limit the amount of water that can invade the tissues of the fingertips, but oddly enough, like the dead portion of the skin, they perform this function partly by soaking up large amounts of water when they are dipped into it. Nails are so porous that they can hold a hundred times as much water as an equivalent weight of skin. The swollen nails later get rid of excess water by evaporation and resume their ordinary size. But all this soaking and drying out, repeated several times a day over a period of months, can have very disruptive effects on the condition of fingernails.

Frequent immersion in water is not the only cause of splits in the nails. Many women use nail polish, removing it periodically with solvents. Both polish and remover can contain irritating chemicals dissolved in liquids that the nails soak up as readily as they do water. If the polish has been applied to hide water-caused damage, the result can be an endless cycle of nail troubles—among them greatly increased brittleness.

Incidentally, some nail polish may be damaging to the skin near the nails. If the polish contains formaldehyde, it may cause a condition called contact dermatitis.

What do your nails reveal about your health?

Before undergoing surgery, women are often asked to remove their nail polish. With the lips covered by an anaesthesia mask, the colour of the nail beds helps the anaesthetist tell whether the patient is receiving enough oxygen. A skilled diagnostician can often learn things about your health just by looking at your nails.

Fine grooves running across all your fingernails may reveal that you suffered a serious illness a few months earlier. That is because illness often slows nail growth and produces ridges in the nail root that are pushed outwards as the nail grows. Misshapen, backward-bent nails may indicate iron-deficiency anaemia.

The colour of the fingernails can also reveal a great deal. A dead-white, opaque nail may on rare occasions indicate cirrhosis of the liver; white bands on fingernails may be signs of mild arsenic poisoning or may be due to unknown causes. Only a physician should interpret such signs; self-diagnosis may lead to groundless pan-

ic. For instance, a harmless knock on the base of your fingernail may cause frightening, but insignificant, dark blood clots under the nail.

What is a hangnail?

A hangnail—a strip of dry skin that has partly split off from the area on either side of a fingernail—can be so painful and distracting as to make ordinary activities difficult.

Hangnails can result from excessive dryness, an improper manicure, or injury. They should be cut—not pulled—off at a point not too close to their base in order to avoid infection. Subsequently, avoid dryness, and apply a moisturizer around the nails.

What causes ingrowing toenails?

A "mere" ingrowing toenail can cause so much pain as to reduce a football halfback to a hobbling, wincing caricature of his normal self. Ingrowing toenails usually come from cutting the nail too close, especially at the edges. As the nail begins to grow, the corners push into the soft, sensitive underflesh, instead of riding up over it like the rest of the growing nail. Tight shoes can also cause ingrowing toenails. In case of infection, do not try to treat it yourself; you should see a doctor.

You can usually prevent ingrowing toenails by cutting the nail straight across and by wearing shoes that give you sufficient room.

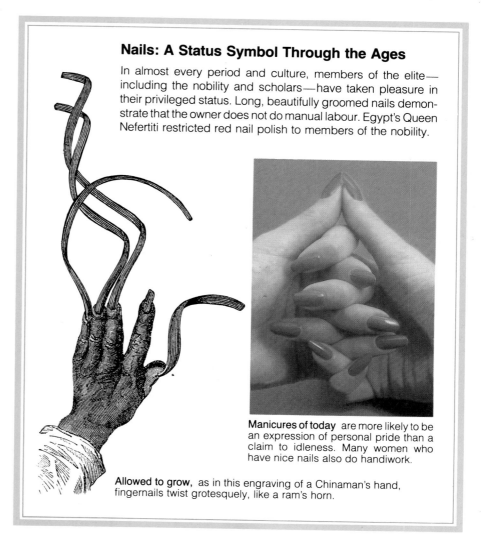

Nails: A Status Symbol Through the Ages

In almost every period and culture, members of the elite—including the nobility and scholars—have taken pleasure in their privileged status. Long, beautifully groomed nails demonstrate that the owner does not do manual labour. Egypt's Queen Nefertiti restricted red nail polish to members of the nobility.

Manicures of today are more likely to be an expression of personal pride than a claim to idleness. Many women who have nice nails also do handiwork.

Allowed to grow, as in this engraving of a Chinaman's hand, fingernails twist grotesquely, like a ram's horn.

Chapter 7

THE BONES & MUSCLES

Everyone knows that if you do not exercise, your muscles turn to flab. Less well known is the fact that unless your bones get exercise, they lose vital calcium.

The Framework of the Body	160
The Secret of Muscular Action	162
Degrees of Flexibility	164
The Casing for the Brain	166
What's Behind Your Smile	168
The Development of Teeth	170
The Spine: Supple or Stiff	172
Straight From the Shoulder	174
The Dexterous Human Hand	176
The Long, Strong Bones and Muscles	178
Feet as a Target of Fashion	179
The Springs on Which You Move	180
Wear and Tear on the Body	182
Strains, Sprains, and Fractures	184
Keeping Fit Through Exercise	186

What do engineers think of the human body?

To an engineer's trained eye, the human body is remarkable, a masterpiece of strength, compactness, and efficiency. For instance, in most people, thighbones are stronger, kilogram for kilogram, than reinforced concrete. When you stride along briskly, your thighbone resists an average pressure of 80 kilograms per square centimetre (half a ton per square inch) with every step. In the meantime, your muscles are using energy six times more efficiently than the engine of the most advanced car.

An engineer might also take note of the body's remarkable girders and scaffolding—the skeleton. It has 206 bones, and it holds upright a mass of muscles and organs that may weigh five times more than the bones themselves. What should by rights be a ramshackle and unsteady framework is actually an often graceful body, lashed together at the joints by tough ligaments and tendons and moved by strong sets of paired muscles.

How old are your bones?

X-rays taken only two months after conception show what looks like a skeleton already in place, so it would seem that the bones are just about the same age as the rest of the body. But as a matter of fact, they are much younger, for the "skeleton" of the two-month-old foetus is not a true bony skeleton, but only a precursor of bones to come.

This precursor is made mostly of cartilage, a tough, whitish, flexible tissue. The resilient quality of cartilage allows the baby's head to be compressed during its passage through the birth canal, and ensures that after the baby is born, it can suffer bumps and knocks without damage to its skeleton.

Some changeover from cartilage to bone is accomplished before birth, some continues afterwards. Calcium, phosphorus, and other hard minerals are deposited year after year in the cartilage, which eventually is replaced by bone. In this process, which is called ossification, large amounts of calcium—all but 1 percent of the body's supply of this essential mineral—are stored in the bones. Later, should the calcium level of the blood drop, calcium is withdrawn from the bones. Calcium is vital to the functioning of the nerves that stimulate muscle contractions, without which you could not move.

Many years must pass before calcium levels rise enough to make the bones really hard. Throughout youth, when people are physically vigorous, the bones remain somewhat flexible, and therefore are less likely to break during rough-and-tumble games. At the age of about 18 in women and 20 in men, the bones are as hard and strong as they are ever likely to be.

Does a baby have as many bones as an adult?

Infants are born with 350 soft bones, roughly 150 *more* than an adult has. But, with the passage of time, many of the infant's bones fuse. For instance, five of the spine's original vertebrae slowly combine to form the solid, single lower-back bone called the sacrum.

When bone fusion is complete, generally by the age of 20 to 25, most adult bodies have 206 hard, permanent bones. But the rule is not hard and fast: some adults go through life with one vertebra or one pair of ribs more than normal.

Can heavy drinking injure your bones?

For many years, doctors were puzzled by evidence that alcoholics have light, easily broken bones. To cautious researchers, this did not mean that drinking *caused* fractures—it seemed to mean only that bone breaks and heavy drinking tended to occur together.

Recently, doctors have definitely isolated heavy drinking as a direct cause of bone breakdown. Alcohol in large quantities, they discovered, prevents certain body chemicals from doing their job, which is to stimulate bone growth. As yet, no one knows why this is so.

How do you learn to walk?

For a baby, learning to walk is a formidable task that must be mastered slowly over many months. The first steps are an exercise in hard knocks. From wriggling on his stomach, the infant progresses to crawling on hands and knees. Then he carefully pulls himself upright, but at the slightest misstep, he topples. Only after a period of trial and error does he learn to make the right moves.

Though he does not realize it, the tottering baby is learning an elaborate series of muscle contractions aimed at keeping his centre of gravity balanced over the leg that is supporting his weight. The contractions are orchestrated by a centre in the brain called the cerebellum. The arms, too, play a key role in keeping the body upright and in balance—especially during running or fast walking.

What does "muscle-bound" actually mean?

The muscle-bound person is one who is unable to make full use of his muscles. This is because the muscles, which work in pairs, have been incorrectly trained. An example is the biceps muscle, on the front of the upper arm, which is balanced by the triceps, which runs along the back of the upper arm. To lift a heavy hammer, you must contract and shorten your biceps, while your triceps relaxes and becomes long. Then, to strike the hammer on a nail, you must tense your triceps while relaxing your biceps. It may sound complicated, but when these paired muscles are both strong, they work together smoothly.

The trouble comes when someone develops enormous biceps by lifting weights unwisely or by heaving heavy objects. In that case, the biceps will be more developed than the triceps. The biceps will then bend the arms slightly inwards even when the body is relaxed, and the muscle man will find it hard to snap his arm straight out. The penalty for being muscle-bound is poor athletic performance and a generally awkward, ill-at-ease stance.

Years ago, would-be body builders bought weights and used them without coaching. Often, the muscles looked impressive, but their development was uneven, and they lacked flexibility. Gym instructors now see to it that weight lifters train for balanced development, making muscles strong and supple.

The Framework of the Body

What do bones do?

The bony framework of the body weighs only 9 kilograms (20 pounds) or so, and in this respect, at least, it might seem unimpressive. Yet bones do much more than allow you to stand and walk. They protect your internal organs: the skull safeguards the brain, while the rib cage shields the heart and lungs.

The marrow inside certain bones produces red blood cells that carry oxygen and nutrients throughout the body, and the marrow in other bones makes millions of white cells that destroy harmful bacteria. Furthermore, bones repair themselves without forming a scar when injured.

What goes on inside living bones?

To get some idea of what living bone is like, imagine you are a surgeon operating on a patient's thighbone. The first part of the bone you come to is a layer of thin, whitish "skin," the periosteum, which is Latin for "surrounding the bone." This skin, packed with nerves and blood vessels, supplies the cells from which the hard bone just beneath the periosteum is built up.

Peeling back the periosteum, you come to the dense, rigid bone proper, known as compact bone. This cylinder-shaped mass is so hard that surgeons must use a saw instead of a knife to cut through it.

Honeycombing the compact bone are thousands of tiny holes and passageways, through which run nerves and blood vessels that supply the bones with vital oxygen and nutrients. When you cut open the compact bone, you discover that it is a cylinder surrounding and protecting spongy bone spicules and a central gelatinous material. This is the bone marrow, which produces white blood cells (which fight infection), red cells (which carry oxygen), and platelets (which help to stop bleeding).

All three bone layers—periosteum, compact bone, and marrow—interact with each other, with nerve signals flashing back and forth and streams of blood coursing between the layers. So so-called dead bone is actually one of the liveliest places in the human body.

Can you feel pain in your bones?

The dense layer of compact bone that supports the weight of the body is composed mainly of calcium and other minerals, so that it feels no pain. But the periosteum that surrounds the compact bone contains nerves and is therefore sensitive to pain. When a bone is broken, injured nerve fibres that run through passageways in the compact bone send messages of distress to the periosteum, which relays the protest to the pain centres of the brain. If the splintered edges of the broken bone rip through the periosteum itself, the victim experiences severe pain.

How can you tell male and female skeletons apart?

If you just happened to find a skeleton in a cupboard some day, you could probably figure out the sex of the person it belonged to by simply looking at the pelvis. A woman's pelvis is wider than a man's and has a large, round birth opening at its centre. A man's has an opening, but it is smaller and heart-shaped. As for other bones, a man's are likely to be bigger and heavier than a woman's.

A woman's breastbone is wider and shorter than a man's. Her skull is more softly contoured, and her wristbones are slimmer. Her jaw is smaller, and she is unlikely to have the heavy brow ridges and somewhat slanted forehead commonly found in a man.

Can your bones endanger your body in any way?

Bones are among the most perfect creations of nature. Each one can withstand four times the weight resisted by a comparable amount of reinforced concrete and about the same weight resisted by aluminium or light steel. The key to the bones' extraordinary strength-lightness ratio is the way atoms of calcium and phosphorus are densely packed together inside the bone in regular, crystalline patterns. Diamonds, which

Early Theories: THE USES OF SKULL SURGERY IN ANTIQUITY

Trepanation (opening holes in the skull) was practised as early as 10,000 B.C. in Europe, South America, and some parts of northern Africa. Skulls were opened by boring, scraping, and cutting. The smooth-edged bones—signs of healing—show that patients lived far more often than they died. Some scholars theorize that trepanning was solely a ritual to free "demons possessing the patient." Other experts suggest that trepanning was used to cure headaches and epileptic

seizures. An anthropologist who worked closely with Algerian tribes in the early 1900s reported that women there actually sought trepanation, and that local practitioners cheerfully obliged. Pieces of bone cut from trepanned skulls were believed to serve as good luck charms for doctors.

This ancient Peruvian skull gives evidence of repeated operations. One specimen from the region had seven different, well-healed holes.

The Internal Scaffolding of the Body

The skull, spine, and rib cage account for 80 of the body's 206 bones, and form the "axial" skeleton. The rest are known as the "appendicular" skeleton and include the shoulder, arms, hands, hips, legs, and feet. The skull has 28 bones, with 8 fused to cover the brain. At the bottom of the skull is a big hole that surrounds the top of the spinal cord. The shoulder group includes the shovel-shaped scapula (Greek for "dig") and the key-shaped clavicle (Latin for "little key"). The 24 ribs anchored in pairs to the spine protect the heart and lungs along with the thick breastbone. The lower half begins with the pelvis and ends with the 26 bones in the ankles and feet.

Cartilage cross-section: in an embryo, the skeleton is all cartilage, which is transformed into bone by calcium.

Bone cross-section: the active, bone-forming cells are shown as dark, circular structures.

SKULL

COLLARBONE (clavicle)

PECTORAL GIRDLE

BREASTBONE (sternum)

SHOULDER BLADE (scapula)

RIBS

HUMERUS

VERTEBRAL COLUMN

RADIUS

PELVIC GIRDLE

ULNA

CARPALS

METACARPALS

PHALANGES

FEMUR

KNEECAP (patella)

Tough, dense, elastic, the cartilage surface of most adult joints has no blood supply of its own; it gets nutrients from tissue fluids. The distribution of cartilage throughout the body is shown here in grey.

FIBULA

TIBIA

TARSALS

METATARSALS

PHALANGES

are the hardest of all natural substances, owe their great density to similar crystalline structures.

Unfortunately, a bone's crystalline patterns are somewhat flawed, and they frequently develop tiny fissures or cracks somewhat similar to the crystalline dislocations that cause "fatigued" metal to collapse. Such cracks in the bone are usually con-

tained and eventually heal; but, in some cases, they can widen and seriously weaken the bone. And a sharp blow to a bone may produce somewhat the same effect as a blow to a diamond, which can split open along its lines of cleavage.

Another hazard is the fact that under certain circumstances, radioactive substances, such as radium, can

accumulate in bone. Once radium is present, even tiny amounts of it become "the enemy within," destroying the surrounding marrow and bone tissue with "tracer bullet" radiation. This occasionally causes fatal tumours. So, ironically, your body's enormously strong inner scaffolding, the skeleton, can become one of its most vulnerable points.

The Secret of Muscular Action

Why is your body like the mast of an old-time sailing vessel?

In high winds and tossing seas, the towering masts of the old-time windjammers were kept erect only with difficulty. Without an elaborate network of chains and ropes—the rigging—all of those masts would have toppled over or snapped off.

Very much the same thing happens when you try to stand in place without moving. No one, not even an army cadet standing at attention, can remain perfectly still for any length of time. You will probably begin to sway forward, but you won't fall. A complex network of rope-like tendons and ligaments, along with the muscles in your back and legs, quickly tighten up and pull you back to an upright position. The same holds true if you sway backward or to either side.

The muscular system does more, of course, than just keep your body upright. Your muscles enable you to carry out thousands of intricate moves—moves as complicated as the ones needed to high jump, do sit-ups, tap dance, or play the piano.

The Major Muscles of the Body

When you throw your head back for a good laugh, you employ the trapezius muscles connecting the head, neck, and shoulders. Lifting your arm to ward off a blow uses the deltoid muscles, which join the upper arm, collarbone, and shoulder blade. Biceps and triceps on the upper arm control the up-and-down motions of your forearm. For coughing and childbirth, you need the rectus and transversus abdominus (midsection) muscles. The strong gluteus maximus muscles (buttocks) are used for standing up; the gastrocnemius (calf) muscles, for walking.

STERNOCLEIDO-MASTOID
CLAVICLE
SERRATUS ANTERIOR
EXTERNAL OBLIQUE
RECTUS ABDOMINUS
QUADRICEPS
TIBIALIS ANTERIOR

PECTORALIS MAJOR
DELTOID
BICEPS BRACHII
TRICEPS
LATISSIMUS DORSI
BRACHIORADIALS
EXTENSOR DIGITORUM
ABDUCTOR POLLICIS LONGUS
FLEXOR CARPI RADIALIS
FLEXOR POLLICUS BREVIS
LUMBRICALS
SARTORIUS
RECTUS FEMORIS
GRACIUS

TRAPEZIUS
GLUTEUS MEDIUS
GLUTEUS MAXIMUS
SOLEUS
HAMSTRINGS
GASTROCNEMIUS
ACHILLES TENDON

A **front view** shows the musculature of a female body.

A **back view** shows the musculature of a male body.

How many kinds of muscle are there?

Watching the play of ripples under the skin of a body builder or a weight lifter, you might think that the body had lots of different types of muscle. In reality, there are only three basic kinds: the striped, or striated, voluntary muscles that move the bones; the smooth, involuntary muscles that line the blood vessels, stomach, digestive tract, and other internal organs; and the muscles of the heart, which are a kind of cross between smooth and striped muscles.

The striped muscles are capable of strong contractions that you control. The smooth muscles have important but ·non-emergency functions, so they do not contract as powerfully. Their movements are involuntary, that is, not under conscious control.

Cardiac, or heart, muscles have stripes, but the stripes are farther apart than in other striped muscles. The muscles of the heart are involuntary—the heart beats at a certain rate whether you like it or not.

What does the inside of a muscle look like?

If you slice through a typical muscle diagonally, you find that it resembles a telephone cable. Inside is a bundle of lesser cables, each bundle enclosing still smaller ones.

The first and largest bundle you come to is made up of muscle fibres in which there are nerves, blood vessels, and connective tissue. Each fibre is built up from smaller strands called myofibrils. Finally, every myofibril contains intertwined filaments of the muscle proteins myosin and actin.

As you grow older, the resilient fibres of the striped muscles that move your bones are slowly replaced by connective tissues, in a process known as fibrosis. Although this new connective tissue is tough, it is not elastic, so the muscle becomes weak and can no longer contract strongly. That accounts for the reduced strength and slow muscular response that comes with old age.

The Basic Muscle Types

Striped (skeletal) muscles come in two types: fast twitch for bursts of energy and slow twitch for efficient oxygen use. Smooth muscles control the body's unconscious functions such as digestion. Cardiac muscles are also involuntary; however, some Indian yogis can influence heartbeat during periods of profound meditation.

Striped (versatile) muscles

Smooth (steady) muscles

Cardiac (powerful) muscles

How do muscles work?

A major achievement of 20th-century science is the discovery of what makes muscles work. The process involves chemical reactions and an exchange of nerve signals. When your arm dangles at your side, the biceps muscle is long, thin, and stringy. But if you clench your fist, and flex your forearm, the biceps muscle becomes tense and bulges out.

Only in recent decades have scientists learned just what happens when muscles tense up in this way. Imagine a small room with movable walls, representing a sarcomere, or unit of muscle contraction. Standing in the middle of the room, you are in the position of a myosin filament and in front of you are two ropes, one attached to the left wall and the other attached to the right wall. These represent thin actin filaments. In muscle contraction, you would be stimulated to pick up the two ropes and pull on them, bringing the walls closer. In relaxation, you'd drop the ropes, and the walls would slide back. What keeps them locked together? The main factors are nerve signals that set off chemical reactions that contribute to the process of contraction.

The point where the message-bearing nerve fibre links with the muscle fibre is called the motor end plate. When a message reaches the end plate, the plate secretes the powerful chemical acetylcholine, which passes into the muscle fibre and produces jolting electrical charges that get the muscle action under way.

What makes the heart muscle so tough?

Tough is indeed the word for the heart, which has seen thousands of people through lives of more than 100 years. In such a case, the heart will have beaten a thousand million times and have pumped 550,000 tonnes of blood. Physiologists think the reason for such durability is that the heart muscle combines the power of the striped, voluntary muscles with the steady reliability of the smooth, involuntary ones. Moreover, the cardiac fibres, unlike those of striped or smooth muscles, connect with each other and create a mutually supportive network of communications. This network enables the cells of the heart to exchange electrical signals and to act in unison.

Degrees of Flexibility

How do joints work?

Given the fact that bones are all rigid, it is remarkable how flexible the body is. The reason you can move so easily is that your bones are linked to each other at intersections that are called joints—an arrangement that allows the muscles to manoeuvre the skeleton into thousands of positions.

There are several types of joints that permit different kinds and degrees of motion. Hinge joints, most notably in elbows and knees, swing back and forth like doors on hinges. Ball-and-socket joints—the shoulder and hip—allow one bone to twist and turn in many directions while remaining firmly connected to another.

What makes joints operate smoothly?

The insides of healthy joints, where bones come together, are miracles of both snug fit and mobility. The ends of adjacent bones are lined with a smooth coating of cartilage. Furthermore, the space between these almost-touching bones contains a thin film of lubricating liquid, called synovial fluid (after the Greek word for "egg white," which the lubricant resembles). In some joints, the space also holds flat discs of cartilage called menisci that act as shock absorbers. The parts of the joint are kept in position by flat or cordlike ligaments.

Which joint is most vulnerable?

The knee is the body's biggest, and heaviest, joint and seems well armoured. It is wrapped in a protective, fluid-filled bag called the synovial capsule. Its parts are lashed together with tendons and ligaments. It is protected by a stout bony shield, the kneecap. And the thighbone is cushioned from contact with the lower-leg bones by shock-absorbing cartilage. Despite all this, the knee is injured more often than any other joint.

When the knee is either knocked or wrenched out of position, and ligaments either tear or are stretched too far, the kneecap is sometimes dislocated, and the cartilage inside the joint may be damaged. One dramatic example is a side-on tackle in rugby football, in which a runner's knee is forcibly rammed sideways.

Are all your joints movable?

You probably associate the word *joint* with vigorous action, but in fact, a joint may be fixed. Such joints are found in the skull, where the bones are joined by layers of tough, dense tissue called sutures. Except for unusual situations, the skull bones stay in place, as if they were a rigid unit.

Another class of joints is capable of slight, gliding movements. The joints that connect the vertebrae of your spine are in this category. When a batsman stands at the crease and drives at the ball, the cumulative effect of the tiny spinal movements rippling up his back permits a broad, sweeping swing.

What is a ball-and-socket joint?

The ball-and-socket joint, the third type of the skeletal articulations, moves freely in almost all directions. A student of anatomy would say that such joints are fulcrums, that the bones they connect are levers, and that the muscles attached to the bones provide the moving force.

If you don't fully appreciate what the hip can do, watch a ballet performance closely, and notice what a truly remarkable range of movement the hip joint (frequently mistaken for a bone) permits. That range is possible because the knob-like, hemispheric head of the thighbone, or femur, fits snugly into a concave receptacle in the pelvis. Nearly frictionless action is made possible by the synovial, or lubricating, fluid that is contained in the membrane lining the hip cavity.

What makes your joints crack?

When you do a deep knee bend, chances are your knees will give off sharp, snapping noises. The same thing happens when you "crack" your knuckles or other jointed bones. One cause of such noises is the loud bursting of air bubbles in the fluid that lubricates your joints. Another cause is the snapping and twanging of stringy ligaments—tightly stretched

---

DID YOU KNOW...?

- **Your muscles can produce tremendous amounts of heat —** by one estimate, a 62 kilogram (9 stone 11 pound) squash player produces enough heat in 7 minutes to bring a litre (1.75 pints) of water to the boil. In fact, that's what shivering is all about. Involuntary contractions of muscles release chemical energy, which produces heat and so warms the body.

- **In isometric exercising,** you strain to move objects that are immovable. When you work with stationary bars or push outwards against a door frame, that's isometrics. In isotonic exercising, you pit your muscles against objects that do move. If you lift weights, for instance, you are exercising isotonically, exerting "constant tension" against the barbell as you lift it overhead.

- **When a baby sucks its thumb,** many parents try to make it stop, for fear that the baby will "spoil" the shape of its mouth. However, dentists say that thumb sucking rarely has anything to do with malocclusion (poorly positioned teeth).

- **Aerobic exercise,** which is designed to increase the efficiency of the body's intake of oxygen, should be done for periods of 20 minutes, three to five times a week. To find your optimum level of exertion, subtract your age from the number 220, then multiply the result by 0.85. This gives you the maximum heart rate for your age. To see if you are achieving the maximum level of exertion, take your pulse for 15 seconds immediately after exercising.

How You Bend, Stretch, Glide, and Swivel

There are three basic kinds of joints: ones that do not move at all, where rigidity is desirable; joints that move very little, as in the joint that connects the pubic bones in the pelvis; and the largest category, the joints that move freely. What determines the joint's range of movement is the shape of the bones, how taut the ligaments are, and the musculature around them. The saddle joints of the wrist and thumb allow movement in two dimensions, at right angles to each other. The term *saddle* describes the fact that each of the bones is concave in one direction, convex in the other. This is what prevents rotation of the joint. Contrast the movement of the thumb to the fingers: like the ankle joint below, the finger joints are capable only of gliding. Elbows and knees are both hinge joints, but the knee is more flexible, capable of some rotation. The ball-and-socket joint of the hip is not as flexible as the comparable joint in the shoulder, but the deeper socket makes dislocation less likely.

Suture joint, in the skull, is inflexible in an adult. The back-lit close-up (left) shows jagged edges.

HINGE JOINT

BALL-AND-SOCKET JOINT

SADDLE JOINT

PLANE JOINT

---

like banjo strings across bony surfaces in the joints—as they slide off one bony surface and onto another.

What does it mean if a person is double-jointed?

Many people can bend their fingers far back, wrap their knees around their neck, and perform other remarkable contortions. The popular belief is that such people have extra joints that make their twistings possible. Actually, there is no such thing as being double-jointed. People who seem to be so gifted simply have the knack of stretching the ligaments that surround the joints and that normally limit movement. An Indian fakir or a circus contortionist was probably born with slack ligaments, and through rigorous stretching and twisting has loosened them still further. Since the truth has less power to draw crowds than the legend about double-jointedness, professional contortionists are in no hurry to dispel the popular notion that they are a very special breed of people.

The Casing for the Brain

Why are infants born soft-headed?

A baby's skull, made of soft bone and gristle-like cartilage, gradually ossifies during the first 18 months of the child's life. At birth, the infant's skull is large relative to the size of the birth opening in the middle of the mother's pelvic girdle. The infant's soft skull may be compressed as it is slowly pushed through the pelvic opening. When the baby emerges into the world, its head may be somewhat flattened, but it is unharmed and in a few days regains its original shape.

The infant's brain is not fully developed at birth. It grows rapidly, and the soft skull expands right along with it, until, at about the age of 18 months, the brain has nearly reached its adult size, and the skull has hardened around it.

What is the function of the skull?

The 28 bones of your skull, separated at birth by membranous soft spots called fontanelles, have by adulthood hardened and fused together to form an almost rigid, almost spherical container that protects your brain, eyes, nose, and ears. The large, dome-shaped portion of your skull, the cranium, is made up of eight tightly

The face of a young girl emerged from this 27,000-year-old skull.

Beauty From Bones: A Blend of Science, Art, and Human Curiosity

It all began back in the 1930s when a young Soviet scientist named Mikhail Gerasimov first observed and recorded the relationship of the flesh to bones. Studying hundreds of skulls and corpses, he noticed that a woman's skull is usually smaller than a man's and that a woman's jaw is more delicate than a man's. He then learned how to determine the age of the person whose skull it was: worn-down teeth and fully merged, ossified bones are sure signs of adulthood. Teeth can also help indicate a person's race. (Asians don't normally have wisdom teeth, for example.) Other subtle clues are left by the bones—for instance, the width of the nose and the depth of the cheek muscles. Improving on Gerasimov's calculations, today's past-finders use ultrasound waves on live people to research the flesh-bone ratios. For reconstruction, chemicals strip away any remaining flesh, and, starting at the forehead, the "muscles" are shaped out of a flexible plastic. How can we be sure Gerasimov's work was accurate? Early proof came when he built the face of a Papua New Guinea circus performer who had died in the late 1800s. The head was ultimately paired with an indisputably authentic photograph of the subject. But are today's anthropological detectives infallible? One noted U.S. specialist says, "If I'd been given the skull of Jimmy Durante, I doubt that I would have given him such a big schnozzle."

The complex mathematical relationship of specific bones to bones and flesh to bones guides the skull builders.

interlocking bones that shield the brain. The front part of the skull, the face, contains 14 bones including the jawbone. At birth, the skull accounts for a quarter of the skeleton's size, but by maturity it makes up only about an eighth of it.

What happens when you hit your head?

The skull is engineered to give ever so slightly—so as to absorb shock—at the seams where the bones come together. Furthermore, the brain is wrapped in three baglike layers of protective tissue, and it floats in a sea of cerebrospinal fluid that serves as a shock absorber. Despite all these factors, the brain is far from invulnerable to injury.

Your skull reacts to a blow much as a church bell responds to the impact of its clapper. When a bell is struck, the force of the blow spreads quickly across the entire surface of the bell. In much the same way, your head "rings" when it is struck as the energy of the blow travels through the arching bones of your skull. Each time the shock wave passes across one of the borders, or sutures, where the skull's 28 bones meet, a little of the wave's force is dampened and absorbed. If the blow is not too hard, its force will soon be dissipated, most likely leaving you with nothing more than a slight ringing sound in the head. However, if the blow is beyond the limit of the elasticity of the bone, you will suffer a fracture.

When is a fractured skull a serious matter?

If the victim of a blow on the head is lucky, the result may be only a severe jarring, or concussion, that lasts for a few hours. Then, perhaps after some nausea and dizziness, the victim recovers. In a more serious case, a damaged artery may leak blood into or around the brain. Without surgery to remove it, the spilled blood may interfere with vital body functions. If the brain itself has been bruised, convul-

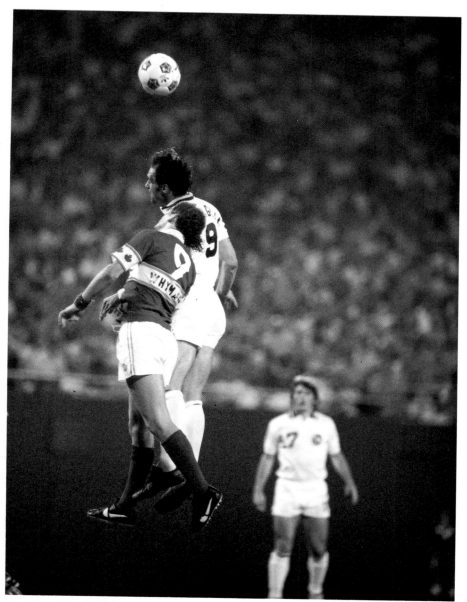

Heading the ball in soccer is spectacular, but not without hazard. Sports doctors say the move should be used sparingly to avoid brain damage.

sions may result. When blood and clear cerebrospinal fluid pour from the mouth, nose, or ears, the base of the skull has probably been fractured. Such an injury may be very serious; the patient may suffer permanent damage, or even die.

Can "heading" a soccer ball cause brain damage?

Soccer is frequently promoted as the "civilized" form of football. But studies show that "heading" the soccer ball—that is, bopping it in midair

with the head—can cause headaches, dizziness, loss of memory, and worse. In a career lasting 15 years, a soccer pro may hit the 425-gram (15-ounce) ball with his head more than 5,000 times. When the leather ball is water-soaked and is travelling at upwards of 120 kilometres (75 miles) an hour, it becomes a formidable missile. As protection against it, doctors have suggested the wearing of helmets and the use of light, non-absorbent plastic balls. They also recommend weight lifting to help players to develop strong, shock-absorbing neck muscles.

167

What's Behind Your Smile

How many muscles are there in the face?

In the small area of the face there are several dozen muscles, which explains why the face is capable of so much expression. When you furrow your forehead, you are using a muscle that runs from the back of the scalp to the top of the eyebrows, but most of the facial muscles are in pairs, one on each side of the face.

Around each eye is a sphincter muscle that contracts when you close your eyelids. Another set of muscles, however, raises your eyelids, and still others draw your eyebrows towards each other when you frown. Six pairs of muscles control the almost constant movements of the eyeballs.

Your nostrils may flare when you are angry, enabling you to take in more air. This dilation is accomplished by one pair of muscles, while an opposing pair constricts the nostrils. When you wrinkle your nose, you can feel both your nose and your upper lip move upward, controlled by a common pair of muscles that lie alongside the nose.

The mouth is the most mobile area of the face. When you pucker up for a kiss, or tighten your mouth over your teeth, you are using the sphincter muscle that forms a large part of the lips. In addition, you have seven pairs of muscles that control those movements of the mouth that turn the corners up or down, in or out. The chin muscles are involved when you

choose to push out your lower lip.

The powerful jaw muscles, which are capable of up to 100 kilograms (200 pounds) of pressure, and the cheek muscles, which you use with the lips when you whistle, are the muscles employed for eating and speaking. Movements of the jaw are controlled by four different pairs of muscles.

Is there a universal language of expression?

Most people are capable of a wide range of facial expressions, the outward reflections of inner emotions and thoughts. Many societies have rules governing the display of feelings—whether it is proper to smile or

---

Gesture Versus Expression

A Tibetan who's glad to see you sticks out his tongue. A Bulgarian means "yes" when his head swings left-right. But tests in 13 industrial, Third World, and preliterate countries have proved that facial expressions are the same worldwide.

When shown pictures, the great majority of people picked the same emotion to express what they saw. And tests measuring the electrical output of facial muscles identified what people were feeling even when they tried to hide it.

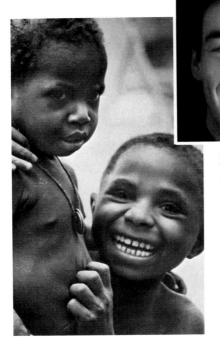

Happiness is one of the six basic expressions. But it incorporates only a few of the 7,000 possible facial movements that have been identified by the behavioural psychologists Paul Ekman and Wallace Friesen. Although both a spontaneous grin and a deliberate smile use lip and cheek muscles, each look involves a different neural pathway from the brain.

Surprise, as a facial expression, is sometimes difficult to distinguish from fear, particularly in preliterate cultures. Researchers have speculated that this may be because surprise and fear go together in these societies. Also, surprise, with its open mouth, wide eyes, and raised eyebrows, is close to the look of fear.

express sorrow in public, for instance. But in an unguarded moment, everyone uses the same facial expressions to show surprise, anger, fear, grief, and other basic feelings. Some facial expressions are ambiguous—grins, for example. They can indicate amusement as well as tension and apprehension. Very slight facial movement can be eloquent—a small frown, a barely perceptible twitch of the mouth.

As you grow older, your habitual expressions become visible on your face; the wrinkles and lines reveal which muscles you use the most.

What is the temporomandibular (TMJ) disorder?

If you have a habit of clenching or grinding your teeth or tensing your jaw from stress, you may suffer from disturbance of the temporomandibular joint, or TMJ. Besides stress, the cause of TMJ syndrome may be misaligned jaws, malocclusion of teeth, or poorly fitting dentures. Symptoms vary, from tenderness in the jaw, clicking noises and pain when you open your mouth to recurring headaches, ringing in the ears, and a feeling of pressure in the eyes.

When your upper and lower teeth, for instance, malocclude—that is, do not fit together properly when you bite—the resulting strain on the TMJ and its supporting muscles can cause agonizing pain. Unfortunately, many people react to tension and stress by clenching their jaw muscles. This strains the TMJ and causes severe shooting pains. If stress is the cause, the solution for most TMJ pain is to learn how to deal with the underlying tension. Short-term treatments that can bring a degree of relief include tranquilizers and analgesics, application of moist heat or ice packs, eating a soft diet, and limiting all jaw movement, including speaking. For long-term relief, your doctor may prescribe special exercises and mouth appliances. But if the problem is only tension, the greatest benefit comes from learning techniques to reduce stress and relax the jaw.

An Ancient Mystery Solved

Until relatively recent times, no one made the connection between pain in the face, neck, and shoulders (usually on one side only); earaches; ringing in the ears, occasional loss of hearing; blurred vision; clenched teeth; and a clicking of the jaw with every movement. We now know that spasms in the temporomandibular joint muscles may be responsible. An attack can be triggered off by yawning, chewing, and even laughing. The cure? Relaxation of the jaw muscles.

The 19th-century French artist Honoré Daumier portrayed the miseries of a headache. From the variety of pains, this could well be TMJ, temporomandibular joint syndrome.

TMJ (temporomandibular joint)

MANDIBLE (lower jawbone)

Opening and closing your mouth is controlled by five pairs of muscles attached to the lower jaw. Prolonged tensing of these muscles puts pressure on the joint where the jaw connects to the skull. TMJ's clicking sounds result from slippage of the bone over cartilage.

The Development of Teeth

What are your teeth made of?

The hardest substance in the human body is one of the four kinds of tissue that make up teeth. It is enamel, and it covers the crown of the tooth, the part you see above the gum, or gingiva. (Enamel is so tough that a dentist's drill has to whir at half a million revolutions a minute in order to cut through it.) A bony material called cementum covers the root, which fits into a socket in the jaw and is joined to it by a membrane. Dentine, a material similar to bone is found under the enamel and the cementum, and it forms the largest part of the tooth. Pulp, the living heart or centre of every tooth, is the last of the four substances. It contains nerves, connective tissue, blood vessels, and lymphatics. When you have a toothache, this is where it hurts.

Why are baby teeth important?

The idea that baby teeth don't matter because they fall out anyway is a misconception. To neglect the baby teeth is to invite a lifetime of dental problems. As the child matures, the primary teeth guide the growth of the jawbones and the second, permanent set of teeth. If the primary teeth are lost prematurely, the jaw may not develop correctly, and the new teeth may come in crooked or crowded.

How do your teeth grow?

You are born with the beginnings of your permanent teeth already in place under the gums, below the buds of the baby, or milk, teeth. The adult teeth develop very slowly, and when they are fully formed, they push up through the gums. The permanent molars erupt behind the primary molars, where the child originally had no teeth at all. The eight bicuspids dislodge and take up the space of the eight primary molars, while the adult incisors and cuspids replace the baby teeth of the same kind. Sometimes a baby tooth is slow to fall out and must be removed by a dentist.

The first permanent teeth are often

The Structure and Types of Teeth

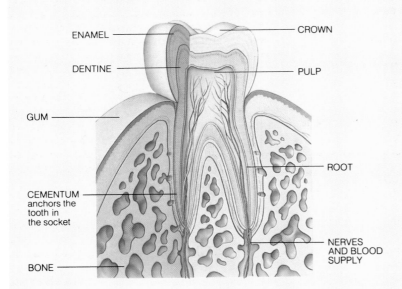

ENAMEL — CROWN
DENTINE — PULP
GUM
ROOT
CEMENTUM anchors the tooth in the socket
NERVES AND BLOOD SUPPLY
BONE

Each tooth consists of a crown and a root, bedded in a socket in the gum. The outer layer of the tooth consists of enamel; a layer of hard dentine surrounds the pulpy central part of the tooth. The pulp contains nerves and blood vessels, which nourish it and provide sensation. Excluding the wisdom teeth, adults have 28 permanent teeth of 4 types, suited for a variety of jobs: 8 incisors, 4 canines, 8 bicuspids, and 8 molars. The sharp incisors at the front of the mouth seize food and sever bite-sized portions. The four canine teeth at the corners of the mouth are pointed, and are capable of tearing hard or tough foods. Next come the bicuspids, for shearing and crushing. Finally, at the back, are the broad, relatively flat molars, which grind and mash.

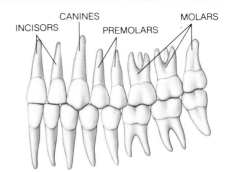

INCISORS CANINES PREMOLARS MOLARS

The permanent teeth begin to appear at about the age of six. There usually are 32 teeth by the age of 21. However, some people never cut four of these: their rearmost molars, or wisdom teeth.

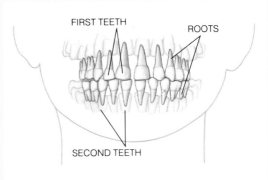

FIRST TEETH ROOTS
SECOND TEETH

The buds of second teeth are already in position when only baby teeth are visible. This illustration shows the teeth of a three- to five-year-old child.

called six-year-molars because they appear at about the age of six. The process of shedding baby teeth begins at about the same age, with the front teeth the first to go. The upper canines are the last of the baby teeth to be lost. By age 13 or so, the 28 permanent teeth are usually in place. The four additional adult teeth, the wisdom teeth, emerge several years later—or, in some cases, not at all.

Why are wisdom teeth so often troublesome?

A good many people have no wisdom teeth, and if you do not have them, don't worry about it. They are certainly not a sign of wisdom: they get their name from the fact that they appear in the late teens or early twenties, when people are physically mature—but not necessarily wise.

By the time the wisdom teeth are due to appear, the other 28 teeth may have preempted all the space in the jaw. In this case, one or more of the last four teeth may remain embedded in the jaw, or impacted, perhaps causing pain and swelling. If wisdom teeth do erupt, they may crowd and damage the other teeth. In addition, the wisdom teeth are prone to decay because they are difficult to reach for thorough cleaning. People who have problems with wisdom teeth should seek prompt treatment.

Why are straight teeth and a good bite important to health?

Occlusion is a favourite word among dentists. It refers to the physical relationship of the upper and lower teeth when the mouth is closed. If your bite is right, the points and facets of the upper and lower jaw mesh just right, so that your molars are able to grind up even small bits of food. Malocclusion means faulty bite; the teeth don't fit together as they should. They may be too widely spaced, because some of them are missing; or they may be crowded together, with some teeth twisted or overlapping.

Crowded teeth are difficult to clean

The Barber of Seville Was Also a Dentist

Old-time dentistry fascinated onlookers, but was very painful for the patient because extraction—without anaesthetics—was the only real solution for infected teeth. Many dentists were itinerants, going from town to town to pull teeth. Barbers, doctors, and pharmacists were also part-time dentists. In 1699, Louis XIV made formal study and testing mandatory in France. But Pierre Fauchard (1678–1761) was the first to encourage the practice of dentistry as an independent discipline. Even so, it wasn't until 1839, in Baltimore, U.S.A., that the world's first College of Dental Surgery was established.

Dentists frequently had to leave town after performing an extraction.

and as a result collect debris that causes tooth decay and gum disease. A defective bite creates pressure and stress that can loosen teeth and lead to imperfect speech, muscle strain, chewing difficulties, as well as disorders of digestion.

Is it worthwhile for adults to straighten their teeth?

Because children's jaws and teeth are still developing, orthodontics—correcting the alignment of teeth—is easiest in the young. But adults, too, can benefit from orthodontic treatment; it can improve their looks and make their teeth last longer.

In children, the orthodontist relies mainly on braces to straighten a twisted tooth or to move it backward, forward, or sideways. Braces are also used to improve the bite of adults, but in addition, the orthodontist may grind down tooth surfaces and build new crowns and bridges. Surgery may be necessary to correct such serious problems as a receding jaw.

Nowadays, orthodontics does not always require the "metal-mouthed" look. Improved adhesives and new metal alloys frequently permit the fastening of braces to the back of teeth instead of the front.

Why do teeth become discoloured?

Some stains on teeth are caused by smoking or by drinking tea or coffee and can be removed by a dental hygienist. Very deep discoloration—from such causes as excessive fluoride, antibiotics, iron therapy, or, in the case of a dead tooth, blood secretion in the dentine—is more difficult to obliterate. A dentist can apply bleaching agents, bond a white sealant to the enamel, or cap the tooth with a porcelain or plastic crown.

What can you do if you lose a tooth?

Missing teeth should be replaced as soon as possible, not only for the sake of appearance but also to keep other teeth from moving into the gap and spoiling the bite.

The most common substitutes for natural teeth are traditional dentures constructed of plastic or metal. Complete dentures replace all of the natural teeth; fixed bridges, which are cemented in place, can substitute for one to four missing teeth if there are natural teeth on either side of the gap. And metal tooth implants, inserted in the jawbone or under the gums are in the experimental stage.

The Spine: Supple or Stiff

How is the spine organized?

Of the 33 bones of the spine, the top 24 are usually categorized into three groups. The seven in the neck area are called the cervical vertebrae. The twelve thoracic vertebrae are found in the chest area, while the five lumbar vertebrae are in the lower back. The sacrum and coccyx (tailbone), which together consist of five and four fused vertebrae respectively, form part of the pelvis. The spinal column is reinforced and held in place by an intricate network of tough muscles, tendons, and ligaments.

At every point, the spine is a marvel of compactness and efficiency. From each vertebra, prongs, or "processes," protrude, to hold the muscles; each has a groove through which the spinal cord descends from the brain, sending and receiving messages along the way. The vertebrae are separated by discs, which are shock absorbers of elastic cartilage that account for about 25 percent of the spine's length. The S-shaped, spring-like form of the spine contributes greatly to its strength and flexibility.

Tucked away at the base of your spine is the sharply tapered, inward-curving bone called the coccyx. Made up of four fused bones, the coccyx has no known use. Ordinarily, you're not even aware of it, unless you bruise or fracture it—perhaps by having the bad luck to slip on an icy surface.

How important is good posture?

If the idea of good posture seems to have fallen into disfavour, the fault lies with well-meaning but overzealous parents and teachers. Decades ago, they used to insist that youngsters adopt the ramrod-stiff, suck-in-your-gut posture then required at military academies.

It is now widely recognized that the command to "straighten your back" is contrary to nature. The human spine is not naturally straight, and no effort, however determined, can ever make it so. It was recognized that exaggerated military postures may pinch neck and back nerves.

As seen from the side, a normal adult spine resembles a double S. Beginning just under the skull, it moves slightly inwards, swoops out at shoulder level, and curves back in behind the stomach. Towards the base, it turns outwards again and then nips back in at the coccyx, or the tailbone.

All of this turning and curving serves a purpose: it makes the spine a kind of spring capable of absorbing the jarring shocks that would otherwise be transmitted straight up your back to your vulnerable brain.

Current theories of good posture are based on balance. The aim is to stand with your head high, but not thrust back. The shoulders are held back just far enough to permit full, free breathing. Try to imagine that a weighted line, dangled from beside your ear, hangs down just in front of your main anklebone. Meanwhile, stand supporting yourself on the ball and heel of the foot.

Why are backaches so common?

Fully 80 percent of Western peoples suffer, off and on, from backaches. So common are they that they often assume that they are inevitable, especially as you get older. But doctors say

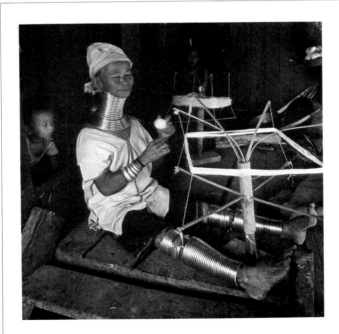

Are people ever born with giraffe-like necks?

The impulse to "improve" the human body is an ancient, widespread phenomenon, ranging from the Chinese practice of binding the feet of young, beautiful girls, to the Mayan practice of changing the shape of a baby's skull by means of flattening boards. The Padaung tribe of Burma artificially created beauty in the form of elongated necks. At five, a young girl was introduced to the stretching process. Rings of metal were wedged around her neck like a collar. As she grew, more rings were added, depressing the shoulders into the torso and making the neck look several times longer than normal. In the eyes of the tribe, this not only enhanced the woman's beauty, it also showed off the family's valuable metal rings. When a long-necked beauty gave serious offence, the tribe removed the rings. Thus she lost her beauty and perhaps her life because her head would droop, like a flower on a weak stalk. Unless someone held her head up and provided some other support, she could choke to death.

The custom of neck stretching has fallen into disfavour. This Padaung woman is among the last of a vanishing breed.

this is not so. Although old age and congenital defects account for some backaches, most result from muscular weakness due to a sedentary existence and from stress.

When people tense up under stress, their flabby, unprepared muscles often go into spasm. This is particularly true of "weekend athletes." The pain of these spasms may be so agonizing that the victim is sure something in his spine must have slipped or possibly broken. Actually, cases in which a disc between two vertebrae slips from its normal position and presses on nerves account for only about 5 to 10 percent of all backaches.

The commonest of all back difficulties is low back pain, which often strikes when you are in your thirties. Most such attacks are what used to be called lumbago: an acute spasm of one of the powerful muscles running along the lower spine. Overweight people or those whose jobs are partly sedentary, partly strenuous—for instance, truck drivers and nurses—may be vulnerable to these spasms. They should be careful to lift heavy loads by letting their legs, not their backs, bear the main weight, and to lower themselves by bending their knees, rather than by leaning over and lifting from the waist.

What makes a person hunchback?

Quasimodo, the central character in Victor Hugo's novel *The Hunchback of Notre Dame*, is perhaps the most famous of all real and fictional sufferers from kyphosis, an abnormal backward bulging of the spine.

The upper section of the normal spine curves outward; kyphosis is an exaggeration of the slight hump everybody has. The typical kyphosis victim is short, with a stooped-over look. The affliction often diminishes lung capacity, and causes shortness of breath and heart problems. Doctors say the condition is idiopathic—that is, "We don't know what causes it." Nevertheless, a doctor must exclude the possibility of other spinal deformities for which specific treatments are available.

What is the key to good posture?

Think of your body parts as building blocks set on top of one another, with ligaments, tendons, and muscles serving as guy wires to keep the structure from toppling over. When the body sections are in perfect balance, each one resting solidly on the one beneath, the body can relax and still maintain its erect position. Alignment, in short, is indispensable to good posture. If you let your shoulders round and slump too far forward, other body parts rearrange themselves accordingly. The pelvis and the stomach thrust forward, the knees bend, and the back muscles tighten up. Poor posture causes chronic strain, general fatigue, and a nagging sense of physical unease. By contrast, a well-aligned body feels buoyant and uses energy efficiently.

CERVICAL (neck) vertebrae

THORACIC (chest) vertebrae

LUMBAR vertebrae

SACRUM

COCCYX

Changing from bare feet to high-heeled shoes tilts the body forward. To counteract the tilt, a woman bends her knees and throws her trunk forward, exaggerating the spine's inward curve.

Cartilage discs that separate the vertebrae in the spine cushion the bones and protect the spinal cord and peripheral nerves. With age, the cartilage becomes thinner and harder. Injury can also displace the disc, resulting in severe back pains.

SPINAL NERVE

DISC

LUMBAR VERTEBRAE

SPINAL CORD

RUPTURED-DISC material pressing on the spinal nerve

Straight From the Shoulder

How do the arms and shoulders work?

If you examine a skeleton, you will see that the arms and shoulders form a kind of independent unit hung from the main skeleton. The large, shovel-shaped scapulas, the "wings" or shoulder blades that stand out on your upper back, are held in place by the long, curving collarbones, or clavicles. Joined to the scapulas by ball-and-socket joints are the arms. The upper arm has one long, thick bone, the humerus. The lower half, or forearm, has two slimmer bones, the radius and the ulna, which connect with the wrist and hand.

The trapezius muscles, which enable you to throw your head and neck back, connect with the shoulders at the back of the neck. The deltoid muscles—which play a crucial role in weight lifting—connect the collarbone with the upper arm bone, the humerus. When you throw up your forearm to ward off a blow from above, you are using a deltoid. The

pectorals, which lie along the upper chest, make a "bear hug" possible. The biceps and the less familiar triceps control the up-and-down movement of your forearm, as when you "make a muscle" on your upper arm.

Is frozen shoulder a cold-weather affliction?

The word *frozen* has several meanings, most of them unrelated to cold or to ice. What happens in the condition known as frozen shoulder, or adhesive capsulitis, is that the shoulder-joint capsule—the envelope of protective tissue that surrounds the joint—becomes greatly inflamed and temporarily immobilizes the shoulder. If the patient (usually middle-aged or elderly) tries to move his shoulder, he suffers agonizing shooting pains. The condition may take months or even years to resolve, but it almost always goes away in time after treatment with drugs and a supervised exercise regimen.

What happens when you dislocate your shoulder?

It's surprisingly easy to dislocate your shoulder. For some people even shrugging on a heavy overcoat can do it, because the socket into which your shoulder bone fits is rather shallow, and it does not take much to pull the bone out. Shoulder dislocations are especially common in adults who have had such a dislocation earlier in life. The reason is that this kind of mishap often stretches the supporting ligaments so that they remain permanently loose.

The telltale signs of shoulder dislocation include pain when you try to move the arm; a lumpy, misshapen appearance around the site, instead of the normal smooth curve of the shoulder line; and an obvious difference in length between the affected arm and the normal one.

If your shoulder gets dislocated, you may be tempted to let a friend force the bone back into place. Don't! It's not as easy as it seems. A joint

Tennis Elbow: A Persistent Problem for Many

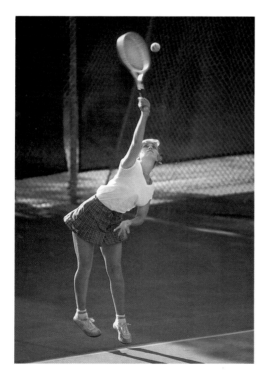

The injury that goes by the name tennis elbow (medically, epicondylitis) is an inflammation of the tendons on the outer side of the elbow joint. It is most common among persons over 30, and despite its name, it is by no means limited to tennis players. It is characterized by steady pain on the outside of the elbow, frequently radiating down the arm to the wrist. The affected area is also extremely tender to the touch. Oddly enough, both inexperienced and professional players are subject to this affliction. The beginner often tries too hard, hits the ball with too much force, and grips the racket too tightly. But the pro has problems, too. According to one sports expert, for pros the cause is sheer overuse of the elbow; there is a correlation between the amount of tennis a pro plays and the frequency of this injury.

During the serve, the player's arm travels at tremendous speeds—often approaching 500 kilometres (310 miles) an hour.

INCORRECT

CORRECT

The whole arm is needed for a correct backhand stroke, not a bent elbow.

dislocation is as serious as a fracture, and only a doctor should deal with it. He will gently replace the bone in its socket, and may then strap it up to reinforce the ligaments that hold the joint in place. Generally, he will also ask you to keep your arm in a sling while the stretched ligaments heal and shorten to their natural length. In all, recovery takes approximately a month.

Why is a blow to your funny bone no laughing matter?

Some people say the funny bone is so called because it is next to the arm bone known as the humerus. The fact is that the funny bone is not a bone at all. The ulnar nerve passes under a bony prominence of the humerus, where it is vulnerable. To find the place, put the point of your right elbow down on the table. Above and to the left of the point, you can feel a big knob. When it is struck, the blow compresses the nerve against the knob, and you feel momentarily paralysed, as if a tiny bolt of lightning had struck your elbow. The last thing you feel like doing is laughing!

What is tennis elbow?

Far more people get tennis elbow from twisting a screwdriver than from swinging a racket. This painful affliction is traceable to a surprising fact about your two forearm bones, the radius and ulna. They run side by side if you hold your forearm straight and palm up. But if, without twisting your elbow, you rotate your forearm until the palm faces down, your radius will lie across your ulna at a shallow angle, forming a long, narrow X.

This rotating capacity is useful, but if you overdo it and strain your muscles, the pain running from your elbow down the back of your forearm can be fierce and disabling. Usually, with rest, the pain goes away, but in some cases your doctor may suggest physiotherapy or local injections.

What is the difference between tendons and ligaments?

Tendons and ligaments have something in common; both are tough connective tissues that don't stretch much (though ligaments generally have more give than tendons). But their functions are different. A tendon is a strong cord attached to a muscle; it transmits the muscle's pulling power to a bone, so as to make it (and your body) move. By contrast, the ligaments—some cord-like, others broad, flat, and shaped like bandages—wrap around your joints, reinforcing them against stresses that might otherwise wrench them out of alignment and cause a sprain or a tear. Injury to tendons or ligaments can be painful and disabling.

Ligaments can be found everywhere in your body, especially around your wrist, ankle, knee, shoulder, and elbow joints. Bandage-flat or shoelace-like ligaments help to keep the bones of the neck and vertebral column braced and aligned.

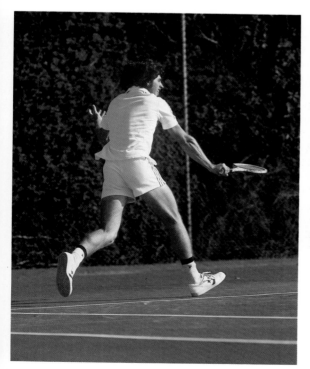

A cause of injury in the backhand stroke is clearly shown: the locked elbow in this one-hand move strains forearm muscles. Generally speaking, a two-handed backhand stroke is less hazardous.

One sure sign of an inexperienced player is a cramped forehand stroke such as this. The player has misjudged the distance, and is too close to the ball. The stroke not only looks awkward, but is stressful to muscles of arm and elbow.

The Dexterous Human Hand

What makes your hands so flexible?

The human hand is so sensitive that it can perform brain surgery, so strong that it can twist a screw deep into wood. Underlying your palm are the five cylinder-shaped metacarpal bones, which extend from your wrist to your knuckles. From the metacarpals rise the finger bones—the 14 jointed, flexible phalanges. In all, there are 27 bones in each of your hands. The bridge between hand and forearm is the wrist, a collection of eight small bones fitted together like cobblestones. Called carpal bones, they are bound together in a glove-like structure of strong ligaments.

Your fingers are controlled primarily by strong muscles in your forearm. These muscles connect with tendons, which are, on the palm side, embedded in long sheaths that extend along each finger. When the forearm muscle contracts, it tugs on the tendon and its sheath, and the finger bends. The thumb contributes to the hand's flexibility because it is opposed to the other fingers, which means you can easily pinch a small object between thumb and finger and pick it up.

What's in a Name?

Thumb is good enough for most of us, but the medical name, pollex, is right on target. It is also the Latin word for thumb and comes from *pollens,* meaning "strong." The little finger comes from minimus, meaning "least." The third finger is annulary after the Latin annulus for "ring," and the middle finger medius, meaning "middle." The forefinger is index, Latin for "pointer." Finger bones are called phalanges, after the ancient Greek word for formations of soldiers in battle.

TENDONS: the power trains connecting bones to muscle

WRIST LIGAMENT: binds nerves and muscles

FOREARM MUSCLES: remote control of fingers and hand

PHALANGES: finger bones

METACARPALS: five bones between the fingers and wrist

METACARPALS

ARTICULAR DISC

ULNA

RADIUS   CARPALS: wrist bones   PHALANGES

Is a mallet finger a serious sports injury?

Probably every village cricketer knows what happens when an inexperienced fielder dives to catch a hard-driven ball. The ball strikes the tip of his unprotected finger, acutely flexing the last joint while the extensor tendon is trying to straighten it. Thus the ball may snap one of the player's extended fingers backwards, damaging a tendon.

If the injured finger is splinted and rested for approximately six weeks, it will heal normally. If it is left untreated, the tendon may repair itself, but it may grow back slightly longer than it was before. In that case, unless it is surgically treated, the top joint of the damaged finger will be permanently bent. The condition is called mallet finger, and it is by no means distressing to everyone who suffers from it. Quite the contrary. Many old-time cricketers disdained treatment for minor injuries, and will show you their crooked mallet finger with obvious pride.

Why is a painful wrist serious?

Athletes do not always realize that the practice of simply strapping up a painful wrist and forgetting about it can lead to some distressing complications. The reason, as any trainer will tell you, is that what an athlete assumes to be simply a sprained wrist is often something more serious: a fracture, a dislocation, or an early symptom of arthritis.

The wrist, or carpus, is a rather

Coloured light (strobe) patterns *prove that hands really can be quicker than the eye. This rapid arpeggio is prac-* *tised until the pianist can perform it without step-by-step instructions from the brain to the hands.*

vulnerable mosaic of delicate bones that allows for great flexibility and suppleness in your hand movements. In a number of sports, heavy falls broken by the heel of the hand are quite routine. The wrist absorbs the shock, and consequently, the carpal bones get rough treatment. If pain persists after an accident, the wrist should be treated by a doctor, and should be X-rayed if necessary.

Is it harmful to crack your knuckles?

As many a parent knows all too well, one of a child's main reasons for cracking his finger knuckles is the fun of seeing grown-ups cringe at the sound. It turns out that the cracking noise is probably caused by the bursting of bubbles inside your knuckles. To keep the bones that form the knuckles from grating against each other, the space between them is filled with a thick lubricant, the synovial fluid, which is kept inside the joint by a strong membrane. The fluid is filled with bubbles so small that they cannot be seen by the naked eye.

As long as the knuckle bones are close together, the fluid is under pressure, and the bubbles remain tiny. But if you clench your fist, the bones pull apart, and the pressure drops. When that happens, the bubbles rush together, coalescing to form one large bubble. As you work your fist, varying the pressure, the big bubble bursts with a loud popping noise.

Doctors are not sure whether or not it is bad for you to crack your knuckles, although some of them believe that frequent cracking makes them large and unsightly.

What is "trigger finger"?

Despite its name, this extremely painful affliction has nothing to do with guns. When you bend a damaged tendon in your finger, it may remain in that position, as if you had just pulled a trigger. When the finger "unfreezes" and extends, it usually gives off an audible snap that may also have something to do with the name of the ailment.

The trouble begins with overwork, injury, or infection. Either the ten-

don becomes swollen or the tendon sheath constricted, and the tendon can no longer glide within the sheath. This makes it impossible for the tendon to move through freely. The doctor may at first prescribe rest and medication for trigger finger, but minor surgery is frequently necessary to release the constriction.

What is Colles' fracture?

The dubious distinction of being one of the commonest kinds of bone injuries belongs to Colles' fracture, a break that frequently occurs when an individual falls forward and then lands heavily on an outstretched hand. Unable to support the weight of the body, the radius, one of the forearm's two bones, snaps at a point 2 or 3 centimetres (about 1 inch) above the juncture of bone and wrist joint. Since the pain from Colles' fracture is considerable, a local or general anaesthetic is necessary before the broken segments are realigned and the limb surrounded by a rigid plaster cast. Full recovery takes approximately three months.

The Long, Strong Bones and Muscles

How do hip, thigh, and knee relate to one another?

The bones of your hip, thigh, and knee are much stronger and heavier than those of your arms, and the muscles that control them are much bigger. At the hips, six bones form the pelvis, a basin-shaped structure that cradles and protects vital organs. At the lower end of the pelvis are two large socket joints into which fit the bulbous upper ends of your thighbones, the longest, strongest bones in the body. The thighbones, in turn, fit into the knee joints, which connect the body's midsection to the shinbones and feet.

What is "housemaid's knee"?

The medical name for housemaid's knee—prepatellar bursitis—refers to the fluid-filled sacs in the knee called bursae (the Latin word for "leather bag"). These sacs are filled with fluid to cushion shocks. Despite its padding, the knee is not designed to withstand hours of kneeling on hard surfaces, as housewives and maids used to do when they got down on hands and knees to scrub floors.

Irritated by friction against the kneecap, the protective bursae swell up, exerting pressure around the knee. Modern cleaning equipment has reduced household drudgery in recent decades, so housemaid's knee has become rarer. But any task that calls for prolonged pressures on the knee—gardening, say—can cause this affliction.

Housemaid's knee is usually only painful if the fluid becomes infected. In this case antibiotic treatment is necessary. Doctors can remove the fluid from the bursa using a small syringe and bandage the knee tightly to prevent further collection of fluid.

What is a locking knee?

To the victim, it's a familiar experience. He's walking along easily, and suddenly his knee joint locks, and he can't move it. Or else his knee folds up right under him, and he nearly falls down. "There goes my knee again," he says.

The classic locking knee starts when a football player is tackled so hard from the side that his lower and upper leg bones get pushed slightly out of line, tearing one of the pads of cartilage that separate these bones. Besides being painful, the injury becomes disabling if a piece of torn cartilage drifts about and impedes the knee's hinge action.

Many sufferers try to live with a trick knee if it isn't too serious, hobbling along when they have to. Others, especially athletes, get the knee fitted with a tight elastic bandage to try to keep it from "going out" at an inconvenient moment. Doctors can temporarily ease the inflammation in the joint with steroids, but this treatment is rarely called for. In some cases, surgery is necessary. The nature of the damage can be shown with an arthrogram, whereby an injection of a dye makes the damaged cartilage visible under X-ray. Arthroscopy is a procedure that allows the surgeon to look inside a joint to diagnose and possibly treat the abnormality.

Can you tell a dead man's height from a single skeletal bone?

Since ancient skeletons eventually dissolve into dust, leaving only a few bony fragments, archaeologists have long tried to devise formulas for calculating height from isolated bones. The Roman architect Vitruvius devised an ingenious set of criteria for determining height from bones. The length of your hand, he said, is one-tenth of your height; and the distance between the fingertips of one outstretched arm to those of the other is about the same as your height.

These approximations worked surprisingly well, but they were not close enough to satisfy modern scientists. Using algebraic formulas, scientists now can quite accurately deduce height from the skeletal remains of the long bones, specifically the thighbone, or femur (the longest, heaviest, and strongest bone in the body), and the heavy shinbone, or tibia.

THE STORY BEHIND THE WORDS...

Getting off on the wrong foot, which means to make a bad start, is based on a superstition of the ancient Romans. They believed that it was bad luck to enter a house with your left foot foremost. So important was this idea that footmen were stationed at the door to see that no one misstepped.

Muscle is a word with an unusual root; it is derived from the Latin word *musculus,* which means "little mouse." To ancient peoples muscular movement seemed like little mice scampering under the skin.

When someone knuckles under, he is submitting to something or giving in. This expression may derive from the old custom of knocking the underside of a table to acknowledge defeat. Or it may go back to the Middle Ages, when the word *knuckle* referred not just to the joints of the fingers, but to the joint that we now call the knee. In this case, to knuckle under can be interpreted as kneeling, or bowing to another's will.

Using elbow grease means to work vigorously—polishing silver or furniture, scrubbing pots and pans. The centuries-old expression was a practical joke, played on naive youngsters, who were sent out by their elders to buy grease so that they could oil their elbows.

Keeping a stiff upper lip means to control your feelings, and not to exhibit any pain or emotion. But the expression is awry, because when you cry, it's the muscles in the *lower* lip that quiver.

Feet as a Target of Fashion

At first, people were sensible. Hittites, who lived on rocky terrain, wore boot-like shoes with curled-up toes to protect their feet. Egyptians, Greeks, and Babylonians had open sandals for comfort. Legionnaires were issued sturdy hobnailed boots. But wealthy Romans wore high-heeled, open-toed slippers with embroidery or beads. By the mid 1300s, rich Europeans treasured narrow shoes up to a metre (1 yard) long with needle-like tips (which supposedly kept witches away) that had to be chained to one's shin in order to walk. In the 1400s, 30-centimetre (12 inch) wide shoes were the rage. Next came shoes with wooden soles 50 centimetres (20 inches) high, which made women look stately, but they couldn't walk without help. Napoleon's Josephine had such fragile shoes, they needed repair after one wearing. Meanwhile, peasants went barefoot or wrapped their feet in whatever was handy. In Spain, they braided grass for "espadrillas." Germans wore a simple square of leather with holes punched in the side for lacing, which became the symbol of peasant revolts. The principal American contributions to footwear have been moccasins and cowboy boots.

The **dainty feet** of this serene Chinese beauty were created by a binding process, now outlawed. An X-ray of the prized "lotus" foot shows the heel forced forward, four toes curled under, and curved instep.

Tiny feet have long been a sign of femininity. (Remember Cinderella? It was her tiny foot in the glass slipper that won the prince and happiness ever after.) At right, an artist's conception of the kind of feet we should have (big toe in the middle) for the shoes we wear.

Although high-heeled shoes (left) are still as popular as ever, they aren't the only footgear in town. Women now wear running or jogging shoes, finally getting on an even footing with men where comfort is concerned.

The Springs on Which You Move

What is the common job of the foot, ankle, and calf?

When you stride along or break into a run, your lower extremities are subjected to five or six times your total body weight—a force in some cases equal to half a tonne or more. Your calf muscles, among the strongest in your body, are equipped to absorb most of the shock. The bones of the calf are the tibia and fibula, and the gastrocnemius is the powerful muscle that runs down the back of the calf. The latter terminates in the Achilles tendon, which is anchored in your heel bone.

The remarkable strength of the foot can be compared to the ancient Roman symbol of power—the fasces—which was made up of dozens of sticks. Any one of the sticks could easily bend or snap, but bound together, they took on tremendous strength. Similarly, the bones of the feet are very fragile, but bound by tough, ropelike tendons and ligaments, they are often extremely strong. The resilience and spring of the foot are enhanced by the arches, which run both crosswise and lengthwise of your foot.

What is your Achilles heel?

When the Greek warrior Achilles was an infant, his mother sought to make him immortal by dipping him in the River Styx. But she held him by the heel, which never touched the water, and this remained his one vulnerable spot. Years later, in battle, Achilles died only because his adversary shot an arrow into his heel.

The Achilles tendon gets its name from this mythological tale. The tendon attaches your calf muscle to your heel bone, puts spring in your step, and helps you stand on tiptoe. Unlike the body's other tendons, the Achilles has no protective covering and is therefore vulnerable to inflammation and injury. If ill-fitting shoes inflame or tear the tendon, you will feel excruciating pain in your heel and ankle. If violent exertion causes the tendon to snap, your leg may be immobilized in plaster six to eight weeks. In some cases, the snapped tendon cannot simply be "set" and allowed to heal, but must be surgically repaired.

What is club foot?

Club foot is the general name for a variety of congenital deformities in which the foot is twisted, cramped and doubled under, or bent up and back. The defect occurs more often in males than in females.

Today, club foot can be corrected in a number of ways. In some cases, beginning soon after birth, the foot is put in a plaster cast. The casts are successively altered until the foot is gradually bent into a normal position. Or the child's feet are put in corrective braces. These braces or splints are removed periodically, and the foot is manipulated. This treatment may take a year or more, but results are generally good. However, in severe cases, surgery may be required to ease the pull of ligaments and tendons that have caused the misalignment of the foot.

What causes flat feet?

Everybody begins life with flat feet. Only as a child begins to walk and ligaments and muscles in the foot strengthen do the bones in the middle of the foot rise to form an arch.

The Marathon: The Most Famous Footrace of All

In the year 490 B.C., Pheidippides, a Greek runner, carried the news of Greek victory over the Persians at Marathon from the field of of battle to Athens. The Olympic marathon event, first held at the 1896 Olympics in Athens, commemorates the feat. Although the distance from Marathon to Athens is 35.5 kilometres (22 miles), the present standard for the event is 42.195 kilometres (26 miles 285 yards). Marathons have since proliferated and have been hugely successful in many major cities.

Runners on this Greek vase exhibit good sprinting form.

New York modern marathoners set out on their gruelling city-wide course.

The process is usually complete by the age of 16, but some people—Olympic athletes included—remain flat-footed all their lives, but nevertheless function perfectly well.

Sometimes arches that were normal in young adulthood later flatten out, which leads to a graceless walk and to intense pain in the arch of the foot. Initially, the pain comes from weakened, stretched ligaments and muscles, but in the later stages of fallen arches, it comes from the bones themselves, with each step. There is some evidence that heredity plays a part in this condition. The best protection against flat feet is a lifetime habit of walking for exercise, and also wearing properly fitting shoes.

Are bunions hereditary?

A bunion is an unattractive, painful bulging of the joint at the base of your big toe. Because bunions occur so often in the middle-aged, people often shrug them off as natural: something inevitable (perhaps hereditary) that you must learn to live with. In fact, there *is* some evidence that a tendency towards bunions runs in families. Three times as many women as men have bunions, but then they are more likely than men to wear ill-fitting shoes.

Even on a normal foot, the joint at the base of the big toe tends to bulge out. Pressure here causes bursitis, inflammation of the lubrication sacs, or bursae, in the joint, and a calcified, bony spur forms. And to make things even worse, corns frequently develop at the same site, and infection may also occur in the bursae. Furthermore, if the big toe presses against the other toes, it may be forced into distorted shapes or positions. Hammertoes—toes curled into clawlike shapes—are yet another result of wearing tight shoes.

The simplest way of dealing with bunions is to begin wearing shoes that are large enough to accommodate the bunion without pressing on it. But if the bunion is too large and tender, it may be necessary to undergo surgery.

How does the foot work?

Your foot is a flexible collection of soft, breakable bones. Yet it can easily handle the jarring weight of your whole body because all of these bones are held firmly in place by a web of sinewy muscles and strong ligaments that have great tensile strength. This combination of bones and bindings makes for an extraordinarily springy, flexible structure. The wide, flat, bandage-like ligaments that encircle the ankle joints act like the ankle supports an ice skater might wear. As the impact of your body weight spreads out through the tarsal bones, the foot's arch softens the shock, turning it into a "bounce" that makes walking much easier.

BROAD LIGAMENTS hold tendons in place, much as tight taping provides support for a sprained ankle or wrist.

SKELETAL MUSCLES help the foot to hold its shape. They also anchor the bones in place and pull on the tendons, thus moving the foot and toes.

CORD-LIKE TENDONS attach your muscles to bones; they pull on the bones like the wires on a marionette.

When a runner lands on his foot, the weight descends from the tibia, a leg bone, into the talus (meaning "ankle bone"). The weight is distributed forward to the tarsals and metatarsals and backward to the heel bone (calcaneus). All of the joints' surfaces are subject to wear, tear, and arthritis. The arches form a "springy" shock-absorbing system.

TIBIA

FIBULA

TARSALS

METATARSALS

PHALANGES

TALUS

CALCANEUS

Wear and Tear on the Body

Is bed rest ever hazardous?

Prolonged bed rest during convalescence from illness makes bones weaken, and after a few weeks of being propped up, idle, a bone in the leg loses a substantial proportion of its bone/calcium content. The same sort of thing happened early in the space program; prolonged missions in the weightlessness of outer space kept the astronauts immobile. The lack of exercise contributed to the bone loss. Now, astronauts follow an exercise regimen while orbiting the earth, and their bones fare much better. All this seems to confirm that lack of exercise is bad for the bones. Certainly, there is plenty of evidence that exercise causes bones to grow sturdier and increases their capacity to store minerals and manufacture blood cells.

Why do bones lose calcium?

Calcium is a mineral that is vital not only for skeletal rigidity but also for blood clotting, nerve function, and muscle activity. If the calcium level in your blood should fall below its normal range, the body will begin to draw on the supply in your bones.

As you grow older, your body's supplies of calcium begin to dwindle. When that happens, the body begins to draw on its store of calcium in the bones. The decline in body calcium seems to be tied to several factors.

First, older people tend to be careless about their diets, and they often fail to eat enough calcium-rich food. Second, they tend to exercise much less than when they were younger, and studies have shown that regular exercise promotes stronger and denser bones. And then, the absorption of calcium is increased by vitamin D. As people grow older, they generally spend more time indoors, away from the ultraviolet rays of the sun, which are required for the body to manufacture its own vitamin D. If this is combined with a dietary deficiency in vitamin D, bone brittleness can result. Finally, after menopause, women lose the protective effect of the hormone oestrogen, and rapid loss of bone calcium occurs.

Many experts believe that calcium-rich foods, dietary supplements, and exercise can usually prevent serious calcium loss, osteoporosis, and other bone-thinning conditions.

What is the biggest threat to your joints?

Traumatic injuries are *not* the principal cause of joint damage. The greatest threat is a degenerative disease called osteoarthritis. This painful and debilitating affliction typically hits hip, spine, and knee joints, because they carry most of your weight, and finger joints because you may use your hands so much. The cartilage repair system in the body is unable to keep up with the wear and tear on the joints, because as tissue becomes more specialized and has a poor blood supply, it heals at a slower rate. Heavily gnarled hands, bulging with bony growths, are a common sight among elderly arthritic men and women who have done heavy manual work all their lives. Most older people probably have some degree of osteoarthritis, though in many cases the symptoms may be so mild as to go unnoticed by the victim.

What happens when osteoarthritis strikes?

Osteoarthritis develops in several stages. First, the cartilage in and around a joint wears down, and the body fails to replace it. Second, the bones that come together at the joint grind together because there is no longer adequate cartilage to buffer them. Third, the friction irritates the periosteum, the thin, sensitive envelope of protective membrane covering your bones. Finally, the periosteum responds to irritation by stimulating the growth of bony outcroppings.

A number of other diseases cause similar symptoms and are related to osteoarthritis. One is gout, a disease famous for causing excruciating pain in the toes. Gout can strike anyone whose body manufactures too much uric acid; when that happens, uric acid crystals may collect in the joints, especially in the big toe, and cause pain. Rheumatoid arthritis is also linked to osteoarthritis. It begins with irritation and inflammation of the synovial membrane, the tissue that holds in the joint's lubricating

"Bankrupt" Bones—Not Just a Problem of Age

The lacy bone at the top has lost the calcium necessary to protect it against stress and other fractures. This condition, known as osteoporosis, is mainly a problem of postmenopausal women. It is common among these older women because not only do they have finer bones than men, but because they cease to produce oestrogen, the female hormone that plays a significant role in forming new bone and retaining established bone. The first sign of osteoporosis is usually a bone broken under conditions that would not break normal bones. It is now recognized that postmenopausal women should consume approximately 1,500 milligrams of calcium per day.

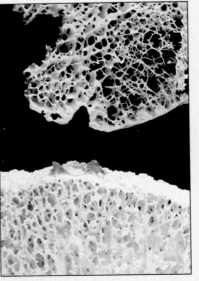

Osteoporosis, top: healthy bone, below.

fluid. The inflamed membrane pours out enzymes that cause the cartilage in the joint to disintegrate, replacing it with fibrous tissue that may then calcify and form bony spurs that fuse the joint and restrict movement. The cause of rheumatoid arthritis is still very much a mystery. However, it is thought to be due to a hereditary breakdown in the immune system that may open the way for an invading virus or cause the body to mistakenly attack its own tissues.

How do doctors replace hips and knees?

The day of bionic man, once a figment of the TV scriptwriter's imagination, is now becoming a reality. When, for instance, a knee or hip joint breaks because of an accident or wears out from arthritis, a surgeon can replace it with a ball-and-socket joint made of metal and plastic and engineered so that it can duplicate the movements of a human joint.

The road to successful joint replacement was a bumpy one. It was easy to make joints that would function well in the laboratory, but when they were implanted in living patients, a number of problems developed. The human body rejected the materials that the artificial parts were made of. The pins that secured the implants to adjacent bones sometimes worked loose, requiring more surgery. In addition, some prosthetic joints didn't work very well, especially the knees. The designers of artificial joints at first made joints that swung back and forth like a simple hinge. Later they realized that the knee also rotates and wobbles when it moves. An artificial joint had to duplicate these movements as well.

Finally, medical pioneers learned to overcome the problem of rejection by making artificial joints of such neutral, non-irritating substances as teflon, Dacron, titanium, and silicone rubber. They have perfected hip and knee replacements so that the present-day implants relieve joint pain and allow recipients to walk with a smoother stride.

Part Plastic—And Pain Free!

Inflamed and disintegrating joints can make putting on a sweater a torture for arthritis victims. But thanks to modern techniques of joint replacement, eight operations, and a lot of courage, the lady below can smile again—and mow the lawn. Without her combination plastic and metal shoulder, elbow, hip, and knee joints, she might have had some relief by being treated with steroids, gold salts, or immunosuppressants. But in severe cases, like hers, pain usually persists, and the treatment may produce negative side effects. Not everyone is a good candidate for such surgery. For best results, the patient should be in general good health and preferably not obese.

THE RIGHT SHOULDER was replaced in October 1978, after her hip joint transplants. A new left shoulder was installed shortly thereafter in November 1978.

THE RIGHT ELBOW was done in October 1979 and the left one in May 1982. Using computers, doctors can now custom-design joints to fit each patient's body specifications.

THE ARTHRITIC LEFT HIP was replaced in June 1976. A new right hip was added in August 1976 along with a shaft to strengthen and stabilize the right leg.

IN BETWEEN WORK on the right and left elbows, new knees were put in—the right one in February 1981, and the left in September 1981.

Strains, Sprains, and Fractures

Not All Bone Fractures Are Equally Serious

Fractures are classified into two main categories: the simple fracture and the compound break, where the skin is pierced, and flesh and bone are exposed to infection. Other kinds of fractures include the greenstick, in which a youngster's still semisoft bone splinters without actually breaking in two; the transverse, which is a break straight across the bone; the oblique, a break on the diagonal; and the comminuted fracture, where there are bone fragments at the break.

SIMPLE FRACTURE

COMPOUND FRACTURE

GREENSTICK

TRANSVERSE

OBLIQUE

COMMINUTED

How do injuries differ?

Rugged as our bodies are, they are all too susceptible to such painful and disabling injuries as strains, sprains, dislocations, and fractures. Of these, the least serious is the strain, an injury that comes from wrenching, twisting, or overstretching muscles or tendons. Muscles in the lower back are particularly subject to strain.

Sprains happen when the strong, ropy ligaments that hold the joints together get torn or wrenched beyond their normal stretching range. Football and other contact sports cause a wide variety of ankle, wrist, and shoulder sprains, though everyday accidents such as falling downstairs account for their share of such injuries. When sudden pressure wrenches a bone clear out of the socket, at a joint, the injury is called a dislocation. Finally, when a bone actually breaks, it is called a fracture.

How does a broken bone heal?

A bone fracture begins to knit almost as soon as it occurs—which is why a broken bone should be set promptly. Within hours, the bone has begun to create its own primitive splint. This is material that bridges the gap between the broken ends and holds them in alignment. This callus, as it is called, is a tough meshwork of collagen, a protein found in the skin, tendons, ligaments, and cartilage, and it slowly replaces the thick blood clot, or haematoma, that has spread through the fracture site. It is there that bone-producing cells called fibroblasts begin to deposit collagen. The callus is eventually replaced by bone.

Do all bones heal at the same rate?

The older a person is, the longer it takes for a bone to knit; a child's recovery may take a few weeks, an elderly person's, several months. At all ages, however, some bones heal faster than others. A broken arm may take a month to mend, but a leg may take as long as six months. Once it is mended, a broken bone usually ends up stronger along the fracture line than it was before.

What is the value of traction?

Traction devices for exerting a pulling force on bones have a long history. Such a mechanism already existed in antiquity, when it was called the Hippocratic bench, or scamnum. It was a sophisticated contraption of cogs, levers, and crankshafts, and today no one is sure exactly how it worked. In the 18th century, traction devices came into wide use to ensure proper bone healing.

Even after a fracture has been set, it is difficult to keep the broken ends in their proper position. The weight of the body can in some cases pull them out of alignment, as can the muscles, which tend to contract and bunch up near the site of the break. In traction, the injured limb is elevated and gently stretched by a system of weights and pulleys to keep the muscles from shortening.

Can sports be harmful for children?

Stress fractures, tiny cracks in the bones and joints caused by the strain of repeated motion, are a little noticed but common phenomenon in young athletes. These fractures can lead to further damage, ending a young athlete's career prematurely.

With the waning of adolescence and the onset of physical maturity, the body's originally rapid formation of new bone changes to a more balanced cycle of formation and reabsorption of bone. Ideally, this balance should continue throughout an individual's life.

Why does a sprained ankle hurt so much?

A badly sprained ankle can be as painful as a fracture. Doctors often insist on seeing X-rays of the affected area, since a number of "sprains"

The Hazards of Exercise

Athletes tend to disregard the pain of aching muscles. Many take pride in enduring pain, believing they are building stronger muscles. According to one theory, the athletes are right: they are building up lactic acid, a product that accumulates during the breakdown of sugar as energy is produced. As the athlete becomes better trained, lactic acid is removed from the tissues more swiftly. But pain can also be a sign of serious tissue injury. Those aches and pains after exercising may be an indication of damage to connective tissue surrounding the muscle, mechanical wear and tear, or of inflammation. One of the most important things an athlete should learn is when he or she is overdoing it.

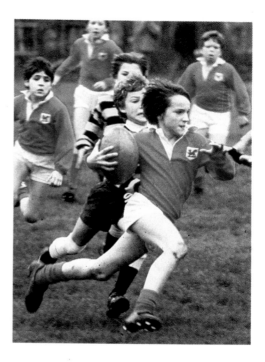

A horrified audience at the 1984 Olympics witnessed Gabriella Andersen-Schiess drag herself across the finish line at the women's marathon, suffering from extreme dehydration.

Growing bones can be seriously damaged when children pursue sports too vigorously. In soccer knees can be damaged; in rugby children's spines may also be at risk.

turn out, in fact, to be fractures. But even an ordinary sprain can be troublesome enough. It occurs when the mesh of taut, tough ligaments that hold the foot, ankle, and lower calf in alignment is suddenly wrenched apart. Blood rushes to the injured parts; and the synovial fluid that lubricates the joint may escape from the capsule that normally contains it. The result is that the ankle puffs up alarmingly and very quickly turns black and blue. In the meantime, injured nerves cause excruciating, shooting pains. Curiously, a slight sprain, in which the ligaments are stretched too far but do not actually tear, frequently causes more pain and swelling than a major sprain.

What happens when you get a "whiplash" injury?

A sudden, intense jolt may cause your head to snap back and then abruptly whip forward. This snap-the-whip effect can damage the muscles, vertebrae, and nerves, causing severe neck pains, headaches, and, in some rare instances, even paralysis. Whiplash injuries are especially common in rear-end car collisions, and they also sometimes occur among rugby players.

Once X-rays have ruled out broken bones and other major injuries, rest, hot packs, massage, and aspirin can be used to relieve pain. A collar worn around the neck to restrict muscle-straining movements of the head may also be helpful.

185

Keeping Fit Through Exercise

What are the benefits of regular exercise?

Exercises that make you breathe hard, such as jogging, bike riding, and swimming, build up your "wind" and help to prevent heart attacks. The point is not to exercise to the point of exhaustion, but to raise your heartbeat significantly. As a minimum, such "aerobic" exercises should be done for at least 20 minutes, three times a week. If you are seriously out of shape, over 35, or have any physical infirmity such as shortness of breath, get a doctor's OK before undertaking an exercise program.

Oddly enough, the long-range effect of exercise on the heart is to slow it down and make it deliver more blood and oxygen to the body with each stroke. A professional athlete may have a heartbeat of 40 strokes a minute, an average person a heartbeat of between 60 and 100 per minute. Exercise also causes the body to produce new capillaries. Exercise makes your muscles grow larger. This is beneficial because a large muscle is more efficient, energy-producing, and flexible than a small one.

Some scientists say that exercise stimulates the release by the brain of pain-killing substances called endorphins. This effect may be the physical basis of the euphoria experienced by many long-distance runners. Other specialists say that when more blood surges through the arteries during exercise, it discourages the build-up of plaque, which can cause heart attacks. It is also possible that such aerobic pursuits as jogging cause bone marrow to release larger than usual numbers of white blood cells, the body's disease fighters. All in all, evidence is mounting daily that moderate exercise keeps you healthy.

Should you be able to bend over and touch your toes?

To some experts, the ability to touch your toes with your fingertips while keeping your knees straight is proof that you are physically fit. But to others, that ability doesn't prove a single thing—except that you can touch your toes!

Those in favour of toe touching as a test of fitness say your performance can expose such weaknesses as a flabby stomach or a stiff spine. Opponents say toe touching causes strain on your Achilles tendon, your hamstring tendon and its muscles, and your vertebrae. Since your muscles are less flexible as you age, there are dangers in toe touching for older people. And it is true that toe touching may cause your knees to lock in a hyperextended position. You should not do anything where your upper and lower

In the year 1902, office workers at the National Cash Register Company in the U.S. went through their paces without removing collars, ties, or waistcoats.

Today, it's recognized that exercise is most effective when you work up a good sweat.

Exercising: Then and Now

Modern fitness programs started in Prussia in the 1800s; group exercises were used to revive national pride after the Napoleonic wars. The feminists took up the idea, to prove that women are not frail. "Callisthenics," coined in 1831, by the headmistress of an American girls' school is from the Greek *kallos*, or "beautiful," and *sthenos*, or "strong."

leg bones grind together. To touch or not to touch your toes is less important than an exercise program that keeps you loose and limber.

Should you always warm up before exercise?

The advantage of a warm-up is that it raises the temperature of your muscles by several degrees, enabling them to make more efficient use of energy. If your muscles are abruptly required to go all out, stretching and squeezing to the limit, the ligaments may tighten up around the joints, and the muscles may begin to contract painfully. In extreme cases, muscles can tear. Standard warm-up exercises include rotating the upper half of the body, stretching the hamstring muscle, rising on tiptoe, and stretching the Achilles tendon. Studies at one major sports medicine centre reveal that some 60 percent of sports injuries are traceable to faulty training methods and to improper warm-up techniques, not to the stresses of sports themselves.

What is your strongest muscle?

To see a squatting weight lifter stand straight up and thrust 250 kilograms (40 stone) over his head is really a spectacular sight. A very different but equally remarkable feat is a race to the 86th-floor observatory of the Empire State Building in New York. Some are able to make it up the 86 flights of stairs (1,575 steps) in less than 12 minutes.

Neither of these feats would be possible without the gluteus maximus, the strongest, largest muscle in your body and the one that accounts for most of the hard flesh in your "seat." It's not just in prodigious exploits that the gluteus maximus becomes important. It comes into play when you straighten up from a stooped posture, climb steep hills, or rise to your feet from a sitting position. When the gluteus maximus contracts, it pulls your thigh into a straight line with your trunk.

Surfers manoeuvre their boards by shifting their weight. Rising from the flat board to a flexed crouch, then riding the wave, takes a highly developed sense of balance.

Why do weight lifters often have pot bellies?

Stomachs so prominent that their owners can hardly read their weight on the bathroom scales are characteristic of many top weight lifters and strongmen. In the case of the weight lifter, however, this natural tendency to develop a pot belly is exaggerated because his body needs the additional stability, provided by such girth, to execute tremendously heavy lifts.

It would be a mistake to think that these "strong men" are obese and out of shape. The proof is in their performances in competition. Without the cage of dense muscles and fatty tissue sheathing their midsections, their vital organs could burst under the tremendous pressures of their lifts. For the same reasons, Japan's big-bellied sumo wrestlers also build bulk. Some weigh about 200 kilograms (30 stone), yet are able to move like lightning.

What does your centre of gravity have to do with posture?

The trick in tightrope walking is to keep the centre of gravity over the rope. A high-wire performer thrills the crowd by lurching, staggering, and otherwise pretending he is about to fall. But careful observation reveals that as he leans and wobbles off to one side of the wire, he is counterbalancing this move by stretching out a leg on his other side. Despite his eye-catching, seemingly accidental movements, he is careful to keep his centre of gravity directly above the wire.

An acrobat is not an exception but a vivid example of postural rules that apply to everyone. Your centre of gravity, just like the acrobat's, is the imaginary but significant point where your weight is equally distributed. The secret of good balance and of good posture is to sense where your centre is at all times, and to keep it in line with whatever is supporting your body at the moment. This applies whether you are simply walking down the street or engaging in some unusually demanding physical activity.

If you are learning to figure skate, for instance, you will find that you can bend over so that your trunk is parallel to the ice as you glide along—but only if you balance yourself by extending one leg behind you, keeping your centre of gravity above the skate on the ice. Similarly, if you think of an Olympic diver turning triple somersaults in mid-air, remember he does it by keeping a keen sense of where his centre of balance is. This lets him enter the water cleanly, with his body properly oriented.

Chapter 8

THE EYE

Our eyes are our windows on the world—a means of learning, a source of pleasure. Better than a camera, the eye continuously records images. Through the marvellous teamwork of eye and brain, we make sense of the world around us: we judge distances, make comparisons, read, interpret, enjoy.

The Workings of the Eye	190
When the Tears Flow	192
The Evolution of Spectacles	193
Bringing the World into Focus	194
Everyday Optical Illusions	196
Visual Tricks and Treats	198
The Amazing World of Colour	200
Limitations of Vision	202
Eye Problems and Remedies	204

Are you right-eyed or left-eyed?

Just as you habitually use one of your hands more than the other, you unconsciously favour the use of one of your eyes. Your dominant eye is the one you use to look into the viewfinder of a camera or to thread a needle.

Try this simple test to determine which of your eyes is dominant: make a circle with the thumb and forefinger of one hand; look through the circle with both eyes at a small object across the room, say a doorknob; close first one eye and then the other. The eye that sees the doorknob within the circle is your dominant eye.

Why do people have different eye colours?

Two brown-eyed parents usually produce a brown-eyed child, and two blue-eyed parents almost always have blue-eyed offspring. But when one parent has blue eyes and the other has brown ones, their children are usually brown-eyed. The fact is that brown eyes are a stronger hereditary trait, so that brown-eyed people far outnumber those who have blue eyes throughout the world.

The iris gives the eye its colour. The pigment that determines the colour is called melanin. Large amounts of the pigment result in brown or hazel eyes, while smaller amounts produce blue or light green eyes. The pink appearance of the eyes of albinos is due to lack of melanin; because their irises are transparent, the pinkish blood vessels of the eyes can be seen through them.

What are floaters?

The small, circular specks and hairlike objects that sometimes drift across your field of vision in one eye are called floaters. If you try to focus your eye on one, it flits away.

Floaters, though annoying, are almost always harmless. These dark spots or wispy filaments are shadows cast on the retina by cellular debris that has collected in the transparent part of the eye (the vitreous humour). Floaters generally appear in adulthood, and are associated with the aging process.

Floaters rarely need treatment. When they first appear, however, it is wise to consult an eye doctor to be sure that they are just floaters and not symptoms of an eye disease.

Can too much reading weaken your eyesight?

From the standpoint of the structure of the eye, there is no such thing as overuse. But reading for long hours, watching television excessively, or working in poor light can result in what is popularly known as eyestrain. This is really fatigue of the eye muscles. Frequent feelings of fatigue and strain may indicate not overuse of the eyes but a structural defect that calls for glasses. Rarely, such strain may be the sign of a serious condition that requires medical attention.

Good lighting helps to prevent eyestrain. When you sit down to read or work, position yourself so that the light comes from behind you and from one side; you should not cast a shadow on what you are looking at. However, mothers who find their children reading under less-than-perfect lighting conditions have no reason to fear that they are doing any actual damage to their eyes.

Why do eyes get bloodshot?

Dust, smoke, or small foreign particles are common causes of red, bloodshot eyes, as are colds and hay fever. Bloodshot eyes can also be a sign of fatigue, and may be a consequence of excessive consumption of alcohol. The condition may cause some discomfort, but it is usually not serious.

Sometimes, however, bloodshot eyes can signal an infection such as conjunctivitis, a highly contagious inflammation affecting the eyelid membrane. Symptoms usually include pain or discomfort and a sticky discharge. If conjunctivitis is suspected, see your doctor.

Is make-up ever a cause of eye inflammation?

Substances in cosmetics cause an allergic reaction in some people; happily, special brands of make-up are available for people with hypersensitive skin. However, there are people who can't wear any make-up at all.

Most eye cosmetics contain preservatives, but over time, the cosmetics may nevertheless become contaminated with skin bacteria transferred by applicators and brushes. Bacteria then multiply in the container. Thus it is prudent to dispose of eye make-up from time to time. Never borrow or lend eye make-up or applicators, and avoid using the eye make-up samples at cosmetic counters.

If your eyes do become infected, stop using all make-up, and dispose of all the cosmetics and paraphernalia that you have been using. This avoids the risk of reinfecting yourself. Also remember that your towels and flannels can carry infection, so be absolutely sure that members of your family avoid touching them.

Does it hurt your eyes to cross them intentionally?

By the time a child is about three, the eye muscles are strong enough to hold the eyes in whatever alignment the child has developed. No matter how often it is done, deliberately crossing the eyes (usually for funny effect or to get a parent's attention) cannot make the eyes "stick."

There is a normal blind spot in your eye, a small area where the optic nerve leads to the brain. To find your blind spot, hold this book at arm's length, cover your left eye, and stare at the red pepper with your right eye. Move the book towards you till the yellow pepper disappears. To find the blind spot in your left eye, cover your right eye, concentrate on the yellow pepper, and adjust the distance of the book till the red one disappears.

The Workings of the Eye

How does the eye compare with a camera?

A camera's adjustable diaphragm works like the iris of the eye to control the amount of light that enters. In both camera and eye, a lens focuses images on a light-sensitive area. Photographic film and the retina of the eye both "see" images or pictures. Together, the eye's lens and iris produce a sharp, well-defined image similar to that produced by a camera's lens and diaphragm.

Unlike the camera, however, the eye "takes" images continuously when you are awake, and transmits them via the optic nerve to the brain. The lens of both the eye and the camera produce an upside-down image. The image is slightly different in each eye. The brain is responsible for the right-side-up, three-dimensional view that most of us see. Images are sorted, stored in the memory, and recalled later by the brain.

What happens when light enters the eye?

Light first passes through the transparent cornea that covers the pupil, which is really the opening of the iris. Then it continues through a chamber of watery fluid called the aqueous humour. Next, light passes through the lens and is focused on the retina, after having passed through the gelatinous centre of the eye, the vitreous (meaning glassy) body. In the retina, light stimulates masses of receptors known as rods and cones (the latter are colour detectors). Impulses from the receptors eventually reach the brain after following a complicated pathway via the optic nerve and brain tracts.

What can an eye doctor tell by looking into your eyes?

The doctor can test your vision with an eye chart. He can examine your external eye and the surrounding area for abnormal signs, and pull down your eyelids to examine their inner surface. He can determine whether the pupils react normally to light and the presence of a nearby object, and check whether the eyes work together normally.

By covering one eye at a time while you stare at a light, he can test for strabismus, commonly called a squint or cross-eyes. An eye that "jumps" when uncovered is evidence of strabismus. The doctor studies internal and external eye tissue with an instrument called a slit-lamp.

The doctor can look into the interior of your eyeball with an ophthalmoscope, a set of special lenses connected to a light, to determine the condition of the retina, blood vessels, and optic disc. Also, the doctor can check your eyes for glaucoma.

What are the different eye specialities?

The doctor who is qualified to diagnose eye disorders and to provide medical and surgical treatment is called an ophthalmologist. (The name is derived from the Greek word for eye.) Ophthalmologists may prescribe glasses but do not provide them. At one time, eye doctors were called oculists, but this term is no longer used.

An optician is not a medical doctor and cannot diagnose or treat eye disorders; he is qualified to measure vision, to prescribe corrective eyeglasses, and to screen for eye diseases such as glaucoma.

An orthoptist often works alongside the ophthalmologist measuring vision and visual fields, and treating children with squints.

Why does the doctor use drops when examining your eyes?

The pupil of the eye expands and contracts with variations in light. The brighter the environment, the smaller the pupil needs to be. In dim light, the pupil widens, letting in as much light as possible. If the doctor tried to examine your eyes in their natural state, the light emanating from his instrument, the ophthalmoscope, would cause the pupil to contract, and he would not be able to see very much.

A few drops of a special medication temporarily paralyses the pupil in a dilated state. The doctor is then able to take his time examining the interior of the eye. The paralysis wears off fully in a few hours, but many people just leaving their doctor's surgery are shocked by the impact of the sunlight on their medicated eyes, thus discovering how wonderful pupillary action usually is.

DID YOU KNOW...?

- **Perfect 6/6 vision** will not in itself get you through the eye test given to air force pilots. Among other things, you must also have "contrast sensitivity" — you must be able, for instance, to see a white cat moving about in the snow.

- **You can get bloodshot eyes from a sneeze.** The bleeding, which spreads out under the conjunctiva, is called a subconjunctival haemorrhage. The blood will be absorbed in about a week; there is no way to hasten the process.

- **Human vision is incredibly keen.** Astronauts orbiting the earth have reported being able to see the wakes of ships in the ocean below.

- **The "black eye"** that blossoms soon after you receive a blow to the face is really not black at all. A "shiner" is actually a mixture of purple, red, and yellow hues, caused by blood under the skin.

- **Babies are born long-sighted.** Their eyes don't focus close up until they are from three to six months old, and it may be a year before their eyes consistently work together, instead of occasionally wandering individually.

What do your pupils reveal about you?

In addition to their function as regulators of light to the retina, pupils are highly expressive of emotions. There is truth in the saying, "His eyes were like saucers." Intense interest is apparently reflected in a widening of the pupils of the eyes. Merchants the world over who sell their wares by bargaining—with offers and counteroffers—watch the eyes of the prospective buyer to judge whether the person is eager to purchase the goods or not; there is some evidence that customers reveal their preferences involuntarily, with widened pupils. In general, one particular series of studies suggests, the pupils seem to grow larger when people look at something that pleases them and seem to grow smaller when they look at something they find distasteful.

Dilated pupils in someone else have an appeal for the person who sees them—whether the observer knows it or not. In a series of tests, men were shown two pictures of an attractive woman, one retouched to enlarge her pupils, the other to make them smaller. When comparing them, none of the men reported noticing the specific difference, but some found the woman with the larger pupils to be "softer" or more feminine looking.

The appeal of enlarged pupils has been known since the Middle Ages, when women put drops of belladonna in their eyes to enhance their attractiveness. In fact, *bella donna* is Italian for "beautiful woman."

The Structure of the Eye in Cross-section

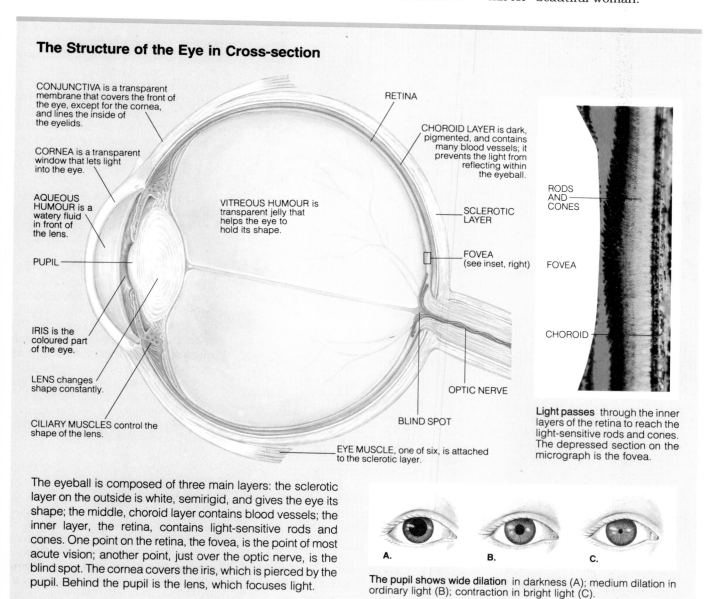

CONJUNCTIVA is a transparent membrane that covers the front of the eye, except for the cornea, and lines the inside of the eyelids.

CORNEA is a transparent window that lets light into the eye.

AQUEOUS HUMOUR is a watery fluid in front of the lens.

PUPIL

IRIS is the coloured part of the eye.

LENS changes shape constantly.

CILIARY MUSCLES control the shape of the lens.

VITREOUS HUMOUR is transparent jelly that helps the eye to hold its shape.

RETINA

CHOROID LAYER is dark, pigmented, and contains many blood vessels; it prevents the light from reflecting within the eyeball.

SCLEROTIC LAYER

FOVEA (see inset, right)

OPTIC NERVE

BLIND SPOT

EYE MUSCLE, one of six, is attached to the sclerotic layer.

RODS AND CONES

FOVEA

CHOROID

Light passes through the inner layers of the retina to reach the light-sensitive rods and cones. The depressed section on the micrograph is the fovea.

The eyeball is composed of three main layers: the sclerotic layer on the outside is white, semirigid, and gives the eye its shape; the middle, choroid layer contains blood vessels; the inner layer, the retina, contains light-sensitive rods and cones. One point on the retina, the fovea, is the point of most acute vision; another point, just over the optic nerve, is the blind spot. The cornea covers the iris, which is pierced by the pupil. Behind the pupil is the lens, which focuses light.

A.   B.   C.

The pupil shows wide dilation in darkness (A); medium dilation in ordinary light (B); contraction in bright light (C).

When the Tears Flow

LACRIMAL GLAND

LACRIMAL DUCTS

LACRIMAL CANALS

LACRIMAL SAC

TEAR

NASOLACRIMAL DUCT

NASAL CAVITY

Where do tears come from?

Almond-shaped lacrimal glands are located above the eyes, under the frontal bones. About a dozen ducts lead from each gland to the eye and eyelids. Tears are normally salty because they are derived from the circulatory system, which has a salt composition of about 0.9 percent. Tears are also sterile because they contain bacteria-destroying enzymes, which provide a measure of protection from infection. When you blink, tears bathe the eyes, keeping the cornea moist. The fluid drains down through the inside corner of the eye into a lacrimal sac and from there into the nasolacrimal duct, which drains into the nasal cavity. Usually, you do not notice this flow, but when tears are copious, from irritation, sorrow, or a cold, they spill onto your cheeks, and your nose runs.

Why do you blink your eyes?

Your eyelids guard your eyes from injury. The inner surface of the upper and lower lids, as well as the eyes themselves, are covered by a transparent membrane called the conjunctiva. This membrane helps to keep the surface of the eye moist so that the eye can move freely. The eyelid sweeps tears over the conjunctiva regularly, like a windscreen wiper, preventing the eye from drying out.

On average, you blink automatically about every two to ten seconds. This reflex blinking regularly triggers the process of lubrication. Closing the eyelids also pushes tears into the inner corner of the eye, where they drain through tear ducts into the nose. Some people—especially older women—suffer from a lack of tears. This painful condition can be remedied by using lubricating eye drops.

You are able to blink your eyes consciously—or wink one eye—but it is difficult to stop reflex blinking for more than a minute at a time.

How many kinds of tears are there?

The film of tears in the eye is composed of three layers, an outer oily layer that is secreted by glands in the eyelid (which prevents evaporation), lacrimal fluid secreted by the lacrimal glands, and a mucous layer that forms an interface between the cornea and the tear film. Any disease that interferes with the constituents of the tear layer can affect vision.

When a speck of dust irritates the eye, or when you cry with grief, the tears change in composition, containing a greater percentage of lacrimal fluid than at other times. In one study, it was discovered that tears of grief have a slightly different chemical composition from other kinds; the cause of this and the consequences (if any) have yet to be discovered.

Is crying good for you?

The act of crying apparently leads to feelings of release from emotional tension. It is only in recent years that scientists have tried to find out who cries and why. In one study, both men and women reported feeling much better after crying at times of emotional stress. Women cried five times as often as men, and many more men than women refrained from tears altogether.

It is difficult to get to the physical basis for crying because our reaction to tears is so strongly influenced by culture. In some parts of the world, men may weep freely; in others, tears are considered a sign of weakness.

Why do you sometimes cry when you laugh?

Psychologically, tears of laughter may be a response to intense emotion—perhaps a feeling of great relief. Physiologically, laughter may actually squeeze tears from your eyes. Really convulsive laughter can be quite violent, with muscle spasms of the abdomen, diaphragm, and facial muscles, inability to speak, gasping for breath, increased heartbeat, and stimulation of the endocrine system. Laughter has been compared to uncorking a champagne bottle—letting off the pressure within you.

Can a speck in the eye be dangerous?

When a foreign particle becomes embedded in the eyeball or scratches the cornea, a doctor should be consulted at once, as this can be very harmful. If it only rests on the inside of the lid, you should also remove it, as it, too, may scratch the cornea.

The Evolution of Spectacles

The earliest recorded use of glass or quartz for magnification goes back to about 2500 B.C. The first glasses were either held in the hand or placed on the object. Credit for inventing spectacles that put two lenses together goes to 13th-century Venetians. Not until the invention of the printing press in the mid-l5th century did the need for glasses become widespread. Later, lenses were made in rough grades of intensity and sold in shops or by peddlers on the street; a customer would try on glasses until he found the right correction. The American statesman and scientist Benjamin Franklin (1706–1790), who had two vision problems (near-sightedness and far-sightedness), became impatient with having to change glasses constantly; he cut two pairs of spectacles apart, fastened the halves together, and thus invented the first bifocals.

The earliest spectacles, worn mainly by churchmen and merchants, were *pince-nez* (French for "pinch-nose"). In this 16th-century Flemish painting, the wearer is a "usurer," or money lender.

Leather-rimmed spectacles were apparently common in 16th-century Italy; in 1967, divers brought up a whole box of them from the wreck of a Venetian vessel that went down in the Adriatic Sea.

Antique glasses. Clockwise from front: wooden frames from China (1700), lunettes (1900), glasses with rigid temple sidepieces (1850), tortoiseshells (1800), lorgnette (1900). In centre, pince-nez.

A soft contact lens. This kind of flexible, worn-in-the-eye visual aid is a lot more comfortable than the first hard contacts, which were developed in Switzerland at the turn of the 20th century.

193

Bringing the World Into Focus

What is normal vision?

If you can read certain-sized letters on the standard eye chart at the prescribed distance of 6 metres (20 feet), you are generally considered to have normal, or 6/6, vision. But the eye test measures only the sharpness of vision, or visual acuity—the ability to see clearly such small things as fine print at a distance. Good vision depends on several other factors as well.

An important aspect of normal vision is accommodation, the eye's reflexive ability to adjust its focus from far to near, or vice versa. The process of focusing the two eyes properly on a close object also involves another re-flex, convergence. Another factor is the eye's sensitivity to differences in the intensity and colour of light. The nerve connections between the eye and the brain, and the brain itself, contribute to vision. It is only when all these processes are working properly that good eyesight results.

It is possible to have 6/6 vision and still need glasses. For instance, long-sighted young people may score perfectly on a simple eye test because their strong near-focusing muscles can correct any refractive defects. The constant use of these muscles, however, may cause eyestrain and eventually require the use of glasses to relieve eye fatigue.

What are the most common visual defects?

Structural faults in the eyeball or lens cause refractive errors, or the irregular bending of light, so that a visual image is not focused perfectly on the retina. The most common refractive errors are near-sightedness, long-sightedness, and astigmatism.

Can the wrong spectacles ruin your eyes?

The sole purpose of spectacles is to focus light rays onto the retina of the eye. Even badly fitted glasses cannot

How do spectacles correct your vision?

In **near-sightedness**, or myopia, the eyeball is too long from front to back. Nearby objects are clearly visible, but light rays from distant objects come to a focal point before they reach the retina, which makes these objects appear quite blurred. Spectacles that are fitted with concave lenses will correct the eye's error and bring the images of far-off objects into sharp focus on the retina.

In **long-sightedness**, or hypermetropia, the eyeball is too short. Distant objects can be seen clearly, but the focal point of light from nearby objects is behind the retina, making it impossible for a long-sighted person to see close objects clearly. To correct this refractive error (the improper bending of light) and improve vision by focusing the light rays correctly, convex lenses can be used.

In **astigmatism**, an irregular curvature of the cornea and the lens causes some light rays to bend more than others and thus prevents them from focusing properly. This results in distorted images at all distances. Cylindrical lenses, which are shaped like slices from a tube, compensate for the structural defects of the eye and bend light rays consistently inward so that they can focus properly.

CONCAVE LENS

CONVEX LENS

CYLINDRICAL LENS

change the structure of the eye in any way. The wrong glasses may irritate your eyes, blur your vision, and cause headaches and even nausea. But in no sense can wearing the wrong eyeglasses ruin your eyes.

What kinds of contact lenses are available?

Hard lenses give superior visual correction, especially when astigmatism is present; they last for years, and are cheaper and easier to care for than other contacts. But you need from a week to as long as a month to adjust to them, and they have to be worn regularly. If the individual stops wearing them for a few days, hard contact lenses usually require another breaking-in period.

Soft lenses are made of water-absorbent synthetic polymers and are often more comfortable than hard lenses. They take less time for adjustment, they do not give the best visual acuity, are easily torn, and need meticulous daily disinfection.

Gas-permeable lenses let the cornea "breathe" by permitting oxygen and carbon dioxide to pass through. Gas-permeables are often recommended for people who cannot tolerate hard lenses.

Bifocal contact lenses have been developed, but they are expensive and hard to fit. Until they have been perfected, some people may prefer so-called "monovision." This technique requires wearing one lens for distant vision along with one for reading. Unconsciously, the wearer adapts to using one eye at a time as the occasion demands.

Are contacts better than glasses?

For people who dislike the looks of spectacles, contact lenses are a great improvement. They also offer excellent peripheral vision; they give near-normal sight after cataract surgery; and they are very useful in sports in which glasses might get broken.

There are some drawbacks, however. Unlike glasses, they require get-

Screening out the sun's rays in the Arctic

Snow reflects sunlight, and when the sun shines in summer in the Arctic region, the cumulative effect can be so dazzling as to cause snow blindness. Your first impulse whenever light is too bright is to squint, thereby cutting down on the amount of light that can strike the retina. Eskimos, for whom the risk of snow blindness is serious because the condition can last for several days, have solved this problem by inventing goggles of bone or wood with just a slit to see through. The effect is much the same as sunglasses.

ting used to, sometimes pop out of the eye for no apparent reason, and are difficult to find if dropped. Finally, they may prove unsatisfactory for those who have allergies, work in dusty places, or need bifocals.

Can contacts harm the eyes?

Properly fitted and used, contact lenses can safely be worn by almost anyone. The most serious hazard is infection, which can lead to corneal ulceration and even blindness. But the danger can be avoided by cleaning lenses daily and by using a sterile wetting solution (not bacteria-laden saliva) when inserting hard lenses.

To avoid scratching the eye, lenses should be put in and taken out gently. If a particle of dirt gets under a lens, the contact should be removed. Only "extended-wear" contacts, specially designed to be kept in place for several weeks, should be worn overnight. Wearing regular lenses too long deprives the eye of oxygen and interferes with the circulation of eye fluids. Some specialists are concerned that even long-wear lenses may cause damage if worn too long or without expert advice. As one authority says, "With extended wear, there should always be extended care."

Do sunglasses really do any good?

Tinted glasses that screen out ultraviolet rays can minimize the possible dangerous effects of intense sunlight. Proper sunglasses are useful to cut down glare at the beach, and are very practical for seeing clearly while driving or skiing.

Why do older people need glasses for close work?

With aging, the lens of the eye loses its elasticity and ability to focus on both near and distant objects. When a person reaches the age of about 40, the lens has difficulty changing from a flattened to a spherical shape in order to focus on nearby objects. The eye gradually becomes focused permanently at a more or less constant distance—a condition called presbyopia. Thus a middle-aged person begins to hold a book farther and farther away in order to read the print.

An older person afflicted with presbyopia must wear corrective spectacles to do close work. Often, bifocal glasses with separate corrections for both close and distant viewing solve the problem. Near-sighted adults may find that as they get older they can read without glasses.

Everyday Optical Illusions

Do you see everything upside down?

Although you always see things right side up—and never get the impression that people are walking on the ceiling—the lens of your eye is actually focusing an upside-down image on your retina. This is due to the special properties of the lens, in relation to the size and shape of the eye. The upside-down image is what is transmitted to the visual centre of the brain via the optic nerve. The brain simply transposes the picture to make it conform to what it knows it should be seeing.

In scientific experiments, people have worn spectacles with special lenses that turned all images upside down. Within a few days they began to "see" the changed images right side up again—despite the distorting lenses they were wearing. When they removed the glasses, their world was topsy-turvy once more, but only briefly; then their brains once again adjusted, and the world returned to its familiar orientation.

The miraculous teamwork of your eye and your brain is exhibited in a number of ways in your everyday existence. When you see an object that is half in sunlight and half in deep shadow, you have no trouble filling in the shaded part of the object—say a car in the street. Very small clues can be used by your eye and your brain to help you get your bearings. For example, one glance at the way sunlight strikes the floor of your living room tells you what time of the day it is. Thus you habitually perceive much more than you actually see.

How do you see in 3-D?

The world is three-dimensional, but the image received by the retina is two-dimensional. If you relied solely on that image, your world would be "flat." Seeing in depth is your brain's interpretation of what you see.

The fact that you have two eyes, separated by your nose, provides you with a large visual field. The ability to see a single scene, even though the images received by the two eyes differ slightly, is called binocular vision. Using its accumulated experience, the brain blends the two overlapping optical images, producing the proper impression of depth and distance in a single image, so that you see three-dimensionally. When a person cannot blend the two optical images, he is said to have double vision.

Highway mirage. *That wet patch you keep seeing on the road ahead on a hot summer day is an illusion. When a layer of hot air lies below a layer of cold air, a reflection (in this case of the sky) appears above the road.*

How do people with "cross-eyes" or "wall-eyes" see the world?

An accurate view of any scene requires the eyes to move in concert. In looking directly at an object, both eyes must remain parallel and focus straight ahead. If an object is to the right, both eyes must move to the right. When eye movement is not co-ordinated, a person sees two dissimilar images, a condition called double vision. In some cases, one image is suppressed, which prevents double vision but causes faulty depth perception. In children, "lazy eye" (amblyopia, or impaired vision) can result if one image is suppressed. If caught early, the condition is reversible.

Is depth perception possible with only one eye?

There are several ways of judging distance with a single eye. When you close an eye and look at a car parked near a building that appears smaller than the car itself, you immediately conclude that the building is farther away than the car. Another clue comes from the shadows cast by objects; they can help you to judge the distance between them. Differences of brightness and image sharpness between objects are also helpful in establishing depth perception; an object closer to you appears brighter and sharper than one farther away.

How do movies move?

When you watch a film, you are staring at a blank screen about half the time. What you see on the screen is a rapid succession of still photographs, each slightly different from the one that preceded it. The images are projected at a rate of up to 72 frames each second. Cinema films—and TV as well—are based on a phenomenon called "persistence of vision." The response of the eye lasts long enough so that the frames are not seen as separate pictures; instead, they fuse with each other, giving the illusion of continuous movement.

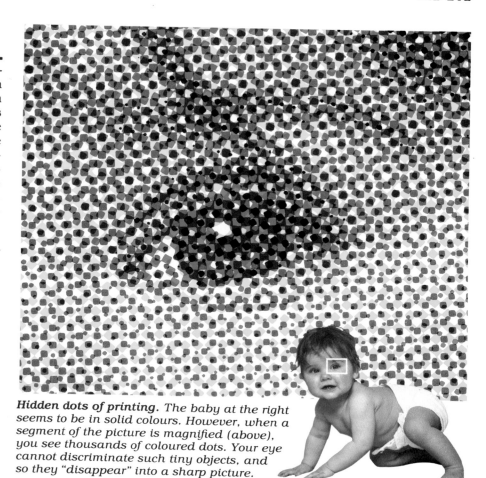

Hidden dots of printing. The baby at the right seems to be in solid colours. However, when a segment of the picture is magnified (above), you see thousands of coloured dots. Your eye cannot discriminate such tiny objects, and so they "disappear" into a sharp picture.

Can a batsman really keep his eye on the ball?

A cricket ball in flight may be so fast that it reaches the batsman within half a second of leaving the bowler's hand. It cannot be tracked by the eyes, although experienced batsmen can pick up early clues from the bowler's run-up and delivery action to aid in shot selection. Once the ball is released, the batsman's eyes make rapid movements, called saccades, constantly jumping ahead to the spot in flight where he expects the ball to be. When it reaches about 1.5 metres (5 feet) from his crease, vision of the ball is lost. Players report seeing it right on to the bat, but this is because the brain "fills in" the intermittent information from the saccadic movements into a continuous picture.

Visual Tricks and Treats

More (and Less) Than Meets the Eye

Essentially, optical illusions are figures that give contradictory information. Visual cues such as perspectives may be shown in ways that don't make sense. Your eye may be baffled by unexpected juxtapositions of objects, and may jump to the wrong conclusion about such things as size, shape, and even, in the case of the mystery spots below, the actual existence of what your eye keeps seeing.

Which centre dot is bigger in these two sets of circles? Although they may not seem so, they are identical.

The persistent grey spots you see at the intersections of these boxes aren't really there—they're only in your mind!

These herringbone lines seem to be going every which way, but put a ruler on the pattern and you'll find that the verticals, horizontals, and diagonals are regular.

Can your brain draw the wrong conclusion?

Optical illusions challenge our expectations. When certain patterns of light fall on the retina, the brain does not know just what to make of them. For example, we expect to find certain kinds of perspective in pictures without our being conscious of it. The brain tries to interpret what it sees in the light of past experience. Sometimes the brain's expectations lead it to faulty conclusions.

Let's say you hand someone two pails with covers on them. One pail is small and filled to the brim with sand. The other pail is much larger but contains the same amount of sand as the smaller pail. Hefting the two, most people would say the small pail weighs more. The explanation for their error: they expected the small pail to weigh less because of its size, and they are so surprised by its heaviness that they immediately overestimate its weight.

Why do some optical illusions seem to flip back and forth?

Given ambiguous information, or contradictory clues, the mind does not choose a single interpretation of what it sees; in effect the brain can't "make up its mind." For example, if you take a close look at the goblet at the far right, you can also see two profiles facing each other. Once the dual aspect of the picture becomes apparent, the brain tends to keep checking the information and to see first one figure and then the other.

Are optical illusions of any practical importance?

It was not just intellectual curiosity—interest in knowledge for its own sake—that led scientists to begin studying visual illusions about 150 years ago. In the 19th century, astronomers and physicists got most of their information about the universe by looking through powerful optical instruments. When they realized that

Three prongs show at the top of this figure, but one of them vanishes on the way down. Put a finger across the drawing to see where the deception takes place.

"Relativity," by Maurits Escher, plays surrealistic tricks with perspective. The human mind can accept all the individual parts of the picture, but it cannot accept impossible situations, such as two people walking on the treads and risers of the same staircase.

everyone makes certain errors of perception, they began to worry that their supposedly scientific conclusions might be distorted. That practical concern was one of the causes of a growing scientific interest in optical illusions.

Nowadays, astronomers and physicists can rely on top-quality photographs as checks on the accuracy of the data they gather visually. But optical illusions are still of practical importance in the field of transportation because they can cause accidents on highways and airport runways.

How can we "see" more than is actually visible?

The answer is startling and more than a little mysterious. Seeing is not simply a matter of a camera-like eye projecting a flat image of the outside world onto the screen-like retina. We know that seeing begins only when the brain gets to work interpreting

this retinal image. The brain uses the image as a kind of scaffolding around which it constructs another, more complete and more useful mental image of reality.

The brain maintains a great memory-storehouse of accurate visual data about the world around us—bits and pieces that come in handy when the retinal image proves incomplete or ambiguous, and needs explanation.

On a battlefield, for instance, an infantryman might risk a split-second look at the terrain ahead. All that his retinal image registers is a clump of foliage and a round object jutting out of the foliage near the ground. Quickly, the soldier's brain dips into its store of data and reasonable hypotheses. Within seconds, he fabricates a vivid mental image-pattern of an enemy tank sitting there well camouflaged by the foliage—except that the tip of its turret cannon and part of its undercarriage are showing. The soldier is seeing not only with his eye but with his brain.

Reversible figures. Often called the profile-goblet illusion, this figure seems to move forward and back because the weight of the dark colours tends to be perceived as a background; thus the lighter goblet comes forward. But the profiles can also be perceived as silhouettes against a lighted background.

199

The Amazing World of Colour

How does the eye see colour?

There are two kinds of light receptors in the retina at the back of the eye, rods and cones. The cones have colour-sensitive pigment within them and are specialized by colour sensitivity—one kind for red, one for blue, one for green. The combined stimulation of these cones produces all the colours you see. It is estimated that most people can recognize 120 to 150 hues; if you count variations in brightness and saturation, the number is even greater than that.

Is your sky as blue as mine?

In all likelihood, people with unimpaired vision perceive particular colours in the same way. But we can never be absolutely certain, because colour is subjective; it is the individual brain's interpretation of light signals. Then too, there's no way of knowing precisely whether the colours one person sees are as bright as those seen by another person.

Does colour affect our moods?

Recent experiments have shown that a room painted bubble-gum pink has a pacifying effect on rowdy children, causing them to stop misbehaving and to fall asleep quickly. Although many psychologists remain sceptical about the colour's calming influence, some 1,500 hospitals, prisons and other institutions in the United States use at least one "passive pink" room to discourage antisocial behaviour. Although some scientists scoff at photobiology, or colour therapy, as a science, the advertising world takes colour seriously. Packaging and advertisements are carefully designed to get attention and to set moods. Detergents are most often packaged in bold primary colours, perfumes in unusual "fashion" colours.

Interior designers customarily discuss colour as mood provoking. A blue and white colour scheme is called cool; brown, orange, and tan are considered by some to produce a warm effect. And some restaurateurs have noted that when restaurant walls are painted red, the customers' appetites appear to increase.

Reactions to colour are strongly influenced by culture. The colours people wear at significant moments of their lives vary worldwide, with white regarded as the appropriate colour for weddings in some cultures and as a sign of mourning in others.

A Negative Afterimage — In Complementary Colours

If you gaze steadily at the dot in the coloured panel at left for a few moments, then shift your gaze to the grey box at right, you will see that the original hues have changed into their complementary colours. The blue appears as yellow, the red as green, the green as red, the yellow as blue. This pairing of colours has to do with the fact that colour receptors in the eye are apparently sensitive as pairs; when one colour is turned off (when you stop staring at the panel), the other colour in the receptor is briefly "turned on." The afterimage effect is especially noticeable when you spend time painting walls or objects in bright colours.

What colours do babies prefer?

Because babies can't answer questions, we have to infer their preferences from their behaviour. Interest in this subject goes back to the turn of the century, when one psychologist observed his nine-month-old daughter and noted that she showed a strong preference for a red toy over a green one.

More recently, when four-month-old infants were shown different colours one at a time, for about 15 seconds each, they spent more time looking at red and blue than at the other colours. And when a pure colour was shown side by side with a blended colour, most babies looked longest at the pure colours.

Why do you sometimes see light even after you close your eyes?

Look at a brightly lit sky through a window at a point where the window-panes meet. Stare for a few seconds and then close your eyes: you will see an afterimage lasting from five to ten seconds. The afterimage is known as a positive one because it appears in much the same brightness of light and colour as the original object.

If, however, you look intently for about ten seconds at a small, coloured object on a light field (say a button) and then look at a piece of plain white paper, you are likely to see a negative afterimage of the pattern in pale, complementary colours, which may last for some 10 to 15 seconds. Like the negative of a photograph, the dark spots in the original pattern appear light in the afterimage, while the light spots look dark.

Afterimages are very much like photo imprints on the retina; if you move your eyes, the afterimage moves with them. Positive afterimages are presumably due to the persistent effect of bright light on the photoreceptors; these continue to stimulate the nerve cells that produce visual images after the light has stopped shining. Negative afterimages are more complex. Here, the interplay between adjacent light receptors is involved.

Why does this picture seem to pulsate? *The red and turquoise colours are complementary; wherever the colours meet, the eye sees shifting afterimages.*

The power of contrast is great. *The blue panel against a yellow field makes the blue look brilliant; an identical blue rectangle set against a purple field takes on a pastel appearance, its brilliance toned down by the deeper colour.*

201

Limitations of Vision

Testing for Colour Blindness

The Ishihara test for colour blindness (right), developed in Japan, is used throughout the world to determine the most common form of colour deficiency—red-green colour blindness. In the first plate (right), those with normal colour vision can hardly distinguish a number at all, but those with a red-green deficiency will see the figure 2. In the second plate (far right), normal subjects will read 74 while those with a red-green deficiency will read 21. Colour deficiency can only be diagnosed by a doctor.

 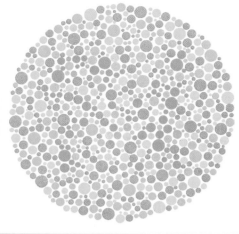

Why is colour blindness usually a misnomer?

Normal colour vision is dependent upon three types of cones. The absence of any one type results in colour blindness for the corresponding colour. Complete colour blindness, which makes a person see everything in shades of grey, is extremely rare. Red-green colour blindness, in which a person can't tell red from green, occurs in about 8 percent of the male population, and is extremely rare in women.

Colour vision defects may be acquired as a result of diseases or injuries to the optic nerve and retina. But usually they are hereditary, due to a defective gene. The daughter of a colour-blind man, although not herself affected, may pass a colour defect on to her son, who is born colour-blind.

Although congenital colour blindness is in most cases irreversible, it does not affect visual acuity and is considered a minor handicap. A motorist with red-green colour blindness is usually able to distinguish traffic lights without trouble because he knows the relative positions of the red, amber and green lights.

Can colour blindness be corrected?

Since congenital colour blindness is an inherited trait, there is no medical cure. But a new contact lens has recently been developed to help persons with red-green colour blindness distinguish these colours. The red-tinted lens, called X-Chron (for X chromosome), is worn in one eye and enhances the brightness contrasts between red and green so that green is seen as the darker colour. The lens does not, however, restore normal colour vision.

How do your eyes adapt to darkness and bright light?

When you enter a dark cinema from a brightly lit lobby, you have difficulty in seeing clearly until your eyes adjust to the darkness. Your eyes may need an hour or more to adapt to darkness completely after long exposure to bright light, but the adjustment from darkness to light requires only a few minutes.

The adaptation of the eyes to light or dark takes place in light-sensitive cells in the retina called rods and cones. Both rods and cones contain light-sensitive chemicals that change on exposure to light and send visual signals through the nervous system to the brain. Cone-shaped cells enhance daylight vision by allowing the eyes to see the details and colours of objects. Rod-shaped cells are concerned with night vision and permit the eyes to make out the outlines of objects, but without any detail or colour. When you go from daylight to darkness, the rods in your eyes become more sensitive; when you return to sunlight, they become less so.

What causes night blindness?

People who can't see images clearly or can't distinguish shades of grey under dim light suffer from night blindness. This condition is commonly caused by a deficiency of vitamin A, which is vital for the proper functioning of the light-sensitive, rod-shaped cells of the retina. In most cases, fortunately, night blindness can be cured by supplemental doses of vitamin A, together with a diet rich in this vitamin.

Can blindness be prevented?

Blindness is defined as partial or total loss of vision. Complete sightlessness is unusual; most blind people are able to see at least some light. The loss of vision does not have to be general. A person may be classified as blind, for example, if his visual field is much reduced, even if objects are still seen sharply. In Britain the statutory definition of blindness is "that a person should be so blind as to be unable to perform any work for which eyesight is essential."

Loss of vision may be caused by a congenital defect of the eye, optic nerve, or brain. Blindness can also result from injury to or a disease of any of these areas. Uncontrolled diabetes is a leading cause of blindness; early detection of the disease can save an individual's eyesight. Glaucoma is another vision-threatening disease that can be prevented in most instances. Regular eye checkups for adults should include the glaucoma test. This painless, quickly performed test measures the pressure within the interior of the eye. If pressure builds up, the optic nerve can be damaged. Early detection and treatment can control the condition.

Blindness can also be prevented by training your children to handle objects such as pencils and scissors with the sharp end or cutting edge pointed downward. They should be told never to run with sticks or sharp objects that could injure the eye if the child fell, and never to jab at their playmates with anything that could do harm. Adults should wear protective goggles while working with power tools that might throw off chips.

Are the other senses of the blind especially acute?

There is no evidence to indicate that the senses of hearing, smell, or touch are intrinsically different in the blind than in the sighted. But it is certain that many blind people make better use of their senses—and their memories—than do the sighted. The blind worker who travels by public transport every day is a marvel of concentration, seldom needing assistance except when the path has been obstructed.

Does alcohol affect eyesight?

Blurred vision is one of the classic signs of excessive alcohol consumption; a person may literally see double because alcohol may interfere with ocular reflexes. In some people, excessive use of alcohol and tobacco can damage the optic nerves.

In daylight, the colour-sensitive cones in the eye are activated, and people with normal vision can see everything clearly, including all shades of colour.

At night, rods take over from the cones. Rods cannot pick up colour or details, so the same scene becomes grey, an indistinct shape against the night sky.

Within your eye, there are millions of these slender, light-sensitive rods, which respond to weak light. Folklore to the contrary, nobody can really see in the dark—there must be some glimmer of light for vision. Rods also give peripheral vision, the ability to see out of the corner of your eye.

Eye Problems and Remedies

What causes cataracts?

A cataract, the gradual clouding of the normally clear lens of the eye, impairs vision by preventing light from reaching the retina. Although cataracts can develop early and for several reasons, the most common cause is the aging process. Senile cataract is the chief cause of blindness in older people and results from gradual degeneration of the lens.

Cataracts develop painlessly and slowly over several years and usually affect both eyes. In some cases the loss of vision is slight and does not warrant any treatment. But advanced cataracts eventually produce a "white" pupil, known as a ripe cataract. Ophthalmologists used to ask patients to wait until their cataracts had fully ripened before removing them surgically, but nowadays, with improved techniques, cataracts can be removed much sooner.

The modern cataract operation is painless and is successful in approximately 90 percent of cases. The opaque lens is removed from the eye, and the patient's vision is restored by means of spectacles, contact lenses, or implantation of a permanent device known as an intraocular lens.

Can the results of cataract surgery be predicted?

The removal of cataracts that cloud the lens of the eye is the most common type of eye surgery. Unfortunately, in approximately 10 percent of cataract patients, the operation does not improve vision. Determining whether or not surgery will help has long been a perplexing problem for eye doctors, in part because it is sometimes difficult to tell whether loss of vision is due to the cataract or to a disorder in the retina, the sensory membrane at the back of the eye.

Now, a new device called a potential acuity meter, or PAM, has become available, which can help the surgeon predict whether the removal of a cataract will actually improve the patient's vision. The instrument shines a tiny beam of light through a fairly clear "window" in the lens and projects the image of an eye chart onto the retina. The patient reads the chart almost as if the cataract did not exist; from the accuracy of the patient's reading, the doctor can determine whether the visual problem is caused by the cataract or by a retinal disorder. In addition to forestalling disappointing cataract operations, PAM shows patients what their vision will be like after cataract surgery.

How is glaucoma treated today?

The two main types of the serious eye disorder known as glaucoma are caused by inadequate drainage of the eyeball's aqueous fluid; there is a blockage or narrowing of the drainage angle at the front edge of the iris. The excess fluid then builds up and exerts too much pressure on the optic nerve and retina. Eventually the condition leads to irreversible blindness.

Chronic glaucoma is a progressive disease associated with aging; it occurs most often in people over 40 years old, and it runs in families. There are no symptoms at first, but the patient eventually notices a loss of peripheral vision. Chronic glaucoma accounts for approximately nine out of ten cases of the disease. It can usually be controlled by eyedrops and other medicines that reduce pressure in the eye.

Acute glaucoma strikes suddenly and may cause blindness within a few days if it is not treated immediately. The victim feels extreme pain in the eye and may see blurred images and haloes of lights. This form of glaucoma, which is fairly rare, can be treated surgically.

How are detached retinas reattached?

If you think of the eye as a room and of the retina as wallpaper, you can visualize how a detached retina occurs; just as wallpaper peels away when water seeps beneath it, so the retina comes loose. The condition begins with a hole in the retina that allows the vitreous fluid in the eyeball to come through and lift up the reti-

Folklore of the Body: THE POWER OF THE EVIL EYE

The belief was once almost universal that the human eye had the power to injure or destroy an enemy. This fear may have arisen from a primitive terror of being watched by wild animals, hostile tribesmen, evil spirits, or jealous gods who resented human success. Remedies for the evil eye abounded, ranging from placation of an evil-eyed man with beer and tobacco in the Congo, to tying red ribbons to the tails of livestock in Scotland.

During the 16th and 17th centuries, when witches were said to destroy their victims by the power of the evil eye, hundreds of women were executed solely on the evidence that someone had died after receiving an angry look from them. The judges who presided at their trials were so fearful of being bewitched by these women when passing sentence, that it was not uncommon for the accused to be led into court backwards.

A small craft in Portugal shows a modern version of the eye, once painted on the bows of Mediterranean fishing vessels to counteract the effect of evil eyes.

How does the world look when vision is impaired?

Normal vision. What an observer sees with good eyes is what a camera captures on film. From the edge of a city park, for instance, a viewer gets a clear picture ahead and to both sides.

Glaucoma, caused by pressure in the eyeball that damages the optic nerve, destroys peripheral vision. Most of the park is blotted out, because the nerve has sent the brain only a partial image.

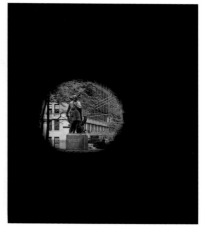

Retinitis pigmentosa (tunnel vision) also causes loss of peripheral sight. In this hereditary, progressive disease, blood vessels in the retina are gradually replaced with scars, and vision narrows.

Macular degeneration, a common condition in the elderly, causes a blind spot in the centre of the visual field. The reason is a decreased supply of blood to the macula, which is part of the retina.

Cataracts cloud the eye's lens, blocking the passage of light to the retina. The photographic clarity of normal vision is lost, and the world looks hazy, very much as if viewed through a frosted window.

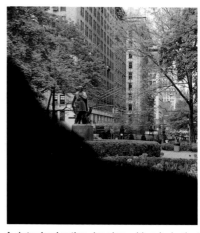

A detached retina begins with a hole that allows fluid to seep through. As wallpaper peels away when water gets under it, so two layers of the retina separate. A dark shadow seems to block the view.

nal layer. The retina is separated from the underlying pigment membrane and choroid layer, which supplies it with nutrients. Without surgery, blindness eventually results.

An eye surgeon can reattach the retina by gluing it back in place with minute patches of scar tissue. The doctor employs a tiny probe of extreme cold, heat, or light for a fraction of a second to "spot-weld" the layers together. A laser beam that focuses a pinpoint of intense light on the detached retina is often used. If surgery is performed promptly, eyesight is restored in about 85 percent of patients with a detached retina.

What is corneal grafting?

The healthy cornea from a recently deceased person can be removed and transplanted to someone whose cornea has been scarred by injury or illness. This operation, the first widely performed tissue transplant, has an excellent record of long-term success. But not everyone with a corneal defect can be helped by a transplant. The main limitations on the operation are the scarcity of donated eyes and the fact that corneas must be transplanted within a short time after the death of the donor, ideally within 48 hours.

Chapter 9

THE EAR, NOSE, & THROAT

This is a very expressive part of the body, a kind of sense-centre, where we take in sound, smell, and sustenance, and from which we send speech and song.

The Ear: A Marvel of Miniaturization	208
The Sounds Around Us	210
Degrees of Hearing Loss	212
Ear Problems and Remedies	214
Hearing Aids: Capturing Sound Waves	215
Keeping Your Balance	216
The "Air Conditioner" of the Body	218
The Smell-Taste Connection	220
Four Sets of Sinus Cavities	222
The Switch From Breathing to Swallowing	224
Miseries of the Nose and Throat	226
The Wonderful Human Voice	228
Overcoming Speech and Hearing Problems	230

Why are the ear, nose, and throat related medically?

You wake up one morning with a sore throat. Before the end of the day, your nose is runny. By the next day, you have a full-fledged cold. Your nose is stuffy, food doesn't seem to have any taste, you're not hearing very well, and you may have an earache.

This familiar sequence of events is one bit of evidence that the ear, nose, and throat are structurally, functionally, and neurologically interrelated. As a result, they fall prey to many of the same irritants and diseases. Discomfort sensed in one part of this tripartite system may originate in another, and when infection occurs in one part, it can spread to the rest of the system. That is why ear, nose, and throat together are the province of a single branch of medicine, usually called by the initials E.N.T.

Can you test your own hearing?

No do-it-yourself test enables you to evaluate your own hearing accurately, but there are several rough checks you can make. If, for instance, you hear better over the telephone than in face-to-face conversation, or if you need to turn up the TV sound when others can easily hear, a specialist's opinion might be valuable. The same is true if you do not hear a tap dripping, or cannot make out the words when the speaker is standing where you cannot see his face.

Do you hear your voice as others hear it?

When you heard your own voice on tape for the first time, you probably could hardly recognize it. You could have sworn your voice was more appealing, and you were sure there was something wrong with the recorder. Chances are that what you heard on the tape is what everyone else always hears when you speak. But when you hear your voice untaped, it sounds very different to you than to others. Your voice reaches your inner ear

Which way is up? In zero gravity conditions, weightless astronauts float around in midair. They not only lose their sense of which way is up, but four out of ten also suffer from motion sickness. The inner ear and muscles that normally rely on the force of gravity for orientation get scrambled signals.

by means of two routes. When it goes through your eardrums, it travels by air. When it goes through your jaw, the medium is bone. By contrast, your voice reaches other people by travelling through air alone. No wonder, then, that without the help of a recording machine, you can't hope to hear your voice as others hear it.

Does one sex have a keener sense of smell than the other?

In tests, women have, as a rule, proved superior to men in their ability to identify smells. This does not prove that women have an innate advantage. Scientists attribute much of the sexual difference in odour sensitivity to the fact that women are more aware of their odour environment.

Can your sense of smell wear out?

Lovers of chocolate may find it very hard to believe, but confectionery workers say that after working with chocolate for hours on end and day after day, they hardly notice its aroma. Whether or not the sense of smell really tires out may still be debatable, but it is certain that people get used to odours and cease to pay much attention to them.

Familiarity tends to weaken the impact of unpleasant smells as well as pleasant ones. Workers in rendering plants, for example, soon develop a tolerance for the smell of rancid fats, an odour that most people regard as objectionable. But sensitivity does not disappear permanently. One rendering plant worker was reported as saying: "The odour was terrible, but I got used to it. It was less annoying when you stayed right with it. When you left for a vacation, you had to come back and get used to the thing all over again."

By the way, varying opinions about what smells good and what smells bad stem not from inborn preferences but from experience and associations. In Africa, members of some tribes like to perfume their hair with rancid oil. In many countries, some people love the smell of such pungent-smelling cheeses as Limburger, while other people respond with an eloquent "Ugh!"

Why do some people get motion sickness?

These days, ships are equipped with stabilizers to keep them from rolling and pitching, and aeroplanes generally fly high enough to avoid turbulence, so that seasickness and airsickness are less common than they used to be. But some people still get motion sickness on a ship or in the air—or while dancing a polka, riding a roller coaster, or even while travelling by car or train.

The apparent cause of motion sickness is overstimulation of the balance mechanism in the inner ear. Fluid sloshes through all three semicircular canals simultaneously and sends contradictory nerve impulses to the brain, which just doesn't know what to make of them. In some people, anxiety probably lowers the threshold of susceptibility to motion sickness. As they grow older and become more seasoned travellers, many people outgrow the affliction.

The symptoms of classic motion sickness are fatigue, sweating, dizziness, nausea, and vomiting. Several drugs have proved helpful, but since some of them cause drowsiness, they should be used only by people who can leave the driving to others. Everyone can reduce the risk of developing motion sickness by getting plenty of rest before setting out, eating lightly before and during the trip, keeping the air as fresh as possible, and not drinking alcohol.

The Ear: A Marvel of Miniaturization

How is the ear constructed?

The ear is really two organs in one: an organ of hearing and one of balance. Amazingly, the inner ear, although no bigger than a hazelnut, contains as many circuits as the telephone system of a good-sized city. The Eustachian tube, which leads from the middle ear to the throat, admits air. This helps to equalize pressure on either side of the eardrum. The diagram below is of an adult ear. During childhood, the Eustachian tube is more nearly level with the throat. It is narrow and easily blocked, which accounts for the tendency of children to have earaches.

SEMICIRCULAR CANALS

COCHLEAR NERVE

EAR CANAL (OUTER EAR)

COCHLEA (INNER EAR)

EARDRUM   ANVIL

HAMMER   STIRRUP

MIDDLE EAR

EUSTACHIAN TUBE

What is the function of the external ear?

Despite the over-all efficiency of the human ear, one part of it is really not very remarkable. If by chance you lost the external ear in an accident (this does happen sometimes), the loss would be mainly cosmetic. You would hear about as well as before, and your equilibrium would not be affected. This is because your external ear is simply a sound-gathering device. It helps to funnel noises into the part of the ear that does the hearing, but it doesn't do so anywhere near as well as a horse's ear or a rabbit's ear, both of which can swivel around.

The external ear consists of a flap of cartilage framing a 25-millimetre (1-inch) long, irregularly shaped canal. The canal inclines slightly upwards to the eardrum, or tympanic membrane, which forms the divider between the outer and middle ear. The passageway is an obstacle course of hairs and some 4,000 wax-producing glands which catch insects, dust, and any other intruders before they can make their way into the hearing mechanism. The canal also serves to moderate the climate inside the ear; the air that reaches the sensitive ear-

The Cochlea: Where Sounds Are Transmitted to the Brain

The cochlea in these micrographs is that of a guinea pig, in structure virtually identical to the cochlea of a human being. The bony covering has been removed, revealing the rows of hairlike cells that line the spirals inside the cochlea. These cells move to one side as vibrations of sound wash over them. Very loud noise, especially over long periods, can damage these fragile cells, causing permanent loss of hearing. The architecture of the cochlea is shown here in progressively closer views. In the two pictures at far right, you can see the contrast between healthy and damaged hairs. Such damage is done not just by working in a noisy factory, but by music played too loudly.

Interior of the cochlea is a spiral.

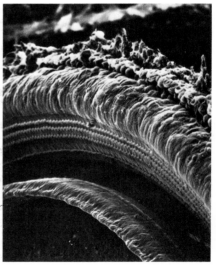

Rows of hair cells line the spiral.

drum remains fairly constant in temperature and humidity, no matter what the conditions are outside.

How does the middle ear work?

In the ear—just as in electronics—miniaturization is the name of the game. The middle ear is a chamber so small that five or six drops of water would fill it. It is filled with air, and contains an amplifying system composed of three linked bones that together take up no more space than a small carpet tack. These bones, so crucial to the mechanical transmission of sound waves, are named according to their shape: the malleus, or hammer; the incus, or anvil; and the stapes, or stirrup, which is the smallest bone in the human body.

The hearing process begins when sound-bearing air waves strike the taut but resonant eardrum and cause it to vibrate. With each tiny inward movement of the membrane, the malleus next to it vibrates in the same rhythm, and by a lever action transmits the message to the adjoining incus. The incus, in turn, transmits the vibrations to the stapes. That bone fits into a membranous opening, called the oval window, on the inner wall of the middle ear and relays the vibration to the inner ear.

As the vibrations move through the middle ear from the relatively large eardrum to the small oval window, the energy behind the vibrations becomes ever more concentrated. Air pressure in the chamber is kept the same as atmospheric pressure by means of a vent (the Eustachian tube), that runs down from the middle ear to the upper part of the throat.

What does the inner ear do?

Surprising as it may seem, you have something very much like a piano keyboard in your inner ear, and it is the seat of hearing. But that is not the only unusual structure in the inner ear; this part of the ear also contains the structures essential for maintaining balance. The complexity of the inner ear, and its important, dual role in human life, may help to explain why it is among the best-protected parts of the body. Located within the rigid skull, it is further safeguarded by a cushion of fluid.

The mechanism that is central to the hearing process is the cochlea, where sound waves are converted to nerve impulses. The cochlea, a small, bony structure, looks like a snail shell and works like a piano keyboard. But there are perhaps 20,000 "keys" in the cochlea, compared with 88 on a piano, and they are made of hairlike sensory cells rather than of ivory. Instead of being laid out flat, they are arranged along a membrane that coils around itself 2½ times.

Sounds transmitted by the stapes to the oval window set fluid pressure waves moving through the spiral of the cochlear canals. Depending on their pitch, sounds have their maximum effect on different segments of the sensory-cell keyboard. Sounds belonging to the lowest frequencies activate the wider, flexible sensory cells at the core of the cochlear spiral; the highest frequency sounds get their maximum response at the end of the spiral nearest the oval window, where the sensory cells are narrow and stiff.

As the sensory cells vibrate, they generate impulses that are picked up by the auditory nerve and then transmitted to the brain. There the signals are "heard" as a particular sound: a voice, a bird call, or whatever experience has taught us to associate with that particular pattern of signals.

A closer view. Note rows at top.

Healthy cochlea has few broken hairs.

Deafness results from loss of hairs.

The Sounds Around Us

What is sound?

When violin strings, vocal cords, tuning forks, and other objects vibrate, or move rapidly back and forth, they produce disturbances in the air on either side of the vibrating object. It is these disturbances that we call sound. They come about when the oscillating movement forces the molecules that make up the air into alternating waves of compressed air—in which the molecules are bunched up under pressure—and rarefied air—in which the molecules are spread out under minimal pressure. The effect is rather like the peaks and valleys of ocean waves.

Sound waves come in a range of frequencies or cycles per second—the lowest piano tone, for example, produces 27 vibrations per second, the highest tone on a piano has a frequency of approximately 4,000 vibrations per second. Sound waves of 70,000 million vibrations per second have been produced in scientific experiments. The pressure waves constitute "sound" as we know it, however, only when they are picked up by the resonating eardrum and sent along to the brain for analysis.

What are the main characteristics of sound?

A single sound produces multiple effects on the ear. When you hear a sound, you are conscious of its pitch, its volume, and its tone quality, or timbre. Pitch simply means the number of vibrations of sound waves each second. A low-pitched sound is one in which the pressure waves are moving very slowly, perhaps only 20 or 30 of them rumbling past your ear each second. Conversely, a high-pitched sound is made up of pressure waves that move rapidly.

Rating Loudness—From Whisper to Take-off

The standard unit for measuring the loudness of sound is the decibel. A sound that is just audible is 10 decibels, a rushing stream 50, a power mower 105. Every increase of ten decibels marks a tenfold increase in the intensity of sound. For example, a 40-decibel sound is 10 times louder than a 30-decibel sound. Noise rated at 80 decibels or higher, if heard for prolonged periods, can cause permanent hearing loss. "Hair cells," says one specialist, "aren't designed for the racket of modern civilization." By one estimate, machinery is making the Western world noisier by one decibel every year.

Sounds carry far in the country because there is little ambient noise.

It isn't the loudness of a pneumatic drill that's damaging but prolonged exposure to it.

SOUND	DECIBELS						
	0	20	50	70	100	120	150
Absolute silence							
Watch ticking							
Country quiet							
Normal conversation							
Car horn nearby							
Pneumatic drill							
Jet take-off							

Loudness varies with distance; these decibel ratings are averages.

Every note in a musical scale has a certain pitch. People who have absolute, or perfect, pitch can hear a single note and say just where in the scale it lies. Most people, however, can say only that a particular note is higher or lower in pitch than a preceding note.

Volume, or loudness, is sound intensity—that is, the degree of pressure the sound waves exert on the nerve cells of the inner ear at a particular distance. The pressure is determined by the amplitude of the sound waves, and is usually expressed in decibels (db). The ear can adapt to a wide range of sound intensities, the softest being perhaps one million millionth as loud as the loudest.

Tone quality is the characteristic sound of a particular voice, musical instrument, or some other sound source. A piano, a trumpet, and a cello, say, may play the same note, at the same degree of loudness, and yet sound totally different from each other. This is because each instrument produces not only the pure, fundamental tone that a musician plays on it but also, and simultaneously, certain overtones: higher tones that vary from instrument to instrument and that blend in with the fundamental tone to make a special sound.

Can we hear all possible sounds?

The "silent" whistles dog trainers use are of course not silent: dogs can hear them even if trainers can't. Most adult human beings are able to detect sounds ranging from some 16 to 20,000 cycles (vibrations) per second, which covers about 10 octaves. People miss out on really high-frequency sounds that animals can hear. Cats, for instance, are good at detecting high-frequency sounds. That is why your cat is better at catching mice than you are; mice utter high-pitched squeaks that are inaudible to you— but not to your cat.

You may (or may not) regret your inability to hear high-pitched mouse squeaks. However, you should be grateful that the human ear cannot hear frequencies below 16 cycles. If it

could, you would never know silence; you would hear, without respite, the sounds of molecules of air colliding with one another.

How does having two ears affect your hearing?

Unless the source of a sound is of equal distance from both ears, the sound reaches one ear before it gets to the other, and it sounds louder in one ear than in the other. You would think that would be confusing. Not so: two-eared hearing greatly enhances your ability to make sense of the sounds around you.

By a remarkable process that hearing specialists call binaural summation, your brain can grasp the subtle differences between the sounds that reach the two ears. Using these differences, it can automatically perform certain mental calculations and so figure out where the sound came from. People who are deaf in one ear do not have a basis for comparing sounds and thus find it difficult to locate the source of sounds.

Can blind people see with their ears?

The blind are often more sensitive to the nuances of sound than the rest of us, not because their ears are different but because they pay more attention to listening and interpreting what they hear than most people do. That increased sensitivity has always been of some help to the blind in locating sound-producing objects. In recent years, scientists have begun to take advantage of blind people's acute hearing in a systematic fashion.

The scientists are developing a device similar to sonar, which is used by the armed forces to detect submarines and other underwater objects. Built into a spectacles frame, it scans all the surroundings with ultrasonic waves. The echoing waves are reflected back to the sonar-for-the-sightless, which turns them into sounds of different pitches audible to the spectacles' wearer through the earpieces.

Locating Sounds

Slight differences in sounds arriving at each ear can indicate the direction it is coming from. Called binaural hearing, this also gives sound a three-dimensional effect.

Each ear gets a different sound from one source. Here, sounds match.

Shifting the head brings the sound to one ear faster, indicating source.

When sounds come from one side, the head creates a sound shadow.

Degrees of Hearing Loss

How is hearing tested?

A specialist can learn a great deal about a subject's hearing acuity just by speaking to him in a whisper. An audiometer, a device that produces tones similar to those made by tuning forks, is more precise. Each tone consists of a single pitch—that is, the sound produced by one particular frequency per second of sound waves. In a soundproof room, the patient dons earphones that conduct a series of tones into one ear at a time. Each frequency is introduced at an inaudible level and increased in loudness until the listener indicates that he hears it. This phase of testing detects conduction deafness—an inability to hear airborne sounds.

The second phase of testing is designed to detect nerve deafness—inability to hear because of nerve damage. This kind of deafness is revealed by difficulty in hearing bone-conducted sounds. The examiner therefore employs earphones that transmit vibrations to the bones of the skull.

What causes deafness?

Some people are born deaf; others become hard of hearing in later life. Physiologists describe two principal types of hearing loss: conduction deafness and nerve deafness.

Conduction deafness results when something interferes with the mechanical transmission of the sound waves to the inner ear. The cause may be as simple as an accumulation of ear wax or an infection that makes the ear canal swell. Or it may be a damaged eardrum, fluid in the middle ear, or otosclerosis (hardening of the ear tissues).

Nerve deafness, sometimes called perceptive hearing loss, occurs because of damage to the nerve fibres that transmit sound to the brain or to the cells in the cochlea. This kind of deafness may be present at birth, perhaps because the mother had German measles, or rubella, in the first three months of pregnancy, perhaps as a consequence of a head injury sustained in a difficult delivery. Nerve deafness can also be due to encephalitis, Ménière's disease, or a tumour. Some prescription drugs may cause it, too, and so may chronic exposure to loud noise. Most people develop some degree of nerve deafness as they get older, because the auditory nerve tends to degenerate. In such cases, the ability to hear high tones may diminish, but low ones may remain clearly audible.

Sometimes you can guess what kind of deafness a person suffers from by noticing the way he speaks. People with conduction difficulties often speak quietly, because their own voices, amplified by the bones of the skull, sound *loud* to them. People with nerve deafness, by contrast, are apt to speak in a loud tone, because their own voices sound *faint* to them.

Can music damage your ears?

"Turn that thing down!" That demand, rarely heeded for long, is often heard from parents fed up with the sound of rock music blaring from their teenagers' rooms. No doubt par-

A Composer Who Couldn't Hear His Own Music.

Ludwig van Beethoven, the great German composer, first noticed a growing deafness in the early 1800s, when he was about 30 years old. Probably all of his symphonies were written after he had experienced some degree of hearing impairment. Tragically, by the time Beethoven had completed what many consider his greatest symphony, the Ninth, he had lost most of his hearing. When he died, in 1827, he was nearly a recluse because of the isolation imposed by his deafness.

Thunderous applause greeted the first performance of Beethoven's Ninth Symphony, in 1824, but the deaf composer did not turn to acknowledge the ovation until one of the musicians gently prompted him to do so.

Modern physicians now believe that Beethoven suffered from otosclerosis, a condition that could not be treated in his own time. Today, it could probably be corrected by a hearing aid or surgery.

ents would like to be able to tell their youngsters they face certain deafness if they keep it up. Unfortunately for parents' nerves and family harmony, the evidence is not conclusive.

The average rock group plays a lot louder than a symphony orchestra. A recent study in Norway indicated that rock music produces a sound pressure level of 120–130 decibels in the listener's ear when heard from a speaker 1 metre (3.3 feet) away. Many researchers have found that some—but not all—of those who listen to rock music suffer at least temporary hearing loss. There is some evidence to suggest, however, that breaks between numbers may give the ears a chance to recover.

Most likely, disc jockeys and musicians in loud-music bands are at greater risk than ordinary listeners. In one study, significant hearing loss was found in one-third of 70 discotheque disc jockeys. The deejays were still in their 20s; at that age, hearing disability is to be expected in less than 1 percent of the population.

Are some people more sensitive to noise than others?

People who engage in activities that injure hearing often tolerate noise levels that others, with their hearing still intact, find uncomfortable. The toleration of loud noise may be a consequence of their impaired hearing.

People who play music at top volume—especially those who use headphones—increase the likelihood of acoustical trauma. And those who are employed in high-level-noise professions—such as manufacturing, construction, mining, and farming—are at a greater risk of sustaining some hearing loss.

By the age of 40, most Westerners have lost some hearing ability, especially in the higher ranges. It is significant, however, that age-associated hearing loss occurs only in the industrialized world. Studies conducted in primitive villages have shown that when people are not constantly exposed to loud noises, hearing loss does not take place.

The pleasures of headphones are many. You can carry your own background music with you or listen to language tapes as you walk. But the joys of headphones are offset by two risks: inattention to the hazards of traffic and possible damage to hearing from turning the sound up too high.

What is tone deafness?

The ability to discriminate fine differences in pitch—to hear a tone and then sing it back on key, to respond with sensitivity to different kinds of music—has little, if anything, to do with the physical characteristics of the ear. Tone deafness is therefore not inherited. Instead, it describes an educational or environmental handicap. A person who has not been taught, or is not motivated, to hear subtleties of sound at an early age is likely to have difficulty if he later tries to develop the skills necessary to hear fully and richly.

Can noise impair your efficiency or your general health?

There is mounting evidence that excess noise can trigger a variety of biochemical reactions, including elevated blood pressure, abnormal glandular function, increased heart rate, shallow breathing, and reduced blood flow to the foetus in a pregnant woman. In addition, emotional stress, learning problems, disturbed sleep, and susceptibility to accidents have been shown to increase measurably in noisy environments. In addition,

research has shown that noise makes workers less productive than they would normally be. For instance, a study of typists in a noisy office indicated that 20 percent of their energy was expended in overcoming the negative effects of the noise. In a similar study of executives, the figure rose to about 30 percent.

Which sense is more important, sight or hearing?

An inability to hear is definitely a grave handicap for everyone who suffers from it—perhaps 1 out of every 2,000 people in the world—because of the isolation it necessarily imposes. Obviously, no one can say which of these two senses is more important. But Helen Keller, who became blind and deaf in early childhood, called deafness "a much worse misfortune" than blindness.

Those who are born deaf are at a greater disadvantage than those who become deaf in later life. Children ordinarily learn to speak by imitating the words they hear others speak. If they are born deaf, they need special training to learn to communicate with others and to ensure normal intellectual development.

Ear Problems and Remedies

What is the most common cause of earaches?

A foreign object lodged in the outer ear, a ruptured eardrum, an impacted wisdom tooth—any of these may give you an earache. But the most common cause of pain in the ear is a middle-ear infection following an infection of the nose and throat.

Earaches often stem from colds, flu, scarlet fever, mumps, measles, or tonsillitis. The viruses and bacteria associated with these ailments travel by way of the Eustachian tube to the closed chamber of the middle ear, where they settle in and then multiply. The infection stimulates the mucous membrane lining of the middle ear to produce defensive fluids, but because the Eustachian tube is inflamed and swollen, the fluids cannot drain out as they should. The result is intense pain due to pressure in this nerve-sensitive area.

Some 80 or 90 percent of all middle-ear infections occur in children under 12. Such infections are potentially dangerous, because the infected material may spread, causing mas-

toiditis, meningitis, or even a brain abscess. However, with modern medications these complications rarely occur. If fever is high, a doctor should be consulted promptly.

Is ringing in the ears cause for concern?

Almost all of us have experienced brief episodes of unexplained ringing, whirring, whistling, cracking, buzzing, roaring, or hissing in one or both our ears. The event is often traceable to too much aspirin, caffeine, alcohol, quinine, or some other drug, or to exposure to extraordinarily loud noise. In these cases, the symptom is usually alleviated once the cause is removed.

But a large number of people live with a degree of auditory noise all the time, for the condition is fairly common. A few are so severely afflicted that they cannot lead normal lives. One unhappy victim described the constant ringing in his ear as like the sound of 5,000 crickets.

This condition is called tinnitus. In

most cases, the cause is not found, but it is more frequent in older people whose hearing has gradually started to deteriorate. The most frequently known cause of tinnitus is job-related noise exposure. Otosclerosis, a form of bone degeneration in the middle ear, allergies, anaemia, diabetes, injuries to the head and neck, high blood pressure, tumours, and stress have also been identified as triggers in some people. However mild your tinnitus is, you should consult your doctor if it persists; it could be an early warning of some more serious hearing disorder.

What can you do if you're hard of hearing?

If Beethoven were alive today, his deafness could perhaps be alleviated by surgery. The composer is now thought to have suffered from otosclerosis, a common form of deafness that immobilizes the stapes, one of the tiny bones in the ear that transmits sound vibrations.

Many cases of hearing disability are not amenable to surgery. But many people who do not hear well can be greatly helped by a modern hearing aid. The early, unsophisticated devices, which amplified all sounds indiscriminately, were often more annoying than helpful to their wearers. Using them was like turning up the volume of a radio without first making sure that it was tuned to the right frequency; the result was louder sound, but no improvement in clarity. Now, however, experts can find out just what kinds of sounds a particular person does not hear and then can design an electronic aid that amplifies only those sounds.

Lip-reading—better called speech-reading because it requires attention to the whole face—is a useful supplement to a hearing aid. Even people with good hearing use it unconsciously if they are in a noisy environment. Instruction from a professional is helpful, but it is possible to teach yourself a great deal by trying to follow television programs with the volume turned down.

Folklore of the Body: READING CHARACTER, FINDING OMENS

From antiquity, ears have been the focus of superstition. The Greeks and other ancients believed ears to be the seat of human intelligence. Small ears were frequently taken as a sign of stinginess; on the other hand, they might indicate refinement. The same sort of message could be read in large ears—in some cases, generosity, in others, coarseness. Any ringing, tingling, burning, or itching meant that the person was being talked about. In some cases, the left ear meant a favourable mention, in others, the right; ill-wishing was then ascribed to sensations in the opposite ear. A modern study of ears reveals that their shape is unique to each individual. They are effective in identification (though seldom used) because the ear remains the same shape throughout life. Of all the fancies about the ear, none has more charm than the notion that the ear can pick up the sounds of the ocean in a seashell. The fact is, what you hear is only an echo.

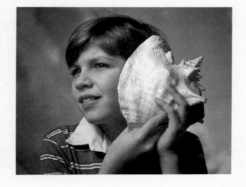

The spiral shape of the conch shell and the smoothness of its inner walls catch and intensify the slightest vibration, even the pulse in your head.

Hearing Aids: Capturing Sound Waves

The earliest hearing aid of all—one we all use—is the cupped hand. A listener can move his hand around until the best effect is achieved, perhaps collecting the conversation of a dinner partner over the din of a busy restaurant. Of course, in the case of serious hearing loss, this doesn't work.

The 17th century saw the first hearing trumpets—various designs that gathered and channelled sound to the ear. But mechanical hearing aids were of limited value. It was not until the 20th century, with the development of electronic hearing aids, that real help was at hand. Electronic aids are superior to the old trumpets because they amplify sound. A microphone picks up the sound and converts it to current, which is amplified and transmitted to an earphone. The sound is of greater intensity than the original. Researchers are working on hearing aids implanted in the cochlea, and their efforts are having considerable success.

This **"conversation tube,"** invented by the German scientist Athanasius Kircher about 1650, amplified the voice, but was incredibly cumbersome.

The stress and rapt attention of speaker and listener alike, as demonstrated in this 19th-century lithograph, was probably the common experience of people who were dependent on trumpets. These primitive hearing aids were hit-or-miss affairs, useless for some kinds of deafness, and exasperating under the best of circumstances.

LONDON HEARING HORN

CORRUGATED EAR TRUMPET

TELESCOPIC EAR TRUMPET shown closed (left), open (right)

WALKING CANE, open for use (left), closed (right). It was inconspicuous but awkward to use

CONVERSATION TUBE for making whispers audible

EAR OF DIONISIUS

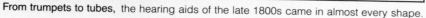

From trumpets to tubes, the hearing aids of the late 1800s came in almost every shape.

The electronic hearing aids of today are a far cry from the early, battery-wired models. Some fit right into the ear canal, and are virtually invisible.

Keeping Your Balance

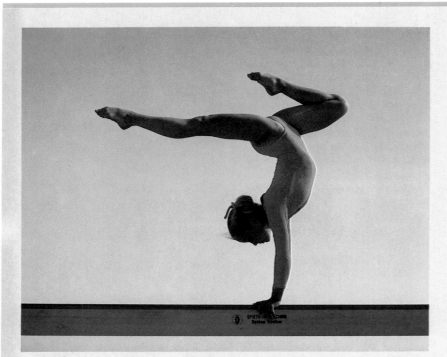

Gymnast in stag handstand. Training is not just to hold balance, but to regain it rapidly.

How the Inner Ear Balances Your Body

A baby who is learning to walk does a great deal of wobbling. First, an arm goes out, then the bottom sags, the shoulders go backwards, and then down he goes. The baby is trying to find and keep his centre of gravity. With the help of the inner ear—and lots of practice—the skill will ultimately be learned. Fluid-filled chambers in the inner ear contain minute, hairlike sensors. As the head moves, the fluids shift, bending the hairs and stimulating nerve impulses; any change in position is transmitted to the brain. The three semicircular canals, which are at right angles to one another, maintain equilibrium while the body is in motion. The lower part of the balance structure, the cochlea, maintains static equilibrium. The sensor cells of the cochlea are slightly different and have tiny particles called otoliths that press on the hairs when the fluid in the chamber shifts. All information about any change in the position of the otoliths and hairs is relayed to the brain, which then signals the body to shift position.

Labyrinth (left) is the name for structures concerned with balance and hearing, chiefly the cochlea and the semicircular canals.

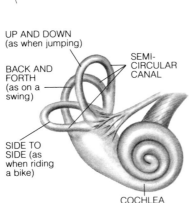

UP AND DOWN (as when jumping)

BACK AND FORTH (as on a swing)

SEMI-CIRCULAR CANAL

SIDE TO SIDE (as when riding a bike)

COCHLEA

How do you keep your balance?

Standing on one leg with your eyes closed is a difficult thing to do. If you can't see where things are in relation to your body, you will have trouble keeping your balance. Vision, however, is not the only factor that affects equilibrium. Much more important is a structure in the inner ear called the labyrinth. Its main features are the semicircular canals, three fluid-filled loops arranged in three different planes so that each canal is at right angles to the other two. The canals are lined with sensory hairs linked to the part of the brain that controls the skeletal muscles.

When your head moves, fluid in one or more of the loops washes over the sensory hairs and stimulates them. They respond by relaying nervous impulses to the brain. If the brain perceives that the body is losing its equilibrium, it will automatically signal some muscles to contract and others to relax until balance is restored.

What is Ménière's disease?

Giddiness—a feeling that your feet are not solidly on the ground—sometimes develops as a side effect of high blood pressure, anaemia, depression, anxiety, too much alcohol, or some other condition in which the brain lacks sufficient oxygen. But when dizziness is extreme—and especially when the patient feels as if he or everything around him is spinning, a symptom called vertigo—the trouble may be Ménière's disease. Besides vertigo, this syndrome can include tinnitus, fluctuating hearing, and a feeling of fullness in the affected ear. In this disturbance of the inner ear, the labyrinth contains too much fluid. The typical sufferer from Ménière's disease is a male over the age of 40. The disease is extremely variable and unpredictable. It can come on gradually or suddenly, be mild or severe, affect one or both ears, and last from a few minutes to months or years, with occasional remissions. In some cases, the disease causes such severe vertigo that ordinary activities are impossible; the patient may stagger, fall, or even lose consciousness.

The underlying cause of the excess fluid is mysterious, and for that reason, there is no single accepted treatment. Many sufferers take medication to ease the symptoms of dizziness and vertigo. For patients who are severely disabled, surgery may be the only solution, though it can be a delicate situation because the surgeon has to operate within millimetres of the brain. But the results of surgery can be dramatic. For instance, the astronaut who made the first American space flight, Alan B. Shepard, Jr., was subsequently grounded by Ménière's disease for eight years; surgery, however, enabled him to return to space as commander of the 1971 moon landing.

Why do your ears pop when you fly?

One function of the Eustachian tube, which connects the middle ear and the throat, is to keep air pressure the same on both sides of the eardrum. When your plane climbs, pressure drops rapidly, and air rushes out of the Eustachian tube; when the plane descends, pressure rises, and air rushes into the tube. You hear the rapid movement of air, whatever its direction, as a popping sound.

Sometimes, your Eustachian tube can't keep up with rapid changes in pressure, especially if the tubes are blocked because of a cold, an allergy, or a sinus infection. In that event, air cannot get through. Pressure in the middle ear no longer matches that in the outside world, and the sensitive eardrum either bulges outward or is sucked inward. What you are experiencing is a mild case of barotrauma, damage to the eardrum that leads to a sense of fullness, pain, and dulled hearing. The symptoms may persist for several hours.

Swallowing, yawning, or chewing gum will sometimes solve the problem by forcing the reluctant valve at the throat end of the Eustachian tube to open and release or admit air as needed. However, it is better to stay

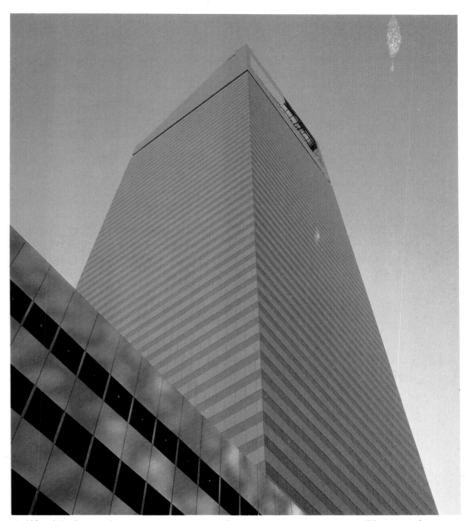

A lift ride in a skyscraper commonly causes ear popping. This unpleasant effect is a serious problem for designers of future, supertall structures.

on the ground if you have a cold or some similar ailment, or to take medication (as directed by your doctor) before taking off.

Incidentally, it is also possible to experience barotrauma when you ski very fast down a steep slope or when you dive into deep water.

Does one-sided hearing loss mean anything special?

Sudden or gradual one-sided hearing loss can occur at any age, and many times the cause is unknown. Some of the known causes include vascular problems such as clots in the small blood vessels. Infections or trauma can also result in a hearing loss. Occasionally, acoustic neuromas—tumours in the passageway

through which the acoustic nerve runs to the brain—are the cause. These growths are not cancerous, but if they are not removed while they are small, they may not only destroy hearing permanently but may also grow until they cause irreparable damage to vital parts of the brain. However, most deaths from acoustic neuromas are preventable.

The distinctive things about such tumours is that they usually occur in one ear only. So this means that you should pay particular attention to any one-sided loss of hearing. Acoustic neuromas normally give other early-warning signs. Among them are ringing in the ear, intermittent pain or loss of sensitivity on one side of the face or in one outer-ear canal, a burning sensation on the tongue, recurring headaches, and dizziness.

The "Air Conditioner" of the Body

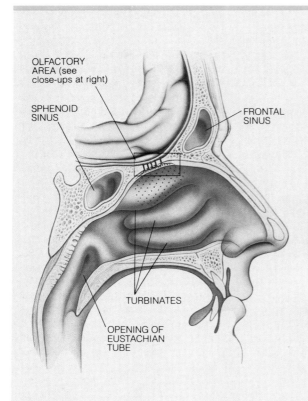

OLFACTORY AREA (see close-ups at right)

SPHENOID SINUS

FRONTAL SINUS

TURBINATES

OPENING OF EUSTACHIAN TUBE

What does your nose do for you?

Beyond its important role as the collector of olfactory information—such as whiffs of smoke that warn of impending danger or smells of cooking which whet the appetite—the nose acts as an air conditioner for the respiratory system. Every day, it treats approximately 15 cubic metres (530 cubic feet) of air, the amount enclosed in a small room. It filters out dust, traps bacteria from the air, brings air to the temperature of the blood, and also adds moisture. And then, the nose has some lesser-known functions. Among them it gives your voice resonance, adding a richness of tone that would otherwise be lacking.

OLFACTORY BULB

CILIA

Odour receptors on the roof of the nasal passages communicate through a bony plate to the olfactory bulbs, which lead directly to the brain.

OLFACTORY BULB — CRIBRIFORM PLATE

CILIA

Hairlike cilia in the smell patch relay messages upward. There are two such patches, together taking up as much space as a postage stamp.

What does the interior of the nose look like?

Architecturally, the nose has an admirable design. The external shape makes good practical sense, since its projecting form enhances its primary function, taking in and venting air. And the nose is strategically located right above the mouth, an ideal place from which its smelling apparatus can gather useful information about food to supplement the data provided by the taste buds in the tongue.

Internally, too, the nose is efficient. Two nostrils provide ready access to the nasal air passages. Lying behind them are two cavities, which are separated by a thin, cartilaginous and bony nasal septum. Other bits of thicker, tougher cartilage and bone form the supporting ridge of the nose.

The lining of the nose, beneath its layer of mucus, is packed with blood vessels that transmit body warmth to incoming air. Assisting in the heating process are three scroll-like "turbinate" bones that project horizontal-ly from the sides of the nose. They function like fins on an air conditioner, enlarging the surface over which the cool external air must pass. A number of tiny openings link the nose to the eyes (through the tear ducts), to the ears (through the Eustachian tubes), and to the nasal sinuses, those air-filled cavities that are scattered through the front and sides of the skull.

How does the nose filter air?

Filtration is a two-stage process. Just inside the entrance to the nostrils, short, stiff hairs screen out airborne pollen, fuzz, grit, and other large particles. Any debris that eludes this first line of defence then encounters even more formidable opposition. It may be summarily ejected if it irritates the nose in such a way as to trigger off a sneeze. Or it may run afoul of the mucous membrane. This membrane, which lines the respiratory passages, secretes a viscous substance called mucus that not only entraps bacteria mechanically but also contains a powerful substance, called lysozyme, which destroys the bacteria chemically.

The nose is producing fresh mucus continuously—as much as 1 litre (1.75 pints), all told, on an ordinary day. To get rid of the old, debris-laden mucus, your nose has thousands of millions of tiny hairlike cilia that poke up through the layer of mucus. With nearly a thousand sweeping strokes every minute, the cilia propel the secretions on their way towards the oesophagus and stomach. There, digestive juices destroy many of the entrapped bacteria.

In a healthy adult, mucus moves at about 6 millimetres (quarter-inch) per minute. However, the rate of clearance is considerably slower in people who smoke, drink alcohol to excess, are dehydrated, or are in general poor health. The slower the movement, of course, the less effectively the nose can defend you against bacteria and other attackers.

Why is it better to breathe through your nose than your mouth?

The mouth is primarily an entry-way for food and water; it has few defences against germs and is not much good at warming and moisturizing the air you breathe. Consequently, if you breathe through your mouth, you are denying yourself the valuable "services" that the nose can perform for you. Of course, there are times—for example, when you have a cold or an allergy blocks your nasal passages—when you have no choice about how to get vital air to your lungs. Then, you can be grateful that nature provided an alternate route, whatever its shortcomings.

Is there a right way to blow your nose?

Blowing your nose seems more like a natural activity than a skill that must be learned. But, in fact, if you apply too much pressure to your nose when you blow it, you can rupture an eardrum or possibly send harmful germs into your ears or into your sinus cavities.

An ear, nose, and throat specialist recommends the following method for safe blowing: clear one nostril at a time by pressing lightly on one side while you blow out the other; blow frequently if the nose is congested, before mucus has a chance to build up; use a soft, disposable tissue, and discard it where no one else will come in contact with it; and daub a little petroleum jelly on the nostrils if they become chapped and irritated.

Very small children have difficulty learning to blow the nose properly. Babies have particular difficulty when they are sucking from the breast or a bottle if they cannot breathe through their blocked nostrils.

You can help the child with a congested nose (and yourself, for that matter) by setting up a humidifier or vaporizer to moisten room air and speed mucus clearance. This may help during dry winter weather. But follow the instructions given for use to the letter. If they are not cleaned and sterilized regularly, humidifiers can breed, and spread, infectious micro-organisms.

Why are some drugs administered through the nose?

Because of the concentration of small blood vessels in the nose, the nasal lining absorbs chemicals at an uncommonly rapid rate. Some drugs reach the bloodstream in three to five minutes if administered through nasal sprays or nose drops; that is why such drugs as replacement hormones for patients whose pituitary gland is malfunctioning are given by this route.

Some pharmaceutical experts predict that more and more medications will eventually be given via the nose. Taking drugs by suppository can be unpleasant or inconvenient. Injections can be painful. Drugs taken orally need a long time to reach the bloodstream—and in the process of going through the digestive system, they lose much of their potency.

What is the effect of a deviated septum?

If the septum, or wall of cartilage between the nostrils, deviates from a straight line, the two air passages that it creates will be unequal in size and shape. So long as the difference is minor, you are not likely to notice it, except, perhaps, when you get a cold and the smaller of the nasal passages is consistently more congested than the other. That problem is insignificant and is best left alone. But if a deviated septum prohibits normal breathing, you may wish to undergo surgery to straighten the divider.

How does the plastic surgeon change the shape of the nose?

Plastic surgery on the nose, or rhinoplasty, has one of two purposes. Some alterations are designed to correct structural deformities that inhibit breathing: children born with a cleft palate require this sort of reconstruction. More often, however, surgery on the nose is cosmetic: it resculpts the exterior of the nose so that it more nearly satisfies the owner's sense of beauty. A hump in the ridge or a bridge that seems too wide can be corrected by removing or adding pieces of bone and cartilage.

Though rhinoplasty requires a delicate touch, it carries few medical risks. Patients usually look bruised and swollen for two weeks or more, with the nose healing to its final shape within a few months.

DID YOU KNOW...?

- **A "drinker's nose," despite rumours to the contrary,** has no known cause. However, this embarrassing condition, in which the nose becomes red, bulbous, and disfigured by enlarged veins, appears to be aggravated by hot and spicy food, hot coffee and tea, excessive cold, wind, and heat, *and* by alcohol.

- **A cauliflower ear** is the result of contusion, frostbite, or severe infection of the outer ear flap. Tiny blood vessels rupture, forming a bloody mass called a haematoma under the skin. Fibrous tissue develops, eventually turning into a dense substance, and the ear becomes deformed, taking on lumpy configurations reminiscent of a cauliflower. Nowadays, cauliflower ears can be prevented by using a needle to withdraw the collected blood before it coagulates.

- **The sense of smell is useful in the practice of medicine.** The author of an article in a respected British medical journal suggests that if doctors would only get closer to their patients, they could often smell the trouble. Certain diseases, he maintains, such as diphtheria, diabetes, and fungal infections, all produce distinctive odours; a patient who smells like whole-wheat bread may have typhoid; the smell of rotten apples goes with gangrene.

The Smell-Taste Connection

How Your Nose Detects Odours

If you want to identify a smell, inhale deeply. You will create swirls of air that will flow upward and pass over olfactory receptor sites at the top of the nasal passages. Mucous secretions in the nose have the effect of dissolving airborne molecules, and, of course, many scents are already in vapour form when you sniff them. It is only in liquid form that an odour can be smelled. When odour chemicals strike the microscopic, hairlike sensors, a chain of impulses is set off, of increasing strength, that eventually travel up the nerve fibres. Amazingly, it has been discovered that a single molecule can trigger this response. The nerve fibres enter the cranium via tiny apertures in the bony plate under the brain, and lead to two olfactory bulbs (see diagram on page 218). It is clear, from this, why medication taken through the nose acts so quickly.

A **micrograph** of olfactory membrane shows cilia fringe at bottom.

A closer view of odour-sensitive cilia shows their densely packed, undulating character.

What is smell?

Insects and animals are better than people at detecting odours. For example, the male silkworm moth can smell the female when she is more than 3 kilometres (2 miles) away. Still, human beings are not dependent on smell to find food or a mate, and most can smell as well as they need to—better than they want to, sometimes. Chances are that you can smell a skunk when just a trace of its characteristic perfume wafts by!

Smell and taste are two chemical senses; they are stimulated by chemical molecules of odour and flavour. Sight and hearing are physical senses, because they respond to physical stimuli: waves of light and sound.

The sense of smell is estimated to be about 10,000 times more sensitive than the sense of taste. The two senses are closely linked; in a way, it is correct to say that you actually smell certain flavours more than you taste them. When your nose fails, as it often does during a cold, you lose about 80 percent of your ability to detect taste. If you can't smell, apples and raw potatoes taste almost exactly alike, while chocolate ice cream tastes like not much of anything.

Where is your sense of smell located?

Each of your primary senses depends on the complex interaction of many specialized body structures. To smell something, you need nerve cells to receive stimuli from odorous substances, a pair of olfactory nerves to transmit those stimuli to the brain, and nerve cells in the temporal lobes of the brain to interpret the stimuli.

The two receptor sites, each smaller than a postage stamp, are patches of yellow-brown, mucus-covered membrane, called olfactory epithelium, in the roof of the nasal cavities. The sites are covered with millions of hairlike antennae which project through the mucus and make contact with air on its way to the throat and lungs.

Ordinarily, only a small part of the air you inhale passes the smell receptors. To get a better idea of an interesting or alarming smell—the bouquet of a fine wine, perhaps, or the odour of escaping gas—you must therefore sniff deeply. Doing so alters the normal air flow so that more air, with its odorous molecules, comes into contact with the receptors.

Perhaps you wonder why your dog is a better smeller than you are. One reason is that his smell receptors are located right along the main airflow route. In addition, his smell-receptor sites are 100 times larger than yours.

Why is it difficult to taste food when you have a cold?

People suffering from a cold frequently complain that they have lost their sense of taste. They are wrong. Laboratory tests of such people have demonstrated that their taste buds are functioning normally. What accounts, then, for the undeniable fact that they cannot taste much of anything that they eat?

Taste and smell are so closely allied that you often label as taste what is really smell. When food is in the mouth, its odours pass through the nasopharynx (the link between the nasal and oral cavities) to the receptors of smell. The olfactory system is thousands of times more sensitive to odours than the taste system is to flavours, so that when your nasal passages are blocked by a cold, it may *seem* as if you had lost the ability to taste. What you are missing, in fact, is the all-important *smell* of food.

Are there primary odours comparable to primary colours?

Scientists (and the rest of us too, for that matter) like to find order by reducing things to their fundamental elements. Experiments have shown that all colours can be derived from three basic hues: red, yellow, and blue. The scientists have also demonstrated that all flavours are made up of four basic tastes: sweet, sour, bitter, and salt. In the realm of the sense of smell, however, their efforts at clas-

Until modern times, many people believed that diseases were caused by miasmas, the malodorous vapours that rise from decaying vegetation in swamps. In fact, the word *malaria* is taken from the Italian words, *mala aria*, meaning "bad air." Though the actual cause of malaria was mosquitoes and not bad air, the atmosphere can indeed trigger off an epidemic. In periods of high temperature and humidity, swamps gave off vapours, and disease-carrying mosquitoes flourished. Other epidemics gave rise to the idea that diseases were transmitted by the breath. There was a basis for this: in addition to the type of plague that is caused by the bite of a flea, there is a virulent respiratory form. The worst bubonic plague, the Black Death of the 14th century, killed off a third of the population of Europe. Frantic and demoralized, people resorted to all manner of remedies—including stenches to drive off disease!

Leather clad from head to toe, a 17th-century German doctor attended plague victims. His protective beak held perfumes and spices.

sification have been less successful.

At the one extreme, some scientists say that there are seven primary odours: floral, peppermint, ethereal (like ether), musky, camphoraceous (like mothballs), pungent, and putrid. At the other extreme, there are scientists who say that *every* odour can be called a primary one. Other experts suggest that there may be as many as 50 or more primary sensations of smell. But, according to one scientist in the field of smell: "Olfaction researchers have yet to demonstrate that smells in different 'categories' are functionally distinct."

How many smells can you smell?

Sensory acuity varies widely from person to person, especially in the sphere of smell. It has been estimated that the average nose can distinguish approximately 4,000 different odours, while an especially sensitive one can recognize as many as 10,000.

Of course, there is more than one way of judging olfactory sensitivity. If you are blindfolded and presented with two smells, it may not be difficult to tell whether they are different from each other or the same. But to identify substances just from their smell alone is much harder.

Until recently, experimental psychologists thought that most people could not recognize more than about 16 substances by scent. Further research has shown that that figure is too low, and that the average person could name more odours if he or she had the right words to describe them.

In studies at Yale University, subjects often seemed to recognize an odour as familiar, but the name of the substance just would not come to mind. Presented with 80 common substances, including sardines, liverwurst, shoe polish, and crayons, subjects could at first correctly identify only 36 of them by smell. After practice sessions in which the odours were specifically labelled, scores improved: the subjects were able to identify an average of 75 items.

Four Sets of Sinus Cavities

Where are the sinuses, and what do they do?

Your eight nasal sinuses are simply holes in your head: air spaces in certain bones of the skull that decrease the weight of those bones and add resonance to the voice. A beautiful singing voice may owe more to the sinuses than to the vocal cords.

One pair of sinuses is located just above the eyebrows. Another set lies beside the bridge of the nose. A third pair is set deep in the head behind the nose. The last, and largest, pair is in the cheekbones. Each sinus is lined with mucous membrane continuous with that of the nose and throat, and when the nose fails to produce enough mucus, the sinuses make up the difference.

Normally, the mucus from the sinuses drains into the nasal cavity through tiny canals. But if the mucous membrane in the sinuses swells and impedes drainage, pressure can build up, squeeze sensitive nerves, and cause severe headaches. Even more troublesome are secondary bacterial infections that sometimes lodge in one or more sinuses, a condition called sinusitis.

How do you recognize sinusitis, and what is the treatment?

An acute sinus infection is almost always preceded by a common cold, the flu, a bout of allergic rhinitis (hay fever), or development of a growth that blocks drainage. The symptoms are similar to those of a cold, only more severe. A general feeling of malaise is common. There may also be a fever, a sore throat, a cough, some tenderness about the face and eyes, and an unusually thick and greenish-yellow nasal discharge, consisting of mucous membrane cells that have been destroyed in the course of fighting infection.

A mild condition may clear up by itself, though it can persist for weeks or months. More severe cases virtually demand attention, because discomfort is great and there is a risk that the infection will spread. For those with a chronic sinus condition, the best approach is to deal with its fundamental causes. If allergies are suspected, treatment can be prescribed. Nose drops can improve drainage; vaporizers may decrease discomfort; antibiotics can clear up an infection. Sinus irrigation is sometimes prescribed as well.

What is allergic rhinitis?

There are only two things wrong with the term *hay fever*: the ailment referred to is not caused by hay, nor is it accompanied by a fever. The correct medical term is allergic rhinitis, which covers a host of allergic reactions that produce symptoms similar to a cold.

Seasonal allergic rhinitis is triggered mainly by pollens from trees, grasses, or plants. Perennial allergic rhinitis is often caused by house dust or particles of animal hair or feathers.

Any airborne allergen—that is, a substance to which the victim is hypersensitive—causes the nasal membrane to release a chemical called histamine. The substance irritates and inflames the nose, sinuses, and eyes, causing them to swell, itch, and become runny.

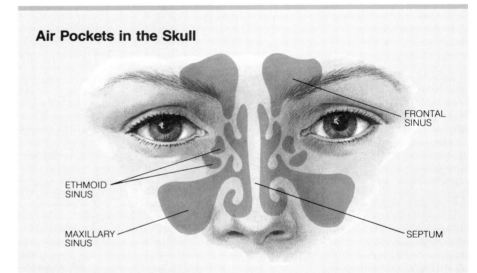

Air Pockets in the Skull

FRONTAL SINUS

ETHMOID SINUS

MAXILLARY SINUS

SEPTUM

FRONTAL SINUS

SPHENOID SINUS

ETHMOID SINUS

MAXILLARY SINUS

The size and shape of sinuses vary from one person to another, but these illustrations show their usual formation. The ethmoid bone contains many small sinuses. The sphenoid sinuses are in the centre of the head. The maxillary, the largest sinuses, and the frontal sinuses account for most sinus trouble in adults. The nasal passage is linked to these three sets of sinuses. When an infection spreads to the sinuses, and their drainage is blocked, they fill with pus and mucus, causing pressure and pain. Sinus drainage can also influence sleep. When you sleep on your side, the nostril on that side becomes congested. The nose signals this fact to the brain, which tells you to change position.

This miserable though not life-threatening affliction is the result of an inherited defect in the immune system. It frequently occurs in several members of the same family, though not necessarily in response to the same allergen. Often stress plays a role in allergy reactions.

Is there any cure for hay fever?

The best way to avoid hay fever, or allergic rhinitis, is to stay away from the allergen that causes it—often easier said than done. The first requisite is a battery of skin tests to find out what substances to avoid. The procedure calls for scratching the skin and then applying common allergens one by one. A subsequent redness of the skin signifies hypersensitivity to a substance. A newer method is a blood test that also can detect what a person is allergic to.

If the problem is pollen from a flowering tree or plant, the victim can perhaps take a holiday in a pollen-free spot during the worst days. If that is impossible, the sufferer can at least take comfort from the fact that the season is short: after a few weeks, the condition clears up until the same time next year. But if the problem is animal hair, house dust, or some other substance in the air all the year round, the solution is not so easy. Antihistamines can counteract the irritating histamines the body produces, but they cause drowsiness and can produce adverse effects in those with high blood pressure, glaucoma, or an enlarged prostate.

Another possible solution is immunotherapy, formerly called desensitization, in which the patient gets a series of injections of the known allergen. The dosage is gradually stepped up until the body is able to tolerate larger and larger quantities of the substance. Although the procedure may be effective against pollen and house dust, the injections themselves carry a risk of sudden collapse or even death. Because of the dangers, most British doctors have now given up the attempt to prevent hay fever by means of immunotherapy.

Scents: The Memory Lingers On

It has long been known that insects influence each other's behaviour by generating odorous substances called pheromones, which signal sexual interest, danger, and such. Some researchers believe that pheromones may play a role in sexual attraction between people, but so far, no human pheromone has been identified. Yet odours are powerful indeed. Certain cooking aromas can call up bygone days, a whiff of perfume the presence of a loved one. And, of course, some smells have a negative association, and produce revulsion. Smell preferences are not universal—they are very much influenced by culture and personal experience.

The ritual use of incense, as here at a shrine in Tokyo, is traditional in many cultures. Incense has been an important trading commodity since antiquity; the gifts of the Magi included two: frankincense and myrrh.

The strong scent of hyssop (a member of the mint family) acts as natural smelling salts. Herbalists valued pungent plants and used this one for many different ills.

What are adenoids?

Masses of lymphoid tissue located at the junction of the nose and the throat are called adenoids. They are glands which function much as your lymph nodes and tonsils do, filtering out and destroying bacteria, particularly those associated with respiratory tract infections.

Adenoids typically keep on developing until a child is five or six years old, and from about the age of nine or ten until puberty, they shrink down to nothing. Generally speaking, they go unnoticed unless, in the process of fighting germs, they become infected, inflamed, painful, and swollen, sometimes interfering with the sense of smell. Once in a while, adenoids become permanently enlarged, threatening the free passage of air from nose to throat or blocking the Eustachian tubes.

Treatment for occasional adenoiditis is usually a course of antibiotic therapy. The surgical removal of infected adenoids was once frequently coupled with removal of the nearby tonsils. These days, however, most doctors advise leaving both tonsils and adenoids intact except when other therapies for adenoiditis and tonsillitis fail repeatedly. One reason is that tonsils and adenoids generally help to protect against bacteria. Also, the adenoids usually tend to shrink naturally before adolescence.

The Switch From Breathing to Swallowing

How is the throat constructed?

Technically called the pharynx, the throat is a muscular tube, lined with mucous membrane, which is approximately 125 millimetres (5 inches) long and extends from behind the nose to the entrance to the oesophagus. It forms part of two different systems, the respiratory and the digestive. Both air and food travel through it, and it is a wonder that this mixed traffic flows so smoothly.

The throat divides naturally into three regions. The uppermost one is the nasopharynx, the part of the tube that begins at the nasal cavity. Here, fresh air and secretions from the nose and sinuses begin their downward journey. The middle region is the oropharynx, the widest segment of the throat. It is here, just below the soft palate in the mouth, that the air passage merges with the food transport system. In the lowest portion of the throat, the laryngopharynx, the respiratory and the digestive passages diverge. Since they cross in doing so, one might expect solid or liquid foods to take the wrong route more often than they do. The air passage, which begins at the back of the throat, takes a curved path to the front. There it becomes the larynx, the site of the vocal cords. The larynx opens into the trachea, or windpipe, which leads to the lungs. Running parallel to the air channel and just behind it is the food transport tube, the oesophagus, which terminates in the stomach.

What keeps food from entering your windpipe?

Your throat contains both an air passage—the windpipe—and a food passage—the oesophagus. If both of these were open when you swallowed, air could get into the stomach and food into the lungs. Fortunately, the windpipe is closed tight during the act of swallowing.

Part of the safety mechanism that seals it off is called the epiglottis, and it comes into play every time you swallow. At the crucial moment, the epiglottis, a little valvelike cartilage, acts as a lid in concert with the larynx. The larynx draws upwards and forwards to close off the windpipe. The combined movement keeps liquids and solid foods out. Then, at the end of each swallow, the epiglottis again moves up, the larynx returns to its original position, and the vital flow of air to the larynx and windpipe resumes.

Once in a while, food may "go down the wrong way," and something solid gets into the air passage and blocks it. Ordinarily, the resulting fit of coughing dislodges the foreign body and re-opens the windpipe. But if coughing doesn't work, only prompt, skilled first aid can prevent the victim from choking to death. (See the emergency action to be taken on page 125.)

Why does a tongue depressor make you gag?

Retching may be most unpleasant, but it can also save your life by preventing you from accidentally swallowing something that would choke you. You cannot help it when you retch; the gag reflex, as it is properly called, is an automatic response. It is triggered off when a foreign body strikes certain nerve endings embedded in the archway that forms the border between the mouth and the middle region of the throat.

The doctor's wooden probe is just such a foreign body. When it touches those nerves, it sets off the reflex, which usually thrusts material about to be swallowed back into the front of the mouth where it can be spat out. Of course, the reflex is unneeded during the doctor's examination of the throat. But its occurrence at least lets you know that this vital response is working right.

What does the little flap at the back of the throat do?

The uvula is that fleshy bit of muscle, connective tissue, and mucous membrane that hangs down from the free edge of the soft palate. It is the part that normally moves upward when you say "Ah." (If instead it moves to one side, the doctor knows that something is wrong.)

It is true that the uvula (Latin for "little grape") flips upwards and helps close off the nasal passages when you swallow. But that function is presumably not too important, since people without a uvula do not complain of food coming out of their noses! Car-

---

THE STORY BEHIND THE WORDS...

Nostril and thrill share a common root, the Middle English word *thrillen,* which means "to pierce." When you are thrilled, you are pierced with emotion. Your nose is also pierced, but with two holes: the *nosethirls,* as the word *nostrils* was originally spelled. Nose is derived from a Sanskrit word, *nasa,* meaning "dual."

If you follow your nose, you are taking a route that lies straight ahead, and is obvious (as plain as the nose on your face). Or else you are going ahead without a plan, following wherever instinct leads.

To hum and haw can be traced to "humys and hays," a phrase that first appeared in print in 1469, and to "hem and hawke," which appeared in 1580. Regardless of spelling or pronunciation, the words suggest the sounds you make when you clear your throat before speaking. Humming and hawing lets you delay before replying. When you hum and haw, you are uncertain, undecided; you are equivocating, and perhaps expressing a certain disapproval.

Keeping your ear to the ground means to be alert to current trends. The phrase harks back to early 20th-century politicians and draws on the frontier lore of pioneers and American Indians who listened for thundering hoofbeats approaching.

toon animators like to depict the uvula as vibrating during singing and shouting, but in fact, the structure has nothing to do with the voice.

What happens when you get a "lump in the throat"?

One thing is certain: the unpleasant sensation of a lump in the throat is hardly ever caused by a tumour or by any other physical obstruction. In almost every case, it is a symptom of nervous anxiety.

The feeling is traceable to a disturbance in the ninth cranial nerve and in the muscles controlling the oesophagus, which sometimes goes into spasm when a person becomes emotionally upset. *Globus hystericus*, as the condition is known medically, is most often a transient symptom associated with a particularly stressful event; if this is the case, time will cure it. However, in rare situations, the lump may persist, and the person should see a doctor. Occasionally, a postnasal drip or excessive stomach acid can cause this symptom.

What does it mean to be tongue-tied?

Although the expression "tongue-tied" is usually only considered to be a figure of speech, it may, in fact, be a reality. A baby's tongue is far less mobile than the tongue of an adult. This is because the fold of mucous membrane called the frenum, or frenulum, which anchors the underside of the tongue to the bottom of the mouth, initially extends nearly the full length of the tongue, so that only the tip is left free.

During the baby's first year, the tip of the tongue grows considerably, and the frenum "ties" a progressively smaller proportion of the tongue. In rare instances, however, the frenum remains restrictive, and the child has difficulty eating and speaking. The doctor will then recommend a simple surgical procedure to trim back the fold enough so that the tongue can move normally.

The Many Functions of the Pharynx

When, at dinner, your food goes down the wrong pipe, four activities are disrupted: inhaling, exhaling, eating, and speaking. A coughing fit demonstrates (however unpleasantly) the importance of the throat, or pharynx, as a passageway. When you inhale, air travels from the nose through the pharynx and into the larynx and then the trachea, at the front of the neck; when you exhale, the order is reversed. When you eat, food travels through the pharynx to the oesophagus.

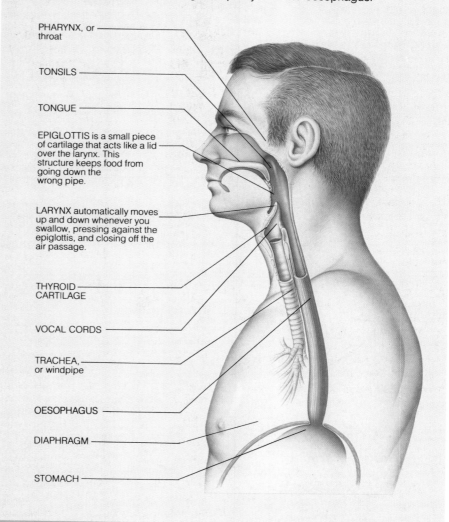

PHARYNX, or throat

TONSILS

TONGUE

EPIGLOTTIS is a small piece of cartilage that acts like a lid over the larynx. This structure keeps food from going down the wrong pipe.

LARYNX automatically moves up and down whenever you swallow, pressing against the epiglottis, and closing off the air passage.

THYROID CARTILAGE

VOCAL CORDS

TRACHEA, or windpipe

OESOPHAGUS

DIAPHRAGM

STOMACH

Can choking be prevented?

Eating and heavy drinking do not go together; large amounts of alcohol can paralyze the swallowing mechanism, causing food to go down the windpipe instead of the oesophagus. However, the majority of episodes of choking come about simply because food just happens to "go down the wrong way," as people so often put it. Talking or laughing with food in your mouth, and taking large bites of food should be avoided.

A few victims of choking may have a long-standing swallowing difficulty without even knowing it until they find themselves gasping for survival. The problem may come from a malformation of the throat or from some other abnormality that was present at birth. Or perhaps the condition may have developed in later life because of a tumour or a muscular or neurological disorder. If you have frequent difficulty in swallowing, ask your doctor, as a preventive measure, to examine your throat carefully.

225

Miseries of the Nose and Throat

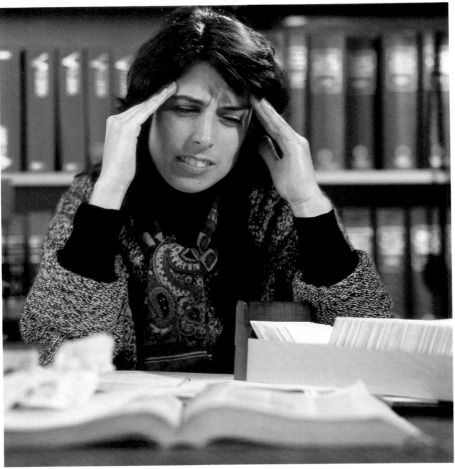

Headaches have many causes, including colds that clog the sinuses. Some people get a headache when they eat ice cream or other cold foods because the nerves in the area where tongue and throat meet may be hypersensitive. Pain is felt not at the site, but is "referred" to the forehead and ears.

What is postnasal drip?

Just as the term suggests: postnasal drip is drainage of secretions from the nasal passages into the throat. It is a normal phenomenon that occurs in all of us and usually passes unnoticed. But sometimes the drip becomes—or seems to become—faster and more copious than the system can comfortably dispose of. You may then need to cough or clear your throat repeatedly.

An annoying postnasal drip is often a symptom of sinusitis, chronic upper-respiratory infection, allergy, or overactive mucus glands in the nose and throat. In such cases, treatment requires identifying and correcting the underlying condition. But in other cases, the problem is simply an overawareness of secretions that are in fact not excessive. The solution in this situation may be to seek reassurance from your doctor that nothing is seriously wrong. Relieved of worry about the condition, you may then learn to ignore it.

Are nasal decongestants ever dangerous?

Most nasal decongestants contain potent ingredients drawn from a class of drugs called sympathomimetics. They reduce congestion by constricting the small blood vessels in the mucus-secreting area of the nose. When the swelling diminishes, the nasal passages open up, breathing becomes easier, drainage improves, and pain diminishes.

Occasionally, the relief is short-lived. The sufferer therefore applies a second and perhaps a third dose in quick succession—with possible adverse effects. The most typical reaction is the rebound syndrome, or *rhinitis medicamentosa*, which means rhinitis caused by medication. Used to excess, decongestants irritate the nasal membranes, and the irritation causes renewed congestion. Damage to the lining of the nose is sometimes permanent. Nasal decongestants are especially dangerous for persons with high blood pressure, glaucoma, diabetes, hyperthyroidism, heart disease, and a variety of emotional and behavioural disturbances.

What are nasal polyps, and are they harmful?

When the nose becomes irritated frequently because of recurring infections or nasal allergies, soft, moist outgrowths called nasal polyps occasionally develop from the mucous membrane and then protrude into the nasal cavity. These polyps are basically harmless, except that large ones can obstruct breathing, press on sensitive nerve endings and cause pain or headache, or close off circulation of odours to the olfactory membrane, so that the sense of smell is impaired. Nasal polyps can be removed only by surgery.

Why do people get nosebleeds?

The most common cause of a nosebleed is nasal trauma. This causes a direct breakage of a blood vessel. Other common causes include excessive dryness making the vessels fragile. This occurs especially in cold weather when homes are heated. Nose picking and excessive nose blowing can also bring on bleeding. Elevated blood pressure either due to stress or medical reasons rarely causes nosebleeds.

To stop a nosebleed, pinch the nostrils up to the bony portion of the nose, and sit upright over a catch basin or bowl. Hold this position for ten minutes, which should be long enough for a blood clot to form. Then let go and see if the bleeding has stopped. If not, repeat the procedure. Refrain from blowing your nose for a day or two.

Don't try to staunch a nosebleed by tilting the head back. This only drains the blood into the back of the throat and leads the victim to swallow it. And don't waste time pressing a cold key to the back of the neck or against any other part of the anatomy. The effect will be nil.

If steady bleeding from the nose continues for more than 20 minutes, if it accompanies haemorrhaging from the ears or from some other part of the body, or if you have frequent nosebleeds, you should seek medical attention. Your doctor will probably insert a gauze pack in the bleeding nostril or cauterize the ruptured vessels to seal it. An underlying cause may have to be sought; it could be a circulatory or blood disorder, or even a fracture of the skull.

Is a sore throat a disease?

Inflammation of the throat seldom occurs as an isolated condition; it is almost always a symptom, not a disorder in itself. The underlying disease is rarely serious. Research has shown that with or without treatment, most sore throats get better within about a week.

The usual cause of a sore throat is the common cold. If the sore throat and other symptoms include fever, headache, general aches and pains, and a dry cough, the cause is likely to be influenza. A sore throat associated with a mucus-laden cough, moderate fever, and difficulty in breathing suggests bronchitis. In each case, the throat irritation is probably due not to bacteria or to a virus but to mucus dripping down the throat. Allergies, hypersensitivity to drugs, smoking, prolonged mouth breathing, overuse of the voice, too much spicy food, and air pollutants are some other possible causes of minor sore throats.

To alleviate ordinary soreness, try sucking a throat lozenge or a boiled sweet. You might also gargle with warm salt water, take aspirin or its equivalent, and add humidity to room air if it is dry. It is also a good idea to cut down on the use of your voice until your throat improves.

What is streptococcal sore throat, and is it dangerous?

One cause of a sore throat, the *Streptococcus* bacterium, is always around. Usually, the immune system holds it in check, but when a cold or other illness weakens natural defences, it may gain the upper hand. The symptoms include a *very* sore throat. You may also be able to see white or yellow spots at the back of the throat, and you are likely to suffer from fever, headache, abdominal pain, and nausea. But only a throat culture can positively identify a strep infection.

In the past strep throat sometimes led to rheumatic fever or glomerulonephritis, a disease of the kidneys. Fortunately such complications are now extremely rare.

Does everyone have an Adam's apple?

Whether you are a man or a woman, you have an Adam's apple, or, to use the technical term, a thyroid cartilage. The Adam's apple is the largest of nine cartilages in the larynx. It is more noticeable in men for two reasons. First, the structure is bigger in men because their larynxes are generally larger, providing space for their larger vocal cords. Second, men usually have less fat in their necks to conceal the Adam's apple from view. The popular name for the thyroid cartilage recalls the biblical story in which Adam and Eve are said to have eaten the forbidden fruit. The visible swelling of the man's larynx was supposedly a mark of shame, the stolen bite remaining forever stuck in the throats of Adam's descendants as a reminder of his transgression.

The Adam's apple is a prominence on the largest cartilage in the larynx

Eve reaches for the apple that caught in Adam's throat. Titian, c. 1570.

The Wonderful Human Voice

How Vocal Cords Move to Produce Speech

These pictures show vocal cords at work. The slitlike opening between the cords is the glottis. Its size and shape change according to your activity. When you breathe, the cords draw apart, allowing passage of air to and from the lungs. If you speak or sing, the folds draw closer together. Speech is produced when you breathe out. The airflow through the glottis causes the vocal cords to vibrate, producing waves of sound. The tautness of the cords determines the frequency of the vibrations and the pitch of the sound.

Following from top to bottom, left to right, you can see vocal cords change in a one-second progression. In pictures 1 to 6, speech stops, cords gradually open. In pictures 7 to 9, speech resumes.

What is speech, and how do we learn to communicate with it?

Over the long reaches of time, many languages have evolved along independent but parallel lines. The organs of speech can produce scores of different sounds, or phonemes, but each language uses only some of them. The flavour of a language depends largely on which sounds it uses; some languages have a musical, flowing quality; others are characterized by guttural sounds; still others are notably nasal or labial.

In a sense, people begin learning to speak at birth. Newborns hear the phonemes and words of the people around them and begin to move their bodies in a rhythmic relationship to them. They then form mental associations between certain frequently heard sounds and certain familiar objects and events. Initially, babies make random cooing and babbling sounds, but very young children soon begin trying to imitate the specific sounds they most often hear. As they come to have a measure of control over the muscles of sound formation, they first master the easier sounds, the vowels. Then they learn a succession of consonants, which are harder sounds and require greater control over the vocal apparatus. Gradually, the sounds youngsters make come more and more to resemble language and to communicate meaning. When adults respond with interest and encouragement, children are motivated to speak more, thus improving their language skills even further.

How do we speak?

Human speech requires both raw sounds and finished consonants and vowels assembled into words. The raw sounds are produced in the voice box, or larynx, by means of air expelled from the lungs and with the help of a pair of elastic vocal cords. The sounds are shaped into speech in the mouth by the teeth, tongue, palate, and facial muscles.

The voice box, approximately 40 millimetres (1.5 inches) long, is part of the upper respiratory tract. It is shaped like a triangular box and is made up of nine cartilages, of which the most prominent is the Adam's apple, or thyroid cartilage. They are linked by muscles and ligaments.

Lying on either side of the glottis (the opening of the larynx behind and below the tongue) are the two folds of tissue that constitute the vocal cords. The cords are attached to the thyroid cartilage at the front and to a pair of smaller cartilages at the back. When you sing or talk, air passes against the vocal cords and causes them to vibrate. Changing the frequency of the vibrations (done by moving the cords with a set of muscles that move the small cartilages) changes the tone of the sounds you make.

Most people talk or sing without giving much thought to how they produce a particular sound. But professional singers, and some actors, too, are well aware that contracting and relaxing the muscles in certain ways will produce certain vocal effects. For example, shortening and tensing the vocal cords will produce high-pitched sounds, while lengthening and loosening the cords will produce low-pitched sounds. Furthermore, the faster and more forcefully air is expelled past the vocal cords, the louder the sound produced.

Why does the voice change in adolescence?

If you happen to pass a crowded schoolyard at break time, or a group of youngsters at play anywhere, you are bound to be struck by the shrill voices of the very young. Their high-pitched shouts and laughter are due less to youthful exuberance than to anatomy. Very short vocal cords produce high-pitched sounds—and little children have very short vocal cords. As adolescence approaches, the larynx in both sexes begins to enlarge, the vocal cords become longer, thicker, and farther apart, and the sounds produced become lower in pitch. The changes are much more pronounced in boys than in girls; their voices deepen markedly, and eventually boys lose the ability to produce high notes. For a while, however, a boy's voice may switch suddenly from low to high and back again— much to the boy's embarrassment. The reason is that it takes him a while to get used to his new, larger voice box; he must learn to adjust the way he uses the muscles that control the tension of his vocal cords.

What causes laryngitis?

When you have laryngitis, you know it, because your voice is hoarse, or whispery—or nonexistent. Ordinarily, you also know *why* you have it. You are suffering from a cold. Or you're smoking too much. Or you talked too much at the party last night, or cheered too enthusiastically at the football game.

There are also other causes of laryngitis, or inflammation of the larynx. If laryngitis is chronic, it may be due to air pollution, to irritation from alcohol, or to tuberculosis. It may also be caused by a growth (benign or cancerous) on the vocal cords. For instance, chronic overuse of the voice can lead to the growth of calluses or "singers' nodes," which are benign.

Acute laryngitis usually gets better if you stop talking for a while. When it persists beyond three weeks or is accompanied by a cough and bloody or pus-laden phlegm, you should have your throat examined by a doctor.

In the case of calluses, prolonged rest and an end to abuse of the voice, should restore the vocal cords to normal. Tumours can sometimes be destroyed by radiation therapy, but if they are large, they may have to be removed by surgery. In the operation known as a laryngectomy, the voice box and vocal cords are excised. The windpipe is then attached to the neck, where an opening is made to permit breathing.

How do you whisper?

When you whisper, you are speaking without using your vocal cords. Whispering makes use of the gentle hiss of exhaled breath, which is shaped, as in normal speech, by the teeth, tongue, lips, and palate. If you choose to whisper, you hold the vocal cords rigid to prevent them from vibrating. If you lose your voice involuntarily from laryngitis, the effect is the same: the cords *cannot* vibrate normally because they are inflamed.

What do opera singers and babies have in common?

A "column of air" is needed for the production of operatic music. A professionally trained singer draws a full breath by expanding the lower ribs and dropping the diaphragm (the muscular wall that separates the chest from the abdomen). As this air is released in song, it seems abundant, powerful, and effortless. On the other hand, singing that comes from the throat, with only shallow breathing to back it up, lacks resonance, control, and may produce hoarseness. When they cry, babies use their diaphragms like opera singers. This natural tendency to use the diaphragm is lost in childhood and must be relearned when an individual takes up professional singing.

Really serious crying is always preceded by a moment of silence while the baby draws in a lungful of air. Breathing from the diaphragm gives staying power.

Overcoming Speech and Hearing Problems

What causes speech disorders?

Among speech defects, the lisp is unique: it is usually considered to be charming, at least when it appears in the very young. In fact, lisping is quite common in small children, and it may unintentionally be encouraged by adults who are amused by it, and repeat the child's lisped words. By school age, it is likely to be a disadvantage, a cause for teasing by other children. However, in 90 percent of all cases, lisping disappears by the time the child reaches the age of eight.

To lisp is to substitute one sound for another, usually *th* for *s* or *z*. The main cause of lisping is poor control of tongue and lip muscles. After the age of eight, continued lisping requires the attention of a speech expert. The reason is that lisping may become a kind of personal norm, no longer heard by the speaker and consequently very hard to correct.

Poor muscle control also results in cluttering, which is characterized by rapid speech in which letters, syllables, and even whole words and phrases are garbled in a habitual rush to voice them. Like chronic lisping, cluttering resists retraining because it entails many long-standing physical and mental habits.

Why do some people stutter?

Most people who stutter (or stammer: the words are interchangeable) involuntarily repeat the first sounds of syllables of words. Stutterers may also suffer from muscle spasms in the throat and mouth that make it very difficult for them to get words out at all. In their efforts to overcome their block, stutterers often grimace or engage in other obvious struggles.

Experts do not agree on the causes of stuttering. Some believe that stutterers have simply picked up bad habits of speech. Other experts have tried to find a physical basis. And there are some who view stuttering as a neurotic response to conflict and stress.

Treatment for stuttering ranges from psychotherapy to drugs. Results are mixed. But almost every method has helped some stutterers to improve their speech or even to conquer their difficulty entirely.

Can anything be done for deaf-mutes?

Children who are deaf at birth or who become so soon afterwards do not learn to speak, at least not in the usual way. Their organs of speech and language formation are intact, as are the neurological pathways. But children normally learn to speak by imitating others, and deaf children cannot hear others' speech.

Long ago, deaf-mutes were generally condemned to a life of isolation. In the 17th century, a sign language

---

How a Ventriloquist Makes Dummies and Puppets Speak

The word *ventriloquist* comes from the Latin word *venter*, meaning "belly," and *loqui*, meaning "to speak," but the sound really comes from manipulation of the tongue. The speaker retracts the tongue, moving only its tip. This elevates and constricts the larynx, narrows the glottis, and puts pressure on the vocal cords. This, in turn, causes a muffling and diffusion of sound, making it seem to come from another source. As the ventriloquist speaks, the breath is released slowly through a slightly open and nearly immobile mouth. The performer distracts the audience by wiggling the dummy or hand puppet, and moving its mouth to synchronize with the sounds. Ventriloquism goes back to ancient Eygpt, when it was practised by high priests who sent forth haunting voices from stones and statues. Nowadays, ventriloquism is just for fun.

Keith Harris's green baby duck Orville seems to have a personality all of his own.

Peter Brough and his schoolboy dummy Archie Andrews are chiefly remembered for the radio program of the 1950s *Educating Archie*. The listeners, of course, unlike the studio audience, could see neither dummy nor ventriloquist.

Voiceprints: A Picture of Speech

Phonemes, the smallest units of speech, show up on a spectrograph in distinctive patterns. These printouts are useful to scientists in a wide variety of studies: analysing speech defects, recording regional accents, discovering how babies acquire language, designing equipment used in communications. The sounds of speech are influenced by many things, including your vocal cords, the shape of your throat, mouth, and nasal passages, if you have a cold or sore throat, and whether or not you are under stress. Voiceprints reveal not just variation in the rhythm of speech but in pronunciation as well.

Note the difference in this voiceprint between the two "l" sounds in "little" and between the "comp" in "compact" and "computer."

was developed. Today, with specialized training, many deaf-mutes can learn oral speech. First they become familiar with speech vibrations by putting their fingers on the teacher's larynx while the instructor is speaking. Then they must try to reproduce these vibrations. They also watch the teacher's mouth and lips and, with the help of a mirror, try to make precisely the same movements. To a greater or lesser degree, they succeed. Their voices usually sound rather monotonous, and their pronunciation is not conventional, but their speech is generally comprehensible.

How do you know if an infant can't hear?

If a baby seems exceptionally "good"—that is, very quiet most of the time—perhaps it can't hear the sounds that would make most babies babble happily or cry in protest. An infant who fails to act startled if you clap your hands behind it may also suffer from a hearing impairment.

Of course, infants cannot be instructed to raise a hand if they hear a test sound. Nevertheless, specialists have devised some reasonably accurate hearing tests for the very young, based on the assumption that an unexpected sound will capture a baby's attention and make it respond in some obvious way.

In one test, the examiner notices whether or not a baby turns its head in the direction of the sound. In case the sound itself might not be interesting enough to make the baby respond, an appealing toy—a drumming bear, perhaps—is displayed as a reward for turning the head. In another test, sound sensors in a crib mattress pick up a baby's every movement. Once a movement pattern is established, a series of beeps are emitted. If the baby's movement pattern remains unchanged following the introduction of sound, it is probably deaf. Yet another test uses electrodes attached to a baby's head to record "evoked potentials," which are special brain waves emitted only if the baby hears a test sound.

If you lose your larynx, do you lose the ability to speak?

The removal of the larynx does not mean permanent loss of the ability to talk, but it does require learning a new way of speaking. Laryngectomy patients (those whose larynx has been removed) can learn oesophageal speech, in which air is swallowed and then expelled to produce speech, or they can be trained by a speech rehabilitation specialist. More recently, a special valve, called a voice prosthesis, has been developed which, when surgically inserted, allows speech in many patients who had their voice box removed.

Chapter 10

THE DIGESTIVE SYSTEM

What's wonderful about digestion is the way the system (a compact, self-renewing conveyor belt) produces body tissues and energy out of a dazzling diversity of materials—from rice to broccoli.

The Food Journey	234
How You Taste Your Food	236
Care of Teeth and Gums	238
Filling Your Stomach	240
What the Stomach Really Does	242
The Paradox of Salt	243
The Liver: A Chemical Factory	244
The Gallbladder and the Pancreas	246
Where Absorption Takes Place	248
The End of the Journey	250
Fuelling the Body	252
Pluses and Minuses of Food	254
Eating: Too Much, Too Little	256

What makes you hungry?

You don't need a stomach to feel hungry; people whose stomachs have been entirely removed continue to experience a periodic craving for food. When the body's nutritional stores are depleted, the brain (which constantly monitors the amount of glucose, amino acids, fats, and other substances in the blood) sends out signals to let you know it is time to eat. The first sign of hunger may be slight restlessness, then perhaps irritability or a feeling of tension, and finally a gnawing feeling in the stomach—plain hunger pangs.

Hunger is affected by the temperature. Extreme heat, which decreases the quantity of fuel needed to keep the body going, discourages hunger; cold, on the other hand, stimulates it, because the body needs more fuel to offset heat loss in a cold environment.

Generally, the body registers hunger when there's a physical need for food, but not always. When people are sick, and food might do them good, they often lose all interest in it. Conversely, people with no need for food sometimes quieten their nervousness by eating, or they may feel hungry simply from habit. Most people are conditioned to eat at certain times of day, and their bodies produce the appropriate feelings on schedule.

Why do you feel thirsty?

Some activities or conditions make you conscious of a dry mouth: physical exertion that causes sweating, prolonged talking, fever, certain medicines, uncontrolled diabetes, or eating sweet or salty foods. But it does not take something special to create thirst; you are losing water all the time through the skin, the lungs, and the functioning of the kidneys.

A healthy person automatically adjusts liquid intake to match output fairly closely, and when necessary, drinks water to supplement the water in foods and beverages. The brain receives the signal that you're thirsty from your blood. Insufficient water in the body reduces the volume of blood, and, therefore, the blood pressure. As water is lost, other substances in the blood vessels become more concentrated, and the parts of the brain that are sensitive to such changes make you experience thirst.

Why does your stomach rumble?

Borborygmi: this word refers to the rumbling, gurgling sounds that come from your insides at the most embarrassing moments. Usually you assume that the stomach is growling, and that it does so because you are hungry. But much of the time the growl is gas moving in the digestive system, frequently in the intestine rather than the stomach.

Does it matter when you eat your biggest meal of the day?

To lose weight, make breakfast your main meal, and eat your lightest meal at night. There is some evidence to back this up, but it is far from conclusive. Similarly, many argue that you will lose more weight eating five small meals a day rather than three large ones. This idea draws some support from research indicating that when you eat a lot at one time, your pancreas secretes extra insulin, a hormone that causes the body to store calories as fat. Much remains to be learned about the relationship of diet and weight, and this is one of many such unanswered questions.

Can mouthwash cure bad breath?

Mouthwash does not *remove* the causes of bad breath—it can only mask the odour. The sources of bad breath (halitosis) include decaying teeth, trapped particles of stale food, infections of the nasal cavity or lungs, and uncontrolled diabetes. More often, however, the cause of bad breath is something much simpler: eating such foods as garlic or onions. Residual oils from those foods pass into the bloodstream and through the lungs; the odour is expelled with each breath.

Does brushing your teeth affect your sense of taste?

If your orange juice tastes somewhat sour or bitter in the morning, it may be because you brush your teeth before breakfast. This odd effect is due to a detergent called sodium lauryl sulphate (SLS) which is contained in some toothpastes. Residues of SLS in the mouth cause the acid in orange juice to taste sour and bitter, and make the sugar in it seem less sweet than usual.

SLS is not the only taste modifier known to scientists. Another sweetness inhibitor is the plant *Gymnema sylvestra*, which grows in India and West Africa. In 1847, a British man living in India reported that when he chewed the leaves of this plant, he could no longer taste the sugar in his

Because honey is made by bees and has a long history as a sweetener (it is mentioned in the Bible), many believe it to be more beneficial than other sugars. In fact, it is much the same—but with a flower flavour.

tea. Almost a century later, an American explorer in West Africa reported on a sweetness inducer already familiar to the natives, who called it the miracle fruit. After eating that fruit, the berry of the *Synsepalum dulcificum* bush, even lemons and rhubarb taste delightfully sweet.

Do you need extra protein when you engage in sports?

Eating steak or taking protein supplements is not the best way to provide energy or guarantee endurance, nor will it give an athlete a winning edge in a sporting event. Strenuous activity does not require unusual amounts of protein. In fact, protein metabolism creates large amounts of waste that must be excreted in the urine. Eating too much protein may cause an excessive loss of fluid from the body, so a high-protein diet can actually interfere with physical performance. The best diet for most sports is basically the same balanced one recommended for everyone.

Is sugar bad for you?

If you drink a 350-millilitre (12-fluid-ounce) can of fizzy drink every day, you consume eight teaspoons of refined sugar per can, which can mean a weight gain of 5 kilograms (12 pounds) a year. When you have a soft drink your blood-sugar level rises abruptly. That stimulates the secretion of insulin, which may result in the storage of excess calories as fat.

Besides being high in calories, table sugar is a major cause of tooth cavities. Sugar in this form, sucrose, is also not particularly nutritious. It is far better to satisfy your craving for sweets with fruits, which contain valuable nutrients along with sugar.

Also more healthy than table sugar are the complex carbohydrates, found in such plant foods as pasta, cereal, potatoes, and other vegetables. The process of digestion breaks down these carbohydrates into glucose, a form of sugar that fuels the brain, nerves, and muscles.

The Food Journey

What happens when you eat?

The digestive system operates like an assembly line in reverse, taking whole foods and breaking them down into their chemical components. The food you eat is broken down by digestive juices into small, absorbable nutrients that generate the energy required to maintain life, replace the cells that are constantly dying, and keep you functioning.

Suppose that you eat a balanced lunch or dinner of meat or fish, vegetables, bread, butter, and fruit. Your meal would contain all the basic elements of food that you need: protein, found mainly in the meat or fish; carbohydrates, principally in the vegetables, bread, and fruit; vitamins and minerals, especially in the vegetables and fruit; and fat, in the meat, fish, and butter.

What does the mouth do?

The mouth is a channel for the breath and the sounds of speech. The mouth is also the place where digestion begins, the first stop on a journey of some 9 metres (30 feet) through the digestive canal. In the mouth, food is pulverized by the teeth and, with the help of the tongue, mixed with saliva. This secretion promotes the first of several chemical reactions that convert food into usable nutrients. During chewing, food reaches a temperature suitable for digestion.

The mouth is bounded by the cheeks, with the hard and soft palate as a roof and the tongue as a floor. The part of the mouth between the lips or cheeks and the teeth is called the vestibule; the rest, between the teeth and the throat, is the mouth proper, or oral cavity. The hard palate at the front of the mouth is composed mainly of bone. The rest is muscle and connective tissue.

Why is saliva important?

To get an idea of what saliva does, chew a piece of bread, paying attention to the way it tastes. When it develops a sweet flavour, you will know that your saliva has begun to convert the complex starch molecules in the bread to a mixture of the simple sugars glucose and maltose. This is accomplished by a digestive enzyme known as salivary amylase, or ptylin.

Saliva does more than break down starches into sugars. Without saliva, you could swallow only with extreme difficulty. The mucus in saliva adheres to food and moistens it so it can be chewed and mixed into a ball that will slide easily down the oesophagus.

A third function of saliva is to help keep your mouth healthy. A mild germicide, saliva kills bacteria, especially the kind that cause tooth decay. It also cleans the mouth by washing away bacteria and bits of food.

Where does your saliva come from?

You have three pairs of salivary glands that secrete about 1.5 litres (2.5 pints) of fluid every day and pour it into your mouth through a system of ducts. Even if you didn't know their name, you may have become familiar with the parotid glands when you were a child: they are the glands that became swollen if you had mumps. Swollen or not, they are your largest salivary glands. The submandibular glands are smaller than the parotid glands, about the size of a walnut, while the sublingual glands are the smallest of the salivary glands.

What prompts salivation?

The aroma of fresh-baked bread— or even just the thought of it—can start your mouth watering. Triggered by the senses and by psychological stimuli, the brain orders the salivary glands to step up production. Depending on the stimulant, the secretion may be a thin, watery substance containing amylase, or a thicker saliva containing mucus. Not surprisingly, you salivate more when you see or smell food that you especially like.

Once you begin to eat, chewing stimulates additional saliva outflows. Smooth objects or a sour taste cause an abundance of saliva, while rough objects call forth a smaller amount. You may also salivate in response to irritation in your stomach or upper intestine. Swallowed saliva helps to dilute or neutralize the irritant.

DID YOU KNOW...?

- **The tradition of drinking milk** before bed as an aid to sleep has long been followed, but not till fairly recently has there been any scientific explanation of why it works. Apparently, the amino acids contained in milk send signals to the brain that release a mildly tranquilizing substance.

- **The average Western European** consumes nearly 40 tonnes of food in a lifetime. This, of course, is a very broad estimate. People vary in body size, degree of activity, and diet.

- **When a pill gets "stuck in your throat,"** it has probably settled into a small pocket between the upper part of the throat and the larynx called the piriform recess. You can avoid this problem by drinking a full glass of water when you take a pill, especially an aspirin or any other tablet with a high acid content.

- **You shouldn't go swimming** for an hour or more after eating because digestion makes heavy demands on your circulatory system. Swimming itself, particularly in cold water, also taxes your circulatory system. Blood is drawn to the digestive system and away from the muscles, and may cause them to cramp.

- **Why do some people love peas but hate beans,** or any other foods? Studies have shown that aversions to certain foods are most often picked up in childhood from parents or siblings. Once you decide you hate something, you are not likely to change your mind—because you will seldom or never give that particular food another chance.

How does your food get down to your stomach?

When you swallow, pressure causes a sphincter, or "purse-string" muscle, at the top of the oesophagus to relax and let food through. Once the food has entered the oesophagus, the muscles contract to close the opening. Muscles behind and in front of the food relax and contract in swift, rhythmic sequence, forcing the food onwards. This so-called peristaltic movement is much like moving a ball through a collapsed inner tube. Once the food reaches the lower end of the oesophagus, another muscle, the cardiac sphincter, relaxes and opens the way into the stomach.

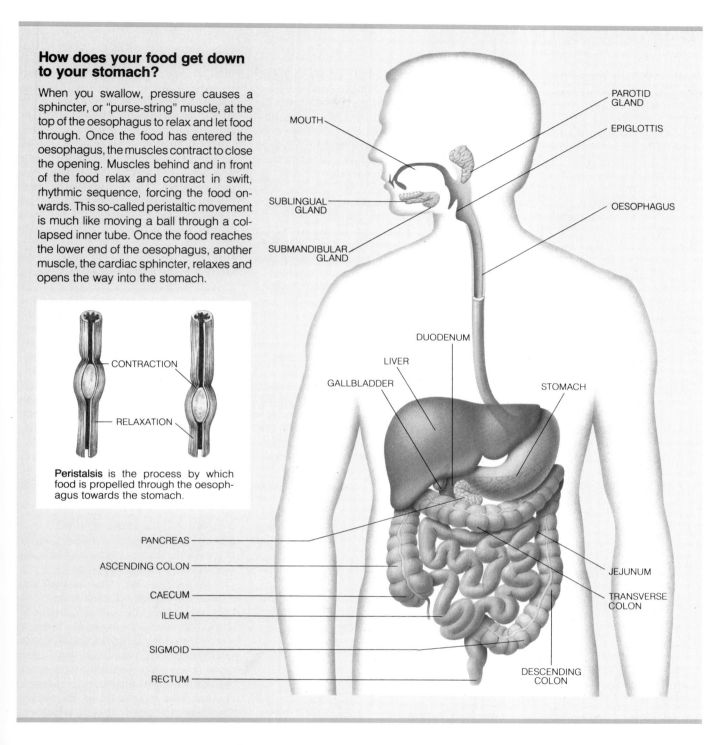

CONTRACTION

RELAXATION

Peristalsis is the process by which food is propelled through the oesophagus towards the stomach.

MOUTH

PAROTID GLAND

EPIGLOTTIS

SUBLINGUAL GLAND

OESOPHAGUS

SUBMANDIBULAR GLAND

DUODENUM

LIVER

GALLBLADDER

STOMACH

PANCREAS

ASCENDING COLON

CAECUM

ILEUM

SIGMOID

RECTUM

JEJUNUM

TRANSVERSE COLON

DESCENDING COLON

How long does it take food to go through the digestive tract?

It may be 24 hours or longer after a meal before its residue is eliminated. And even then, some of the residue is retained in the bowel and is mixed with waste from subsequent meals.

Much of the time, the muscles of the large intestine are inactive, yet contractions do occur there. In the colon, churning and kneading movements take place. They are sluggish, but in a period of 12 to 14 hours, they mix the contents so that each part of it comes in contact with the intestinal wall, through which fluids are absorbed. Three or four times a day, mass movements also occur. These propulsive waves force the wastes along and into the rectum (which is empty most of the time). Many people experience such a mass movement after breakfast. When faeces distend the rectum, the internal anal sphincter opens, and you feel the urge to defecate. Because you learned to exercise control over the external anal sphincter, you can postpone defecation to a suitable moment.

235

How You Taste Your Food

What does your tongue do?

One of the body's most versatile organs, the tongue plays an important role in speaking and in eating. It is also the bearer of taste and tactile sensations and so gives us pleasure in eating. It gives warning of possible injury by registering pain when foods are too hot, and revulsion when they are spoiled. In its role as manipulator, the tongue takes food into the mouth, moves it between the upper and lower teeth for chewing, and then moulds the crushed and moistened particles into a ball, or bolus, for swallowing. When the tongue moves up and back, pressing against the hard palate, it propels the bolus to the back of the mouth and into the oesophagus.

What does a healthy tongue look like?

Composed mainly of muscles, the tongue is covered, on top, with a thick layer of mucous membrane, which is studded with thousands of tiny projections called papillae. Inside these are the sensory organs and nerves for both taste and touch. On a healthy tongue, the papillae are usually pinkish-white and velvety smooth, and are crossed by slits or fissures that reveal the red tongue beneath.

How do you taste food?

The first requisite for tasting is moisture. The organs of taste can detect the pleasant tasting chemicals in food only when they are dissolved in saliva. If your mouth were dry, you could not taste a thing.

The structures that pick up the flavours from the food you eat are the taste buds, which are found mostly on the tongue, although there are also some elsewhere in the mouth and in the throat. Each bud is comprised of receptor cells, from which taste hairs, or microvilli, project. The cells are linked to a network of sensory nerves that relay messages about taste sensations experienced in the mouth to the taste centres of the brain, which are located principally in the thalamus and cortex. At the same time, other nerves notify the brain about sensations of temperature, texture, and pain, which are also experienced in the tongue, as well as about the smells that come from food. The brain coordinates all these data and interprets them as a single taste or flavour.

What are the primary tastes?

Although they combine to make a myriad different flavours, there are believed to be only four primary tastes: salty, sweet, sour, and bitter. These come from the chemical compounds in foods (or in other substances that you may put in your mouth). Various parts of the tongue have taste buds which are especially sensitive to one of the basic sensations. You taste salty and sweet mainly on the front of the tongue, sour on

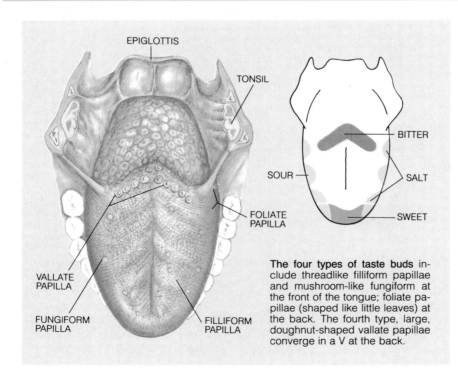

The four types of taste buds include threadlike filliform papillae and mushroom-like fungiform at the front of the tongue; foliate papillae (shaped like little leaves) at the back. The fourth type, large, doughnut-shaped vallate papillae converge in a V at the back.

On the Tip of Your Tongue

Licking ice cream is by far the best way to enjoy it since the taste buds that transmit sweetness to your brain are on the tip of your tongue. But three other factors affect your reaction: smell, nutritional needs, and experience. Much of what we call taste is smell. The olfactory cells in each nostril react thousands of times more strongly to food than our taste buds do. These cells are stimulated only by molecules carried in the air (odour), which, in turn, can cause us to salivate—a precondition for tasting food. Nutritional needs are also important. Animals that have been injected with excess insulin will automatically choose the sweetest of the available foods to create the proper bodily balance. Finally, we react to what we remember. If a person becomes sick right after eating a certain food, he often will not want to eat it again—even though the illness may have had nothing to do with the item eaten. Conversely, some foods are enhanced by happy memories.

the sides, and bitter at the back. The middle of the tongue registers almost no taste. Curiously, at least to some people, a single substance may taste sweet when it enters the front of the mouth but taste bitter by the time it reaches the back; one such substance is saccharin.

Of the four primary tastes, the one that is most easily distinguished is the bitter. Its unmistakable taste serves as a protective mechanism. Many deadly toxins taste bitter, and their unpleasantness usually makes a person spit them out before they can do any damage.

Can every taste bud sense every taste?

Each taste bud in your mouth is predominantly sensitive to a single primary taste. Research has shown, however, that some of your taste buds can be stimulated—at least to a small degree— by one or more of the other primary tastes.

Do particular foods taste the same to everyone?

Taste is highly individual. This means not only that people like different foods but that the same foods may produce different taste sensations in different people. Part of the explanation is heredity. Some people's genes make their receptors for bitterness especially keen. In these people, saccharin is likely to produce a strong sensation of bitterness.

And then, too, each person's saliva has its own special taste, which affects, in turn, the taste of food. If, for example, your saliva has a low sodium content, foods containing a given amount of salt taste saltier to you than to a person whose saliva is high in sodium. Influences as diverse as exercise, dehydration, and illness can affect the composition of saliva.

Food preferences, as distinct from the actual taste sensations that foods give rise to, are determined not only by those sensations but also by culture and experience. People tend to prefer foods that they are accustomed to eat, particularly when the foods are associated with joyous holidays or with happy family mealtimes. There is also some evidence that at times people like—and perhaps crave— foods that supply specific nutrients needed by their bodies.

Is the sense of taste sharper in infancy or in adulthood?

Babies have many more taste buds than the average adult, and they have taste buds almost everywhere in the mouth, including the cheeks. Thus sensitivity to taste apparently decreases from infancy to adulthood.

Nevertheless, because of acquired tastes, which develop with experience, adults enjoy many more flavours than babies, who dislike all bitter tastes and prefer bland foods. In general, the food prejudices of childhood disappear slowly. Many adults can easily remember the days when they detested coffee or artichokes.

When something is very bitter, taste buds at the back of the tongue cause gagging. Many people gag on coffee the first time they taste it.

Tiny papillae (magnified) can be thick or thin and contain up to five taste buds that send messages to the brain.

Care of Teeth and Gums

Why do your teeth decay?

If you consume a lot of sugar and other carbohydrates, you risk tooth decay, or dental caries. Carbohydrates react in a special way with mouth bacteria to form acid that destroys tooth tissue and causes cavities. When you eat, a thin, sticky, transparent film called plaque, composed of mucus, food particles, and bacteria, forms on the surface of the teeth. The acid produced by the chemical interaction of the food and the bacteria eats away at the tooth's enamel. As the hardest substance in the human body, the enamel does not yield easily, but once acid penetrates it, the bacteria can invade the softer layer of dentine. Unless you visit your dentist promptly to have the cavity filled, tooth decay proceeds, ending in an infection of the pulp.

The plaque that forms on teeth (above, under high magnification) contains a dense tangle of hard-to-remove bacteria and cocci.

Under magnification, the tooth surface (left) is revealed as rough terrain; it's easy to see where food particles can stick.

What causes a toothache?

The early Egyptians were sure they knew the reason for a toothache: it meant the gods were angry. Today's experts have a more mundane explanation. According to them, the aching is due to pressure on the nerve in the pulp. When a tooth is badly decayed, white blood cells rush to the pulp to fight off the infection. Their presence enlarges the blood vessels, which then press on the nerve.

Can tooth decay be prevented?

Though fluorides, which have been added to some communities' drinking water as well as to some tooth preparations, are known to strengthen tooth enamel and to make teeth more resistant to acid, unfortunately there is as yet no foolproof way of preventing all tooth decay. However, there are several steps you can take that will help to protect your teeth.

First, avoid foods that contain refined sugar, or limit your consumption of them. If you do eat sweets, do so only once a day. It takes just a little sugar to start the process of plaque formation. If you eat sweets or other sugary snacks several times a day, however, you will subject your teeth to repeated acid attacks.

Second, brush your teeth after each meal (if this is not possible, rinse your mouth with water, and brush as soon as possible); bacteria turn sugar to acid within moments of contact. At least three times a day, clean your teeth thoroughly to remove the plaque before it has a chance to harden. Ask your dentist about the most effective way to brush and to use dental floss.

Third, see your dentist for regular checkups, probably every six months. That allows him to find and fill cavities while they are small, remove tartar, and treat any gum disease.

How do fluorides work?

The single most effective and least expensive measure to prevent tooth decay is fluoridation of the public water supply. Children who drink fluoridated water while their teeth are still forming gain a tremendous lifelong advantage, since fluorides combine with calcium to become part of the structure of their teeth. This strengthens the enamel and makes it three times more resistant to erosion by acid than it would otherwise be.

Fluorides also protect fully formed teeth. The initial effect of acid on teeth is to weaken the enamel by causing it to lose calcium and phosphate. Fluorides increase the rate at which these minerals are restored to the teeth, thus enabling the enamel to repair itself. In addition, fluorides impair the ability of bacteria to produce acid. These effects can obviously benefit people of all ages, even adults who were not exposed to fluorides in their early years. Moreover, fluorides apparently protect not only enamel but also the cementum which covers the roots of the teeth. Exposure to fluorides is thus valuable for adults whose gums have receded and exposed the roots.

Are fluorides dangerous?

Studies show that the most significant effect of fluoridating water to the recommended level (1 part in 1 million parts of water, the equivalent of 1 drop in 50 litres (10 gallons)) is a dramatic decrease in dental caries.

However, if your water supply is fluoridated, dentists do not recommend that you take fluoride supplements. Among children whose teeth are in the process of formation, excessive fluoride can mottle the enamel or cause more serious harm to the teeth and even the bones. Once children are old enough to clean their teeth they no longer require additional fluoride supplements because they will swallow fluoride in the toothpaste.

Patients with kidney disease should be cautious about water for dialysis, because the process exposes them to 50 to 100 times more fluoride than people normally consume.

What if a toothache goes away on its own?

When a toothache disappears all by itself, it means that the nerve fibres in the pulp have died. Even so, the infection that originally caused the pain is still there, and it can cause an abscess around the tip of the root. The infection may eventually spread to the jawbone and could possibly cause blood poisoning.

Can a dead tooth be saved?

A dead tooth is not necessarily useless; modern root-canal therapy can keep it functioning for years. In this procedure, the dead pulp is removed from the tooth, and the space it occupied is filled.

What is the major dental problem of middle age?

If you have a cavity in a tooth, the dentist can usually restore it and save the tooth. But if gum disease destroys the tissues that hold a tooth in place, there is no lasting solution; you will most likely lose the tooth, even if it does not have a single cavity in it.

Gum disease is the major cause of tooth loss in adults. (It affects two out of three middle-aged persons.) In its early stages, when it is called gingivitis (inflammation of the gums), it does not usually cause pain. However, you may notice that your gums are no longer as firm and pink as they once were but rather soft and red, with a purple tinge. The gums may not fit tightly around the teeth, and they may bleed easily. This may lead to periodontitis (inflammation around the tooth), in which pockets form between the teeth and gums and bacteria attack the bone and tissues that support the teeth.

Periodontal disease can be caused, or aggravated, by poor oral hygiene, by the use of tobacco, poor dental work, malocclusion, and a habit of grinding the teeth.

What can you do about gum disease?

If you suffer from periodontal disease, the remedy is an intensive regimen of brushing and flossing. In addition, you will probably need deep scaling every few months. This is the procedure in which the dentist or dental hygienist uses a fine instrument to reach deep down under the gums and scrape away tartar and diseased tissue. This is different from an ordinary cleaning mainly in requiring deeper probing with finer instruments. Usually this procedure brings about improvement, but if it does not, surgery may be recommended. The surgeon cuts back the gum to get at and remove infected material so deeply buried that it cannot be reached by simple scaling. Then he shapes the gums to fit more tightly around the teeth.

How and Why You Should Floss Your Teeth

Running dental floss through your teeth at least once a day cleans the sides of your teeth, removes food particles, and helps prevent the build-up of plaque, the major cause of gum disease. Use a 50-centimetre (18-inch) length of floss (either waxed or unwaxed), wound around the middle fingers of each hand and controlled with the thumbs and forefingers. Guide the floss between the centre of the two upper front teeth. Slide the floss firmly but gently down the side of each tooth, taking special care at the gum line. Repeat the flossing against the adjacent teeth. As you proceed, wind the floss from one middle finger to the other so as to gain a clean, strong piece of floss. After flossing between all the upper teeth, repeat the procedure between all the lower teeth. After flossing, rinse your mouth, drawing the water through your teeth.

Proper dental hygiene is difficult and time consuming in the beginning, but it soon becomes easy and routine.

Filling Your Stomach

Liquefying and Storing Food

The openings at each end of the stomach are guarded by sphincter, or "purse-string," muscles. These lead into tubes: the oesophagus at the top upper end, the duodenum at the bottom. Each ball of food, or bolus, enters the part of the stomach called the fundus and pushes food previously eaten down and out towards the stomach walls. The fundus and the main body of the stomach serve as a storage area, holding food until it is time for it to move along to the antrum and duodenum. The digestive tract is constructed in layers: the innermost is composed of mucous membrane that lubricates the tube; the next layer contains a network of blood vessels that nourish the structure, as well as nerves that activate glands and muscles; in the third layer are the muscles that move food, and, in certain parts of the system, soften it and mix it with chemicals; the last layer is a protective covering.

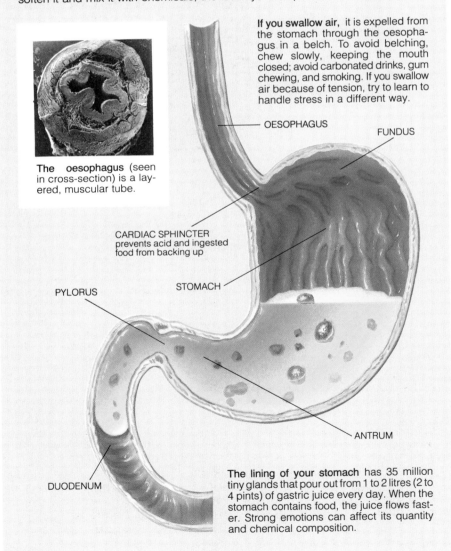

The oesophagus (seen in cross-section) is a layered, muscular tube.

If you swallow air, it is expelled from the stomach through the oesophagus in a belch. To avoid belching, chew slowly, keeping the mouth closed; avoid carbonated drinks, gum chewing, and smoking. If you swallow air because of tension, try to learn to handle stress in a different way.

OESOPHAGUS

FUNDUS

CARDIAC SPHINCTER prevents acid and ingested food from backing up

STOMACH

PYLORUS

ANTRUM

DUODENUM

The lining of your stomach has 35 million tiny glands that pour out from 1 to 2 litres (2 to 4 pints) of gastric juice every day. When the stomach contains food, the juice flows faster. Strong emotions can affect its quantity and chemical composition.

Why is it important to chew your food thoroughly?

The major purpose of chewing is to make each bite easy to swallow. Chewing also mixes the food with saliva. Crushing and moistening food ease its passage through the digestive tract and simplify the stomach's task of macerating and liquefying it. Digestion in the mouth, however, is not very efficient. Saliva only *starts* the digestion of complex carbohydrates. In addition, chewing stimulates the senses of taste, touch, and smell; the longer you chew, the more pleasure you derive from eating.

What happens when you swallow?

For the few seconds it takes to swallow, you can neither breathe nor talk. In the first phase of swallowing, which is the only part of the process that is under voluntary control, the tongue pushes food into the pharynx. Once food gets this far, it is too late to change your mind and decide you don't want that particular mouthful; from this point on, swallowing is a reflex act. To prevent food or liquid from going up into the nose (which can happen if you laugh or try to talk as you swallow), the soft palate moves to close off the nasal cavity, and the pharynx rises and widens to accommodate the food. At the same time, the entrance to the windpipe is blocked by the epiglottis, folded over the larynx, and the vocal cords, which are closed. Food is thus prevented from getting into the lungs. The sphincter that guards the oesophagus, usually closed to keep out air, now opens, and muscles of the pharynx send food down the gullet.

Does swallowing depend on gravity?

When you eat, you are usually sitting upright. It is not surprising, then, that gravity facilitates swallowing. What *is* surprising, perhaps, is that it is not absolutely essential to have the help of gravity to get food from your mouth to your stomach; the oesophagus can do the job all by itself if necessary. Remember that astronauts can eat even when the weightless conditions of space turn them upside down.

Is "heartburn" a misnomer?

Heartburn is a painful burning sensation behind the breastbone, at the junction of the oesophagus and the stomach. Although it is felt near the heart, it has nothing at all to do with that organ. It comes, instead, because the highly acidic contents of the stomach flow back into the oesophagus. This regurgitation occurs when pressure from an overextended stomach opens the muscular valve of the gullet, the one named the "cardiac sphincter"—solely because of its position near the heart.

You are most likely to experience heartburn when you are bending over or lying down. It is frequently triggered by overeating, emotional upsets, wearing tight clothing, smoking, or consuming coffee, chocolate, garlic, onions, or alcohol. Chronic heartburn occasionally signals a serious condition, but in the vast majority of cases, it is harmless.

Why are hiatus hernias often misdiagnosed?

Even doctors sometimes confuse heart disease or ulcers with a hiatus hernia because their symptoms are remarkably similar. The main complaint of the patient is a burning sensation in the general region of the heart. In some cases, the pain radiates to the arm.

The diaphragm, which is the breathing muscle that separates the chest from the abdomen, contains a hiatus, or opening, through which the oesophagus passes to reach the stomach. Occasionally part of the stomach protrudes through the hiatus, creating a hernia that permits the backflow of acid from the stomach to the oesophagus. The result is often the pain known as heartburn.

A Living Laboratory for Observing Digestion

In 1822, when a Canadian fur trapper, Alexis St. Martin, was accidentally shot at close range, the blast left a gaping hole in his side. The army doctor who attended him, William Beaumont, did not expect his patient to live. But the 18-year-old St. Martin survived, burdened thereafter with a 60-millimetre (2.5-inch) hole in his stomach. Beaumont realized that this presented an opportunity to discover how the stomach digests food. For eight years, he used St. Martin as a human guinea pig, withdrawing gastric juices, and lowering food samples into his stomach at intervals to monitor the digestive process.

St. Martin's wound led to the discovery of hydrochloric acid in gastric juices. Between tests, St. Martin covered his wound with gauze and worked as a handyman.

What is the commonest misconception about the stomach?

Many people believe that the stomach lies just behind the navel, but it is actually much higher up. As a matter of fact, the upper end of it is not far beneath the heart. Most of the stomach rests behind the lower rib cage, under the diaphragm on the left side of the body.

What does your stomach do to food?

No food is nutritious in the form in which you eat it. The carbohydrates, fats, and proteins in food are too complex in their chemical structure to be of any use to the body until they have been digested, or broken down into their components.

Much of this process goes on in the stomach. There, food is transformed into a partly digested, semiliquid pulp called chyme before being moved along into the duodenum, the first part of the small intestine. To form chyme the stomach kneads, tosses, turns, and churns the food, mixing it with gastric juices that do much of the work of chemical simplification.

The wall of the stomach contains three layers of muscles. The presence of food in the stomach causes rhythmic contractions: they are weak in the upper part of the stomach, but they intensify to vigorous force in the lower part. These contractions—the slowest being about three per minute—combine the food with gastric juices, bringing it to a fine consistency, and moving it gradually to the small intestine.

What causes an upset stomach?

Indigestion is a common, but usually minor, complaint that produces a wide variety of symptoms: nausea, belching, gas, bloating, heartburn, abdominal cramps, and sometimes diarrhoea or constipation. It is often caused by eating too much or too fast, by overly rich or fatty foods, or by tension and anxiety.

What the Stomach Really Does

How long does food stay in the stomach?

It takes three to six hours for a meal to be converted from solids to semiliquids in the stomach. The rate at which the stomach moves food along is controlled primarily by the duodenum. This sphincter releases hormones that control the muscle movements of the stomach and thus regulate the rate of digestion. As a result, the duodenum receives the chyme gradually, in just the right amount for optimum digestion and absorption. However, the stomach does exert some control over how quickly food travels through it. When it is especially full, it signals for the release of the hormone gastrin, which speeds up digestion.

Fluids pass rapidly out of the stomach, but solid foods need time to disintegrate. Large chunks take longer than do thoroughly chewed ones. Other factors that slow the passage of food through the stomach include low temperatures, as in ice cream, and strenuous exercise after a meal, which diverts blood from the abdomen to the heart and muscles. Emotional stress, too, may alter the rate of digestive activity, either slowing it down or speeding it up.

Why doesn't the stomach digest itself?

The hydrochloric acid the stomach secretes is corrosive enough to dissolve a razor blade or annihilate living cells. Sometimes it actually eats into the stomach itself and creates ulcers. Usually, however, the stomach remains impervious to attack.

First, the gastric lining is coated with mucus, which forms a barrier between the acid and the stomach wall. The mucus, somewhat alkaline, neutralizes the acid and thus helps to keep the stomach from digesting itself. Furthermore, food in the stomach dilutes the acid, making it less corrosive. Also, the lining of the stomach sheds cells at the rate of half a million every minute and replaces them so rapidly that the stomach has what amounts to a new lining every three days. Even if hydrochloric acid does damage the cells, the stomach makes repairs automatically.

How much food will the stomach hold?

The stomach is expandable, like a soft-sided holdall. When it has no food in it, it is shaped like a big capital J. When it is full, it takes the shape of a boxing glove. When filled to capacity, the average stomach can hold up to 1.5 litres (2.5 pints) of food.

What do gastric juices do?

You can digest food even if you have no stomach because most of the digestive process takes place *after* food has left the stomach. Still, the stomach has a role to play, and the gastric juices are an important element in it.

In addition to hydrochloric acid, the major ingredients in gastric juice are gastrin, mucus, intrinsic factor, and pepsin. The hydrochloric acid destroys bacteria in food, making the stomach almost germ free. It also helps to soften protein foods and fosters the secretion and effectiveness of pepsin, an enzyme that breaks proteins down into simpler chemical substances. Mucus buffers the acid and provides lubrication, while gastrin, a hormone, stimulates the production of gastric juice. Intrinsic factor enables your body to absorb vitamin B_{12}, required for production of normal blood cells and the normal function of nervous system.

What happens when you vomit?

Vomiting is an effort to get rid of material that you cannot digest. Its cause may be spoiled food, motion sickness, or emotional distress. But more often it is something much simpler: you ate or drank too much.

When you vomit, the muscles of your stomach and oesophagus relax, as does the cardiac sphincter muscle; and the muscles of the diaphragm and the abdomen contract in powerful spasms, squeezing the stomach and forcefully ejecting its contents. Sometimes the pyloric sphincter also opens, and the contents of the duodenum are expelled.

THE STORY BEHIND THE WORDS...

"Let us eat and drink; for tomorrow we shall die" is from the Bible (Isaiah 22:13), a warning that life is brief indeed. The Egyptians used a similar saying at banquets, and displayed a skeleton to make the point more emphatically. "Eat, drink, and *be merry*" is a modern corruption of the expression.

Sandwiches owe their existence to the Earl of Sandwich (1718–1792), who was so intent on gambling that he was unwilling to sit down to eat a regular meal. He had the waiter bring him a piece of cold meat between two pieces of bread. He would undoubtedly be at home in the 20th century, where people frequently "grab a sandwich" or some other fast food.

A lily-livered coward was someone whose liver contained no blood. The expression harks back to the days when the liver was regarded as the seat of life and the organ in which blood was manufactured. In ancient Mesopotamia, priests examined the livers of sacrificial animals to predict the future. Models of sheep livers have been found with carved instructions for reading signs. Before going into battle, the Greeks and Romans sacrificed animals to the gods. When the liver was examined, if it was healthy and the blood was bright red, victory was at hand. A diseased liver or pale blood was a prediction of defeat.

Gourmet and gourmand sound alike, and both were borrowed from the French (though not from the same root—gourmet originally meant "wine taster" and had no connection with food). The difference is that a gourmet is a connoisseur of food, and a gourmand is a hearty eater (and may also be a bit of a gourmet).

The Paradox of Salt

Throughout most of recorded history, salt has been in short supply. In ancient Abyssinia, slabs of rock salt were used as currency. Caravans carried salt vast distances, often trading it for gold, measure for measure. Salt is essential to life—the impulses that travel along nerve cells are carried by sodium ions, which are contained in salt (sodium chloride). Insufficient salt causes weakness, weight loss, muscle cramps, and can even result in death. It is effective as a preservative, and also works as an antiseptic. The most important item always placed first on a Roman soldier's allowance of rations was salt—*sal* in Latin—which gave rise to the word "salary." If salt was spilled during the Middle Ages, it was a sign of impending doom. Today, not only are we able to mine the vast supplies in the earth and collect it in commercial salt pans, it is no longer the chief means of food preservation. Now the problem is a surplus of salt—a tendency to use too much. It has become a health hazard, particularly for people with high blood pressure.

The Dead Sea (above) is so saturated with salt that encrusted "pillars" form above it, a product of evaporation. Before refrigeration, salting was one of the few ways to preserve food. In biblical times, it became a symbol of the covenant between God and the Jews. When Lot's wife broke God's commandment not to look back at Sodom, she was punished by being turned into a pillar of salt (right).

The daily intake of salt in many industrialized nations is ten grams, or three times as much as necessary. In one region of Japan, the intake reaches 30 grams (1 ounce) a day.

This Cleveland salt mine is 600 metres (2,000 feet) down. Salt pillars support the ground above.

The Liver: A Chemical Factory

Is it true that the liver does 500 different things?

Important as vitamins are, you could let a year or two go by without taking in any vitamin A, and you might not show ill effects. You could go as long as four months without consuming vitamins B_{12} or D, and, again, you would probably not suffer

—not if you were well-nourished and your liver were functioning properly. For the liver banks these and other vitamins when the body takes in more than its current needs, and it releases them into the bloodstream when supplies get low.

That is just one of the 500-odd functions performed by the liver. Others include manufacturing glycogen,

stabilizing the body's blood-sugar level, detoxifying poisons, and inactivating drugs. It builds enzymes, processes digested fats and proteins, removes waste products, manufactures bile and cholesterol, and constitutes an important source of heat. No wonder the amazingly versatile liver is frequently likened to a chemical processing plant.

The Remarkable, Regenerating Liver

The liver is the largest organ inside the body, weighing about 1.5 kilograms (3 pounds). Protected by the lower rib cage, it is found on the right side of the upper abdomen, its left lobe overlying the stomach where it joins the oesophagus. Its right lobe is much larger than the left, and

it is subdivided into three sections. The liver can function even if as much as 90 percent of it is removed. If it should be entirely destroyed by disease, the only hope for survival would be a liver transplant. Because of its many functions, it is unlikely that a machine could do its work.

RIGHT LOBE

LIVER

FALCIFORM LIGAMENT

LEFT LOBE

Vitamins A, B, D, E, and K are stored in the liver. All but the B vitamins are soluble in fats and are therefore absorbed into the body with fatty materials. The detergent action of bile in the small intestine breaks down these fats, along with the vitamins, into suspended globules that are absorbed through the intestinal wall and get into the blood via lymph vessels. Without bile, the body would be deficient in its vital stockpile of vitamins.

PANCREATIC DUCT

HEPATIC DUCT

COMMON BILE DUCT

CYSTIC DUCT

PANCREAS

GALLBLADDER

AMPULLA OF VATER

DUODENUM

Low-power magnification of a section of human liver shows the typical arrangement of the hepatic cells.

What is the role of the liver in digestion?

Every day the liver manufactures a half to one litre (1 to 2 pints) of a bitter substance known as bile. A viscid, alkaline, yellowish-green fluid, it is stored in the gallbladder, connected with the liver, and it plays an important role in the digestion of fats.

Bile is more than 97 percent water. Its most important components are bile salts. Released into the small intestine, the bile salts work like a detergent, emulsifying fatty materials, breaking up globules of fat so more of their surface is exposed to chemical conversion by enzymes, and preparing the fats so they can be absorbed into the body. Because bile is alkaline, it helps neutralize the acidic chyme that comes from the stomach.

What is so remarkable about liver cells?

A single extraordinary structure in the liver, the hepatic cell, is responsible for nearly all of the liver's vital accomplishments, from storing nutrients, to removing waste products, to creating new liver cells as old ones die off. The liver is composed of some 300 thousand million of these cells.

To our eyes, the surface of the liver appears smooth and rubber-like. In fact, it is comprised of 50,000 to 100,000 little lobules, each of which has a central vein at its core. From each vein radiate hundreds of hepatic cells, interwoven with a network of microscopic bile ducts and blood capillaries. The latter are minute blood channels, which are called sinusoids, which act rather like the holes in a sponge and serve to carry oxygenated and nutrient-laden blood to the hepatic cells.

How much does the liver filter in a year?

When the body needs blood, it calls on the reserves in the liver. The amount of blood flowing to the liver is impressive, amounting to a quarter

Is drinking the only cause of cirrhosis of the liver?

In cirrhosis, the liver cells die and are replaced by scar tissue. At the onset of the disease, the liver enlarges. As the disease progresses, the patient's skin may take on the yellowish hue of jaundice. Fluid accumulates in the legs, and frequently the abdomen as well. In the "end stage" of this chronic inflammation, the liver shrivels and can no longer function effectively; the damage is irreversible. Such patients become vulnerable to infection among other complications. Although excessive

use of alcohol is considered a primary cause of cirrhosis, the relationship of alcohol to the disease is not fully understood. Poor nutrition—particularly insufficient protein in the diet—can play a part. Cirrhosis also occurs in people who never drink; occasionally, it follows viral hepatitis, exposure to toxins, such as carbon tetrachloride (dry cleaning fluid), congestive heart failure, or inflammation of the biliary tract. The disease most often strikes men, especially those between the ages of 40 and 60.

Degas' painting *Absinthe*, was named after the alcoholic drink, which is now banned for its harmful effects.

of the body's total supply. It filters over a litre (1.75 pints) of blood a minute when the body is at rest. This adds up, in a year, to an enormous quantity—by one estimate enough blood to fill 23 milk tankers.

The liver is the only organ that is bathed in blood from two sources. First, the hepatic artery from the aorta supplies the liver with fresh blood to oxygenate the cells. Second, the portal vein delivers the nutrient-rich blood from the stomach and intestines to the liver. As portal blood is filtered through the cells of the liver, the nutrients are extracted, chemically processed, stored, or returned to blood circulation by way of the inferior vena cava.

At the same time, the liver plays a role in regulating the composition of the blood. Along with the spleen, it helps to retire old red blood cells. The liver metabolizes a portion of the haemoglobin molecule from the used blood cells and converts it to a water-soluble form of bilirubin, a component of bile, to be excreted as a waste product. The Kupffer cells of the liver,

which line the sinusoids, remove bacteria that can pass occasionally into the blood from the colon.

How does the liver maintain the blood sugar level?

The liver is a kind of magician. It can turn sugars and fats into protein. It can also make sugar out of protein (specifically, from amino acids) and out of fat (the glycerol of fat stored in adipocytes). In addition to manufacturing sugar, the liver serves as the receiving centre and storage area for most of the glucose absorbed from the small intestine. After a meal, when the blood sugar level is high, insulin causes the liver to convert glucose to glycogen and store it. A few hours later, when the blood sugar level takes a dip, the liver converts glycogen back into glucose and returns it to the blood so it will get to the parts of the body that need it. The brain, for instance, requires a steady supply of glucose, and the liver makes sure that the supply is adequate.

The Gallbladder and the Pancreas

Why does liver disease turn you yellow?

A healthy liver removes a yellow pigment called bilirubin from the blood, converts it to a form which can be excreted into bile, and eliminates it from the body. A diseased liver, however, cannot do that; the pigment remains in the bloodstream, and the skin and the whites of the eyes take on the yellowish tinge called jaundice.

When people talk about "yellow jaundice," incidentally, they are repeating themselves, because the term *jaundice* is derived from a word that means "yellow."

Bilirubin is a waste product from the destruction of worn-out red blood cells. Under normal conditions, it gives the stool its characteristic colour. When a person has jaundice, the urine and the tears darken, but the stool becomes lighter.

Is there more than one kind of viral hepatitis?

Hepatitis, or inflammation of the liver, is sometimes caused by alcohol or by certain drugs or chemicals, but in many instances it is the result of one of three viruses, known as Type A, Type B, and "non-A, non-B." That awkward designation for the third virus comes from the fact that the specific agents have yet to be identi-

Water Cures: Conditioning the Body Inside and Out

This ornate stained-glass skylight is typical of the lavish architecture of old European health spas.

Naturally occurring mineral springs have attracted visitors for at least 2,500 years. Hippocrates, the father of medicine, practised hydrotherapy on Kos, one of the Greek Isles. Later, the Romans took up curative bathing, spreading the practice to the far reaches of their empire—to Bath in England, Tiberias in Israel, and elsewhere. Mineral baths went into decline after the fall of Rome, but the Renaissance brought them back with renewed vigour. Patronage by royalty—ranging from Tsar Peter the Great of Russia to Kaiser Wilhelm II of Germany—encouraged their development as health resorts. Taking the cure meant, on the one hand, drinking the water for its mineral content, and on the other, bathing in it. Some springs were especially suited to the treatment of gastrointestinal diseases; waters with high magnesium content were recommended for liver complaints. Other claims for mineral waters included laxative properties, diuretic effect, and balm for the nerves! Mineral baths, whirlpools, steam baths, wet packs, alternating hot-and-cold baths, pool exercises, packs, rubs, and sprays are considered by many to be equally therapeutic.

Modern health spas like this one (Leuze in Stuttgart, West Germany) offer all the traditional cures, plus long-term fitness programs.

fied; doctors know only that it isn't either A or B.

Primarily a disease of children and young adults, hepatitis A (formerly called infectious hepatitis) is spread through faecally contaminated food, water, or objects. Although victims may feel miserable, the illness almost never has lasting consequences.

Type B hepatitis, on the other hand, causes chronic liver inflammation in about 10 percent of all patients and can be serious for the elderly or those in poor health. Serum hepatitis, as this ailment used to be called, is transmitted through blood transfusions, injections with unsterile needles, or intimate contact: Type B virus is present in such body fluids as saliva, semen, and tears.

Regardless of type, viral hepatitis results in a common set of symptoms, which includes fever, headache, sore throat, nausea, aching joints and muscles, loss of appetite, weakness, pain in the upper right abdomen, and jaundice. Though no medicine exists for treating viral hepatitis, bed rest, a nourishing diet, and avoidance of alcohol are generally prescribed.

Where is the gallbladder, and what does it do?

About the size and shape of a small pear, the gallbladder lies on the underside of the liver. As its name suggests, it is a sac for storing bile, or gall, a substance the body needs in order to digest fats completely.

In the liver, hepatic cells continuously secrete bile, which then travels through a system of small ducts to feed into the larger hepatic duct. That channel leads, in turn, to the cystic duct, which carries bile to the gallbladder. By concentrating bile, the gallbladder can hold as much of it as the liver cells manufacture in half a day. Fat and protein entering the duodenum cause the hormone cholecystokinin to be released and sent to the gallbladder by way of the blood. That hormone triggers off the gallbladder's muscles to contract and discharge bile into the duodenum to aid in the digestion of fat.

Can you live without your gallbladder?

After the gallbladder has been removed, bile flows directly from the liver to the small intestine and promotes the digestion of fat exactly as it did when the gallbladder was intact. In short, you do not need a gallbladder to live and to enjoy good health.

What does the pancreas do?

Resembling a fish, with a large head and a long tail, the pancreas extends across the body, behind the stomach, in the upper left side of the abdomen. The larger end of it rests next to the duodenum. The function of the pancreas is to secrete enzymes and hormones, including insulin, that are needed for the digestion and absorption of food. Insulin is manufactured by cells known as the islets of Langerhans, which are scattered like little islands throughout the pancreas. The pancreas is sometimes described as two organs in one: the exocrine cells of the pancreas secrete digestive enzymes into the duodenum; the endocrine cells release two hormones, glucagon and insulin, into the blood. Insulin regulates the utilization of glucose in the body. All body tissues except the brain require insulin for the absorption of glucose. If the pancreas fails to produce insulin, or secretes it in insufficient quantities, the result is a serious disease called diabetes mellitus.

How does the pancreas promote digestion?

Like a stalk with clusters of grapes attached to it, the pancreas has a long duct running down its centre. The "grapes" on it are clusters of exocrine cells known as acinar cells. They secrete enzymes that flow through ducts into the chief pancreatic duct and then into the duodenum, where they digest proteins, carbohydrates, and fats. Also, the pancreas produces an alkaline solution that neutralizes the acid in chyme in the duodenum,

Solid, pebble-like masses, gallstones cause great pain, which may be relieved only by removal of the gallbladder. They are more likely to occur in women than in men.

protecting the small intestine and creating an environment in which the enzymes can function efficiently.

The pancreas is amazingly accurate in producing the right enzymes at the right times and in exactly the quantities required to digest the food you have eaten. The entry of food into the duodenum signals the pancreas to begin pouring out its juices. The food mixture stimulates the release from the duodenal wall of special hormones that travel through the blood and stimulate the pancreas.

Can the pancreas digest itself?

The Greek name *pancreas*, meaning "all flesh" or "all meat," is descriptive of the protein composition of this small but mighty organ. If its protein-digesting enzymes are activated while in the pancreas, they are powerful enough to digest the pancreas itself! This condition, known as acute pancreatitis, can occur if the pancreatic duct is obstructed and the digestive enzymes are forced to accumulate in the pancreas. When this happens, the substances that normally inhibit the activation of the enzymes are overwhelmed, and the pancreas may be damaged and may even be destroyed by its own juices.

Where Absorption Takes Place

How large is the small intestine?

If it were not looped back and forth on itself, the small intestine could not possibly fit into the abdominal space allotted to it. In the average adult, it measures 5 to 7 metres (16 to 23 feet), which makes it roughly four times longer than the average person is tall. It takes the form of a 3-part tube 2.5 to 4 centimetres (1 to 1.5 inches) in diameter. First comes the duodenum, the receiving area for chemicals and partially digested food from the stomach. Next is the jejunum, where most nutrients are absorbed; and last, the ileum, where the remaining nutrients are absorbed before the residue moves into the large intestine.

ASCENDING COLON

TRANSVERSE COLON

JEJUNUM

CAECUM

DESCENDING COLON

APPENDIX

SIGMOID

ILEUM

RECTUM

VILLUS

The absorption area of the small intestine, (shown in the micrograph at left) is three times the entire surface area of the human body.

What happens to food in the small intestine?

The fragmentation of food that begins in the mouth is completed in the small intestine. As food enters the duodenum from the stomach, it stimulates four different organs to release the chemicals needed to finish digestion. The small intestine pours forth mucus to protect the duodenum from damage by gastric acid. It also produces hormones that stimulate the liver, pancreas, and gallbladder to release digestive substances. Bile from the gallbladder and alkaline juice from the pancreas neutralize acid. Digestive enzymes, secreted by the pancreas and small intestine, break down food into simple components that the body can use. Carbohydrates are converted to glucose and protein to amino acids. Fat is also partially digested prior to absorption. Most of these materials are absorbed; at the end of the ileum, little but indigestible cellulose and a small amount of water are left for disposal.

How are nutrients absorbed into the body?

Each day the intestines process approximately 10 litres (18 pints) of food, liquids, and bodily secretions. If enough nutrients are to be absorbed into the body, the food must come into contact with huge numbers of the intestinal cells. Arranged in circular folds, like those of a gathered skirt, the lining of the intestinal wall is studded with millions of tiny finger-like projections called villi, and each villus is studded with microscopic microvilli. In just 3 square centimetres (0.5 square inches) of the small intestine are some 10,000 villi and 5,000 million microvilli.

Each villus has a lymph channel at its centre, glands at the base that secrete intestinal juice, and a network of capillaries and blood channels that bring in fresh, oxygenated blood and remove nutrient-enriched blood. Like plantlife under water, the villi sway incessantly, stirring up the liquefied food and connecting with the absorbable nutrients, which pass through the membranes of the villi and then enter the blood or lymph vessels. From there, fatty nutrients journey through the lymphatic system, while glucose and amino acids travel in the blood to the portal vein and on to the liver.

Are all intestinal movements alike?

When food is in the small intestine, the muscles that encircle the tube constrict about 7 to 12 times a minute, segmenting the tube so it resembles a chain of sausages. These rapid contractions move the food back and forth, churning it, kneading it, and mixing it with the digestive juices. Besides these mixing movements, the small intestine also makes propulsive, or peristaltic, movements: waves that move food through the system. In this part of the gastrointestinal tract, peristaltic movements are usually weak and infrequent. This ensures that food will stay in one place long enough to be absorbed. Only when toxic substances enter the small intestine are the propulsive movements strong and swift, to expel the poisons rapidly.

Why are some foods more quickly digested than others?

Carbohydrates pass through the system quickly. The digestion of carbohydrates begins in the mouth and is completed in the small intestine, where carbohydrates usually remain for less than an hour.

When you eat a fat-rich meal, you feel full and satisfied for a long time, because fats take longer than other foods to digest, remaining in the gastrointestinal tract for hours. The digestion of fats does not begin until food reaches the small intestine, and ten hours may go by before a fat-rich meal is fully digested and absorbed.

In the small intestine, fat globules are emulsified, or broken into tiny droplets by bile salts, so that they can be digested by a pancreatic enzyme

Invaders of the Digestive Tract

Eating raw or undercooked beef, pork, or fish is risky—tapeworm larvae may be present, ready to take up residence. The adult worm ranges in length from 2 metres (6.5 feet) to 9 metres (30 feet). As it grows, the worm sheds segments, each able to produce eggs. Tapeworms do not, as many think, cause voracious appetites or weight loss. But they can live for ten years or more, and fish tapeworms can cause pernicious anaemia. Infestations are detected by the presence of eggs in the victim's faeces. Once discovered, the tapeworm can be expelled by drugs.

A tapeworm's head (called scolex) attaches to the wall of the intestines by means of hooks and suckers.

called lipase. Most fats consist of triglycerides, which the lipase converts into diglycerides, free fatty acids, and glycerol. These are ferried by bile to the villi for absorption. Once inside the intestinal cells, the simple components of fat unite with a bit of protein and reform into complex substances that pass into the lymph channels of the villi to enter the bloodstream.

Protein-rich foods such as meat are also relatively difficult to digest, and remain for quite a while in the gastrointestinal tract. Partial digestion of protein occurs in the acid environment of the stomach. In the small intestine, pancreatic enzymes split the proteins into smaller units that can cross the intestinal wall.

Do the bacteria in your digestive tract hurt you?

Normally, a multitude of bacteria flourish in both the small and the large intestines. In the small intestine, certain kinds of bacteria foster the breakdown of food molecules into chemical substances that the tissues can absorb. The bacteria that inhabit the small intestine also prevent any harmful organisms in the large intestine from entering the ileum, the end of the small intestine. In the large intestine, some bacteria supplement the diet by manufacturing vitamins.

On occasion, especially when you

are travelling, alien bacteria invade the intestines and cause "traveller's diarrhoea," known by a variety of local names. Very often the bacteria that trigger off such holiday-spoiling illnesses are not inherently harmful. They may inhabit the bodies of the native population without causing trouble, while you get sick because your body is not used to them.

Does the appendix serve a purpose?

The vermiform appendix is a pouch 5 to 8 centimetres (2 to 3 inches) long near the juncture of the small and large intestines on the lower right side. There are a number of theories about why we have an appendix, but so far, it has no known function. The appendix is significant only if it becomes diseased.

The pain of appendicitis is severe, and the danger is that the inflamed appendix will burst, scattering infectious matter throughout the abdomen. Abdominal pain should be diagnosed promptly, and until it is, no laxative, medication, food, or drink should be given for fear of rupturing the appendix and causing fatal infection. If the diagnosis is appendicitis, appendicectomy, or surgical removal of the appendix, is almost always recommended. The operation is simple and usually entails little risk if the organ has not ruptured.

249

The End of the Journey

Is the large intestine really large?

Very little of what you eat goes to waste. More than 95 percent of it is absorbed into the body to provide you with the fuel you need to live; the rest is eliminated through the large intestine. The bowel, as the large intestine is also called, does not have to be big to hold that small residue. Actually, compared to the small intestine, the bowel is large in only one dimension; in diameter, it measures about 60 millimetres (2.5 inches), as against 25 millimetres or so (1 inch) for the small intestine. The bowel is the shorter of the two intestines: roughly 2 metres (6.5 feet) compared with about 6 metres (20 feet).

How does the large intestine fit into the body?

Inside the abdominal cavity, the large intestine takes the shape of a horseshoe and forms a kind of border enclosing the coils of the small intestine. Because the muscle that runs along the length of the bowel is shorter than the bowel itself, the large intestine is gathered into bulging, pouchlike segments.

As food makes its way through the large intestine, it travels up, across, down, and back. The small and large intestines are connected in the lower right abdomen by means of a valve that prevents the contents of the large intestine from backing up into the small intestine.

The two major parts of the large intestine are the colon and the rectum. The caecum is the pouchlike segment at the beginning of the large intestine. The ascending colon carries waste up the right side of the abdomen, the transverse colon moves it across the body just under the rib cage, and the descending colon takes it down the left side of the lower abdomen. Next comes the sigmoid colon, which makes an S-shaped turn leading to the rectum, a tube 130 millimetres (5 inches) long leading to the anal canal and the anus. The chief function of the first half of the colon is the absorption of fluids; the second half is basically a storage vessel.

What are faeces made of?

The large intestine is sometimes called the garbage dump of the body, because the food residues that reach it are of little use to the body. The large intestine's job is to remove fluid from these residues and to solidify them. Intestinal chyme is a liquid when it enters the colon, but as it travels through the bowel, the fluid is gradually absorbed through the intestinal wall and recycled through the bloodstream. What is left is compacted into semisolid faeces. Mucus secreted by the large intestine binds the material together, and also lubricates and protects the colon, and facilitates the passage of the faeces.

The amount and composition of faeces depend on what you eat. Consuming a large amount of fibre increases the quantity of residue, while a highly refined diet reduces it. The average Western European eats 7 to 10 litres (12 to 18 pints) of food a day, but only about 350 millilitres (12 fluid ounces) of residue enters the large intestine. This includes food and digestive juice residues plus some water. Of the material that you eliminate—the faeces— roughly three-quarters is water. The rest generally consists of protein, inorganic matter, fat, undigested food roughage, plus dried remainders of digestive juices and cells shed by the intestine, and dead bacteria.

How can you prevent wind?

You cannot hope to be entirely free of wind, gas, or flatus. Considerable quantities of it form every day in the normal intestine. Moreover, doctors have not found any foolproof way of helping people who form too much of it and cannot control its expulsion.

Much of the gas in the large intestine results from the fermentation of food wastes by the bacteria that thrive in every healthy colon. Normally, a large part of the gas is absorbed through the intestinal wall, but some people expel it through the rectum. One reason is too-frequent peristaltic movements that do not allow time for

A **close-up view of the colon** reveals its convoluted, porous surface. By the time the chyme reaches this point, all nutrients have been extracted. It is here that water is reabsorbed; from here, the semisolid mass moves into the rectum.

Cleansing the System

Purging the intestines, even in ancient times, included both enemas and cathartics. American Indians practised a combination of herb and "magic" medicine, but their tools demonstrate a use of enemas for both cleaning and a kind of primitive intravenous feeding. Egyptian "bowel specialists" existed as early as 2500 B.C., and records from 500 B.C. note Egyptians clearing their bowels, with a variety of enema fluids including ox bile, three consecutive days each month to avoid diseases that seemed to be food related. Around A.D. 196, Chang Chung Chin, regarded as China's Hippocrates, recorded his preference for enemas—presumably because they were fast, efficient, and easier on the system than cathartics. The Greeks favoured enemas but used simpler (and medically correct) solutions of water or saline. We also owe the word itself, meaning "to send in," to the Greeks. In the Middle Ages, practitioners returned to elaborate ingredients, and by the late 1600s, using enemas to poison enemies was common. Now, enemas are a presurgery must to avoid contaminating the operating table because the sphincter relaxes under anaesthesia.

By the 17th century, enemas were such an important element of medicine that Dutch painters, who were known for depicting everyday life, included the practice in their work.

Indians used this carved bone enema tube and rubber bulb syringe. The pottery figure is holding an enema syringe.

---

absorption of the gas. Another cause is the consumption of foods known to produce immoderate amounts of gas: beans, for instance, contain certain sugars that the body cannot digest. Reaching the colon intact, these sugars are the perfect food for gas-forming bacteria. Some people lack the enzyme for digesting lactose, so dairy products cause gas.

What causes the odour of faeces and flatus?

Bacteria in the colon are useful—to a degree. They manufacture vitamin K and several of the B vitamins. But they also feed on protein residues, particularly those that contain sulphur, to form odoriferous chemicals, that emanate from the intestinal gases and faeces that we expel. The nature of the odour depends on the food consumed and on the micro-organisms dominant in a particular person's bowel.

Does constipation matter?

Only rarely is constipation a symptom of a disease or an infection. There is wide variation in how frequently healthy people evacuate their bowels, ranging from two or three times a week to two or three times a day. It is true, however, that constipation can be a problem for the bedridden and the elderly, because physical activity is essential to colonic movement.

When the dry, hard, difficult-to-pass stools that indicate constipation occur, it is frequently because the individual habitually fails to heed the urge to defecate, whenever it is felt. If faeces remain too long in the rectum and colon, they become hard and dry. It is very important to establish a regular time for elimination. Your daily diet should include plenty of fibrous material and liquids, as well as some fat. And you should exercise regularly to improve muscle tone in your abdominal area. Relying on laxa-

tives is unwise. They inhibit the defecation reflexes, and they can even *cause* constipation.

What causes diarrhoea?

Mild and transient diarrhoea comes from a variety of causes: too much food or alcohol, over- or under-ripe raw fruits or vegetables, slightly contaminated foods, allergic reactions to foods, emotional responses to tension and stress, or bacterial or viral infection. Whatever the specific trigger, diarrhoea occurs because irritation has stimulated greater-than-usual waves of movement in the intestinal tract. These waves sweep the faecal matter rapidly out of the digestive system, while allowing too little time for the absorption of nutrients and fluids. The danger of diarrhoea, which can quickly become life threatening for an infant or a young child, is dehydration.

251

Fuelling the Body

What is a Calorie?

In the field of human nutrition, the caloric, or energy, values of food are measured in kilocalories (1,000 calories or 1 Calorie with a capital "C"). The accepted international unit of energy is the kilojoule (1 Calorie equals 4.184 kilojoules).

Different foods provide different amounts of energy, and so have different caloric values. Fat generally supplies nine Calories per gram, and carbohydrates and proteins supply four Calories per gram, while water and cellulose (fibre) have no calories. That is why foods high in fat are highest in calories, and foods high in cellulose and water (such as fresh vegetables) are lowest in calories.

In ordinary life, it is impossible to calculate either the precise number of calories in the food you eat or the exact number of calories you use up. Nevertheless, there are charts that show the approximate calorie count of particular foods, and an estimate of how many calories are expended in such activities as walking, doing housework, and typing. Calorie counting can help in a weight-reducing program. Every kilogram (2.2 pounds) of body weight equals roughly 8,500 Calories. If, every day for a week, you eat 500 Calories less than you expend, you will lose about 500 grams (1 pound). If, for a year, you eat 100 Calories a day more than you burn, you will gain roughly 5 kilograms (10 pounds).

What foods should you eat daily for proper nutrition?

You need energy not only to split wood or to run a marathon but also to watch television and even to sleep. Without energy, the heart will stop pumping; all bodily processes cease, the cells die. While plants get their energy from exposure to the sun, human beings get theirs from eating.

Food is composed of three basic nutrients: proteins, carbohydrates, and fats. It also contains vitamins and minerals that play a vital role in all the chemical processes that go on in the cells. While lean meats are mainly protein, vegetables largely carbohydrate, and oils pure fat, most foods are a mix of the three nutrients.

What is your ideal weight?

If you're thin, you're in, and if you're stout, you're out—at least as far as the trendsetters in fashion are concerned. But medical experts are less sure about the health benefits of thinness and the presumed dangers of overweight. They do not even agree on the precise meaning of overweight. Many doctors would say that if you weigh 10 to 20 percent more than your "ideal" weight on the charts developed by insurance companies, you are probably overweight, and that if you weigh more than 20 percent above your chart weight, you are obese. Obesity, the experts agree, is dangerous for people with high blood pressure, diabetes, and heart disease. But new research suggests that people who are moderately overweight by the charts live longest.

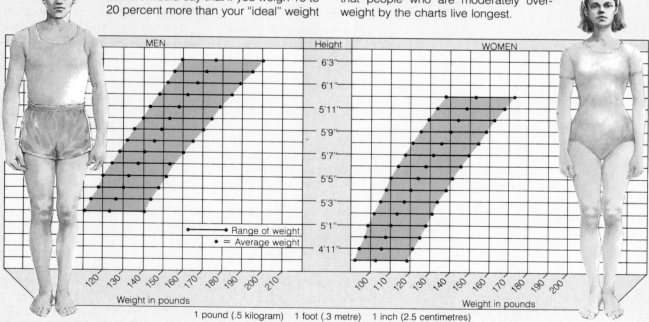

1 pound (.5 kilogram)   1 foot (.3 metre)   1 inch (2.5 centimetres)

Higher levels of desirable weight were recently set by the Metropolitan Life Insurance Company tables (above). These show ideal weights by height and frame for those 25 to 59 years old, in 1-inch-heel shoes, 5 pounds of clothing for men, and 3 pounds for women.

Proteins are the vital building blocks of body tissue, and are required for the growth and repair of cells and for the production of hormones and enzymes. Carbohydrates and fats are your prime source of energy. Fats also perform significant functions in energy storage and insulation.

If you eat a variety of foods, your diet will probably be well balanced, and you will get all the nutrients your body requires. Food is divided into five basic essential groups. This is a guide to a balanced daily intake:

Group 1—Milk products: 600 millilitres (1 pint) for children and expectant and nursing mothers; half this amount for others

Group 2—Poultry, fish, meat, eggs, nuts, and pulses: at least one serving

Group 3—Fruit and vegetables: four varied servings per day

Group 4—Bread, cereals, and other grains: three or more servings per day

Group 5—Fats and oils: no more than 30 grams (1 ounce) per day

How much protein do you need?

The solids of your body are three-quarters protein. Every day, from 20 to 30 grams of protein are needed to make the other chemicals that sustain life. At a minimum, then, you have to consume at least that much protein daily. Health authorities recommend a protein intake of 44 grams a day for the average woman and 56 grams for the average man. (A pint of milk contains 20 grams, an egg 6 grams, 1 chicken breast 52 grams.)

What is "high-quality" protein?

Proteins are made up of amino acids. Most of the 22 we need can be synthesized in the liver, but eight amino acids must be consumed daily in food. These eight are called "essential amino acids." Meat, eggs, milk, and other animal foods contain all 22 amino acids, and they are high-quality protein sources. Because it lacks one or more of the essential amino acids, the protein in plants is incomplete. But if the right combination of plant foods is eaten at one meal, they complement one another and provide complete protein. Rice and beans, or sweet corn and dried peas, are such complementary foods.

How much fat should you eat?

Most people in industrialized societies eat too much fat. Nutritionists recommend a diet that is 10 to 15 percent protein, 55 percent carbohydrate, and 35 percent fat. Most nutritionists advise limiting intake not only of fats in general but of saturated fats in particular. These are fats from animal foods, and are believed to raise the level of cholesterol in the blood, which apparently increases the risk of heart disease. Polyunsaturated fats come from poultry, fish, and vegetables, and may reduce blood cholesterol. However, the subject of cholesterol is very complex, and its role in diet is not fully understood.

The Sailor's Curse and Other Vitamin Deficiency Diseases

In the days of the great sailing vessels, sailors had more to contend with than high seas and stern captains. Scurvy could kill half a ship's crew because the dried foods eaten on long voyages lacked vitamin C. Symptoms included exhaustion, loose teeth, and bleeding from weakened capillaries and membranes around joints. It was long known that fresh fruit cured the condition, but it wasn't until naval doctor James Lind published his book on the subject in 1753 that such foods were provided on British vessels—and British sailors came to be known as "limeys." Japanese sailors were laid low by beriberi from eating polished rice, which lacked the vitamin B of whole rice. Nowadays, scurvy and beriberi are rare in industrialized societies—as well as rickets, a disease caused by a lack of vitamin D in the diet and lack of sunlight. These days, vitamin deficiencies have been replaced by a tendency of some people to take too many!

The tragic consequences of insufficient vitamin D in infancy are seen in this deformed adult skeleton.

If children choose their food, will they eat what is good for them?

You've prepared a delicious, balanced meal: turkey, vegetables, and a salad. But your youngest child clamours for a peanut butter sandwich. Or he eats the turkey but won't touch anything else. It happens often, and you worry about his nutrition. But you needn't be concerned.

If your child is a picky eater, you may feel reassured to know that malnutrition among children is seldom, if ever, caused by a child's food fads. When experimenters have given children the freedom to make their own selections from among a wide array of foods, the youngsters selected, over a period of weeks, the nutrients they needed, even though their choices for particular meals or days were limited. While proper nutrition is vital to a child's growth, a balanced diet can be achieved over a time span of days rather than at every meal.

Pluses and Minuses of Food

What is fibre, and why is it good for you?

You may call it roughage, but by whatever name, fibre is that part of plant food that is not digested. Fibre includes the cellulose, hemicellulose, pectin lignin, mucilage, and gum in vegetables, fruits, and cereals that pass through the digestive tract and into the large intestine unchanged. Fibre is not nutritious, but it is nevertheless useful, even essential.

If you are on a weight-loss diet, fibre-rich food fools you into thinking you're eating more than you are, because they are chewy, and you get a full feeling from them. Fibre absorbs fluid and swells in the body, thereby adding bulk to residues in the intestinal tract, and stimulating the waves of muscular movement that sweep faeces out of the body. This is why dietary fibre helps prevent constipation. It also reduces the straining during bowel movements that may cause haemorrhoids.

Can you consume too much fibre?

Too much of a good thing, even fibre, can have harmful results. The abrupt addition of large amounts of fibre to the diet sometimes causes gas, nausea, and an inability to absorb certain vitamins and minerals. If you decide to eat more fibre, do it gradually. And keep in mind that a high-fibre diet requires no more than 5 grams (0.2 ounces) of fibre daily, about the amount in two slices of whole-wheat bread and a large unpeeled apple. Raw, unpeeled fruits, salads, and whole grain cereals give you vitamins and minerals as well as fibre, so they are preferable to bran, which contains no nutrients.

Do you need vitamin supplements?

Vitamins are complex organic compounds that help you utilize other nutrients. Your body manufactures some but not all vitamins, usually in insufficient quantities; that is why you must get them from food. Vitamins C and B-complex should be in your daily diet because they are quickly excreted. Vitamins A, D, E, and K may be stored in the body for weeks. If you eat a varied, balanced diet, you probably get the vitamins and minerals you need; if you think you lack them, consult a doctor.

Are vitamin megadoses helpful or harmful?

The idea that huge doses of vitamins can prevent disease, or cure everything from the common cold to

A Case History of Overeating

Early in his reign, Henry VIII was "an athletic king, vigorous enough to tire out horses in the chase and opponents on the tennis court." He was a tireless dancer, and was able to drink his courtiers under the table. But his marvellous constitution could not stand up to the day-in, day-out feasting at court. Even ordinary meals were enormous; the menu for one particular day lists a first course of several salads plus cold dishes of "stewed sparrows, carp, capons in lemon, larded pheasants, duck, gulls, brews, forced rabbit, pasty of venison from fallow deer, and pear pasty." The second course of hot dishes included "stork, gannet, heron, pullets, quail, partridge, fresh sturgeon, pasty of venison from red deer, chickens baked in caudle and fritters." This was followed by a lavish array of desserts, and a cordial of spiced wine. Injuries in athletic contests over the years limited the king's activities. Small wonder that he swelled to a grotesque size. When he died, Henry VIII had kidney disease, gout, circulatory disorders, and a "torturously painful" leg ulcer. Although famous for having problems with his wives (six in all, two beheaded), Henry's real trouble may have been food.

Corpulent King Henry VIII, who ruled England from 1509 to 1547, was a victim of too much food.

schizophrenia and cancer, seems to be spreading. So many people are prescribing vitamins for themselves, and doing themselves harm in the process, that a special word—*hypervitaminosis*—has been coined for the condition that results from toxic amounts of vitamins. Vitamin overdoses are especially dangerous for children: they are known to have caused brain dysfunction and even death. Medical researchers are investigating the possible value of vitamin therapy for disease. Right now, however, the consensus of well-informed scientists is that megadoses of vitamins may be an expensive waste, or worse, a threat to your health.

Are the additives in foods dangerous?

Those ingredients that are not naturally present in foods but that are added in processing are called additives. Many enhance the colour, texture, flavour, or body of foods; some are leavening agents that cause baked goods to rise; others are nutrients added to enrich foods. Primarily, however, additives are placed in foods as preservatives, maintaining freshness and flavour, and most important, keeping foods edible and unspoiled.

The readiness to attribute blame for a variety of disorders to additives has not been matched by scientific evidence. Some additives are natural substances, others are synthetics, but they are allowed only in particular manufactured foods in amounts not exceeding stated maximum concentrations. Any of the foods we now take for granted could not be produced without the use of food additives. These range from such common substances as salt and spices to those that are more controversial, such as artificial colours, caffeine and the sweeteners mannitol, sorbitol, and saccharin.

In most industrialized countries refrigeration, dehydration and canning are used extensively to preserve foods, but additives still hold a place. Some people would prefer to avoid them altogether but, to give examples, free-flowing salt, sausages, prepared meats, salad dressings, processed cheeses, and peanut butter could not be packaged without them.

Is caffeine harmless?

If you need a cup of coffee to get going in the morning, you know the virtues of caffeine. A major component of coffee, it is a drug that stimulates the central nervous system and can reduce fatigue and increase alertness. You may have discovered that it can also lead to insomnia, nervousness, and irritability. But you may not know that it can speed up and make the heart beat irregularly, and constrict blood vessels in the brain.

Doctors believe that healthy adults can safely drink the equivalent of one or two cups of coffee a day. Pregnant women, breast-feeding mothers, diabetics, and people with coronary disease or hypertension are advised to avoid caffeine. If you decide to give it up, it might be best to proceed gradually, since it can lead to dependency and withdrawal symptoms; these will disappear when your body is used to doing without it.

Folklore of the Body: FOOD FACTS AND FALLACIES

Is fish brain food? In the 19th century, one scientist discovered that the brain contains phosphorus, and another found that fish are rich in phosphorus. From this, the Swiss naturalist Jean Louis Agassiz concluded that fish is good for the brain. Not so. Nutrients entering the blood reach all parts of the body, not just the brain. Another belief that *seems* logical is that vegetable seeds can cause appendicitis. In an appendicectomy, a small pellet is often found, which resembles a grape stone but is likely to be compacted faecal matter.

The idea that mushrooms are edible if they are white or have a ring at the foot of the stalk is a fallacy. Neither colour nor smell is a reliable guide. Mushrooms should be identified by using an illustrated reference. When in doubt, do not eat it.

HORSE MUSHROOM (*Agaricus arvensis*)
DEATH CAP (*Amanita phalloides*)

A comparison of two species of wild mushrooms, the "safe" horse mushroom and the poisonous death cap, shows how similar they are. The main difference is below the ground.

Can food really poison you?

Abdominal cramps, diarrhoea, vomiting, and sometimes fever and prostration, are signs of food poisoning. The ailment, which can be inconsequential or, occasionally, fatal, comes not from food itself but from bacteria in food that is spoiled. The bacteria, usually either staphylococci or salmonella, are spread by food handlers, by contaminated utensils, or by improper storage or cooking.

Beware of foods that can carry staph germs: cream or egg sauces, salad dressings, salads such as chicken, tuna, and potato, and pastries filled with cream. These are not good picnic foods on a hot summer day unless you have a way of refrigerating them en route to your picnic spot.

Botulism is the most dangerous kind of food poisoning; it can cause muscle paralysis and death. The bacteria that cause botulism grow only in the absence of air. Their usual habitat is canned food that was not properly heated during the canning process. If you can food at home, you should follow to the letter the preparation advice of a reliable authority.

255

Eating: Too Much, Too Little

Do diets really work?

Every year, thousands of people go on weight-control diets and lose thousands of kilograms—and then gain them right back. In some studies, only 5 percent of dieters managed to lose 10 kilograms (22 pounds) and keep them off.

Why should weight loss be so difficult? Some nutritionists believe that everyone has an internal set point, a natural weight established by a kind of body thermostat that a dieter can override only with difficulty, if at all. According to this theory, your body has "decided" how fat you will be, and you will stay at that level, or come back to it, no matter what you eat. Intriguing as this idea is, it is only a theory. Other experts believe that overweight is caused by biochemical defects in the body mechanisms that control appetite and metabolize food.

The main reason most popular diets do not work is simple: they run counter to nutritional and psychological realities. Some fad diets are so monotonous that no one could be expected to stay on them for long. Others are so low in calories that dieters cheat out of sheer hunger. As for crash diets, they do cause an initial drop in weight, but the loss is misleading; you lose water, not fat.

Is exercise effective against fat?

If you exercise more, you are very likely to lose weight—even if you don't eat less. Physical activity not only burns calories, thus reducing the number that can be stored as fat, but also increases your basal metabolic rate, causing your body to burn off additional calories. Exercise suppresses appetite, reduces the depression and anxiety that cause some people to overeat, and builds lean muscle tissue, which uses up more calories than does fat.

Experts recommend sustained activity at least every other day for a minimum of 30 minutes each time. Whatever you do should be strenuous enough to increase your pulse rate and respiration and make you perspire. Fast walking, running, swimming, cycling, skating, skiing, and stair climbing can all fill the bill.

Is there any sensible way to lose weight?

Most successful dieters eat well-balanced meals, cutting down on extremely fattening foods, and consuming enough calories to keep them from feeling unsatisfied. Instead of trying to become unrealistically slim, these people have generally set rather modest weight-loss goals for themselves. And instead of trying to lose large amounts of weight in a short time, they have allowed themselves time to lose the weight gradually. Some people seek the psychological support of weight-loss groups, which often prove helpful. Other people take advantage of behaviour-modification techniques—they may take note of situations that lead to overeating and

Sumo wrestlers carry on a 2,000-year-old Japanese tradition. Most wrestlers retire by 35; some weigh up to 200 kilograms (30 stone). Balance, agility, and a low centre of gravity are essential to their success.

try to avoid them. For instance, they may avoid shopping for food when they are hungry and therefore likely to overbuy. They may form the habit of postponing second helpings for 20 minutes—long enough to realize that they don't need any more to eat.

Nutrition experts from a leading U.S. medical school have two useful bits of advice: "Don't try to live on grapefruit, lettuce, and iced tea. It just won't work in the long run for most people." And "Preventing weight gain is ultimately the best defence against obesity...Focus on *not gaining* rather than slimming down."

When does loss of appetite become dangerous?

Perhaps in response to media emphasis on thinness, increasing numbers of young women are voluntarily starving themselves to the point of malnutrition and sometimes even death. This condition is called anorexia nervosa, which translates as "nervous lack of appetite." Once a very rare affliction, anorexia nervosa is now thought to affect as many as one of every 100 girls aged 14 to 18. Boys and adults suffer from it only occasionally.

The ailment is a psychosomatic illness characterized by a refusal to eat, sometimes accompanied by strenuous exercising, self-induced vomiting, and the taking of laxatives and diuretics to cause further weight loss. Symptoms include loss of up to 25 percent of normal weight, along with a distorted self-image: although an anorexic may come to look skeletal, she may insist that she looks repulsively fat. As weight loss continues, symptoms of starvation begin to appear. The patient stops menstruating. Her heart rate slows, and she feels cold continually. In the worst cases, the anorexic may hallucinate.

Believed to be psychological in origin, anorexia nervosa often stems from disturbed family relationships and inner conflicts about the physical changes of puberty, the emotional stresses of growing up, and the prospect of becoming independent. Recent research suggests the possibility of some physiological basis (hormonal and hypothalamic abnormalities) for the ailment. Early medical attention is essential to keep the patient from starving to death, and psychotherapy is usually needed to help resolve underlying emotional problems.

What is bulimia?

The average individual consumes roughly 2,000 to 3,000 Calories a day; a bulimic may take in from 10,000 to 20,000 Calories at one time, and occasionally as many as 50,000 Calories in one day. But bulimia is much more than an abnormal craving for food. It has been characterized as a binge/purge cycle, in which the victim first consumes enormous quantities of food and then purges herself or himself through self-induced vomiting, laxatives, diuretics, and punishing amounts of exercise.

The vast majority of bulimia sufferers are females in their teens and twenties. By some estimates, from 1 to 4 percent of today's young women are full-blown bulimics, while another 15 to 30 percent binge and purge occasionally. Bulimia has been variously described as an obsession, an addiction, and an emotional illness. By any name, it is disabling and terrifying to its victims. They feel out of control and deeply ashamed, and invariably keep their bulimic behaviour a closely guarded (and often very expensive) secret.

Bulimia often begins with extreme dieting, which is sometimes triggered off by an emotional loss. Then, feeling deprived and hungry, the dieter first goes on an eating binge and then seeks to get rid of the kilojoules and at the same time regain some sense of self-control.

Most bulimia victims are attractive, intelligent young women, perfectionists who present a successful facade while suffering from a poor self-image. Group therapy is sometimes thought to be the most effective treatment. Its aim is generally to teach the patients to turn to people rather than food for solace and support.

Anorexia Nervosa: A Disease of Self-Loathing?

The questions asked, over and over, by parents and friends of anorexia nervosa victims (most often teenaged women) are: Why is she starving herself to death? How can she think herself too fat, when her bones are sticking out? In some cases, the individual has a history of obesity; by means of dieting—usually a fad diet—she has lost weight. But instead of resuming normal eating after her acceptable weight has been reached, she continues dieting to the point of starvation. One theory holds that the victim is expressing a desire to control her life, another that she has low self-esteem, and another that she does not want to grow up (the anorexia victim has a childlike figure and ceases to menstruate). Whatever the cause, the only known cure is intensive medical counselling.

This **classic case** of anorexia nervosa (above) was reported in the British medical journal, *The Lancet,* in 1888. The then-rare disorder was nevertheless successfully treated; the young woman is shown six months later (right), fully recovered.

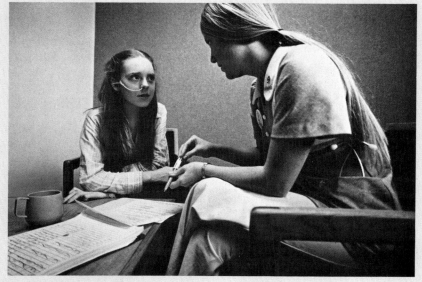

A **present-day anorexia nervosa victim** is treated medically (note feeding tube in the patient's nose). Unless she can also be reached emotionally, the outlook is bleak.

Chapter 11

THE URINARY & REPRODUCTIVE SYSTEMS

Though linked by location, these two systems have vastly different functions. One regulates our fluid balance, the other ensures our survival as a species.

Maintaining Your Fluid Balance	260
The Composition of Urine	262
Urinary Problems and Remedies	264
The Male Reproductive System	266
The Production of Sperm	268
Causes of Impotence	270
The Female Reproductive System	272
The Functioning of the Uterus	274
Understanding the Female Body	276
Sexually Transmitted Diseases	278
The Changing Nature of VD	280
The Timing of Fertility	282
Marriage: The Ceremonies Vary, but the Meaning Is the Same	283
Dealing With Infertility	284
Methods of Contraception	286

What is the most surprising characteristic of urine?

After urine is eliminated, it is easily contaminated by bacteria, but at the moment it leaves a healthy body, it is sterile. As a matter of fact, urine has been used as an antiseptic in emergency situations in which no conventional disinfectant was available. Moreover, people stranded in the desert have been known to survive by drinking their own urine. It is also clear that even when severe dehydration threatens the body, the kidneys continue to draw water from the tissues to produce urine.

How does what you consume affect your need to urinate?

When you drink coffee, tea, or cola, or consume anything else that contains caffeine, your need to urinate is greater than it would otherwise be, because caffeine is a diuretic: it increases the amount of urine the kidneys produce. When you drink a lot of water or other beverages, your kidneys work to maintain a constant level of fluids in your body: you eliminate the excess promptly.

When is it especially important to drink plenty of fluids?

If you have a fever that makes you perspire profusely, or suffer from persistent vomiting or diarrhoea, your body tends to become dehydrated. That is why you are often told to "drink plenty of fluids" when you are ill; water is vital to kidney function. It is also important to replenish lost fluids when you engage in strenuous exercise or hard physical work, particularly in warm weather.

Why does nervousness sometimes produce an urge to urinate?

In an emotionally stressful situation, some people feel a strong need to relieve themselves even though the bladder contains little fluid. The reason is simple but surprising. When people are nervous and upset, the bladder may, in a sense, become "nervous," too. That is, the muscles of the bladder may lose the capacity to relax. It is the tightened muscle that brings on the urge to urinate.

Why does the colour of urine vary?

Urine gets its yellow colour from a pigment called urochrome. The exact hue, however, varies with the changing composition of urine. When the kidneys excrete a large amount of water, the urine is diluted and therefore pale. But when the body needs to conserve liquid, the kidneys produce a more concentrated and therefore darker urine which contains less water than usual. One of the times this happens is during sleep, when consumption of food and fluids ceases and the body processes slow down. That is why the day's first urine is generally dark.

Do the kidneys have anything to do with hangovers?

If you drink a lot of water when you drink alcohol, you may avoid some of the effects of a hangover. Alcohol dilates the blood vessels and has a diuretic effect; it increases the flow of blood through the kidneys and stimulates them to produce more urine than usual. When this happens, the body may excrete more water than it is taking in. The resulting dehydration causes the dry mouth and aching head of a hangover.

Are over-the-counter medications harmful to the kidneys?

Aspirin and other pain relievers should not be taken casually, since they may cause kidney damage if used excessively. When taken in large amounts, antacids or bicarbonate of soda may also harm the kidneys. Moderate amounts of these preparations, however, taken when really necessary, will not cause problems.

In some cultures, a baby is trained before it is even able to sit up. But in other cultures, parents believe it is better to wait and enlist the baby's cooperation—which usually occurs between the ages of two and three.

At what age do children learn to control their bladders?

For infants and young children, relieving themselves is a reflex action: as the bladder fills, its walls expand, the bladder muscle contracts, the sphincter muscle opens, and urination occurs automatically. When children are about two and a half years old, however, they begin to exert conscious control over urination, and, by the age of three, most children can initiate or prevent the emptying of their bladders at will. Despite their parents' zealous attempts, children cannot be completely "toilet-trained" much before that, according to the experts, because the higher centres of the brain have not yet taken over control of the urinary function.

Is there any connection between diet, weight, and reproduction?

Proper nourishment is essential to the fertility of both husband and wife. Body fat also plays a key role in ensuring fertility. The ovaries manufacture the female hormone oestrogen from the fatty substance cholesterol; when a woman is seriously underweight, she produces less oestrogen and may lose the ability to ovulate and menstruate. (That helps to explain why many weight-conscious ballet dancers menstruate irregularly or not at all.) When a woman is grossly overweight, the effect is similar; changes occur in her hormone levels that cause failure to ovulate. Obesity may also adversely affect the ability of a man to sire offspring. Excess fat may cause overheating of the testicles, which sometimes leads to underproduction of sperm.

What is the menopause?

By the time a woman is 45 years old, about 450 of her ovarian follicles have ripened and ovulated; only a few are left to secrete oestrogens and progesterone. Over the following months or years, these too will be used up, until her production of feminizing hormones is essentially zero, and her two ovaries have ceased to function as glands. Not only do a woman's monthly cycles now come to an end, but as her body attempts to adjust to the radical change in its hormonal environment, she may suffer from flushing, sweating, irritability, fatigue, anxiety, and depression for months, sometimes for years.

Is there such a thing as "male menopause"?

Men's testes undergo a gradual decline, but usually continue to produce sperm throughout life and never cease their production of testosterone altogether. Men sometimes have an emotional "mid-life crisis" but, unlike women, it is nothing to do with declining hormone production.

Maintaining Your Fluid Balance

How does your body respond to thirst?

If the concentration of salt in the blood is too high, or if you are dehydrated, specialized cells called osmoreceptors, located in the hypothalamus, will sense these changes and signal the posterior pituitary gland to secrete a hormone called antidiuretic hormone (ADH). ADH increases the amount of water that the kidneys reabsorb. In addition, the release of a hormone called angiotensin signals the hypothalamus in the brain to produce a sensation of thirst by ordering the salivary glands to reduce their secretions. The dry mouth and throat that you then experience lead you to drink until you have restored your body's depleted water reserves. Curiously, as soon as you have ingested enough fluid, the sensation of thirst disappears—even though it takes as long as an hour for the body to absorb the water you drink.

What is the role of the kidneys?

The main task of the kidneys is to cleanse the blood of poisons and impurities, but they do much more than just filtering and purifying the blood. They regulate its volume, recycle water, minerals, and nutrients, and adjust the chemical composition of the blood—making sure that it contains the right balance of constituents.

The kidneys are reddish brown in colour and are bean-shaped. Each one of the pair is not much bigger than an extra-large bar of soap, yet together they receive about a litre (1.75 pints) of blood a minute, pumped into them from the aorta. Without the kidneys, or a substitute for them, you would die: from poisoning by your own wastes, from lack of vital nutrients, or from drowning in excess body fluids.

How do the kidneys function?

Each kidney contains about a million microscopic units called nephrons, which filter blood, reabsorb wa-

ter and nutrients, and produce urine to carry off wastes. In the many twists and turns of their tiny tubes, the nephrons process about 180 litres (40 gallons) of fluid every day. Of this amount, only a litre (1.75 pints) or so is eliminated as urine.

Your blood pours into the kidney through the renal artery and is forced under pressure into a ball of capillaries called the glomerulus. That structure is the part of the nephron that filters out the blood cells, platelets, and protein, and allows some of the plasma, the liquid portion of the blood, to pass through, as filtrate, into Bowman's capsule, a container that surrounds and sheathes the sieve-like glomerulus. To picture this part of the nephron, imagine a child's hand cupped around a golf ball, and think of the hand as Bowman's capsule and the glomerulus as the golf ball, with a network of threadlike capillaries inside. The filtrate, which will become urine, passes out of Bowman's capsule through the nephron's convoluted tubule and a hairpin-shaped structure known as the loop of Henle. Then it travels back out to

the renal cortex and down through the collecting duct, finally exiting as urine at the renal pelvis. As the fluid drains through the nephron, it is surrounded by capillaries that reabsorb the materials the body needs. The renal vein is the conduit for blood flowing out of the kidney.

How does an artificial kidney work?

When people's kidneys fail, their own wastes will poison them unless impurities in the blood can be removed by other means. That is precisely what the machine known as an artificial kidney accomplishes. This device is used in cases of kidney failure, giving the patient's own kidneys a chance to heal and resume normal function. Many people whose kidneys have been removed or destroyed have been kept alive for years by an artificial kidney.

The process of purifying the blood by means of an artificial kidney is called haemodialysis. Two or three times a week, for four to eight hours

During kidney dialysis, the patient's blood is protected from clotting by the addition of an anticlotting substance, heparin. As the blood is returned, an antiheparin substance is added, thus protecting the patient from bleeding.

at a time, the patient is connected to the machine. The waste-laden blood flows into a tube, made of semi-permeable cellophane, submerged in a chemical solution that is kept at body temperature. Microscopic waste particles pass through the cellophane into the solution, and purified blood is returned to the patient's body.

Some haemodialysis machines are small enough and simple enough to be used at home, and some patients are even able to sleep during the process. But haemodialysis is not without risk, and a trained person (who may be a spouse or another family member) must be on hand at all times to be sure nothing goes wrong.

In peritoneal dialysis, blood purification takes place inside the patient's body. The dialysing solution is channelled into the abdominal cavity, and diffusion of wastes from the blood into the solution occurs across the peritoneum—the membrane that lines the cavity. The procedure takes from 24 to 48 hours each week and requires close medical supervision.

Are kidney transplants usually successful?

Organ transplants are feasible only when donor and recipient are closely matched in tissue and blood type. The prospects of success are greatest when the donor is the patient's identical twin; the next best choice is a brother, sister, or some other close relative. Since the body rejects foreign tissue, the major obstacle to success in an organ transplant is the patient's immune system. For months or years after a transplant, the patient must take drugs that block the body's immune system—unfortunately making the patient vulnerable to infections. However, recent advances in surgical techniques, cross-matching techniques, and the introduction of the immunosuppressive agent cyclosporine prolong the survival of transplanted kidneys. A kidney donated by a relative will have a 90 percent chance of surviving two years, while a kidney from a cadaver has a 75 percent chance of surviving two years.

Where are your kidneys, and what do they do?

The kidneys lie one on each side of the spinal column, at the back just above the waist. The outer part of the kidney is called the cortex, the inner part, the medulla. A concave recess on the surface of each kidney is the place where the kidney is connected to the rest of the body. It is here that blood flows in and out, and through which urine (manufactured in the kidney) is excreted. The medulla consists of 12 to 18 conical structures called renal pyramids; these drain into the renal pelvis. From here, urine passes through the ureter to the bladder.

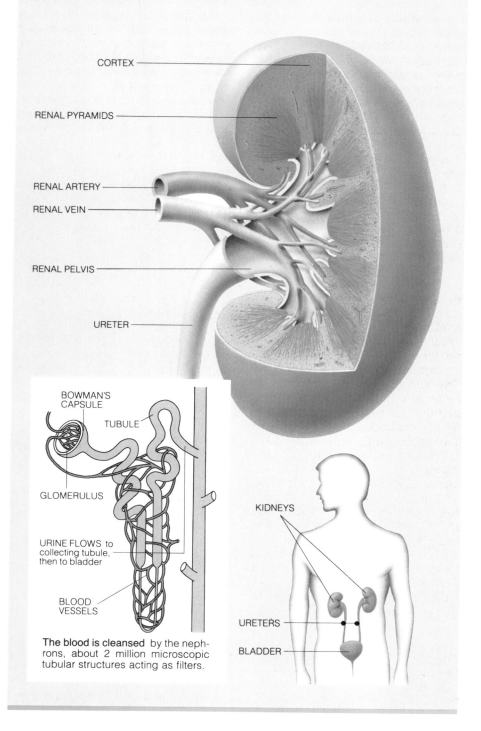

CORTEX

RENAL PYRAMIDS

RENAL ARTERY

RENAL VEIN

RENAL PELVIS

URETER

BOWMAN'S CAPSULE

TUBULE

GLOMERULUS

URINE FLOWS to collecting tubule, then to bladder

BLOOD VESSELS

The blood is cleansed by the nephrons, about 2 million microscopic tubular structures acting as filters.

KIDNEYS

URETERS

BLADDER

The Composition of Urine

What is urine made of?

When the cells of your body burn calories to create energy, they produce waste products that would destroy you if they were allowed to accumulate in your tissues. Instead, the wastes stream into the blood and are transported to the kidneys, which reclaim the valuable components of the blood and manufacture urine to get rid of injurious or unnecessary materials. Produced continuously, urine serves as the primary channel for expelling waste products containing nitrogen. These include urea, uric acid, and creatinine, formed as the result of the breakdown of protein, nucleic acid, and creatine in the body cells. Excess sodium, potassium, chloride, calcium, magnesium, iron, sulphate, phosphate, and bicarbonate are also deposited in the urine for excretion.

The major component of urine is water. Though the exact percentage of water in the urine varies, depending on your general health, what you have been eating and drinking, and whether you exercise, urine is generally about 95 or 96 percent water.

How is urine eliminated?

Urine, which is continuously produced by the kidneys, trickles down 24 hours a day through two 250- to 300-millimetre (10- to 12-inch) long tubes called ureters, connecting the kidneys to the bladder. About 6 millimetres (a quarter of an inch) in diameter, the muscular walls of the ureters often constrict, creating waves of movement that force the urine into the bladder. This expandable receptacle for storing urine contracts to initiate urination, and to close off the

What stimulates urination?

As urine accumulates in the bladder, the elastic walls are stretched. Sensors in the tissues trigger off the urge to urinate when the bladder contains about 500 millilitres (1 pint) of urine. Though urination is voluntary, once started, it takes place in a series of reflex actions. The bladder muscles contract to squeeze out the urine, and the sphincter muscle that closes off the urethra opens to let urine pass through.

EPITHELIAL CELLS of contracted bladder

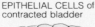

EPITHELIAL CELLS of stretched bladder

URETERS are 250 to 300 millimetres (10 to 12 inches) long, leading from kidneys to bladder

OPENINGS of ureters into bladder

SPHINCTER MUSCLES

URETHRA

At most, a bladder holds almost a litre (1.75 pints).

The contracted bladder wall, shown in a micrograph, is tough and muscular.

When stretched to full capacity, the same tissue is only a few cells thick.

ureters to prevent urine from flowing back to the kidneys. Urine is expelled from the body through a small tube called the urethra.

Do you eliminate the same amount of fluid that you take in?

No matter how much fluid you take in, the total amount of water in your body remains fairly constant. The kidneys keep it that way by adjusting the amount of water in the urine, either increasing or decreasing it, in order to keep your body fluids in balance. In other words, your daily output of water matches your input.

What causes an increase or a decrease in the volume of urine?

The amount of urine that you eliminate is largely determined by the body's need to maintain its equilibrium. Water is the most important constituent of the body, accounting for nearly 60 percent of the weight of a lean adult; the percentage is smaller in a fat person. The body eliminates excess fluid through a variety of channels: water escapes in the breath, evaporates through the skin, is exuded by the sweat glands as perspiration, and is excreted in the faeces. Sometimes the body loses excessive amounts of water as a result of hot weather, exercise, or an illness that causes perspiration, vomiting, or diarrhoea. At such times, the kidneys are called upon to conserve the body's liquid resources.

Like the manager of a city's water-supply system when a shortfall of rain gives warning of a possible drought, the hypothalamus (a tiny organ in brain) keeps a close watch over the quantity of fluids in the body. When it detects a lowering of water volume, it signals the pituitary gland to release the antidiuretic hormone (ADH) into the bloodstream, thus increasing the capacity of the kidneys to reabsorb and recycle water. On the other hand, if the body is receiving more fluid than is necessary, the hypothalamus decreases the secretion of ADH.

Folklore of the Body: GOUT AS A SIGN OF HIGH LIVING

Gout sufferers are often pictured as gluttonous, heavy-drinking folk, who, more than likely, have brought their affliction on themselves, a portrayal that adds insult to injury. The fact is that a tendency to gout is inherited. And while the disease can be aggravated by certain foods and alcohol, gout is a form of arthritis caused by a metabolic disorder. Victims of gout cannot properly metabolize purines, which are uric-acid-forming substances found in food and also manufactured by the body. In gout sufferers, high levels of uric acid accumulate in the blood, then precipitate out, forming deposits in the joints. Gout strikes suddenly, causing agonizing pain and swollen joints. Attacks can be brought on by trauma, fatigue, an infection, a low-carbohydrate diet, stress, or strenuous exercise. Gout most often afflicts middle-aged men. It is an ancient disease, still being treated by an ancient remedy: a herbal drug called colchicine.

The big toe is where gout is commonly felt. It causes swelling and pain akin to torture.

Another mechanism that regulates water and salt is a feedback system that begins and ends with the kidneys. Blood pressure drops when the level of sodium in the blood falls. As soon as such a sodium deficiency occurs, the kidneys secrete an enzyme named renin that initiates a chain of chemical events in the kidneys and the bloodstream. The result is the formation of a hormone called angiotensin that stimulates the adrenal gland to release aldosterone, which promotes the reabsorption of sodium. Angiotensin also constricts the blood vessels, thus raising the blood pressure and increasing the rate at which blood filters through the kidneys. It also prods the hypothalamus to trigger off the release of ADH and to create a sensation of thirst. The restoration of blood pressure and sodium concentration in the blood to normal levels then turns off renal renin secretion.

How do the male and female urinary systems differ?

There are major fundamental differences between the urinary tracts of men and of women. In women, the urethra is a tube about 40 millimetres (1.5 inches) long, which serves the exclusive function of conveying urine from the bladder out of the body. The bladder of the female lies in front of the vagina and uterus.

In men, the urethra is a tube approximately 200 millimetres (8 inches) in length which passes through the prostate gland and for most of its length through the penis; it serves the dual purpose of expelling both seminal fluid and urine. When a man urinates, the process automatically closes the opening into the urethra for seminal fluid, thus allowing only urine to flow through. The bladder of the male lies immediately in front of the rectum.

Urinary Problems and Remedies

Why is it important to treat minor urinary tract infections?

Cystitis, or inflammation of the bladder, is a very common bacterial infection usually caused by germs that spread from the intestinal tract through the urethra and into the bladder. It is more prevalent among women than among men, because the female urethra is short and because its opening is so near the anus and vagina.

Symptoms include a frequent, urgent need to urinate, even when there is little fluid in the bladder, and a burning sensation when the urine passes. Some people develop a fever, and blood may appear in their urine. Cystitis is not dangerous in itself, and it can be quickly and successfully treated with antibiotics. In fact, the symptoms often clear up so rapidly that the patient believes the infection is over and stops taking the prescribed medication too soon. Then the micro-organisms may travel up the ureters to the kidneys and cause pyelonephritis, which is potentially more dangerous than cystitis. That is why patients should finish the full course of antibiotics prescribed for them even if they think they're cured.

Why do some children wet their beds?

About 15 percent of children over five years old wet their beds occasionally, boys more often than girls. Most doctors believe that bed-wetting is generally caused by a late-maturing nervous system or by a small bladder. Most of these children will gain control of their bladders by the age of ten. Bed-wetting is primarily psychological in origin in 20 to 30 percent of cases—the result of conflict between parent and child or some other emotional difficulty. Psychotherapy may help these youngsters. In 20 percent of the cases, infections or anomalies of the lower urinary tract may be the cause of bed-wetting. Limiting fluid intake at bedtime and using a moisture-activated buzzer device may help in these cases.

What are kidney stones?

Most kidney stones are composed of calcium, which has precipitated out of urine and crystallized. Victims of gout sometimes form stones made of uric acid. Certain people are particularly at risk of developing stones: those who become dehydrated from living in a tropical climate or doing strenuous physical work, those with an inherited predisposition to forming stones, and those who lead a sedentary life, and who accumulate excessive calcium in their blood.

Kidney stones may be minuscule in size, or as large as 25 millimetres (1 inch) or more in diameter. Eighty-five percent of all kidney stones are small enough to move through the urinary tract and out of the body without surgical intervention. A large stone that becomes lodged in the renal pelvis, the ureter, or the bladder causes agonizing pain and obstructs the kidney. There is not much a doctor can do to facilitate a stone's passage through the urinary tract except to give the patient painkillers and plenty of fluids.

Is surgery always necessary to relieve kidney stones?

Doctors can now dissolve or remove most stones that are causing their patients problems without performing open surgery. By using a machine that generates shock waves, a doctor can pulverize stones in the kidney and upper ureter into sand-like particles that can be easily passed in the urine. Alternatively, a kidney stone can be removed by inserting a special type of endoscopic instrument called a nephroscope into the kidney through a small incision, allowing the renal stone to be visualized, pulverized to a smaller size with ultrasonic waves, and removed from the kidney. Stones that are lodged in the ureter near the bladder can be removed with a ureteroscope which is introduced through the urethra and bladder into the ureter.

Some types of kidney stones lend themselves to dissolution. Uric acid

THE STORY BEHIND THE WORDS...

Male and female are such obviously paired words that you would expect them to originate from a common source, but such is not the case. Though in the biblical story Eve does spring from Adam, the word *female* does not stem from the word *male*. Female comes from the Latin *femella*, and male comes from the Latin *masculus*. Woman and man, however, are related words; woman is a combination of *wif* and *man,* the words for "wife" and "human being" in Old English.

Venereal, which comes from the name of Venus, the Roman goddess of love, may be defined as "relating to sexual pleasure," though, in practice, it is almost never used in that sense. Venereal is now used almost exclusively in the phrase "venereal disease," where it means a "sexually transmitted" condition.

Virility is sometimes thought to be synonymous with fertility, but the two are not the same. A man can be virile or potent—that is, capable of erection and ejaculation—but still be infertile because his sperm are malformed, or are poor swimmers, or are too few in number.

Androgynous, which means having the characteristics of both male and female, and androgens, which are male sex hormones, are words that are easily confused. *Androgynous* stems from two Greek words: *andro,* meaning "man," and *gyne,* meaning "woman." (Gynaecology is the branch of medicine that deals with the specific functions and dysfunctions of the woman's reproductive system.) Androgen, on the other hand, stems from *andro* and from another Greek word, *genus,* which means "birth." *Genus* is also the root for such words as *gender, progeny,* and *generation.*

Urinalysis: Valuable in Diagnosis

Ancient Greek, Roman, and Arab doctors used six basic diagnostic measures: the patient's behaviour, the location of the pain, the intensity and type of pain, swellings, foul odours, and urine analysis. The urine's colour, smell, consistency, sediment content, and taste helped identify the ailment and determine treatment. Today, urine continues to provide vital medical guidance. An early-morning specimen is preferred because it is concentrated. Subsequent analysis, including a microscopic search for bacteria, can show potential kidney malfunctions through the level of acidity or abnormal proteins, blood cells, or crystals. Excess sugar is a sign of diabetes. A high white cell count can indicate a urinary-tract infection. Poisons and drug use can also be detected in a urinalysis.

This medieval medical chart, showing various urine colours and sediment contents, suggested possible maladies from which the patient could be suffering.

Bile pigments give urine a greenish-yellow or golden brown colour and can be a symptom of liver problems.

The 17th-century Dutch genre painter Gerard Dou recorded urine examination in *The Dropsical Woman*.

---

stones are very soluble in sodium bicarbonate solution and can be dissolved by irrigation for several days with this substance. Unfortunately, stones containing calcium are not safely soluble.

If a stone should obstruct the kidney, renal damage may result if the stone does not pass spontaneously or is not removed. When a stone is very large and occupies a large portion of the kidney, these more conservative methods of stone removal may not work, and most likely the stone will have to be removed surgically. If an obstructing kidney stone is present in association with a urinary infection, a life-threatening situation exists, requiring antibiotics and immediate relief of the obstruction.

How can kidney stones be prevented?

There are a number of ways to prevent the formation of stones. One very effective and inexpensive method is to drink abundant fluids daily. Specific medications are also available to prevent the formation of most kidney stones, once the patient is stone free.

The Male Reproductive System

What is the structure of the testicles?

White in colour and shaped like an egg, each testicle is divided into 250 to 400 lobules that contain the tiny seminiferous tubules in which the sperm are produced. So coiled, twisted, and convoluted are the tubules that, although their total length can be well over 200 metres (650 feet), they are contained in a testicle only 40 to 50 millimetres (1.5 to 2 inches) long. Interspersed among the tubules are the interstitial cells of Leydig, which secrete testosterone. Another group of structures, the Sertoli cells, are rich in glycogen and are believed to provide nutrients for the developing spermatids.

Why does the scrotum lie outside the abdomen?

If it seems surprising that the testicles, which produce life-initiating sperm, should lie in a vulnerable position outside the male body, there is a simple explanation: it's too hot inside the body. Sperm production is best accomplished when the temperature is three to five degrees below body temperature. Normally, the scrotum muscles are relaxed, and the testicles lie in a cool position, away from the abdomen and thighs. But if it gets too cool there, the muscles of the scrotum contract and bring the testes close to the warm trunk. The right temperature for producing spermatozoa is so important that even such a seemingly harmless practice as wearing tight clothing has been known to affect the fertility of the male.

What are the main parts of the male reproductive system?

A pair of testicles, or testes, which lie outside the abdominal cavity in the pouch called the scrotum, produce sperm, which fertilize the female eggs. This is the means by which the male's genes are passed on to his offspring. The testes also manufacture testosterone, the hormone that regulates masculine development. The penis conveys sperm from male to female. Less familiar but nevertheless essential parts of the male reproductive system include the epididymis, a thin, coiled tube located in the scrotum alongside each testicle, where sperm mature; and the vas deferens, a duct where sperm are stored and through which they are transported to the urethra. The bulbourethral glands, the seminal vesicles, and the prostate are also essential parts of the male reproductive system; all secrete substances that make up the sperm-laden semen.

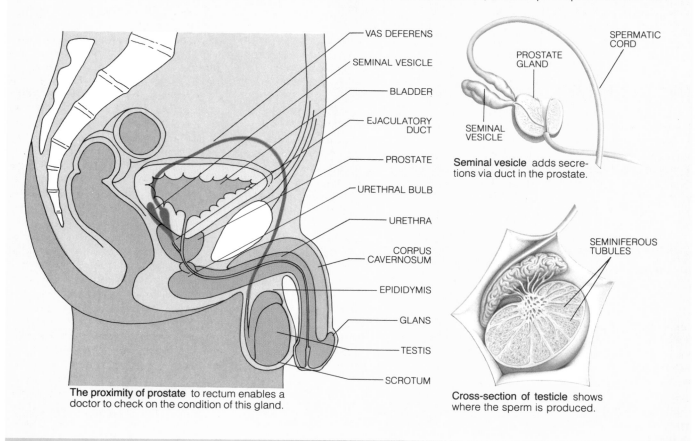

VAS DEFERENS
SEMINAL VESICLE
BLADDER
EJACULATORY DUCT
PROSTATE
URETHRAL BULB
URETHRA
CORPUS CAVERNOSUM
EPIDIDYMIS
GLANS
TESTIS
SCROTUM

PROSTATE GLAND
SPERMATIC CORD
SEMINAL VESICLE

Seminal vesicle adds secretions via duct in the prostate.

SEMINIFEROUS TUBULES

The proximity of prostate to rectum enables a doctor to check on the condition of this gland.

Cross-section of testicle shows where the sperm is produced.

What leads to an erection of the penis?

The passageway for semen to the external world is the urethra, a channel inside the penis that transfers sperm from male to female. The penis lies just in front of the scrotum. It is cylindrical in shape and contains three masses of sponge-like erectile tissue, resembling columns, that run through it lengthwise. These spaces, which are sometimes called "cavernous" tissue, fill up with arterial blood whenever the male becomes sexually aroused. The result is an enlargement and a hardening of the usually limp penis to permit penetration of the female vagina.

What happens during ejaculation?

The climax of the reproductive act is orgasm, which for the male entails the ejaculation, or discharge, of semen. During orgasm, the heart rate increases, blood pressure rises, and emotional excitement reaches a climax. In the male, orgasm begins with emission, the movement of sperm cells into the urethra by means of rhythmic contractions of muscles in the testes, epididymis, and vasa deferentia. At the same time, muscles of the prostate gland and the seminal vesicles contract, pouring their secretions into the urethra. When the penis is filled with the sperm and the secretions, contractions of muscles at its base cause ejaculation. Then the erection of the penis subsides.

Is the prostate gland related to sexual performance?

The prostate gland lies directly below the neck of the male urinary bladder. The narrow channel that runs through the prostate is the urethra, which may be partly blocked off by any disease that affects the prostate. Since semen as well as urine pass through the urethra, any prostate troubles that affect that channel are likely to cause sexual as well as urinary difficulties.

Circumcision, the removal of the foreskin of males, is a Mosaic religious requirement set forth in the book of Genesis. Jesus' circumcision is here portrayed by the 15th-century painter Andrea Mantegna.

Why is the prostate so often a source of trouble for older men?

After the age of 50 or 60, the prostate gland tends to increase in size. As it does, it may compress the urethra, restrict the flow of urine, create a frequent, urgent need to empty the bladder, and make urination difficult. Moreover, retention of urine can cause inflammation of the bladder and possible kidney damage. It is sometimes necessary to perform surgery in order to remove the enlarged section of the prostate.

Does surgery for an enlarged prostate affect sexual functioning?

The prostate gland produces a fluid that provides the necessary alkaline environment for sperm. When a benign growth of the prostate is surgi-

cally corrected, most of the gland itself remains, and a man's potency is rarely affected. In some cases, however, surgery may cause retrograde ejaculation: during orgasm, semen may pass into the bladder rather than out through the urethra.

Why do doctors examine the rectum to detect an enlarged prostate?

If a man has an enlarged prostate, he need not worry that it will lead to cancer: the two conditions are unrelated. Nevertheless, prostate cancer is common, and doctors recommend a rectal examination for any man over the age of 50. Since the prostate is located immediately in front of the rectum, changes in the gland are easily detected during a rectal examination. When prostate cancer is diagnosed and treated soon after its onset, the prognosis is quite good.

What is the reason for circumcision?

Circumcision is the surgical removal of the foreskin, or prepuce, a flap of tissue that usually covers the glans, or head of the penis. The great majority of North American males, as well as many boys in other parts of the world, are circumcised soon after they are born. For Jews and Muslims, circumcision is a religious rite. Some doctors advise circumcision as a hygienic measure for all male infants, partly on the ground that it reduces the risk of infection by preventing the accumulation of smegma, a secretion of the glans, under the foreskin, where bacteria frequently breed. These doctors also believe that circumcision may ultimately prevent cancer, both of the penis and of the cervix of the female sexual partner.

Many experts, however, state that circumcision is not only unnecessary for most males but that it causes severe pain, can cause complications such as bleeding, and may be psychologically damaging to infants. Doctors in Britain hold that circumcision is not medically necessary.

The Production of Sperm

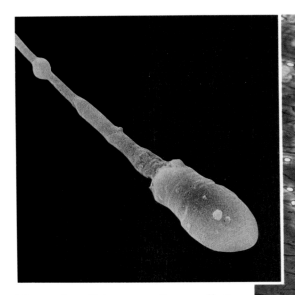

The male cell is among the smallest of all human cells, yet it carries the father's full legacy to the child.

Streams of sperm, propelled by lashing tails, line up in the direction of an egg. In the absence of an egg, no such formations are seen.

How are sperm produced?

Spermatogenesis, the process of making sperm, begins with germ cells called spermatogonia that were formed during foetal life and have been stored ever since in the tubules of the testes. Each of these cells carries 46 chromosomes bearing a full complement of genes. Under the influence of hormones, the germ cells go through several transformations, eventually becoming spermatozoa, or mature sperm. Each sperm contains 23 chromosomes, or half of the man's genetic code. If and when a sperm unites with an ovum, which also carries 23 chromosomes, the result is a fertilized egg containing 46 chromosomes, all the hereditary information needed to create a human being.

How many sperm does the male release in each ejaculation?

An enormous number of sperm—about 400 million—are contained in the average ejaculation. Of course, actual figures may vary widely from the average ones. However, the fertilization of an egg is a chancy thing: innumerable factors can prevent it. The more sperm there are, the better the odds in favour of fertilization.

What is semen for?

Male fertility requires more than sperm. Also needed are the secretions in which the sperm are suspended. These secretions, products of several male glands, provide nutrients for the sperm, neutralize the acidity of vaginal secretions, and induce contractions in the female uterus and Fallopian tubes to speed sperm on their way to meet the egg.

About 60 percent of the seminal fluid is supplied by the seminal vesicles. They secrete a thick alkaline material containing fructose, vitamins, and amino acids to nourish the sperm. The material also contains mucus for lubrication and prostaglandins, which are believed to cause uterine contractions. Lying behind the bladder, each seminal vesicle joins the vas deferens in a single ejaculatory duct that leads into the urethra through the prostate.

Frequently likened to a chestnut in size and shape, the prostate gland is under the bladder. It secretes a thin alkaline fluid to counteract acidity in both the vas deferens and the vagina.

Under the prostate are two yellow, pea-sized glands, one on each side of the urethra, known as the bulbourethral, or Cowper's, glands. Before ejaculation, they secrete an alkaline, mucous fluid that lubricates the urethra and cleanses it of any acidic urine that might linger and might damage the sperm. The glands of Littre, which line the urethra, also secrete mucus for lubrication.

Do semen and urine ever mix?

Since the acid in urine is lethal to sperm, the male reproductive system prevents the two from coming together. Although both urine and semen are discharged through the urethra, they cannot be released at the same time. During sexual intercourse, nervous reflexes prevent urination. And before ejaculation occurs, alkaline liquid secreted by the bulbourethral glands flushes any traces of urine out of the urethra.

Are nocturnal emissions normal?

An erection of the penis is a reflex that can occur as the result of pressure from tight clothing or from a full bladder, as a reaction to tactile stimulation or to changes in the body's hormone levels, or as a response to provocative thoughts and dreams. It is normal for males to experience erections during sleep, and spontaneous ejaculation during sleep is quite a common experience among healthy adolescents and occasionally among adults as well.

Is self-examination of the testicles necessary?

For every 100,000 men, two to three develop cancer of the testicles every year. Young, white, adult males between the ages of 20 and 40 are at the greatest risk. Fortunately, with the wide availability of chemotherapeutic drugs today, the majority of testicular tumours can be cured, even when they have metastasized to other sites in the body.

Of course, the best chance for cure exists when tumours are discovered early. It is therefore important for all males to become familiar with the shape and size of their testicles, and to check them regularly. Any change in the size or consistency of either testicle should be immediately reported to a doctor for evaluation. In cases where the tumour does not appear to have spread beyond the testicle itself, chemotherapy may be avoided, if careful follow-up examinations reveal there is no recurrence.

Do all testicular masses represent tumours?

A mass or swelling of the testicle should be brought to a doctor's attention immediately so that its nature can be determined and it can be treated. There are several causes of testicular masses besides tumours. Hydroceles are collections of watery fluid between the layers of tissue that cover the testicle (these are usually benign, but may be associated with testicular tumours). Varicoceles are dilated varicose veins surrounding the testicle, while haematoceles are collections of blood usually associated with trauma or a tumour. An infection of the epididymides may lead to a painful hardening of the testicle, which must be distinguished from a tumour, which is usually not painful. A painful situation resulting from the twisting of a testicle that causes obstruction to its blood supply, testicular torsion is associated with swelling and hardening of the testis and epididymis, and requires surgical correction immediately if the testicle is to be saved.

Who is at greatest risk to develop a tumour of the testis?

Each testis has its origin near the kidneys. Most often, the testes descend into the scrotum by the time the baby is born, but if not by then, almost always within the first year of life. Males whose testes do not descend have a much greater risk of developing a tumour of the testis than do males whose testes spontaneously descended into the scrotum. Undescended testes should be surgically brought down into the scrotum at one to two years of age if descent has not occurred. This operation does not necessarily prevent the development of a tumour, but it does make the tumour easier to diagnose. Testicular self-examination is strongly recommended for any man who has a history of undescended testes.

Why is mumps dangerous for men?

About 85 percent of mumps cases occur before the age of 15. The painful swelling of the salivary glands that characterize this contagious viral infection lasts about a week, and so many think of it as a mild disease. But when mumps strikes adolescent or adult males, it may cause swelling in the testicles. Known as acute orchitis, the inflammation may lead to atrophy of the affected testicle, causing sterility.

The bandage on a mumps victim was to ease the pain of swollen glands.

Causes of Impotence

Do many men suffer from sexual impotence?

Probably every man has had transient episodes of impotence, or an inability to attain and maintain an erection adequate to complete sexual intercourse. In such instances, the cause is usually something as simple as fatigue, illness, or stress.

What are the most frequent causes of chronic impotence?

Not too long ago, the physiological causes of impotence were largely ignored by the medical profession, but in recent years doctors have begun to pay more attention to them. Potency depends on the healthy functioning of many parts of the body—not just the reproductive system but also the brain, spinal cord, and nerves; the pituitary, thyroid, and adrenal glands; and the vascular system. In addition to drugs, which can impair potency by causing hormonal imbalances or enlarging vessels, certain diseases sometimes inhibit the ability to sustain erection—among them, neurological diseases, diabetes, arteriosclerosis, cancer, radical prostate surgery, and genitourinary injuries and infections.

Psychological factors, once considered almost the *only* cause of potency problems, remain the most frequent source of difficulty. Stress, depression, marital problems, and anxiety (particularly anxiety centred on sexual performance) are often implicated in persistent impotence. Whether the cause is physiological or psychological, however, many cases of chronic impotence can be cured by treatment tailored to the cause of the particular dysfunction. The types of treatment range from psychotherapy, marital counselling, and sex therapy to medication and surgery.

Can drugs make a man impotent?

Impotence is one of the more unfortunate side effects of numerous medications. Among them are certain antidepressants, tranquilizers, narcotics, diuretics, vasodilators, and certain drugs used to treat hypertension and ulcers. Addictive as well as prescription drugs can be linked to impotence. Alcoholism—capable of increasing oestrogen levels by affecting the liver, decreasing testosterone levels by causing testicular dysfunction, and depressing the central nervous system—can also make a man chronically impotent. And too much drinking at any one time may temporarily prevent erection.

How do doctors find out what causes impotence?

Increasingly, doctors try to rule out physical causes of impotence before assuming that a man's potency problems stem from emotional difficulties. A physician may test hormone levels in the blood to determine if the glands are functioning properly and check for a possible impairment in circulation that may be impeding the flow of blood to the male organ. There is also a special test, using a recording device attached to the penis, to learn whether or not a man experiences nocturnal penile tumescence. Men usually have three or four erections a night, lasting a total of about 90 minutes, while asleep. If that is so in a particular case, or if a man reports having morning erections, it is likely (though not certain) that his problem is not organic. In such cases, he is referred to a sex therapist or to a specialist in emotional disorders.

Can premature ejaculation be prevented?

Sex therapists have devised a simple behavioural technique for delaying ejaculation, and most males can learn to use it. Generally, a man's doctor can make a referral to a specialist in sexual problems who can explain the technique.

Is sexual intercourse safe after a heart attack?

For some patients, sexual activity after a heart attack must be avoided or curtailed. In individual cases, only the doctor can advise the patient. However, most heart attack victims can safely resume all or most of their regular activities—including a normal sex life.

Can a vasectomy cause impotence?

A vasectomy is a simple, 20-minute procedure in which a surgeon severs and ties off the vasa deferentia, the

---

DID YOU KNOW...?

- **The biologists' symbol** for the female derives from the hand mirror of Venus (♀), and the symbol for the male is from the shield and spear of Mars (♂).

- **A nephrologist is a doctor specializing** in diseases of the kidneys; a urologist deals with problems of the urinary tract, as well as with the male reproductive system; a gynaecologist specializes in the female reproductive system.

- **Everyone is conscious of thirst** when it's hot, but few realize that dehydration can be a problem in the cold. In one study, workers in the Arctic became seriously dehydrated — and very inefficient — without realizing they needed to drink water.

- **Less than half of a single kidney** can successfully take over all the tasks that two kidneys usually accomplish together.

- **The record holder for most children born to one mother** is a Russian woman who produced 69 children between the years 1725 and 1765. Wife of a peasant named Feodor Vassilyev, she produced 16 pairs of twins, 7 sets of triplets, and 4 sets of quadruplets. The modern record holder is Leontina Albina of Chile, who, by 1980, had produced 44 children (including 5 sets of triplets).

Aphrodisiacs: The Search for a Food of Love

Do potions exist that will increase sexual prowess or arouse a partner's passion? Despite centuries-old claims, the answer is no. The word *aphrodisiac* comes from Aphrodite, the Greek goddess of love. Honey was thought by the ancient Greeks to produce erotic effects, as was hair from a wolf's tail and snake bones. The French candidate was the tomato, called *pomme d'amour*, or "apple of love." Perhaps in response to this, the Puritans declared tomatoes to be poisonous. Nowadays, oysters are favoured by the hopeful. There is some evidence that alcohol and certain drugs may temporarily increase sexual drive by depressing inhibitions, but these substances tend to backfire and can even cause impotence over the long term. Love foods, if effective, operate through the power of suggestion—it's all in the mind.

Mandrake root, a legendary aphrodisiac, irritates the urinary tract when eaten, thus *reducing* sexual desire.

Ginseng probably got its reputation as an erotic stimulant from its root's shape, which bears some resemblance to the human body.

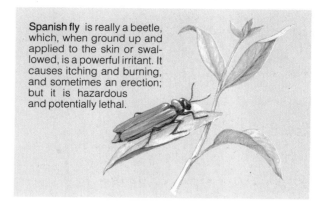

Spanish fly is really a beetle, which, when ground up and applied to the skin or swallowed, is a powerful irritant. It causes itching and burning, and sometimes an erection; but it is hazardous and potentially lethal.

Saddest of all is the absurd belief that ground rhinoceros horn increases sexual power; this erroneous notion has put the species on the endangered list.

tiny tubes that transport sperm out of the testicles. After a vasectomy is performed, the seminal fluid no longer contains sperm, but the operation has no effect on a man's production of either sperm or hormones, and it has no bearing on his physical ability to attain an erection and achieve orgasm. Some men experience impotence for psychological reasons after a vasectomy, but they usually recover their potency as soon as they understand that a vasectomy cannot possibly cause physical impotence.

Sterilization—vasectomy is a form of sterilization—is unquestionably the most effective means of contraception, but a man should not undergo the surgery unless he is prepared to consider it permanent. If he changes his mind and wants to have children, there is at best a 70 percent chance that microsurgery could reverse the operation.

A single report that vasectomy may increase the risk of heart disease has not been confirmed by additional investigations. At present, it is felt that a vasectomy does not increase the risk for heart disease.

The Female Reproductive System

What are the major functions of the ovaries?

Oval in shape and 25 to 40 millimetres (1 to 1.5 inches) in length, the ovaries are the primary female reproductive organs and are analogous in function to the man's testes. They secrete the hormones responsible for female development and produce the ova, or eggs, that contain a woman's genetic heritage and that develop into new human life when fertilized by sperm. The ovaries lie in the pelvis, one on either side of the uterus, and each is anchored to the uterus by an ovarian ligament.

How many eggs do the ovaries contain?

To ensure the survival of the human race, nature is lavish with reproductive cells. When a girl is born, her ovaries contain about 2 million primordial ova, or potential eggs. About three quarters of these degenerate before puberty, and of the remaining hundreds of thousands, only 400 or 500 develop into mature ova. Every month from puberty to menopause, one ovary or the other releases a single egg that is ready for fertilization.

What is the structure of the uterus?

The uterus, or womb, is a life-support system, the place where the fertilized ovum becomes implanted, receives nourishment, and develops, over a period of nine months, into a human being. The uterus lies behind the bladder and, in a nonpregnant woman, is the shape and size of an upside-down pear approximately 75 millimetres (3 inches) long and 50 millimetres (2 inches) at its widest. The upper, wide part of the uterus is known as the body; the lower, narrow neck is called the cervix, and leads into the vagina.

Before pregnancy, the cavity of the uterus is small and narrow. Its muscular walls have an outside, protective layer called the perimetrium; a middle, thick layer of muscles known as the myometrium; and an inner, vascular lining, the endometrium. Every month, this lining thickens in preparation for the implantation of a fertilized egg. But if a woman does not become pregnant, the unneeded endometrial cells degenerate, and the uterus sheds them through the process of menstruation.

How does ovulation come about?

At puberty, every girl has myriads of potential eggs resting in the germinal outer layer of her ovaries. In the process that is known as oogenesis,

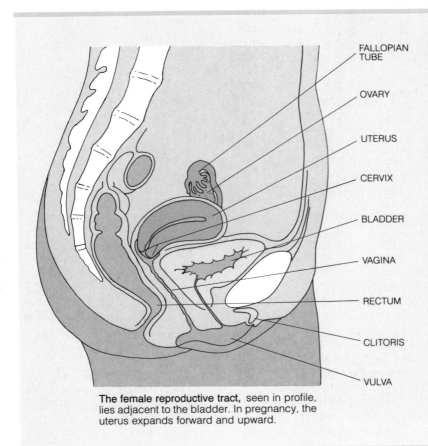

The female reproductive tract, seen in profile, lies adjacent to the bladder. In pregnancy, the uterus expands forward and upward.

FALLOPIAN TUBE
OVARY
UTERUS
CERVIX
BLADDER
VAGINA
RECTUM
CLITORIS
VULVA

What are the principal parts of the female reproductive system?

While the male reproductive system plays a vital role only in conception, the female reproductive system contains all the essential elements not only for conception but also for the development of the foetus, for childbirth, and for nurturing the infant after it is born. New life grows inside the woman, and her major reproductive organs—the vagina, the uterus, the uterine, or Fallopian, tubes, and the ovaries—are also inside, instead of outside like a man's. However, the accessory organs of female reproduction—the mammary glands and the vulva—are external.

Vaginal secretions, which increase during sexual arousal, provide lubrication that facilitates intercourse. Such secretions are more apparent during pregnancy, and just before and after menstruation as well. In addition, the vulva is moistened by the lesser vestibular glands and by paraurethral glands that surround the urethral opening. Although glandular secretions may stain underwear, they are normal, and do not cause odour or discomfort, and can thus be distinguished from discharges caused by infection. The vagina maintains a hygienic environment through the action of useful bacteria that normally inhabit the canal. These bacteria acidify the mucus in the vagina; this inhibits the growth of harmful micro-organisms.

several of these "eggs" begin to ripen every month, but, with rare exceptions, only one comes to full maturity. Enclosed in what is called a Graafian follicle, the ripe ovum reaches the surface of the ovary. At about the midpoint of the monthly cycle, ovulation occurs: distended with fluid, the follicle that holds the egg bursts and discharges the egg into the peritoneal cavity, from which it moves into the Fallopian tube.

What is the function of the vagina?

The vagina, a tube 100 to 150 millimetres (4 to 6 inches) long, connects the uterus with the external world. Amazingly expandable, it serves as a receptacle for the male penis and sperm and as a corridor for the emergence of the baby into the outside world. Composed of muscle and fibroelastic connective tissue, the walls of the vagina are usually folded inward, but they can expand to form a passageway 100 millimetres (4 inches) or more in diameter, enough to accommodate an infant.

The vagina is behind the urethra and bladder and in front of the rectum. At first, a thin mucous membrane called the hymen covers the vaginal opening, either partly or entirely. The hymen, however, eventually breaks, sometimes during sports or another activity, sometimes during the initial act of sexual intercourse.

The vagina and vestibule are moistened by Bartholin's glands, one on each side of the vaginal opening, and by mucus secreted by the cervix. Every month, at the time of ovulation, the secretions become thin, watery, and more profuse, helping the sperm move up through the vagina and uterus. During the remainder of the monthly cycle, the mucus is thick and more difficult to penetrate.

What is the vulva?

The most obvious of the woman's external genital organs, collectively called the vulva, is the mons pubis, or mons veneris. It is the rounded pad of fatty tissue that covers the pubis, or pubic bone. Extending downward from the mons veneris are the labia majora, or "larger lips," two folds of fatty tissue that reach almost to the anus and protect the genitals within. Just inside the labia majora are the labia minora, or "smaller lips," which enclose the vestibule containing the tiny opening of the urethra and the larger mouth of the vagina. At their upper end, the labia minora form a small projection called the prepuce, which shelters the clitoris. The clitoris is a highly sensitive organ with specialized nerve endings, and like the penis, it contains cavernous tissue that becomes engorged with blood during sexual arousal.

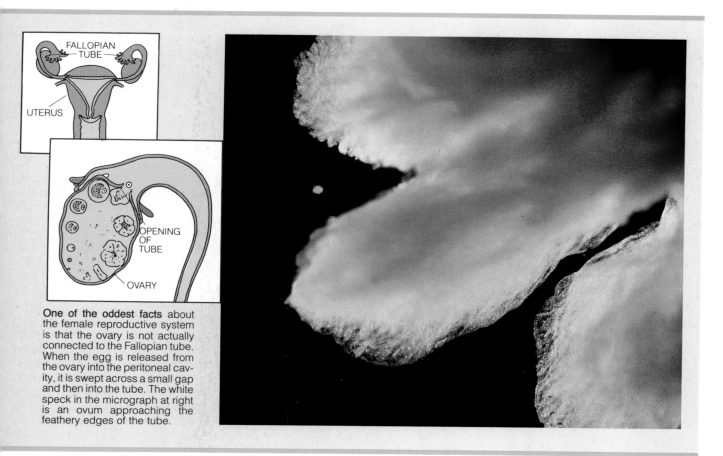

One of the oddest facts about the female reproductive system is that the ovary is not actually connected to the Fallopian tube. When the egg is released from the ovary into the peritoneal cavity, it is swept across a small gap and then into the tube. The white speck in the micrograph at right is an ovum approaching the feathery edges of the tube.

The Functioning of the Uterus

Why are regular cervical smears advisable?

Among women, cervical cancer is the second most common cancer of the reproductive system (after breast cancer). Since the cervix does not contain any nerve endings that sense pain, the disease may be well advanced before symptoms appear. Fortunately, there is a quick, painless, and reliable test that can detect cervical cancer early, when it is nearly always curable. Usually referred to as a cervical smear, the test has saved many women's lives since its development in the 1940s by Dr. George N. Papanicolaou.

Taking a smear is part of a routine gynaecological examination. An instrument called a speculum is inserted in the vagina to keep it open and expose the cervix. Using a small wooden spatula or some similar device, the doctor collects samples of tissue from three areas of the cervix and vagina, which are sent to a laboratory for microscopic examination. The cells will be classified in one of five ways: Class I negative, meaning the cells are normal; Class II negative, meaning some cells are slightly atypical, perhaps because of infection;

Class III, meaning that a premalignant condition is suspected; Class IV positive, indicating a possible malignancy; and Class V positive, signifying a probable malignancy.

What is a D and C?

Dilatation and curettage is a frequently performed surgical procedure in which the cervix is temporarily widened to permit scraping of the uterine lining. In a D and C, as it is called, the patient is anaesthetized, and a series of dilators, increasing in size, are inserted through the vagina into the cervix to enlarge the opening. Then a curette, a spoonlike instrument, is used to scrape the endometrium, or lining of the uterus.

A D and C can be used for both diagnosis and treatment. Examination of the cells scraped from the uterus can reveal the cause of infertility or excessive menstrual bleeding and can confirm the presence of uterine cancer or pelvic tuberculosis. The procedure can also be used to remove polyps and other benign growths, to effect an abortion in early pregnancy, or to remove remnants of the placenta after childbirth or miscarriage.

Why are fibroids removed?

Fibroids are benign tumours which develop in the wall of the uterus, usually in a woman's thirties or forties. They do not lead to cancer, and they are often so small that they cause no symptoms. Moveover, they generally get smaller, or disappear, after the menopause. But sometimes a fibroid grows larger than an orange, and one or more may fill the uterus, impinge on nearby organs, or perhaps cause profuse bleeding. Generally, fibroids can be removed by myomectomy—that is, by scooping out the tumours and preserving the uterus—but when the fibroids are very large, a hysterectomy is sometimes necessary.

What is removed in a hysterectomy?

Technically, the word *hysterectomy* refers to the removal of the uterus, which brings an end to menstruation and childbearing, but the ovaries and the Fallopian tubes are sometimes taken out at the same time. If a premenopausal woman has her ovaries removed, she experiences the hormonal changes that normally occur at menopause, but the resulting discomfort can often be alleviated by hormone replacement therapy.

In many instances, most notably in cases of cancer, the operation is lifesaving. It may also be advisable when miscarriage, childbirth, endometriosis, or infection has seriously damaged the uterus or when fibroid tumours in the uterus cause bleeding and pressure on other organs.

What is the psychological effect of a hysterectomy?

How a woman reacts to a hysterectomy depends on her physical and mental health before the operation. Some women are deeply disappointed at losing menstrual function and the capacity to bear children; others welcome these changes with relief. Those who have experienced pain and a sapping of their strength as a result of an

A Continuing Cycle in the Uterus

Every month, the blood-enriched uterine lining, the endometrium, awaits the arrival of an egg. It comes from one of a woman's ovaries and gets to the uterus through a Fallopian tube. If the egg has not been fertilized and the woman, therefore, is not pregnant, the egg and endometrium leave her body as the menstrual flow.

The **28-day cycle** begins with bleeding. Then the uterine wall builds up to receive the egg.

Menstruation: An Ancient Mystique

Superstition, myth, and ignorance have surrounded the menstrual period since time immemorial. Rooted in a primitive fear of blood, taboos about it have existed in virtually every society, from the Africans who believe that food cooked by a menstruating woman will make them sick, to employers who think that menstruation adversely affects a woman's job performance. The very word *taboo* may derive from the Polynesian word for menstruation. Not all the myths are negative: A girl's first menses is greeted with celebration in some areas, for it means she can now bear children. Magical properties have been ascribed to menstrual blood, notably as an antidote to infertility. Research into the premenstrual syndrome and strides made by the women's movement have helped to dispel some of the myths and taboos, but even as the 21st century looms, some women still regard the menses as "the curse."

A veil of caribou skin was worn by girls of Canada's Naskapi tribe during their first menses.

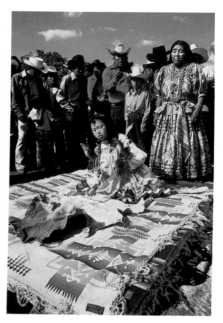

Kneeling on a "sacred" deerskin provided some relief in a fatiguing four-day menses ceremony for this Apache girl.

The Hebrew language has a word, *niddah*, for a menstruous woman, and because the ancient rabbis thought her unclean, her activities were strictly regulated by Jewish law. When her period was finished, she had to wait seven days and then cleanse herself in a *mikvah*, or ritual bath, as shown here in an 18th-century German engraving. Some Orthodox Jewish women still observe this rule.

enlarged uterus often feel restored to health and vitality after surgery.

A woman need not experience any significant change in her sex life after a hysterectomy, though the experience of orgasm may be somewhat different for women whose climax was heightened by movements of the cervix and uterus. A hysterectomy does not alter the vagina or change the essence of a woman's sexual appeal and femininity.

Is premenstrual discomfort all in your mind?

About 40 percent of all women suffer from a mild form of premenstrual tension, characterized by emotional unpredictability, slight depression, weight gain from fluid retention, and tenderness of the breasts. In perhaps 5 percent of women, these symptoms are greatly magnified. In this so-called premenstrual syndrome (PMS),

there may be inexplicable and uncontrolled bouts of anger, unusual food cravings, migraines, severe depression, and spells of crying.

Some doctors say the symptoms are signs of an unstable personality or a stressful environment. But others attribute the syndrome mainly to chemical changes that take place in women's bodies before menstruation and which are more pronounced in some women than in others.

Understanding the Female Body

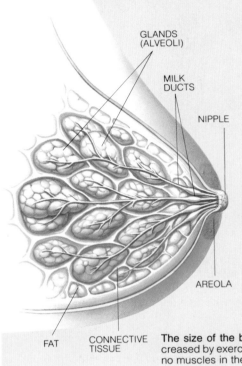

GLANDS (ALVEOLI)

MILK DUCTS

NIPPLE

AREOLA

FAT CONNECTIVE TISSUE

What is the structure of the breast?

The female breast is divided into 15 or 20 lobes that radiate outwards from the nipple and contain clusters of milk-producing glands. Each cluster drains into its own duct, which leads into a small storage space near the nipple and then into the nipple. At the tip of the nipple are 15 or 20 tiny duct openings. The pigmented circle around the nipple is known as the areola. The nipples themselves contain erectile tissue which can be stimulated by breast feeding, by sexual activity, and by cold.

The breasts are composed not only of glands but also of fat and fibrous tissue, which provides support and contains nerves as well as blood and lymphatic vessels.

The size of the breasts cannot be increased by exercise because there are no muscles in the breast to develop.

What if you find a lump in your breast?

If you discover a lump in the breast, it will probably prove to be benign; most lumps in the breast are not cancerous. But you should see a doctor right away to be sure. To establish that a tumour is benign, a biopsy—surgical removal and close study—may be needed to exclude the possibility of cancer. Prompt action is necessary because a malignant growth can invade neighbouring tissue and spread through the body by way of the lymph system and the blood.

There are several types of benign breast tumours. The most prevalent is the fibroadenoma, a firm lump that moves freely under one's fingers; it may grow large enough to be a cosmetic problem. The next most common kind of lump is the result of fibrocystic disease, characterized by cysts filled with fluid and surrounded by thick fibrous tissue. Yet another harmless lump, which may appear

How to Examine Your Breasts

Two to three days after each menstrual period, a woman should examine her breasts. Putting your arm behind your head makes it easier to detect unusual lumps, knots, or thickenings. Large-breasted women may find that lying down with a towel or pillow under the shoulder helps the breast flatten out.

Look for scaling, lack of symmetry, or a discharge from the squeezed nipple.

It takes time to know your breasts; ask the doctor if you're unsure about them.

Using a mirror, look for bulges, puckered or dimpled skin, and changes in the size and shape of your breasts and nipples.

Begin at the top, and gently press around the edge. An increased firmness at the bottom is normal glandular structure.

Move towards the centre, about a 3-finger width, and begin another circle. Repeat process until you have reached the nipple.

The breast also extends up towards the armpit so be sure to feel that part of each breast carefully as well.

276

under the nipple, is called an intra-ductal papilloma. This small growth may discharge a cloudy or bloody fluid through the nipple. Somewhat different from these tumours is the haematoma, which is a transient, blood-filled swelling under the skin caused by an injury that bruises the breast.

What is cystic breast disease?

After ovulation occurs, hormones flow through the body, stimulating the glands and tissues of the breasts to develop in preparation for possible pregnancy. Some women's breasts are particularly sensitive to these changes and become painful and swollen each month during the premenstrual phase. If the hormonal stimulation is not followed by the usual regression when menstruation begins, nodules may develop. In time, they often become fluid-filled, fibrous cysts that enlarge each month and then subside. Though these lumps are benign, they should be diagnosed and treated by a physician. Generally, the fluid in a fibrous cyst is withdrawn through a needle, in a simple procedure called aspiration, and the lump then disappears. The cystic fluid is examined to rule out malignancy. Some studies suggest that smoking and caffeine can contribute to fibrocystic disease, and that cutting out both brings relief.

Does the size of the breast affect its nurturing capacity?

The fatty tissue deposited at puberty determines the size of the breasts, but it is the glandular tissue that produces milk. The amount of milk the mammary glands secrete is therefore not related to breast size. The size of the breasts is set mainly by your genetic heritage, though if there is an overall increase in body fat, the breasts will reflect it. The breasts enlarge greatly during pregnancy, and slightly in the premenstrual phase, when extra blood flows into the breasts and the tissues retain more water than usual.

What happens when a woman experiences sexual arousal?

Whether or not a woman is in the mood for intercourse depends on a variety of psychological and physiological factors, ranging from her emotional response to her partner to the hormone level in her blood, from her reactions to physical stimuli bombarding her senses to thoughts and fantasies filling her mind.

Hormones, including oestrogen and progesterone, are not believed to play a key role in a woman's sex drive, but androgens, male sex hormones also produced in small quantities by women, are especially powerful stimulators of sexual desire. The release of hormones can be triggered off by emotional responses, by thoughts about love and sex, and by foreplay.

During sexual arousal, whether it is caused by psychological stimuli or by the touching of a woman's erogenous zones, parasympathetic nerve impulses cause physical changes in the pelvic area. The supply of blood to the sexual organs is increased; the clitoris becomes erect; the vaginal walls are distended; and the cervical glands and Bartholin's glands at the entry of the vagina secrete extra mucus for lubrication.

Why is the female orgasm important?

The female climax, or orgasm—which may be single or multiple—is similar to that of the male except that there is no ejaculation. As sexual excitement reaches its peak, muscle tension also increases. At orgasm, muscles in the uterus and the vagina contract involuntarily, and the engorgement of the genitals with blood subsides, leading to feelings of peace and fulfilment. The female orgasm is important physiologically, to relieve congestion in the pelvic area, and psychologically, to give emotional satisfaction. In addition, some believe that the female orgasm promotes fertility by increasing movement in the uterine area, thus helping to carry the sperm to the ovum.

Red, irritated "jogger's nipples" can be prevented with a supportive bra. So can strain and stress on fibrous tissue, a cause of sagging breasts.

Can frigidity be cured?

Applied to female sexuality, the term *frigidity* means failure to enjoy the entire range of normal sexual feelings, from arousal to orgasm. The psychological causes of frigidity are varied. A woman who is often left unfulfilled may lose her desire for sex. A marital rift may leave the wife indifferent to sex. Some remain inhibited because of taboos imposed on them in childhood. Stress, fatigue, depression, or anxiety about becoming pregnant can also prevent a woman from enjoying her sexuality.

Illness is often a factor in frigidity, especially in cases of diabetes or anaemia. Reduced sex drive can be related to the hormonal changes of pregnancy, childbirth, or menopause. Most women experience some fluctuation in their sex drive in the course of the monthly hormonal cycle.

Every healthy human being has at least the latent capacity to enjoy sexual relations and can be helped to overcome problems that prevent sexual satisfaction. Professional counselling, sex therapy, and sex education have proved effective in awakening or restoring sexual responsiveness.

Sexually Transmitted Diseases

What diseases are sexually transmitted?

Around the world, sexually transmitted diseases pose a major health problem. In Britain, there are five such diseases which are particularly troublesome. The most widespread, and the least known, is chlamydia which causes non-specific urethritis. Gonorrhoea, the second most common, is easy to cure in its initial stages; however, it can be difficult to detect. Genital herpes, although not life threatening, is recurrent and, so far, incurable. Fourth, there is syphilis, which can cause serious damage to many organs of the body, but which is curable. Lastly, there is AIDS, or Acquired Immune Deficiency Syndrome, a disease which is rapidly spreading throughout the world with devastating effect.

Other rarer conditions include chancroid, a localized ailment resulting in soft ulcers and venereal warts, which are caused by a virus that attacks chiefly women. Trichomoniasis is a common kind of vaginitis which rarely causes symptoms in males.

Which sexually transmitted disease often causes sterility?

Chlamydia, the most widespread of the sexually transmitted infections, is a major cause of sterility in women, and, less frequently, in men. Like all the sexually transmitted diseases, chlamydia spreads through contact with infected tissue. The organism that causes it is called *Chlamydia trachomatis*. It invades the body through the vagina, urethra, rectum, eyes, or mouth. In men, it usually infects the urinary tract; if infection

---

An Upswing in Sexually Transmitted Diseases

Time was when syphilis and gonorrhoea were the only sexually transmitted diseases we had to worry about, both of which respond to treatment by antibiotics. Now, however, there are 25 or more diseases that are spread by sexual contact, for some of which there are as yet no cures. These include chlamydia, herpes, and AIDS (Acquired Immune Deficiency Syndrome). Some of these diseases may not have any symptoms in their early stages. Except for AIDS, which is spreading among both men and women, the long-term victims of most of these new diseases are women and their babies.

Syphilis mimics so many diseases it is called "the great imitator."

Gonorrhoea, called a "preventer of life," can cause sterility.

AIDS virus attacks the body's natural immune system.

Chlamydia is part of a large family of related diseases.

reaches the testicles, sterility may result. In women, the organism infects the cervix and may cause pelvic inflammatory disease. In addition, the germ causes conjunctivitis, an eye inflammation, in adults and newborn babies, who pick up the germ during their passage through the mother's infected birth canal. In some infants, the infection may also cause pneumonia.

Is it easy to tell if you have chlamydia?

In many cases, there is no mistaking the fact that something is wrong. A man experiences a frequent desire to urinate, pain when urinating, and a discharge from the penis; a woman notices a vaginal discharge and pain on urination. These symptoms can come from either gonorrhoea or chlamydia, which complicates the problem of diagnosis. In some cases, moreover, chlamydia initially causes *no* symptoms—though even when the infection is "silent," it may invade the reproductive organs and may be transmitted to others. When diagnosed, it can be cured by antibiotics.

Are all herpes viruses sexually transmitted?

The herpes family is a large one, and most forms are not sexually transmitted. The herpes virus that infects children with chickenpox—varicella zoster virus—is the same that causes shingles in adults. The herpes virus that causes glandular fever is called Epstein-Barr virus. A third herpes virus, known as cytomegalovirus, may cause birth defects and seems to be associated with diseases of the nervous system.

There are two forms of herpes simplex virus: herpes simplex virus 1 (HSV-1) is known primarily for causing cold sores or fever blisters, though it may also infect the eyes, brain, and genitals; herpes simplex virus 2 (HSV-2) is the sexually transmitted form of the disease. It causes clusters of small red swellings which

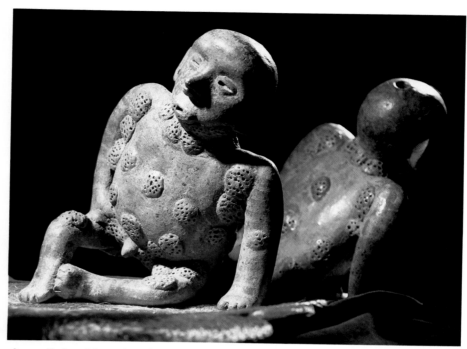

A pre-Columbian clay figure with syphilis pustules records the existence of the disease in the New World. Many historians now question that Columbus's crew carried syphilis back to Europe; they believe it was already present.

turn into painful blisters on the sexual organs, buttocks, lower abdomen, or thighs. This form is now relatively common. The child of a woman with genital herpes may also contract herpes because the infection can be acquired during passage through the birth canal.

Can genital herpes be prevented?

Anti-viral drugs may help in the first attacks of genital herpes, and medication can help to relieve the pain. Although the infection may lie dormant from time to time, it is likely to flare up repeatedly. Victims of genital herpes can help themselves and should be sure to protect others from contagion.

First, they should be very careful about hygiene when their symptoms are acute. Herpes simplex virus 2, which causes the infection, can be carried on the hands and thus transmitted to others. Second, victims can best protect others by abstaining from sexual contact when their infection is active: genital herpes is trans-

mitted mainly by intercourse; rarely is it transmitted when the infected person has no symptoms.

Can you contract venereal disease by using public toilets?

The experts are all but certain that venereal disease in adults can be transmitted only from person to person, and then almost always through intimate physical contact. (AIDS and, very rarely, syphilis can be transmitted by contaminated blood.) The micro-organisms known to cause chlamydia, gonorrhoea, syphilis, and AIDS are parasitic to human cells; outside the warm and moist environment of the human body, they soon die. It is virtually impossible to contract these infections from objects in public toilets or elsewhere. However, the herpes simplex virus that causes genital herpes can survive outside the body for some hours on such objects as towels, toilet seats, and medical instruments. Whether a person can acquire the infection by touching these objects is not known.

The Changing Nature of VD

A Brilliant Life Tragically Destroyed by Syphilis

The great French artist Edouard Manet (1832–83) began, in his midforties, to be troubled by pain in his left foot. First thought to be rheumatism, it was in fact a disorder of the nervous system called locomotor ataxia, which sometimes occurs in advanced stages of syphilis. Exuberant and outgoing all his life, Manet was forced into seclusion by lengthy bouts of fatigue, depression, and excruciating pain.

There were occasional respites when his energies returned, and in 1881 he began a canvas depicting the Parisian nightlife he had so long enjoyed. He struggled for months, and in 1882, *Bar at the Folies-Bergère* was unveiled, considered by many to be his greatest painting. When gangrene developed in 1883, doctors amputated the leg. But it was too late; ten days later Manet was dead at age 52.

Cut down before his time, Edouard Manet (in a sketch by Degas) was the prime force in modern art. Paul Gauguin said of his influence: "Painting begins with Manet."

The strangely wistful barmaid at the Folies-Bergère was the last face Manet ever painted.

What is pelvic inflammatory disease?

One of the major, and increasingly common, causes of infertility is something called PID, or pelvic inflammatory disease. Also known as salpingitis, PID is an infection of the Fallopian tubes, the links between the ovaries and the uterus. Any of several bacteria can cause PID, but it generally begins with one of two sexually transmitted diseases, gonorrhoea or chlamydia, which can spread upward through the cervix. The use of an IUD (intrauterine device) for contraception increases the risk of PID.

Pelvic inflammatory disease can be cured, but unless it is treated promptly, it may leave the Fallopian tubes scarred or damaged. The result may be infertility and increased risk of ectopic pregnancy.

What are the characteristics and dangers of syphilis?

Syphilis is a highly contagious and an extremely dangerous infection. If treated in its early stages, syphilis can almost invariably be cured by antibiotics. However, if it is not treated, it can cause heart disease, blindness, mental illness, and even death.

The primary stage of syphilis begins 10 to 90 days after sexual contact with an infected partner. A small, hard, and usually painless nodule or chancre forms on the skin at the site of infection, which is usually a sexual organ, and lymph glands in the genital area may become swollen and tender. After ulcerating, the chancre heals spontaneously, but that is not the end of the disease.

In the secondary stage, which usually begins four to eight weeks after the chancre develops, a rash appears all over the body. The victim feels sick, and may suffer from a sore throat, aches in the muscles and joints, and other symptoms. At this stage, the disease is still highly contagious—but it is still curable.

The third stage may begin anywhere from a year to 30 years after the second. At this point the disease is no longer infectious: it cannot be transmitted to others. But the probability is that it has spread and done irreparable harm to the body. Syphilis can attack any tissue or organ, from the skin and bones to the liver and stomach, from the reproductive organs to the eyes. The greatest danger is to the heart and the central nervous system.

Can syphilis be inherited?

Although syphilis can be passed on by an infected mother to an unborn child, it is not carried by the genes, and therefore cannot be inherited.

Congenital syphilis is preventable. For that reason, pregnant women are routinely tested for syphilis. If the disease is treated before the fourth month of pregnancy, the foetus will probably not be affected. But if a woman has untreated syphilis beyond that time, the baby may die in the womb or shortly after birth. If the infant survives, it will probably suffer from scaling of the skin, bone deformities, especially in the nose and shins, and dental abnormalities. As time goes on, other organs may be damaged, the liver and lungs in particular, and the baby may become deaf or blind.

Why is gonorrhoea sometimes difficult to detect?

The early signs of gonorrhoea include a frequent and urgent need to urinate, pain during urination, and a heavy discharge. Unfortunately, a minority of infected men and a majority of infected women never experience any early symptoms. As a result, they may not know they are infected until the disease has spread through the blood to the bones, joints, skin, tendons, or other parts of the body.

How does gonorrhoea spread?

Gonorrhoea is almost always transmitted by contact with the sexual organs of an infected partner. Not completing the sex act is no safeguard against contracting it; the bacteria that cause it may enter the body through the urethra, the cervix, the rectum, or the mouth. The first symptoms normally appear within two to seven days, though there is occasionally a delay of up to a month.

Why is early treatment of gonorrhoea important?

In its initial stages, gonorrhoea is easy to cure with penicillin or other types of antibiotics. Left unchecked, however, the infection can cause serious damage.

In men, the bacteria may invade the urethra, obstructing urination, or the prostate gland and the other structures important in semen production, causing sterility. In women, the disease may spread to the uterine tubes and the ovaries, causing pelvic inflammatory disease and infertility. In its most advanced stages, gonorrhoea may attack not only the urinary and reproductive systems, but also the skin, bones, joints, tendons, and other organs of the human body.

Who is most likely to catch AIDS?

AIDS (Acquired Immune Deficiency Syndrome) renders the immune system powerless to fight off infections. Lacking resistance to disease, people who suffer from AIDS frequently fall prey to pneumonia and other illnesses. AIDS is always fatal.

AIDS can be transmitted in three ways only: from infected semen or vaginal secretions in sexual intercourse; from blood to blood contact; and from an infected mother to her unborn baby. Anyone who has had several sexual partners is at risk of catching AIDS, as are drug addicts who share needles and syringes.

Is there any chance of soon finding a cure or a vaccine for AIDS?

Scientists are putting all their efforts into developing a cure for AIDS and a vaccine against the virus, but neither is likely to be generally available in the near future. However, much can be done to alleviate the symptoms of the many different diseases that can afflict AIDS sufferers.

The Long Search for a Cure

In hope and desperation, many substances were tried as cures for syphilis. One long-standing course of treatment employed mercury in various forms— ointments, vapours, and the like. The efficacy of mercury was widely touted, but the poisonous side effects could be even more agonizing than the affliction itself. The search for cures extended to the far corners of the earth. Sir William Johnson, superintendent of Indian affairs in North America from 1755 to 1774, on advice from an Iroquois Indian friend, sent a blue flower to England as a remedy—to no avail. Not until the 20th century, and the discovery of penicillin, did science at last triumph over the disease.

High hopes for the blue lobelia gave rise to its scientific name, *Lobelia syphilitica*.

The Timing of Fertility

How many days a month is a woman fertile?

It is rarely possible to say just when a woman is fertile, because the female cycle is seldom strictly regular. Ovulation takes place 13 to 15 days before menstruation begins. The egg can be fertilized for at most 24 hours after ovulation, and only while the egg is moving through the uterine tube. The chances of conception are greatest when intercourse occurs some hours before ovulation, so that sperm are in the tube when the egg appears. After ejaculation, most sperm remain fertile for about 24 hours, though some may last 72 hours. Therefore, there are no more than two or three days each month when intercourse may lead to pregnancy.

What is the role of female hormones in fertilization?

At the time a woman ovulates, hormones produced by her ovaries prepare her organs for conception. One thing the hormones do is to make the vagina receptive to sperm; ordinarily, its acidity is destructive to them. Usually, the mucus from the cervix is thick enough to block entry to the uterus; the hormones thin the mucus out and increase its quantity, which helps the sperm to move rapidly through the cervix. In addition, the hormones prepare the endometrium, or uterine lining, for the implantation and nourishment of the ovum. In some women, a hormone deficiency or imbalance may prevent these changes from taking place, but hormone therapy can usually correct the difficulty and restore fertility.

How does age affect fertility?

Women are capable of reproduction from menarche to menopause—that is, from the age of about 13 to about 45 or 50—but they are more likely to conceive at some stages of life than at others. During their late teens and twenties, women reach a peak of fertility. After the age of 30, a woman's fertility declines, and the risk of miscarriage or of bearing a baby with birth defects increases. The primordial eggs stored in a woman's ovaries developed before she was born. As these eggs age, they decline in quality and are less easily fertilized. Whereas a woman produces 1 egg a month and is fertile for only a day or so in every cycle, a man may produce from 100 million to 200 million sperm every day and continue to do so all his life.

How long does it take sperm to mature?

A man produces sperm continuously in each testicle from puberty onward. The transformation from germ cells, or spermatogonia, into mature sperm, or spermatozoa, takes approximately 74 days. But the spermatozoa still cannot fertilize eggs until they undergo a ripening process of about ten days that takes place in the epididymis, the coiled tube connected to the testis.

From each of the epididymides, ripened sperm move into the vas deferens, where they may remain fertile for as long as six weeks. (If sperm are not ejaculated, they degenerate and are absorbed.) The vasa deferentia are long, thin tubes that travel up from the scrotum, pass in front of the pubic bone, and continue across the bladder and down into ampullae. These are storage areas which empty into a pair of ejaculatory ducts opening into the urethra.

Can a woman become pregnant while breast feeding?

When a woman breast-feeds her baby, the hormones her body produces sometimes prevent ovulation and, therefore, conception. However, this is not a reliable form of birth control. Infertility during lactation is most likely when all of the baby's nourishment comes from the mother, but it is not inevitable even then. Perhaps 15 to 40 percent of nursing mothers will, over a period of a year, become pregnant.

The Fertility Goddesses of Prehistoric Times

Among the earliest known pieces of art in the world are the so-called "Venuses" of Stone Age Europe. These figures—about 130 have been discovered from France to the southern U.S.S.R.—are characterized by pendulous breasts, enormous bellies, exaggerated buttocks, and minimized extremities. Scholars believe them to be charms or talismans—an offering or appeal to the spirits to ensure fertility. It is hard for us today to imagine the precariousness of life in Paleolithic times, when people lived in small, scattered tribes, lacking remedies for disease or injury. Life was short, and the renewal of life was urgently prayed for.

The Venus of Willendorf, discovered in Austria, is 105 millimetres (4.1 inches) and is about 20,000 years old.

Marriage: The Ceremonies Vary, but the Meaning Is the Same

Marriage is a universal ritual, the "first bond of society," said the Roman orator, Cicero. Whether it is an elaborate Hindu ceremony or performed by a civil marriage celebrant, its basis in ancient tribal law is the same: community approval of a couple who will live together and produce children. Many of our Western customs, such as throwing confetti at the bride, have come down through the ages. The wedding ring, according to one theory, is a vestige of a time when brides were shackled; it is worn on the third finger of the left hand because—or so the Romans believed—a nerve led directly from that finger to the heart.

Painted in 1434 by Jan van Eyck, this Flemish couple are exchanging vows. It was not until 1563 that a religious ceremony was required. This woman is not pregnant but is padded to appear so, since pregnancy was an admired state.

In an unusual role reversal, the young women of the nomadic Bororo tribe of West Africa pick their own husbands (left). The event takes place in September, when the young men dance before the women to display their physical beauty. Once the choices are made, the marriage does not immediately follow. The couples live together first.

Ornate rings given to Jewish brides were symbols that they belonged to their husbands.

Every bride and groom on their wedding day are a royal couple, said the Archbishop of Canterbury, when he married Prince Charles and Lady Diana.

Dealing With Infertility

How can a tubal infection prevent pregnancy?

Contractions of the uterus and of the Fallopian tubes help propel the sperm towards the ovum. But the two cannot meet if scar tissue or some other obstruction in the tiny uterine tube prevents passage of the sperm or the egg, or if cilia in the tube cannot move freely to sweep up the egg after it leaves the ovary. Although occasionally caused by a congenital defect, a blocked Fallopian tube is more frequently the result of pelvic inflammatory disease caused by bacterial infection. In some cases, the obstruction can be removed by reconstructing the tube surgically or by blowing it open.

When are fertility drugs effective?

A woman may menstruate, yet still not produce eggs that are ready for fertilization. When failure to produce mature eggs is caused by a hormonal imbalance, as is often the case, hormone therapy—the administration of fertility drugs—can induce ovulation. (Rarely, these drugs are so effective that they cause release of several eggs at once, and a multiple birth results.) Some women do not ovulate because of a growth on the ovary; in such cases, surgery may restore the ovary's reproductive function.

What are the two major causes of female infertility?

When ovulation takes place, one egg is released from the ovary and is then swept up into the Fallopian tube. This is the passageway through which the egg travels to the uterus. If a few hundred healthy sperm are in the tube as the egg appears, fertilization is likely. All of the waiting sperm secrete an enzyme that removes the protective layer from around the egg so that one sperm can penetrate and unite with it. Fertilization cannot take place if ovulation does not occur or if the Fallopian tube is obstructed. These are the two most frequent causes of female infertility, and fortunately, both are treatable.

What is the most frequent cause of male infertility?

A man's fertility depends on three conditions. He must produce enough sperm: at least 10 million in each ejaculation. A majority of the sperm must be normal in shape and structure. And the sperm must be capable of self-propulsion, that is, able to "swim" through the woman's reproductive tract to meet the woman's ovum. Unless all these conditions are met, fertilization is unlikely to occur.

When a couple find they cannot have a child, the difficulty lies with the man in about 30 to 40 percent of cases. The most common problem is poor sperm production, which may be caused by a varicocele, a swollen or varicose vein surrounding one of the testes. (In some men, however, varicoceles cause no problems.) Fertility is usually restored when the varicocele is surgically tied off or closed up by a non-surgical method called balloon occlusion.

What other factors affect male fertility?

Perhaps the most important point to be made about infertility in men is that most of the problems that cause it can be remedied. Many genital defects, such as an undescended testicle, can be corrected in early youth. Life-style factors that may lead to infertility—and that can easily be changed—include drinking too much alcohol, using marijuana or cocaine, or taking other drugs. Oddly enough, wearing tight, heavy clothing can also impair fertility temporarily. Sperm mature at 34° C to 35° C (94° F to 95° F). The temperature in the testicles may rise above this optimum level if a man takes frequent hot baths, works in an overheated environment, or wears

---

Early Theories: THE MYSTERY OF HUMAN REPRODUCTION

The first efforts to understand reproduction as a natural process—not a matter of magic—go back to the first century A.D. The Greek scholar Soranus wrote *Gynaecology,* a series of treatises on midwifery, based on observation. Over the centuries, many strange theories gained favour. Leonardo da Vinci's sketches of the uterus indicate that he credited an ancient notion that menstrual blood was retained during pregnancy and converted into milk by the breasts. Even new scientific information could launch outlandish ideas. After Leeuwenhoek and one of his students made their landmark discovery of spermatozoa, in 1677, their contemporaries decided that tiny men must be curled up inside each male sex cell. Some even claimed to see small horses in horse sperm. Facts about fertilization of the female egg took much longer to discern, and it wasn't until the mid-19th century that the great miracle of life was finally understood.

Paracelsus, the 16th-century Swiss chemist, believed that if you cooked human sperm and horse dung for 40 days, you could make a small man, albeit one without a soul.

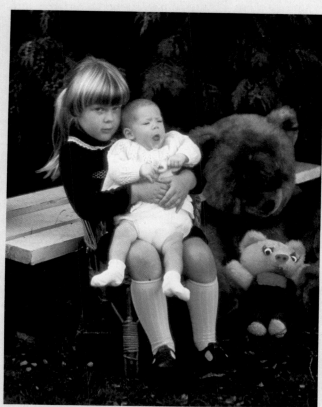

Louise Brown's birth has encouraged other couples to try this method. Her sister Natalie (above) was also conceived *in vitro*.

Successful Fertilization Outside the Body

The technique known as *in vitro* fertilization had its first success in Bristol, England, in 1978. It involves uniting sperm and ovum in a petri dish, a standard laboratory container (not a test tube). The mother-to-be received daily hormone injections to accelerate the production of eggs. (Normally, only one is produced at a time.) The eggs were then surgically removed. Six hours later, the father's sperm was added; the fertilized eggs incubated for two days before one was implanted in the mother's womb. In this procedure, it is not known for about ten days whether or not the egg has lodged in the uterus.

Two days after conception, the cell has divided; it is at this stage that the egg is implanted in the mother's uterus.

underclothes that are too warm.

Of course, some causes of male infertility are not easy to remedy. These include overexposure to X-rays or other types of radiation, certain chronic diseases, and some of the drugs used to treat high blood pressure, heart disease, and other ailments.

What is an ectopic pregnancy?

Usually, a human egg is fertilized in one of a woman's two uterine tubes, after which it makes its way to the uterus. But sometimes it becomes implanted elsewhere, most commonly in a uterine tube. The result is an ectopic pregnancy. The cause of a tubal pregnancy is usually an abnormality of the tube that blocks movement of the egg through it. Early diagnosis of an ectopic pregnancy

is urgent, since the growing embryo may rupture the tube, endangering the mother's life. If the pregnancy is discovered soon after conception, a surgeon may be able to leave the tube intact while removing the embryo.

When is artificial insemination useful?

Artificial insemination may be considered when a wife is able to conceive and bear children but her husband is either impotent or infertile. Insemination is also a possibility when some physical problem in the woman prevents the meeting of egg and sperm. In such cases, the husband's semen is collected and deposited with a syringe in his wife's vagina or uterus. If the man is sterile, an anonymous donor may contribute the semen.

How does test-tube conception circumvent infertility?

Louise Brown is probably well known to newspaper readers around the world, but she is often mistakenly identified as a test-tube baby. That term refers to a baby that developed, as a foetus, outside the womb—an impossibility with today's scientific capability. Louise Brown was, rather, the first baby to come into the world as a result of "test-tube conception." She was conceived in a laboratory: the egg and sperm from which she grew came from her legal parents and were united in a laboratory. Then the fertilized egg was implanted in her mother's uterus. The baby developed there and was born in the usual fashion. With Louise's birth, test-tube conception became a real, if rare, alternative for treating infertility.

Methods of Contraception

What are the main methods of contraception?

Although the popularity of the Pill has declined somewhat, it is still the most widely used artificial contraceptive in Great Britain. It works by using synthetic female hormones to suppress ovulation. The IUD, or intrauterine device, prevents implantation of the egg in the uterus; barrier methods of contraception (the condom, the diaphragm, spermicidal agents, and the vaginal sponge) either keep sperm from passing through the cervix, or, in the case of the condom, prevent sperm from even entering the vagina.

Natural methods of contraception, all unreliable, have been practised for centuries. They include *coitus interruptus*, or withdrawal of the penis from the vagina before ejaculation;

breast feeding; and the rhythm method, which requires sexual abstinence on the days when a woman is believed to be most fertile. The only sure way to prevent pregnancy is by sterilization; conception is impossible if a man has had a vasectomy or if a woman has had a tubal ligation (sealing the Fallopian tubes).

How do barrier methods of contraception work?

Barrier methods are just what their name suggests: physical barriers that either keep sperm out of the woman's body entirely or prevent it from penetrating very far into the woman's reproductive system. The effectiveness of the best of these methods depends to a large degree on how conscientiously a couple uses them. They are

inexpensive, simple, and have the major advantage of causing almost no serious side effects. The most popular barrier is the condom, a sheath of rubber, plastic, or animal membrane that is worn over the penis during intercourse to receive the semen when it is ejaculated. The condom also reduces the risk of spreading sexually transmitted diseases, including AIDS.

The diaphragm, a cup-like ring of thin rubber that fits over the cervix to block entry of sperm, should be fitted for the first time by a doctor or nurse. As an added safeguard, it is covered with a spermicide before insertion; and it should not be removed for at least six hours after intercourse.

Spermicidal agents are creams, jellies, foams, and suppositories used with a condom or diaphragm or,

Natural Methods of Family Planning

The calendar, or rhythm, method of family planning requires sexual abstinence on the days that a woman is fertile. Failure of this system is very common because it is difficult to predict exactly when a particular woman's ovulation will occur.

The temperature method involves taking one's temperature daily and keeping accurate records. The body temperature takes a slight dip just before ovulation, then rises a day later. The problem here is that other things can influence a woman's temperature, including illness, stress, and even a holiday.

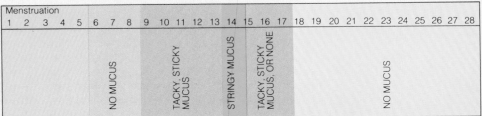

The mucus method is based on the fact that the mucus secreted by the cervix thins and increases in quantity at ovulation. The woman checks daily for the stickiness of the discharge. Finding a woman's fertile days can be as useful for couples who are trying to have a baby as for those who are not.

286

much less effectively, by themselves. Put into the vagina before each act of coitus, these agents are intended to form a protective barrier over the cervix; they are also meant to destroy sperm chemically. Foam and suppositories are sometimes said to provide slightly better protection than jellies or creams. The newest barrier method is the disposable vaginal sponge, which, like the condom and spermicides, is available without prescription. It, too, covers the cervix and contains spermicidal agents.

Is the IUD safe?

Intrauterine devices, or IUD's—small pieces of plastic or metal, often moulded into a loop, spiral, or T-shape—are in place in the bodies of some 15 to 20 million women around the world. One reason for the popularity of the device is its effectiveness. About 3 percent of women who use IUD's become pregnant, but in most cases, the IUD causes the expulsion of a fertilized egg from the uterus. Another advantage of the IUD is its semi-permanence. Once inserted by a medical professional, it can stay in place for at least a year.

But there are disadvantages. When the IUD is initially put in, sometimes it causes cramping and excessive menstrual bleeding; and some women cannot tolerate the device. More important, the IUD increases the risk of pelvic inflammatory disease, which can cause sterility. It also increases the chances of ectopic pregnancy.

How does the Pill prevent pregnancy?

Except for sterilization, the "combined" Pill is by far the most effective method of contraception yet invented. The Pill contains synthetic forms of two female hormones, oestrogen and progestin, which prevent ovulation. In the bloodstream, these synthetic sex hormones simulate pregnancy. The hypothalamus and the pituitary gland, behaving as they would if the woman were actually

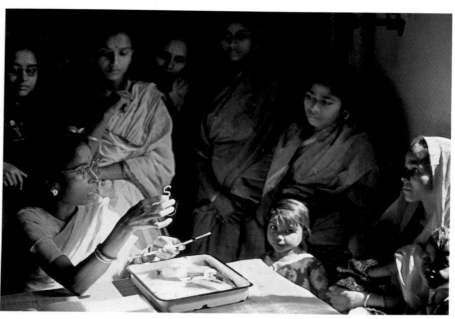

The intrauterine device, here being explained by an Indian health official, is for long-term birth control. It must be fitted (or removed) by an expert.

pregnant, fail to secrete the hormones that would normally stimulate the ovaries to release an egg. The so-called combined pill must be taken for 21 days, then omitted for 7, during which menstrual bleeding occurs. The same pill-taking schedule must be followed for as long as the woman wants to avoid becoming pregnant.

There is also a "minipill," containing progestin alone, which is taken every day. Experts believe that the minipill works not by suppressing ovulation but by preventing the egg from attaching itself to the uterine lining and perhaps by thickening the cervical mucus to prevent passage of sperm. Although the minipill is not as effective as the combined pill, it is recommended for those women who might be adversely affected by supplementary oestrogen.

Is the Pill safe for everyone?

Experts agree that certain women should not take the Pill, including those with a personal or family history of cardiovascular, liver, or kidney disease; breast or uterine cancer, or migraine headaches. The Pill is also considered dangerous to women over

the age of 40, or, if they are heavy smokers, over the age of 30. The combination of smoking and long-term use of the Pill is believed to be particularly hazardous to the cardiovascular system. The decision to rely on oral contraception must be made only after consultation with a doctor.

Is sterilization by tubal ligation reversible?

One way of sterilizing a woman is to seal off her Fallopian tubes from the uterus so that the egg and the sperm cannot meet. To accomplish this, the tubes are tied, cut and cauterized, or closed by applying clips or bands. The operation is sometimes called "Band-Aid" or "belly-button" surgery if the surgeon avoids a long abdominal incision and instead makes one or two tiny cuts near the navel, just big enough to insert instruments.

In some 70 percent of cases, tubal interruption, or ligation, cannot be reversed. Even when an unobstructed passageway through the tubes can be restored, full-term pregnancy may be impossible. However, the operation has no physical effects on a woman's sexuality or femininity.

Chapter 12

PREGNANCY, BIRTH, & GROWTH

Whether you will have brown eyes or blue, be short or tall, be male or female—all these attributes and more are determined in the momentous instant of conception.

When Conception Takes Place	290
The Early Stages of Pregnancy	292
Protecting the Unborn	294
How the Baby Grows	296
The Mother-Child Relationship	298
The Phenomenon of Twins	300
The Marvel of Multiple Births	301
The Different Ways of Giving Birth	302
Potential Problems of Pregnancy	304
The Onset of Labour	306
The Miracle of Birth	308
After the Baby Is Born	310
The Best Food for the Infant	312
A Growing Awareness	314
Milestones of Development	316

How is the expected birth date figured out?

Gestation, the period from fertilization to birth, has an average duration of 38 weeks from conception to birth, or 40 weeks from the last menstrual period. The due date is usually figured by a convenient rule of thumb: count back three months from the day the last menstrual period began, then add a year and a week. The date you come up with is just a guide: the baby may arrive anywhere from two weeks earlier to two weeks later.

Doctors speak of pregnancy as divided into three trimesters of three months each, some of the doctors using lunar months of 28 days, others sticking to calendar months. Yet, whether you measure by moon or by calendar, pregnancy is precisely nine months long in only a few women!

What is the difference between an embryo and a foetus?

At about eight weeks of age, a baby graduates from embryo to foetus. This name change signifies a change in the baby's level of development. While an embryo, the baby looks very much like a tadpole, but as a foetus, it has a distinctly human appearance. The tail has disappeared. Instead of the lumps and folds that only an expert could recognize, it has distinguishable ears, arms and hands, legs and feet, as well as the fingerprints and footprints that will set it apart from other human beings all its life.

The sex of the foetus, established at conception, will be apparent in a matter of a few weeks. This little 25-millimetre (1-inch) being weighs only about a gram (0.04 ounces), and might fit comfortably in a nutshell.

Is delayed parenthood risky for the foetus?

Overall, about 3 percent of newborn babies have a birth defect of some kind. (However, not all birth defects are major, life threatening, or permanent.) After mothers reach the age of 30, the probability that the baby will have a defect begins to increase. The incidence of Down's syndrome, a form of retardation, correlates strongly with the mother's and the father's age. One in 300 children born to mothers in their mid-thirties will have the disorder, 1 in 100 for women aged 40, and a startling 1 in 30 for women in their mid-forties. This disorder is most often caused by an abnormality in the chromosomes of the particular egg that happened to be fertilized. A mother who has one Down's child will not inevitably have another; many of her eggs may be perfectly normal.

The risk of a baby's inheriting a genetic disease caused by an abnormality of the genes of the parents does not change with age. For instance, among parents at risk for producing a child with sickle cell anaemia or haemophilia, both heritable diseases, the chance that the baby will inherit the disorder is neither greater nor lesser if either parent is over 30.

What if pregnancy lasts longer than nine months?

Everyone knows that premature birth is dangerous for the baby, but few people know that postmature, or postterm, babies are also subject to risk. The aging placenta cannot always provide the baby with sufficient nutrients or oxygen. To rescue an overdue baby, the doctor sometimes induces labour, giving the mother a hormone that stimulates uterine contractions. In other cases, a Caesarean section may be performed.

Is there such a thing as a "nesting" instinct?

The urge to decorate the house, clean the cupboards, or stock up the kitchen with food is commonly experienced as delivery nears. Though the theory doesn't lend itself to laboratory research, you don't have to accept the idea of a true *instinct* (an innate drive or tendency) for nest building to believe the testimony of many women.

With the baby's descent into the pelvis in the last weeks of pregnancy, there is literally more room for the mother's lungs to expand, and it becomes easier for the mother to breathe. This "lightening" also eases indigestion and back strain, and the woman may feel just too energetic and well to sit still.

What is "witches' milk"?

In the first few days after birth, drops of milk are sometimes seen oozing from the tiny breasts of both boy and girl babies. This "witches' milk" got its name at a time when no one understood the phenomenon. Now, however, it is known that the milk of newborns is produced under the influence of hormones in the mother's blood, which prepare her

Cuddling is essential for an infant's healthy development. The utter helplessness of babies evokes an urge to fondle and protect them. Thus it is that babies have the power to ensure their own survival.

own breasts to feed her infant. Reaching the foetus through the placenta, these same hormones also make the newborn's genitals look swollen in the early days of its life.

Can the baby sense its mother's emotions?

When a mother is furious or frightened, part of her adrenaline and other hormones that she secretes when under tension reach the foetus through the placenta and cord, spilling some of the chemical effects of stress into her baby. In one study, the physical activity of unborn babies increased several hundred percent during periods that were emotionally disturbing for their mothers.

Some researchers theorize that the women who are chronically unhappy or fearful during pregnancy give birth to more than their share of crotchety babies. But a cautionary note is in order. There is no *proof* that the mother's stress-related hormones influence the way their babies behave after birth. It is entirely possible that women who are anxious during pregnancy make anxious mothers, and that the mothers' anxiety creates psychological tensions that make the babies crotchety. Nevertheless, the old-fashioned attitude towards pregnant women just may make sense: pamper them; don't upset them.

Can anything be done about morning sickness?

Morning sickness is a misnomer. It can occur at any time of day—or all the time. It is worse on an empty stomach. Frequent small meals of non-greasy foods, plus a few dry biscuits and a glass of milk from time to time between meals, seem to reduce the queasy feeling. If that doesn't work, wait. Morning sickness almost always goes away before the fourth month. Certain drugs used for prevention of morning sickness in the past are no longer on the market, because some of them may have caused severe birth defects.

When Conception Takes Place

How soon can pregnancy be detected?

Usually, a woman doesn't suspect she's pregnant until her period is two weeks late—by which time the embryo may have been implanted in her uterus for three weeks, and its heart is already beating.

From the eighth or ninth week after the last menstrual period, an experienced doctor can be pretty sure that conception has occurred. Upon physical examination, the doctor finds a uterus which is already rounder, plumper, and softer than normal, as well as a cervix that has become bluish in colour because of pelvic congestion. By the same time, the pregnant woman herself may have noticed that her breasts have become heavy and tender, with sensitive, tingling nipples. Some women experience a sense of fullness of the abdomen and "morning sickness."

How is a pregnancy test done?

One of the hormones secreted by the placenta is human chorionic gonadotropin (HCG). Fortunately for the woman who needs to know if she is pregnant, HCG gets into her blood very quickly and is excreted by her kidneys. Two weeks after conception, the most sensitive laboratory tests can detect the increased hormonal secretion. Most of the commercial pregnancy tests are designed to show a positive reaction to the hormone 10 to 14 days after a missed period. The home urine tests are more variable in sensitivity. But be careful: if you do the test yourself, or have irregular periods, false results, negative or positive, are quite possible.

Why doesn't the mother have periods during pregnancy?

The young embryo needs the secretions of the uterine lining, normally sloughed off during menstruation, for nutrition. The hormone HCG, first produced by the embryo as it burrows into the uterine lining, is very much like the hormone that is responsible for maintaining ovarian hormone production that in turn maintains the lining between periods. When conception occurs, a woman is at the stage in her cycle when her hormone production should fall. If it did so, the uterus would shed the embryo's food supply, along with the embryo itself. However, the embryo releases HCG, which circulates exactly as the crucial female hormone usually does. Her endocrine system has no way of determining the source of this chemical message, so the lining is retained—as is the life that is dependent on it. The body changes during pregnancy are also a 100 percent contraceptive. You cannot conceive again while pregnant.

How does a baby begin?

The beginning of a baby occurs at the moment when a sperm cell (spermatozoon) penetrates a woman's egg. This event, called conception or fertilization, takes place in the woman's oviduct, or Fallopian tube, through which her ripened ovum, after its release from the ovary, passes on its way to the womb. The sperm cells come from the opposite direction to meet the egg, moving, within five minutes of intercourse, from the vagina into the uterus and from there into the oviduct. Fertilization probably takes place within 24 hours of the release of the egg.

The penetration of the egg by a sperm cell has an immediate effect on the surface of the egg: the condition of the outer coating of the egg changes, so that no other sperm cell can enter. In the fertilized ovum, the 23 chromosomes that are carried in the sperm now unite with the 23 chromosomes in the egg, providing the new individual with a full complement of 46 chromosomes, which determine its inheritance and direct its growth and development.

How does a fertilized egg get into the uterus?

The oviduct, where the sperm cell meets the egg, is very narrow; there is no room for a fertilized egg to grow into a baby. To find more space the fertilized egg must make its way to the uterus, which has the capacity to

A sperm moves within the Fallopian tube *past a patch of waving cilia. The cilia create a current of fluid against which the sperm swims vigorously, whirling its long tail to propel itself towards an egg that may lie ahead.*

How a Fertilized Egg Develops

After fertilization, the single cell divides into 2 new cells, which continue to divide about every 12 hours, becoming 4, 8, 16, 32, 64, 128 cells. As the clump of cells emerges from the oviduct into the uterus, the organism secretes fluid that pumps it up into a hollow ball called a blastocyst. Over the next few days, the ball becomes organized into two layers. The hollow sphere encloses a little fluid and a cluster of cells heaped up at one side. The wall of the sphere is destined to become the placenta and the amniotic sac; the cells within, the baby. So far there has been no growth; the tiny sphere, though considered an embryo, is no bigger than the original egg. Finally, on the ninth day after the egg was released from the follicle, the embryo penetrates into the uterine lining to begin receiving the nourishment from its mother that will enable it to grow.

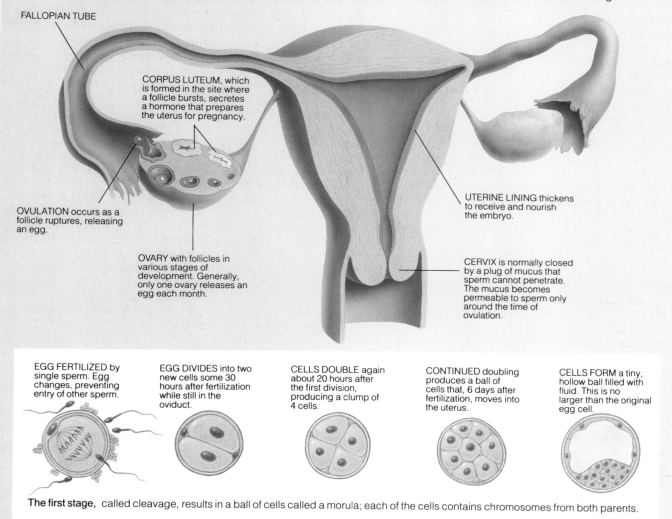

FALLOPIAN TUBE

CORPUS LUTEUM, which is formed in the site where a follicle bursts, secretes a hormone that prepares the uterus for pregnancy.

OVULATION occurs as a follicle ruptures, releasing an egg.

OVARY with follicles in various stages of development. Generally, only one ovary releases an egg each month.

UTERINE LINING thickens to receive and nourish the embryo.

CERVIX is normally closed by a plug of mucus that sperm cannot penetrate. The mucus becomes permeable to sperm only around the time of ovulation.

EGG FERTILIZED by single sperm. Egg changes, preventing entry of other sperm.

EGG DIVIDES into two new cells some 30 hours after fertilization while still in the oviduct.

CELLS DOUBLE again about 20 hours after the first division, producing a clump of 4 cells.

CONTINUED doubling produces a ball of cells that, 6 days after fertilization, moves into the uterus.

CELLS FORM a tiny, hollow ball filled with fluid. This is no larger than the original egg cell.

The first stage, called cleavage, results in a ball of cells called a morula; each of the cells contains chromosomes from both parents.

---

grow in response to foetal needs. The egg is helped to its destination by contractions of the oviduct. (These movements are similar to those that occur in the digestive system.) The egg is also moved along by the activity of cilia, fine hairs lining the tube, which propel the fluid inside the oviduct. The egg reaches the uterus about four days after ovulation.

What determines a baby's sex?

The sex of the unborn child is decided at the instant of fertilization, and it is the father's sperm cell that is decisive. Every ovum, or egg, that a woman produces is female in the sense that it contains an X, or a female, sex chromosome. In a man, only half of the sperm cells carry an X chromosome, while the other half carry a Y, which is the male sex chromosome. If an X sperm cell happens to enter the X ovum, the result is a fertilized egg with two X chromosomes that will become a girl. If, however, a Y spermatozoon fertilizes the egg, the result is a fertilized egg that has one X chromosome and one Y chromosome, and will become a boy.

291

The Early Stages of Pregnancy

What is the job of the placenta?

The placenta is only a temporary organ, which will be discarded after the baby is born. But before that time, it performs many vital functions. Its main task is to permit the diffusion of nourishment from the mother's blood to the baby's and the disposal of waste products from the baby's blood to the mother's. A creation of the embryo, the placenta begins to form when the fertilized ovum becomes embedded in the uterus.

The cells of the embryo begin to grow rootlike projections into the uterine lining, where they branch and form a dense network. These projections grow into maternal blood vessels and so become bathed in maternal blood. The embryo's own blood vessels grow into this network, and embryonic foetal blood comes close to maternal blood, but the blood of mother and baby never actually mix. Oxygen and nutritive chemicals can pass through the two layers of foetal cells separating maternal from embryonic blood; meanwhile the waste products can pass outward from the

How an Embryo Implants in the Uterus

By the time that the embryo has emerged from the oviduct into the uterus, it has become a two-layered ball of cells that is called a blastocyst. The outer sphere, known as the trophoblast, will form the placenta, the inner cluster of cells, the baby. In the process called implantation, the blastocyst secretes enzymes that penetrate the thick, soft lining of the uterus, creating a space in which it will become implanted. The lining of the uterus seals over, enclosing the embryo and its covering completely within the nourishing lining. Later, the placenta emerges attached at this point.

DAY 4 to 5

Blastocyst reaches womb.

DAY 6

Blastocyst implants in uterus.

The trophoblast "roots" into the lining, extracting nutrients from the mother's blood and allowing the embryo to grow. It grows more complex as it grows larger. Cells which were originally identical change, or differentiate, becoming different kinds of tissue: the ectoderm (to be skin), the endoderm (to be inner organs), and the mesoderm (to be muscle and bone).

DAY 9

Blastocyst develops cavities.

DAY 13 to 15

Endoderm forms yolk sac.

DAY 16

Mesoderm appears.

The embryo, a three-layered disc, detaches from the trophoblast. It will remain attached to the source of its nourishment only by a stalk which will become its umbilical cord. Meanwhile, the fluid-filled amniotic sac expands to surround the embryo completely, cushioning it from injury. The yolk sac will disappear.

DAY 20

Embryo separates from trophoblast.

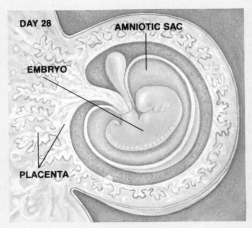

DAY 28

Embryo exhibits recognizable organs.

embryonic to maternal blood to be carried away and be disposed of through maternal lungs and kidneys.

The placenta does the work of several organs that the developing foetus possesses in only rudimentary form. It serves as a lung for the baby, exchanging the foetus's carbon dioxide for the mother's oxygen. It serves as an intestine, absorbing food molecules from the mother's blood. It functions as a kidney, filtering urea and other waste products from the foetal blood and delivering it to the mother for disposal; as a liver, processing the mother's blood cells for the iron they contain; and as an endocrine gland, supplying the hormones that maintain the pregnancy.

Hormones produced in the placenta help the mother's body to maintain the pregnancy and to prepare the breasts for the production of milk after the birth. And that's not all. The placenta forms a barrier against bacteria and viruses but permits the passage of certain maternal immunoglobulins that provide protection against infection in the foetus and in the newborn, too.

To do its job, the placenta keeps growing. Initially, it is bigger than the embryo. At 4 months, when the foetus is roughly 180 millimetres (7 inches) from head to toe, the placenta is a disc about 75 millimetres (3 inches) in diameter. By the end of pregnancy, it has grown to 200 millimetres (8 inches) in diameter and weighs about 0.5 kilograms (1 pound).

How is the umbilical cord formed?

Though formed from an egg, human embryos do not depend on egg yolk for nourishment. The human egg does include a yolk sac, but it degenerates early in pregnancy. Instead the embryo forms a connection to the cells that will become the placenta via a body stalk, which later becomes the umbilical cord. Remnants of the yolk sac and amniotic membrane cover the umbilical cord. Running between the placenta and the abdomen of the foetus, the rope-like cord is the new organism's life-

line. It contains two arteries and one vein, through which the baby's heart pumps blood carrying nutrients or wastes to and from the placenta. The cord is about 12 millimetres (0.5 inches) in diameter and is usually some 300 to 900 millimetres (12 to 35 inches) in length—a little longer than the average baby.

Where does the fluid in the amniotic sac come from?

Within the womb, the foetus moves and floats within the enclosed fluid-filled amniotic sac. Some of the amniotic fluid, which protects and cushions the foetus against physical injury, seeps through the placenta and through the wall of the sac (which is only two cell layers thick) from the uterus. But most of it comes from foetal blood by way of the baby's lungs and kidneys.

The amniotic sac is more like a circulating bath than a pool. By the time the baby is fully developed, the sac holds approximately a litre (1.75 pints) of fluid, of which about a third is recycled hourly. In the latter part of pregnancy, the foetus swallows a

good deal—approximately 500 millilitres (18 fluid ounces)—of this clear, sterile liquid daily.

Is spontaneous abortion common after the first trimester?

Only a quarter of all miscarriages take place after the first three months of pregnancy. Late miscarriages are sometimes caused by structural abnormalities in the uterus itself, damage to the placenta or to the umbilical cord, or, much less frequently, by functional problems in the mother's endocrine system leading to overproduction or underproduction of some hormone. A common structural problem is that of a uterus divided by a partial partition that makes the available space too small for the embryo to develop. Another common difficulty is an "incompetent cervix" that begins to open too soon.

Hormones can be adjusted, wombs can be repaired, and a cervix that threatens to dilate prematurely can be sutured to keep it closed. As many as 90 percent of women who have had a miscarriage for any reason can carry another pregnancy to term.

THE STORY BEHIND THE WORDS...

A Caesarean section, which means surgery for delivery of a baby, was not named after Julius Caesar, the Roman emperor, as legend would have you believe. According to myth, he was born by Caesarean section, and the surgical procedure was, therefore, named after him. The procedure is more likely named after the ancient Roman law, *lex caesarea,* which decreed that a woman who was dying in the last weeks of her pregnancy be operated on to save the child. Another theory is that the name comes from the Latin *caedere,* "to cut."

Pregnant and prenatal stem from the same Latin roots: *prae,* which means "before," and *nasci,* which means "to be born." *Nasci* is also the origin for such words as *nature, innate,* and *native.* Not many years ago, the word *pregnant* was seldom used in polite society; a woman's pregnancy was referred to by euphemisms such as "expecting," being "in the family way," or "a mother-to-be," "awaiting a blessed event."

To cut the umbilical cord, when the phrase is applied to an adult, means to become independent of parental support. The navel, which after birth is all that remains of the umbilical cord, is a word that stems from *nave* (*nafe* in Anglo-Saxon), meaning "the hub of a wheel." The navel, or the "little nave," was so named because it was thought to be the centre of the human body.

Protecting the Unborn

How important is good nutrition?

Without a doubt, nutritious food is very important for pregnant women. Although excessive weight gain (more than 16 to 18 kilograms, or 35 to 40 pounds) is undesirable, pregnancy is no time for dieting. Mothers-to-be should eat enough so they do not feel hungry. But they should avoid junk food, so called because it is nutritionally poor. A balanced diet, with plenty of milk, meat, fruit, cereals, greens, and cheese, that adds up to about 2,500 Calories a day constitutes a good supply of food for both foetus and mother. Any excess fat the woman accumulates in her own tissues will be used to produce milk when she nurses her baby.

World War II provided a natural nutrition experiment in several countries. In the Netherlands, where food was scarce under the German occupation, there were more than the usual number of premature births and stillbirths, and babies tended to be born small. When the war ended, however, the statistics returned to normal. Today, there are similar findings in those underdeveloped countries where there is poor nutrition.

Does a mother's intake of alcohol affect her baby?

One writer on pregnancy has compared the placenta to a farmyard fence: "impermeable to horses but permeable to mice." What this means is that big things—blood cells and bacteria—cannot get through the placenta, while small things—oxygen molecules, small viruses, and most drugs—can. Alcohol is one of the drugs that cross the placental barrier. When a pregnant woman drinks, it is as if the baby drank too. An alcoholic woman's baby may already be addicted to alcohol in the womb. In industrialized Western society, one or two of every thousand newborns is so afflicted. Experts do not agree on how much alcohol is *too* much in pregnancy. Some say that up to 60 millilitres (2 fluid ounces) a day is probably not harmful; others believe a pregnant woman had best limit herself to an occasional glass of wine. As for addictive drugs such as heroin, the hazards to the child are great; the infant born to an addicted mother suffers from withdrawal.

There is a positive side to the semipermeability of the placenta. Some of the mother's antibodies can cross over, along with the hazardous substances. In short, the unborn baby shares the hazards of its mother's body chemistry, but also gains, temporarily, from her defences.

Is it safe to take drugs during pregnancy?

A woman who is taking drugs of any sort should discuss the matter with her doctor if she is planning to have a baby. After she knows that she

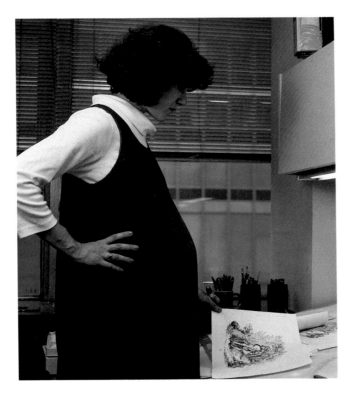

How long should a woman continue with her job during pregnancy?

This question probably was never asked before the mid-20th century. Until that time, women worked because they had to, whether they were pregnant or not. Some returned to work—often in the fields—without any period of recuperation. Nowadays, depending on the physical demands of her job, a healthy woman usually can work up to the very end of her pregnancy—but she may not want to. The baby gets too big for comfort. A bulging belly makes bending difficult, and the sheer weight strains the back. The enlarging uterus pushes the other internal organs around, sometimes causing indigestion, heartburn, and other discomforts. Loosening pelvic ligaments can make walking wobbly. Pressure may also give rise to varicose veins; the most effective relief is putting the feet up—which may not be possible in the job situation. However, some companies provide a place where pregnant women can lie down. By the end of pregnancy, the average woman has gained 9 to 12 kilograms (20 to 25 pounds). Although books and doctors can offer useful advice for relieving discomfort, no one can help a woman to carry those extra kilograms.

Many women prefer to work through to the end of their first pregnancy, rather than sit at home. Sudden feelings of fatigue are commoner in early pregnancy than later on.

is pregnant, she should take only those drugs that the doctor considers absolutely essential.

Drugs are most dangerous to the foetus during the first three months of pregnancy, when the heart, brain, limbs, and facial features are forming. The most severe defects date from the third week of gestation (when the mother is not yet aware that she is pregnant) to the tenth week. A few drugs are harmful if taken in the final weeks, or even during labour itself.

Even very small quantities of some drugs can be extremely hazardous. It is well to remember that just one thalidomide pill containing a mere 100 milligrams of that sedative was enough to produce gross limb deformities in babies.

Could intercourse hurt the growing baby?

A foetus floating in its watery bubble is rarely hurt even by a fall, much less by intercourse. The baby is cushioned from any bump; give it a poke, and it floats away. However, women prone to miscarriage are sometimes advised to avoid intercourse, particularly when they would ordinarily be due to menstruate. Some experts believe that sexual relations are undesirable for all women during the third trimester of pregnancy. But there is no proof of danger, except in complicated pregnancies or when there is an infectious venereal disease.

How much of a woman's weight gain is the baby itself?

The average baby weighs about 3 kilograms (7 pounds) at birth, and its paraphernalia—placenta and the membranes, amniotic fluid, and umbilical cord—weigh another 1.5 to 2 kilograms (3 to 4 pounds). A pregnant woman, however, gains much more than 5 kilograms (11 pounds). Her breasts gain approximately 1 to 1.5 kilograms (2 to 3 pounds), her uterus another kilogram (2 pounds). Under the influence of steroid hor-

Folklore of the Body: CRAVINGS DURING PREGNANCY

What is it about being pregnant that causes a woman to feel an urgent desire for such foods as pickles and ice cream? According to many authorities, there is no specific nutritional need that would be asserted in this way. Generally, they put cravings down to hysteria; or to a bid for sympathy. However, there *is* a craving, called pica, in which a person—often a pregnant woman—develops a craving for non-foods such as dirt, plaster, or coal. Such cravings are thought to be a sign of iron deficiency, and can be treated by foods or drugs containing iron. The ice cream kind of craving does little harm, but if anyone craves non-foods, it's time to see a doctor.

Satirizing a pregnant woman's craving for meat, French artist Honoré Daumier depicts her gnawing on a butcher boy's arm in this 1839 cartoon.

mones, her body retains an extra 3 kilograms (6 pounds) or so of fluids, which she loses as urine in the first few days after the baby is born.

The baby's weight is related to the mother's weight gain. Taller mothers tend to have bigger babies, and bigger babies do better. Women who gain less than 5 kilograms (11 pounds) or so have more premature and low-birth-weight babies than do the women who gain more weight.

How does a woman's body change during pregnancy?

In most cases, a pregnant woman's uterus expands to 20 times its previous size. Her breasts more than double in volume, her vagina enlarges, and, as ligaments slacken, her pelvis widens. Blood volume increases by about 30 percent, which means the woman has roughly an extra litre

(1.75 pints) of blood in her body, and her heart has to work harder than usual to pump it. Her breathing rate increases so that she takes in 20 percent more oxygen, and there is an increase in urine production.

Does having a baby spoil a woman's figure?

After the baby is born, a woman's appetite, generally heartier during pregnancy, usually returns to normal. Although nursing mothers must eat more so that their bodies are not drained of important nutrients, they need not gain weight. In fact, most can return to their prepregnancy weight without dieting. Breasts can sag if the new mother neglects to support them with a good bra. The protruding belly button typical of the last months before delivery soon sinks back in place.

How the Baby Grows

From 2 Weeks to 15 Weeks

As the baby grows in size, it changes in proportion, and becomes more recognizably human in feature. At first, with its big head and small tail, it resembles a comma. By the time limb buds have developed knee and elbow joints at seven and a half weeks, facial features are recognizable, and the body is less top-heavy. Shoulders can be discerned the 31st day; two days later, there are budding fingers, and by the 36th day, thumbs. The following day, the nose and ears are developed enough to make out certain inherited peculiarities, such as attached or unattached ear lobes. Invisible but no less important, nerves and muscles develop rapidly, so that by the ninth week, when the baby still looks embryonic, it is capable of automatic movements. By 12 weeks, the baby is growing nails; it is 75 millimetres (3 inches) long and weighs 30 grams (1 ounce).

- 14 days
- 18 days
- 24 days
- 4 weeks
- 6½ weeks
- 7½ weeks

The embryos are shown in their actual size.

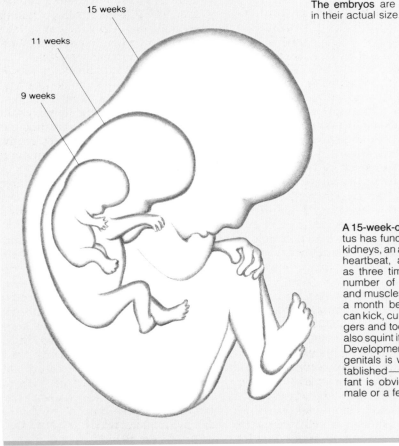

15 weeks
11 weeks
9 weeks

A 15-week-old foetus has functioning kidneys, an audible heartbeat, as well as three times the number of nerves and muscles it had a month before. It can kick, curl its fingers and toes, and also squint its eyes. Development of the genitals is well established—the infant is obviously a male or a female.

What does the unborn baby look like one month after conception?

Four weeks after it comes into existence, the future baby is called an embryo. The embryo is shaped like a tadpole and is 5 millimetres (0.2 inches) long, about the size of a pea. Its heart has been beating for about a week. The head is defined, with eyes and rudiments of ears visible, and inside there is the beginning of a brain. So far, there are no bones. Tiny bumps are beginning to bulge where arms and legs will form.

A week later, the embryo has grown to the size of a bean, the limb buds will have grown into little paws. The head has enlarged to accommodate the rapidly growing brain. The arms and hands become recognizable before the legs. Movements start almost as soon as the limbs are formed, though the mother will not feel them yet. The eyelids arise after the fifth week and gradually close over the eyes, but reopen during the seventh or eighth month.

How does the baby spend its day?

Between naps, a foetus exercises, practising, in a sense, for its life to come. At seven to eight weeks, its first movements become apparent. They are jerky, as though the foetus were a marionette dangling from strings, but during the following months, it gains in grace and coordination. Well before the mother can feel the baby's movements, at 16 to 20 weeks, it is opening its mouth, touching its face, waving its arms, and kicking its feet. Like the manoeuvres of an astronaut floating freely in space, linked only by a line to the spacecraft, the movements of the foetus, tethered only by its umbilical cord, send it tumbling in slow motion inside the amniotic sac.

Does the foetus sleep?

Although the unborn child is physically active, it sleeps, too, and there is every reason to believe that it dreams, though of what we can only guess. By ultrasound, the foetus can be seen yawning and stretching. Some babies in the womb sleep sprawled on their tummies, others curled up on one side, some with head tucked to chest, others with head tilted back. In the last third of pregnancy, there is no more space for sprawling, and most babies lie curled up in the womb, usually with head down.

How can we know any of this? Partly through ultrasound pictures of the foetus, partly from electroencephalograms, or recordings of brain waves, made before the child is born. These tracings show the distinctive brain activity that characterizes the known stages of human sleep, including the REM (rapid eye movement) period that accompanies dreaming.

How is development completed?

From the third month onwards, nature puts all sorts of finishing touches on the foetus. Fingernails appear around the ninth week (and grow eventually so much that some babies come into the world with scratches on their faces and nails in need of trimming). Eyelids, formed at the beginning of the third month, seal the eyes shut like a newborn kitten's while their development is completed. Facial features gradually shift to more familiar locations, the eyes closer together and the ear lobes up where they belong from their earlier position low on the foetal head. Lips form, cheeks fill out, taste buds develop on the tongue, and salivary glands come into being. In a girl the ovaries, and in a boy the testes, begin to produce the primitive eggs and male germ cells that are the seeds for the next generation; even as a woman is becoming a mother, her baby is preparing to make her a grandmother.

How soon does the baby grow hair?

About the beginning of the third foetal month, the baby grows fine hairs on its eyebrows and whiskers on its upper lip and hair on the palms

A three-month foetus, eyelids fused shut and skin transparent, floats weightless in the amniotic sac tethered by its long umbilical cord.

of its hands and the soles of its feet. By 20 weeks, the foetus has developed a fine coat of soft hair, called lanugo, over its body. Secondary hair grows in the fifth and sixth months from new hair follicles, gradually replacing lanugo. The foetus sheds most of the lanugo in the succeeding month, but its downy remains can sometimes be seen fuzzing the scalp, eyebrows, and the rims of a newborn's ears.

When can a foetus live on its own?

Provided a baby has grown normally in the uterus, it can, in many instances, live outside the womb from about the 28th week of gestation. The baby's chances of survival improve with every week it is nurtured within the womb, and with every gram it gains before birth. Today, a baby weighing at least 1.5 kilograms (3.3 pounds) has an excellent chance of survival, particularly if it is treated in a specialized unit for premature babies in the hospital. The youngest babies to survive have been only 25 weeks old. At that age, a baby weighs little more than 0.5 kilograms (1 pound).

It is customary to define preterm infants as those whose gestational age is under 37 weeks or whose weight at birth is under 2.5 kilograms (5.5 pounds). It is important to note that many premature babies grow up to be healthy adults. (Winston Churchill was premature.) But some are retarded, autistic, or handicapped in other less serious ways. And many die as infants.

In England, one baby in every 100 is stillborn or dies before reaching the age of one week. For low-birthweight babies the rate is higher: 4.2 out of a hundred for infants weighing 2 to 2.25 kilograms (4.5 to 5 pounds), and 24 out of a hundred for those babies who weigh only 1 to 1.5 kilograms (2.2 to 3.3 pounds).

The vulnerability of preterm infants comes from the fact that their organs are immature and may therefore function imperfectly. The inability to breathe properly is one of the principal causes of death in premature infants. These babies are vulnerable to haemorrhage in the brain and lungs, and they are less developed in a number of other ways. They are not yet padded with the fat that keeps full-term babies warm, and their alimentary tract has not yet developed all the enzymes necessary to digest artificial baby food.

The Mother-Child Relationship

When does the mother first feel her baby's movements?

In the second month after conception, readings from recording equipment placed on a pregnant woman's abdomen reveal that the foetus is already moving around. But the mother can't feel her baby's movements until roughly four months of pregnancy have passed, when the foetus is large enough to bump into her belly. Mothers who have borne children before can usually feel the baby's movements one or two weeks earlier than mothers carrying their first baby.

Between the eighth week, when the foetus begins moving its limbs, and the end of the twelfth week, the baby triples in length. The growth rate tapers off as the pregnancy advances, and it takes about eight to nine weeks for the baby to triple in length again. In the 20th week of gestation (when the foetus is 18 weeks old), it measures about 250 millimetres (10 inches) from head to toe, or nearly half the length it will be at birth. At that size, its movements no longer send it lightly floating in its amniotic sac, but bumping into the surrounding uterine wall. The mother feels gentle flutterings, and as the weeks pass, increasingly hard belly raps from her baby. When delivery is close, the baby's kicking can actually overturn a glass of water balanced on the mother's abdomen. In the last few months of pregnancy, a woman may puzzle over a particularly odd kind of movement, felt as slight jolts repeated 15 to 30 times a minute and lasting as long as half an hour. That may be the baby hiccuping.

The awareness of movement appears to be mutual. Towards the end of pregnancy, the unborn baby will respond to the mother's prods. If she gives it a push, or changes her position rapidly, it will move.

Why do babies kick the most when the mother lies down?

The reason may be that rocking soothes babies before birth just as much as after they are born. By the seventh month, the baby is so large

A little girl lays her head against her mother's belly to feel the unborn baby kicking. Through such intimacies, a relationship begins months before a new sibling is born.

that it presses against many of the mother's organs and can feel its mother's movements. Her bustling activity may rock her baby to sleep, and her lying down to rest may wake the baby up. Another explanation is that a mother engaged in her daily activities is less aware of her baby's movements than a resting mother is.

Can babies see and hear inside the womb?

When the sealed eyelids of the foetus open at about seven to eight months of pregnancy, the eyes are well developed, and, by then, there is something to see. Light penetrates the mother's stretched abdomen, and if the mother happens to be sunbathing in a bikini, light will bathe the baby in dim ruddiness like the glow of a hand held before a candle. The sense of hearing is fully developed too. The foetus hears the thumps of its mother's heart, the rumblings of her intestine, the sound of her voice, and even slamming doors and symphonies. Research indicates that loud noises can provoke movement by the

foetus and alter its heartbeat. Photographs taken by ultrasound show unborn babies turning towards the tinkling of a bell or the flashing of a light.

When does excretion first occur?

By the middle of the fifth month in the womb, the foetus begins to urinate into the amniotic fluid, and at term the foetus may excrete up to 450 millilitres (16 fluid ounces) daily. The urine is sterile and so doesn't contaminate the amniotic fluid.

Solid waste, a by-product of swallowed amniotic fluid and bile, accumulates in the baby's intestine and stays there until after birth. The solids passed in the first few days after birth are called meconium and are dark green in colour.

Do babies learn before birth?

Unborn babies seem to learn to recognize both sounds and rhythms. Studies indicate that as early as 36 hours or less after birth, babies are able to recognize their mother's voice, preferring it to that of another woman. This suggests that the preference developed before birth. Stronger evidence comes from a study in which 16 women read the story *The Cat in the Hat* twice a day to their foetuses during the last weeks of pregnancy. After birth, the babies seemed to prefer that story's familiar cadence to the different metre of another tale or rhyme. The babies showed their preferences by sucking an electronically rigged nipple. If they sucked in one rhythm, they could hear their mother reading the familiar story heard in the womb. If they sucked differently, the device turned on a recording of a voice or poem they'd never heard.

A Japanese study shows that the foetus can also learn to ignore one annoyance of ordinary life: the roar of an aeroplane overhead. Infants born to women who lived beneath the flight path of Osaka airport were five times more likely to sleep through the noise than were babies whose mothers lived elsewhere.

Can a mother find out about her baby's temperament before birth?

Some foetuses move about vigorously and often; others are relaxed. One may startle at sudden noises, while another is not bothered at all. Some people say that a baby that becomes active in the womb when its mother lies down to sleep will be active later on when its mother puts it down in its crib to sleep, and one that is quiet in the womb will sleep quietly in the nursery. Studies monitoring the activity level of the same babies before and after they are born tend to confirm this assumption.

What are the odds that a pregnant woman will bear a boy?

About 106 boys are born for every 100 girls. An even higher proportion of embryos are male: an estimated 130 for every 100 females. Sperm cells (spermatozoa) bearing the Y chromosome are thought to move more rapidly than sperm cells bearing the X, or the female, chromosome, probably because the Y chromosome is smaller and lighter than the X. It may be that the disproportion between male and female embryos is caused by the greater motility of Y-bearing sperm cells, which gives them a much better chance of reaching the egg. However, fewer males than females survive in the uterus, so that a woman is almost as likely to give birth to a daughter as to a son.

When is the sex of the baby apparent?

For the first nine or ten weeks, embryos look very much alike. The genitals develop from a slit with a little round bud in the middle and a swelling on each side of it. At 12 to 13 weeks, in the foetus destined to become a girl, the bud develops into the clitoris, the swellings into the labia; in a boy, the bud grows into the penis, the swellings into the scrotum.

How does the baby change in the last three months?

In the final third of pregnancy, the foetus becomes capable of life outside the womb. Subcutaneous fat begins to accumulate, filling out the scrawny body and preparing the baby to stay warm in the outside world. (One reason premature babies need incubators is that they cannot maintain optimum body temperatures to support body functions.) The average foetus gains about 1.5 kilograms (3 or 4 pounds) during the eighth and ninth months. At the time of normal birth, the foetus is so big that it has almost outgrown its food supply; the placenta, which stops growing in late pregnancy, cannot keep up the supply of ever-increasing demands for nutrients to the foetus indefinitely.

Throughout the last three months, the brain is developing rapidly, and in the last two months, myelinization begins. That is, a fatty substance known as myelin, which insulates the transmission of nervous impulses, forms a sheath around nerve fibres.

All the while the baby is becoming more attractive because of its new plumpness. It sheds the lanugo hairs that covered much of its body for the past couple of months. And then, the hair on its head often grows remarkably long—long enough, sometimes, that an admiring mother can tie a ribbon on it, right after birth.

Looking in on the Unborn Baby

From the woman's standpoint, an ultrasound examination is a simple, comfortable procedure that takes about a half an hour to perform. She lies on her back, and oil is rubbed on her lower abdomen. A sound transmitter, which resembles the head of a stethoscope, is moved gently over her abdomen, bouncing sound waves against the uterus and the baby from various angles. The images that are displayed on a television screen, and also photographed, are cross-sections. They are hard for the patient to interpret, but to the trained examiner, they reveal such details as the size and location of the placenta, the baby's head and spine, and even the inside of the foetal heart. Ultrasound scans are especially helpful when a multiple pregnancy is suspected.

Ultrasound scans are a non-invasive way to study a baby while it is still in the womb.

The Phenomenon of Twins

Why are twins often born early?

Twins are often born early compared with single babies. This is partly because they take up more room in the womb, and partly because the mother's circulatory system cannot always cope with the burden of providing nutrition for two babies. Although nobody knows for sure what starts labour, mechanical stretching of the uterus may promote uterine contractions and thus trigger off labour prematurely in twin pregnancies. Bed rest is suggested to prevent or delay premature birth.

How do twins come about?

Identical twins begin as a single egg, fertilized by a single sperm cell. During the early divisions, the developing organism splits into two parts. Since the cells have not yet begun to form organs or specialize, each of the parts can become a complete person. The result is two babies that resemble each other very closely in the genetically determined characteristics. Though twins develop as separate individuals, they have identical genes and are of the same sex, and they often share the same placenta; about one-third of all twins are of this kind.

Fraternal twins, which account for 70 to 80 percent of all twin births, come from two eggs that have ripened during the same monthly cycle and have been fertilized by two different sperm cells. Each embryo makes its own placenta, and the babies are no more alike than siblings conceived and born at different times.

Twinning rates vary in different lands, and twins are born in about 1 in every 50 to 300 births, but there are possibly three times as many twin conceptions that produce only a single baby. One of the embryos fails to grow, and is resorbed, leaving the surviving baby undisturbed.

What are Siamese twins?

Twin babies which are joined together at birth are the result of a single fertilized egg that failed to divide completely into identical twins. Such births are rare—1 in 100,000. Surgical separation of the babies is extremely difficult if they share major organs, such as the liver.

Why do fertility drugs cause multiple births?

Fertility drugs work by stimulating follicle ripening and ovulation. Sometimes they work *too* well, causing "superovulation," or the ripening of more than one egg at a time. Women who are treated with fertility drugs are thus more likely to conceive more than one child at a time. The babies of such women are as individual as ordinary brothers and sisters, since each came from a separate egg.

Of course, multiple births occurred before fertility drugs came into use, though not as often. Probably there are many people who can remember the sensation created by the Dionne quintuplets' birth in 1934; they were the first set of five to live more than 15 days. Despite medical advances since 1934, multiple births still pose hazards for both mother and babies. Among other things, the infants are likely to be born prematurely because their combined weight and bulk overstretch the uterus. They may also be poorly nourished, because the mother's body is not always able to supply enough nutrients for several babies at once and her heart may not be able to pump enough blood through several placentae. That difficulty can be forestalled, at least in part, if the multiple pregnancy is diagnosed early and the mother rests and takes dietary supplements.

DID YOU KNOW...?

- **Until it has been bathed,** a newborn infant looks and feels somewhat oily. A whitish substance called *vernix caseosa* protects the delicate skin of the foetus and keeps it from getting waterlogged. The waxy material begins to appear in the fifth month, and is like the grease on a long-distance swimmer. It is made of sebum, an oily substance secreted by the sebaceous glands of the hair follicles.

- **By the time they are five or six months old,** virtually all babies babble. That is, they utter sequences of alternating vowels and consonants, such as "ba ba ba." Deaf infants may babble exactly as hearing infants do. And babies of all nationalities make the same babbling sounds; some researchers say that infants spontaneously produce all the sounds of all languages.

- **The mother's womb shrinks back** to half its pregnant weight before the newborn is a week old. By the time the baby is a month old, the uterus may be as small as it was the day the embryo first moved in.

- **Expectant fathers may experience** some of the symptoms of pregnancy— morning sickness, backache, weight gain, cravings, and depression. This phenomenon, called *couvade* from the French word meaning "to hatch," has been recognized officially in some cultures. In parts of Africa and New Guinea, rituals take these feelings into account. In industrialized societies, however, men have been reluctant to acknowledge these feelings, and it is only recently that scientists have even assembled data on the subject.

- **Scientists have tried to categorize** the early behaviour of babies. In one study of newborns, 65 percent of the babies had consistent behaviour patterns. About 10 percent were classified as difficult: they cried a lot, screamed when bathed, spat out new foods. Another 15 percent were described as slow to warm up; they tended to be withdrawn, wary in new situations. Some 40 percent were classified as easy babies because they were cheerful most of the time and adapted readily to new foods, people, and circumstances. Since these temperamental differences showed up very early in life, it is reasonable to infer that they are at least partly innate. But personality in later life depends on both innate temperament and on environmental influences—the individual's own experience.

The Marvel of Multiple Births

Twins are born in 1 out of about 100 births in Britain. They are rarer among the Chinese, whose rate is 1 in 300, but surprisingly common among the Yoruba of Nigeria, who have a set of twins for every 22 births. The different rates are accounted for by an inherited tendency to release more than one egg a month, resulting in non-identical siblings born at the same time. Identical twins are born at the rate of about 4 per 1,000 births regardless of ethnic background or family history, for the tendency of a single egg to separate into two is not inherited. Triplets, quadruplets, and sextuplets may be fraternal or identical, and sometimes a combination of both.

Legend has it that the twin founders of Rome, Romulus and Remus, were nursed by a she-wolf—after surviving an attempt to drown them.

The Dionne quintuplets, shown here with their physician, Dr. Dafoe, were born in a farmhouse in Ontario on May 28, 1934. So rare was the survival of quintuplets that their childhood was blighted by the glare of publicity.

The English village of Leominster (population 8,000) leaped into fame with an unexplained boom in twin births. Although there are no more twins than usual among the adults, there are 28 sets of twins in the present generation of school-age children.

The Van Hove-Gadeyne sextuplets of Belgium are celebrities, but public attention is far more rational than it was for the Dionnes.

The Different Ways of Giving Birth

Delivered at home, a baby is introduced to the whole family in the intimate setting of the parents' bedroom. Though disapproved of by some doctors, home birth is an option in some localities if no complications are expected.

When should a woman choose a birthing method?

A woman in labour is in no position to argue about procedures. She should make all her decisions about how she wants to be treated during labour and how she wants her baby ushered into the world well ahead of time. And she should be sure the people and institutions she will be relying on share her views. She also should make sure that her views are rational and not merely emotional. After all, she takes on the responsibility for the well-being of her baby which may be crucial for its entire life. If she asks questions early, she may discover that the doctor, or hospital, she had selected is strongly opposed to something very important to her and will alter routine procedures only reluctantly, or not at all.

What is the difference between a midwife and a doctor?

More than three quarters of the babies born every year around the world are delivered with the help of midwives. In the past, most midwives were laypersons who learned about childbirth by serving an apprenticeship. Today, many of the world's 800,000 or so midwives are trained professionals, but in large parts of the world, the birth attendants still lack any formal training. In Britain they are registered nurses with midwifery training.

Since midwives do not have medical degrees, they cannot perform Caesareans or use surgical forceps. But they are well-prepared to handle normal labour and delivery and to perform an episiotomy, a minor operation to enlarge the vaginal opening. They are trained to recognize when things aren't going well and the patient needs specialist medical help.

Can a woman choose to have her baby delivered at home?

A few doctors, some midwives, and a small but growing number of pregnant women in Western countries prefer their homes to the hospital for giving birth because they feel they benefit from the comforting presence of family and friends and want to share the joy of childbirth with them. In general, home deliveries give precedence to comfort over technology.

They dispense with many of the hospital procedures that annoy women in labour, including intravenous tubes, electronic monitoring of the mother's contractions and the foetus, and a multiplicity of staff.

Childbirth at home is suitable only for women whose delivery is expected to be uncomplicated. This rules out women expecting twins, or those who have diabetes, hypertension, placenta praevia, or other special problems.

Does natural childbirth ensure painless delivery?

Prepared childbirth (a more accurate term than natural childbirth) is often misunderstood. Its goal is not to eliminate pain but to reduce it, in part by reducing fear. Proponents claim that preparation for delivery helps mother and newborn form close ties with each other.

Interestingly enough, the varieties of prepared childbirth now current in many parts of the world have their origins in the Soviet Union. In the 1930s and 1940s, doctors in that country began applying Pavlov's techniques of conditioning to women in labour. Their aim was to condition expectant mothers to react to their labour contractions not by experiencing pain and fear but by breathing in special ways.

The prepared childbirth movements hold meetings and classes in many communities. The methods are by now the traditional alternative to delivery under heavy sedation or anaesthesia. A pregnant woman attends classes with a partner whose task during labour will be to help the mother concentrate on breathing, relaxing, and massage routines they have learned together during the weeks preceding the birth.

The focus of the Leboyer method is the baby. To minimize the shock of its exit from the womb, lights are dimmed, and the new baby is almost immediately bathed in a small tub of lukewarm water. One should keep in mind, however, that the shock of cold air is necessary to make the baby inhale air. Since the first minutes after birth are the most crucial moments in a baby's life, the wisdom in tampering with the natural stimuli that initiate its normal function in its new environment is doubtful.

What can go wrong in the last months?

Premature labour is a serious complication of pregnancy; it accounts for the largest percentage of infant deaths within a short time of birth. In some instances, when the mother and baby are otherwise doing fine, drug therapy may be administered to forestall premature birth. To guard against preterm birth, the mother should see a doctor or midwife regularly throughout her pregnancy.

Another hazard of the later stages of pregnancy, which occurs in a small percentage of women, is a form of high blood pressure called pre-eclampsia, or, in its most serious form, eclampsia. Another complication is placenta praevia, in which the placenta has developed low in the uterus, sometimes spanning the cervix, stretching it, and causing bleeding. Both of these conditions usually require hospitalization, since they threaten the welfare of both the mother and the foetus. Many instances of placenta praevia require a Caesarean section, because the baby cannot be born without dislodging the placenta first, causing severe bleeding.

Why are so many babies delivered by Caesarean section these days?

Until electronic monitoring of the foetal heartbeat came into use in hospitals, doctors had little detailed information about how the baby was bearing up as its mother was bearing down. Nurses couldn't keep an ear to the mother's belly continuously, or discern the nuances of sound picked up by an electronic ear and delicately scrawled along yards of paper tape. Those recordings reveal when a foetus is in distress because it is not getting enough oxygen, and they signal the need for a prompt delivery by

Caesarean section to save the baby. Electronic monitoring may therefore account for the recent increase in Caesarean births. In addition, the statistics may reflect an increase in the number of foetuses at risk because the mother is a teenager, over the age of 30, in poor health, or undernourished.

Some critics say that there are too many Caesareans, and they advance another possible explanation for the increase: Caesareans, they argue, are more convenient for doctors, enabling them to arrange the time of birth. Whatever the truth of the matter may be, mothers-to-be who prefer not to miss out on the experience of vaginal delivery may wish to defer choosing an obstetrician until they know the attitude of that particular doctor.

Can a mother give birth normally after she's had a Caesarean?

Whether or not a mother can deliver a child vaginally once she's had a Caesarean depends on two things. First, the reason she had a Caesarean must be a one-time thing, such as a breech presentation, rather than a permanent condition, such as a pelvis too narrow for a baby's head. Second, the Caesarean scar must be a strong one: a scar from a long, vertical incision is more likely to tear during labour contractions than one from a short, horizontal cut. In Britain doctors are usually willing to let the woman try for a normal labour although sometimes doctors plan repeat Caesareans after the first one.

Giving Birth Sitting Up

Until about 200 years ago, most women gave birth in a vertical position, either squatting or sitting upright on a birthing stool. The custom was discouraged by 18th-century physicians because new techniques, particularly the use of forceps, were more efficient if the mother-to-be lay flat on her back. Now vertical birth is experiencing a comeback. In a more normal position to push, and with the help of gravity, women who have used the modern version of a birthing chair claim to deliver more comfortably and quickly. Such chairs may be motorized so that the doctor can adjust the position during delivery.

Compared to a medieval birthing chair, the modern moulded and motorized chair is a triumph of comfort and convenience.

Potential Problems of Pregnancy

What does "spotting" mean during pregnancy?

Though the expression *threatened miscarriage* is frequently used when a little bleeding occurs for a day or two during the first few months of pregnancy, such spotting usually isn't a prelude to anything at all. This bleeding tends to occur when the woman's period would ordinarily be expected, and it is soon over. In 85 percent of such cases, pregnancy continues uneventfully, and the baby is born perfectly normal.

Heavy bleeding, or spotting that continues for longer than a week, marks the beginning of a spontaneous abortion, or miscarriage. By the time the warning signs appear, the foetus has probably been dead for some weeks, and the uterus is beginning to shed its lining just as it would do during a menstrual period. Later in gestation, spotting or bleeding may be the sign of placenta praevia; this situation requires close supervision by the doctor.

What causes miscarriage?

It is sometimes thought that miscarriages are nature's way of correcting reproductive errors. In perhaps two out of every three spontaneous abortions, the foetus is grossly abnormal. The causes of foetal abnormality are legion. In their primordial form, at least, a woman's eggs are as old as she is; it is unlikely that every one is in perfect condition when it is released at ovulation. And then, a normal egg may be fertilized by a damaged sperm. Even if an embryo is normal, it can be damaged by the mother's ill health, malnutrition, or exposure to drugs or toxic chemicals in the natural environment or in the workplace. Certain diseases, including German measles and toxoplasmosis (an infection spread through cat faeces), can also harm the embryo.

Miscarriages can occur even when there is nothing wrong with the foetus; in these cases, which usually occur during the second or third trimester, the difficulty is usually an abnormality in the uterus. Many psychiatrists believe that psychological reasons—perhaps an unconscious fear of pregnancy or motherhood—also may underlie some miscarriages. One thing to remember: despite the impression you may get from popular fiction or movies, spontaneous abortion rarely results from a fall, an automobile accident, or a sudden emotional shock.

It is impossible to know precisely how often spontaneous abortions occur; many "late periods" are actually early miscarriages—so early that the women do not know they are pregnant. One frequently heard estimate is that nearly one in every five pregnancies ends in miscarriage.

Is amniocentesis safe?

Amniocentesis is a technique used to diagnose foetal abnormalities by drawing a sample of amniotic fluid into a hollow needle inserted through the mother's abdomen into the uterus. Less than 1 percent of the time, the procedure triggers off uterine contractions and miscarriage, or causes other complications. Yet the risk may be worth taking if there is reason to suspect a birth defect or hereditary disease that could not otherwise be diagnosed in time to permit an abortion—if the parents wish it—or prenatal treatment—if that is possible. Amniocentesis is usually advised for women over the age of 35, whose babies are most likely to suffer from birth defects.

Amniotic fluid contains cells and

Difficult foetal presentations, including twins, appear in a 12th-century manuscript, based on the work of Soranus of Ephesus, a physician of the first century A.D. He originated a method (still in use today) of gently turning the baby in the womb from a transverse to a safer position for delivery.

molecules shed by the foetus. Cultured in the laboratory, those cells can reveal such defects as Down's syndrome (formerly called mongolism), spina bifida, and muscular dystrophy. But amniocentesis cannot guarantee a healthy baby even if findings are negative. This is because many genetically caused abnormalities cannot yet be detected.

Can you find out your baby's sex before it is born?

If amniocentesis is performed, the doctor, at least, will know whether the baby is a boy or a girl because its sex chromosomes will be visible in the cells withdrawn in the sample of amniotic fluid. (Some parents ask the doctor to keep the baby's sex a secret from them. And no doctor will perform amniocentesis just to satisfy the curiosity of the parents.)

Does the umbilical cord ever tangle?

Since the umbilical cord averages about 0.5 metres (1 foot 8 inches) in length, and since foetal movements include frequent somersaults, one might expect the cord to keep tangling. In fact, this rarely happens. The baby's heart pumps blood through the umbilical cord at the rate of 6 kilometres (4 miles) an hour—fast enough to carry the blood through the foetus and the placenta, and back to the cord again, in only 30 seconds. Moreover, the speed creates enough pressure to keep the cord stiff, like a garden hose with water flowing through it.

Not that the cord *cannot* tangle; about one out of three foetuses *have* managed to get the umbilical cord wrapped around them, in some cases as many as three times. If that happens, the cord can get pinched during a contraction, between the bones of the mother's pelvis and the baby's bony head or shoulder. While the cord is compressed, the flow of blood to the baby is impeded, along with the baby's supply of oxygen, and the foetal heartbeat slows. This is a common

Treating the Unborn

Medical technology has made it possible to detect foetal abnormalities at an early stage of the child's development. This has opened a new frontier of medicine: treating sick babies before they are born. Already, infants with various disorders have been saved from severe illness, retardation, and even death, by adjustment of the mother's diet. Until recently, the only access to the foetus has been through the placenta. A new technique allows some deficiencies to be corrected by injection into the amniotic fluid; the foetus swallows the medication. Now pioneering doctors, guided by ultrasound images and using sensitive instruments, have given transfusions to babies while they are still in the uterus. In other cases, they have drained excess fluids from the baby's brain (when there is evidence of hydrocephalus), and they have even successfully performed foetal surgery.

Amniocentesis, in which a sample of amniotic fluid is removed for diagnostic tests, has allowed doctors to identify and sometimes correct problems before birth.

event during delivery, and the foetus usually recovers quickly as soon as the pressure is relieved. The pressure on the cord can often be relieved by having the mother lie on her side, get up on her hands and knees, or move about. If the situation seems dire, the baby can be rescued by doing a Caesarean section immediately.

What is "false" labour?

During the month preceding birth, all pregnant women experience what are called the Braxton-Hicks contractions, which, though painless, are sometimes mistaken for active la-

bour. As pregnancy advances, the increasingly irritable uterus contracts from time to time, sometimes quite powerfully. These contractions serve a very important purpose: by pushing the baby against the cervix, they "efface" it, that is, shorten and thin it so it can later open and let the baby out.

Women who have never been in labour before wonder whether or not the contractions mean that the baby is on the way. A simple way to differentiate true labour from false is to get up and walk around. If the contractions subside, they are not the real thing. But if they become longer, closer together, and more and more intense, then labour is really under way.

The Onset of Labour

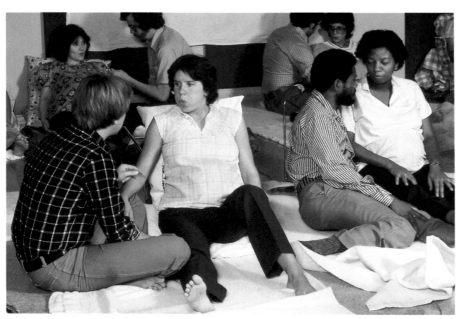

Couples learn together the relaxation and breathing techniques needed in natural childbirth. The husband's role is to accompany and support his wife.

What makes the uterus contract?

During most of gestation, the uterus grows to accommodate the growing foetus. But near the end of pregnancy, its growth ceases, and the uterine wall becomes stretched as the baby continues to grow. When muscles are stretched, their power to contract increases, and they sometimes become more irritable. Thus, just by growing, the baby stretches the uterine muscles and may stimulate the uterus to contract. The baby's descent into the pelvis and the pressure of its head against the cervix apparently set off contractions by stimulating nerves that send signals to the mother's brain to release the hormone oxytocin, a uterine stimulant.

Hormonal as well as mechanical influences are at work. The uterus becomes progressively more sensitive to oxytocin, which is secreted by both the foetus and the mother's pituitary gland. This hormone is a very powerful stimulant of uterine contractions, and labour probably begins when the uterus responds to critical levels of this hormone in the blood.

In fact, this hormone works so well that when a doctor decides to induce labour, he is very likely to administer synthetic oxytocin. But induced labour has become less common than it used to be. Nowadays, the best medical opinion holds that labour should be started artificially only when specific medical conditions in the mother or the foetus absolutely require it. Labour should not be induced just to suit the convenience of mother or doctor.

The foetus itself gives signals to the mother's body to start labour. The sequence of biochemical events is complex: the maturation of the hormone-producing organs sets off a chain of chemical reactions that ultimately leads to the synthesis of substances called prostaglandins within the uterus itself. Prostaglandins have the capacity to stimulate uterine contractions, and they are also produced in the human uterus during labour. Oxytocin and prostaglandins probably work in tandem to ensure well-coordinated contractions that dilate the cervix without undue stress on the baby.

What are the signs that labour is beginning?

The onset of labour is seldom extremely painful or dramatically sudden. In about 6 percent of pregnancies, labour begins with the leaking of fluid from the amniotic sac. Although many women worry in advance about a gush of water that might embarrass them in public, they usually lose, at first, only a couple of spoonfuls or so—the amount of fluid that collects between the baby's head and the cervix. Another frequent signal that labour will soon begin is a show of blood-tinged mucus. This happens because the cervix softens as the time for delivery nears and loses its grip on a mucous plug that has sealed it.

Most commonly, a woman knows that her long period of waiting is over because she begins to experience labour pains, painful contractions of her uterus. At first, the contractions may come only every half-hour and last less than 30 seconds. But gradually, they occur closer together, last longer, and feel more intense. Eventually, the mother-to-be cannot walk or talk as long as a contraction continues.

How long does labour last?

Labour for first-born infants can last anywhere from 8 to 24 hours. In subsequent pregnancies, the time is often reduced considerably, to 6 or 8 hours. Average figures don't tell a particular woman what to expect, however. First labours can be as short as 4 hours, or as long as 24, or longer. If birth isn't imminent by then, the doctor may use forceps to hasten delivery, or perform a Caesarean. This is because unduly prolonged labour not only exhausts the mother but may be dangerous to the baby.

Is there a natural way to shorten labour?

Medical interventions, such as the deliberate rupture of the amniotic sac or the administration of oxytocin, shorten labour by increasing the duration and the strength of the uterine contractions. Sometimes they also can make labour more difficult for the baby and more painful for the mother. For the shortest possible labour without harmful consequences, remain upright and active for as long as possible, don't take medications, and don't be afraid.

Painkilling drugs can slow down labour or even stop it temporarily, especially if they are administered during the early stages of labour, when the cervix is gradually opening. But there are exceptions: a local or regional anaesthetic sometimes facilitates labour if a woman is unusually frightened by the experience of childbirth. Fear and anxiety may prolong labour because they can interfere with uterine contractions. However, a painkiller is generally not the best defence against apprehension. Fear is least when the mother understands what is happening at every stage of labour, has chosen the birth method most congenial to her, and is supported by loving family or friends.

Is there a danger of "dry labour" if the sac of water breaks early?

Once the amniotic sac has broken, labour usually begins within 12 hours, but it is no more "dry" than any other labour: only a fraction of the waters escape after the rupture of the membranes, and amniotic fluid continues to be replaced right up to delivery.

Usually, labour begins without rupture of the sac. In about 60 percent of these cases, the sac breaks at the end of the first stage of labour, the period when the cervix dilates to let the baby through. In other cases, the sac remains intact until the second stage, during which the baby is moving through the birth canal, or even holds fast until delivery. An unbroken sac makes labour easier on the baby. Like a water-filled balloon, it cushions the baby against mechanical injury. It also helps to prevent compression of the umbilical cord, through which the baby gets its oxygen. An intact sac therefore helps to keep the baby's blood well oxygenated, which usually means an alert baby at birth. On the other hand, breaking the sac usually speeds up sluggish labour, which also is a benefit to the baby, and the birth attendant must decide the optimal time for doing it.

Victorian ladies took to their beds or chaises longues at the slightest provocation.

The Importance of Exercise During Pregnancy

During past centuries, when it was considered improper for well-born ladies to exercise, eat heartily, or even expose themselves to sunlight, women faced the physical demands of pregnancy in a state of general weakness and poor health. By one account, women lived in "a dark-papered room behind heavily curtained windows, drinking vinegar against the 'green sickness' and living on toast and tea to enhance a white skin." The result was a high rate of maternal and infant mortality. It is now recognized that exercise is vital to the pregnant woman's health. Good muscle tone, limber joints, and general fitness aid not only in carrying the pregnancy comfortably, but also ease labour. Abdominal muscles and those supporting the backbone and pelvic floor are under particular stress; specific exercises for these muscles can easily be learned. Swimming is an excellent general exercise. Extra weight is buoyed up by water, and the large muscle groups are involved in smooth, unstressful movement. With a doctor's approval, bicycling, tennis, and running have also been found safe during pregnancy. As pregnancy progresses, there is more weight to carry, and it is distributed differently. Pace, rhythm, and balance must be adjusted to compensate. If there is any pain, or if the woman experiences spotting or other unusual symptoms, she should stop that exercise and consult with her doctor before continuing.

An individualized exercise regime may be suggested to correct poor posture, a frequent cause of lower back pain, and other discomforts of pregnancy.

The Miracle of Birth

Is labour always painful?

For most women, yes. Contracting muscles are like cramping muscles: they hurt. There are a lot of women who begin worrying about the pain of labour as soon as they know they are pregnant, and, wisely, they frequently ask the doctor about anaesthesia on one of their early visits. These days, doctors have a wide variety of painkillers to choose from, and experienced practitioners can be relied on to use those that carry the least risk to the baby.

A small percentage of women do not find labour particularly painful. Of the rest, many discover that they can manage the pain—in some cases more easily than they endured severe menstrual cramps—by concentrating on the relaxation and breathing routines that they learned in prepared childbirth classes. Women seem to find labour least painful when their partner, or a midwife or another trained person, stays with them throughout the birth process to offer advice and support.

These days, entirely unmedicated labour has become common even in developed countries where drugs to relieve pain are easily available. (In a recent study in the Netherlands, 52 percent of all women reportedly gave birth without anaesthetics.) Part of the explanation may be that labour pain isn't steady, like the pain of a toothache or appendicitis. It builds gradually to a peak with each contraction, remains at that peak for seconds only, and then subsides. Between contractions, no pain is felt, and the mother can rest or move about to recuperate until the next wave. The hardest part is the approximately 30-minute transition between stage-one labour, in which the cervix stretches until it is fully open, and stage-two labour, in which the baby is pushed through the cervix and vagina. Unpredictable transition contractions come 1 to 5 minutes apart, last 15 to 90 seconds, and sometimes hit more than one painful peak.

Although stage two is theoretically the most painful part, women don't experience it that way. Once the baby begins to move into the birth canal, the urge to push with every ounce of strength becomes irresistible, and the pain is like a signal announcing that delivery is approaching.

Why are most babies born headfirst?

During the final three months of pregnancy, the foetus may turn many times before settling into the head-down position. Then it will so nearly fill the womb that somersaults are a thing of the past; now it can turn only from side to side. In 19 out of 20 cases, its head, the heaviest part of its body, sinks down and fits snugly in the pelvic inlet. There, pillowed upside down, most babies stay put, more or less, until it is time for delivery. The baby is in position for a headfirst (cephalic) delivery, which is easiest on both the mother and the child because the head has the largest circumference of the baby's body. Once the head has wedged open the birth canal, the rest of the baby's body can follow easily. In the last month of pregnancy, the cervix softens, and it begins to dilate, getting the birth

Stages in a Normal Birth

During the final month of pregnancy, more than 95 percent of babies move into the head-down position. From this position, an infant can assist in its own delivery, first by pressing the cervix open with its large, strong head, then by turning and twisting past the mother's pelvic bones. The duration of a normal labour nevertheless varies greatly. First-time mothers may require 16 hours to give birth, whereas later children may be born in half that time. The longest stage in labour is the first, during which the cervix is dilated and the baby's head descends past it into the vagina. Stage two, when the mother pushes the baby through the birth canal and out into the world, generally takes no more than an hour and a half for a first baby, and a half hour for later children. The third stage, delivering the placenta, lasts about 15 minutes.

In a normal position for delivery, the baby is upside down in the uterus, with the head "engaged" within the mother's pelvis.

During the first stage of labour, contractions of the uterus press the baby's head against the cervix, thinning and gradually opening it.

canal ready for the ensuing ordeal.

Of course, the pelvic inlet also holds the buttocks comfortably, and buttocks-first is the second most common birth position. Those babies who have kept their heads up now squat down for a breech delivery.

Why is a breech birth more difficult than a normal one?

You might say that babies positioned head down assist in their own delivery. The cervix is something like the tight neck of a T-shirt. The baby's skull fully stretches the opening, so that once the head is in the birth canal up to about its ears, the rest of the baby's body follows easily.

The situation is different with a breech presentation, in which the baby's buttocks or feet enter the birth canal first. Narrow buttocks do not open the cervix fully, which makes the passage of the baby's head more like struggling out of a tight shirt than easing into it.

Once through the cervix, every baby must get around the bend formed by the pubic bones, a problem akin to getting a foot into a boot. The head-first baby negotiates the curve by arching its neck forward and then turning its head to the side. Breech babies can't do that, which makes their trip longer and more hazardous. The newborn mortality rate is higher in breech presentations than in normal headfirst ones because the baby may suffocate before its head finally emerges. Sometimes a doctor can manipulate a woman's abdomen before labour begins and turn the baby around so that its head will emerge first.

Can forceps injure the baby?

Obstetrical forceps, long-handled, spoon-shaped devices to draw the baby out of the birth canal, were invented about 1630 by Peter Chamberlen, one of a family of English surgeons. The Chamberlens, whose patients included the wives of kings, made a fortune from Peter's invention, and in order to preserve their financial advantage over their competitors, they kept their design a secret for over a hundred years. In many instances, they concealed the device in a gilded box, and before entering a delivery room with it, they made sure the patient was blindfolded.

Today, there is nothing secretive about forceps. In Britain, for example, they are used to deliver one out of ten babies, some doctors using them more than others. The likelihood of injury depends on when the instrument is used. High forceps, used before the cervix has opened all the way, and mid-forceps, used just as the baby is poised to descend through the birth canal, can cause head injuries. If the baby is having that much trouble getting through the cervix, a Caesarean is usually preferred to a forceps delivery.

Low and outlet forceps help the baby through the opening of the birth canal. When the mother's muscles are too weak to let her push hard, they are used to lift the baby's head out from under the pubic arch. Neither low nor outlet forceps is likely to cause any injury more serious than bruises to the baby.

The first stage of labour is over as the baby's head dilates the cervix completely. The baby now turns its head to the side.

With neck flexed to slip around the mother's pelvic bone, the baby descends the birth canal and begins to emerge.

Once the head is free, the shoulders and the rest of the body follow easily. The final stage of labour ends with expulsion of the placenta.

After the Baby Is Born

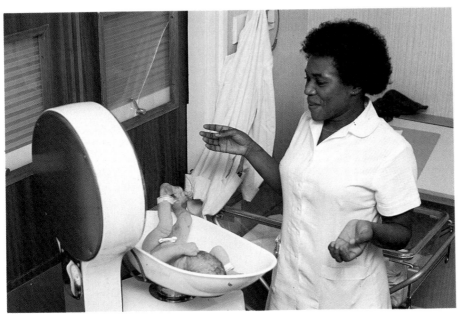

After the birth the newborn will be weighed. Normal birthweight varies with several factors, but most European babies born in the 40th week weigh 2.5–4.2 kilograms (5.5–9.25 pounds).

is impossible to know whether that cry is merely a reflex, or is an expression of distress as well. Being born may or may not be physically painful; we cannot tell. Certainly the baby is mightily squeezed during delivery. But the baby's head, at least—the part that is squeezed most of all—is also protected from both pain and damage. The sides, back, and top of the head remain numb until after birth. The five bony plates that will eventually fuse to form the skull can be pushed together, and may even overlap, as the head is propelled through the birth canal, yet both skull and brain remain undamaged.

Whatever its meaning, if any, the baby's crying during its first week or so is useful, because it helps to clear fluids from the respiratory tract. It is also very reassuring for the mother; by crying the baby tells her that it survived the birth process!

Is it easy for the newborn baby to breathe?

As soon as a baby is born, its need for air is urgent. Every newborn infant suffers from some degree of hypoxia, or oxygen deficiency. At the time of delivery, there may be no oxygen at all in the umbilical blood; at best, the blood may have 70 percent of the oxygen it contained during pregnancy. Soon after the cord is exposed to air, the umbilical circulation ceases, so the baby can no longer get any oxygen from its mother.

Complicating the problem is the fact that before birth the lungs of the foetus contain fluid. Some of it is forced out in the final moments of delivery, because after the head is born, the birth canal exerts pressure on the infant's chest. Yet at birth the lungs still contain some fluid (which is later absorbed), along with thousands of uninflated air sacs that must fill up with air.

The baby's task is not easy. Someone has figured out that the newborn's first breath requires five times more effort than any ordinary breath. To stimulate respiration, the doctor or nurse may draw blood and mucus

from the baby's nose and throat with a suction device, rub the infant's chest and slap the soles of its feet, or administer oxygen. In most cases, however, special efforts are not required. The relative asphyxia, or lack of oxygen, at birth and the cool room air stimulate the baby to inhale, and the average healthy newborn begins to breathe within seconds after it is born—even before the cord is cut, separating it from its mother.

Does a newborn cry because the experience of birth is painful?

A new baby has a lot to cry about. Violent physical upheaval has ended the security it knew for nine months and expelled it from a haven in which its every need was satisfied. In its new world, it must accomplish for itself much that the mother, and the placenta, did for it, and it must adjust to the onslaught of bright lights, loud noises, and chilly temperatures.

Most babies utter a cry just after their initial intake of air, because the air strikes the partly closed glottis (the space between the vocal cords) as the babies exhale for the first time. It

Does the baby feel anything when its umbilical cord is cut?

After a baby is born, it sometimes gets what is known as a placental transfusion: the infant is held below the level of the mother's vagina while foetal blood from the placenta (which is still inside the uterus) is allowed to drain through the umbilical cord into the baby. Only then is the cord cut, usually leaving a stump 50 to 75 millimetres (2 to 3 inches) long attached to the baby. After two or three days, the stump dries and drops off. The remaining scar is of course the navel.

There are no nerves in the umbilical cord, and therefore the baby feels no pain when the cord is cut. Nor does the cord bleed. Its blood vessels are embedded in a jelly-like substance that expands when the cord is exposed to air and, like a tourniquet, squeezes the vessels shut. A valve in the newborn's heart that has been open until this moment is forced to shut, forcing much more blood to flow to the lungs than during pregnancy. From that instant, the baby's oxygen supply depends not on the umbilical cord but on the infant's own heart and lungs.

From Swaddling Clothes to Overalls

We know from the Bible that Jesus was wrapped in swaddling clothes. So too were infants throughout the world, down through the ages. One theory was that this helped babies' limbs to grow straight. The practice has long been abandoned by all but a few cultures. Hopi Indians of the American Southwest still bind their infants to cradle boards for the first year. Studies show the babies' motor skills are not affected; they start walking at the same age as children in other cultures. Except for early infant dress, children's clothing used to be drab—miniatures of adult clothing. Nowadays, the child's comfort and mobility take precedence—and the cheerful expression of bright colours.

Diego Velazquez, the great Spanish court painter, captured the heavy formality of children's clothing in this 1660 portrait of a prince (right). The wish to impose formality on children was strong until the late 18th century, but even in the 20th century, little boys were required to be models of starchy propriety (below).

A terra-cotta medallion by Andrea della Robbia portrays a swaddled infant. The figure adorns the facade of a children's hospital in Florence founded in 1416.

Newborns are still swaddled according to the old Russian custom. The belief is that this makes babies feel more secure.

How much blood does the mother lose during childbirth?

It is natural—but wrong—to assume that labour ends when the child is born. In fact, the birth of the baby is followed by stage-three labour, in which the placenta is delivered. This event takes place anywhere from 10 to 45 minutes after the baby emerges.

The hour after the child is born is the most dangerous period of pregnancy, the time when haemorrhage, a principal cause of maternal death, may occur. By this time, the placenta has served its purpose. The contracting uterus shears it off from the uterine wall, leaving open and bleeding the pools of blood that formed so many months earlier. But each uterine vessel that feeds into the placenta in pregnancy is surrounded with a figure-eight of muscle which, like a tightening rubber band, stems the flow. On average, a mother loses 350 millilitres (12 fluid ounces) of blood during labour. The amount would have to reach 500 millilitres (18 fluid ounces) before it would be classified as a haemorrhage.

311

The Best Food for the Infant

When can a baby first suckle?

By the time a baby is born, it already knows how to suckle: it has been sucking its own thumb for weeks. Yet if put to the breast immediately after delivery, the newborn may merely lick its mother's nipple. But if the mother guides the nipple into the baby's mouth, it will soon grab it and begin to suck. The sucking accomplishes two things. By stimulating nerves at the base of the nipple, sucking triggers off the release of oxytocin from the maternal pituitary gland. Oxytocin stimulates uterine contractions that shut off bleeding vessels, thus helping to forestall any excessive bleeding from the uterus. At the same time, oxytocin acts on the mother's breasts, forcing colostrum—the early milk—out of its storage area in the breast and into the ducts that lead through the nipple, to make it available for the baby.

Can a small-breasted woman make enough milk for her baby?

The size of the breasts before pregnancy has nothing to do with the amount of milk a woman can produce. Whether breasts are large or small before pregnancy mainly depends on the amount of fat and connective tissue they contain. What counts in milk production is not fat but glandular tissue. *All* women's milk glands grow and mature during pregnancy. The amount of milk they produce depends on how much the infant stimulates the breasts by suckling: the more the baby suckles, the more milk the breasts give. Thus, supply and demand are usually in equilibrium. Ordinarily, a mother can produce 1 litre (1.75 pints) or more of milk every day, but if she has twins to feed, her output can rise to 2 to 3 litres (3.5 to 5 pints).

How much milk is enough?

A disadvantage of bottle feeding is that mothers usually urge their babies to finish all the formula milk

Breast feeding fosters emotional ties between mother and baby. To many, it is the essence of maternal care—a time of loving and giving.

prepared for them. What the mothers don't recognize is that if the baby leaves some, it may be because it doesn't want or need any more. With breast feeding, babies can decide for themselves how much they want.

Why do most newborns lose weight?

Though mothers often worry about it, the newborn's initial weight loss is normal. In the first two or three days after they are born, even healthy babies lose from 5 to 20 percent of their birth weight. Most of the loss is fluid; newborns lose body fluid about seven times more rapidly than adults do.

The drop in weight is also attributable to the fact that babies generally eat little or nothing for the first day or so. Initially, they live mainly on fats and proteins stored in their bodies, and show few signs of being really hungry until perhaps their third or fourth day—just when a good supply of mother's milk becomes available.

How does breast milk differ from cow's milk?

Breast milk contains specific antibodies that coat the newborn baby's intestines and respiratory tract and fight off infection. It has more fat and milk sugar but less protein than cow's milk, and its mineral content is lower. Yet that does not make human milk inferior: quite the contrary. If the mother is eating a balanced diet, breast milk contains all the nutrients that a baby needs in its first six months or, some authorities say, in its first year. The possible exception is iron; many doctors advise an iron and vitamin supplement for babies born prematurely.

An infant's system cannot readily absorb the fats and casein in cow's milk, and its liver is not efficient at converting all cow's milk proteins into usable forms. By contrast, a baby can digest up to 98 percent of the fat in mother's milk. And while the high level of cholesterol in human milk might be bad for adults, in infants it seems to promote the secretion of enzymes that keep cholesterol levels down for life. Cholesterol and the special fats present in human milk are needed for the development of the brain that takes place in the first year of life. The fat and the proteins in mother's milk are precisely tailored to the needs of the baby's rapidly developing nervous system, and the low salt content of human milk is also just right for the baby's immature kidneys. Breast milk provides all the calcium and phosphorus that the baby needs for its rapidly growing skeleton. And though human and cow's milk are both low in iron, breast milk is more easily absorbed in an infant's body than cow's milk.

Are nutritional advantages the only reason for breast feeding?

If you were to write down everything you and the baby gain from breast feeding, you would find it a persuasive list. The prime consideration, of course, is the nutritional excellence of breast milk: its special suitability for babies during their first 6 to 12 months. Besides, mother's milk contains antibodies and other anti-infective factors that help protect infants against gastroenteritis, respiratory-tract ailments, ear infections, eczema, and other allergies. The psychological benefits of breast feeding are important, too; the experience of giving and receiving milk from the breast promotes a special emotional closeness between mother and baby. Less significant—but still worth noting—are the practical advantages: no need to prepare formula milk or to worry about sterilizing bottles to ensure purity, and, of course, breast feeding does not cost anything.

Are there many women who can't breast feed their babies?

Physiologically, most women can breast-feed, but psychologically, a lot of women may need help and advice. To succeed at breast feeding, you must really want to feed your baby, and you must know the best ways to develop a good supply of milk. Lactation is a natural process, of course, but in some ways it is not an entirely automatic one. You can get helpful advice from a sympathetic doctor or midwife, and from such advocates of breast feeding as the National Childbirth Trust. All these sources will probably tell you that women who have their hearts set on breast feeding are rarely disappointed. In fact, if you try to breast-feed, the chances of success are higher than 95 percent.

Should breast feeding be supplemented with bottles?

The amount of milk a nursing mother has in her breasts at a particular feeding depends on how much her baby suckled at its previous meal. While the baby suckles, the mother's nipples send signals to the brain which result in a surge of prolactin, the hormone that stimulates milk secretion. When babies are given a bottle, they begin to suck less at the breast, and the mother's supply of

milk soon diminishes or dries up entirely. Even if a baby does not seem to get enough milk at the breast in the very beginning, it is best not to offer formula milk. Instead, the hungry baby should be put to the breast more often. That is the only way the mother's body can meet the baby's needs. Also, anxiety can diminish the maternal milk supply; if this occurs, the

mother should be given reassurance.

Once lactation is well established, the mother may then substitute one bottle of formula milk for one breast feeding a day without endangering her own supply. These "top-ups" give the mother a chance to go out if she wants to, to sleep longer at night, or just to take a break from the routine of regular feedings.

How long do babies usually sleep?

Babies can be trusted to regulate their own sleep. Some newborns spend 80 percent of the time sleeping, others only 16 hours a day. For the first weeks, the total hours of sleep are usually divided among seven or eight naps, often not longer than four hours. By six weeks, many babies begin to sleep up to six hours at a time; this is at night. Half of a newborn's sleep is rapid-eye-movement, or REM, sleep, usually associated with dreaming. By the age of two, the proportion of REM sleep drops to one-quarter, and by five, to one-fifth, the average for adults. The increased brain activity that goes with REM sleep may stimulate development of the infant's brain.

Babies spend an extraordinary amount of their sleep in REM, or dream, sleep.

Put down on its tummy to sleep, a baby automatically turns its head to one side and tucks its knees into a foetal position. A pillow should not be provided at this age.

A Growing Awareness

Are there tests to tell if the baby is normal?

Even as the newborn is taking its first breaths, the midwife or the doctor is observing its physiological condition and adding up its Apgar score. A perfect score of ten includes two points each for skin tone; strong, regular breathing; a heart rate of more than 100 beats a minute; active movement and well-flexed arms and legs; and a cry along with the normal reflex response, spreading the toes when the foot is tickled. Pale or bluish skin, a weak or an absent heart rate, and other signs of difficulty result in lower scores.

A doctor examines a baby a few hours after birth to check that the child is normally developed. He will usually do this at the mother's bedside so that she can observe her infant's abilities for herself. A baby may turn its eyes and head to follow the movement of a red ball, but prefer to gaze at a face. It may pay attention to a new sound, but ignore it after several repetitions; be startled or cry when disturbed, but then calm down; fuss or doze when ignored, but become alert when held or spoken to. After examining a newborn baby, the doctor can reassure the mother that all is well or, if necessary, arrange any further investigations or examinations that might be required: checking, for example, to make sure that the baby's hip joints are not dislocated.

What can parents do to prevent cot death?

When an apparently healthy infant suddenly dies in its sleep, its distraught parents often react with overwhelming guilt. What did they do wrong? they ask themselves. Why didn't they recognize that something was the matter? The facts are that there is no way of anticipating cot death, and no way of preventing it. It is never the result of something parents failed to do or did wrong.

Today, doctors refer to cot death as Sudden Infant Death Syndrome, or SIDS, and it is a leading cause of death in babies under a year old. Though much studied, SIDS remains a mystery. Many causes have been suggested; not one has been proved. Possibilities include immaturity of the part of the brain that controls breathing, or some unknown abnormality that makes a baby unable to cope with an infection that is ordinarily trivial. Parents and doctors once assumed that at least some victims died because they inhaled vomitus, or because bedclothes asphyxiated them, but such factors have now been ruled out. Doctors are also convinced that the cause does not lie with birth control pills, fluoridated drinking water, or any other new environmental factor, because cot death was known in biblical times, and it does not seem to be any more common today than it was centuries ago.

Is all crying alike?

No one needs to be told that babies cry a lot. Infants spend only about 30 minutes of every four hours in a state

The Amazing Capabilities of Newborn Babies

The ability to imitate facial expressions has long been regarded as a landmark in an infant's early development. For many years, it was believed that this behaviour did not become established until the baby was from 8 to 12 months old. However, recent studies have produced surprising new evidence that the imitative ability is present very early in life, that, in fact, it is innate and not learned. In one set of experiments, newborns 12 to 21 days old were clearly able to imitate a variety of facial expressions. Facial expressions are unlike hand movements or other gestures because the baby can see gestures and compare them with another person's, but the baby has no way of knowing that its facial expression matches that on another face.

In repeated tests, infants consistently imitated three specific expressions: sticking the tongue out, opening the mouth, and puckering the lips.

The delicate head and neck of the new baby is protected in a frontal pouch (left) while the mother shops. At a later stage, the baby's increased weight is more easily carried on the back—and the baby gets to see what's ahead.

of quiet alertness. During the rest of their waking time, they eat, squirm, kick, or cry. To the average person, one cry sounds like another. But parents notice distinct differences depending on what is bothering the infant. One experimenter has differentiated three crying patterns. The cry of pain begins with a shriek and is interrupted periodically while the baby gets its breath. The angry cry is unmistakably that. The basic cry, generally signalling hunger, gets louder and more rhythmic as it continues. In malnourished infants, the basic cry is often noticeably high-pitched; in brain-damaged ones, it is likely to be less rhythmic.

Are babies genetically programmed to smile?

Babies everywhere begin to smile in response to a face, or some other stimulus, at about the same age. The first real smiles can appear as early as a few days after birth or as late as 7½ weeks, but the average is 5 weeks. A factor that influences the time a baby starts to smile seems to be the baby's age from conception rather than age from birth. Premature babies generally smile later, and late babies earlier than full term babies. This suggests that an infant's smiling may be determined by the genes. Nevertheless, environmental influences have a lot to do with how often babies smile, and studies have shown that they soon stop smiling if they are brought up in institutions where no one plays with them.

What makes babies smile?

When a baby smiles for the first time, parents begin to feel that their sleepless nights are worthwhile. Yet the conclusion to be drawn from the hundreds of published research papers on infant smiling is that a baby's earliest smiles don't necessarily mean what his parents imagine they mean.

Developmental psychologists have observed three kinds of smiling in infants. Reflexive smiling occurs in newborns, usually when they are asleep, or nearly so. The reflexive smile lacks the crinkling around the eyes that marks a true smile and is really a fleeting grimace in response to no particular stimulus. Contrary to popular opinion, the earliest smiles have nothing to do with the gas that forms after feeding.

Non-selective social smiling begins from two to eight weeks after birth. The smile is now a full-scale, crinkly-eyed one that comes when the infant is wide awake. At this point, the baby smiles indiscriminately: at parents and family, at strangers, and, amazingly, even at a piece of cardboard with two dark circles suggesting eyes. Finally, at the age of five or six months, babies reach the stage of selective social smiling: most of their smiles are now reserved for their familiar caretakers.

Some psychologists argue that a baby's smiling is often not a social response at all but an expression of the infant's delight in learning that his own behaviour can make something happen—for instance, he may smile when he discovers that every time he flings up his arms, someone gives him a playful poke in the ribs.

315

Milestones of Development

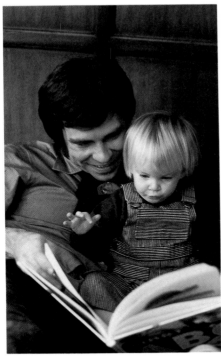

A father's participation in the care of children is beneficial to the whole family. The intimacy of moments such as these—storytime with a toddler—pays dividends later on.

What do babies know, and when do they know it?

The word *infant* comes from the Latin for "incapable of speech." Until about a generation ago, most people assumed that babies lacked not only the ability to talk but the capacity to do much of anything except eat and sleep. Now scientists know better; one of their favourite expressions these days is "infant competency," which turns out to be impressive indeed.

Most newborns turn their heads at the sound of a rattle, and infants only three days old can tell the difference between their mother's voice and that of a stranger. Babies a day old look longer at patterned surfaces than at plain ones, and when they're a few days old, they follow moving lights with their eyes. When shown pictures of a human face and a blank square, a newborn only one minute old may turn 180 degrees so that he can keep the face in view.

When a sweet liquid is dropped on a newborn's tongue, he licks and sucks with obvious pleasure, while a sour liquid makes him purse his lips and wrinkle his nose. The newborn turns away from the smell of ammonia or vinegar, but he clearly enjoys the smell of vanilla, chocolate, bananas, and mother's milk. If two pads, one soaked with a stranger's milk and one with his mother's, are placed on either side of a two-day-old's head, he shows no preference for one or the other. But by the time he is ten days old, he quickly turns to his mother's milk, demonstrating a sense of smell that is keen enough to detect a very subtle difference.

What determines growth?

Many parents know about the adolescent growth spurt from watching their own offspring, so they may be surprised to learn that children grow fastest not during adolescence but in infancy. Ordinarily, children reach half their adult height by the age of 2 years. There is not much correlation between a baby's size at birth or the rate of growth in childhood and actual height in adulthood. A child who shoots up rapidly may stop growing early and end up short; a youngster who grows more slowly but for a longer period of time may be taller than average as an adult. Among the conditions influencing growth, heredity and nutrition are the most important determinants of a person's ultimate height.

How does a child grow?

Over the years, body proportions change radically. At birth, the head makes up about one-quarter of the body's length, but in adulthood, it contributes only about one-eighth to the average person's height. When a baby is born, its head is disproportionately large compared with an adult body, and its legs are disproportionately short. Between birth and adulthood, a person's head just about doubles in size. By contrast, the trunk triples in length, the arms qua-druple, and the legs grow to about five times their original length.

The body grows, in both size and complexity, from the head downwards. The sequence—head, trunk, arms, legs—governs not only physical development but also the baby's control over his body. That is why babies can hold their heads up before they can sit, and it is the reason that in crawling, they at first propel themselves with their upper bodies and only later get assistance from their legs. The head-to-toe sequence also accounts for the fact that even before they can walk, babies may be able to control their hands and fingers so well that they can pick up a barely visible bit of lint.

When do most babies learn to walk?

A baby's first staggering steps mark some of the most exciting moments in the lives of young parents. But several notable milestones precede walking. You can find a timetable listing all of them in just about any book on young children. But if you consult several books, you may find minor discrepancies, since different experts tend to base their expectations for development mainly on the particular group of babies they happen to have studied.

One frequently cited study gives the age of the first milestone, raising the head while the infant lies on its stomach, as one month. At four months, babies can often sit up, provided someone supports them, and at seven months, they can frequently sit alone. They are likely to be capable of standing, with assistance, at eight months, of creeping at ten months, walking when led at 11 months, pulling themselves up to a standing position by holding on to a piece of furniture when they are a year old, and climbing stairs on their hands and knees at 13 months. Babies can usually stand alone, if a bit precariously, at about 14 months. Walking alone, though the gait is sure to be unsteady, commonly happens at the age of 15 months.

Is it a bad sign if your baby walks later than the average child?

Averages refer to groups of people, not to individuals. Suppose that you read that the average child walks at 15 months. That figure was derived by adding up the ages at which a number of children walked and dividing the total by the number of children in the group. It is possible that not one child actually walked at 15 months. Some may have done so at 10, 11, 12, 13, or 14 months, others at 16, 17, or 18 months. In short, for each developmental milestone, there is a wide range of normal ages.

You should also know that for all children the sequence of developmental stages is usually the same, but not invariably so. Stages may be skipped, or reversed: some children never crawl at all, while others walk before they crawl. And then, there is no correlation between physical development early in life and intelligence later on. It may be reassuring to know that Einstein was slow in learning to talk—so slow that his parents were afraid he was retarded.

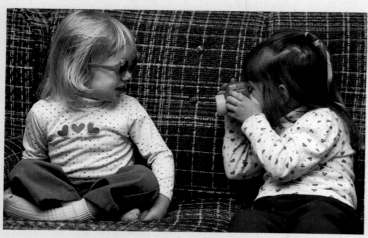

Around three, children love make-believe. A toy camera in the hands of one little girl is all that's needed to bring out the film star in her friend.

Taking Giant Steps

The journey each child takes from helpless infancy to self-expression is truly amazing. In the often hectic daily life of a family, it is easy to lose sight of just how much a child achieves every month, every week, every day. The random babbling of babies turns into words, then commands, then opinions! From baby steps to lessons in dance or gymnastics. The gradations of accomplishment blur from one stage to the next. To the young, childhood may seem eternal, but for those who shepherd the young towards maturity, the time is fleeting. It's worthwhile to stop and share your children's laughter and tears along the way—before they vanish into solemn adulthood.

At four to five, the child puts almost explosive energy into exercising.

By seven to eight years of age, many children are good readers. Though often preoccupied with school, playing with friends, or watching TV, children who enjoy reading frequently find it to be a refuge from stress.

INDEX

A

Abrasions, 28, 141, **141**
Absinthe (painting by Degas), 245, **245**
Acceptable weight, 252
Acetylcholine, in nerve transmission, 163
Achilles, 37
Achilles heel, tendon, **162,** 180
Acinar cells, 247
Acne, 134, 144, **144,** 148
    androgens and, 81
Acoustic neuromas, 217
Acquired immune deficiency syndrome
    (AIDS), 44, 101, 278, **278,** 279, 281
ACTH, 84, 85
Actin filaments, 163
Acupuncture, 70, **70**
Adam and Eve (Titian), 227, **227**
Adam's apple (thyroid cartilage), **225,** 227,
    227
Adenoids, 223
Adenosine triphosphate. *See* ATP.
ADH. *See* Antidiuretic hormone.
Adolescence
    acne and, 134, 144, **144**
    emotions of, 82
    rapid growth during, 80
    voice change during, 81, 229
Adrenal cortex, 84, 85
Adrenal glands, 77, **77,** 81, 84
    function of, 84
Adrenaline, 78, 84, 89, 289
    medical uses of, 85
Adrenal medulla, 84, 85
Adrenocorticotrophic hormone.
        See ACTH.
Adrian, Edgar, 57
Aerobic exercise, 164, 186
Afterimages, 200, **200,** 201, **201**
Aggression, 54–55, 66
Aging, genes and, 21
AIDS. *See* Acquired immune deficiency
        syndrome.
Air pollution, 31, **31,** 126–127
Airsickness. *See* Motion sickness.
Albinos, 131, 136
    eye colour in, 188
Alcohol
    brain and, 68
    choking and, 225
    cirrhosis and, 245
    and damage to bones, 159
    impotence and, 270
    pregnancy and, 294
Allergen, 122, **122,** 222, 223
Allergic rhinitis, 122, **122,** 222–223
Allergies, 123, **123,** 140, 141
    hay fever (allergic rhinitis), 122, **122,**
        222–223
    inherited, tendency to, 122
    and the sinuses, 222–223

Alopecia. *See* Baldness.
Altitude sickness, 126, **126**
Alveolar duct, **115**
Alveoli, 114, 115, **115,** 124, **124**
Alzheimer's disease, 72
Amblyopia (lazy eye), 197
American Indian pipe, 128, **128**
Amino acids, 234, 253
Amnesia, 63
Amniocentesis, 304, 305, **305**
Amniotic sac, 292, **292,** 293, 307
Ampulla of Vater, 244
Amygdala, 53, **53**
Anaemia, 108, 157, 249. *See also specific
        types of anaemia.*
Anaesthesia, 70–71
Andersen-Schiess, Gabriella, 185, **185**
Androgens, 277
    acne and, 81
    hair and, 152
    in men, 80–81
    origin of word, 264
    in women, 80–81
    See also Hormones.
Androgynous, origin of word, 264
Aneurysm, 102
Angel dust (PCP), 66
Anger, 66
Angina pectoris, transdermal patch and,
        139, **139**
Angiogram (coronary arteriograph), 103
Angiotensin, 260, 263
Ankh-per-hor, 45, **45**
Ankle, 180
    joint of, 165, **165**
Anorexia nervosa, 256–257, **257**
Antacids, effect on kidneys of, 259
Anthrax, 30, **30**
Antibiotics
    development of, 28
    drug-resistant bacteria and, 36
Antibodies, 29, 100
Antidiuretic hormone (ADH), effect on
        kidneys of, 260
Antigens, 29, 96, 100
Antihistamines, 122, 223
Antimetabolites, 33
Antisepsis, 134
Antitoxins, 28, 100
Antrum, 240, **240**
Anvil (incus), **208,** 209
Anxiety
    depression and, 66
    hypochondria and, 24
    lump in the throat (globus hystericus)
        and, 225
    motion sickness and, 207
Aorta, 91, **91,** 92, **115**
Aortic semilunar valve, **91**
Apache Indian menses ceremony,
        275, **275**
Apgar test for newborns, 314
Aphrodisiacs, 271, **271**

Aplastic anaemia, 108
Apoplexy. *See* Stroke.
Appendicitis, 31, 249
    folklore of, 255
Appendicular skeleton, 161, **161**
Appendix, 249, **249**
Appetite, loss of, 256–257
Aqueous humour, 190, 191, **191,** 204
Areola, 276, **276**
Aristotle, 82
Arm, 174
    in backhand tennis stroke, 174–175,
        174–175
    role in balance, 159
Armpits, bacteria and, 134
Arrector pili, 150, **150**
Arteries, 105, **105, 110,** 133
    coronary, 90, 104, 105
    difference between veins and, 92
    origin of word, 99
    pulmonary, 91, **91**
    renal, 93
Arterioles, 93, **93**
Arteriosclerosis. *See* Atherosclerosis.
Arthritis, 30, 31, 45
    gout as form of, 263
    joint replacement in, 183, **183**
    osteoarthritis, 182–183
    rheumatoid, 182–183
Arthrogram, 178
Arthroscopy, 178
Artificial insemination, 285
Artificial kidney, 260–261
Artificial limb, 45
Artificial respiration
    mechanical, 125
    mouth-to-mouth, 125
Artificial skin, 143, **143**
Asbestos, 31, **31,** 127
Ascending colon, **235, 248,** 250
Asphyxia, 124, 310
Asphyxiation, 124
Aspiration, 277
Aspirin
    effect on kidneys of, 259
    uses and dangers of, 40
Asthma, 122–123
Astigmatism, 194, **194,** 195
Astrology, 26, **26**
Astronauts, 207, **207**
Atheroma, 104, 105
Atherosclerosis (hardening of the arteries),
        31, 104, 105, **105**
    in antiquity, 45
    gangrene and, 107
    stroke and, 106–107
Athlete's foot, 31, 134, 144–145
ATP, 27
Atrium, 90, 91, **91**
Attention, 60, 73
Audiometers, 212
Auditory nerve, 209, 212
Auditory noise, 214
Auscultation, 116
Autism, 55

Page numbers in **boldfaced** *type refer to the illustrations.*

Autoimmune disease, 30
Autoimmunity, 101
Autonomic nervous system, 48
Awareness, 60–61
Axial skeleton, 161, **161**
Axon, 50, **50**, 51, **51**
Axon terminal, 50, **50**, 51, **51**

B

Babies
    babbling of, 300
    behaviour of, 300
    carriers for, 315, **315**
    colour preferences of, 201
    crying of, 229, **229**, 314–315
    cuddling of, 289, **289**
    depth perception of, 61, **61**
    hearing and, 231
    importance of touching, 138, 289, **289**
    "infant competency," 316
    sleep and, 313, **313**
    smiling in, 315
    walking and, 316, 317
    weight and health of, 312
    See also Newborns.
Baby teeth, 170, **170**
Backaches, 172–173, **173**
Backhand stroke in tennis, 174–175,
    174–175
Bacteria, 30, **30**
    diseases caused by, 28
    first person to see, 28, **28**
    function in digestion, 249, 251
    as producers of hormones, 43
    on skin, 134, 135, **135**, 144
    and viruses compared, 29
Bad breath (halitosis), 233
Balance, 187, **187**
    ear and, 207, 209, 216, **216**
Baldness (alopecia), 152, **152**
Ball-and-socket joints, 165, **165**, 174
Bar at the Folies Bergère (painting by
    Manet), 280, **280**
Barber of Seville, 171
Barbiturates, 32
Barotrauma, 217
Bartholin's gland, 273
Basal cell carcinoma, 145
Basal layer of skin, **133**
Basal metabolic rate, 86, 256
Bat, 30, **30**
BEAM (brain electrical activity mapping),
    57
Beard, 151, **151**
Beaumont, Dr. William, 241, **241**
Bed rest, effect of, 182
Bed-wetting, 264
Bee, 140, **140**
Beethoven, Ludwig van, 212,
    212

Belching, 240
Belladonna, 191
Bending, 165
Bends, 127
Bennett, Henry, 71
Benson, Dr. Herbert, 36
Berger, Hans, 57
Beriberi, 253
Berylliosis, 127
Biceps, 174
Bicuspid (mitral) valve, **91**
Bicuspids, 170, **170**
Bifocals, 193, 195
Bile, 244, **244**, 245, 247
Bile duct, common, **244**
Bilirubin, 245, 246
Binaural hearing, 211, **211**
Binet, Alfred, 64
Binge-purge cycle, 257
Binocular vision, 196
Biological clocks, 75
Birth
    forceps and, 309
    at home, 302, **302**
    midwives and, 302
    natural, 302
    positions, 304, **304**
    record holders, 270
    stages of, 308–309, **308–309**
    See also Pregnancy.
Birth-control pills, 106, 287
Birth defects, plastic surgery and, 147
Birthing chair, 303, **303**
Birthing methods, 302, **302**
Birthmark, 136
Black Death, 221. See also Bubonic plague.
Blackhead, 144, **144**
Black-lung disease, 127
Bladder, 261, **261**, 262, **262**, 266, **272**
    control, 259
Blastocyst, 292, **292**
Blindness, 195, **195**, 202–203, 205
    colour, 202
    glaucoma as cause of, 32, 204
    night, 202
    sensitivity to sound and, 211
Blind spot, testing for, 189, **189**, 191
Blinking, 192
Blood, 89, 90, 91, 92–97, **92**, 106, 108, 110
    altitude and, 95
    arterial, 94
    bleeding, 98-99, **98**
    cancer of, 32
    kidneys' role in cleansing, 93, **93**, 260
    oxygenation of, 113, **113**, 114
    pumped in lifetime, 163
    Rh factor in, 96–97
    in spleen, 110, **110**
    strokes and, 106
    venous, 94
Blood-brain barrier, 48
Blood brothers, origin of phrase, 99
Blood cells. See Red blood cells; White blood
    cells.
Blood clots, 95, 98–99, **98**

Blood clots (contd.)
    atherosclerosis and, 104, 105, **105**
    stroke and, 106–107
Blood counts, 97
Blood groups. See Blood types.
Blood: "In cold blood," origin of phrase, 99
Blood letting, 104, **104**
Blood lipids, 102, **105**
Blood pressure, 20, 84, 90
    hypertension (high blood pressure),
        102–103, 106
    hypotension (low blood pressure),
        102–103
    normal, 102
Bloodshot eye, 189, 190
Blood transfusions, 96–97, **97**,
Blood types, 90, 96–97
Blood vessels, 84, 88, 90, 92, **92**, 93, 96,
    96, 98, 104, 132, **133**, 136
    and blushing, 131
    diseases of, 104
    See also Arteries; Capillaries; Veins.
Blue blood, origin of phrase, 99
Blushing, 131
Body
    components of, 22
    flexibility of, 164
    of the future, 44–45
    internal environment of, 27
    symmetry of, 22, **22**
    systems of, 22–23, **23**
Body builders, 159, **159**
Body paint, 149, **149**
Body stalk, 292, **292**
Boils, 144
Bol, Manute, 79, **79**
Bone, 96, **96**
    age of, 158, 159
    artificial, 183
    babies', 159
    calcium loss from, 182
    calculating height from, 178
    cross-section, 96, **96**, 161, **161**
    fractures of, 184, **184**
    healing of, 184
    injuries to, 161, 177
    lack of exercise and, 182
    major, 161, **161**
    marrow, 160
    pain in, 160
    scintigram of, 80, **80**
    strength of, 160
    structure of, 160
Bone marrow, 96, **96**, 160
Bones, specific
    carpal, **161**, 176, **176**, 177
    finger, **161**, 176, **176**,
    foot, **161**, 181, **181**
    metacarpal, **161**, 176, **176**
    spinal, 172
    thigh, 158, 178
Bones and muscles, 158–186
Borborygmi (stomach rumbling), 233
Bororo tribe, 283, **283**
Botulism, 29, 255

Bound feet, 179, **179**
Bowel, 235, **235**, **248**, 250, **250**
Bowman's capsule, 260, **261**
Braces, teeth, 171
Brain, 46–73, **49**, **53**
  appearance of, 48
  Broca's area of, 52
  cells of, 48, **48**, 50, **50**
  cerebellum, 48, 49, **49**, **53**, 68
  cerebral cortex, 49, **49**, 66
  cerebrum, 48, 49, **49**, **53**
  and communication with the body, 78
  disorders of, 72–73
  fissures, 49, **49**
  functions of, 46, 49
  hearing and, 208, 209, 211
  lobes, 49, **49**
  motor cortex, 49, **49**
  painkillers and tranquilizers produced by, 20
  role of, in hunger and thirst, 232
  role of, in sense of taste, 236
  sex differences in, 54
  skull as protection for, 166–167
  somatosensory cortex, 49, **49**
  sports injuries to, 167
  stroke and, 106
  structure of, 49, **49**
  vision and, 196, 197, 198–199
  Wernicke's area, 52
Brain death, 57
Brain electrical activity mapping (BEAM), 57
Brain scans, 52, 56–57, **56–57**
Brain specialization, 52, 53, **53**, 55, 73
Brain stem, 48, 49, **49**, **53**, 57
Brain surgery, ancient, 160, **160**
Brain tumour, 72
Brain waves, 57
  during sleep, 58, **58**
Braxton-Hicks contractions, 305
Breast feeding, 277, 312–313, **312–313**
  as method of contraception, 282
Breast milk, 312
Breast reconstruction, 147
Breasts
  cancer of, 33
  erectile tissue of, 276
  examination of, 276, **276**
  lumps in, 276–277
  size of, 277
  structure of, 276, **276**
  tumours in, 276
Breath, out of, 112
Breathing, 112, 113, 114, 116, **116**, 117, 118, 120, 125, 224–225
  artificial respiration, 125
  difficulty in, 126–127
  effect of weather on, 126
  at high altitudes, 120, 126, **126**
  hyperventilation, 124
  maximal breathing capacity, 116, **116**, 117
  rate of, 114

Breathing (*contd.*)
  through nose or mouth, 219
  See also Respiration.
Breech birth, 309
Bridge (dental), 171
Broca's area, 49, **49**
Bronchiole, 114, **115**
Bronchitis, 122
Bronchoscope, 116
Bronchus, 114, **115**
Brough, Peter, 230, **230**
Brown, John, 63
Brown, Louise and Natalie, 285, **285**
Brown lung, 127
Bruise, 88
Bubonic plague, 31, 34, 221
Bulbourethral glands, 266, **266**, 268
Bulimia, 257
Bunion, 181
Burns, 143, **143**
Bursae, 178

C

Caecum, **235**, **248**, 250
Caesarean section, 289, 303, 305
  origin of phrase, 293
Caffeine, 255
  as diuretic, 258
Calcaneus. *See* Heel bone.
Calcium, 77, 130
  amount stored in bones, 159, 160
  kidney stones and, 264
  loss from bones, 182
Calf muscle, 162, **162**, 180
Calisthenics, 186, **186**
Callus, 141, 229
Callus, bone, 184
Calories, 252
Cancer, 32–33, 128–129
  asbestos and, 31, **31**
  breast, 147
  causes of, 32, 33
  cell membrane and, 26
  cervical, 274
  heredity and, 32
  Hodgkin's disease, 111
  lung, 113, 123, 128–129
  lymphomas, 110–111
  metastatic, 33
  origin of word, 36
  possible vaccination against, 45
  skin, 136, 145
  treatment of, 33
  types of, 32
  viruses and, 29
Candida albicans, 36
Canines, 170, **170**
Capillaries, 88, 92, **92**, 93, 94, 98, **98**, **111**
  in lungs, 114, 115, **115**

Capillaries (*contd.*)
  lymphatic, 110, **111**
Capsulitis, adhesive, 174
Carbohydrates, 252–253
Carbon dioxide, 112, 115, 124
Carbon monoxide, 126, 128
Carbuncle, 144
Carcinogens, 32
  tobacco tar, 128
Carcinoma, 32. *See also* Cancer.
Cardiac muscle, 163, **163**
Cardiac sphincter, 240, **240**, 241
Cardiovascular disease, 104–105, 107
  test for, 103, **103**
Cardiovascular system, the Pill and, 287
Carpal bones, **161**, 176, **176**
Carriers of genetic disorders, 40, 43
Cartilage, 158
  cross-section of, 161, **161**
  discs in back, 173, **173**
Castiglione, Arturo, 45
Castrati, 81
Cataracts, 204, 205, **205**
Cathartics, 251
Cats, allergy to, 123, **123**
CAT scans, 45, **45**, 56, **56**
  in study of mummies, 45, **45**
Cauliflower ear, 219
Cavities in teeth, 238
Cell
  compared to a city, 27, **27**
  energy of, 27
  life span of, 26
  parts of, 26, 27, 38, **38**
  as smallest living body components, 22, 26
  viruses and, 29
Cell dedifferentiation, 32
Cell differentiation, 26, 42
Cell division, 38, 40
Cell membrane, 26
Cell nucleus, 26, 27, **27**, 38, **38**
Cells of Leydig, 266
Cementum, 170, **170**
  fluoride protection and, 239
Central nervous system, 48
  caffeine and, 255
Centre of gravity, 187
Cerebellum, 48, 49, **49**, **53**, 68
  role in walking, 159
Cerebral cortex, 49, **49**, 66
Cerebrospinal fluid, 167
Cerebrum, 48, 49, **49**, **53**
Cervical cancer, 274
Cervical smear test, 274
Cervix, **272**, 291, **291**, 309–310, **309–310**
  incompetent, 293
Chancroid, 278
Chang Chung Chin (China's Hippocrates), 251
Chaplin, Charlie, 55
Chapped skin, 139, 142
Charlatan, origin of word, 36
Charles, Prince, 283, **283**

*Page numbers in **boldfaced** type refer to the illustrations.*

Chemical skin peel (chemosurgery), 148
Chemotherapy, 32, 33
Chest
  cavity, 114–116, **115**
  examination of, 116
  X-ray of, 116–117
Chewing, 234, 240
Chickenpox, 29, 279
Childbirth. *See* Birth; Pregnancy.
Childbirth fever, 134
Childhood diseases, 29
Children
  clothing of, 311
  development of, 317, **317**
  food preferences of, 253
  growth of, 316
  swaddling of, 311, **311**
  toilet training of, 259
Children and parents, resemblance of, 38, 39
"Chip off the old block," origin of phrase, 36
Chlamydia, 278–279, **278**, 280
Chlorine, hair and, 155
Choking, 124–125, 224
  pill in throat, 234
  prevention, 225
Cholera, 35
Cholesterol, 21
  breast feeding and, 312
  heart disease and, 104–105, **105**
Choroid, 191, **191**, 205
Chromosomes, 27, **27**, 38, **38**, 39, 40, 268, 290
  Down's syndrome and, 289
  sex and, 291
Chyme, 241, 250
Cilia, 120, 218, **218**, 220, **220**
Ciliary muscle, 191, **191**
Circadian rhythms, 75
Circulation, smoking and, 128
Circulatory system, 23, **23**, 88–111
  disorders of, 106–107
  kidney and, 93, **93**
  See also Blood.
Circumcision, 267, **267**
Cirrhosis, 157, 245
Civil War, American, 37
Clare, Rose, 79, **79**
Cleavage, 291
Clemens, Alonzo, 47, **47**
Clitoris, **272**, 273
Cloning, 44
Clothing, children's, 311, **311**
Club foot, 180
Club hair, **150**
Cluttering, speech, 230
Cocaine, 32
Coccyx, 172, **173**
Cochlea, 208, **208**, 209, **209**, 216, **216**
Codeine, 118
Coitus interruptus, 286
Colchichine, 263
Cold, common, 119–120, **119**, 206
  immunity to, 120
  in infancy, 120

Cold, common (*contd.*)
  sense of taste and, 221
  sore throat and, 227
  viruses and, 120
  vitamin C and, 113
  wet feet and, 119
Cold-blooded, 89
Cold cream, 132
Collagen, 98, **98**, 133, **133**, 146, 148
Collarbone, **161**
Colles' fracture, 177
Colon, 235, **235**, **248**, 250, **250**
Colostrum, 312
Colour
  effect on mood of, 200
  how eyes see, 200
  of eyes, 39, 188
Colour blindness, 41, 202, **202**
Computer and brain compared, 47
Conception, 290
  determination of sex, 290, 291
  in vitro, 285, **285**
Concussion, 167
Conditioning, 60, **60**
Condom, 286
Cones, 190, 191, **191**, 200, 202, 203
Congestion, nasal, 119–120
Conjunctiva, 190, 191, **191**, 192
Conjunctivitis, 189, 279
Connective tissue, 22
Constipation, 251, 254
Contact dermatitis, 140, 157
Contact lenses, 193, **193**, 195, 202, 204
  for colour blindness, 202
Contraception
  barrier methods of, 286–287
  coitus interruptus, 286
  condom, 286
  diaphragm, 286
  douching, 286
  intrauterine devices, 287, **287**
  Pill, 287
  rhythm method, 286
  spermicidal agents, 286–287
  sterilization, 271, 286
  tubal ligation, 286, 287
  vaginal sponge, 287
  vasectomy, 270–271, 286
Contraceptive pills. *See* Birth-control pills.
Cook, Captain James, 34
Cooley's anaemia, 108
Corn, 141
Cornea, 190, 191, **191**, 192, 205
Corneal grafting, 205
Corneal layer of skin, 133, **133**, 156, **156**
Coronary arteriograph (angiogram), 103
Coronary artery disease. *See* Atherosclorosis.
Coronary embolism, 104
Coronary thrombosis, 104, 105
Corpus callosum, **53**
Corpus cavernosum, **266**
Corset, 117, **117**
Cortex. *See* Adrenal cortex.
Cortex, hair, **150**
Cortex, kidney, 93, **93**, 261, **261**

Corticotrophin-releasing hormone (CRH), 85
Cortisol. *See* Hydrocortisone.
Cosmetic surgery. *See* Plastic surgery.
Cot death. *See* Sudden Infant Death Syndrome.
Cough, 118, 122
  smoker's, 128
Cough medicines, 118
Couvade, 300
Cowper's glands. *See* Bulbourethral glands.
Cranium, 166–167
Craving, 295, **295**
Cricket. "Keeping your eye on the ball," 197, **197**
Cross-eyes (strabismus), 189, 190, 197
Crown of tooth, 170, **170**
Crying, 192
  babies', 229, **229**, 314–315
Cryosurgery, 33
Cuddling, 289, **289**
Cuticle, 150, 156, **156**
Cuts, 98, **98**
Cyclosporine, 45, 261
Cystic breast disease, 277
Cystic duct, **244**
Cystitis, 264
Cytomegalovirus, 279
Cytoplasm, 26, 27, **27**

D

D and C. *See* Dilatation and curettage.
Dandruff, 151
"Dangerous triangle," 107, **107**
Daumier, Honoré, 169, **169**, 295, **295**
Daydreams, 72
Day (night) vision, 203, **203**
Dead Sea, 243, **243**
Dead tooth, 239
Deaf-mutes, 230–231
Deafness, 212–213
  and blindness compared, 213
Death. *See* Brain death.
Decibels, 210, **210**, 211
Decongestants, 226
Degas, Edgar, *Absinthe*, 245, **245**
Degenerative disease, 30
Dehydration
  caused by alcohol, 259
  in cold weather, 270
  diarrhoea as cause of, 251
  fluids to prevent, 258
Déjà vu experiences, 63
Della Robbia, Andrea, 311, **311**
Deltoid, 162, **162**, 174
Dendrites, 50, **50**
Dental caries. *See* Tooth decay.
Dentine, 170, **170**, 238
Dentistry, 171, **171**
Dentures, 171
Deoxyribonucleic acid. *See* DNA.

Depression, 66, 73
Depth perception, 197
  in babies, 61, **61**
Dermabrasion, 148
Dermis, 132, 133, **133**, 136, **138**, 143, **143**,
  146, 148
Descartes, René, 76
Descending colon, **235**, **248**
Desensitization. *See* Immunotherapy.
Detached retina, 204–205, **205**
Deviated septum, 219
Devil's pinches, origin of phrase, 99
Diabetes
  blindness and, 203
  urinalysis as test for, 265, **265**
Diabetes mellitus, 30, 87, **87**, 247
  sugar consumption and, 75
Dialysis. *See* Haemodialysis.
Diaphragm, 114, 115, **115**, 116, **116**, **125**,
  225, 286
  hiatus in, 241
Diarrhoea, causes of, 251
  travellers', 35
Diastolic pressure, 102
Did You Know. . .?
  of the bones and muscles, 164
  of the brain and nervous system, 72
  of the digestive system, 234
  of the ear, nose, and throat, 219
  of the endocrine system, 85
  of the eye, 190
  of the heart and circulatory system, 90
  of the human body (Chapter 1), 40
  of pregnancy, birth, and growth, 300
  of the respiratory system, 120
  of the skin, 132
  of the urinary and reproductive systems,
    270
Diet, role of iodine in, 86, **86**. *See also*
  Nutrition.
Dieting, 256
  hair loss and, 152
Digestion, 84, 232–251, **235**, **240**, **244**,
  248, **250**
  observation of, 241, **241**
  time required for, 235, 249
Digestive enzymes, 248
Digestive system, 23, **23**, 232–257
Digitalis, 36, 107, **107**
Dilatation and curettage (D and C),
  274
Dionne quintuplets, 300, 301, **301**
Discoloration of teeth, 171
Discs, 172, 173, **173**. *See also* Cartilage.
  Merkel's, **138**
Diseases, 28–29
  acute and chronic compared, 31
  of antiquity, 44–45
  body's defence against, 100
  of childhood, 29
  contagious and infectious compared, 31
  early theories on transmission of, 221
  geography of, 34–35
  lethal viruses and, 44, **44**

Diseases (*contd.*)
  psychosomatic, 25
  tropical, 34
  types of, 30
Dislocation, 184
  of shoulder, 174–175
Diving, deep-sea, 127, **127**
Dizziness and the ear, 216–217
DNA (deoxyribonucleic acid), 22, 33, 38,
  38
Doctor, origin of word, 36
Dou, Gerard, *The Dropsical Woman*, 265,
  265
Double-jointedness, 165
Double vision, 196, 197, 203
Down's syndrome, 30, 40, 289, 305
Dreaming, 58, 59
"Drinker's" nose, 219
Drinking, alcohol
  damage to bones and, 159
  liver and, 245
Dropsical Woman, The (painting by Dou),
  265, **265**
Drugs
  abuse of, 32, **32**
  administration through nose, 219
  fertility, 284
  impotence and, 270
  prescriptions for, 36
  timing of treatment, 75
  transdermal patch for
    administering, 139, **139**
Dry labour, 307
Duc de Berry, 26
Duodenum, **235**, 240, **240**, 241, 242, **244**,
  248
Dust mite, 122, **122**
Dwarfism, 78, 79, **79**, 85
Dyslexia, 55

Ear, 206–217
  folklore about, 214
  as means of identification, 214
  popping of, 217
  ringing in (tinnitus), 214
  structure of, 208, **208**, 209, **209**, 216, **216**
  surgery on, 217
  wax in, 212
Earache, 214
Eardrum (tympanic membrane), 208, **208**,
  209
  damage to, 217
Ear: "Keeping your ear to the ground," origin
  of phrase, 224
Early Theories
  "Bleeding as a Remedy," 104, **104**
  "Ill Winds and Killing Exhalations," 221,
    221

Early Theories (*contd.*)
  "The Influence of Stars and 'Humours',"
    26, **26**
  "The Mystery of Human Reproduction,"
    284, **284**
  "Reading the Skull," 52, **52**
  "The Pineal Gland and the Human Soul,"
    76, **76**
  "The Uses of Skull Surgery in Antiquity,"
    160, **160**
Eat: "Eat, drink, and be merry," origin of
  phrase, 242
Eating, 233, 234, 236
  without weight gain, 86–87
ECG. *See* Electrocardiogram.
Echocardiogram, 103
Eclampsia, 303
Ectoderm, 292, **292**
Ectopic pregnancy, 285, 287
EEG. *See* Electroencephalograph.
Egyptian cosmetics, 149, **149**
Einstein, Albert, 60, 65, **65**
Ejaculation, 267
  number of sperm in, 268, 284
  premature, 270
Ejaculatory duct, **266**
Elastic fibres, **133**
Elastin, 133
Elbow, 164, 165, **165**
Elbow: "Using elbow grease," origin of
  phrase, 178
Electrocardiogram (ECG), 103
Electroencephalograph (EEG), 57
Elizabeth I, Queen, 132
Embolus, 106
Embryo, 288, 292, **292**, 296, **296**
  chromosomes in, 38
Emotions, 66, 73
  facial expressions and, 168
  illness and, 66
  psychosomatic disorders and, 25
  stress on heart and, 89
  thoughts and, 68–69
Emphysema, 116, 124, **124**
Employment during pregnancy, 294, **294**
Enamel, 170, **170**
Endocardium, 90
Endocrine, origin of word, 76
Endocrine diseases, 30
Endocrine gland, 77, **77**. *See also*
  Endocrine system; *specific glands*.
Endocrine system, 20, 23, **23**, 74–87
Endoderm, 292, **292**
Endometrium, 272, 274
Endoplasmic reticulum, 27, **27**
Endorphins, 70
  and exercise, 186
Enema, 251, **251**
Energy, control of, 86–87
Enkephalins, 70
Enzyme, 40, 43
Epicardium, 90
Epidemic, definition of, 40
Epidermis, 98, **98**, 132, 133, **133**, 136, 137,
  137, **138**, 142, 143, **143**, 145, **150**
Epididymis, 266, **266**, 269, 282

Page numbers in **boldfaced** *type refer to the illustrations.*

Epiglottis, **115**, 224, **225**, **235**, **236**
Epilepsy, split-brain operation and, 52
Epinephrine, 84. *See also* Adrenaline.
Epiphyses, 79
Episiotomy, 302
Epithelial cells, 98, **98**
Epithelial tissue, 22
Epstein-Barr virus, 279
Erection, 267, 270
Erythrocytes. *See* Red blood cells.
Escher, Maurits, "Relativity," 199, **199**
Escherichia coli, 35
Eskimos (Inuits), 34, 195, **195**
Ethmoid sinuses, 222, **222**
E.T. The Extra-Terrestrial, 79, **79**
Euripides, 38
Eustachian tube, 208, **208**, 209, 217, 218
Evil eye, 204, **204**
Exercise, 186
  aerobic, 186
  effect on heart of, 186
  for fitness, 186–187, **186**
  hazards of, 185, **185**
  in 19th century, 186, **186**
  pregnancy and, 307, **307**
  pulse rate and, 93
  for toning skin, 147
  warming up before, 187
  and weight control, 256
Exertion, optimum level of, 164
Exocrine glands, 76
Expectorants, 118
Extracellular fluid (ECF), 27
Eyck, Jan van, 283, **283**
Eye, 188–205
  black, 190
  bloodshot, 189, 190
  brain and, 52–53
  and camera, compared, 190
  colour and, 200
  colour of, 39, 188
  dominant, 188
  muscles of, 189, 191, **191**
  problems and remedies, 204–205
  pupils, 191, **191**
  specialists, 190
  speck in, 192
  structure of, 191, **191**
  vision of single, 197
  See also Blindness; Vision.
Eyedrops, 190
Eyelids, 147, **147**, 190, 192
Eyelid surgery, 147, **147**
Eye make-up, 189
Eyestrain, 189, 194

Face, 167
  bacteria on, 144
  expressions of, 168, **168**
Face (*contd.*)
  muscles in, 168
Face lifts, 146–147, **146–147**
Facial expressions as universal language, 168, **168**
Factor VIII, 99
Fad diets, 256
Faeces, 235, 250, 251
Falciform ligament, **244**
Fallen arch, 181
Fallopian tubes, **272**, 273, **273**, 290, **290**, **291**
  blockage of, 284
  ligation of, 287
  See also Pelvic inflammatory disease.
False labour, 305
Family planning, 286, **286**. *See also* Contraception.
Farmer's lung, 127
Fathers and infants, 316, **316**
Fatigue, chronic, 21
Fats in diet, 253
Fear, response to, 84–85
"Feed a cold, starve a fever," 119, **119**
Female, origin of word, 264
Femur (thighbone), **161**, 164, 178
Fertility
  age and, 282
  nutrition and, 259
  prehistoric goddess of (Venus of Willendorf), 282, **282**
Fertility drugs, 284, 300
Fertilization, 38, 284
  development of egg after, 291, **291**
  outside body, 285, **285**
  role of hormones in, 282
  sex determination and, 291
Fever, 40, 119, **119**, 139
Fibre, 250, 254
Fibrin, 98, **98**
Fibroadenoma, 276
Fibroblast, 98, **98**, 184
Fibrocystic disease, 276–277
Fibroids, 274
Fibrosis, 163
Fibula, 161, **161**, 181
"Fight-or-flight" response, 84
Filliform papillae, **236**
Fingernails, 156–157, **156**, **157**
Fingerprints, 132, 136–137, **137**
Fingers, 138, **138**, 176, **176**
Fitness and exercise, 186–187, **186**
Flat feet, 180–181
Flatus, 250–251
Flavours. *See* Taste, sense of.
Floaters, 188–189
Flossing, 239, **239**
Flu. *See* Influenza.
Fluid balance, 260–261
Fluid elimination, 263
Fluoridated water, 239
Fluorides
  dangers of, 239
  to prevent tooth decay, 238, 239
Fly ash, 31, **31**
Flying, popping of ears and, 217
Foetus
  ability of, to see and hear, 298
  abnormalities in, 305
  appearance of, 296, **296**, 297, **297**, 299
  development of, 297
  distinguished from embryo, 288
  first movements of, 296, 298
  mother's emotions and, 289
  position of, before delivery, 308
  sex of, 299
  See also Embryo; Pregnancy.
Foliate papillae, **236**
Folic acid, 108
Folklore of the Body
  "Cravings During Pregnancy," 295, **295**
  "Feed a Cold, Starve a Fever," 119, **119**
  "Food Facts and Fallacies," 255, **255**
  "Gout as a Sign of High Living," 263, **263**
  "The Power of the Evil Eye," 204, **204**
  "Reading Character, Finding Omens," 214, **214**
  "Saving Salves and Ointments," 145, **145**
  "Searching for Heart Remedies," 107, **107**
Follicle, 273, 274, **274**
Fontanelle, 166
Food
  amount consumed in lifetime, 234
  aversions, 234
  chewing of, 240
  facts and fallacies about, 255
  storing of, 240
  time in digestive tract, 235
Food additives, 255
Food poisoning, 255
  See also Botulism.
Food preferences, 236, 237, 253
Foot, 180, 181, **181**
  fashion and, 179, **179**
  structure of, 181, **181**
Foot: "Getting off on the wrong foot," origin of phrase, 178
Footprints, 137
Forceps, 309
Forehand stroke in tennis, 175, **175**
Fovea, 191, **191**
Foxglove, 107, **107**
Fractures, types of, 184–185, **184**
Freckle, 136, **136**
Frederick III, 41, **41**
Frenulum, 225
Frenum, 225
Fright, 75, **75**, 84, **84**
Frigidity, 277
Frontal lobe, 49, **49**
  and control of emotions, 68–69
Frontal sinuses, **218**, 222, **222**
Frostbite, 142
  gangrene and, 107
Fundus, 240, **240**
Fungi, 134
Fungiform papillae, **236**
Funny bone, 175

G

Gage, Phineas, 68–69, **69**
Gag reflex, 224
Gall, 247
Gall, Franz Joseph, 52
Gallbladder, **235**, 244, **244**, 247
Gallstones, 247, **247**
Gamma globulin, 35, 100
Gangrene, 107
Gastric juice, 240, 242
Gastrocnemius 162, **162**, 180
Gastrointestinal diseases, 246
Gene, 38–43, **38**
  in cell nucleus, 26, 27, **27**
  dominant and recessive, 39, 40, 41, 42
  maximum life span and, 21
  origin of word, 66
Gene splicing. *See* Genetic engineering.
Genetic disorders, 30
  colour blindness, 41
  Down's syndrome, 40
  haemophilia, 41
  Huntington's chorea, 40, 43, **43**
  near-sightedness, 42
  number of, 40
  PKU, 40
Genetic engineering, 43, 45
Genital herpes, 278, **278**, 279
Genitals, 266–277, **266, 272**
Genius, origin of word, 66
Genus, origin of word, 264
Gerasimov, Mikhail, 166
German measles (rubella), 212
  birth defects and, 304
Germ cells, 38, 40
Germs, 28–29, 31. *See also* Bacteria; Viruses.
Gestation, 288
Giantism, 78, 79, **79**
Gibson, Eleanor, 61
Gigantism. *See* Giantism.
Gingivitis, 239
Ginseng, 271, **271**
Glands, endocrine, 74–75, 76
Glands, exocrine, 76
Glands of Littre, 268
Glandular fever, 107, 279
Glans, 266, **266**
Glasses. *See* Spectacles.
Glaucoma, 32, 203, 204, 205, **205**
Glial cells, 65
Globus hystericus (lump in the throat), 225
Glomerulus. *See* Nephron.
Glottis, 228, **228**
Glucagon, 77, 87, 247
Glucocorticoids, 84, 85
Gluteus maximus, 162, **162**, 187
Goitre, 86, **86**
Golgi complex, 27, **27**
Gonorrhoea, 278, **278**, 280

Goose flesh (goose pimples), 132, 151
Gould, Stephen Jay, 65
Gourmand, origin of word, 242
Gourmet, origin of word, 242
Gout, 182, 263, **263**, 264
Graafian follicle, 273, 274, **274**
Growing pains, 85
Growth, 316
Growth hormone, 77
  in adolescence, 80
  in adults, 80
  deficiency of, 81, **81**
  dwarfism and, 78, 79, **79**
  giantism and, 78, 79, **79**
  metabolism and, 80
Gum disease, 239
Gums, 170, **170**
Guthrie, Woody, 40
Gymnastics, 216, **216**
Gynaecologist, 270
Gynaecology, origin of word, 264

H

Haematocele, 269
Haematoma, 184, 277
Haemodialysis, 260–261, **260**
Haemoglobin, 88, 94, 108, 128
Haemophilia, 41, 108, 109, **109**, 289
Haemorrhage, 98
Haemorrhoids, 254
Hair, 84, 132, 138, 150–155, **150, 151, 152, 153, 154–155**
  colour of, 131, 154
  dyeing of, 154–155, **154–155**
  functions of, 150
  growth of, 132, 150–151, **150**
  growth of, before birth (lanugo), 151, 297, 299
  heredity and, 39
  loss of, 152
  strength of, 154
  structure of, 150, **150**
  texture of, 151
  vellus, 151, 152
Hair follicle, **133**, 144, **144**, 150–151, **150**
Hairs: "To split hairs," origin of phrase, 148
Hair transplants, 152, 153, **153**
Halitosis, 233
Hammer (malleus), **208**, 209
Hammertoe, 181
Hand, 130–131, 139, 141
  flexibility of, 176
  number of bones in, 176
  speed of movement, 177, **177**
  structure of, 176, **176**
Hangnail, 157
  origin of word, 148
Hangovers, 259
Happy expression, 168, **168**

Hapsburg dynasty, 41, **41**
Hardening of the arteries. *See* Atherosclerosis.
Harris, Keith, 230, **230**
Hats, importance in cold weather of, 89, **89**
Hay fever (allergic rhinitis), 122, **122**, 222, 223
Headache, 72, 169, **169**, 226, **226**
  sinuses and, 222
Heading ball in soccer, 167, **167**
Headphones, 213, **213**
Healing, **98**, 99, 141, **141**
Health
  in advanced and primitive societies, 35, **35**
  definitions of, 24
  laughter and, 20, 21, **21**
  stress and, 25
Health spas, 246, **246**
Hearing, 42
  disorders, 212–213, 214, 217, 230–231
  sense of, 206–207, 211–215, 230–231
Hearing aids, 214, 215, **215**
Hearing loss, one-sided, 217
Hearing tests, 206, 212, 231
Heart, 88–111
  beat, 90, 102, 112, 163
  disease, 103, 104–105
  location of, 88
  murmur, 91
  structure of, 91
Heart attack (myocardial infarction), 104–105, 124, 125
  exercise and prevention of, 186
  life expectancy and, 105
  sexual intercourse and, 270
Heartburn, 241
Heart disease (cardiovascular disease), 103, 104–105
  smoking and, 128, 129
Heel bone (calcaneous), 181, **181**
Height, 42
  of parents and children compared, 85
Helicopters, medical evacuation by, 37, **37**
Helix, 38, **38**
Henry VIII, 254, **254**
Hepatic artery, 245
Hepatic cell, 244, **244**, 245. *See also* Liver.
Hepatic duct, **244**
Hepatitis, 246–247
Heredity, 38–43
  albinism and, 136
  baldness and, 152, **152**
  cancer and, 32
  colour blindness and, 202
  environment and, 21
  eye and hair colour and, 39, 188
  family resemblance and, 38–39, 41, **41**
  freckles and, 136
  haemophilia and, 289
  hay fever and, 223
  hearing and, 42
  height and, 42, 85
  high blood pressure and, 103
  intelligence and, 64

Page numbers in **boldfaced** *type refer to the illustrations.*

Heredity (*contd.*)
  maximum life span and, 21, 42
  PKU and, 40
  polydactylism and, 42
  psoriasis and, 145
  sickle cell anaemia and, 289
  vision and, 42
Heroin, 32
Herpes, 45, 278, 279
Herpes virus, 278, **278**, 279
Hiatus hernia, 241
Hiccups, 114
High blood pressure (hypertension),
    102–103, 106
  atherosclerosis and, 105, **105**
  cholesterol and, 105
  coronary artery disease and, 104
  stroke and, 106–107
High-density lipoprotein (HDL), 105
High-heeled shoes, 173, **173**, 179, **179**
Hildebrandt, Greg and Tim, 39, **39**
Hinge joint, 164–165, **165**
Hip, 164, 178, 183, **183**
Hippocampus, 53, **53**, 63
Hippocrates, 26, 28, 37, **37**
    46, 68, 246
Histamines, 222, 223
Hodgkin's disease, 111
Home delivery, 302, **302**
Homoeostasis, 20, 24
Home urine tests for pregnancy, 290
Honey, 233, **233**
Hormones, 74–87
  acne and, 144
  and aggression, 55
  angiotensin, 260, 263
  baldness and, 152
  brain and, 54
  as cause of cancer, 33
  cholecystokinin, 247
  definition of, 74
  fertility and, 282
  function of, 77
  gastrin, 242
  growth and, 81, **81**
  heart disease and, 104
  number of, 76
  origin of word, 76
  ovarian, 272
  See also Sex hormones; *specific hormones.*
Hospitals, history of, 33, **33**
"Hot labs," 44, **44**
Housemaid's knee, 178
Hudson, Jeffery, 85
Human body, 20–45
Human chorionic gonadotropin (HCG),
    290
"Hum and haw," origin of phrase, 224
Humerus, 174
Humours, in ancient medicine, 26, **26**, 28,
    119
Hunchback, 173
Hunger, 232
Huntington's chorea, 40, 43, **43**
Hydrocele, 269
Hydrochloric acid (gastric juices), 241, 242

Hydrocortisone, 85
  to treat keloids, 148
Hymen, 273
Hypermetropia (far-sightedness), 190, 194,
    194
Hypertension. *See* High blood pressure.
Hyperthyroidism, 86–87
Hyperventilation, 124
Hypervitaminosis, 255
Hypnosis, 63, **63**
  amnesia and, 63
  enhancing memory, 63, **63**
  origin of word, 66
Hypochondria, 24–25
Hypothalamus, 48, 53, **53**, 77, **77**, 84
  and cold weather, 132
  function of, 78, **78**
  as monitor of temperature, 89
  relationship of, to pituitary, 78, **78**
  role of, in fluid balance, 263
Hypoxia, 126, **126**
Hyssop, 223, **223**
Hysterectomy, 274–275

I

Iatrogenic disease, 30
ICF. *See* Intracellular fluid.
Idiot savants, 47
Ileum, **233**, 248, **248**, 249
Illness, factitious. *See* Münchhausen's
    syndrome.
Images, non-verbal, 60
Immune system, 100–101, 261
  development of, 100
  glucocorticoids and, 85
  thymus gland and, 100, **100**
Immunity, sexually transmitted diseases
    and, 281
Immunization
  against influenza, 120, 121, **121**
  in preparation for travel, 35
Immunology, 45
Immunotherapy, 223
Impotence. *See* Sexual impotence.
Inbreeding, 41, **41**
Incense, 223, **223**
Incisors, **170**, 170
Incompetent cervix, 293
Incus (anvil), **208**, 209
Indigestion, 241
Infancy, rapid growth during, 80
"Infant competency," 316
Infants
  birthmark in, 136
  congenital immune deficiency in, 101
  danger to, if mother smokes, 129
  footprinting versus fingerprinting,
    137
  immune system of, 100
  lung collapse in, 124
  skin of, 135

Infants (*contd.*)
  soft heads of, 166
  touching and, 138
  See also Babies.
Inferior vena cava, 91, **91**, 245
Infertility, 278, 280
  causes of (female), 284
  causes of (male), 284–285
  tight clothing and, 284–285
  See also Pelvic inflammatory
    disease.
Inflammation, role in healing of, 99
Influenza (flu), 31, 120, 121, **121**, 227
  A virus, 121, **121**
Ingrowing toenail, 157
Inner ear, 208, **208**, 209, **209**
  balance and, 207, 209, 216, **216**
Insanity, 67, **67**
Insect bites and stings, 85, 140
Insecticides, 37
Insect odours (pheromones), 223
Insomnia, 59
  origin of word, 66
Insulin, 76, 87, **87**, 247
  produced artificially by genetic
    engineering, 43
Intelligence
  definition of, 64
  environment and, 65
  measurement of, 64–65, **64**
  heredity and, 64–65
Interferon, 33, 45
Intestine, large, 235, **235**, 248, **248**, 250,
    251
Intestine, small, 235, **235**, 248, **248**, 249,
    250
Intestines, amount of food processed daily in,
    248
Intracellular fluid (ICF), 27
Intraductal papilloma, 277
Intraocular lens, 204
Intrauterine devices (IUD), 286, 287, **287**
  risks of, 280, 287, **287**
Inuits (Eskimos), 195, **195**
In vitro fertilization, 285, **285**
Iodine, 86
I.Q. (Intelligence quotient). *See* Intelligence,
    measurement of.
Iris (eye), 188, 190, 191, **191**
Iron-deficiency anaemia, 108
Ishihara test, 202, **202**
Islets of Langerhans, 76, 87, 247
Isometric exercise, 164
Isotonic exercise, 164
Itching, 138–139
IUD. *See* Intrauterine devices.

J

Jack the Ripper, 55
Japanese tattoos, 149, **149**
Jaundice, 246

Jaw
   muscles of, 168
   pain in, 169
   temporomandibular syndrome (TMJ), 169, **169**
Jejunum, **235**, 248, **248**
Jenner, Edward, 101, **101**
Jet lag, 74−75
Jogger's nipple, 277, **277**
Jogging shoes, 179, **179**
Joints
   ankle, 165, **165**
   artificial, 183, **183**
   ball-and-socket, 164, 165, **165**
   cracking of, 164
   effect of osteoarthritis on, 182
   functioning of, 164
   hinge, 165, **165**
   plane, 165, **165**
   saddle, 165, **165**
   suture, 165, **165**
Juvenile-onset diabetes, 87, **87**

"Keeping a stiff upper lip," origin of phrase, 178
"Keeping your ear to the ground," origin of phrase, 224
Kekulé, Friedrich von Stradonitz, 60
Keloid scar, 148
Kerotin, 141, 156
Kidney, 93, **93**, 95
   artificial, 260−261
   description of, 260, 261, **261**, 270
   hangovers and, 259
   over-the-counter medications and, 259
   See also Bladder; Urine.
Kidney disease
   fluoridated water and, 239
   haemodialysis and, 260, **260**, 261
Kidney stones, 264−265
   excess calcium and, 77
Kilojoules, 252
Kissing, muscles used in, 168
Kissing disease. *See* Mononucleosis.
Knee, 161, 164, 165, **165**, 178
   cracking of, 164
   dislocation of, 165
   replacement of, 183, **183**
   vulnerability of, 164
Knee jerk, 51
Knuckles, 164
   cracking of, 177
Knuckles: "When someone knuckles under," origin of phrase, 178
Korean War, 37, **37**
Korsakoff's syndrome, 68
Kwashiorkor, 30
Kyphosis, 173

Labia majora, 273
Labia minora, 273
Labour, 305−309, **308−309**, 311. *See also* Birth.
Labyrinth, 216, **216**
Lack of exercise, 182
Lacrimal canals, ducts, glands, sac, 192, **192**
Lactic acid, 185
Landsteiner, Karl, 96
Langer's lines, 146−147, **146−147**
Language ability and the brain, 52
Lanugo hairs, 151, 297, 299
Large intestine. *See* Intestine, large.
Laryngectomy, 229, 231
Laryngitis, 229
Larynx, **115**, 224, 225, **225**, 228, 229
   removal of, 231
Laser beams
   to remove tattoos, 148
   in treatment of atherosclerosis, 105, **105**
   in treatment of cancer, 33
Lassen, Niels, 57
Laughing gas, 71, **71**
Laughter
   health and, 20, 21, **21**
   tears and, 66, 192
Laxatives, 251
Lazy eye (amblyopia), 197
Learning
   before birth, 298
   practice and, 60−61
Leboyer method of childbirth, 302
Leeches for blood letting, 104
Leeuwenhoek, Anton van, 28, **28**, 284
Left-handedness, 55
Leg
   phlebitis in, 106
   varicose vein in, 106, **106**
Legionnaires' disease, 44
Lens, 190, 191, **191**, 194, **194**, 195, 196, 204
Lenses, corrective, 194, **194**, 195
Leominster, England, 301, **301**
Lethargy, origin of word, 66
Leucocytes. *See* White blood cells.
Leukaemia, 32
Lice, 135, **135**
Life span, maximum, 21, 42, **42**
Ligaments, 162, 175, 176, **176**, 181, **181**, 184
"Lily-livered coward," origin of phrase, 242
Limbic system, 53, **53**, 63, 68
Limeys, 253
Lip, 139
Lipid, 27, **27**
Lip-reading. *See* Speech-reading.
Lipsitt, Don R., 25

Lisping, 230
Liver, **235**, 244, **244**, 245−247
   blood circulation in, 245
   blood-sugar level and, 245
   capacity to regenerate, 244
   function of, 244
   hepatic cells, 244, **244**
   lobes of, **244**
   regeneration of, 27
   role in digestion, 245
   storage and manufacture of glucose, 245
   vitamin storage in, 244
Liver, diseases of
   cirrhosis, 157, 245
   hepatitis, 246, 247
   jaundice, 246
Livingstone, David, 70
Lobelia syphilitica, 281, **281**
Lobes
   of brain, 49, **49**
   of lung, 115, **115**
Locking knee, 178
Long-sightedness (hypermetropia), 190, 194, **194**
Loudness, 210, **210**, 211
Low back pain, 173, 184
Low-density lipoprotein (LDL), 105
Lumbago, 173
Lump in the throat, 225
Lung, 90−92, **91**, 94 112−118, **114**, **115**, **116**, 124, **124**, 125, **125**, 127
   amount of air in, 116−117
   cancer of, 123, 128−129
   collapse of, 124
   functioning of, 114
   occupational hazards and, 127
   smoking and, 128−129
Lymphatic system, 110−111, **111**
Lymph duct, 111, **111**
Lymph node, 110, 111, **111**
Lymphocytes. *See* White blood cells.
Lymphoma, 110−111
Lysosomes, 27, **27**

Mabaans of Africa, 35, **35**
Macrophages, 94−95, **94−95**, 105
Macular degeneration, 205, **205**
Malaria, 31, 34, 35
   early theories of, 221
Male, origin of word, 264
Male menopause, 259
Malingerers, 25
Mallet finger, 176
Malleus (hammer), **208**, 209
Malnutrition, 31, **31**
Malocclusion, 169, 171
Mammary glands, 277
Mandible, **169**

Page numbers in **boldfaced** *type refer to the illustrations.*

Mandrake root, 271, **271**
Manet, Edouard, *Bar at the Folies-Bergère*, 280, **280**
Mantegna, Andrea, 267, **267**
Marathons, 180, **180**
Marie Antoinette, 154
Marijuana, 32, **32**
Marlborough, Duke of, 153, **153**
Marriage ceremonies, 283, **283**
Marrow. *See* Bone marrow.
Masai warrior, 103, **103**
Massage, 147
Matrix, 156, **156**
Maturation, sexual, 82, **82**
Maturity-onset diabetes, 87
Maxillary sinuses, 222, **222**
Maximilian I, 41, **41**
Meals, timing of, 233
Measles, 34
Meconium, 298
Medical breakthroughs, 45
Medicine, determining dosage of, 36
Meditation, 72
Medulla
    of adrenal gland, 84
    of brain, 48
    of hair, **150**
    of kidney, 261, **261**
Meiosis, 38
Meissner corpuscle, **138**
Melanin, 131, 133, **133**, 136, 142, 144, **144**, 145, 154, 188
Melanocyte, 131, 133, **133**, **150**
Melanoma, malignant, 136, 145
Melatonin, 76
Memory, 60, 61, 62 – 63, **62**
Menarche, 82, 275, **275**
Ménière's disease, 216–217
Menopause
    effect on bones of, 182
    excessive hair and, 153
    female, 259
    hair loss and, 152
    male, 259
    sexual interest after, 83
Menses. *See* Menstruation.
Menstrual cycle, 274, **274**
Menstruation, 272
    absence of, during pregnancy, 290
    discomfort and, 275
    first, 82, 275, **275**
    hormones and, 74
    myths of, 275, **275**
Mental illness, depression and, 66
Mental retardation, 40
Merkel's discs, **138**
Mesoderm, 292, **292**
Metabolism, hormones and, 80
Metacarpals, **161**, 176, **176**
Metastasis, 32
Metatarsal bones, **161**, 181, **181**
Michelangelo, 55
Microbes, discovery of, 28
Microscopes, early, 28, **28**
Microsurgery, 33, **33**
Microvilli, 27, **27**, 248, **248**

Midbrain, 48
Middle ear, **208**, 209
    infection of, 214
Midgets, 78, 79, **79**, 85
Midwives, 302
Mikvah, 275, **275**
Milk, 234
Milk ducts, 276, **276**
Mind, brain and, 46–47
Mineral baths, 246, **246**
Mineralocorticoids, 84
Minipill, 287
Mirage 196, **196**
Miscarriage, smoking and, 129. *See also* Spontaneous abortion.
Mite, 135, **135**
Mitochondria, 27, **27**
Mitosis, 27, 38
Mitral valve, 91, **91**
Molars, 170, **170**
Mole, 136
Mongolism. *See* Down's syndrome.
Monoclonal antibodies, 33, 45
Mononucleosis (glandular fever), 107
Mons pubis, 273
Mons veneris, 273
Moods, 66
Moon, plans for settlement on, 45
Morning sickness, 289, 290
Morphine, 32
Morula, 291
Motion sickness, 207, **207**
    transdermal patch and, 139, **139**
Motor cortex, 49, **49**, 53, **53**
Motor end plate, 48, **48**, 163
Mountain sickness, 126, **126**
    in aeroplanes, 126
Mouth, 168, 169, **169**
    function of, 234
Mouth-to-mouth resuscitation, 125
Mouthwash, 233
Movies, smoking and, 129, **129**
MRI scan, 56, 57, **57**
Mucous membrane, 119, 120, 122
Mucus
    and cold viruses, 120
    produced by nose, 218
    produced by sinuses, 222
Multiple births, 284, 300, 301, **301**
    fertility drugs and, 300
Multiple sclerosis, 31
Mummies, 44, 45, **45**
Mumps, 29, 269, **269**
Münchhausen's syndrome, 25, **25**
Muscle
    cardiac, 163, **163**
    energy, use of, 158
    functioning of, 84, 163
    heat production by, 164
    involuntary, 163
    major, 162, **162**
    origin of word, 178
    smooth, 163, **163**
    striped, 163, **163**
    strongest, 187

Muscle (*contd.*)
    structure of, **92**, 163
    voluntary, 163
Muscle-bound, 159
Muscles, specific
    biceps, 159, **162**
    deltoid, 162, **162**, 174
    facial, 168
    foot, 181, **181**
    gastrocnemius, 162, **162**, 180
    gluteus maximus, 162, **162**, 187
    heart, 163, **163**
    jaw, 168, 169, **169**
    mouth, 168, 169, **169**
    pectorals, 162, **162**, 174
    rectus abdominus, 162, **162**
    sphincter, 240, **240**
    transversus abdominus, 162
    trapezius, 162, **162**, 174
    triceps, **162**
Muscle tissue, 22
    and blood supply, 92, **92**
    length of cells, 26
Muscular system, 23, **23**, 162–163, **162**
Mushrooms, 255, **255**
Mushroom worker's lung, 127
Music and the brain, 52, 55, **55**
Myelinization, 299
Myocardial infarction. *See* Heart attack.
Myocardium, 90
Myofibril, 163
Myomectomy, 274
Myometrium, 272
Myopia (near-sightedness), 42, 194, **194**, 195
Myosin filament, 163

N

Nail polish, 157, **157**
Nails, 156–157, **156–157**
Nappies, baby in, 259, **259**
Narcolepsy, 59
Nasal cavity, 192, **192**
Naskapi Indian menstrual mask, 275, **275**
Nasolacrimal duct, 192, **192**
Natural childbirth, 302–303, 306–307
Navel, origin of word, 293
Near-sightedness (myopia), 42, 194, **194**, 195
Neck
    Hodgkin's disease and, 111
    stretching, 172, **172**
Neoplastic diseases. *See* Cancer.
Nephrologist, 270
Nephron, 93, **93**, 260, 261, **261**
Nerve, 48, **48**, 49, **49**, 50–51, **50**
    inability to reproduce, 27
    length of cells, 26
    in skin, 132, 133, **133**, 138, **138**, 139
    tissue, 22

Nerve ending, 138, **138**
Nervousness, 51
Nervous system, 23, **23**, 74
    main parts of, 48, 49, **49**
"Nesting" instinct, 289
Nettle, stinging, 140, **140**
Neurotransmitter, 50, 51, **51**, 72
Newborns
    Apgar test for normalcy, 314
    breathing difficulties, 310
    cot deaths, 314
    cry of, 310
    examination of, 310, **310**
    mortality rate of, 297
    responsiveness of, 314, **314**
    self-regulatory mechanisms of, 24
    weight loss in, 312
Niddah, 275, **275**
Night blindness, 202
Night (day) vision, 203, **203**
Nightmares, 59, **59**, 90
Nipple, 276, **276**
Nitrogen, 127
Nitroglycerine patch, 139
Nocturnal emissions, 269
Noise
    damage to ear from, 208, **208–209**, 210,
        210
    general health and, 212–213
Non-rapid-eye-movement (NREM) sleep,
    59
Non-specific urethritis, 278
Non-verbal images, 60
Noradrenaline, 78, 84
Norepinephrine. *See* Noradrenaline.
Nose, 218–223, **218**, 226–227
    blowing of, 219
    deviated septum, 219
    "drinker's," 219
    drug administration through, 219
    functions of, 218
    hair in, 120
    plastic surgery on, 147, 219
    sneezing and, 118
Nosebleed, 226–227
Nose: "Follow your nose," origin of phrase,
    224
Nostalgia, 63
Nostrils, 218, 224
    origin of word, 224
Now, Voyager, 129, **129**
NREM. *See* Non-rapid-eye-movement
    sleep.
Nuclear scanning, 103
Nucleolus, 27, **27**
Nucleus. *See* Cell nucleus.
Nutrition
    absorption of nutrients, 248–249
    children's preferences and, 253
    fertility and, 259
    first menstruation and, 82
    food requirements, 252–253
    importance of, in pregnancy, 294
Nutritional disease, 30, 31, **31**

Page numbers in **boldfaced** *type refer to the illustrations.*

Obesity, 252, 256
    diabetes and, 75
    snoring and, 113
Occipital lobe, 49, **49**, 52
Occlusion, 171
Oculist, 190
Odours
    effect of familiar, 207
    preferences for certain, 223, **223**
    primary, 221
    See also Smell.
Oesophageal speech, 231
Oesophagus, 115, 224, 225, **225**, 235, **235**,
    240, **240**
Oestrogen, 80, 85, 152, 259
    menopause and, 182, 259
    in the Pill, 287
    secreted by testes, 81
    sex drive and, 277
Old age, self-regulatory mechanisms of,
    24
Olfactory system
    bulbs, 218, **218**, 220
    cells, 236
    membrane, 220, **220**
    nerves, 220
    sensitivity of, 221
Oncologist, origin of word, 32
Oogenesis, 272–273
Opera singers, 229, **229**
Ophthalmologist, 190
Ophthalmoscope, 190
Opium, 32
Optical illusion, 196–199, **196–199**
Optician, 190
Optic nerve, 190, 191, **191**, 203, 204
Oral contraceptives, smoking and, 128
Oral hygiene, 239
Organelles, 26, 27, **27**
Organs, 22–23
Organ transplants
    kidney, 261
    role of cyclosporine in, 45, 261
Orgasm
    female, 275, 277
    male, 267
Orthoptist, 190
Osmoreceptor, 260
Ossification, 159
Osteoarthritis, 182–183, **183**
Osteoporosis, 182, **182**
Otosclerosis, 212, 214
Ovaries, 38, 77, **77**, 81, 272, **272**, 273,
    273, 291, **291**
Overeating, 254
Overweight. *See* Obesity.
Oviducts, 290–291, **291**. *See also* Fallopian
    tubes.
Ovulation, 272–273, 282
    fertility drugs and, 284

Ovum, 38, 268, 272, 273, **273**
Oxygen, 95, 126
    in blood, 90, 91, **91**, 94
    exchange in lungs, 93, 112, **113**, 114, 115,
        115, 124, **124**, 125, 126, 128, 129
    at high altitudes, 126
    pure, dangers of, 114, **114**
    stroke and, 106
    use of, by house plants, 120
    yawning and, 113
Oxygen deprivation and the brain, 48–49
Oxytocin, 78, 306, 312

Pacemaker
    artificial, 90
    natural, 90
Pacinian corpuscle, **138**
Padaung tribe, 172, **172**
Pain, 69–72
    referred, 226
    temporomandibular (TMJ) syndrome,
        169
Pain clinics, 71
Pain threshold, 69
Palpation, 116
Pancreas, 76, 77, **77**, 87, **235**, 244, **244**,
    247
Pancreatic duct, **244**
Pancreatitis, 247
Pandemic, definition of, 40
Papillae, 236, **236**, 237, **237**
Papillary layer of skin, **133**
Paracelsus, 284
Parathormone, 77
Parathyroid glands, 77
Parenthood, delayed, 288–289
Parietal lobe, 49, **49**
Parkinson's disease, 72
Parotid glands, 234, **235**
Passive smoking, 113
Pasteur, Louis, 28
Patent medicines, 145, **145**
Paternity, blood type as proof of, 97
Pavlov, Ivan, 60, **60**
PCP (angel dust), 66
Pectoral muscles, **162**, 174
Pelvic inflammatory disease (PID), 280,
    284, 287
Pelvis, **161**, 178
Penicillin, 36, 37
Penis, 266, **266**, 267
Pep, 20
Pericardium, 90
Perimetrium, 272
Periodontitis, 239
Periosteum, 96, **96**, 160, 182
Peripheral nervous system, 48
Peristalsis, 235, **235**, 249
Permanent teeth, 170, **170**
Pernicious anaemia, 108, 249

328

Perspiration, 84
PET scan, 56, **56**
Phalange, **161**, 176, **176**, 181
Pharynx (throat), 115, **115**
    function of, 224–225, **225**
Pheidippides (Greek runner), 180
Phenylketonuria. *See* PKU.
Pheromones, 223
Philip IV, 41, **41**
Phlebitis, 106
Phobias, 68, **68**
Phrenology, 52, **52**
Physical fitness. *See* Exercise.
PID. *See* Pelvic inflammatory disease.
Pigment. *See* Melanin.
Pill. *See* Contraception.
Pill stuck in throat, 234
Pimples. *See* Acne.
Pineal gland, 77 ,**77**
    early theories of, 76, **76**
Pinel, Philippe, 67, **67**
Pipes, 128, **128**
Pitch, 210–211
Pituitary gland, 77, **77**, 78, **78**, 80, 84
PKU (phenylketonuria), 40
Placebo effect, 36
Placenta, 292–293, **292**, 294, **309**
    delivery of, 311
Placental barrier, 294
Placental transfusion, 310
Placenta praevia, 303, 304
Plane joint, **165**
Plaque, 105, **105**, 238, **238**, 239
Plasma, 94
    transfusions of, 37, **37**
Plastic surgery, 146–147, **146–147**, 148
    on nose, 147, 219
    during World War I, 37
Platelets (thrombocytes), 28, **28**, 94, 95, 96,
    98, 105, **105**
Pleura, 115, **115**
PMS. *See* Premenstrual syndrome.
Pneumonia, 28
Pneumothorax, 124
Poliomyelitis, 35
Pollen, 122–123, **122–123**
Pollution, environmental, 31, **31**
Polygenes, 42
Polymerization, 146
Polyps, nasal, 226
Polyunsaturated fats, 253
Ponce de León, Juan, 42, **42**
Pons, 48
Pore, 135, **135**, 144
Portal vein, 245
Port-wine stain, 136
Postmature babies, 289
Postnasal drip, 226
Posture, 173, **173**, 187
Pot belly
    in sumo wrestlers, 187
    in weight lifters, 187
Potential acuity meter (PAM), 204
Pre-eclampsia, 303
Pregnancy, 288–311
    alcohol and drugs during, 294, 295

Pregnancy (*contd.*)
    breast feeding and, 282
    changes in body during, 295
    complications of, 303
    cravings and, 295, **295**
    detection of, 290
    duration of, 288
    early stages of, 292–293
    employment during, 294, **294**
    exercise and, 307, **307**
    false labour and, 305
    morning sickness and, 289, 290
    nutrition during, 294
    Rh factor and, 97
    sexual intercourse and, 295
    smoking during, 129
    spotting during, 304
    syphilis and, 281
    trimesters of, 288
    tubal infection and, 284
    See also Birth; Embryo; Foetus; Labour.
Pregnancy tests, 290
Pregnant, origin of word, 293
Premature babies, 297, 299
Premature ejaculation, 270
Premenstrual syndrome (PMS), 275
Premolars, **170**
Premotor cortex, 49, **49**
Prenatal, origin of word, 293
Prepuce, 273
Presbyopia, 195
Prickle cells, 133, **133**
Priestley, Joseph, 71
Primary teeth, 170, **170**
Primary visual cortex, 52
Primordial eggs, 282
Printing, close-up of, 197, **197**
Progesterone, 277
    production of, 81
Progestin, 287
Prolactin, production of, 81, 83
Prosopagnosia, 55
Prostaglandin, 306
Prostate gland, 266, **266**, 268
    aging and, 267
    cancer of, 33
    sexual performance and, 267
Proteins, 252–253
    deficiency of, 26
    DNA and, 38, **38**
    effect on athletic performance, 233
    function of, 27
    manufacture of, 26
    quantity needed, 253
Psoriasis, 145
Psychosomatic disorders, definition of, 25
Psychosomatic illness, 256–257, **257**
Puberty
    growth of hair during, 151
    production of sex hormones, 80
    voice change and, 81
Public toilets and venereal disease, 279
Pulmonary arteries, 91, **91**, 92, 115, **115**
Pulmonary arteriole, 115
Pulmonary function tests, 117
Pulmonary veins, 91, **91**, 115

Pulp, 170, **170**
Pulse, 93, 102, **102**
Pupil, 190, 191, **191**
Pus, 99
Pygmies, 79
Pyloric sphincter, **240**, 242

Quack, origin of word, 36
Quasimodo, 173
Quinine, 145

Rabies, 30, **30**, 31
Räderscheidt, Anton, 73, **73**
Radiation
    anaemia and, 108
    bone damage and, 161
    as cause of cancer, 32
    from chest X-rays, 116
    as treatment for cancer, 33
Radius, 137, **161**, 174, 175, **176**, 177
Raleigh, Sir Walter, 128, **128**
Rapid-eye-movement (REM) sleep, 58–59
    in babies, 313, **313**
    in foetus, 297
Rasputin, 109, **109**
Receptor, 51, **51**
Recombinant DNA technology. *See* Genetic
    engineering.
Reconstructive surgery. *See* Plastic Surgery.
Rectum, **235**, 248, 250, 251, **272**
    examination of, 267
Rectus abdominus, 162, **162**
Red blood cells (erythrocytes), 26, 88, 90, 91,
    91, 92, **92**, 94–96, **94**, 96, **96**, 98, **98**,
    108, **108**, 110, 126
    anaemia and, 108
    number of, 94
    sickle cell anaemia and, 108
Referred pain, 226, **226**
Reflexes, 130, 131
"Relativity" (painting by Escher), 199,
    199
REM. *See* Rapid-eye-movement sleep.
Renal arteries, 93, **93**, 261
Renal pelvis, 261, **261**
Renal pyramids, 261, **261**
Renal veins, 93, **93**, 261. *See also* Kidney.
Renin, 263
Reproduction
    early theories of, 284
    effect of diet on, 259
Reproductive system, 23, **23**, 259, 266–287
    female, 272–277, **272**, **274**, **276**
    male, 266–269, **266**

Respiration, 112–129
    artificial, 125
    See also Breathing.
Respiratory system, 23, **23**, 112–129
    structure of, 115, **115**
    See also Lung.
Restak, Richard, 59
Retardation, mental, 47
Reticular layer of skin, **133**
Retina, 191, **191**, 194, **194**, 199, 205
    cataracts and, 204
    compared to camera film, 190
    detached, 204–205, **205**
    floaters and, 188
    rods and cones in, 200, 202
    upside-down images on, 196
Retinitis pigmentosa (tunnel vision), 202,
    205, **205**
Reye's syndrome, 40
Rh factor, 96–97
Rheumatoid arthritis, 30, 101, 182, 183
Rhinoceros horn, 271, **271**
Rhinoplasty, 147, 219
Rib cage, 114, 115, 116, **116**, 161, **161**
Ribonucleic acid. *See* RNA.
Ribosomes, 27, **27**
Rickets, 253, **253**
Ringworm, 132
RNA, 22
Rods, 190, 191, **191**, 200, 202, 203,
    203
Romanovs, 109, **109**
Romulus and Remus, 301, **301**
Root of tooth, 170, **170**
Roughage, 254
Royal Society, 29
Rubella. *See* German measles.
Ruffini ending, **133**

Sabin oral polio vaccine, 100
Saccharin, 237, 255
Sacrum, 172, **173**
Saddle joint, 165, **165**
St. Martin, Alexis, 241, **241**
Salary, origin of word, 243
Saliva, 234, 237, 240
Salt, 243, **243**
    antidiuretic hormone and, 260
    in Dead Sea, 243, **243**
    high blood pressure and, 103
    snoring and, 113
Sandwiches, origin of word, 242
Sarcoma, 32. *See also* Cancer.
Scab, 98, **98**
Scabies, 135, 148
Scaling, 239
Scalp, 151
Scan, ultrasound, 299, **299**

Scanners, brain, 45, **45**, 56–57, **56, 57**
Scanning electron microscope, 28, **28**
    scintigram, 80, **80**
Scapula, 161, **161**, 174
Scar, 148, 149
Scents, 223, **223**
Schistosomiasis. *See* Snail fever.
Schizophrenia, 56, **56**, 72
Scintigram, 80, **80**
Sclerotic layer of eye, 191, **191**
Scrotum, 266, **266**
Scurvy, 253
Seashell, sounds in, 214, **214**
Seasickness. *See* Motion sickness.
Sebaceous glands, **133**, 134, 144, **144**, 150,
    150
Second teeth, 170, **170**
Semen, 266, 268–269
Semicircular canals, **208**, 216, **216**
Seminal fluid, 268
Seminal vesicles, 266, **266**, 268
Seminiferous tubules, **266**
Semmelweis, Ignaz, and childbirth fever,
    134, **134**
Sense receptors, **133**, 138, **138**, 139
Septum 90, **90, 222**
Serotonin, 66
Sertoli cells, 266
Sex chromosomes, 40–41
Sex determination, 305
Sex differences
    in aggression, 54–55
    in behaviour, 54
    in brain, 54, 80
    in disorders, 55
    in hormone production, 80
    in sense of smell, 207
    in skeleton, 160, 166
    in urinary system, 263
    in vulnerability to genetic disorders,
        40–41
Sex hormones
    growth and, 80
    secreted by adrenal cortex, 84
    secretion of, before birth, 80
    sexual behaviour and, 82–83
Sexual activity
    hormones and, 82–83
    old age and, 83, **83**
Sexual arousal (female), 277
Sexual impotence, 270–271
Sexual intercourse
    pregnancy and, 295
    after prostate surgery, 267
Sexually transmitted diseases (STD),
    278–281, **278, 279, 281**
Sexual maturation, 82, **82**
Shell, sounds in, 214, **214**
Shepard, Alan B., 217
Shinbone (tibia), **161**, 178
Shingles, 29
Shivering, to produce heat, 164
Shock, from blood loss, 98
Shoes. *See* Foot.

Shoulder, 161, **161**, 174–175
    dislocation of, 174–175
    frozen, 174
Siamese twins, 300
Sickle cell anaemia, 30, 108, **108**, 289
SIDS. *See* Sudden Infant Death
    Syndrome.
Sigh, 40
Sight compared with hearing, 213. *See also*
    Vision.
Sigmoid colon, **235**, 248, **248**, 250
Silence, degrees of, 211
Silicosis, 127
    in antiquity, 45
Sinuses, 218, **218**, 222–223, **222**
Sinusitis, 222
Sinusoids, 245
Skeletal system, 23, **23**, 160–161, **161**
Skeleton, 161, **161**
    number of bones in, 158–159
    vulnerability of, 161
    weight of, 160
Skin, 23, **23**, 130–157
    aging of, 146
    artificial, 143, **143**
    chapped/dry, 139, 142
    cleanliness of, 134
    colour of, 131, **131**
    cross-section of, **133**
    disorders of, 144–145, **144**
    on fingers, lips, and ears, compared, 137,
        137
    healing of, 98, **98**
    as protective mantle, 130
    structure of, 132, 133, **133**
Skin cancer, 136, 142, 145
Skin grafts, 143, **143**, 147, 148
Skin: "To get under your skin," origin of
    phrase, 148
Skull, 161, **165**, 166–167, **166**
    effect of blow to, 167
    fractures of, 167
    function of, 166–167
    phrenology, 52, **52**
    reconstruction of ancient, 166, **166**
    surgery on, 59, 160, **160**
Sleep, 58–59, **58, 59**, 72, 313, **313**
    before birth, 296–297
"Sleeping like a log," origin of phrase, 66
Sleeping sickness, 34
Sleepwalking, 66
Slit-lamp, 190
Small intestine. *See* Intestine, small.
Smallpox, 100, 101, **101**
    eradication of, 29
Smegma, 267
Smell
    in medical diagnosis, 219
    memory and, 63
    sense of, 63, 218, 219, 220–221
    compared to sense of taste, 220–221
    sex differences and, 207
    wearing out of, 207
    See also Odours.
Smiling, 168, **168**
    in babies, 315

*Page numbers in **boldfaced** type refer to the illustrations.*

Smoking, 113, 123, 127, 128, **128**, 129, **129**
    cholesterol and, 105, **105**
    cigarettes and cigars, 128, **128**, 129
    coronary artery disease and, 104
    passive, 113
    during pregnancy, 129
    stopping, 129
    stroke and, 106
Snail fever, 34, **34**
Sneeze, 118, **118**, 120
Snooperscope, 24
Snoring, 112–113
Snow blindness, 195, **195**
Soccer injuries, 167, **167**
Socket, 170, **170**
Somatic system, 48
Somatosensory cortex, 49, **49**, 53, **53**
Somatotrophin. *See* Growth hormone.
Somnambulism, somniferous, somniloquy,
    somnolent, origin of words, 66
Sonar for the blind, 211
Sore throat, 227
Sound, 210, **210**
    location of, 211, **211**
    loudness of, 210, **210**
Sound waves, 210, 211, **211**
Space colonies, 45
Spanish fly, 271, **271**
Spanish influenza, 40, 121, **121**
Spectacles, 189,190,193, **193**, 194–195,
    204
    bifocals, 193,195
    goggles, 195, **195**, 203
    sunglasses, 195, **195**
    See also Contact lenses.
Speech, 228, 230, 231, **231**
Speech-reading (lip-reading), 214
Sperm, 38, 266–269, **268**, 290, **290**
    infertility and, 284
    maturation of, 282
Spermatozoa. *See* Sperm.
Spermicidal agents, 286–287
Sphenoid sinuses, **218**, 222, **222**
Sphincter, 168, 240, 262, **262**
Sphygmomanometer, 102
Spinal column, 172
Spinal cord, 49, **49**
Spine, 161, **161**, 172–173, **173**
Spirometer, 117
Spleen, 110, **110**, 245
    Hodgkin's disease and, 111
Split-brain research, 52
Spontaneous abortion, 293, 304
Sports
    dangers of, 167, **167**, 184, 185, **185**
    influences on performance, 54
Sprained ankle, 184–185
Sprained wrist, 176–177
Sprains and strains, 184–185
Squamous cell carcinoma, 145
Squint, 190
Stammering. *See* Stuttering.
Stapes (or stirrup), **208**, 209
Staphylococcus, 30, **30**
Staphylococcus infections, 36, 134, 144,
    255

STD. *See* Sexually transmitted diseases.
Sterility. *See* Infertility.
Sterilization
    tubal ligation, 287
    vasectomy, 271
Steroids, 145, 153
    to treat trick knee, 178
    types of, 84
    use by athletes, 75
Stethoscope, 116, 120
Stirrup (stapes), **208**, 209
Stomach, **225**, 235, **235**, 240–242, **240**
    capacity of, 242
    effect on food of, 241
    location of, 241
    muscles in, 241
    rumbling of, 233
    upset, 241
    why it doesn't digest itself, 242
Story Behind the Words, The
    bones and muscles, 178
    brain and nervous system, 66
    digestive system, 242
    ear, nose, and throat, 224
    heart and circulatory system, 99
    human body, 36
    pregnancy, birth, and growth, 293
    skin, 148
    urinary and reproductive systems, 264
Strabismus, 190. *See also* Cross-eyes.
Straightening teeth, 171
Strained wrist. *See* Sprained wrist.
Strawberry mark, 136
Strep throat, 227
Streptococcus, 36, 227
Stress, 66, 120
    endocrine system and, 85
    health and, 25
    heart disease and, 89
    pain and, 70
    pain in jaw and, 169, **169**
    stroke and, 107
Stress fracture, 184
Stroke, 106–107
    atherosclerosis and, 105, **105**
    recovery from, 53, 73, **73**, 107
Stuttering, 55
    treatment for, 230
Subconjunctival haermorrhage. *See*
    Bloodshot eye.
Subcutaneous tissue, 133, **133**, 143, **143**,
    146, **146**
Sublingual glands, 234, **235**
Submandibular glands, 234, **235**
Sudden Infant Death Syndrome (SIDS),
    314
Sugar
    balance of, 86–87
    dangers of, 233
    diabetes and, 75
Sumo wrestlers, 187, 256, **256**
Sunburn, 133, **133**, 142, **142**, 145
Sunglasses, 195, **195**
Suntan, 136, 142
Superior vena cava, 91, **91**
Surfing and balance, 187, **187**

Surgery
    foetal, 305
    Hippocrates and, 37, **37**
    psychological preparation for, 69
    in space, 45
Surprised expression, 168, **168**
Suture joint, 164, 165, **165**
Swaddling, 311, **311**
Swallowing, 224, 225, **225**, 235, **235**,
    240–241
Sweat glands, 132, **133**, 134, 135, **135**
Sweating, 130–131, 132
Swimming after eating, 234
Swivelling (ball-and-socket joint), 165,
    165
Swollen glands, 110
Symmetry, facial, 22, **22**
Synapse, 50, **50**
Synaptic cleft, 51, **51**
Synovial capsule, 164
Synovial fluid, 164
Synovial membrane, 182
Syphilis, 278, **278**, 280, **280**
    characteristics and dangers of, 280–281
    cures for, 281
    Edouard Manet and, 280, **280**
    pre-Columbian evidence of, 279, **279**
Systems, interdependence of body, 23, **23**
Systolic pressure, 102

T

Tailbone (coccyx), 172, **173**
Talus, 181, **181**
Tapeworms, 30, 249, **249**
Tar, 128
Tarsal bones, **161**, 181, **181**
Taste, sense of, 220–221, 236–237, **236**,
    237
    in adulthood, 237
    in infancy, 237
    role of smell in, 236
Taste buds, 236, **236**, 237, **237**
Tastes
    acquired, 237
    basic, 221
    primary, 236–237, **236**
Tattoos, 148, 149, **149**
TB. *See* Tuberculosis.
Tears, 192, **192**
    laughter and, 66
Teeth, 238–239, **238**
    cavities in, 238
    dead, 239
    flossing of, 239, **239**
    structure of, 170, 170
    surface of, 238, **238**
Teeth, types of
    baby, 170, **170**
    bicuspids, 170, **170**
    buds, 170, **170**
    canines, 170, **170**

Teeth (*contd.*)
 incisors, 170, **170**
 molars, 170, **170**
 permanent, 170, **170**
 wisdom, 166, 170, **170**, 171
Temperature, normal, 89
Temporal lobe, 49, **49**
Temporomandibular (TMJ) syndrome, 169, **169**
Tendon, 162, 175, 176, **176**, 180, 181, **181**
 in trigger finger, 177
Tennis elbow, 174–175, **174–175**
Testes. *See* Testicles.
Testicles, 38, 77, **77**, 81
 masses in, 269
 mumps and, 269
 self-examination of, 269
 structure of, 266, **266**
Testosterone, 75, 85, 266
 aggression and, 55
 sex drive and, 83
"Test-tube" babies, 285, **285**
Thalamus, 48, 53, **53**
 pain and, 69
Thalassaemia, 49
Thermography, 24, **24**
Thighbone, 178
 strength of, 158
Thirst, 232–233
 body's response to, 260
 during cold weather, 270
Thoracic duct, 110, 111, **111**
Thorax, 116
Thoughts
 emotions and, 68–69
 without words, 60
Throat (pharynx), 224–225, **225**, 227
Thrombocytes. *See* Platelets.
Thrombus, 106
Thumb sucking, 164
Thymosine, 45
Thymus, 77, **77**, 100, **100**, 110
Thyroid cartilage. *See* Adam's apple.
Thyroid deficiency, 86
Thyroid gland, 77, **77**, 86, **86**
Thyroid-stimulating hormone (TSH), 86
Thyroxine, 86
TIA. *See* Transient ischaemic attack.
Tibia, **161**, 178, 180, 181, **181**
Tickling, 130
Ticks, 140
Tightrope walking, 187
Timothy grass, 122, **122**
Tinea pedis. See Athlete's foot.
Tinnitus, 214
Tissues, types of, 22
Titian, *Adam and Eve,* 227, **227**
TMJ. *See* Temporomandibular syndrome.
Tobacco smoke, cancer and, 32
Tobacco tars, 128
Toenails, 156–157
Toes, ability to touch, 186–187
Toilet training, 259
Tone, 211

Tone deafness, 213
Tongue, 236, **236**, 237, **237**
Tongue-tied, 225
Tonsils, 223, **225**
Toothache, 239
Tooth brushing, 233, 238
Tooth decay, 238
Touch, sense of, 138, **138**, 289, **289**
Toxic shock syndrome, 44
Toxins, 28, 29
Toxoplasmosis, 304
Trachea (windpipe), 114, 115, **115**, 124, 125, **125, 225**
 See also Throat.
Traction, 184
Traits, 42
Trance, origin of word, 66
Tranquilizers
 in combination with alcohol, 32
 fatigue and, 21
Transdermal patch, 139, **139**
Transient ischaemic attack (TIA), 106
Transplants
 brain tissue, 72
 cornea, 205
 hair, 153, **153**
Transverse colon, **235, 248,** 250
Trapezius, 162, **162,** 174
Travel, medical preparations for, 35
Traveller's diarrhoea, 35, 249
Treadmill test, 103, **103**
Trepanation, 160, **160**
Très Riches Heures, Les, 26, **26**
Triceps, 162, **162,** 174
Trichomoniasis, 278
Tricuspid valve, 91, **91**
Trigger finger, 177
Triiodothyronine, 86
Trophoblast, 292, **292**
Tryrosinase, 136
Tsetse fly, 34
TSH. *See* Thyroid-stimulating hormone.
Tubal infection, 284
Tubal ligation, 286, 287
Tuberculosis (TB), 34, 123
Tumours
 benign and malignant, compared, 32
 brain, 72
 breast, 276, **276**
 ear, 212, 217
 fibroid, 274
 pituitary, 78
 testicular, 269
 vocal cords, 229
 See also Cancer.
Tunnel vision (retinitis pigmentosa), 202, 205, **205**
Turbinate bones, **218**
Twins, 300, 301, **301**
 fingerprints of, 137
 identical, 39, **39**
Tympanic membrane. *See* Eardrum.
Type A personality, 90
Typhoid fever, 35

U

Ulna, 137, 174, 175, **176,** 177
Ultrasound, 299, **299**
Ultraviolet rays, 130, 131, 133, 142, 147
Umbilical cord, 292, 293, 305, 307, 310
Umbilical cord: "To cut the umbilical cord," origin of phrase, 293
Upset stomach, 241
Ureter, 93, **93,** 261, **261**
Urethra, 262, **262,** 263, 264, **266,** 273
Urethral bulb, **266**
Urinalysis, 265, **265**
Urinary system, 23, **23,** 258–265
Urinary tract, 264–265
 infections of, 264
Urination, 262, **262**
 before birth, 298
 effects of nervousness on, 258–259
Urine
 bile pigments in, 265, **265**
 effect of caffeine on, 258
 colour of, 259, 265, **265**
 composition of, 258, 262
 elimination of, 262–263
 role in eliminating poisons, 93
 volume of, 262, 263
 See also Kidney.
Urochrome, 259
Urologist, 270
Uterus, 272, **272, 273,** 290–291, **292,** 300
 contractions of, 306
 removal of, 274–275
 structure of, 272, **272,** 273, **273**
Uvula, 224–225
 role in snoring, 112

V

Vaccination, 29, 100, 101, **101**
Vaccine, 100
Vagina, 272, **272,** 273
Vaginal sponge, 287
Vaginitis, 278
Vallate papillae, **236**
Van Hove-Gadeyne sextuplets, 301, **301**
Varicella zoster virus, 279
Varicocele, 269, 284
Varicose veins, 106, **106**
 of testes, 269, 284
Vas deferens, 266, **266,** 268, 282
Vasectomy, 270–271
Vasopressin, 77, 78
VD. *See* Venereal disease.
Veins, 90, 92–93, **92,** 98, 107, 110, **133**
 difference between arteries and, 92
 phlebitis and, 106
 pulmonary, 91, **91**
 varicose, 106, **106**
 venules, 92, 93, 111

Page numbers in **boldfaced** *type refer to the illustrations.*

Velazquez, Diego, 311, **311**
Venereal, origin of word, 264
Venereal disease (VD), 278–281, **278–281**
  pregnancy and, 295
Venereal warts, 278
Ventricle, 90, 91, **91**, 92, 93, 102
Ventriloquism, 230, **230**
Venus of Willendorf, 282, **282**
Vernix caseosa, 300
Vertebrae
  cervical, **173**
  coccyx, 172, **173**
  lumbar, **173**
  sacrum, 172, **173**
  thoracic, **173**
Victoria, Queen, 52
  haemophilia and, 109, **109**
Villi, 248, **248**
Violence. *See* Aggression.
Virility, origin of word, 264
Viruses
  and bacteria compared, 29
  as cause of cancer, 32
  common cold and, 119–120
  diseases caused by, 29, 30
  influenza and, 120, 121, **121**
  lethal, 44, **44**
  warts and, 140–141
Vision
  binocular, 196
  blurred, 203
  brain and, 52–53, 196, 198, 199
  contrast sensitivity in, 190
  correction of poor, 194, **194**
  defects in, 194
  double, 196, 197, 203
  heredity and, 42, 202
  normal, 194, 205, **205**
  peripheral, 203, 205, **205**
  persistence of, 197
  6/6, 190, 194
  two-dimensional image, 196
  upside-down image, 190, 196
  See also Eye.
Visual cliff, 61, **61**
Visual memory, 62, **62**
Vitamin A, 244
  night blindness and, 202
Vitamin B, 244, 251, 253
Vitamin B$_1$, 253
Vitamin C, 253

Vitamin C (*contd.*)
  colds and, 113
Vitamin D, 130, 131, 142, 244
  bones and, 182
Vitamin D$_1$, 253, **253**
Vitamin E, 244
Vitamin K, 244, 251
Vitamins, 253, 254
  megadoses of, 254–255
Vitreous humour, 189, 190, 191, **191**, 204
Vocal cords, 116, 225, 228, **228**, 229
Voice, 228–229
  hearing your own, 206–207
  prosthesis to restore, 231
  role of sinuses in, 222
Voiceprints, 231, **231**
Volume (loudness), 211
Vomiting, 242
Vulva, 272, **272**, 273

Wadlow, Robert, 79, **79**
Walk, Richard, 61
Walking
  learning, 159, 316, 317
  to prevent flat feet, 181
Wall-eye, 197
Warm-blooded, 89
Wart, 140–141
Wasp, 140, **140**
Water
  amount of, in body, 263
  in urine, 262
  polluted, 29, **29**
Water cures, 246, **246**
Weather
  breathing and, 126
  temperature inversion and, 126
Wechsler adult intelligence scale, 64
Wedding ceremonies, 283, **283**
Weight, acceptable, 252, **252**
Weightlessness, 182
  motion sickness and, 207, **207**
Weight lifting, 159, 164, 167, 187
Weight loss
  diabetes and, 87
  hyperthyroidism and, 86–87

Wernicke's disease, 68
Wexler, Nancy, 43, **43**
Whiplash, 185
Whispering, 229
White blood cells (leucocytes), 26, 94, **94**, **95**, 98, **98**, 99–101, 110
  number of, 95
  types of, 94, **94**, **95**
Whitehead, 144
Wigs, 153, **153**
Wind, intestinal, 250, 251
Windpipe. *See* Trachea.
Wisdom teeth, 166, 170, **170**, 171
"Witches' milk," 289
Womb. *See* Uterus.
Wordlore. *See* Story Behind the Words.
World Health Organization, 24, 29
World War I, 37, **37**, 121, **121**
World War II, 37, **37**
Wounds, healing of, 98, **98**, 99
Wrinkles, 146–147, **146–147**, 148, 169
Wrist, painful, 176–177

X-rays, 108
  anaemia and, 108
  of brain, 56
  to treat scars, 148
Xinguano Indians of Brazil, 35

Yawning, 113, **113**
Yeasts, 134
Yolk sac, 292, **292**

Z

Zodiac and the body, 26, **26**

CREDITS & ACKNOWLEDGMENTS

We wish to express our gratitude to the many people who contributed to this book. Hundreds of publications were consulted, notably Human Anatomy and Physiology *by Alvin Silverstein, published by John Wiley & Sons;* Basic Physiology and Anatomy *by Ellen E. Chaffee and Ivan M. Lytle, published by J.B. Lippincott;* Textbook of Medical Physiology *by Arthur C. Guyton, M.D., published by W.D. Saunders;* Cecil Textbook of Medicine, *edited by James B. Wyngaarden, M.D., and Lloyd H. Smith, Jr., M.D., published by W.D. Saunders; and* Scientific American *Medicine, published by Scientific American, Inc. Particular thanks are due to the Gillette Research Institute, Rockville, Maryland, for its assistance on the section on hair, and to Bruce Abernethy of the University of Queensland. We also acknowledge with pleasure the contribution of the following artists and photographers:*

TABLE OF CONTENTS

3 Jane Hurd Studio. **4** Judy Skorpil. **6** Dr. R.P. Clark, Mervyn Goff, AMPA, AIIP, ARPS/Science Photo Library/Photo Researchers. **7** Warren Anatomical Museum, Harvard Medical School. **8** *left* National Library of Medicine; *right* James A. McInnis. **9** Judy Skorpil. **10** *left* Courtesy of the Fashion Institute of Technology Library; *right* Enid Kotschnig. **11** *left* Musée du Louvre; *right* E. Kairinen, Gillette Research Institute. **12** Jane Hurd Studio. **13** Dave Stock/Focus West. **14** *left* David Lees; *centre* Reproduced from *Ishihara's Tests for Color Blindness*, published by Kanehara & Co. Ltd., Tokyo. **15** Mette Ivers. **16** D.L. Cramer, Ph.D.; *right* Scala/Art Resource. **17** From *Behold Man* by Lennart Nilsson, published by Little, Brown and Company, Boston. **18** Scala/Art Resource. **19** Scala.

CHAPTER 1

21 Brett Froomer/The Image Bank. **22** James A. McInnis. **23** Jane Hurd Studio. **24** Dr. R.P. Clark, Mervyn Goff, AMPA, AIIP, ARPS/Science Photo Library/Photo Researchers. **25** The Bettmann Archive. **26** Giraudon/Art Resource. **27** George V. Kelvin. **28** *upper left* The Bettmann Archive; *upper right* Rijksmuseum-Stichting, Amsterdam; *bottom* A. Appel and A. Stein, IBM, Yorktown Heights, New York. **29** Philadelphia Museum of Art, given by Mrs. William H. Horstmann. **30** *upper left* Manfred Kage/Peter Arnold, Inc.; *bottom left* Centers for Disease Control, Atlanta; *right* Sdeuard C. Bisserot/Bruce Coleman Ltd. **31** *left* UNICEF; *upper right* Dee Breger/Lamont-Doherty Geological Observatory/Phototake; *bottom right* Dr. G.L. Fisher/Science Photo Library/Photo Researchers. **32** Britt-Mari Norberg. **33** *top* The Granger Collection, New York; *bottom* Tom Tracy/Medichrome/The Stock Shop. **34** Centers for Disease Control, Atlanta. **35** *top* © 1963 Arthur Leipzig; *bottom* Charles May/Shostal Associates. **37** *upper left* Scala/Art Resource; *top right* National Library of Medicine; *bottom left* Tim Page; *lower right* U.S. Army Photo. **38** *top* Judy Skorpil, based on a diagram by M.E. Challinor from "Genetic Gibberish in the Code of Life" by Graham Chedd, *Science 81*, November 1981, courtesy of the American Association for the Advancement of Science; *bottom* George V. Kelvin. **39** © Harvey Stein 1978. **41** *top left* Bildarchiv d. Ost. Nationalbibliothek/Courtesy of the Austrian Press and Information Service; *lower left* Kunsthistorisches Museum, Vienna; *right* Scala/Art Resource. **42** *left* The Bettmann Archive; *right* John Launois/Black Star. **43** *top* © Steve Uzzell 1982; *bottom* © Fred Burnham

1983. **44** Centers for Disease Control, Atlanta. **45** Wayne Sorce.

CHAPTER 2

47 *left* Driscol Gallery; *right* Driscol Gallery, photo by William Carter. **48** Eric V. Gravé/Photo Researchers. **49** Jane Hurd Studio. **50–51** Laszlo Kubinyi. **52** The Bettmann Archive. **53** Jane Hurd Studio, based on an illustration from "Brain Function and Blood Flow" by Lassen, Ingvar and Skinhøj, *Scientific American*, October 1978. **54** Michael Philip Manheim/Photo Researchers. **55** © 1981 Eiji Miyazawa/Black Star. **56** *top* Dan McCoy/Rainbow; *bottom* Brookhaven National Laboratory. **57** © Howard Sochurek 1984. **58** James A. McInnis. **59** Archivio Casiraghi. **60** Tass from Sovfoto. **61** Steve McCarroll. **62** Paul Weller. **63** The Bettmann Archive. **64** *upper* Numerical and word puzzles reproduced courtesy of Mensa; *lower* Max Menikoff, based on designs from *Introduction to Psychology*, Seventh Edition by Ernest R. Hilgard, Richard C. Atkinson, and Rita L. Atkinson, © 1979 by Harcourt Brace Jovanovich, Inc., by permission of the publisher. **65** AP/Wide World Photos. **67** *top left* Scala/Art Resource; *middle left* National Library of Medicine; *middle right* The Bettmann Archive; *bottom* Rapho Division/Photo Researchers. **68** © 1981 Jim Sugar/Black Star. **69** Warren Anatomical Museum, Harvard Medical School. **70** Peabody Museum of Salem, photo by Mark Sexton. **71** National Library of Medicine. **73** Courtesy of Giselle Räderscheidt.

CHAPTER 3

75 © Jeff Lowenthal 1980/Woodfin Camp & Associates. **76** The Bettmann Archive. **77** Jane Hurd Studio. **78** Robert J. Demarest. **79** *upper left* © 1982 Maureen Lambray/Sygma; *upper right* The Bettmann Archive; *bottom left* The Bettmann Archive; *bottom right* Jacqueline Duvoisin/*Sports Illustrated*. **80** Gruppo Editoriale Fabbri-Bompiani. **81** *left* Eddie Adams, © 1982 *Discover* Magazine, Time Inc.; *right* Mallinckrodt Institute of Radiology at Washington University Medical Center. **82** Ray Skibinski, based on photos from *Life Span Development* by Jeffrey S. Turner and Donald B. Helms © 1979 by W.B. Saunders Company. **83** The Photo Library, Sydney. **84** *left* James A. McInnis; *right* Ray Skibinski. **86** *left* UNICEF; *right* Robert J. Demarest. **87** *left* Martin Dohrn/Science Photo Library; *upper right* Peggyann Grainger, courtesy of the American Diabetes Association; *bottom right* Miles Laboratories, Inc.

CHAPTER 4

89 Richard Laird/Leo de Wys, Inc. **91** Judy Skorpil. **92** From *Behold Man* by Lennart Nilsson, published by Little, Brown and Company, Boston. **93** Edward Malsberg. **94** *left* From *Corpuscles* by Marcel Bessis, Springer-Verlag, Berlin, New York © 1974. **94** *right* **and 95** From *Behold Man* by Lennart Nilsson, published by Little, Brown and Company, Boston. **96** *left* Judy Skorpil; *right* From *Behold Man* by Lennart Nilsson, published by Little, Brown and Company, Boston. **97** The Bettmann Archive. **98** *upper left* E. Bernstein and E. Kairinen, Gillette Research Institute; *bottom* Judy Skorpil, © Copyright 1967, CIBA Pharmaceutical Company, division of CIBA-GEIGY Corporation; adapted from CLINICAL SYMPOSIA; all rights reserved. **100** Ray Skibinski. **101** *bottom left* Culver Pictures; *upper right* National Library of Medicine; *bottom right* Sally and Richard Greenhill. **102** *left* Ray Skibinski; *bottom right* James A. McInnis. **103** George V. Mann, M.D. **104** The Granger Collection, New York. **105** *bottom* Leonard Dank, © 1982 *Discover* Magazine, Time Inc.; *remainder* George Schwenk, © 1984 *Discover* Magazine, Time Inc. **106** Ray Skibinski. **107** *top* James A. McInnis; *bottom* Library, New York Botanical Garden, Bronx, New York/Photo by Allen Rokach. **108** Courtesy of Marion I. Barnhart et al., Wayne State University School of Medicine. **109** *top* The Royal Collection, Lord Chamberlain's Office, Copyright Reserved; *bottom left* The Bettmann Archive; *bottom right* Culver Pictures. **110** Edward Malsberg. **111** Ray Skibinski.

CHAPTER 5

113 Syndication International/Photo Trends. **114** Focus on Sports. **115** Judy Skorpil, based on an illustration from "The Mechanism of Breathing" by Wallace O. Fenn, *Scientific American*, January 1960. **116** Ray Skibinski. **117** *left* Courtesy of the Fashion Institute of Technology Library; *right* Effects of lacing on the female body from *The Unfashionable Human Body* by Bernard Rudofsky. **118** © 1984 Al Francekevich. **119** The Wellcome Institute for the History of Medicine. **121** *top* Phototake; *middle left to right* Judy Skorpil; *bottom* National Archives. **122** *left* Leonora Box; *upper right* © Phil Harrington/Peter Arnold, Inc.; *bottom right* Dr. Jeremy Burgess/Science Photo Library. **123** *left* © Yoav/Phototake; *right* Jane Burton/Bruce Coleman Inc. **124** Kenneth A. Siegesmund, Ph.D., Department of Anatomy, Medical College of Wisconsin. **125** Ray Skibinski, © Copyright 1967, CIBA Pharmaceutical Company, division of CIBA-GEIGY Corporation; adapted from CLINICAL SYMPOSIA; all rights reserved. **126** Alex Stewart/The Image Bank. **127** *left* © 1978 Flip Schulke/Black Star; *right* Max Menikoff, © Copyright 1967, CIBA Pharmaceutical Company, division of CIBA-GEIGY Corporation; adapted from CLINICAL SYMPOSIA; all rights reserved. **128** *left* The New York Public Library, Arents Collections; *upper right* Iconographic Collection, State Historical Society of Wisconsin. **129** Movie Star News.

CHAPTER 6

131 White/Pite/International Stock Photo. **133** *bottom left* Farrington Daniels, Jr., M.D.; *remainder* Judy Skorpil. **134** *left* Courtesy of International Museum of Surgical Science, International College of Surgeons, Chicago/Photograph by Ron Testa; *right* World Health Organization. **135** *top* From *Behold Man* by Lennart Nilsson, published by Little, Brown and Company, Boston; *bottom left* P. Bagavandoss/Photo Researchers; *bottom right* Dr. Clifford E. Desch, University of Connecticut, Hartford Branch. **136** Mel Di Giacomo/The Image Bank. **137** *upper and bottom right* Phillip A. Harrington/Fran Heyl Associates; *remainder* Ray Skibinski. **138** Judy Skorpil. **139** *upper* Alastair Black/Focus on Sports; *bottom* CIBA-Geigy Corporation. **140** *left* Ann Savage; *right* Guy Michel. **141** Judy Skorpil, © Copyright 1967, CIBA Pharmaceutical Company, division of CIBA-GEIGY Corpora-

tion; adapted from CLINICAL SYMPOSIA; all rights reserved. **142** Farrington Daniels, Jr., M.D. **143** *upper* Ray Skibinski; *bottom* Dan McCoy/Rainbow. **144** Judy Skorpil. **145** The Granger Collection, New York. **146–147** Ray Skibinski. **149** *top* Musée du Louvre; *bottom left* Morton Beebe/The Image Bank; *bottom right* Rene Burri/Magnum. **150** *bottom right* The Oregon Health Sciences University; *remainder* Judy Skorpil. **151** James A. McInnis. **152** Ray Skibinski. **153** *left* Peter Williams/Camera Press; *upper right* Courtesy of Hudson's Bay and Annings Ltd.; *bottom centre and right* Norman Orentreich, M.D. **154** Courtesy of Redken Laboratories. **155** *bottom right* Tony Brain/Science Photo Library/Photo Researchers; *upper middle and right* Courtesy of Redken Laboratories; *remainder* E. Kairinen, Gillette Research Institute. **156** Judy Skorpil. **157** *left* The Bettmann Archive; *right* James A. McInnis.

CHAPTER 7

159 James A. McInnis. **160** Lee Boltin. **161** *upper left* Photo Trends; *lower left* Manfred Kage/Peter Arnold, Inc.; *right* Jane Hurd Studio. **162** Jane Hurd Studio. **163** Judy Skorpil. **165** *top left* From *Behold Man* by Lennart Nilsson, published by Little, Brown and Company, Boston; *upper right* National Library of Medicine; *remainder* Jane Hurd Studio. **166** *upper* S. Petrov, © 1982 *Discover* Magazine, Time Inc.; *bottom* George V. Kelvin. **167** Antonio Suarez/Leo de Wys, Inc. **168** *left and centre* Courtesy of Human Interaction Laboratory, University of California, San Francisco, from *The Face of Man* by Paul Ekman; *upper centre and right* James A. McInnis. **169** *top* Culver Pictures; *bottom* Judy Skorpil. **170** Robert J. Demarest. **171** National Library of Medicine. **172** Bruno Barbey/Magnum. **173** *upper right* Ray Skibinski; *remainder* Robert J. Demarest. **174** *left* Dave Stock/Focus West; *right* Ray Skibinski. **175** *left* Lorraine Rorke; *right* Dave Stock/Focus West. **176** *upper left* Robert J. Demarest; *bottom right* Judy Skorpil. **177** Yale Joel, *Life* Magazine © Time Inc. **179** *upper left* The Bettmann Archive; *top right* Courtesy of the Essex Institute, Salem, Massachusetts.; *bottom left and right* James A. McInnis; *remainder* Bernard Pfriem's drawing of a foot that fits the shoe from *The Unfashionable Human Body* by Bernard Rudofsky. **180** *left* The Metropolitan Museum of Art, Rogers Fund, 1914; *right* Jim Anderson/Woodfin Camp & Associates. **181** *top* Robert J. Demarest; *bottom* Judy Skorpil. **182** Michael J. Klein, M.D. **183** Michael Melford/Wheeler Pictures. **184** Ray Skibinski. **185** *left* Focus on Sports; *right* Mike Powel/Allsport. **186** *left* NCR Corporation; *right* D. Walker/Gamma-Liaison. **187** Darrell Jones/The Stock Market.

CHAPTER 8

189 Morris Karol. **191** *upper right* F. M. de Monasterio, M.D., and E. P. McCrane, National Eye Institute, National Institutes of Health, Bethesda, Maryland; *remainder* Judy Skorpil. **192** Ray Skibinski. **193** *upper left* Opera Museo Stibbert; *bottom left* Dane A. Penland; *upper right* David Lees; *bottom right* Bausch & Lomb. **194** Ray Skibinski. **195** The Photograph Collections of the Episcopal Church in The Archives of the Episcopal Church, Austin, Texas. **196** Peter Menzel/Stock, Boston. **197** *top and lower right* The Image Bank; *bottom* The Photo Library, Sydney. **198** *top* Max Menikoff, based on illustrations from *Optical Illusions and the Visual Arts* by R.B. Carraher and J.B. Thurston © 1966 by Reinhold Book Corp., by permission of Van Nostrand Reinhold Company; *bottom* Max Menikoff, based on an illustration from "Visual Illusions" by Richard L. Gregory, *Scientific American*, November 1968. **199** *top left* Max Menikoff, based on an illustration from "Pictorial Perception and Culture" by Jan B. Deregowski, *Scientific American*, November 1972; *top right* © 1985 Sotheby's, Inc.; *bottom right* Max Menikoff, based on an illustration after Rubin, 1915, from *Psychology Today: An Introduction*, CRM Books, Del Mar, California, by permission of Random House, Inc. **200** Max Menikoff, based on an illustration from

Introduction to Psychology, Seventh Edition by Ernest R. Hilgard, Richard C. Atkinson, and Rita L. Atkinson, © 1979 by Harcourt Brace Jovanovich, Inc., by permission of the publisher. **201** *top* Lent by James and Mari Michener, The Archer M. Huntington Art Gallery, The University of Texas at Austin; *bottom* Max Menikoff, based on illustrations from "The Elements of Color," a treatise on the colour system of Johannes Itten based on his book *The Art of Color* © 1970 by Otto Maier Verlag by permission of Van Nostrand Reinhold Company. **202** Reproduced from *Ishihara's Tests for Color Blindness*, published by Kanehara & Co. Ltd., Tokyo. **203** *bottom* Toichiro Kuwabara, M.D., National Eye Institute, National Institutes of Health, Bethesda, Maryland; *remainder* James A. McInnis. **204** The Image Bank. **205** James A. McInnis.

CHAPTER 9

207 NASA. **208** *top* Robert J. Demarest. **208** *bottom* **and 209** Molly Webster, *Discover* Magazine © Time Inc. **210** *left* James A. McInnis; *right* Dewitt Jones. **211** Ray Skibinski. **212** The Bettmann Archive. **213 and 214** James A. McInnis. **215** *top* National Library of Medicine; *bottom right* James A. McInnis; *remainder* The Bettmann Archive. **216** *top* John Dominis/Wheeler Pictures; *bottom* Judy Skorpil. **217** Michael Melford/Wheeler Pictures. **218** *left* Robert J. Demarest; *right* Judy Skorpil. **220** From *Behold Man* by Lennart Nilsson, published by Little, Brown and Company, Boston. **221** The Bettmann Archive. **222** *upper* Ray Skibinski; *bottom* Judy Skorpil. **223** *upper* Richard Kalvar/Magnum; *lower* Mette Ivers. **225** Robert J. Demarest. **226** James A. McInnis. **227** *left* Giraudon/Art Resource; *right* Judy Skorpil. **228** G. Paul Moore. **229** *top* © Jack Vartoogian; *bottom* © Erika Stone 1984. **230** *upper* Pictorial Press; *bottom* Pepperfoto. **231** Courtesy of AT&T Bell Laboratories.

CHAPTER 10

233 J R M Media Inc. **235** *left* Judy Skorpil; *right* Jane Hurd Studio. **236** *left* Ray Skibinski; *right* Judy Skorpil. **237** From *Behold Man* by Lennart Nilsson, published by Little, Brown and Company, Boston. **238** Manfred Kage/Peter Arnold, Inc. **239** American Dental Association. **240** *top* Jane Hurd Studio; *lower left* Dr. Richard G. Kessel, Department of Biology, University of Iowa; *lower right* D.L. Cramer, Ph.D. **241** The Bettmann Archive. **243** *top* Bullaty-Lomeo/The Image Bank; *lower left* Russ Kinne/Photo Researchers; *lower right* Culver Pictures; *bottom* The Bettmann Archive. **244** *left* Judy Skorpil; *upper right* Jane Hurd Studio; *bottom right* Dr. Edith Robbins. **245** Scala/Art Resource. **246** *top* Volker Corell/Black Star; *bottom* Margot Granitsas/Photo Researchers. **247** Dianora Niccolini/Medichrome/The Stock Shop. **248** *top* Jane Hurd Studio; *middle* Judy Skorpil; *bottom* Roland Birke/Peter Arnold, Inc. **249** Biophoto Associates/Photo Researchers. **250** From *Behold Man* by Lennart Nilsson, published by Little, Brown and Company, Boston. **251** *right* The Bettmann Archive; *remainder* Ray Skibinski. **252** Ray Skibinski. **253** Department of Medical Illustration, St. Bartholomew's Hospital, London. **254** Scala/Art Resource. **255** Brenda Katté. **256** John Launois/Black Star. **257** *bottom* Paul Fusco/Magnum; *remainder* National Library of Medicine.

CHAPTER 11

259 James A. McInnis. **260** Al Paglialunga/Phototake. **261** *left top and bottom* Judy Skorpil; *right top and bottom* Jane Hurd Studio. **262** *left* Judy Skorpil; *right* Manfred Kage/Bruce Coleman Ltd. **263** The Granger Collection, New York. **265** *lower left* Giraudon/Art Resource; *top right* National Library of Medicine; *lower right* Miles Laboratories. **266** *left* Judy Skorpil; *right* Robert J. Demarest. **267** Scala/Art Resource. **268** *left* Gower Scientific Photos; *right* From *Behold Man* by Lennart Nilsson, published by Little, Brown and Company, Boston. **269** The Bettmann Archive. **271** *top left* Library, New York Botanical Garden, Bronx, New York/Photo by Allen Rokach; *lower left* Kenneth W. Fink/Bruce Coleman Inc.; *upper right* IL HWA American Corporation; *lower right* Ray Skibinski. **272** Judy Skorpil. **273** *left* Judy Skorpil; *right* From *Behold Man* by Lennart Nilsson, published by Little, Brown and Company, Boston. **274** Judy Skorpil. **275** *top left* Peabody Museum, Harvard University; *top right* Bill Gillette; *bottom* Hebrew Union College Library. **276** *top* Robert J. Demarest; *bottom* Ray Skibinski. **277** Courtesy of Bonne Bell Cosmetics. **278** *bottom left* Prof. Luc Montagnier, Institut Pasteur/CNRI/Science Photo Library; *upper right* Eric Grave/Photo Researchers; *remainder* Centers for Disease Control, Atlanta. **279** Collection of Dr. and Mrs. William F. Kaiser, Berkeley, California. **280** *left* The Granger Collection, New York; *right* Courtauld Institute Galleries, London (Courtauld Collection). **281** Gwen Leighton. **282** Courtesy of Douglas Mazonowicz/The Gallery of Prehistoric Art, New York. **283** *upper left* Victor Englebert; *top right* Reproduced by courtesy of the Trustees, The National Gallery, London; *bottom left* Scala/Art Resource; *bottom right* Wally McNamee/*Newsweek*. **284** The Bettmann Archive. **285** *left* Denis Waugh, *Life* Magazine © 1982 Time Inc.; *right* Alexander Tsiaras/Science Source/Photo Researchers. **286** Max Menikoff, based on a chart courtesy of the Meredith Corporation from the Better Homes and Gardens publication *Woman's Health and Medical Guide* edited by Patricia J. Cooper, Ph.D. **287** Marilyn Silverstone/Magnum.

CHAPTER 12

289 Sandra Lousada/Susan Griggs Agency. **290** From *Behold Man* by Lennart Nilsson, published by Little, Brown and Company, Boston. **291** Jane Hurd Studio. **292** Judy Skorpil. **294** James A. McInnis. **295** National Library of Medicine. **296** Ray Skibinski. **297** From *Behold Man* by Lennart Nilsson, published by Little, Brown and Company, Boston. **298** James A. McInnis. **299** Shaun Skelly/International Stock Photography Ltd. **301** *top* Alinari/Art Resource; *middle left* Courtesy of Stan Guignard; *middle right* Figaro/Gamma-Liaison; *bottom* Deville/Gamma-Liaison. **302** © Joel Gordon 1984. **303** *left* Ray Skibinski, based on a photo courtesy of Barbara J. Franzese, St. Vincent's Hospital and Medical Center of New York; *right* The Bettmann Archive. **304** The Granger Collection, New York. **305** Howard Sochurek. **306** © J.T. Miller 1985. **307** *top* The New York Public Library, Picture Collection; *bottom* © Joel Gordon 1983. **308–309** Ray Skibinski. **310** Sally and Richard Greenhill. **311** *left* Courtesy of Suzanne E. Weiss; *upper middle* Courtesy of the Picture Gallery of the Art History Museum, Vienna; *top right* Scala; *bottom* Tass from Sovfoto. **312** Erika Stone. **313** *upper* Mimi Cotter/International Stock Photography Ltd.; *bottom* James A. McInnis. **314** From "Imitation of Facial and Manual Gestures by Human Neonates" by A.N. Meltzoff and M.K. Moore, *Science*, October 7, 1977, reprinted courtesy of the American Association for the Advancement of Science. **315** *left* John Howard/Science Photo Library; *right* © 1983 Joel Gordon. **316** Suzanne Szasz. **317** *upper and bottom right* James A. McInnis; *remainder* Judy Skorpil.

Efforts have been made to contact the holder of the copyright for each picture. In several cases, these sources have been untraceable, for which we offer our apologies.

40-187-1